D1807427

The Role of the Judiciary in Environmental Governance

Energy and Environmental Law & Policy Series
Supranational and Comparative Aspects

VOLUME 4

Editor

Kurt Deketelaere

Professor of Law, University of Leuven, Belgium,
Honorary Professor of Law, University of Dundee, UK; Chief of Staff,
Flemish Minister for Public Works, Energy, Environment and Nature

Editorial Board

Professor Philip Andrews-Speed, University of Dundee
Professor Michael Faure, University of Maastricht
Professor Gunther Händl, Tulane University, New Orleans
Professor Andres Nollkaemper, University of Amsterdam
Professor Oran Young, University of California

The aim of the Editor and the Editorial Board of this series is to publish works of excellent quality that focus on the study of energy and environmental law and policy.

Through this series the Editor and Editorial Board hope:

- to contribute to the improvement of the quality of energy/environmental law and policy in general and environmental quality and energy efficiency in particular;
- to increase the access to environmental and energy information for students, academics, non-governmental organizations, government institutions, and business;
- to facilitate cooperation between academic and non-academic communities in the field of energy and environmental law and policy throughout the world.

KLUWER LAW INTERNATIONAL

The Role of the Judiciary in Environmental Governance

Comparative Perspectives

Edited By

Louis J. Kotzé
B.Com, LLB, LLM, LLD
Professor of Law
North West University
South Africa

and

Alexander R. Paterson
B.Soc.Sci, LLB, LLM
Attorney of the High Court of South Africa
Senior Lecturer
University of Cape Town
South Africa

 Wolters Kluwer
Law & Business

AUSTIN   BOSTON   CHICAGO   NEW YORK   THE NETHERLANDS

Published by:
Kluwer Law International
PO Box 316
2400 AH Alphen aan den Rijn
The Netherlands
Website: www.kluwerlaw.com

Sold and distributed in North, Central and South America by:
Aspen Publishers, Inc.
7201 McKinney Circle
Frederick, MD 21704
United States of America
Email: customer.care@aspenpubl.com

Sold and distributed in all other countries by:
Turpin Distribution Services Ltd.
Stratton Business Park
Pegasus Drive, Biggleswade
Bedfordshire SG18 8TQ
United Kingdom
Email: kluwerlaw@turpin-distribution.com

Printed on acid-free paper.

ISBN 978-90-411-2708-2

© 2009 Kluwer Law International BV, The Netherlands

All rights reserved. No part of this publication may be reproduced, stored in a retrieval system, or transmitted in any form or by any means, electronic, mechanical, photocopying, recording, or otherwise, without written permission from the publisher.

Permission to use this content must be obtained from the copyright owner. Please apply to: Permissions Department, Wolters Kluwer Legal, 76 Ninth Avenue, 7th Floor, New York, NY 10011-5201, USA. Email: permissions@kluwerlaw.com

Printed in Great Britain.

For
Wendy, Ruby and Lucy Paterson
and
Willemien du Plessis

Table of Contents

Chapter 2
Belgium   **85**
Luc Lavrysen

Chapter 3
Germany **123**
Eckard Rehbinder

Chapter 4
United Kingdom   **151**
Karen Morrow

Chapter 5
United States of America   **181**
Nicholas Robinson

Chapter 6
Canada   **209**
Jamie Benidickson and Heather McLeod-Kilmurray

Chapter 7
Brazil   **249**
Ingo Sarlet and Tiago Fensterseifer

Chapter 8
Argentina   **269**
Juan Carballo

Chapter 9
Paraguay   **295**
Sheila Abed

Chapter 10
Australia **321**
Linda Pearson

Chapter 11
New Zealand   **355**
Klaus Bosselmann

Chapter 12
Pakistan   **381**
Parvez Hassan and Jawad Hassan

Chapter 13
The People's Republic of China **411**
Qun Du

Chapter 17
Nigeria   527
Muhammed Ladan

Chapter 18
South Africa   557
Louis Kotzé and Alexander Paterson

Chapter 19
Eritrea   **603**
Zerisenay Habtezion

Preface

The role of the courts is especially important in the context of the protection of the environment and giving effect to the principle of sustainable development. The importance of the protection of the environment cannot be gainsaid. Its protection . . . is vital to life itself. It must therefore be protected for the benefit of the present and future generations. The present generation holds the earth in trust for the next generation. This trusteeship position carries with it the responsibility to look after the environment. It is the duty of the Court to ensure that this responsibility is carried out. Indeed, the Johannesburg Principles adopted at the Global Judges' Symposium underscore the role of the Judiciary in the protection of the environment [. . .] Courts therefore have a crucial role to play in the protection of the environment. When the need arises to intervene in order to protect the environment, they should not hesitate to do so. (*Fuel Retailers Association of Southern Africa v. Director-General: Environmental Management, Department of Agriculture, Conservation and Environment Mpumalanga Province, and Others* 2007 (6) SA 4 (CC) at paras 39G-40F as per Ngcobo J).

With these words, the South African Constitutional Court recently reaffirmed the all-important role courts play in (re)shaping the environmental governance landscape. The significance of this statement should not be underestimated: it is indicative of increased environmental awareness in the ranks of the judiciary and serves as a signal to all that environmental protection and the achievement of sustainability are paramount considerations in modern society; considerations which courts will not hesitate to entrench and uphold in current endeavors to achieve sustainable environmental governance. The Constitutional Court's explicit reference to the *Johannesburg Principles on the Role of Law and Sustainable Development* adopted at the Global Judges Symposium held in Johannesburg, South Africa, 2002, underscores the assumption that this commitment to achieving sustainability should similarly pervade the attitude of the judiciary in all countries that endorsed these universally-applicable principles. At this Symposium, judges from all over the world confirmed that: '... members of the Judiciary, as well as those contributing to the judicial process at the national, regional and global levels, are crucial partners for promoting compliance with, and the implementation and enforcement of, international and national environmental law.' By way of emphasis, the judges emphatically stated that:

> ... the fragile state of the global environment requires of the Judiciary as the guardian of the Rule of Law, to boldly and fearlessly implement and enforce applicable international and national laws, which in the field of environment and sustainable development will assist in alleviating poverty and sustaining an enduring civilization, and ensuring that the present generation will enjoy and improve the quality of life of all peoples, while also ensuring that the inherent rights and interests of succeeding generations are not compromised.

These statements made it abundantly clear that as far as the future involvement of courts in environmental governance was concerned, it would be 'business unusual'. To this extent, four principles were adopted, namely: (1) 'A full commitment to contributing towards the realization of the goals of sustainable development through the judicial mandate to implement, develop and enforce the law, and to uphold the Rule of Law and the democratic process'; (2) 'To realize the goals of the Millennium Declaration of the United Nations General Assembly which depend upon the implementation of national and international legal regimes that have been established for achieving the goals of sustainable development'; (3) 'In the field of environmental law there is an urgent need for a concerted and sustained programme of work focused on education, training and dissemination of information, including regional and sub-regional judicial colloquia'; and (4) 'That collaboration among members of the Judiciary and others engaged in the judicial process within and across regions is essential to achieve a significant improvement in compliance with, implementation, development and enforcement of environmental law'.

The past six years have seen many global, regional and national initiatives aimed at achieving these bold undertakings made in 2002. Most of these initiatives are continuing and new strategies to augment the role of courts in environmental governance are being contemplated for the future. It is in this context that the idea for the current book was born. Given the mammoth task that still lies ahead to realize fully the commitments enshrined in the Johannesburg Principles, we considered this an opportune moment to gather the thoughts of leading environmental law scholars from across the globe into a single volume which exclusively focuses on the role of the judiciary in environmental governance. The principal objective of this book is to present the cumulative research and experience of these eminent scholars, and to provide a well-represented, comprehensive, informative and critical exposition of the current issues relating to the judiciary and environmental governance in nineteen different countries situated in Europe, North America, South America, Australasia, and Africa.

The investigation is comparative in nature and aims to distil current judicial trends, identify best practices, and formulate proposals for reform of environmental laws, governance structures and approaches to environmental governance. It is hoped that the proposals in the chapters of this book will ultimately contribute to ameliorating several deficiencies inherent in the current role of the courts in facilitating sustainable environmental governance. The complexity presented by the study's theme makes the comparative legal method particularly useful since the book draws from experiences in selected countries which are representative of the different geographical regions, legal systems and legal cultures around the world.

Each chapter, dedicated to a specific jurisdiction, follows a similar basic structure. The chapter proceeds with a brief introduction to the environmental challenges facing the country, a discussion of the country's principal environmental laws and governance structures, and an analysis of the structure, composition and general role of its judiciary. This overview provides a general contextual background for the subsequent detailed analysis of the country's court judgments of environmental relevance. These judgments are critically surveyed and key findings regarding the role of the courts in environmental governance are highlighted. Each chapter concludes with a critical reflection on the opportunities and challenges facing the judiciary in the specific jurisdiction, and suggestions for reforms which may shape its future endeavors in environmental governance and ultimately the attainment of sustainability. For fear of unfairly presenting a too generalized view of the entire book's conclusions, we briefly summarize below some of the main highlights of each of the chapters.

Chapter 1:   The Netherlands

Verschuuren points out that until 2005, the *actio popularis* existed in Dutch environmental law procedures. It was however abolished following a fierce political debate in which the prevailing argument was that non-governmental organizations and local citizens had become too powerful and were obstructing government attempts to stimulate the economy. Currently, any person who is able to show an interest in a matter can seek to challenge administrative action, including decisions made by environmental authorities. Legislative acts (by parliament and orders in council) cannot, however, be tested in the Dutch courts owing to the separation of powers doctrine entrenched in the Dutch Constitution. Notwithstanding the abolition of the *actio popularis*, Verschuuren highlights recent Dutch jurisprudence which indicates that environmental non-governmental organizations are generally considered to have an interest in most environmental decisions. The above approach accords with the 1998 Aarhus Convention on Access to Information, Public Participation in Decision-making and Access to Justice in Environmental Matters (Aarhus Convention), and with European Union law implementing the Convention. He argues that the Dutch courts accordingly appear to be fairly liberal when deciding whether applicants have an interest in a matter or not, and generally speaking, grant sufficient opportunities to business corporations, non-governmental organizations, and individual citizens to bring environmental matters before the courts. Verschuuren discusses how the recent decisions of the Dutch courts in environmental matters have, however, been the subject of increased criticism from all spheres. Business organizations and local authorities feel that courts frequently go too far in testing government decisions; whereas non-governmental organizations and local residents are of the view that courts test decisions too marginally. He considers a survey of recent court decisions which appears to suggest that the latter view is the reality, and that the courts' apparent deference to the executive will probably continue in line with Dutch legal and administrative culture. However, since European Union law sets legal boundaries for domestic administrative decisions on practically every environmental issue, he argues that the Dutch courts are constantly compelled to measure administrative decisions against European Union law, policies and standards. The result, according to Verschuuren, is that the Dutch courts practically promote the implementation of European Union environmental law, albeit indirectly, and aid in forging a balance between environmental and other competing interest groups in the Netherlands.

Chapter 2:   Belgium

Lavrysen argues that, as is the case in other member States of the European Union, most of Belgium's domestic environmental laws are the result of legislative developments at European Union level. The Belgian Constitution contains a reference to sustainable development and recognizes a right to the protection of a healthy environment. Despite the existence of a comprehensive environmental legal framework, Belgium has no specialized environmental court and it is up to 'ordinary' courts to deal with environmental issues. The Constitutional Court has, however, over the years opened its doors to citizens and non-governmental organizations seeking to protect environmental interests. A rich jurisprudence has accordingly developed regarding the constitutional right to the protection of a healthy environment, the right to respect for private and family life, and the equality clause. The author indicates, however, that access of non-governmental organizations to ordinary courts and the Supreme Administrative Court remains somewhat problematic due to very strict or varying interpretations of the notion of 'legal interest', and that these interpretations appear to be somewhat at odds with the tenor inherent in the Aarhus Convention. A further trend evidenced in Belgium is the marked increase in the number of environmental cases heard before the criminal courts, and the apparent improvement in the quality of the judgments in these matters. This may be attributable to the improved training of judicial officers, greater sensitivity to environmental protection and an extension of the available legal remedies. Partly under the influence of international, European and constitutional developments, the courts are no longer inclined, when faced with conflicting interests, to automatically sacrifice environmental interests in favor of economic interests. Lavrysen points out, however, that this is not always the case and that considerable differences remain from one court to another. Key challenges are also posed by the enormous case backlogs plaguing various courts, most notably the Supreme Administrative Court. He accordingly recommends that the Belgian government would be well-advised to revisit the current judicial system and to implement reforms to further expand on existing structures and to create specialized judicial units to exclusively adjudicate environmental matters.

Chapter 3: Germany

Rehbinder focuses particularly on the role of the German judiciary in reviewing administrative action of relevance to the environment. He finds that the judicial review of administrative action in Germany is founded on the protection of individual rights and that the requirements for standing aim to exclude plaintiffs acting in the public and/or environmental interest. He highlights how the grounds and scope of review in Germany are governed by the protective law theory and that environmental laws that protect the public against unacceptable risks of pollution are in principle protective laws. He indicates that although there is a certain tendency towards broadening standing requirements in Germany, access of affected third parties (as opposed to addressees of administrative decisions) to the courts in environmental matters remains limited. The adoption of a rights-oriented concept of standing in Germany has also had the result of precluding access to an array of administrative law remedies by public interest organizations. The author discusses how the traditional paradigm of judicial review of administrative action is constituted by particularized conflicts between the State and an isolated and abstract individual. This paradigm, he argues, has several shortcomings in the environmental field. First, the systematic distinction between the addressee of an administrative decision and third parties amounts to a discrimination of the latter's role in environmental conflicts. Secondly, the collective nature of environmental conflicts (or diffuse interests) is systematically ignored. Thirdly, the interest of parties in controlling the proper functioning of the executive in environmental matters or exercising democratic participation rights effectively falls outside the scope of judicial review. Rehbinder nonetheless points out that the German rights-based approach is, however, less monolithic than it may appear as the interests of individuals, whose rights are fairly comprehensive, may, and does in practice, bring to the fore environmental issues which third parties are precluded from bringing to court in the public interest. It furthermore, at least indirectly, also serves to control the proper functioning of the administration in environmental matters and thereby contributes to promoting the public interest. Based on a broader understanding of the division of powers between the judiciary and the executive, German administrative courts have also succeeded in addressing orders to the administration and to a certain extent substitute their opinion for that of the administration. Rehbinder also highlights the key role the German courts play in clarifying and interpreting broad statutory terms inherent in environmental laws, and developing these laws where appropriate. The latter role is particularly served by the German courts in acting as a first filter for controlling the national implementation of European Union environmental directives. He indicates that although the German judiciary originally took a rather reserved position towards European Union environmental law, in the recent past, it has developed a more open stance. The author concludes that Germany has a well-functioning and powerful judiciary and that its principal shortcoming in the field of environmental protection lies in the rights-based concept of judicial review. He argues that this considerably reduces the problem-solving capacity of the judiciary. Rehbinder points out, however, that the recent trend inspired by European Union law towards opening the concept of subjective rights, including the recognition of procedural rights, should culminate in the reform of the German rights-based approach and ultimately open up the current restrictive standing requirements. Finally, he advocates the introduction of a direct review mechanism for all generic decisions (such as regulations and qualified administrative rules) and argues that these reforms will improve environmental governance by: better controlling the functioning of the administration; enforcing effective democratic participation in decision-making; and comprehensively protecting citizens' environmental rights.

Chapter 4:   United Kingdom

Morrow indicates that the judiciary in the United Kingdom is faced with an ever increasing caseload dealing with an expanding range and complexity of environmental issues. She highlights how the situation is further complicated by: the overlapping domestic, regional and international environmental regimes at play in the United Kingdom; and the complex division of labor within the United Kingdom on environmental governance between the constituent parts of the Kingdom, national and local government, and between environmental policy makers and administrators. Morrow states that as a result of the above, environmental law and governance has never been more complex in the United Kingdom and that all branches of government, including the judiciary, are under constant and intense public scrutiny. Morrow further states that the nineteenth century saw an activist and innovative judiciary pushing the boundaries of the common law to tackle environmental problems, though ultimately their scale and prevalence necessitated government intervention. She is of the view, however, that recent cases demonstrate an apparent reluctance on the part of the judiciary at the highest level to fully pursue the potential of the common law as a tool of environmental protection, and are indicative of judicial over-deference to statute law where the environment is concerned. The author finds that in other areas, notably those which involve the interpretation of environmental legislation, the story is a rather different one. In the context of judicial review and human rights cases, Morrow is of the view that the British judiciary appears willing to adopt open-minded and innovative means to explore new avenues to address environmental issues. She discusses several key cases to illustrate how judicial creativity has flourished in these areas. Morrow furthermore reflects on how remarkable this development has been given the profound pressures being exerted on the judiciary through a broad constitutional reform project currently being undertaken by the government. Morrow concludes that there is further potential for developing the role of the judiciary in environmental governance in the

United Kingdom, if the ongoing and wide-ranging debate on the creation of specialist environmental courts or tribunals ultimately comes to fruition.

Chapter 5: United States of America

Robinson points out that since the 1960s, federal and State judicial branches of government in the United States of America continue to affect the implementation of environmental law. He highlights how early federal decisions, in particular those cases enforcing the environmental impact assessment procedures prescribed by the *National Environmental Policy Act* of 1969, provided the foundation for the congressional enactment of the several statutes that authorize citizens to bring suits to enforce environmental laws. Robinson indicates that the role of the judiciary in criminal enforcement of environmental law is strong and that decisions by leading State supreme courts (such as those in California, Minnesota and New York) have provided sound judicial guidance on the interpretation and application of domestic environmental law. The author is of the view, however, that since the 1980s, most federal appellate decisions are not as insightful. Many of the rulings in cases brought by applicants with industrial interests appear to retard the implementation of environmental statutes by aggressively critiquing administrative agency implementation and remanding matters back to the agencies for reconsideration. Robinson argues that the lack of any federal constitutional right to the environment retards federal judicial decision-making and that the Supreme Court guidance regarding federal constitutional protection of private property has curbed federal judicial recognition of public rights to the environment. He suggests that while the United States of America needs to enact an environmental constitutional amendment, this is an unlikely prospect at present. He juxtaposes the federal approach to that of many States which have enacted environmental rights within their respective constitutions. Using New York as an example, he argues that it has ensured strong judicial protection of wilderness areas in the State. Moreover, he refers to procedural innovations enacted by various States, such as shifting burdens of proof to provide a legal foundation for a judicially enforceable 'land ethic', as proposed by the ecologist Aldo Leopold. Robinson recommends that such salutary procedural reforms are needed in all States, also with a view to strengthening judicial review of federal environmental statutory norms, and that laws that provide for 'technology forcing' would similarly afford the courts a role in ensuring that environmental remedial ends are attained.

Chapter 6: Canada

Benidickson and McLeod-Kilmurray trace the evolution of judicial contributions to environmental protection in Canada, from the early days of the federation to the current challenges faced by judges and the innovative approaches they have forged to deal with them. The authors outline the advantages and disadvantages of using litigation as a tool for resolving environmental dilemmas. They emphasize that judicial contributions include both the practical impact courts have on the law, as well as their more intangible role in expressing deep-rooted and evolving societal attitudes toward the environment and the kind of environmental governance Canadians aspire towards. Benidickson and McLeod-Kilmurray also briefly highlight sometimes overlooked judicial contributions, such as by leading royal commissions and public inquiries into significant environmental problems. Proceeding with a discussion of some remarkable early decisions based on common law principles such as riparian rights, the authors highlight the leading Supreme Court of Canada decisions on environmental law. These decisions span several areas of law including the common law, administrative law, criminal law and international law. This overview of significant decisions leads the authors to a critical thematic survey of the contribution of the Canadian judiciary to environmental governance. These themes include judicial elucidation of fundamental environmental values; tackling the problem of federalism and the environment; strengthening environmental legislation through judicial interpretation; judicially-created procedural innovations to facilitate environmental litigation; attempts to reconcile environmental and aboriginal rights; creative approaches to environmental sentencing; and missed opportunities such as the resistance to expanding the field of toxic torts. Benidickson and Mcleod-Kilmurray conclude that the Canadian judiciary has been an influential force in environmental governance. They argue that it has seized its role as a powerful, independent and well-respected public institution and has had a significant impact in interpreting, enforcing and adding strength and effectiveness to environmental law in Canada. The authors point out, however, that the judiciary continues to struggle with reconciling environmental and aboriginal rights. Also, despite aggressive and creative enforcement of common law principles in defense of the environment, the courts more recently have shown significant deference to government action and a reluctance to allow the expansion of private law causes of action as effective tools in environmental governance. The authors predict that future challenges for the judiciary will include finding their appropriate place amid new tools such as voluntary measures, economic approaches and other alternatives to traditional litigation; and adapting to the increasing influence of international law on domestic environmental governance. They are of the opinion, however, that the history of commitment, innovation and a central role for the judiciary in the effort to achieve justice and sustainability is likely to continue, and this judicial commitment will allow Canadian courts to continue to make important contributions as a central, independent and powerful institution of environmental governance.

Chapter 7:   Brazil

Sarlet and Fensterseifer approach their inquiry into the role of the Brazilian judiciary in environmental governance from a purely rights-based perspective. They demonstrate that environmental and other socio-economic rights play an overriding role in environmental governance and protection in Brazil. Their chapter analyses the adjudicatory role of the judiciary (specifically the Supreme Court), in contributing to a better understanding of the State's environmental protection duties in relation to the fundamental right to a healthy environment. They argue that the Brazilian courts, generally speaking, have expanded their adjudicatory role in terms of applying and interpreting, in a more protective way, environmental laws as well as constitutional provisions relating to environmental protection. Drawing on an analysis of various judgments considering constitutional provisions of relevance to environmental protection, the authors conclude that judicial intervention, whilst including control and oversight of private parties' conduct, primarily concerns the control of the executive and the legislative branches of government where their actions or omissions violate the fundamental right to a healthy environment. They also demonstrate that within these judgments there is a fine interplay between property rights and environmental protection, socio-economic rights and the environmental right, and the intrinsic value of environmental objects (such as animals) and environmental protection.

Chapter 8:   Argentina

Carballo illustrates how the judiciary has played, and continues to play, an important role in further developing and promoting environmental governance in Argentina. He argues that the inferior courts, and more specifically the Supreme Court, have contributed significantly over the years to entrench environmental protection in Argentina's legal system and to mold approaches to environmental governance. The author provides examples of the courts willingness to: force government agencies to heed their environmental protection duties even in the absence of statutorily prescribed duties; show support for the protection of cultural and environmental rights of indigenous communities; allow parties without a direct interest in an environmental matter to approach a court for redress; not strictly abide by formal and traditional court procedures and rules where environmental problems require innovative and tailor-made solutions and methods of conflict resolution; support the establishment of extra-judicial and non-governmental institutions to promote environmental protection; accept that in some highly technical environmental cases they do not have the necessary expertise and therefore require specialist advice and opinions from experts to make informed decisions; and broaden public participation in judicial processes. Carballo further reflects on the increasing tendency of the courts to step outside their traditional domain and intervene in matters of environmental policy (primarily the task of the executive branch of government) especially where these policies are incomplete, inadequate or not enforced. The author concludes by highlighting key challenges facing the judiciary such as: its tendency to dispose of matters on procedural grounds rather than dealing with substantive issues; the need to improve its understanding and integration of social and cultural issues when dealing with environmental disputes; how to correctly manage non-legal knowledge and technical information of relevance to judicial decisions; and where to draw the line between judicial activism and an undue undermining of the separation of powers doctrine.

Chapter 9:   Paraguay

According to Abed, one of the most visible characteristics of environmental governance in Paraguay is the central role played by criminal law. She indicates that the judiciary has played a key role in this regard but that the exaggerated reliance placed on criminal law has resulted in no civil law environmental disputes being brought to court to date. In the author's view, this has hampered the development and application of civil measures that could improve the overall environmental governance effort in Paraguay. Moreover, she argues that it has resulted in the judiciary being more interested in the imposition of criminal sanctions than the application of civil mechanisms to stop the damage-causing event and/or to impose liability on the offender to rehabilitate the damaged environment. Abed confirms that administrative law also plays an important part in environmental governance, especially as regards environmental impact assessment, and that the courts have been called upon to resolve disputes relating to due compliance with public participation requirements and the scope of decision-makers mandates. She concludes, however, that the current extensive role played by environmental criminal law needs to be matched with increased activism, by both citizens and the courts, in the field of administrative and civil law. Abed further analyses two important aspects which she considers to constitute the backbone of the development of Paraguayan environmental law, namely: the environmental right and access to environmental justice by means of the *actio popularis*. She illustrates that Paraguayan courts are increasingly willing to fuse these two aspects in mutual support of one another with the aim of providing broader access to justice and increased recognition and protection of environmental rights. Despite these positive developments, the author concludes that the Paraguayan judiciary has done relatively little to reform vigorously environmental governance. In her view, many judges remain traditional in their approach and somewhat reluctant to intervene in efforts to promote environmental governance in Paraguay. Abed concludes that the need to improve the role of the Paraguayan judiciary in environmental governance is closely related to the broader imperative of building and ensuring good democratic governance in the country. Both necessarily imply broad-based participation and citizen control over governmental structures and processes, as well as an emphasis on the training of governmental officers, including judges.

Chapter 10:   Australia

Pearson reflects on the diverse array of Australian federal and State courts, including specialist environmental courts in certain States, in which environmental disputes fall to be determined. Thereafter, she highlights a diverse array of instances in which these courts have contributed to the overall environmental governance effort in Australia. First, she discusses the key role the judiciary has played in delineating the division of responsibility for environmental legislation and implementation, in many instances through challenges in the High Court to the constitutional validity of Commonwealth or State legislation. Secondly, she considers the contribution of the judiciary in interpreting environmental legislation and through providing a check on administrative action and decision-making. She illustrates the trend prevalent since the early 1990s, for Australian environmental legislation to include reference to the principles of ecologically sustainable development, and the manner in which the courts and tribunals have sought to analyze these principles and enforce legislative directions to factor these principles into the decision-making process. She argues that despite the judiciary generally adopting a generous interpretation to statutory and common law standing requirements, the costs and risks associated with environmental litigation continue to pose a constraint to would be litigants. Regarding specific challenges facing the judiciary, Pearson highlights the somewhat limited availability of suitable legal remedies available to the courts to address environmental matters brought before them. Pearson concludes that the developing jurisprudence of the specialist environmental courts and tribunals plays a significant role, both in providing a model for good decision-making in merits review, and in setting the boundaries and expectations for decision-makers in judicial review.

Chapter 11:   New Zealand

Over the past twenty years, New Zealand has undergone dramatic legislative reform with regard to its environmental and resource management laws. According to Bosselmann, this legislative reform was directly informed by the 1987 Brundtland Report, which has meant that New Zealand's new environmental and natural resource regime is underpinned by the concept of sustainable development, albeit in its more narrow form, 'sustainable management'. He argues that the concept of sustainable management effectively sets ecological limits to the use and development of New Zealand's natural and physical resources. As part of the reform, the office of the Parliamentary Commissioner for the Environment was established to act as an environmental watchdog. Furthermore, a special Environment Court with jurisdiction over all environmental cases was established to enhance the expertise of judges (assisted by environmental commissioners). The New Zealand system of environmental governance is widely regarded as the world's most advanced. Accordingly to Bosselmann, this may be true with respect to the aspirations underpinning the system, but not with respect to the system's actual performance. He is of the opinion that as in many Western countries, New Zealand's government, administration and judiciary have been reluctant to move beyond traditional resource management and accordingly concludes that the promise of sustainability remains unfulfilled.

Chapter 12:   Pakistan

Hassan and Hassan illustrate how Pakistan's courts have interpreted and implemented the country's various laws, rules and regulations aimed at facilitating improved environmental governance. They describe how specific Environmental Tribunals have been established in Pakistan, with exclusive jurisdiction to try serious environmental offences and to hear appeals in this respect, to complement the role played by the Supreme Court and Provincial High Courts. These tribunals were notably established following a direction by the Supreme Court. The foregoing judicial institutions are further aided by District and Session Courts, Environment Magistrates, and *quasi*-judicial forums. Through an analysis of relevant environmental jurisprudence, the authors highlight how the Pakistani courts have contributed to environmental governance by: affording a wide interpretation to constitutional provisions thereby extending their application to the environmental context (in the absence of an explicit environmental right); recognizing the importance of international environmental law principles and instruments (despite the fact that some of these instruments do not formally form part of Pakistani law); relaxing and in some instances even removing procedural constraints to allow and expand public interest litigation; taking *suo motu* action to rectify environmental wrongs; formulating and imposing innovative measures to address pollution; appointing special judicial commissions to resolve complex environmental issues; and using their jurisdiction to protect the poor and marginalized communities from the adverse effects of environmental degradation. The authors conclude that despite these positive developments, various challenges remain, including: a lack of judicial capacity and resources; inadequate enforcement; the prevailing idea that economic growth imperatives outweigh ecological imperatives; and lack of political will to promote the environmental agenda.

Chapter 13:   People's Republic of China

The People's Republic of China, one of the fastest-developing economies in the world, is subject to unprecedented environmental degradation. The Chinese judiciary accordingly has a particularly important potential role to play in stemming the demise of the nation's landscapes and natural resources. According to Qun Du, the judiciary, following a protracted period of judicial reform, currently enjoys a relative degree of freedom and independence and is frequently called upon to adjudicate environmental matters. The author considers the recent record of the Chinese judiciary in adjudicating environmental civil matters (with specific emphasis on pollution torts), administrative review cases and criminal cases concerning environmental pollution control and natural resource protection. She concludes that the judiciary is currently a vital agent in guiding the implementation of environmental laws, enforcing these laws and promoting the active participation of civil society in environmental governance. Qun Du does, however, acknowledge that there is room for improvement, specifically a need for the judiciary to expand the protective jurisdiction in civil law matters, perform a more activist role when adjudicating administrative actions of government, and improve the review and enforcement of environmental impact assessment laws. The author also highlights the need to sensitize judges on environmental issues, create more specialized tribunals exclusively dedicated to resolving environmental disputes, and curb government meddling in the work of the courts.

Chapter 14:   Kenya

Kameri-Mbote highlights the prevalence of both formal and informal mechanisms for resolving disputes, including environmental disputes, in Kenya. Regarding the formal judiciary, she states that it has been traditionally conservative in its approach to allowing persons to bring environmental matters to court, insisting on a narrow construction of *locus standi*. However, the author illustrates how, through statutory and institutional reforms undertaken in the course of the past decade, the role of the formal judiciary has grown with an increasing number of environmental cases being adjudicated by Kenyan courts. She further indicates how the above has been reinforced and supported by non-judicial, informal and non-traditional mechanisms and institutions for environmental dispute resolution, such as community organizations. The author analyses recent jurisprudence and is of the view that there is a progressive jurisprudence evolving from Kenyan courts on issues of *locus standi*, the right to a healthy environment, and suits against governmental agencies. She, however, opines that while the High Courts have been able to provide direction in implementing the framework and sectoral environmental laws, the lower courts, where most environmental cases are heard, still lack the requisite resources and expertise to adjudicate environmental matters. Kameri-Mbote concludes that while several capacity building programmes have been recently carried out for the benefit of both the judiciary and legal practitioners, these need to be expanded and complemented by aggressive public awareness campaigns and the promotion of traditional dispute resolution institutions as key role players in environmental governance.

Chapter 15:   Uganda

In this chapter, Kasimbazi provides a synopsis of environmental issues in Uganda and notes that the country's wealth and diversity of natural resources is under significant threat from human activity. The author is of the view that the Ugandan judiciary currently plays a significant role in environmental governance by: developing, enhancing and interpreting environmental laws; giving effect to the principles, standards and rights contained therein; protecting public environmental interests; and supporting the governance efforts of Uganda's environmental authorities. In coming to this conclusion, Kasimbazi considers a diverse array of court decisions dealing with: the application of common law principles and remedies; *locus standi*; environmental impact assessment; the application of the public trust doctrine and the precautionary principle; access to information; and the grant of appropriate remedies. The author notes, however, that the Ugandan judiciary's current and future positive contribution to environmental governance is somewhat undermined by: its over-reliance on technicalities; limited judicial activism; the high costs of litigation; undue political interference; inadequate financial resources; poor case flow management; and the lack of specialized environmental knowledge. In order to overcome these challenges the author recommends that: first, the jurisdiction of the courts in respect of applications under the Constitution be extended to Magistrates' Courts to reduce the case backlog in the High Court; secondly, the judiciary be more flexible in its interpretation of the law in matters of public importance; thirdly, the government urgently increases its funding to the judiciary; and fourthly, in cases where it is clear to the court that the applicant is acting *bona fide* out of an interest for the environment, the judiciary exercises its discretion and relieves the applicant from having to file a bond of security and pay statutorily prescribed court fees. Kasimbazi concludes by emphasizing the importance of judicial independence and observes in this respect that even if the foregoing reforms are implemented, a failure by the executive to consistently support and respect the decisions of the judiciary will not only undermine democracy in Uganda, but also the key role of the courts in environmental governance.

Chapter 16:   Tanzania

Mainland Tanzania enacted its first framework environmental management legislation in 2004 and owing to its relative novelty, this new legal framework is yet to be applied or tested by the Tanzanian judiciary. Kabudi notes, however, that this is not indicative of a failure by the Tanzanian judiciary to recognize its key role in environmental governance. He illustrates how, owing to the absence of an express environmental right in the Constitution of the United Republic of Tanzania, the Tanzanian judiciary has been compelled to creatively infer such a right through other entrenched constitutional rights, specifically the right to life. As regards *locus standi*, he discusses the liberal approach of the courts to standing, especially in cases dealing with the application and interpretation of constitutional rights, such as the right to life and its extension to include the right to live in a clean, safe and healthy environment. He illustrates how the judiciary has been prepared to dispense with the orthodox common law rules on standing, particularly in the context of constitutional litigation; affirm the value of public interest environmental litigation; apply the orders of *certiorari*, *mandamus* and prohibition in environmental cases; and creatively use comparative jurisprudence to circumvent domestic statutory deficiencies. Kabudi is accordingly of the view that the Tanzanian judiciary is neither ill-equipped nor ill-adapted to hear and determine environmental disputes. The author argues that if anything, the judiciary has shown it can be relied upon to ply its role with remarkable intellectual vigor and erudition, and with deep social conscientiousness and commitment to wider issues of social justice. The author concludes by suggesting an array of reforms for improving the current role of the Tanzanian judiciary in environmental governance, notably: building capacity in the judiciary; sensitizing judges on matters of environmental law;

raising public awareness on environmental issues; and encouraging public interest environmental litigation.

Chapter 17: Nigeria

Ladan demonstrates that Nigeria's formal environmental law regime has developed significantly in the past decade. He emphasizes that facilitating access to justice and the prudent application of legal remedies are key issues through which the judiciary can play an important role in improving environmental governance. Ladan examines the role the Nigerian courts have played in this respect by reflecting on recent jurisprudence delineated according to various themes including: procedural and jurisdictional issues; *locus standi* and representative actions; human rights and the environment, pre-action notices and statutory limitations; prescription in civil claims; the application of torts; and burden of proof and special damage claims. Through this analysis, the author illustrates that: the courts require strict adherence to procedural rules in environmental matters; current rules on *locus standi* are not conducive to promoting efficient public interest environmental litigation; the courts are increasingly willing to recognize the importance of environmental rights; the courts are prepared to apply torts in the environmental context; and the courts are fairly flexible regarding representative actions and pre-action notice procedures in environmental matters. The author concludes with various recommendations on ways to improve the role of the Nigerian judiciary in environmental governance.

Chapter 18: South Africa

Kotzé and Paterson argue that South Africa currently has a comprehensive environmental governance framework underpinned by an extensive array of environmental laws. As in most countries, however, the interpretation, application and enforcement of these laws remain a challenge. They indicate that this challenge is compounded in South Africa by the need to balance competing socio-economic needs with pressing environmental imperatives, and that it is mainly up to the three branches of the South African government (namely the executive, legislature and the judiciary) to address these challenges. The focus of their chapter is on the judiciary and the manner in which it has contributed to this process. Owing to the absence of a specialized environmental court, they highlight how it has accordingly been left to the general courts to fashion their role in environmental governance. Judging from the environmental jurisprudence which has emerged during the course of the past twelve years following the country's transition to a constitutional democracy, the authors find that the judiciary is increasingly asserting itself in the realm of environmental governance through: interpreting environmental legislation; pronouncing on the validity of relevant executive and legislative action; resolving civil environmental disputes between citizens, and/ or citizens and the State; and sanctioning non-compliance with environmental legislation. Kotzé and Paterson conclude that the South African judiciary is clearly playing a significant role in environmental governance. It has demonstrated a clear willingness to grapple with the elements of, and challenges posed by, South Africa's fledging environmental regime by seeking to: give content to the environmental right; define the mandate of environmental authorities; facilitate administrative justice; promote access to environmental information; extend *locus standi* in environmental matters; interpret anomalies in environmental legislation; link land reform and environmental matters; facilitate criminal enforcement; and apply and develop common law remedies to resolve environmental disputes. Despite these positive developments, the authors are of the view that the judiciary's performance relating to environmental governance in South Africa remains 'chequered' and they suggest a number of reforms necessary to improve its role in environmental governance.

Chapter 19:   Eritrea

Habtezion discusses Eritrea's fledgling judiciary and its role in environmental governance, with a specific focus on recent jurisprudence relating to the country's forestry and wildlife sectors. The author discusses the relevant laws, policies, institutions and governance structures of direct and indirect relevance to the environment, and provides a historical overview of the Eritrean judiciary, elaborating on its evolution, status and current structure. Habtezion focuses his analysis on the fundamental challenges currently undermining the role of the judiciary in environmental governance, specifically emphasizing legislative gaps, jurisdictional issues, structural constraints, judicial capacity constraints, and the lack of public awareness and political will. The author concludes that Eritrea is the youngest state in Africa and it is still struggling to assert itself within the African and international arena after a period of prolonged armed conflict. As a result, the Eritrean judiciary is also in its infancy. He argues that the court decisions relating to forestry and wildlife resources provide testimony to the fact that the structure and jurisdiction of the judiciary is constantly evolving to reflect Eritrea's economic and political transition. Ongoing evolution provides opportunities for change and in the Eritrean context, numerous opportunities and prerequisites exist for improving the role of the judiciary in environmental governance. By way of summary, these include: soliciting political will; prescribing a comprehensive environmental law regime; facilitating capacity building and training for the judiciary and prosecution authorities; providing the judiciary and prosecution authorities with requisite resources; and improving civil society participation. Habtezion highlights that the biggest toll on Eritrea's environment is arguably attributable to the military's ongoing activities. He indicates that this is worrying given the limited jurisdiction of the High Court and regional courts to pronounce on these activities, and the reticence of the military courts to sanction their own personnel. The author suggests that resolving these jurisdictional gaps appears to be a final key prerequisite for establishing the Eritrean judiciary as a force in the country's environmental governance effort.

We trust the insights presented in this collection of national experiences will contribute to a better understanding of the environmental law and judicial systems of various countries, a better understanding of the connection between environmental governance and the judiciary, and ultimately, an increased awareness of the manner in which sustainable environmental governance may be achieved by way of judicial intervention.

The Editors
Louis J. Kotzé
Alexander Paterson

Foreword

In the context of growing environmental degradation, the need to create effective environmental governance structures is receiving increased international, regional and national attention from governments, courts, practitioners, academics, civil society and the private sector. In most countries, 'governance', in its broadest sense and from the public sector perspective, is usually executed by the legislative (law-makers), executive (parliament/cabinet) and judicial authorities (courts). This also applies to environmental governance which is one of the many components of the broader science of 'governance'. Environmental governance is a concept which encompasses a number of elements, institutions, processes and mechanisms and is yet to be precisely defined. What is clear is that domestic courts are playing an increasingly important role in environmental governance.

This publication *The Role of the Judiciary in Environmental Governance: Comparative Perspectives* which I have the pleasure to present, has as its primary objective to survey current trends in the development of environmental governance, focusing specifically on the role played by the judiciary in developing environmental law in various countries around the world. However, developing environmental law is an oversimplification, since courts, through a much more complex process of adjudication and judicial intervention also interpret, apply and enforce laws, including environmental laws. It is specifically by executing these latter functions in the context of environmental law that the judiciary may contribute to the development of effective and sustainable environmental governance practices and precedents.

This publication is unique because it investigates the broader concept of environmental governance and the role that the judiciary plays in this process. It specifically focuses on the judiciary as an important component of developing environmental law in the broader quest for sustainability. In addition, it investigates court structures and adjudication processes in the environmental law context in various countries, representing different regions, legal systems, and legal cultures around the world. In doing so, this book distils comparative trends, new developments, and best practices in adjudication endeavors; highlights the benefits and shortcomings of the various approaches followed by courts in the selected countries; and thus contributes to a better understanding of the manner in which sustainable environmental governance may be achieved by way of judicial intervention.

Written by a broad array of leading academics and practitioners, the book provides a broad overview of relevant content together with critical commentary, and thus serves its primary objective to survey current trends on the role of the judiciary in environmental governance across various jurisdictions based on a comparative law methodology.

I have no doubt that this publication will be an invaluable tool for judges, decision makers, environmental law scholars and private sector actors from around the world to further advance their knowledge of environmental law and governance development, reform, and implementation at the national, regional and international levels.

Dr. Alejandro Iza
Head, IUCN Environmental Law Programme
Director, IUCN Environmental Law Centre (Bonn, Germany)
November 2008

Acknowledgements

The editors wish to extend their sincere thanks to the following individuals and institutions for their valuable assistance and contribution to this publication:

- Dr. Tanya du Plessis (University of Johannesburg, South Africa), for her impeccable editorial assistance and tireless efforts in preparing the final typeset manuscript. Her exceptional professionalism, attention to detail and uncompromised ethics bear testimony to her diligent efforts and high standard of work.

- Prof. Kurt Deketelaere (Flemish Ministry of the Environment and professor, University of Leuven, Belgium), for his valuable insights and guidance during the initial planning phase, and for his continued support of the publication.

- Our publishing team at Kluwer Law International (Netherlands), specifically: Karel van der Linde, Publishing Manager; Vincent Verschoor, Developmental Editor; and Hanneke Verbeek, Publishing Assistant; for their encouragement and professional assistance throughout the publishing process.

- The Faculties of Law, University of Cape Town and North West University, South Africa, for their encouragement and financial contribution towards the publication and for having supported the editors throughout this project.

- Prof. Alan Brimer, professor emeritus, and former Head of the English Department at the University of Durban-Westville, South Africa, for his assistance in language editing.

- Our families and friends for their unwavering understanding and support.

- Ultimately, our contributing authors who have managed to set aside time in their demanding schedules to contribute to this publication and without whom this book never would have materialized.

Author Biographies

Sheila Abed

Sheila Abed is the current chair of the Commission on Environmental Law of the World Conservation Union (IUCN). She is the founder and Executive Director of IDEA (*Instituto de Derecho y Economía Ambiental*), a non-governmental organization operating in Asuncion (Paraguay) and Montevideo (Uruguay). She is professor of law at the Asuncion Catholic University and a guest professor at several international universities. She has represented the Paraguayan government in the negotiation of multilateral environmental agreements. Her research focuses primarily on trade and the environment, and environmental governance. Sheila is co-author of various publications and her work has been recognized at the national and international level through numerous awards.

Jamie Benidickson

Jamie Benidickson teaches environmental law, water law and legal history at the Faculty of Law, University of Ottawa, Canada, where he is a member of the Environmental Law Group. He is a former co-director of the IUCN Academy of Environmental Law and has served as an expert and advisor with a number of Canadian royal commissions and public inquiries, including the Walkerton Inquiry on drinking water security in Ontario. His publications include *Environmental Law* (Irwin Law, 2008); *The Culture of Flushing: A Social and Legal History of Sewage* (UBC, 2007); *Idleness, Water and A Canoe: Reflections on Paddling for Pleasure* (University of Toronto, 1997); and *The Temagami Experience: Recreation, Resources and Aboriginal Rights in the Northern Ontario Wilderness* (University of Toronto, 1989).

Klaus Bosselmann

Klaus Bosselmann is professor of law and Founding Director of the New Zealand Centre for Environmental Law at the University of Auckland. He previously taught at the Freie Universität in Berlin and in 1987 co-founded Germany's first Institute for Environmental Law in Bremen. He is a member of the IUCN Commission on Environmental Law, currently chairing its Ethics Specialist Group; a member of the IUCN Academy of Environmental Law; and co-chair of the Global Ecological Integrity Group. He has published fifteen books and eighty book chapters and journal articles. His latest books are *Reconciling Human Existence and Ecological Integrity: Science, Ethics, Economics and Law* (co-edited with L. Westra and R. Westra, Earthscan, 2008) and *The Principle of Sustainability: Transforming Law and Governance* (Ashgate, 2008).

Juan Carballo

Juan Carballo is currently a lecturer in the Department of Natural Resources and Environmental Law at the National University of Córdoba, Argentina. He is a Fulbright Fellow and studied at Delaware University in the United States of America. He has participated in numerous academic *fora* in Argentina, Uruguay and the United States of America. He has also worked for various non-governmental organizations and has been legal advisor to the Environment and Sustainable Development Secretary of Córdoba City. He is presently the coordinator of the Global Governance Program at the Center for Human Rights and Environment, Córdoba, Argentina. He is also a member of the Environmental Law Alliance Worldwide.

Qun Du

Qun Du is professor of law in the Faculty of Law at Wuhan University, People's Republic of China. She is also the deputy director of the Institute of Environmental Law located within this institution. Her research focuses on Chinese environmental law, natural resource policy and law, energy law, and general international environmental law. She has published various papers and a number of books on these issues. She is a board member of the Environmental and Resource Law Association of the China Law Society, a member of the IUCN Commission on Environmental Law, and co-chair of the IUCN Commission on Environmental Law Specialist Group on Sustainable Use of Soil. She is also a member of the IUCN Academy of Environmental Law.

Tiago Fensterseifer

Tiago Fensterseifer is a public defender in the State of São Paulo, Brazil. His research focuses on social, economic, cultural and environmental rights and questions related to human dignity and access to justice. He has extensively published on these issues, and his most recent publication is *Direitos fundamentais e proteção do ambiente: a dimensão ecológica da dignidade humana* [Fundamental Rights and Environmental Protection: the Ecological Dimension of Human Dignity] (Porto Alegre: Livraria do Advogado, 2008).

Zerisenay Habtezion

Zerisenay Habtezion is a senior lecturer at the Faculty of Law, University of Asmara, Eritrea, where he teaches environmental law and intellectual property law. He is the secretary of the Academic Commission of the Faculty of Law. His research interests include biosafety, biotechnology and intellectual property law. He has published and acted as consultant to national and international organizations on these issues. He has drafted numerous laws for the Eritrean government related to forestry, wildlife, biosafety, water, integrated coastal area management, and pesticides. He is a member of the Natural Resources and Environment Research Centre (Environment and Water Resources Research Team), and the Association of African Environmental Law Lecturers from African Universities.

Jawad Hassan

Jawad Hassan is a partner at Hassan & Hassan (Advocates) in Lahore, Pakistan. He holds an M.A. (Economics) and LLB from Punjab University, and an LLM from Pace University, United States of America. Jawad has authored a book on Pakistan environmental law as well as various publications in national and international law journals. He teaches environmental law at various institutions in Pakistan. He is the secretary of the Pakistan Environment Law Association.

Parvez Hassan

Parvez Hassan is the senior partner at Hassan & Hassan (Advocates) in Lahore, Pakistan. His legal education includes an LLB from Punjab University, an LLM from Yale Law School and an SJD from Harvard Law School. He has had extended associations with various institutions including the IUCN (also as the Chair of its Commission on Environmental Law), 1990-1996; LEAD International and LEAD Pakistan (Chair, 1995-2001); World Wildlife Fund for Nature Pakistan; and the Asia-Pacific Forum for Environment and Development. He is the president of the Pakistan Environmental Law Association.

Palamagamba John Kabudi

Palamagamba John Kabudi is an associate professor of law at the University of Dar es Salaam, Tanzania, where he is the current Head of the Department of International Law. His research focus areas include environmental law and intellectual property law. He is a consultant in the Vice-president's Office and other ministries in Tanzania on areas of environmental and natural resource management and was responsible for drafting many of Tanzania's environmental laws including: the *Environmental Management Act, Cap.* 191, 2004; the *Environmental Impact Assessment and Audit Regulations*, 2005; and the *Strategic Environmental Assessment Regulations*, 2008. He also serves as the vice-chair of the Board of Legal and Human Rights Centre, Tanzania and is a member of the Board of Trustees of ACODE, Uganda.

Patricia Kameri-Mbote

Patricia Kameri-Mbote is an associate professor of law at the University of Nairobi, Kenya. She studied law in Nairobi (LLB), Warwick (LLM in Law and Development), Zimbabwe (post-graduate diploma in women's law) and Stanford (JSM and JSD with environmental law specialization). She is an advocate of the High Court of Kenya; director and founder of the International Environmental Law Research Centre; member of the Kenya National Academy of Sciences, the IUCN Academy of Environmental Law, and the IUCN Commission on Environmental Law (CEL). She is also chair of the Kenya Seeds and Plant Varieties Tribunal. Patricia has published widely on environmental law, women's rights and property rights. Her publications and co-editorial works include: *Environmental Governance in Kenya: Implementing the Framework Law* (East African Educational Publishers, 2008); *Globalisation and Environmental Challenges: Reconceptualising Security in the 21st Century* (Springer-Verlag, 2007); *Land Use for Sustainable Development* (Cambridge University Press, 2007); and *Property Rights and Biodiversity Management in Kenya* (ASTS Press, 2002).

Emmanuel Kasimbazi

Emmanuel Kasimbazi is an advocate, a legal consultant, researcher and a senior lecturer at the Faculty of Law, Makerere University, Uganda. He teaches environmental law at pre-and post-graduate level. He has authored the *Environmental Law and Energy Law Monographs for Uganda* published by Kluwer Law International. He is a member of the IUCN Commission on Environmental law and the IUCN Academy of Environmental Law. He has published extensively in areas of international law, environmental law, water law, energy law and forestry law. He has also consulted to various international and national organizations including: the World Bank, the African Development Bank, the United Nations Environment Programme, the United Nations Office for Project Services, the Nile Basin Initiative, the European Union, the United Nations Development Programme, the Food and Agricultural Organisation, Germany Technical Cooperation, the United States Agency for International Development, the Norwegian Agency for Development Cooperation (NORAD), and the Danish International Development Agency (DANIDA).

Louis Kotzé

Louis Kotzé is professor of law at the Faculty of Law, North West University, South Africa. He teaches environmental law at pre- and post-graduate level. He is the co-coordinator of the LLM in Environmental Law and Governance at the Faculty of Law. His research focuses on European, international and domestic environmental law, and more specifically environmental governance, constitutionalism and the environment, and comparative environmental law. He has published extensively on these issues, and has co-authored and co-edited various national and international environmental law textbooks. He also serves on the executive editorial boards of several international and national environmental law journals. He is a member of the IUCN Academy of Environmental Law, the IUCN Commission on Environmental Law and its Specialist Group on Environmental Governance, the Global Ecological Integrity Group, the International Network for Environmental Compliance and Enforcement, the Executive Council of the Association of Environmental Law Lecturers from African Universities, and the South African Environmental Law Association.

Muhammed Ladan

Muhammed Ladan is professor of law at the Department of Public Law, Faculty of Law, Ahmadu Bello University, Nigeria. He specializes in the areas of human rights and the administration of criminal justice; comparative jurisprudence; humanitarian, gender and development law; environmental law; and security law. Muhammed is a member of the World Jurist Association (United States of America); IUCN Academy of Environmental Law; Association of Environmental Law Lecturers from African Universities, and the Nigerian Society of International Law. He is also a Hubert Humphrey Fellow in the United States of America and visiting professor at the Faculty of Law, Usman Dan Fodio University, Sokoto. Muhammed has authored various books as well as publications in scientific journals focusing, among others, on: migration, trafficking, human rights and refugees, humanitarian law, environmental law, reproductive health rights, maternal mortality, HIV/AIDS, election violence, women and children's rights, and human rights law and practice.

Luc Lavrysen

Luc Lavrysen is a judge in the Belgian Constitutional Court and part-time professor teaching European and national environmental law at Ghent University, Belgium. He is director of the Environmental Law Centre of the University, editor-in-chief of the *Tijdschrift voor Milieurecht* [Flemish Environmental Law Review], and scientific adviser to the Belgian Federal Council for Sustainable Development (a multi-stakeholder advisory body). He was a member of the Inter-University Commission for the Revision of Environmental Law in the Flemish Region. As a judge, he is involved in the United Nations Environment Programme Global Judges Project on Sustainable Development and the Role of Law, UNECE's training initiatives for judges on the Aarhus Convention, and the IUCN Commission on Environmental Law Judiciary Specialist Group. He is also a founding member and current president of the European Union Forum of Judges for the Environment. He has published various books and articles on environmental law in Dutch, French and English.

Heather McLeod-Kilmurray

Heather McLeod-Kilmurray holds an SJD from the University of Toronto, and an LLM first class from the University of Cambridge. She was law clerk to Chief Justice Isaac of the Federal Court of Appeal of Canada and practiced as legal counsel at Environment Canada, and as assistant solicitor at the Sheffield City Council in England. She is a member of the Environmental Law Group at the Faculty of Law, University of Ottawa, Canada, and is actively involved in the IUCN Academy of Environmental Law. Her research interests include environmental procedure, such as class actions and pre-trial injunctions; the role of environmental principles and ethics in judicial approaches to environmental problems; and particular environmental problems such as the legal regulation of genetically modified foods. She has published several papers on these issues. She teaches environmental law, torts, legal writing, administrative law and *fondements de la common law*.

Karen Morrow

Karen Morrow is professor of environmental law at the School of Law, Swansea University, United Kingdom. She has taught environmental law at under-graduate and post-graduate levels in law and non-law programs in a number of United Kingdom universities. She is the co-director of the Centre for Environmental and Energy Law and Policy in the School of Law. Her research interests include: the theory of environmental law, environmental governance, environmental torts and a range of aspects of domestic, European and international environmental law. She has published extensively on these issues. She serves on the editorial board of the *Environmental Law Review* and acts as deputy convener of the Environmental Law section of the Society of Legal Scholars. She is a member of the IUCN Academy of Environmental Law.

Alexander Paterson

Alexander Paterson is an admitted attorney of the High Court of South Africa. Having practiced law in South Africa for a number of years he joined the Institute of Marine and Environmental Law, Faculty of Law, University of Cape Town, where he currently convenes the environmental law programmes at the pre and post-graduate levels. His research interests include incentive-based regulation, biodiversity, and protected areas. He has published widely on these issues in international and local journals and books. Alexander serves on the board of various regional and national institutions such as the Executive Council of the Association of Environmental Law Lecturers from African Universities and the Environmental Law Association of South Africa. He is furthermore a member of the IUCN Academy of Environmental Law; IUCN Commission of Environmental Law, and the Joint Task Force on Protected Areas of the World Commission on Protected Areas.

Linda Pearson

Linda Pearson is senior lecturer in the Faculty of Law, University of New South Wales, Australia. She teaches environmental law and administrative law. She is also a judicial member of the Administrative Decisions Tribunal of New South Wales. Linda has researched and written on planning law, local government law, and administrative review. She is the Natural Resources Editor for *Australian Administrative Law*, and is a member of the Environmental Consultative Committee of the Legal Aid Commission of New South Wales, and the IUCN Commission on Environmental Law.

Eckard Rehbinder

Eckard Rehbinder is professor emeritus of economic law, environmental law and comparative law, and a member of the Research Centre for Environmental Law at the Law Faculty, Goethe-University Frankfurt am Main, Germany. His research focuses on general environmental law, the regulation of chemicals, and comparative environmental law. He has published extensively on these topics and a number of other environmental law issues, and has co-authored a textbook on German environmental law and various interdisciplinary studies. He also serves on the executive editorial board of a leading German journal on environmental policy and law. He was a member of the German Advisory Council on Environmental Policy. He is currently Regional Governor of the International Council of Environmental Law and a member of, among others, the IUCN Commission on Environmental Law and its Specialist Group on Forestry; the IUCN Academy of Environmental Law; and the European Council of Environmental Law.

Nicholas Robinson

Nicholas Robinson's scholarship draws on his experiences litigating environmental cases in State and federal courts in the United States of America, and collaborating with courts around the world. During his chairmanship of the

IUCN Commission on Environmental Law (1996-2004), he: lectured at the United Nations Environmental Programme's judicial symposia for the 2002 World Summit on Sustainable Development (Johannesburg), for South Asia (Colombo), and Southeast Asia (Manila); convened the UNEP/IUCN judicial symposia for West Europe (London) and Eurasia (L'viv); organized the Commission on Environmental Cooperation's judicial symposium for North America in 2004 (White Plains, New York); and lectured at the 2005 symposium (Mexico City). His leadership of the Asian Development Bank/IUCN seminars for law professors, *Capacity Building for Environmental Law in the Asian and Pacific Regions* (1996-1998), and his editing of the *traveaux préparatoire* for the 1992 Rio Earth Summit, Agenda 21 and the UNCED Proceedings (six volumes), afford him a unique inter-regional perspective on how courts shape environmental law. Founder of Pace University's environmental law specialization (www.law.pace.edu), he serves on the board of Pace's environmental litigation clinic. In 2008, he stepped down as the founding chair of the IUCN Academy of Environmental Law.

Ingo Sarlet

Ingo Sarlet is professor of law at the Faculty of Law, Pontifical Catholic University in Porto Alegre, Brazil. He teaches constitutional law and fundamental rights theory at pre- and post-graduate level. He is coordinator of the LLM and Doctoral Program in Public and Procedural Law and coordinator of the Research Center at the Faculty of Law and the Research Group on Fundamental Rights. His research focuses on social, economic, cultural and environmental rights and more specifically, issues related to human dignity and human rights. He has published extensively on these issues, and has co-authored, edited and co-edited various national and international books, chapters and articles in various national and international law journals. He also teaches in the LLM and Doctoral Program in Human Rights and Development at the University Pablo de Olavide, Seville, Spain, and has spent various periods as visiting scholar and researcher at the Max Planck-Institute for Foreign and International Social Law, Germany; the Georgetown Law Center, United States of America; and Harvard law School, United States of America. He serves on the executive editorial boards of various international and national law journals. He also serves as a State Judge in Porto Alegre, Brazil and teaches at the Judges Academy in Porto Alegre. He has coordinated the Department for Public Law at the Academy since 1998.

Jonathan Verschuuren

Jonathan Verschuuren is professor of international and European environmental law at Tilburg University, Netherlands. He is currently the Vice-dean for Research, as well as the director of the Tilburg Graduate Law School. In 1993, he received his PhD degree entitled: *Constitutional Right to Environmental Protection (cum laude)*. His research mainly focuses on the role of international and European Union environmental law in legal practice. Jonathan has written more than

200 publications in the field of environmental law, including several books and various articles in refereed scientific journals throughout the world. He is a member of the IUCN Commission on Environmental Law, and the IUCN Academy of Environmental Law. He is also a deputy judge at the District Court of Arnhem (on criminal environmental law cases). He is a visiting professor at the University of Connecticut (United States of America), North West University (South Africa), and University of Leuven (Belgium).

Chapter 1
The Netherlands

*Jonathan Verschuuren**

1   INTRODUCTION

Although Dutch administrative courts are considered to test government decisions in a rather marginal manner, and despite the abolishment of the *actio popularis* in 2005, the judiciary does play a central role in environmental governance. The fact that European Union (EU) environmental law is of significant importance in day-to-day decision-making in the Netherlands, is almost entirely due to the judiciary. Owing to the existence of an efficient court system that grants sufficient opportunities to companies, non-governmental organizations (NGOs) and individual citizens, many environmental cases are brought before the judiciary; arguably far more than in all other countries in the EU. These are some of the remarkable findings that are discussed throughout the course of this chapter.

---

*   Parts of this chapter have previously been published in J.M. Verschuuren, 'The Netherlands', in *Access to Justice in Environmental Matters and the Role of NGOs. Empirical Findings and Legal Appraisal*, ed. N. de Sadeleer, G. Roller & M. Dross, (Groningen: Europa Law Publishing, 2005), 97-117.

Louis J. Kotzé and Alexander R. Paterson (eds), *The Role of the Judiciary in Environmental Governance: Comparative Perspectives*, pp. 55–83.
© 2009 Kluwer Law International BV, The Netherlands.

2   ENVIRONMENTAL ISSUES AND ENVIRONMENTAL
           GOVERNANCE STRUCTURES

2.1   ENVIRONMENTAL ISSUES

With 16.4 million people living on only 41,029 km^2 of land, the disruption of the
environment and especially nature is enormous. Construction and operation of
industries, railroads, airports and so forth, not only cause stress on the available
space, but also on nature and the environment. The Netherlands Environment
Assessment Agency publishes annual reports on the state of the nation's environment.[1] These reports show that the following are the most important sources of
environmental degradation in the Netherlands:

- Industry: The Netherlands is a heavily industrialized state with large scale
  chemical industries scattered across the country. Refineries and the energy
  industry sector cause significant environmental problems. During the
  period 1980-1990 the most polluting industries have, however, heavily
  invested in environmental protection measures. Attention therefore shifted
  to other sources of environmental degradation, although renewed interest is
  now being paid to the industrial sector as a consequence of climate change.
- Traffic and transport: Since the Netherlands (because of its situation at the
  Rhine estuary and the North Sea) is an important transit route to Germany,
  infrastructure has extensively been developed. This is true for transport by
  air, ship and road. The increasing mobility has led to a rise in the use of
  private cars and to a growth of air traffic. Since 2005, air pollution caused by
  the transport sector is considered one of the major environmental challenges, especially because of its negative impact on people's health.
- Agriculture: Due to the increased input of nutrients, pesticides, energy and
  (ground) water, and the development of new techniques in farming and
  livestock breeding, agricultural production and consequently pollution
  have escalated. Agriculture in the Netherlands is the most intensive in
  Europe and negatively impacts the nation's flora and fauna.

Apart from these specific issues, the Fourth National Environmental Policy Plan
lists seven of the most important environmental challenges in the Netherlands.[2]
Loss of biodiversity: many plant and animal species are severely threatened by
habitat fragmentation frequently caused by infrastructure projects and intensive
forms of agriculture (such as land parcelling and the application of pesticides and
fertilizers). Climate change: industry and traffic are the most important sources of
greenhouse gas emissions. Global climate change causes wetter and milder winters
in the Netherlands, as well as periods of extreme rainfall, resulting in severe

---

1. Each year, the agency produces the Nature Balance and the Environmental Balance, see MNP,
   'MNP aktueel', <www.mnp.nl>, 3 June 2008.
2. See Dutch Ministry for the Environment, 'National Environmental Policy Plan',
   <www2.vrom.nl/pagina.html?id=7377>, 3 June 2008.

flooding. With almost half of the country lying below sea level, sea level rise and increased storm activity are of great concern to the Netherlands. Over-exploitation of natural resources: current production and consumption patterns in the Netherlands lead to increased environmental pressures abroad, especially in developing countries. Threats to human health: hazardous substances in the environment cause threats to human health, some of which have not yet properly been mapped out. Threats to external safety: the use, storage and transportation of hazardous substances in a densely populated country like the Netherlands lead to a high risk level of accidents. Damage to the quality of the living environment: excessive exposure to air pollution and noise leads to a decline in the quality of living organisms. Possible unmanageable risks: rapid technological developments, such as genetically modified organisms (GMOs) and nanotechnology, may pose significant future environmental problems.

2.2   Principal Environmental Laws[3]

Environmental law has its foundation in the Dutch Constitution. Article 21 of the Constitution charges the government with the duty to care for the protection and improvement of the environment.[4] The government has, until now, mainly fulfilled this task by promulgating legislation. One of the main sources of Dutch environmental law is, therefore, statutory law. This does not only include formal legislation (legislation by government and parliament), but also regulation by decentralized bodies (provinces and municipalities) and delegated legislation at the level of the central government (ministerial ordinances). Dutch environmental law is largely influenced by EU law. Apart from statutory law, self-regulation has become increasingly important over the last two decades. This means that instruments like covenants have become rather important as sources of law, while industries have gained increased freedom and responsibility from obeying environmental rules when voluntary environmental management systems are in place.[5]

Dutch environmental legislation has traditionally been dominated by sectoral acts: one act for every type of pollution (noise, air, waste and chemical waste). Since the 1980s, however, the strong tendency towards an overall environmental

---

3. For a more extensive overview of Dutch environmental law and policy, see E. Bohne, *The Quest for Environmental Regulatory Integration in the European Union* (The Hague: KLI, 2006), 293-332, and J.M. Verschuuren, 'Environmental Law', in *Introduction to Dutch Law*, ed. E.H. Hondius, 4th ed. (The Hague: KLI, 2006), 369-397.
4. See J.M. Verschuuren, 'The Constitutional Right to Protection of the Environment in the Netherlands', *AJPIL* 46 (1993): 67-77, and J.M. Verschuuren, 'The constitutional right to protection of the environment in the Netherlands', *Revue Juridique de l'Environnement* (1994): 339-347.
5. See R. Seerden, 'Legal Aspects of Environmental Agreements in the Netherlands, in Particular the Agreement on Packaging and Packaging Waste', in *Environmental Contracts: Comparative Approaches to Regulatory Innovation in the United States and Europe*, ed. E.W. Orts & K. Dekeletaere (The Hague, KLI, 2001), 179-197.

policy has impacted on legislative developments. The most important environmental act is the *Environmental Management Act* (EMA).[6] This act incorporates
matters of procedure that used to be dealt with in sectoral acts. The EMA contains
provisions on, inter alia: the application and granting of permits for installations,
environmental impact assessment (EIA), waste, environmental planning, environmental quality standards, general provisions concerning appeal and enforcement of
environmental laws, financial provisions, and provisions on emissions trading.

The EMA has not resulted in the total integration of environmental legislation.
Although it covers a considerable area of environmental governance issues, it does
not regulate the entire environmental law system. There exist a number of laws in
addition to the EMA, such as the *Soil Protection Act,*[7] the *Air Pollution Act,*[8] the
Nuclear Energy Act,[9] the *Pesticides Act,*[10] the *Nature Conservation Act,*[11] and the
Flora and Fauna Act.[12] Although the plethora of sectoral laws was considerably
reduced by the adoption of the EMA, these laws continue to regulate a number of
major environmental issues.

In 2009, the environmental permit system will be further integrated by the
Environmental Law (General Provisions) Bill.[13] When the Act takes effect, a total
of 25 permits, ranging from the environmental permit under the EMA to the
building permit and the mining permit, will be procedurally integrated. A person
who initiates a project that is regulated under more than one statute will only be
required to send one digital permit application to one authority (the so-called 'one-
stop shop'). This authority will then ensure that all procedures under each relevant
statute are carried out by the various competent authorities (where there are
multiple competent authorities).

Another important and complex integration project is the assimilation of
several statutes regulating water issues (marine and fresh water, groundwater
and surface water, as well as statutes dealing with the protection against flooding)
into a new *Water Act.* Under this new statute, six permits regulating water issues

---

6. Act of 13 June 1979, latest amendments *Staatsblad* [Bulletin of Acts and Orders] 2008, No. 173.
7. Act of 3 July 1986, latest amendments *Staatsblad* [Bulletin of Acts and Orders] 2007, No. 152.
8. Act of 26 November 1970, latest amendments *Staatsblad* [Bulletin of Acts and Orders] 2005, No. 532.
9. Act of 21 February 1963, latest amendments *Staatsblad* [Bulletin of Acts and Orders] 2006, No. 11.
10. In 2007, the original *Pesticides Act* (1962) was totally revised and renamed *Pesticides and Biocides Act* of 17 October 2007, *Staatsblad* [Bulletin of Acts and Orders] 2007, No. 387.
11. Act of 25 May 1998, latest amendments *Staatsblad* [Bulletin of Acts and Orders] 2005, No. 705.
12. Act of 25 May 1998, latest amendments *Staatsblad* [Bulletin of Acts and Orders] 2007, No. 449.
13. In December 2007, the Bill was introduced in the Senate after it had passed in the Lower House. See *Kamerstukken* [Parliamentary Documents] I, 2007-2008, 30 844, A. For the text of the Bill and further information on this project, see Ministry of the Environment, 'Kennisplein Omge-vingsvergunning', <omgevingsvergunning.vrom.nl>, 3 June 2008 (in Dutch), as well as some additional information available in English at Ministry of the Environment, 'Minister reduces environmental administrative burden', <international.vrom.nl/pagina.html?id=11102>, 3 June 2008.

will be integrated into a single water permit.[14] The Water Bill will probably take effect in 2009.[15]

2.3   INSTITUTIONS AND GOVERNANCE STRUCTURES

Responsibility for national environmental policy in the Netherlands rests with four ministers. The minister primarily responsible for environmental matters is the Minister of Housing, Spatial Planning and the Environment. In addition, this minister has to co-ordinate the environmental policies regarding traffic and water management (for which the Minister of Transport, Public Works and Water Management is responsible); pollution by the agricultural sector and the conservation of nature; (for which the Minister of Agriculture, Nature and Food Quality is responsible); and energy; (for which the Minister for Economic Affairs is responsible). The implementation of environmental policies and laws occurs at provincial and municipal level by provincial and municipal administrative authorities.[16]

3   OVERVIEW OF THE COURT SYSTEM

3.1   INTRODUCTION

Most environmental matters fall within the scope of administrative law, for which the *General Administrative Law Act* (GALA)[17] prescribes procedural rules. However, NGOs and citizens also have the possibility to initiate court proceedings under civil law and criminal law. For most administrative law cases, there are administrative sectors within the District Courts, with the possibility of appeal to the Administrative Law Division of the Council of State. However, until 2009, in almost all environmental cases, legislation provided for immediate appeal to the Administrative Law Division of the Council of State (i.e. appeal in first and only instance). When the Environmental Law (General Provisions) Bill comes into force in 2009, statutory decisions taken under it can be addressed by courts in two instances pursuant to regular administrative law. Civil and criminal law cases can be addressed in three instances. Decisions of the District Courts (both in tort and criminal cases) can be reviewed by Courts of Appeal. The Supreme Court can be approached for a cassation procedure in which only questions of law are reviewed (and then only in civil law, tax law, and criminal law cases). The possibilities for

---

14. In March 2008, the Bill was introduced in the Senate after it had been passed in the Lower House. See *Kamerstukken* [Parliamentary Documents] I, 2007-2008, 30 818, A.
15. The integration of the water permit and the new integrated permit under the Environmental Law (General Provisions) Bill is not considered for the purpose of this contribution.
16. For an extensive overview of the governance structure and the administrative style in the Netherlands, see Bohne, *supra* n. 3.
17. Act of 4 June 1992, latest amendments *Staatsblad* [Bulletin of Acts and Orders] 2008, No. 20.

approaching the above courts in environmental matters are discussed below; as too are the non-judicial procedures for resolving environmental disputes.

3.2   PROCEDURES BEFORE ADMINISTRATIVE COURTS

Until 2005, environmental permits (integrated permits issued under the EMA and other permits such as those issued under the *Pollution of Surface Waters Act* (PSWA),[18] were granted applying the so called 'extensive public preparation procedure'.[19] Other decisions were usually taken applying the 'public preparation procedure'. Following a strong call for deregulation in 2005, the public preparation procedure and the extensive public preparation procedure were integrated and renamed the 'uniform public preparation procedure'.[20] The following section turns to a discussion on developments leading to the integration of both preparation procedures and its most important consequence: the limitation of access to courts in environmental matters. It then discusses the remaining opportunities for approaching the administrative court in environmental matters.

3.2.1   The Abolishment of the *actio popularis*: From 'Anyone' to 'Interested Parties'

Decision-making processes on applications for all environmental permits are now regulated by the uniform public preparation procedure. According to Article 8.1 of the EMA, it is forbidden to set up, operate or change the setup or operation of an installation unless one has a permit to do so. A company has to apply for such a permit with the competent authority. The uniform public preparation procedure applies to these permits, as well as to several other decisions (for instance, permits to discharge waste into surface waters). After the application and the draft-decision have been published, *anyone*, including advising bodies, such as the Inspectorate for the Environment, can submit written or oral objections. The term 'anyone' implies that all groups of citizens, environmental NGOs and even non-interested individuals have a right to participate in environmental decision-making relating to permits. There is no need to demonstrate a special interest in this procedure. The final decision has to reflect that the objections have been taken into consideration.

   Once the uniform public preparation procedure has been completed, there is no need to object to the same administrative authority. Instead, one can directly address an appeal to the Administrative Law Division of the Council of State. This right, however, is reserved for *interested parties*, being those that can show a special interest in the decision. This differs from the public participation phase

---

18. Act of 13 November 1969, latest amendments *Staatsblad* [Bulletin of Acts and Orders] 2008, No. 28.
19. S. 3.4 GALA.
20. *Staatsblad* [Bulletin of Acts and Orders] 2002, No. 54.

that is open to anyone. It is trite that environmental NGOs are considered to usually have an interest in most environmental matters.

Prior to the legislative amendments affected in 2005,[21] there existed a so-called 'indirect *actio popularis*' in Dutch administrative environmental law. Once a person or a group of people or NGO had entered the decision-making process, they had a right to go to court as well, as long as they objected on the grounds raised by them in the decision-making process. They were not allowed to introduce new arguments in court. In 2005, parliament accepted the proposal to abandon the *actio popularis*.[22] As a consequence, only interested parties are allowed to go to court. Two important additional procedures that were open to anyone to bring matters to court have similarly been limited to interested parties, namely: the right to request an update or withdrawal of a permit when this is necessary to protect the environment;[23] and the right to request an administrative body to take enforcement action when it fails to do so.[24] The decision relating to such requests can be reviewed by the judiciary. This has effectively abolished the *actio popularis* in the Netherlands, a remedy which existed for more than twenty-five years. Cabinet thought it no longer justified to have a special regime for environmental matters, although they admitted that the abolishment of the *actio popularis* would probably not significantly reduce the number of court cases, since research suggests that usually only interested persons object to relevant decisions.[25] Non-interested persons simply do not seem sufficiently interested to institute legal proceedings regarding environmental matters. Still, cabinet argued that in times of deregulation and decreasing administrative burdens such as these, maintaining an *actio popularis* would send the wrong signal to society.[26] In general, it is often thought that court procedures, especially those instituted by NGOs and individual citizens, are time-consuming and expensive. The national government that was installed following the May 2002 elections took the view that:

> It has become easier to obstruct decisions than to take a decision; as a consequence, public authorities often cannot solve social problems. The Cabinet will look into proposals to . . . streamline procedures and abolish the so called *actio popularis*, in order to increase decisiveness of the authorities.[27]

The proposal to abandon the *actio popularis* met severe criticism. Some feared an increase of the administrative burden because now competent authorities as well as courts, in each and every case, have to decide whether or not the applicant is an

---

21. *Staatsblad* [Bulletin of Acts and Orders] 2005, No. 282.
22. *Kamerstukken* [Parliamentary Documents] II, 2003-2004, 29 421.
23. Art. 8.22vv EMA.
24. Art. 18.14 EMA.
25. A.A.J. de Gier et al., *De actio popularis in het ruimtelijke ordenings- en milieurecht* (Utrecht: Utrecht University, 1999), 48.
26. *Kamerstukken*, *supra* n. 22, No. 3 at 4.
27. *Regeerakkoord* [Coalition agreement] of 3 July 2002, see Ministerie van Algeme Zaken, 'Regeerakkoord 2002', <www.minaz.nl/Onderwerpen/Regeringsbeleid/Regeerakkoord/Regeerakkoord_2002>, 7 December 2007, at 24.

interested party.[28] In addition, the changes to legislation might be considered contrary to the Aarhus Convention on Access to Information, Public Participation in Decision-Making and Access to Justice in Environmental Matters.[29] Although the Aarhus Convention does not explicitly necessitate an indirect *actio popularis*, it still is rather odd to reduce access to justice in environmental matters, whilst the Aarhus Convention in its preamble clearly states that access to justice must be improved. Some even argued that once someone has entered the participation process, he or she becomes a member of the 'public concerned' and acquires a 'sufficient interest' as meant in Article 9(2) of the Aarhus Convention, thus allowing this person to go to court. This line of reasoning is to be found in current literature,[30] and in the UN/ECE Aarhus Implementation Guide.[31]

In parliament, it is even frequently suggested to drop the presumption that environmental NGOs have an interest when the environment is at stake.[32] A few authors and politicians have claimed that NGOs should not be granted access to justice, not even in administrative law cases, as NGOs have no direct interest in environmental matters.[33] The decision to grant an environmental permit to an industrial plant is a matter between the competent authority and the company that applied for the permit and, possibly, one or two people living in the vicinity of the plant. NGOs should only be able to interfere with the political process, for instance, by urging the city council to look into the decision of the competent authority. Courts should not be able to annul a decision taken by a democratically legitimized public authority following arguments of a non-democratically legitimized NGO.[34] The latter suggestion has not been adopted by the legislature, as it would clearly violate both the Aarhus Convention and the EU Directive implementing the Aarhus Convention.[35] Both state that environmental NGOs, that fulfil certain conditions, are considered to have an interest in environmental matters.

---

28. J.C.A. de Poorter, 'Van actio popularis naar kringen van belanghebbenden', *Bouwrecht* 43 (2006): 312.
29. (1999) 38 ILM 517. In April 2004, the ratification process of the Aarhus Convention was well under way (*Kamerstukken* [Parliamentary Documents] II, 2002-2003, 28 835, Nos 1-2), see J.M. Verschuuren, 'Internationaal milieurecht en de Awb', in *De grootste gemene deler: Opstellen aangeboden aan prof.mr. Th.G. Drupsteen*, ed. M. Lurks et al., (Deventer: Kluwer, 2002), 235-244.
30. F. de Lange, *Beyond 'Greenpeace': Courtesy of the Aarhus Convention*, YEEL, vol. 3, (Oxford: OUP, 2003), 239.
31. S. Stec, S. Casey-Lefkowitz & J. Jendroska, *The Aarhus Convention: An Implementation Guide* (New York: UN, 2000), 108.
32. A motion to that extent was introduced as recently as 22 May 2008 by two of the major political parties, see *Kamerstukken* [Parliamentary Documents] II, 2007-2008, 31 472, No. 4.
33. J.M.H.F. Teunissen, 'De algemeen belangorganisatie als bestuursrechtelijk (pseudo) Openbaar Ministerie?', *Gemeentestem* 7179 (2003): 61-69.
34. E.g.: Teunissen, *supra*, 30, annotation under Administrative Law Division of the Council of State, 13 November 2002.
35. Directive 2003/35/EC providing for Public Participation in Respect of the Drawing up of Certain Plans and Programmes relating to the Environment and Amending with Regard to Public Participation and Access to Justice Council Directives 85/337/EEC and 96/61/EC, OJ L156/17, 2003.

In addition, standing for environmental NGOs is often considered to be a consequence of the constitutional right to environmental protection. The large number of environmental cases that are won by NGOs against public authorities illustrates that public authorities are not always inclined to correctly apply environmental legislation. Therefore, NGOs play an important role in environmental governance.[36] Additionally, abolishing the right of NGOs to go to court in administrative law would probably lead to the same number of court procedures, this time initiated by directly involved individual citizens that take up positions prepared by NGOs.[37] From a legal point of view, the separation between a group of local citizens that have joined forces in an association and NGOs is not clear. Courts, in each instance, will have to go into the matter of admissibility, which, in turn, leads to delays. In addition, the number of tort procedures was expected to increase after having made administrative courts less accessible for NGOs.[38]

3.2.2 Procedures against Environmental Permit Decisions Since 2005

Since the abolishment of the *actio popularis* in procedures against environmental permits, standing requirements for all environmental decisions are more or less the same since the uniform public preparation procedure applies to most decision-making processes, such as: permits issued under environmental laws, nature protection laws, construction laws and environmental ordinances; and decisions relating to administrative enforcement. There are on occasion specific processes not included in the GALA and differences between the procedures leading to the various decisions depending on which Act has to be applied. However, in most cases interested parties have a right to participate in the decision-making process.

After an environmental decision has been taken, one has the right to lodge a notice of objection against the decision. When the uniform preparation procedure has been followed, any person has a right to raise objections.[39] The objection has to be lodged with the same administrative authority that took the original decision. After the notice of objection has been received the issuer of the notice and other concerned parties have an opportunity to be heard. The administrative authority determines whether the complaints are well-founded. If the administrative body agrees with the objections raised, it can overrule the original decision and substitute a new decision. No administrative fee may be imposed by the administration. Moreover, judicial assistance is not needed which means that expense does not generally stand in the way of the participation in or the commencement of the above procedures.

---

36. M.P. Jongma & F.C.M.A. Michiels, 'Het beroepsrecht van milieu-organisaties moet blijven!', *NJB* (2002): 2238-2239.
37. *Ibid.*
38. *Ibid.*
39. Art. 13.3 EMA read with Art. 3:15 GALA.

As stated above, an appeal against the decision relating to such an objection can only be lodged by a party whose interest is directly involved with the environmental decision. Legal entities are deemed to have an interest if their objectives and actual activities seek to specifically protect such an interest. Article 1:2(3) GALA states:

> As regard legal persons, their interests are deemed to include the general and collective interests which they specially represent in accordance with their objectives and as evidenced by their actual activities.

In general, case law shows that courts are rather lenient towards NGOs when applying this clause.

The appeal must be addressed to the Administrative Law Division of the Council of State where the decision is based on the EMA or the acts mentioned in Article 20.1 of EMA.[40] Appeal against a few other decisions, such as those based on the *Flora and Fauna Act*,[41] must be addressed to the administrative sector of the competent District Court. In these cases, after appealing to the District Court, higher appeal usually is possible to the Administrative Law Division of the Council of State. As already mentioned above, as of 2009, the latter system of appeal will in two instances also be applied to permits granted under the new Environmental Law (General Provisions) Bill.

The Council of State has very extensive powers since it can, besides quashing a decision to grant a permit, also take a new decision if it decides that this is warranted in the circumstances. Otherwise, it can rule that the administrative body has to take a new decision. It can also change some of the conditions attached to the permit, or draw up new conditions. In some instances, compensation for damages can be awarded. However, it must be noted that usually the Administrative Law Division of the Council of State only tests government decisions in a rather marginal way. Allegations by administrative bodies that administrative courts sometimes show 'legal activism' are taken seriously, both by the legislator (by initiating deregulation programmes) and by the courts. This means that the Administrative Law Division of the Council of State usually annuls a decision on formal grounds, generally leaving the task of adopting a new decision to the administrative authorities.

---

40. I.e., *Nuclear Energy Act* of 21 February 1963, latest amendments *Staatsblad* [Bulletin of Acts and Orders] 2006, No.11, *Noise Abatement Act* of 16 February 1979, latest amendments *Staatsblad* [Bulletin of Acts and Orders] 2007, No. 349, *Groundwater Act* of 22 May 1981, latest amendments *Staatsblad* [Bulletin of Acts and Orders] 2005, No. 530), *Air Pollution Act* of 26 November 1970, latest amendments *Staatsblad* [Bulletin of Acts and Orders] 2005, No. 532, *Pollution of Surface Waters Act* of 13 November 1969, latest amendments *Staatsblad* [Bulletin of Acts and Orders] 2007, No. 248, *Pollution of the Sea Act* of 5 June 1975, latest amendments *Staatsblad* [Bulletin of Acts and Orders] 2007, No. 248, *Soil Protection Act* of 3 July 1986, latest amendments *Staatsblad* [Bulletin of Acts and Orders] 2007, No. 152, *Antarctic Protection Act* of 5 March 1998, *Staatsblad* [Bulletin of Acts and Orders] 1998, No. 220, EC Regulation on Shipments of Waste (Regulation (EC) 1013/2006, OJ 2006, L 190).
41. Act of 25 May 1998, latest amendments *Staatsblad* [Bulletin of Acts and Orders] 2007, No. 449.

The above procedures are characteristically inexpensive. Although parties can be held liable for procedural costs, they do not have to provide financial security in advance. The final decision, including judicial review, usually takes no longer than one and a half years. Judicial assistance is not obligatory and there are no strict formal rules for the formulation of complaints or letters of appeal. There are government-financed bureaus of legal aid, some of which specialize in environmental matters. They specifically assist local and regional environmental organizations.

It must be noted, however, that there are various decisions against which no appeal is possible. These include all forms of legislation, including orders in council, ministerial orders and national environmental policy plans. Since in many cases environmental permits have been replaced by general rules for certain categories of installations laid down in orders in council (75% of all installations no longer require a permit), this can be criticized from the point of view of access to justice.

Finally, it is important to note that since 1992 Legal Aid Service Centres have been armed with environmental lawyers tasked with providing free legal assistance to indigent individual citizens and NGOs. These environmental lawyers can even represent them in court should the need arise. However, to reduce costs associated with the legal aid system in the Netherlands, access to environmental legal aid was considerably reduced in 2005. Presently, only a few centres remain that provide legal aid in environmental matters, although not entirely free of charge.[42]

3.3 PROCEDURES BEFORE CIVIL COURTS

Activities causing environmental harm can be unlawful under the general law of torts. Any individual who claims to be the victim of a wrongful act has access to justice in civil cases where his or her specific interest is affected. The Dutch Civil Code contains an explicit provision that deals with group actions. The legal requirements for admissibility of organizations in civil law proceedings prescribes that one should be a legal person, have relevant objectives under the articles of association and have members with similar interests.[43] Environmental NGOs explicitly fall under the scope of this article. The State has access when a private party commits a wrongful act against it and the civil action does not violate the rules for compliance as laid down in basic public law. As mentioned above, any individual citizen and environmental organization can request the competent authority to enforce environmental legislation.

The Dutch Civil Code contains two bases for the requisition of environmental damage: personal liability stemming from a wrongful act; and qualitative liability.

---

42. See SMN, 'Stichting Milieurechtsbijstand Nederland', <www.milieurechts bijstand.nl>, 3 June 2008.
43. *Civil Code*, Act of 1809, latest amendments *Staatsblad* [Bulletin of Acts and Orders] 2007, No. 395. See Art. 3:305a.

Personal liability is determined by applying the general law of torts.[44] The essential requirements for succeeding with an action of this nature are: unlawfulness, accountability, damage, and a causal connection between unlawful actions and the damage. The requirement of unlawfulness in satisfied in the instance of an infringement of (subjective) rights, when the action or omission violates legal duties, or when there is a violation of unwritten law or a failure to take due care. The qualitative liabilities in the Dutch Civil Code include liability for dangerous substances, liability of the owner of a waste disposal site and liability of the operator of a drill hole.[45] In cases of environmental damage, it is very often difficult to point out exactly who caused the damage. In such instances, courts consider the most likely responsible party to be the party primarily responsible and thereafter it is up to that party to prove someone else caused the damage. When there are additional responsible parties, each of them may be held jointly and severally liable for the damage.

Individuals, NGOs and the State can ask for a judicial injunction or prohibition. This is possible in the situation of an (impending) breach of right or breach of law. Individuals and the State can also ask for compensation for the damage they suffered. NGOs cannot request (financial) compensation for damage to the environment in general (such as *res nullius* or *res communes omnium*). Costs incurred in restoring or preventing damage to the environment (such as clean-up costs) can be recovered if the claimant can show an interest in the matter (this may also include an environmental organization). This is mostly damage to persons or objects and is therefore fairly easy to establish. However, when restoration to the original condition or the creation of an equal situation is not possible, it is not possible to order damages covering ecological loss in general.[46]

The aforementioned also applies to governmental decisions. NGOs sometimes institute a tort procedure when they feel that a governmental body violates legal duties, for instance, under international or EU law. In cases where administrative courts have no legal jurisdiction, the civil court can function as 'a way out'. When factual acts, juridical acts under private law or decisions excluded from appeal (such as regulations from decentralized authorities, orders in council, and so forth) are legally questionable, one can approach the civil sector of the District Court if it is a matter of tort. An individual or an organization has to prove that the administrative authority has committed a wrongful act against them by the action concerned. A famous example of this in Dutch case law is discussed in section 4 below.

The costs of proceedings before a civil court are rather high in the Netherlands. In civil procedures, parties are obliged to seek legal representation before the court: they cannot be their own attorney. These costs are usually considerable. Moreover, the party who loses the case also risks paying the costs of the opposing party. This risk

---

44. Art. 6:162.
45. Art. 6:175/177.
46. This has explicitly been laid down for tort actions initiated by NGOs in Art. 3:305a(3) of the Civil Code.

undermines the use of (rather uncertain) environmental liability procedures, especially by cash-strapped environmental organizations who think twice before going to court. In addition to the above economic constraints, civil litigation is generally extremely time-consuming and it can take anything from a few months to a few years to get a final judgment.

3.4 PROCEDURES BEFORE CRIMINAL COURTS

The public prosecutor has the competence to decide whether to prosecute or to refrain from prosecution. The Dutch legal system is fairly familiar in dealing with environmental matters by transaction, settlement and dismissal. In exchange for being renounced from penal prosecution, the public prosecutor can set several conditions, the fulfilment of which can prevent penal prosecution. These so-called 'transactions' generally result in the offender paying a certain amount of money determined by the prosecutor. In principle, no other authority or judge checks whether the decision to refrain from prosecution is correct or justified. However, an important legal right is afforded to parties that are directly interested in the above 'transactions' in that they can have the decision to refrain from prosecution tested by a court of law. A directly interested party is defined as someone whose interest will be affected if a prosecution should not be instituted.[47] An NGO which, according to its objectives and as it appears from its factual activities looks after a certain interest, has that same right to complain to the court when that particular interest is directly affected by the decision not to prosecute. It needs to be stressed that environmental NGOs are considered promoters of the interest of victims of environmental crimes. 'Victims' are not only those that experience disadvantage because of environmental degradation, but also natural resources (in those instances where no humans are injured).

NGOs are therefore able to provoke a prosecution by complaining to the court even where the public prosecutor initially decided to renounce the offender from prosecution.[48] If the court considers the complaint to be reasonable, it can order the public prosecutor to commence with the prosecution. The court will turn down the complaint if it decides that the refusal to prosecute is in the common interest.

3.5 NON-JUDICIAL PROCEDURES

Article 9:1 of the GALA grants anyone the right to submit complaints against all acts by any public authority in a non-judicial procedure. The GALA sets out what procedures need to be followed in lodging such complaints. When the complaint has not been dealt with satisfactorily, the complainant can address either

---

47. Art. 12(2) of the *Code of Criminal Procedure Act* of 15 January 1921, latest amendments *Staatsblad* [Bulletin of Acts and Orders] 2007, No. 575.
48. Art. 12(1) of the Code of Criminal Procedure.

the Ombudsman of the competent decentralized authority or the National Ombudsman.[49] The Ombudsman has the responsibility to investigate complaints that are forwarded to it concerning governmental bodies that allegedly have not acted properly towards a natural or legal person. The Ombudsman is not entitled to act if another legal recourse or remedy is available, or has been available but has not been used. Before going to the Ombudsman, the plaintiff must have at least attempted to exhaust all available internal remedies against the administrative authority. If mediation between the Ombudsman and the authority fails, an inquiry will be initiated which will result in a written report. This report must be made publicly available. Only a few environmental cases have been referred to the Ombudsman. However, this procedure plays an important complementary role to those described above. The influence of the Ombudsman extends beyond particular cases as its findings may be confirmed by the Minister, in which instance they may in turn result in the adoption of new policies and rules.

4   SIGNIFICANCE OF THE JUDICIARY: SOME EMPIRICAL DATA

4.1   INTRODUCTION

In 2002, a comprehensive empirical research project was conducted to determine some statistics as to court procedures in environmental cases.[50] Since these statistics are useful when assessing the significance of the judiciary in environmental governance, the most important findings of the project are presented here. Because virtually all administrative environmental law cases are decided in the first and only instance by the Administrative Law Division of the Council of State, data collection was focused on this court.[51]

---

49. Art. 9:17 GALA.
50. J.M. Verschuuren, 'Country Report and Case Study: The Netherlands', in *Access to Justice in Environmental Matters Vol. II*, ed. N. de Sadeleer, G. Roller & M. Dross, (Brussels: CEDRE, 2002).
51. Data has been compiled using the annual reports of the Council of State and the internet database containing all important cases by Dutch district courts (De Rechtspraak, 'The judiciary system in the Netherlands', <www.rechtspraak.nl>, 3 June 2008). Case law by the Administrative Law Division of the Council of State has been made available since April 2002. This database has been used to conduct the searches necessary to find the data on a number of cases. Therefore, in addition, cases published in the various traditional sources (for instance the environmental law reviews), as well as on CD-ROMs, have been studied covering the years 1997-2002. Finally, interviews with key persons within the Administrative Law Division of the Council of State and NGOs were carried out to check the data obtained through other sources.

4.2   DECLINE IN ENVIRONMENTAL AND PLANNING CASES

Since 1997, the number of cases before the Administrative Law Division of the Council of State has declined. The number of cases that were pending on 1 January 1997 dropped from 4,834 in 1997 to 2,846 in 2001; and to 1,847 in 2002.[52] These are cases in which the Administrative Law Division of the Council of State decides in the first and only instance. It is estimated that about 80% of these cases are related to environmental and planning law in a 2:1 ratio. The same trend is evident with regard to the number of preliminary (suspension) procedures. The sharp decline can largely be attributed to a series of changes in legislation to reduce legal procedures. The most important change is that about 75% of all installations that originally required an environmental permit have been brought under national regulations. These installations have to comply with environmental rules laid down in an order by council. They no longer have to apply for a permit to local or regional authorities. Since individual decisions no longer exist for these installations, the opportunity for appeal has been nullified.

A dramatic further decline took place in 2002 owing to a political assassination. On 6 May 2002, the leader of a new right wing political party, Pim Fortuyn, was assassinated by someone working for an environmental NGO, *Vereniging Milieuoffensief*. This particular NGO mainly sought through court procedures to challenge environmental permits issued to cattle-raising installations. *Vereniging Milieuoffensief* accounted for about 50% of all cases in this field of environmental law that were brought before the Administrative Law Division of the Council of State. Its legal activities practically came to a halt after the assassination, inactivity which appears to have rubbed off on other environmental NGOs.

At the same time, the political climate in the Netherlands has turned against environmental policy. This has amplified the decline in the number of cases brought before the Council of State. People accordingly seem to be reluctant to institute court procedures on environmental issues.

A third reason for the decline in 2002 is the effect of court procedures. NGOs feel that they often win cases on legal grounds, but that the practical effect of a successful court action is very limited. The competent authority usually simply makes a new decision, this time without formal procedural irregularity, and the plan or project goes ahead thereafter. This is a consequence of the rather formal approach adopted by the Administrative Law Division which tends to annul decisions which have not been carefully prepared (for example, without thorough research into environmental effects) or because they are inadequately motivated. When a decision has been adequately-prepared and well-motivated, administrative courts usually test it in a very marginal way. Since 2002, the number of cases

---

52. Figures taken from the annual reports of the Council of State, see Raad van State, 'Council of State: Advisory Body and Administrative Court', <www.raadvanstate.nl>, 3 June 2008.

decided by the Council of State in environmental and planning matters more or less stabilized around 1,800 per year.[53]

4.3   NUMBER OF CASES BROUGHT BY NGOS AND OTHER PARTIES

About 55% of environmental and planning law cases are brought before the Administrative Law Division by local residents or groups of local residents. The remainder of cases is more or less equally shared by environmental NGOs (25%) and operators of installations (20%). Non-interested parties hardly ever approach the courts (less than 1%). If one combines these figures with the number of cases mentioned above, it can be concluded that NGOs brought 966 cases before the Administrative Law Division in 1997, a figure which diminished to 569 cases in 2001 and 370 cases in 2002.

4.4   CIVIL LAW CASES

To distill an estimate of the number of civil law cases, this chapter relies on the information contained in the internet database mentioned above. From the 199 environmental cases initiated by NGOs which are listed in the database, only four are civil law cases. This means that about 2% of all cases brought before courts by NGOs are civil law cases, a statistic which has remained fairly constant for many years now. There are various reasons for the low prevalence of civil cases, most notably their expense and the fact that there exists a good system of cheaper and more informal administrative procedures (see the discussion above). It is interesting to note, however, that according to the lawyer of the *Stichting Natuur en Milieu*, a co-ordinating organization for all environmental NGOs in the Netherlands, NGOs often send a summons threatening to institute a civil law suit. This usually leads to negotiations with the relevant company without a lawsuit ultimately being pursued. Given the fact that the majority of cases are not subsequently pursued in court, one may conclude that these negotiations lead to a result that is satisfactory to the NGOs.

4.5   NUMBER OF CASES WON AND LOST BY NGOS AND LOCAL
               CITIZEN GROUPS

The president of the Environmental Law Chamber of the Administrative Law Division of the Council of State estimates that NGOs win between 30% and

---

53.   In 2006, for instance, a total of 1,838 cases were decided. See Raad van State, 'Annual report 2006', <www.raadvanstate.nl/publicaties/jaarverslagen/>, 3 June 2008, 180.

40% of all cases, a figure which equates with the success rate of individual citizens and groups of local residents. Research through the database suggests a slightly better result for NGOs, namely 50%. It was, however, pointed out that the above success rate does not necessarily imply that the environment is better protected. NGOs (as in the case of individuals or other interested parties) frequently win a case on a legal technicality only for the matter to be referred back to the competent authority which in turn rectifies its error and approves the project.

It is remarkable that the data shows that some NGOs are more successful than others. Jongma and Michiels,[54] in 2002, researched the number of cases won by one specific environmental NGO, *Vereniging Milieuoffensief.* This particular NGO is a non-typical NGO because it almost exclusively uses court procedures to achieve its goals in contrast to others which approach the court as a last resort. In addition, this NGO only deals with environmental and animal welfare problems relating to the bio-industry. Jongma and Michiels determined that this NGO initiated 2,200 court applications between 1992 and 2002. According to the NGO's own records, it won 80% of these cases. When considering the cases initiated by *Vereniging Milieuoffensief* as decided by the Administrative Law Division of the Council of State between April and November 2002, the NGO won 52% of the fifty cases that were decided. The authors conclude that the quality of decisions regarding livestock farms taken by public authorities is poor. The present author's own research supports this conclusion. For instance, of the sixty-eight cases by *Vereniging Milieuoffensief* in 2002, this NGO won thirty-four plus an additional six partly-won cases. They lost twenty-six cases, and were declared inadmissible in two cases. They won more than 60% of their cases. Greenpeace, on the other hand, lost five of its six cases.[55]

For local citizen groups, the situation is radically different. Of the 199 cases studied, thirty-seven cases were initiated by local groups. In only seven cases these groups acted on their own without a regional or national NGO being an additional plaintiff. Local groups won only 30% of the cases. The latter estimate also applies to cases brought by individual citizens.

The above data makes it abundantly clear that Dutch administrative courts usually only test government decisions in a very marginal way. Of the ninety-six cases won by NGOs and local citizen groups, almost 70% were won on formal grounds. The quality of appeals by NGOs is much higher than the quality of appeals by individual interested parties. According to the president of the Environmental Law Chamber of the Administrative Law Division, legal claims by NGOs usually oblige the court to go into the matter more profoundly, thereby enhancing the quality of case law.

---

54. Jongma & Michiels, *supra* n. 36, 2238.
55. See details in the report, *supra* n. 50.

5   ANALYSIS OF SIGNIFICANT ENVIRONMENTAL
           JUDGMENTS

5.1   INTRODUCTION

To illustrate the relevance of individual court decisions for environmental governance in general is, from a methodological point of view, not an easy task. It is
difficult, if not impossible, to prove that a certain development or change observed
in society is indeed caused by court decisions. For this contribution, the author did
not conduct the empirical research that is necessary to find the shreds of such
evidence. What follows is a short description of two landmark cases on environmental issues in the Netherlands that, beyond doubt, were of greater significance
than just the specific disputes in question. The first is a civil law case and the
second an administrative law case.[56] Both cases are several years old and this
enables some conclusions to be drawn regarding their possible impact on environmental governance in the Netherlands. However, these conclusions are based on
limited available empirical research conducted by the author and others and should
not accordingly be considered as scientifically undisputable.

5.2   ADMINISTRATIVE LAW CASE ON EU HABITATS DIRECTIVE

A landmark case as far as environmental governance is concerned, is a nature
conservation case that was in court for several years around the turn of the
century.[57] The case involved EU nature conservation law, laid down in Directive
79/409/EEC on the Protection of Wild Birds (Wild Birds Directive),[58] and
Directive 92/43/EEC on the Conservation of Natural Habitats and of Wild
Fauna and Flora (Habitats Directive).[59] The case concerned plans to construct a
transboundary business park on the German/Dutch border near the cities of Heer-
len and Aachen to combat regional unemployment in the area. However, the site
hosted one of the last populations of the common hamster (*Cricetus cricetus*) in the
Netherlands and in Western Europe. This species is listed in Annex IV of the
Habitats Directive, and therefore falls under the protection of Article 12 of the
Habitats Directive. As a consequence, it is prohibited to capture or kill specimens

---

56. This civil law case is selected because of its great environmental relevance. However, it is a
     rather exceptional case. Because of the effective system of (administrative) judicial review, and
     because of the fact that civil procedures are very costly, the number of cases brought before a
     civil court by NGOs is extremely low (probably only 2% of all cases brought before a court by
     NGOs). The author has nevertheless decided to select this civil law case because of the impact
     it has had on environmental law. Civil environmental law cases decided by the Dutch Supreme
     Court sometimes significantly influence environmental law in the Netherlands as fundamental
     issues are generally at stake and the decisions of the Supreme Court carry significant weight.
57. The most important decision being Administrative Law Division of the Council of State,
     15 January 2001, (2001) *Milieu en Recht* 73-78.
58. OJ L 103/1, 1979.
59. OJ L 206/7, 1992.

of this species, or to damage or destruct its breeding sites or resting places. Article 16 of the Directive offers a way out as far as these prohibitions are concerned in that a derogation may be granted under strict conditions, such as: the condition that there are no satisfactory alternatives, that the derogation is not detrimental to the maintenance of the species concerned at a favourable conservation status, and that the derogation is necessary for imperative reasons of overriding public interest.[60]

In a series of judgments, the Administrative Law Division of the Council of State found that the competent authorities in the Netherlands had not rightfully applied the derogation clauses because they had failed to demonstrate that:

– There were no satisfactory alternatives. The authorities had only assessed other possible locations for the business park. They should have also considered options for upgrading existing business parks or the possibility of creating jobs in other sectors, such as education or health care.
– The derogation was not detrimental to the maintenance of the populations of the species at a favourable conservation status in their natural range. The authorities neither showed that population dynamics data indicated the species would maintain itself on a long-term basis as a viable component of its natural habitat if the business park was constructed, nor that the natural range of the species would not be reduced as a consequence of the decision to construct the business park; and
– The derogation was necessary for an imperative reason of overriding public interest. According to the Council of State, combating regional unemployment can be an imperative reason for overriding public interest. However, in this case, the Council of State found that the authorities had used outdated unemployment figures, and, therefore, had not established that the construction of the business park was an imperative reason for overriding public interest.

This case, and several other cases that were in court during the same period, almost all dealing with EU environmental law and mostly with both nature conservation directives, received overwhelming media attention. The cases have had an enormous impact on all types of development projects throughout the country. They make it very clear that the provisions of the Birds and Habitats Directives must be very carefully applied when making decisions relating to building permits, environmental permits, allowances for the construction of roads and allowances for the exploration of fossil fuels.

5.3   CIVIL LAW CASE ON EU NITRATES DIRECTIVE

In July 1995, the European Commission sent a formal notice to the Netherlands, reprimanding the country for not having implemented Directive 91/676/EEC

---

60. See more extensively, J.M. Verschuuren, 'Effectiveness of Nature Protection Legislation in the EU and the US: The Birds and Habitats Directives and the Endangered Species Act', *YEEL* 3 (2003): 310-311.

concerning the Protection of Waters against Pollution Caused by Nitrates from Agricultural Sources (Nitrates Directive).[61] In December 1997, several environmental NGOs requested the national government to take all necessary measures to implement the Nitrates Directive. One year later, the European Commission again sent a formal notice to the national government owing to its poor implementation of the Directive. In 1999, the NGOs filed a lawsuit against the national government for not having implemented the Nitrates Directive.

The NGOs requested the court to declare that the State had acted unlawfully towards the NGOs by not having implemented the Directive and to compel the State to issue measures to ensure that the goals of the Directive were met.

The District Court of The Hague first dealt with whether the NGOs had the power to institute the claim in that particular court.[62] The State had argued that the NGOs' claim was inadmissible. The court ruled, however, that the claims were admissible. The NGOs fell under the scope of Article 3:305a(2) of the Dutch Civil Code as they were legal associations that had as their objective the protection of the environment. The fact that the NGOs had been discussing the implementation of the Nitrates Directive with the government for many years also demonstrated that these NGOs had a specific interest in the implementation of this Directive. Moreover, both their statutory objectives and their actions in practice showed that they had an interest as defined under Article 3:305a of the Civil Code.

Secondly, the court rejected the State's argument that it was not competent to address this case because the European Commission had initiated an infraction procedure against the Netherlands. According to the State, the District Court had to wait until the European Court of Justice (ECJ) had rendered its decision in the above dispute so as to prevent contradictory decisions on the same matter. However, the Dutch District Court found that the Commission had at that particular time not (yet) referred the case to the ECJ.

The third question dealt with by the court was whether the Nitrates Directive had direct effect.[63] According to the court it had in that the obligations laid down in the Directive, such as the obligation to achieve a limit value of 50mg nitrate in groundwater, were very specific and clear. Since the State admitted it could not guarantee that this objective had been or would be met on time, the court concluded that the Directive had taken direct effect and that the State did not comply with the provisions of the Directive. Thus, the court held that the Netherlands State had acted unlawfully against the NGOs by not guaranteeing that the objectives of the Nitrates Directive were met. The NGOs had also submitted further arguments (for example, that failure to implement the Directive was contrary to the precautionary principle and the principle of sustainable development), but these were rejected by the court.

---

61. OJ L 375/1, 1991.
62. District Court The Hague, 24 November 1999, (2000) 27 *Milieu en Recht* 63-67.
63. Only when a directive has direct effect does it confer rights on individuals, see J.H. Jans & H.H.B. Vedder, *European Environmental Law*, 3rd ed. (Groningen: Europa Law Publishing, 2008), 168.

The final question dealt with by the court was whether it could order the State to implement the Directive since this *de facto* meant that it would compel the legislature to establish acts and regulations. The State argued that such an order would infringe the separation of powers doctrine. The court rejected this argument. According to the court, the State would only be ordered to terminate the unlawful act and could choose its own means to do so.

The Netherlands State appealed this decision to the Court of Appeal. In its decision of 2 August 2001, this higher court overturned the decision of the District Court on two main grounds.[64] First, the Court of Appeal considered it undesirable for national courts to interfere with similar cases when an infraction case was pending before the ECJ (on 28 August 2000, the European Commission had referred the nitrates case against the Netherlands to the ECJ) as this could lead to conflicting judgments. According to the Court of Appeal, the national courts should abstain from giving a decision until the ECJ had delivered its judgment. Secondly, the Court of Appeal agreed with the State's argument that the order to ascertain the goals of the Directive implied that the current *Animal Manure Act*[65] had to be amended, or that new legislation had to be established. In the Netherlands the legislature decided whether or not, and within which timeframe, new legislation should be established. It accordingly held that courts did not have the power to interfere with the legislature as a consequence of the doctrine of the separation of powers.

The NGOs then referred the case to the Dutch Supreme Court. The Dutch Supreme Court gave its view on the case on 21 March 2003.[66] In its judgment, the Supreme Court followed the Court of Appeal's decision. According to the Supreme Court, national courts are indeed not allowed to force the State to enact legislation implementing EU law. It is a political decision whether to implement an EU Directive, a decision in which the (national) judiciary cannot interfere. The Supreme Court did not refer to Article 10 of the EC-Treaty,[67] although the NGOs argued that this article does not allow a Member State to decide *not* to implement a Directive. The Supreme Court argued that this point of view did not limit the rights of citizens, because individual citizens could still, in administrative procedures, invoke provisions that had direct effect. The Supreme Court concluded its judgment by stating that the ECJ, in an infraction procedure, could in fact force the State to enact legislation. Since this has been regulated in the EC-Treaty, the court held that there was accordingly no need for national courts to do the same. Interestingly, in October 2003, the ECJ condemned the Netherlands for not having implemented the Nitrates Directive. In its decision, the court made it

---

64. Court of Appeal The Hague, 2 August 2001, (2001) *Milieu en Recht*, 258-261.
65. Act of 27 November 1986, latest amendments *Staatsblad* [Bulletin of Acts and Orders] 2006, No. 64.
66. Netherlands Supreme Court, 21 March 2003, (2003) *Milieu en Recht*, 314-315.
67. Treaty of 25 March 1957, see EurLex, 'Access to European Union Law: Treaties', <eur-lex.europa.eu/en/index.htm> 3 June 2008.

perfectly clear that the Dutch policy with regard to animal manure was entirely inadequate to fulfil the obligations laid down in the Directive.[68]

The environmental effectiveness of this case has been limited because of the judgment of the Court of Appeal. Since the Supreme Court took the same position as the Court of Appeal, NGOs therefore do not have a powerful new weapon to force authorities to implement EU Directives. This finding is further discussed in the section below.

6   CRITICAL SURVEY

The Netherlands had a liberal system of access to justice in environmental matters. Over the years, this system has gradually been eroded to the minimum requirements of the Aarhus Convention. By bringing installations under the obligation to follow orders in council rather than having them apply for an individual permit, many cases can no longer be brought before courts. This has caused an enormous decline in the number of environmental cases brought before the courts.

This development was followed in 2004 by the abolishment of the *actio populated*. This does not appear to have led to a further reduction of cases as non-interested parties account for less than 1% of all litigants. NGOs win about 40%-50% of their cases. This is higher than groups of local residents which win about 30% of their cases brought to court. The latter figure applies to individually interested citizens as well. Only 30% of these matters was won on substantive grounds. The quality of appeals by NGOs is higher than the quality of appeals by individually interested parties. Legal claims by NGOs usually oblige the court to go into the matter more profoundly, which enhances the quality of case-law.

In addition, administrative courts tend to only marginally test government decisions, leaving them as much room as possible, within the limits of the law, to set their own policies. Civil courts do the same, as was shown by the *Nitrates Directive* case discussed above. This case also shows that civil law does not comprehensively provide powerful instruments to NGOs or local residents combating environmental degradation, even in cases were EU environmental law is at stake. In the District Court's view in this case, NGOs should also have the ability to initiate a procedure under civil law generally to order the State to implement an EU Directive. Obviously, the threat of such civil law procedures may force the authorities to seriously and timeously consider EU law obligations. Unfortunately, this view was rejected on appeal. The Court of Appeal's judgment has been severely criticized on both its arguments, not only by NGOs, but also in scientific literature. It has been pointed out that under EU law, national courts have the obligation to apply provisions of directives that take direct effect. They cannot ignore EU law simply because the European Commission has started an infraction procedure

---

68. *Commission v. The Netherlands*, Case No. C-322/00 [2003] ECR I-11267.

against the Member State in question.[69] Tort procedures under national law are of an entirely different nature than infraction procedures at the EU level. Moreover, adopting the view that courts cannot interfere with the legislative process, not only implies that the State is allowed to act unlawfully *vis-à-vis* these NGOs, but also that the Nitrates Directive (or any other directive for that matter) has no real effect within the national legal system. It is clear that these questions are important ones. They deal with fundamental issues concerning the division of powers and the role of EU law in national law. As evidenced by many other earlier administrative and civil cases, NGOs often bring forward fundamental legal issues of this nature.

The *Nitrates Directive* case also illustrates how 'democratic' aspects often permeate disputes concerning access to justice. In this matter the State argued that the legislature and not the judiciary had the power to establish a set of rules governing the behaviour of farmers. In other words, it was the legislature that had to transpose the provisions of EU Directives into national law, not the judiciary. The State argued that NGOs should not have the power to approach a civil court in a tort procedure to force the State to take actions to implement EU law. Implementing EU law was up to democratic institutions, such as the legislature. NGOs should interfere in this process through their regular political influence, not through court procedures. NGOs took the opposite position. In their view, the State acted illegally by not transposing the Directive. The duty to implement this Directive was a legal duty that follows from the EC-Treaty.[70] The ability of NGOs to ensure that public authorities observe the law has been somewhat undermined by this jurisprudence.

As was stated above, the main argument against access to justice for a significant number of people (including NGOs), stems from socio-economic considerations. It is argued that it has become too easy to obstruct socially desirable projects by going to court. Relating to the case of the *Nitrates Directive*, the court's order to impose the strict objectives of the Nitrates Directive would have had numerous consequences for the agricultural sector in the Netherlands. As shown above, the court's order was later reversed by the Court of Appeal and the Supreme Court. The ECJ did, however, subsequently condemn the Netherlands for not having adequately implemented the Nitrates Directive and, as a consequence, the socio-economic effect was even more profound. The Minister for Agriculture has been compelled to withdraw the current national policy and legislation and create a new policy in line with the Directive. The EU law did therefore ultimately have an impact in this instance, not through national courts, but through the ECJ.

How different are the *Habitats Directive* cases that were decided by administrative courts! As is evident from the above analysis, these cases show the direct impact of administrative court decisions dealing with EU law on environmental governance. The importance of these cases cannot be overestimated. Although most EU environmental law saw a slow start in the EU Member States, national

---

69. J.H. Jans & J.M. Verschuuren, *Case note*, District Court The Hague, 24 November 1999; *supra* n. 61, 67.
70. Arts 10 and 249 of the EC-Treaty, *supra* n. 67.

cases like these may make a substantial difference to legal practice at domestic level. Cases like the ones discussed above made all relevant actors realize that the Habitats Directive is not only an important instrument to regulate and dictate means for the conservation of biodiversity, but also to provide constraints (of varying degrees) on decision-making for projects that may harm biodiversity. Owing to the persistence of the European Commission, which continues to institute infringement procedures against EU Member States for their failure to fulfil obligations under the Wild Birds and Habitats Directives, but the willingness of national courts, at least in the Netherlands, to test projects against the provisions of the Directives, the impact of EU environmental law on decision-making has increased enormously. Since 2000, a similar development took place with regard to EU air quality law. It is expected that recent EU water law will receive a similar strict treatment by the Dutch courts. Dutch courts consider the duty to strictly and carefully follow EU law to be very important and are willing to test government decisions against it. Since EU environmental law nowadays covers almost the entire spectrum of environmental policy, this approach has had an enormous impact on environmental governance in the Netherlands.[71]

NGOs have successfully seized the opportunities offered by EU Directives to approach the courts and seek remedies to combat the loss of biodiversity and to promote other environmental issues. Initially, they were very successful. The reason for the initial success of NGOs is simple: administrations were not accustomed to providing the amount of data and following the legal procedures that are now required before approving environmentally deleterious project (for instance those prescribed under the Habitats Directive). Courts tend to find administrative decisions inadequate when the authorities are unable to present sufficient data. However, authorities, as well as developers, now recognize that they need to develop their plans so as not to deteriorate, for example, protected areas or harm populations of endangered species. Their efforts must be applauded. As a consequence, it can be concluded that governmental decision-making has become better informed and thus of a higher quality.

Another consequence, at least as far as decision-making with regard to the EU Wild Birds and Habitats Directives is concerned, is that larger projects increasingly are negotiated by all parties involved, including environmental NGOs, by also looking into biodiversity protection for an entire region in an integrated fashion, and drawing up restoration plans to rehabilitate lost habitats. The fact that NGOs

---

71. It must be noted, however, that this is certainly not the case throughout the EU. There still are countries in which courts do not take EU law very seriously. As is apparent from the above discussion, this has consequences for the level of implementation of EU law into national legal practice. This conclusion also follows from a comparative study into the implementation of EU air quality directives in several Member States, see R.B.A. Koelemeijer et al., *Consequences of EU Air Quality Directives for Spatial Development Plans in Various EU Countries* <www.mnp.nl/en/publications/2005/Consequences_of_EU_air_quality_directives_for_spatial_development_plans_in_various_EU_countries.html>, 3 June 2008 (Bilthoven: NEAA, 2005).

are backed by court decisions affords them a strong position in such processes of cooperative governance.[72]

7   THE WAY FORWARD

Courts in the Netherlands are often criticized for their decisions in environmental cases. Business organizations and local authorities often feel that courts go too far in testing government decisions, whereas NGOs and local residents feel courts test decisions too marginally, leaving too much room for the authorities to act. The political discussions leading to the abolishment of the *actio popularis* show that a liberal system of access to justice is no longer a Dutch trademark. Hence, courts are trying to balance these opposing and often conflicting positions. They test government decisions rather marginally and will probably continue to do so in the future. This is in line with Dutch legal and administrative culture. Negotiations and talks between the various actors involved are firmly embedded in daily legal and administrative practices. Courts, however, test the legality of the decisions reached by the authorities. Since there exists EU law on practically every environmental aspect, such a test often results in testing decisions against EU law. Hence, courts (albeit indirectly) promote the implementation of EU environmental law in legal practice. They thus help to develop a level playing field for businesses and a high level of protection of the environment in the EU and in the Netherlands.

BIBLIOGRAPHY

Bohne, E. *The Quest for Environmental Regulatory Integration in the European Union*. The Hague: Kluwer Law International, 2006.

De Gier, A.A.J., et al. *De actio popularis in het ruimtelijke ordenings- en milieurecht*. Utrecht: Utrecht University, 1999.

De Lange, F. *Beyond 'Greenpeace': Courtesy of the Aarhus Convention*. Yearbook of European Environmental Law, vol. 3. Oxford: Oxford University Press, 2003.

De Poorter, J.C.A. 'Van actio popularis naar kringen van belanghebbenden'. *Bouwrecht* 43 (2006): 303-312.

De Rechtspraak. 'The judiciary system in the Netherlands'. <www.rechtspraak.nl>, 3 June 2008.

---

72. See for further examples substantiating this conclusion, W. Snape III, et al., 'Protecting Ecosystems under the Endangered Species Act: the Sonoran Desert Example', *Washb. L. J.* 41 (2001): 14-49, and more recently J. M. Verschuuren, 'The Case of Transboundary Wetlands Under the Ramsar Convention: Keep the Lawyers Out!', *Colo. J. Int'l Envtl L. & Pol'y* 19, no. 1 (2007/2008): 49-127.

Dutch Ministry for the Environment. 'National Environmental Policy Plan'. <www2.vrom.nl/pagina.html?id=7377>, 3 June 2008.

EurLex. 'Access to European Union Law: Treaties'. <eur-lex.europa.eu/en/index.htm> 3 June 2008.

Jans, J.H. & H.H.B. Vedder. *European Environmental Law*, 3rd ed. Groningen: Europa Law Publishing, 2008.

Jans, J.H. & J.M. Verschuuren. *Case note*. District Court The Hague, 24 November 1999.

Jongma, M.P. & F.C.M.A. Michiels. 'Het beroepsrecht van milieu-organisaties moet blijven!'. *Nederlands Juristenblad* (2002): 2238-2239.

Koelemeijer, R.B.A. et al. *Consequences of EU Air Quality Directives for Spatial Development Plans in Various EU Countries*. <www.mnp.nl/en/publications/2005/Consequences_of_EU_air_quality_directives_for_spatial_development_plans_in_various_EU_countries.html>, 3 June 2008. Bilthoven: Netherlands Environmental Assessment Agency, 2005.

Ministry of the Environment. 'Kennisplein Omgevingsvergunning'. <omgevings vergunning.vrom.nl>, 3 June 2008.

Ministry of the Environment. 'Minister reduces environmental administrative burden'. <international.vrom.nl/pagina.html?id=11102>, 3 June 2008.

Ministerie van Algeme Zaken. 'Regeerakkoord 2002'. <www.minaz.nl/Onderwerpen/Regeringsbeleid/Regeerakkoord/Regeerakkoord_2002>, 7 December 2007.

MNP. 'MNP aktueel'. <www.mnp.nl>, 3 June 2008.

Raad van State. 'Council of State: Advisory Body and Administrative Court'. <www.raadvanstate.nl>, 3 June 2008.

Raad van State. 'Annual report 2006'. <www.raadvanstate.nl/publicaties/ jaarverslagen/>, 3 June 2008.

Seerden, R. 'Legal Aspects of Environmental Agreements in the Netherlands, in Particular the Agreement on Packaging and Packaging Waste'. In *Environmental Contracts: Comparative Approaches to Regulatory Innovation in the United States and Europe*, edited by E.W. Orts & K. Deketelaere. The Hague, Kluwer Law International, 2001.

SMN. 'Stichting Milieurechtsbijstand Nederland'. <www.milieurechtsbijstand.nl>, 3 June 2008.

Snape III, W. et al. 'Protecting Ecosystems under the Endangered Species Act: the Sonoran Desert Example'. *Washburn Law Journal* 41 (2001): 14-49.

Stec, S., S. Casey-Lefkowitz & J. Jendroska. *The Aarhus Convention: An Implementation Guide*. New York: United Nations, 2000.

Teunissen, J.M.H.F. 'De algemeen belangorganisatie als bestuursrechtelijk (pseudo) Openbaar Ministerie?'. *Gemeentestem* 7179 (2003): 61-69.

Verschuuren, J. M. 'The Case of Transboundary Wetlands Under the Ramsar Convention: Keep the Lawyers Out!'. *Colorado Journal of International Environmental Law and Policy* 19, no.1 (2007/2008): 49-127.

Verschuuren, J.M. 'Country Report and Case Study: The Netherlands'. In *Access to Justice in Environmental Matters Vol. II*, edited by N. de Sadeleer, G. Roller & M. Dross. Brussels: CEDRE, 2002.

Verschuuren, J.M. 'Effectiveness of Nature Protection Legislation in the EU and the US: The Birds and Habitats Directives and the Endangered Species Act'. *Yearbook of European Environmental Law* 3 (2003): 305-328.

Verschuuren, J.M. 'Environmental Law'. In *Introduction to Dutch Law*, edited by E.H. Hondius, 4th ed. The Hague: Kluwer Law International, 2006.

Verschuuren, J.M. 'Internationaal milieurecht en de Awb'. In *De grootste gemene deler: Opstellen aangeboden aan prof. mr. Th.G. Drupsteen*, edited by M. Lurks et al. Deventer: Kluwer, 2002.

Verschuuren, J.M. 'The Constitutional Right to Protection of the Environment in the Netherlands'. *Austrian Journal for Public and International Law* 46 (1993): 67-77.

Verschuuren, J.M. 'The constitutional right to protection of the environment in the Netherlands'. *Revue Juridique de l'Environnement* (1994): 339-347.

Verschuuren, J.M. 'The Netherlands'. In *Access to Justice in Environmental Matters and the Role of NGOs. Empirical Findings and Legal Appraisal*, edited by N. de Sadeleer, G. Roller & M. Dross. Groningen: Europa Law Publishing, 2005.

TABLE OF LEGISLATION

European Union

Directive 2003/35/EC Public Participation in Respect of the Drawing up of Certain Plans and Programmes relating to the Environment and Amending with Regard to Public Participation and Access to Justice Council Directives 85/337/EEC and 96/61/EC, OJ 2003, L156

Directive 79/409/EEC Protection of Wild Birds, OJ 1979, L 103

Directive 91/676/EEC Protection of Waters against Pollution Caused by Nitrates from Agricultural Sources, OJ 1991, L 375

Directive 92/43/EEC Conservation of Natural Habitats and of Wild Fauna and Flora, OJ 1992, L 206

Regulation (EC) 1013/2006 Shipments of Waste, OJ 2006, L 190

The Netherlands

Algemene wet bestuursrecht [General Administrative Law] Act of 4 June 1992
Burgerlijk Wetboek [Civil Code] Act of 1809
Flora- en faunawet [Flora and Fauna] Act of 25 May 1998

Gewasbeschermingsmidddelen- en biocidenwet [Pesticides and Biocides] Act of
    17 October 2007
Grondwaterwet [Groundwater] Act of 22 May 1981
Kernenergiewet [Nuclear Energy] Act of 21 February 1963
Meststoffenwet [Animal Manure] Act of 27 November 1986
Natuurbeschermingswet 1998 [Nature Conservation] Act of 25 May 1998
Staatsblad [Bulletin of Acts and Orders] 2007, No. 449
Staatsblad [Bulletin of Acts and Orders] 1998, No. 220
Staatsblad [Bulletin of Acts and Orders] 2005, No. 530
Staatsblad [Bulletin of Acts and Orders] 2005, No. 532
Staatsblad [Bulletin of Acts and Orders] 2005, No. 705
Staatsblad [Bulletin of Acts and Orders] 2006, No. 11
Staatsblad [Bulletin of Acts and Orders] 2006, No. 64
Staatsblad [Bulletin of Acts and Orders] 2007, No. 387
Staatsblad [Bulletin of Acts and Orders] 2007, No. 152
Staatsblad [Bulletin of Acts and Orders] 2007, No. 248
Staatsblad [Bulletin of Acts and Orders] 2007, No. 248
Staatsblad [Bulletin of Acts and Orders] 2007, No. 349
Staatsblad [Bulletin of Acts and Orders] 2007, No. 395
Staatsblad [Bulletin of Acts and Orders] 2007, No. 575
Staatsblad [Bulletin of Acts and Orders] 2008, No. 173
Staatsblad [Bulletin of Acts and Orders] 2008, No. 20
Waterwet, Kamerstukken [Water Bill, Parliamentary Documents] I, 2007-2008, 30
    818, A
Wet algemene bepalingen omgevingsrecht, Kamerstukken [Environmental Law
    (General Provisions) Bill, Parliamentary Documents] I, 2007-2008, 30 844, A
Wet bescherming Antarctica [Antarctic Protection] Act of 5 March 1998
Wet bodembescherming [Soil Protection] Act of 3 July 1986
Wet geluidhinder [Noise Abatement] Act of 16 February 1979
Wet luchtverontreiniging [Air Pollution] Act of 26 November 1970
Wet milieubeheer [Environmental Management] Act of 13 June 1979
Wet verontreiniging oppervlaktewateren [Pollution of Surface Waters] Act of
    13 November 1969
Wet verontreiniging zeewater [Pollution of the Sea] Act of 5 June 1975
Wetboek van strafvordering [Code of Criminal Procedure] Act of 15 January 1921

TABLE OF CASES

Administrative Law Division of the Council of State 15 January 2001, (2001)
    Milieu en Recht 73-78
District Court The Hague 24 November 1999, (2000) 27 *Milieu en Recht* 63-67
Court of Appeal The Hague 2 August 2001, (2001) *Milieu en Recht* 258-261
Netherlands Supreme Court 21 March 2003, (2003) *Milieu en Recht* 314-315
Commission v. The Netherlands Case No. C-322/00 [2003] ECR I-11267

ABBREVIATIONS

EC	European Community
ECJ	European Court of Justice
EMA	Environmental Management Act
EU	European Union
GALA	General Administrative Law Act
MNP	Mileu en Natuur Planbureau
NGO	Non-governmental Organization
OJ	Official Journal
PSWA	Pollution of Surface Waters Act
SMN	Stichting Milieurechtsbijstand Nederland
UN/ECE	United Nations/Economic Commission for Europe

Chapter 2

Belgium

Luc Lavrysen

1   INTRODUCTION

1.1   THE TRANSFORMATION OF BELGIUM INTO A FEDERAL STATE[1]

The Kingdom of Belgium is a small country in Western Europe. It has a land surface area of 30,528 km² and a population of around 10.4 million people. Of this number, around six million live in the Flemish Region within an area of 13,522 km², around 3.4 million people live in the Walloon Region within an area of 16,844 km², and around one million people in the Brussels-Capital Region within an area of 161 km². Brussels, which also hosts the main institutions of the European Union (EU), is the federal capital. Belgium became an independent State in 1830. Until 1970 it was a unitary decentralized State. From the early 1960s a State reform process started which gradually transformed Belgium into a complex federal State. In 1963 a so-called language border was established. The law recognized four language areas: the Dutch area, the French area, the German area, and the bilingual Brussels-Capital Region. In 1970, these areas were enshrined in the Constitution.[2] On the Flemish side, there was an increasing conviction that language equality as

---

1. See on this issue: A. Alen & R. Ergec, *Federal Belgium after the Fourth State Reform 1993*, 2nd ed. (Brussels: MFA External Trade and Cooperation for Development, 1998), 80.
2. Art. 4.

Louis J. Kotzé and Alexander R. Paterson (eds), *The Role of the Judiciary in Environmental Governance: Comparative Perspectives*, pp. 85–122.
© 2009 Kluwer Law International BV, The Netherlands.

such was not sufficient. It was considered that the difference in language was accompanied by a difference in culture. This led to the demand for independent authority on cultural matters without the intervention of French-speaking politicians and government officials. A so-called cultural autonomy was established in response to these Flemish demands. In 1970, the Constitution in Article 2, recognized three cultural communities: the Dutch, the French and the German cultural communities. In the following years, the cultural communities were granted their own parliaments (cultural board), their own governments (committee of ministers), and their own administrations. In 1980, the cultural communities became the present communities: the Flemish, French, and German-language communities. Their powers were extended to certain aspects of health care and social policy. In 1989, they also became competent for virtually all matters concerning education.

The industrialization of Belgium began and was most intensive in Wallonia, with specific emphasis on the coal and steel industry. The decline first of the coal-mining industry, and later of the steel industry, in the 1960s and 1970s, induced Walloon regionalism. The impression in Wallonia was that the unitary state, which was also governed by Flemish politicians and officials, was not sufficiently concerned with the economic crisis suffered in Wallonia at a time when Flanders was flourishing economically. Furthermore, there was little trust in the financial and economic decision-making centres elsewhere, particularly those situated in Brussels. Wallonia expressed the desire to obtain its own decision-making powers in socio-economic matters. In response to this demand in Wallonia, three regions were created. In 1970, the principle of three regions was enshrined in the Constitution: the Flemish Region, the Walloon Region and the Brussels-Capital Region.[3] This principle was first elaborated for a provisional period (1974-1975), and acquired a more permanent character in 1980, at least as regards the Flemish and Walloon Regions.

Owing to the coexistence of the communities on the one hand, and the regions on the other hand, the Belgian federal system is very complex. Hitherto, each new round of State reforms raised the question in Belgium whether the new State structure was a federal system or not. The fourth reform of the State (1993) leaves no room for doubt that it is. The new Article 1 of the Constitution now actually stipulates that 'Belgium is a Federal State constituted of Communities and Regions'.

Following the federal general elections of June 2007, difficult negotiations started between political leaders in the North and the South to review the actual shape of the State structures. So far it is unclear, however, to which reforms these negotiations will lead.

---

3. Art. 3.

1.2   FEDERAL GOVERNMENT[4]

At the federal level, there is a federal government, a federal parliament (with two chambers) re-elected every four years, a federal administration (comprising different ministries or so called Federal Public Services) and different federal institutions, such as the Federal Planning Bureau and the Federal Agency for Nuclear Control.

Although powers have considerably been devolved to the regions and communities, the federal authority still holds some important powers. Federal government has all the powers which are not allocated to the regions or communities. Federal competencies include: police and civil protection; justice (including courts and tribunals); civil law; penal law; monetary policy (in the framework of the European Economic and Monetary Union); economic, financial and trade law (including consumer protection law, public procurement regulations, and maximum State aid); some aspects of energy policy (nuclear power, power stations investment planning, heavy infrastructure for storing, distribution and production of energy, tariffs); traffic regulations (land, water, air); and some aspects of environmental policy, such as product standards, protection against ionizing radiation and the protection of the North Sea.

1.3   REGIONS AND COMMUNITIES[5]

Each community and region has its own legislative assembly (council or parliament), and executive body (government), the composition and functioning of which are determined by the Constitution and special majority federal laws enacted in implementation thereof. Since the communities and regions overlap, the composition of the community parliaments is based on that of the regional parliaments, the sole exception being that of the Council of the German-speaking Community, which is directly and independently elected.

The communities and regions are vested with legislative power equal to that of the federal legislature. In many areas, the communities and regions have sole authority to legislate by decrees (or ordinances in the Brussels-Capital Region), having the force of statutes throughout the territory for which they are responsible. Decrees may repeal, amplify, amend or replace statutory provisions in force in the allocated areas of responsibility. Like statutes, they escape review by the ordinary courts and the administrative courts. For this reason they have been placed under the control of the Constitutional Court.

---

4. See in this respect, Belgium Government Portal. 'Official Information and Services'. <www.fgov.be>, 4 August 2008.
5. See Flanders, 'The Official Portal Site', <www.vlaanderen.be>, 4 August 2008; Wallonie, 'Le site du Gouvernement wallon', <www.gov.wallonie.be>, 10 September 2008, and CIBG, 'Living in Brussels', <www.irisnet.be>, 4 August 2008.

The legal equality of federal, community and regional statutes is a distinguishing feature of the Belgian federal system and averts the incidences of concurrent jurisdictions found in certain federal States which operate on the *Bundesrecht bricht Landesrecht* principle. In fact, in Belgian public law, concurrent jurisdictions are the exception to the general rule of exclusively divided jurisdictions between the federal authority and the federated entities.

The responsibilities of the communities and regions, albeit restrictively allocated, are very broad. The communities have responsibility for cultural affairs, education, personalized services, and the use of languages in certain matters. The regions have exclusive or partial jurisdiction over land use and planning, environmental and water policy, rural redevelopment and nature conservation, housing, agricultural policy, economic policy, energy policy, local authorities, employment policy, public works and transport.

The State reform of 1993 vested the communities and regions with extensive jurisdiction in internal relations, which some observers claim has left a confederate imprint on the State set-up.

2   ENVIRONMENTAL ISSUES AND PERFORMANCE

With 10.4 million people, Belgium has a high population density of 341 inhabitants per km^2. The country is characterized by a wide scattering of quasi-urban settlements on rural land. The five largest cities, Brussels, Antwerp, Ghent, Liège and Charleroi, form a part of larger conurbations of at least one million inhabitants. Belgium is situated along an axis of regions extending from England to the north of Italy that have been densely populated and developed since the Middle Ages. The Belgian economy is one of the most open in the Organization for Economic Cooperation and Development (OECD) area. The per *capita* gross domestic product (GDP) is well above the OECD European average. Services account for more than 52% of GDP and manufacturing almost 22%; of the latter, food products (4.1% of GDP) and chemicals (3.8%) are the major branches. Agriculture, hunting, forestry and fishing represent 2.1% of GDP. Belgium is the world's ninth biggest exporter. Exports of goods are dominated by machinery and transport equipment (90% of the cars made in Belgium are exported), other manufactured goods (for example, gemstones) and chemicals.[6] The United Nations Development Programme (UNDP) Human Development Index 2005 for Belgium is 0.946, which ranks the country seventeenth out of 177 countries for which data is available.[7]

In a country as densely populated and economically developed as Belgium, pressures on the environment are significant. As much as one-fourth of the territory is built-up or covered with dense networks of roads, railways and navigation canals. Industry, heavy freight and passenger traffic, and intensive livestock production and crop cultivation also result in increased pressure on the air, soil, water

---

6. OECD, *Environmental Performance Reviews: Belgium* (Paris: OECD, 1998), 35-39.
7. UNDP, 'Human Development Report 2007/2008', <hdr.undp.org/en>, 4 August 2008.

resources and natural environment. In this context, making development economically, environmentally and socially sustainable is a challenge. Because of
Belgium's very open economy (exports reaching 83% of GDP and imports
81%) and its location, there are many physical and economic interdependencies
between Belgium, its European partners and beyond.[8]

According to the 2007 OECD Environmental Performance Review, Belgium
is still catching up on its historic environmental backlog.[9] The challenge now will
be to pursue efforts to implement environmental policies effectively and efficiently, further integrate environmental concerns into economic and social decisions,
and meet the country's international environmental commitments.[10] After periods
of uncertainty and of major environmental reforms associated with the process of
federalization of the country, Belgium's federal and regional authorities were,
during the last decade, able to build stable environmental institutions with a
clear division of responsibilities and mechanisms for co-operation, implementation
of EU environmental legislation as well as the country's international commitments, and co-operation and partnership with industry, trade unions and environmental non-governmental organizations (NGOs). Total expenditure on pollution
abatement and control grew significantly, attaining about 1.7% of GDP. Nature
conservation progressed as well, with the extension of protected areas in the context of the Natura 2000 Network, despite the very high densities of population,
activities and infrastructure of the country. Improved environmental governance
was achieved through a mix of policy instruments, including economic instruments, information campaigns, agreements (between the regions, provinces and
municipalities), regulations (which were codified or streamlined) and voluntary
actions (taken by industry). Inspection authorities also improved their effectiveness and efficiency. Progress with single permitting and the use of environmental
impact assessment (EIA) was noteworthy. All these efforts have helped partly to
repay the country's outstanding environmental debt. However, a number of indicators show that the results remain insufficient. Energy use, material use and
pollutant emission intensities (i.e. per unit of GDP) remain relatively high. Indicators of densities of environmental pressures (i.e. per km^2) are also very high.
Addressing this issue will require Belgium to strengthen and/or extend its environmental efforts and to make them more cost-effective by increasing the use of
economic instruments (such as taxes, charges, and emission trading mechanisms)
and economic analysis (for example, cost-benefit analysis), notably for air, water
and waste management. Belgium made progress over the last decade in decoupling
environmental pressures from economic growth for some conventional pollutants
(such as SOx and NOx emissions) and for water abstractions.[11] Growth in

---

8. OECD, *Environmental Performance Reviews: Belgium* (Paris: OECD, 2007).
9. In the 2008 Environmental Performance Index drawn up by Yale and Columbia Universities,
   Belgium lags behind most other EU countries with a 57th place worldwide. See EPI, 'Environmental Performance Index', <epi.yale.edu>, 10 September 2008.
10. *Ibid.*
11. Virtually all emission reduction targets for air pollutants, more particularly with respect to SO_2,
    NH_3 and VOS, were attained or even exceeded. The emission reduction target for NO_x will

household waste for final disposal was also decoupled from economic growth due to high rates of recycling. There is, however, still a need to decouple road freight transport from economic growth, as the increase in road freight transport is of great concern. Energy intensity (total primary energy supply per unit of GDP) is still considerably higher than in neighbouring countries and integration of environmental concerns into energy policy is lagging behind. Energy prices should incorporate environmental external costs and pressures on water and soil resources (from water abstractions, nitrate and pesticides) are among the highest in the OECD. The targets to expand organic agriculture also have not been met. A number of tax concessions led to perverse effects on the environment. No action has started on a green tax reform as recommended in the first OECD environmental performance review. The effectiveness and economic efficiency of the country's subsidy schemes for rewarding environmental behaviour may therefore also require review. Moreover, quantitative targets are needed and cost-benefit analysis should be used more systematically for setting priorities.[12]

3   ENVIRONMENTAL LAW FRAMEWORK[13]

3.1   Significant Impact of European Environmental Law

As in the other Member States of the EU, most of Belgium's domestic environmental legislation implements European (or International) environmental legislation at the federal and the regional levels. Where European environmental directives simply regulate the main principles of a given problem, federal or regional environmental law will of course be more specific and detailed. There is also proper domestic legislation in areas where European environmental legislation is currently insufficient. Although the European Court of Justice (ECJ) is competent to condemn (and even penalize) Member States that do not implement European legislation, or that do not implement or enforce it properly, the direct (as regards regulations) or indirect (as regards directives that are implemented in domestic legislation) enforcement of European environmental legislation is, as is the case with the enforcement of domestic environmental legislation, the competence of the Member States.[14] The EU has no environmental inspectors, no

---

probably not be attained, while special efforts will have to be made to achieve reductions of PM_{10} and $PM_{2.5}$ levels. The number of households connected to the wastewater treatment infrastructure has risen in the last ten years from 26% to 46%. The reduction targets that have been set by the International North Sea Conference were attained for twenty-five of the thirty-seven substances.

12. *Ibid.*
13. For an overview, see: E. De Pue, L. Lavrysen & P. Stryckers, *Milieuzakboekje 2007* (Mechelen: Wolters Kluwer, 2007), 958; K. Deketelaere (ed.), *Handboek Milieu- en Energierecht* (Brugge: Die Keure, 2006) 1801; L. Lavrysen, *Handboek Milieurecht 2006*, (Mechelen: Wolters Kluwer, 2006), 643.
14. J.H. Jans & H.H.B. Vedder, *European Environmental Law,* 3rd ed. (Groningen: Europa Law Publishing, 2008), 150-115.

dedicated police force and no authority to directly penalize infringements of European law by national subjects. Enforcement of environmental law, through environmental inspectorates, police forces and judicial action, is therefore an internal matter for the Member States.

3.2 CONSTITUTIONAL PROVISIONS

In the Belgian Constitution, there currently is reference to environmental protection in two different provisions. Article 7b, the recently introduced single provision of Title Ib 'General Policy objectives of Federal Belgium, the Communities and the Regions' of the Belgian Constitution, introduced by the Constitutional Amendment of 25 April 2007, states that:

> In the exercise of their respective competencies the Federal State, the Communities and the Regions foster the objectives of sustainable development in their social, economic and environmental aspects, taking into account the solidarity between generations.

This provision is the only Constitutional provision that sets policy objectives for the different authorities, since it calls for integration of sustainable development concerns in the different policies of the authorities concerned.[15] The fundamental rights of Belgians are established in Title II of the Constitution. One of the provisions of that title deals with the so-called social, economic and cultural rights. Article 23 of the Constitution, introduced by the Constitutional Amendment of 31 January 1994, provides in this respect that:

> Everyone has the right to lead a life in conformity with human dignity. To this end, the laws, decrees [...] guarantee, taking into account corresponding obligations, economic, social and cultural rights, and determine the conditions for exercising them. These rights include notably: [...] the right to enjoy the protection of a healthy environment...

This article of the Constitution was extensively debated by the constitutional legislator, yet the right to the protection of a healthy environment was given relatively little thought. What is certain, though, is that the term 'healthy environment' is broadly interpreted. As appears from the parliamentary preparations, every person has 'the right to a decent, healthy and ecologically balanced environment',[16] and:

> [t]he government has a special responsibility to ensure that future generations still have a liveable environment. Its task in this respect is a very broad one.

---

15. B. Jadot, 'Pour une meilleure prise en compte de l'environnement et les enjeux environnementaux dans la Constitution', in *En hommage à Françis Delpérée: Itinéraires d'un constitutionnaliste*, ed. Bruylant (Brussels: Bruylant, 2007), 668.
16. *Parl. St.* [Senate] BZ 1991-1992, n. 100-2/3, 20; *Parl. St.* [House of Representatives] BZ 1991-1992, n. 391/1, 12. According to certain case law, protection may even cover the aesthetic aspect of the environment: Justice of the Peace, Marche-en-Famenne, *JLMB* 21 February 1995: 1301,

It not only covers conservation, but also the controlling of water, air and soil pollution, a proper planning of the available space and of farming and stock-breeding activities, and the promotion of environmentally-friendly technologies in industry and communications.[17]

It was however repeatedly *mille fois répétée*[18] emphasized that since the rights mentioned in that article have no direct effect, no subjective rights can be derived from them.[19] They are primarily meant to serve as guiding principles for government policy and to instruct the legislature.[20] However, the provision also has other legal effects. First, the parliamentary preparation of Article 23 of the Constitution suggests that the fundamental economic, social and cultural rights are supposed to produce a *standstill* effect.[21] Environmental policy should pursue not only a healthy environment, but also an environment with a standard of health no lower than the existing one. The standstill principle is an intrinsic element of fundamental social rights.[22] The government has a wide margin of appreciation, though only in a certain direction. An impairment of the existing level of protection can be sanctioned by the courts. A second meaning in positive law (to a certain extent similar to the standstill effect), lies in a combination of the economic, social and cultural rights with the principles of equality and non-discrimination, which are guaranteed by Articles 10 and 11 of the Constitution. Under these articles, the recognition of socio-economic rights must be ensured without discrimination. According to the parliamentary preparation, an infringement of these provisions by a legislative rule qualifies for review by the Constitutional Court.[23] Even though the rule protects a healthy environment for two distinct categories of persons, it must not unwarrantedly offer a lesser degree of protection to one category than to the other. In this way, too, a *lower limit* is set to the government's margin of appreciation.

---

     note by M.C. Coppieters. Cf. *Schweren* CS 75.557, 6 August 1998, *Dossogne* CS 77.497, 9 December 1998.

17. *Parl. St.* [Senate] BZ 1991-1992, n. 100-2/1, 10.

18. P. Martens, 'L'insertion des droits économiques, sociaux et culturels dans la *Constitution*', *RBDC* 1 (1995): 7.

19. See *Parl. St.* [Senate] BZ 1991-1992, n. 100-2/1, n. 100-2/3, 4 and 11, and n. 100-2/4, 5, 14, 20, 70-74, e.g., at 5: 'The fundamental social rights, on the other hand, must not have direct effect, and the working party felt that this had to emerge unequivocally and explicitly from the text of the proposal, and it will be repeated whenever necessary.'

20. *Parl. St.* [Senate] BZ 1991-1992, n. 100-2/3, 13. See also *Parl. St.* [Senate] n. 100-2/4, 13 and 41, and *Parl. St.* [House of Representatives] BZ 1991-1992, n. 381/1, 9.

21. *Parl. St.* [Senate] BZ 1991-1992, n. 100-2/3, 13. See also *Parl. St.* [Senate] BZ 1991-1992, n. 100-2/4, 85-87, and *Parl. St.* [House of Representatives] BZ 1991-1992, n. 381/1, 8. On *standstill*, see I. Hachez, 'L'effet de *standstill*: Le pari des droits économiques, sociaux et culturels', *APT* 24 (2000): 30-57, and G. Maes, 'Het standstillbeginsel in verdragsbepalingen en in art. 23 G.W.: progressieve (sociale) grondrechtenbescherming', *RW* 69 (2005-2006): 1081-1094.

22. Maes, *supra* n. 21, 464.

23. *Parl. St.* [House of Representatives] BZ 1991-1992, n. 381/1, 9. See also *Parl. St.* [Senate] BZ 1991-1992, n. 100-2/4, 39, and *Parl. St.* [House of Representatives] BZ 1991-1992, n. 218/3, 18.

A third legal meaning of the economic, social and cultural rights, according to the parliamentary preparation, lies in a Constitution-compliant interpretation of laws, decrees and other rules. Where they are open to several interpretations, a court of law is obliged to follow the interpretation that is compatible with the Constitution.[24] This means that, in case of doubt, an environmentally-friendly interpretation is recommended in principle: *in dubio pro natura*. According to Benoît Jadot,[25] this rule of interpretation is also capable of reducing the public authorities' margin of appreciation in the granting of licenses for activities that are a potential threat to the environment. A license should be refused if human or environmental health will be affected. The same author also holds the view that the right of action should, in light of Article 23 of the Constitution, be broadly interpreted when the protection of the environment is at stake.[26] A right (to the protection of a healthy environment) without a right of action would be pointless.[27]

3.3   FEDERAL ENVIRONMENTAL LEGISLATION

The main body of environmental legislation at the federal level consists of: the Act of 15 April 1994 on the *Protection of the Population and of the Environment against Hazards arising from Ionizing Radiation and on the Federal Agency for Nuclear Control*; the Act of 21 December 1998 on *Product Standards to Promote Sustainable Production and Consumption Patterns and to Protect the Environment and Public Health*; the Act of 13 February 2006 on the *Environmental Impact Assessment of certain Plans and Programs and on the Involvement of the General Public in the Elaboration of Plans and Programs in connection with the Environment*; and the Act of 20 January 1999 on the *Protection of the Marine Environment in Maritime Areas under the Jurisdiction of Belgium*. The majority of these laws are implemented by a whole series of Royal Decrees. The federal authorities also play a major part in the enforcement of not only federal, but also regional environmental legislation, since the police, the prosecuting authorities and the courts are the responsibility of the federal government. This not only means that the procedural rules of these judicial authorities are established at the federal level, but also that a series of general rules from the Penal Code, for instance, are

---

24. *Parl. St.* [Senate] BZ 1991-1992, n. 100-2/3, 13, and *Parl. St.* [House of Representatives] BZ 1991-1992, n. 381/1, 9.

25. B. Jadot, 'Le droit à l'environnement', in *Les droits économiques, sociaux et culturels dans la Constitution*, ed. R. Ergec (Brussels: Bruylant, 1995), 263.

26. *Ibid.*, 264-267. See, however, *Vzw Réserves naturelles* CS 133.834, 13 July 2004; and *Vzw Grez-Doiceau, Urbanisme et Environnement* CS 135.408, 24 September 2004, *JT* (2005): 117 and 119, note by Jadot, *supra* n. 25. See also on this subject T. Hazeur, 'L'intérêt à agir des associations de défense de l'environnement devant le Conseil d'Etat: quelle liberté pour le juge et quel rapport à la nature?', *Amén* (2006): 105-114.

27. L. Lavrysen & J. Theunis, 'The Right to the Protection of a Healthy Environment in the Belgian Constitution: Retrospect and International Perspective', in *Constitutional rights to an ecologically balanced environment*, ed. I. Larmuseau (Ghent: 2Mpact, 2007), 9-29.

applicable to environmental offences, even if those offences are defined in regional legislation. In the area of enforcement, the federal government has given the various public authorities, environmental organizations and indirectly, individuals, the ability to take action in private law against environmental offences in pursuance of the Act of 12 January 1993 on the *Right of Action for the Protection of the Environment.*

3.4   REGIONAL ENVIRONMENTAL LEGISLATION

As mentioned above, the main responsibility for environmental policy and therefore for environmental legislation in Belgium, lies with the three regions. This means not only that the bulk of environmental legislation in Belgium is of a regional nature, but also that this legislation differs across the three regions, although European environmental legislation ensures a certain and necessary degree of harmonization. Although there are undeniable differences between the three regions, there is still a fair amount of common ground, either on account of the common European origin of the regulations, or because national legislation from the time when environmental policy had not yet been devolved to the regions, is taken as a basis for further development.

In the Flemish Region there is, first, the Decree of 5 April 1995 on *General Provisions of Environmental Policy.* This was conceived as a basic decree which, in the long term, is meant to develop into a kind of environmental code in which all basic environmental regulations are brought together. This move toward codification is still far from complete since there are several individual decrees which have not yet been incorporated in this Environmental Code. Currently, the Decree of 5 April 1995, as repeatedly amended, contains regulations in connection with objectives and principles of environmental policy, environmental policy planning, environmental quality standards, internal corporate environmental protection, EIA and safety reporting, environmental conditions, strategic counselling, prevention and repair of environmental damage, and enforcement. A second important decree is the Decree of 28 June 1985 on *Environmental Licences,* supplemented by a series of implementing orders, which regulates in detail the licensing and environmental conditions for environmentally harmful establishments. There are also a number of sector-specific regulations, such as the Act of 26 March 1971 on the *Protection of Surface Waters against Pollution*; the Decree of 24 May 2002 on *Water Intended for Human Use*; the Decree of 18 July 2003 on *Integrated Water Management*; the Decree of 27 October 2006 on *Soil Remediation and Soil Protection*; the Decree of 22 December 2006 on the *Protection of Water against Pollution from Fertilizers*; the Decree of 2 July 1981 on the *Prevention and Management of Waste*; and the Decree of 21 October 1997 on *Nature Conservation and the Natural Environment,* to name the most important ones. Detailed implementing orders have been enacted for most of these decrees. Town and country planning and urban development are covered by the Decree of 18 May 1999 on the *Organization of Town and Country Planning.*

A similar process of codification of environmental law has started in the Walloon Region. Pursuant to the Decree of 27 May 2004, *Livre I^e du Code de l'environnement* [Volume I of the Walloon Environmental Code] was brought into effect. It currently contains regulations in connection with the principles of environmental law, the central advisory body, environmental information and awareness, environmental policy planning in the context of sustainable development, EIA, and environmental covenants. By a Decree of the Walloon Government of 3 March 2005, this Code was supplemented with *Livre II du Code de l'environnement contenant le Code de l'eau* [Volume II Environmental Code containing the Water Code]. This contains regulations on principles and organizational structures, integrated management of the natural water cycle, management of water for human use and the financing thereof, and the enforcement of said regulations. The system of environmental licensing for environmentally harmful establishments is covered by the Decree of 11 March 1999 on *Environmental Licences* and its implementing orders. In addition, there is also a fair amount of sector-specific legislation. The main sector-specific laws include: the Act of 12 July 1973 on *Nature Conservation*; the Decree of 27 June 1997 on *Wastes*; the Decree of 1 April 2004 on the *Remediation of Polluted Soils and the Rehabilitation of Economic Sites*; and the Decree of 10 November 2004 *Establishing a System of Negotiable Emission Rights for Greenhouse Gases, Setting up a Walloon Kyoto Fund and on the Flexible Mechanisms of the Kyoto Fund*. Town and country planning and the protection of architectural and natural heritage is regulated by the *Code wallon de l'aménagement du territoire, de l'urbanisme en du patrimoine* (CWATUP) [Walloon Code on Town and Country Planning, Urban Development and Architectural and Natural Heritage].[28]

In the Brussels-Capital Region, environmental licenses are covered by the Ordinance of 5 June 1997 on *Environmental Licences* and its implementing orders. Other horizontal environmental measures are set out in the Ordinance of 25 March 1999 on the *Detection, Reporting, Prosecution and Penalization of Environmental Offences*; the Ordinance of 18 March 2004 on *Environmental Impact Assessment for Plans and Programs*; the Ordinance of 18 March 2004 on *Access to Environmental Information in the Brussels-Capital Region*; and the Ordinance of 29 April 2004 on *Environmental Covenants*. Sector-specific regulations are laid down in the Ordinance of 13 May 2004 on the *Management of Polluted Soils*; the Ordinance of 25 March 1999 on the *Assessment and Improvement of Ambient Air Quality*; the Ordinance of 17 July 1997 on *Combating of Noise Pollution in Urban Areas*; the Ordinance of 7 March 1991 on the *Prevention and Management of Wastes*; the Ordinance of 29 August 1991 on the *Protection of Wildlife and Hunting*; and the Ordinance of 27 April 1995 on *Nature Conservation and Protection*. The Brussels-Capital Region also has a Brussels Code on Town and Country Planning (Ordinance of 13 May 2004).

---

28. B. Lombaert et al., *Mémento de l'environnement* (Waterloo: Kluwer, 2006).

3.5   Legislation through Cooperation Agreements

In a number of cases, the competent authorities chose to jointly address certain environmental issues through so-called cooperation agreements rather than by establishing separate arrangements. Once these agreements are approved by the respective parliaments, they acquire the force of law. Examples of such agreements include the Cooperation Agreement of 5 April 1995 between the Federal State, the Flemish Region, the Walloon Region and the Brussels-Capital Region on International Environmental Policy; the Cooperation Agreement of 30 May 1996 between the Regions on the Prevention and Management of Packaging Waste; and the Cooperation Agreement of 21 June 1999 between the Federal State, the Flemish Region, the Walloon Region and the Brussels-Capital Region on the Management of the Risks of Major Accidents Involving Dangerous Substances.

4   THE COURT SYSTEM[29]

4.1   The Constitutional Court[30]

The Constitutional Court was originally created in 1984 as an arbitrator between the federal and regional legislators. By having its powers extended over time, it has become a constitutional court in its own right. The Constitutional Court has exclusive competence to review regulations that have the force of law. By 'regulations having force of law' is meant both substantive and formal rules adopted by the federal parliament (which are called acts) and by the parliaments of the communities and regions (which are called decrees or, as far as the Brussels-Capital Region is concerned, ordinances). All other regulations, such as Royal Decrees, decrees of governments of communities and regions, ministerial decrees, regulations and decrees of provinces and municipalities, as well as court judgments, fall outside the jurisdiction of the Constitutional Court. Article 142 of the Constitution affords the Constitutional Court (which owes its original name (Court of Arbitration) to its original function as federal arbitrator), the exclusive authority to review regulations having the force of law for compliance to the rules that determine the respective powers of the State, the communities and the regions. The Constitutional Court also has jurisdiction to pronounce judgment on any violation by a regulation having force of law of fundamental rights and freedoms guaranteed in Title II of the Constitution (Articles 8 to 32) and of Articles 170 (legality principle in tax-related matters), 172 (equality in tax-related matters) and 191 (protection of

---

29. See: A. Alen (ed.), *Treatise on Belgian Constitutional Law* (Deventer: Kluwer Law and Taxation Publishers, 1992), 95-115; see also: L. Lavrysen, J. Van den Berghe & K. Van den Berghe, *Report to the European Union Forum of judges for the Environment (EUFJE) on the Belgian situation concerning Criminal Enforcement of Environmental Law* (Brussels: EUFJE, 2007).
30. M. Bossuyt, 'Constitutional Court', <www.const-court.be>, 4 August 2008.

foreign nationals). The Constitutional Court can therefore also review laws relating to the environment for compliance with the Constitution. Around 8% of the Court's cases deal with environmental law and town and country planning.

4.2 THE ORDINARY COURTS

Belgium is judicially organized on the basis of a territorial subdivision with one Court of Cassation (Supreme Court) for the whole country, five jurisdictions (Courts of Appeal and Labour Courts), twenty-seven districts (Courts of First Instance, Labour Tribunals and Commercial Courts), and 225 sub-districts (Justices of the Peace and Police Courts). The public prosecution is largely organized based on the same subdivision, although there currently is also a Federal Prosecutor dealing with special types of organized crime.

The Court of Cassation[31] is the highest court of law and oversees the correct enforcement of the laws by the courts and tribunals. The Court of Cassation does not deliver judgment on the facts, but verifies whether the court deciding questions of fact, has correctly enforced the law. A lawsuit can therefore only be brought before the Court of Cassation after it has already been adjudicated by the court hearing the main action and by the appeal court. When the Court of Cassation establishes that the court has infringed the law, it will quash the judgment and refer the case to a court of law at the same level as the court that passed the unlawful judgment. That court will have to hear the case *de novo*. The Court of Cassation has a *ministère public* [department] composed of thirteen judicial officers, who advises the Court on the performance of its duties. This department is headed by the Attorney-General seated at the Court of Cassation.

Belgium is furthermore divided into five jurisdictions, each with a Court of Appeal and a Labour Court (Antwerp, Brussels, Ghent, Liège and Mons). These are the appellate bodies for the courts in the districts of their jurisdiction. A Court of Appeal has three types of divisions. There are the divisions for civil cases, which hear appeals against judgments delivered in the first instance by the civil divisions of the courts of first instance, and the commercial courts. These divisions are composed of one or three justices, as the parties choose. Then there are the penal divisions, which decide in criminal cases on the appeal against sentences passed by the corresponding divisions of the courts of first instance. Finally, there are the juvenile divisions, which concern themselves with the judgments of the juvenile judges at the court of first instance. The divisions of the court of appeal are usually composed of a president and two justices. In order to reduce the backlog of cases, it is permitted to only have one justice sitting in the division (except in criminal cases). Each Court of Appeal and Labour Court has a prosecution department headed by an Attorney-General.

---

31. Juridat, 'Le portail du Pouvoir judiciaire de Belgique', <www.cass.be>, 4 August 2008.

In Belgium, there are twenty-seven Courts of First Instance, one for each district. A court of first instance has three types of divisions. Civil divisions have jurisdiction in all cases that have not exclusively been assigned to other courts of law. These divisions also rule on appeals against judgments delivered by the Justices of the Peace and the Police Courts in civil matters. Penal Divisions (also called criminal courts or *tribunaux correctionnels*) decide on offences that have not been assigned to the Police Court or the Court of Assizes (a criminal court for very serious crimes). They also rule on appeals against sentences passed by the Police Courts in criminal cases. The juvenile divisions (or Juvenile Courts) rule on protective measures towards minors or take repressive measures against juvenile offenders. The divisions may be composed of three judges or one judge, usually according to the parties' choice. The Court of First Instance is the ordinary court and has general jurisdiction. This means that it is authorized to rule on all matters that are not reserved for another court of law. It is especially the Court of First Instance that tries environmental cases of a criminal as well as civil nature. The president of the Court of First Instance has his or her own special powers in urgent cases. He or she may decide in interim injunction proceedings on urgent matters which would take too long for the full court to hear. Judgments delivered by the Court of First Instance (except for cases that are already an appeal against a decision of a Justice of the Peace or a Police Court), are open to appeal before a court of appeal.

Each sub-district has one Justice of the Peace Court and a Police Court. The Justice of the Peace Court stands closest to the legal subject. A Justice of the Peace hears all cases where the value of the petition does not exceed EUR 1,860.00. In addition, the Justice of the Peace has extensive powers in rent disputes, family matters, expropriations, easements, agricultural affairs and the mentally ill. The Justice of the Peace is known especially as a family judge. Judgments delivered by a Justice of the Peace are open to appeal before the Court of First Instance or the Commercial Court (in commercial cases), depending on the type of case. Each judicial sub-district also has a Police Court. These courts punish traffic offences and minor offences (night-time noise, intentional damage to property, and so forth). All these courts have the competence to hear environmental matters depending of course on the nature of the case before them.

4.3   THE ADMINISTRATIVE COURTS

The Council of State[32] is the supreme administrative court and was set up to rule on certain disputes in its capacity as an administrative court. The Administrative Jurisdiction Division protects the citizen against unlawful government decisions. Insofar as there are no other competent courts, all natural and legal persons can bring an action for annulment before the Council of State against unlawful

---

32.   Council of State, 'Welkom bij de Raad van State', <www.raadvst-consetat.be>, 4 August 2008.

administrative acts that have caused them detriment. As the highest administrative court, the Council of State acts as an appeal body against judgments of lower administrative courts deciding on certain matters. The rulings of the Council of State are not open to appeal. The Council of State, however, faces a backlog of several years, which means that the legal protection it is supposed to offer is often theoretical. The average backlog is nearly five years. It is not exceptional for a ruling to follow more than nine years after the action for annulment has been brought, by which time, in the instance of, for example an environmental license, the challenged license has already long been executed. By the Act of 1989, the Council of State was empowered to suspend the implementation of a challenged administrative decision. An action for cessation may be brought along with the action for annulment. The Council of State may suspend the challenged decision if the grounds for annulment are found to be valid; if there is an urgent necessity; and if the immediate implementation of the challenged act or regulation may cause detriment that is difficult to remedy. However, a petitioner who obtains no interim relief from the Council of State, will often conduct a drawn out action at the end of which the ruling will often have been overtaken by events. The suspension of implementation and the annulment of administrative acts (individual legal acts and regulations) that are contrary to the legal rules in force, are the main duties of the Council of State. The Council of State boasts a certain degree of specialization because the same divisions deal with cases in the same sphere. For instance, some divisions handle cases in the sphere of town and country planning, while other divisions handle environmental cases. In addition, the judge advocates who advise the Council of State handle the same matters, so that they too have a certain degree of specialization. Environmental cases and town and country planning cases account for about 22% of the general cases (without counting the very high number of immigration law cases). This is quite a significant proportion.

5   ENVIRONMENTAL JURISDICTION

5.1   INTRODUCTION

It follows from the division of powers between the different courts and tribunals that they all, to a greater or lesser extent, have to try environmental disputes. Where such disputes concern questions of compatibility of federal and regional laws with the constitutional rights and freedoms, or with the division of powers between the federal State and the regions and communities, they will have to be settled by the Constitutional Court in the context of an action for annulment or a question referred for a preliminary ruling.[33] When such a question arises in a dispute that is pending before another court of law, the latter court cannot settle this question. It must instead refer the case to the Constitutional Court for a preliminary ruling, unless the Constitutional Court has already settled this question on the

---

33.   Art. 142 of the Constitution; Special Act of 6 January 1989 on the Constitutional Court.

occasion of a similar preliminary issue referred in another case. The courts are bound by the ruling given by the Constitutional Court on the preliminary issue. It is important to note that the Constitutional Court, in its review of compliance with the Constitution and the power-assigning rules, also verifies (albeit indirectly) conformity with treaty provisions that are binding on Belgium and secondary European law (directives and regulations). When the Constitutional Court concludes that an act, decree or ordinance infringes the constitutional rules, whether or not in combination with international or European law, the courts will have to refrain from applying that particular provision. In the context of an action for annulment,[34] the Court can wholly or partly annul an act, decree or ordinance, whereupon the nullified provisions are removed from the legal system with retroactive effect, except where the Court decides to maintain the effects of a nullified provision for the past or for a specific period in the future, for instance in order to allow the relevant legislature to adopt new legislation that complies with the Constitution.

The application of federal and regional environmental legislation leads to the establishment of, on the one hand, a whole series of administrative regulations, by means of which the federal and regional governments implement these acts, decrees and ordinances, and, on the other hand, of a whole series of 'individual administrative acts' adopted by various administrative authorities, including local and provincial authorities. The bulk of these individual administrative decisions consist of the granting or refusal of environmental licenses, conservation licenses, planning permissions and all sorts of other approvals and authorizations. Actions for annulment can be brought before the Administrative Jurisdiction Section of the Council of State against such regulatory and administrative acts within sixty days after publication or after obtaining knowledge of an interested party.[35] This would certainly be the case when no further administrative appeal is possible to a higher administrative authority. If there is a risk that the judgment on the merits will not be delivered timeously, an action for cessation can be brought as part of so-called administrative interim injunction proceedings.[36] The Council of State is empowered to review the legality of administrative acts, in other words, their compliance with higher legal standards, and more particularly international and European law, the Constitution, statutes, decrees and ordinances, and with general legal principles, including the principles of good governance and the formal obligation to justify individual administrative acts.[37] When the Council of State finds an illegality, it will wholly or partly annul the challenged administrative decision, causing this decision to be removed from the legal order with retroactive effect, unless the Council decides to maintain all or part of the effects of the nullified decision.

---

34. Anyone who can prove an interest within six months after publication in the *Belgisch Staatsblad* (Belgian Official Journal) can bring an action for annulment before the Constitutional Court against a regulation having force of law. An action for cessation can be brought within three months.
35. Art. 160 of the Constitution; Art. 14 of the coordinated laws on the Council of State.
36. Art. 17 of the coordinated laws on the Council of State.
37. Imposed by the Act of 29 July 1991 on the express justification of administrative acts.

The Council of State may also suspend an administrative act in administrative interim injunction proceedings pending the hearing of the case on the merits, and may also order provisional measures. Under certain conditions it can also impose a penalty payment in order to enforce compliance with its rulings.

In Belgian law, breaches of environmental law usually are punished with penal sanctions. These penal sanctions – which in more recent environmental legislation tend to be more severe in comparison with earlier environmental laws – are usually defined in such a way that they relate to offences that belong to the jurisdiction of the *tribunaux correctionnels* [criminal courts].[38] Such offences can be brought before the criminal courts at the suit of the public prosecutor, following a complaint by a third party claiming damages before the examining magistrate or by means of direct summons by the aggrieved party. The Criminal Court rules on the criminal law aspect of the case by investigating whether the offences are proven and the defendant is guilty, and by imposing the appropriate penalties and safeguard measures. When the aggrieved party brings an action for damages, the court will also have to rule on the compensation to be awarded to the aggrieved party. Judgments of the criminal courts are open for appeal to the Court of Appeal. An appeal can also be brought before the Supreme Court.

Civil law disputes belong to the jurisdiction of the civil courts. In the first instance they are heard by the Justice of the Peace or by the Civil Division of the Court of First Instance, depending on the monetary value involved in the dispute. Judgments delivered in the first instance are respectively open to appeal before the Court of First Instance or the Court of Appeal. Following that, an appeal can still be brought before the Supreme Court. In very urgent cases, the President of the Court can order provisional measures in interim injunction proceedings. The President of the Court of First Instance also has special powers for the protection of the environment. In accelerated proceedings, the public prosecutor, an administrative authority, or an environmental organization with legal personality, can request the President to order the cessation of actions that constitute, or threaten to constitute, an obvious breach of environmental law.

Obviously, within the scope of this contribution it is not possible to provide a complete picture of the Belgian environmental jurisdiction. The bulk of the more than 1,000 judgments that are delivered each year in environmental law cases are closely connected with specific parts of domestic law which have fairly limited relevance for the purposes of comparative law.[39] This contribution therefore restricts itself to a discussion of certain themes of more than mere domestic relevance.

---

38. Arts 1, 7 and 25 of the Penal Code. The Police Courts are competent to try a specific category of environmental offences which are connected with traffic legislation.
39. For a broader survey, see: CEDRE, *Les juges et la protection de l'environnment* (Brussels: Bruylant, 1998); L. Lavrysen (ed.), *Milieurechtspraak* (Mechelen: Kluwer, 2002). See also the specialist journals on environmental law: *Tijdschrift voor Milieurecht, Tijdschrift voor Ruimtelijke Ordening en Stedenbouw, Aménagement, environnement et droit foncier* and *Milieu-en energierecht*. The more general legal journals also occasionally focus on environmental case law.

5.2   CONSTITUTIONAL JURISDICTION

5.2.1   Clarification of the Division of Powers

The Constitutional Court has greatly assisted to clarify the division of powers between the federal government and the regions in the area of environmental protection, with respect to which much ambiguity existed, particularly during the period 1980 to 1993. In doing so, the court removed a number of obstacles to the future development of environmental policy and law.[40] What is remarkable in this respect is that the court actually influenced this division of powers in that, in some cases, certain solutions which the court had formulated for certain disputes, subsequently became expressly enshrined in the statutes regulating the division of powers. For example, in 1988 the court,[41] in a dispute relating to a Walloon tax on the collection of water to be made drinkable for 'export' to the two other regions, ruled (although this was not mentioned anywhere in those exact terms) that the Belgian State system is based on an economic and monetary union in which the free movement of goods and production factors between the different constituent regions must be guaranteed. From this, the court deduced that import and export duties of equivalent effect between the regions are prohibited.[42] When later in that same year the *Special Act* of 8 August 1980 on Institutional Reform (regulating the division of powers between the federal government, the regions and communities) was reviewed by the *Special Act* of 8 August 1988, it was expressly provided in this act that the regions, both in economic and in other matters,[43] and according to the subsequent case law of the Constitutional Court, the communities also exercise their powers 'in accordance with the principles of free movement of persons, goods, services and capital and of freedom of commerce and industry'.[44]

5.2.2   Environmental Protection, Property Rights and Freedom of Enterprise

The majority of the actions for annulment that are brought before the court against federal or regional environmental legislation are instituted by owners or owners' associations, or by polluters or associations of polluters, who believe that the new environmental regulations constitute an excessive infringement of their fundamental rights. Besides a far-reaching infringement of property rights, an

---

40. L. Lavrysen, *De ontwikkeling van het Europese, Belgische en Vlaamse milieurecht in een wijzigende institutionele context* (Antwerp: Kluwer Rechtswetenschappen, 1998), 217-317; F. Tulkens, 'La cour d'arbitrage et la protection de l'environnement', in *Les juges et la protection de l'environnement* ed. CEDRE (Brussels: Bruylant, 1998), 146-154.
41. *Council of Ministers v. Walloon Government* CC 47/88 25 February 1988.
42. Subsequently repeatedly confirmed in connection with various regional environmental taxes; see e.g., *Municipality of Kraainem v. Flemish Government* CC 32/91 14 November 1991; Tulkens, *supra* n. 40, 149-150.
43. Same judgment.
44. Art. 6, § 1, VI.

infringement of the freedom of commerce and industry is invoked in particular. What emerges from the case law is that the Constitutional Court has no intention whatsoever of counteracting the development of environmental law. So far, the court has always considered the restrictions on ownership resulting from the challenged environmental laws to be justified and not disproportionate to the objectives of the public interest pursued, even though the (at times far-reaching) ownership restrictions did not give rise to compensation from the government.[45] The court also argues that the quasi-constitutional freedom of commerce and industry in Belgium is not unlimited, and that an effective environmental policy necessarily implies that activities, which cause an environmental nuisance, are monitored and regulated. In the court's view, there can only be an infringement of the aforementioned freedom if restrictions are imposed without there being any necessity for doing so, or if the restriction is entirely disproportionate to the objective being pursued.[46] Virtually all restrictions introduced by environmental legislation have so far been deemed compatible with the freedom of commerce and industry clause. There is only one exception to this general trend, namely the permitted noise levels in Brussels which were on a particular point found to be contrary to the aforementioned principle when it materialized that in the present state of technology, these penal sanctioned permitted noise levels could not possibly be observed during certain stages of construction and demolition works, whereas it did not appear to be the intention of the Brussels regional legislature to prohibit all construction work in Brussels.[47]

5.2.3 Constitutional Right to a Healthy Environment

Appeals lodged with the Constitutional Court by environmental groups are significantly less in number. Obviously, these groups essentially lodge appeals if they are of the opinion that a particular piece of legislation insufficiently safeguards the environment or the participation rights of citizens, or that the law is wrongly relaxed. Their appeals usually are based on an infringement of the constitutional right to the protection of the environment, the constitutional right to the protection of private and family life and/or the constitutional principle of equality and non-discrimination, usually in combination with international and European environmental regulations.[48]

An illustrative example of this is the case brought by *Inter-Environnement Wallonie*, the umbrella environmental NGO for the Walloon Region, which concerned the so-called 'deferred development zones of an industrial nature'. Such zones were introduced over time in many regional land use plans of the

---

45. See, e.g., *Nv Hazegras cs v. Flemish Government* CC 41/95 6 June 1995.
46. See, e.g., *Nv Obourg Cement cs v. Flemish Government* CC 35/95 25 April 1995; *Vzw BEMEFA cs v. Flemish Government* CC 55/92 9 July 1992.
47. *D Costanza cs v. J. Boton* CC 29/96 15 May 1996; F. Tulkens, *supra* n. 40, 150-152.
48. L. Lavrysen, 'European Environmental Law Principles in Belgian Jurisprudence', in *Principles of European Environmental Law*, ed. R. Macrory (Groningen: ELP, 2004), 75-92.

Walloon Region. The development of these zones was, before the contested amendments to the Walloon Town and Country Planning Code, conditional upon the existence of a municipal planning scheme for the entire area. Failing that, the zone could not be developed. Because of the amendments, such a zone could be developed without such a prior municipal planning scheme for the whole area, and permits could be granted for all economic activities with the exception of 'agro-economic neighbourhood activities' and 'wholesale distribution'. *Inter-Environnement Wallonie* criticized the challenged decree provision for abolishing the municipal planning scheme as an instrument for the development of these zones, and for failing to put an equivalent document in its place. This abolition and failure were thought to undermine the procedural guarantees and thus constitute a violation of the standstill obligation in terms of the right to the protection of a healthy environment, as guaranteed by Article 23 of the Belgian Constitution. Furthermore, Articles 10 and 11 of the Constitution were also thought to have been infringed insofar as the local residents of such a zone would neither see this area being developed in accordance with the relevant standards and regulations, nor obtain an EIA of the programming measures for the area in question, and have any say in the way in which the area would be developed. The court followed *Inter-Environnement Wallonie* in this reasoning and found a violation of Article 23 of the Constitution, taking into account Articles 3 to 6 of Directive 2001/42/EC of the European Parliament and the Council of 27 June 2001 on the Assessment of the Effect of Certain Plans and Programmes on the Environment, and Articles 7 and 8 of the Convention on Access to Information, Public Participation in Decision-making and Access to Justice in Environmental Matters.[49] The court held that:

> The guarantees which the challenged provision puts in their place, more particularly the obligation of justification in the light of the elements referred to in the fourth paragraph of the challenged provision, cannot make up for the loss of the substantive and procedural guarantees that are linked to the preparation of a municipal planning scheme. Consequently, local residents of such areas are confronted with a significant deterioration in the level of protection that was offered by the previous legislation, a deterioration that on the basis of the aforementioned provisions of European and international law cannot be justified by the reasons of public interest underlying the challenged provision.[50]

---

49. 38 *ILM* 517 (1999). Signed in Aarhus on 25 June 1998 and ratified by Belgium on 21 January 2003. Hereafter, Aarhus Convention.

50. The court had previously already annulled a substantial simplification of the screening procedure for projects applied in the Walloon Region as part of environmental impact reporting. The court held that the equality principle had been breached at the expense of parties who are potentially disadvantaged by such projects, since the strongly simplified procedure offered insufficient guarantees in terms of public consultation and impartiality of the investigation (*Inter-Environnement v. Walloon Government* CC 11/2005 19 June 2005; *Inter-Environnement v. Walloon Government* CC 83/2005 27 April 2005).

5.2.4 Right of Respect for Private and Family Life

In a number of cases, environmental organizations have also brought an action for annulment of legislation which in their view offered insufficient protection for the environment, on the strength of Article 22 of the Constitution (whether or not in conjunction with Articles 10 and 11 of the Constitution), which concern the principle of equality and the prohibition of discrimination. Article 22 of the Constitution concerns the right to respect private and family life which, according to the Constitutional Court, should be given the same scope of application as Article 8 of the European Convention on Human Rights. In a dispute relating to the Regional Airport of Liège,[51] the court applied the case law of the European Court of Human Rights including *Powell and Rayner v. United Kingdom*[52] and of *Hatton v. United Kingdom*,[53] which themselves build on the judgments of, among others, *Lopez Ostra v. Kingdom of Spain*[54] and *A.M. Guerra v. Italian Republic*.[55] The court partially annulled a regional statute that instituted different noise protection zones around the airport, depending on the expected noise levels when the airport would be operated at maximum capacity. In the 'A-zone' (with an average expected noise exposure level of 70 dB(A) or more expressed in day-night level (LDN)) the owners have the right to oblige the government to buy their houses so that they can relocate to another area. In the 'B-zone' (with an average expected noise exposure level between 65 dB(A) and 70 dB(A)), there is no such purchasing obligation, but the owners and occupiers of the houses in that area can ask the government to bear the cost of soundproofing. The organization of neighbours of the airport argued that the inhabitants of the 'B-zone' were discriminated against as far as their fundamental right to the protection of private and family life was concerned in comparison with the inhabitants of the 'A-zone', and accordingly demanded the annulment of these provisions. The court partially upheld their demand, stating that none of the scientific reports presented to the court permitted it to conclude that the people living in the 'B-zone' will be able to live in their homes without their right to private life being inordinately affected. As a result of this judgment, the Walloon Region was obliged to extend the purchasing obligation to the 'B-zone'.[56]

---

51. *L Beckers and others and Vzw Net Sky and others v. Walloon Government* CC 51/2003, 30 April 2003.
52. ECHR 21 February 1990.
53. ECHR 2 October 2001; see also *Hatton v. United Kingdom* ECHR (Grand Chamber) 9 June 2005.
54. ECHR 9 December 1994.
55. ECHR 19 February 1998.
56. After the court subsequently annulled a rather too broad exception to the maximum permissible noise levels created by aircraft on the ground for infringement of Art. 22 of the Constitution (*P Thiry cs v. Walloon Government* CC 101/2005 1 June 2005), the subsequently adjusted zoning was deemed compatible with Arts 10, 11, 22 and 23 of the Constitution (*Vzw Net Sky cs and R. Deneye cs v. Walloon Government* CC 189/2005 14 December 2005).

5.3   ACCESS TO COURTS[57]

5.3.1   Ordinary Courts

The general rule in Belgium is that a party must prove an interest in order to gain access to the courts; *actio popularis* is not permitted. The question arises as to what should be understood by 'interest' and whether, for example, environmental organizations can invoke a collective interest in order to take legal action to protect the environment.

In the 1970s, a trend could be discerned whereby the civil courts and the criminal courts (as far as actions for damages are concerned) increasingly acknowledged that environmental groups could rely on such a collective interest.[58] This trend stemmed from the Supreme Court in the so-called *Eikendael* judgment of 19 November 1982.[59] In this judgment the court held, in accordance with Article 17 of the Judicial Code, no legal action is admissible if the plaintiff has no interest in bringing such an action. According to the court, unless the law provides otherwise, legal proceedings instituted by a natural or legal person were not admissible if the plaintiff had no personal and direct interest, in other words, no interest of its own. The court left no doubt that public interest does not amount to 'own interest'. The own interest of a legal person is only that which affects its existence or its tangible and intangible assets, its property, honour and reputation. A corporate purpose, even if this be the protection of the environment, was in the court's view not an own interest. The implications of this judgment soon made themselves felt, and the majority of the lower courts concurred with this position, particularly in the first few years after the judgment.[60] Since then, the Supreme Court had no further opportunity to rule expressly on this issue, taking into account, for example, the potential implications of Article 23 of the Constitution (see the discussion above). This precedent accordingly still stands, although it may be inferred

---

57. See C. Larssen & M. Pallemaerts (eds), *L'accès à la justice en matière d'environnement – Toegang tot de rechter in milieuzaken* (Brussels: Bruylant, 2005), N. De Sadeleer, G. Roller & M. Dross, *Access to Justice in Environmental Matters and the Role of NGO's: Empirical Findings and Legal Appraisal* (Groningen: ELP, 2005).
58. See H. Bocken (ed.), *Vorderingsbevoegdheid voor milieuverenigingen/Le droit, pour les associations de défense de l'environnement, d'ester en justice* (Brussels: E. Story-Scientia, 1988), 232-248; P. Lemmens & J. Verlinden, 'Toegang tot de rechter in milieuzaken', in *Rechtspraktijk en milieubescherming, referatenboek van het Antwerpse juristencongres 1991*, ed. CBR (Antwerp: Kluwer, 1991), and J. Van den Berghe, 'Het vorderingsrecht van burgers en milieuverenigingen', in *Rechtspraktijk en milieubescherming, referatenboek van het Antwerpse juristencongres 1991*, ed. CBR (Antwerp: Kluwer, 1991), 225 et seq. and 267 et seq.; B. Jadot, 'L'intérêt à agir en justice pour assurer la protection de l'environnement', in *Les juges et la protection de l'environnement*, ed. CEDRE (Brussels: Bruylant, 1998), 16.
59. *Nv S. v. Vzw Werkgroep voor Milieubeheer Brasschaat* SC 19 November 1982, confirmed by, SC 25 October 1985 *RW* 1985-1986, 2411 ('Neerpede' judgment).
60. However, certain lower courts did not endorse this position which they felt was not in tune with the spirit of the times (see Jadot, *supra* n. 58, 19). In recent years we have seen a growing dissension: see the overview of 'dissident' case law in P. Lefranc, 'Is het collectief belang een persoonlijk of eigen belang in het strafprocesrecht?', *TMR* (2005): 106-107.

from a judgment of 14 September 2004[61] that the court might be willing to reconsider its position.[62]

The *Eikendael* judgment caused a great deal of controversy and eventually resulted in action being taken by the legislature in the form of the aforementioned Act of 12 January 1993, which allows environmental organizations that satisfy certain requirements[63] to bring an action for cessation of acts that constitute a breach of the protection of the environment. It is unclear whether the legislature expressly saw their reform as a response to the aforementioned judgment. It is a fact, however, that the rulings of that same court largely helped to make this act a particularly effective instrument for the protection of the environment. So far, the court has dismissed all interpretations that sought to construe the Act restrictively.[64] In a judgment of 8 November 1996,[65] the Supreme Court considered that the purpose of the Act was not only to prevent damage to the environment, but also to ensure a viable environment for the population, so that the protection of the environment also extends to protection of town and country planning. According to the court, the Act not only makes it possible to order the cessation of illegal works that impair the environment, but also that the works already completed be undone, if such an injunction is necessary to prevent further damage to the environment. The compulsory reconciliation attempt is not required on pain of nullity.[66] Not only environmental organizations, but also administrative authorities such as municipal authorities, can bring actions for cessation. This led to an interesting development on the basis of Article 271 of the *New Municipal Act*. This provision allows one or several residents of a municipality to act on behalf of the municipality if the mayor and aldermen fail to do so. It was soon accepted in the case law that this provision could be combined with Act of 12 January 1993, so that individual citizens are able to bring such an action themselves on behalf of a defaulting municipal authority by taking the place of the municipality that refuses to bring such an action.[67] This judgment was soon endorsed by the Supreme Court when it considered that it follows from the joint reading of the two aforementioned articles that if the mayor and aldermen fail to take action under those circumstances, one or several residents can take legal action on behalf of the municipality in order to protect the environment.[68] No interest needs to be demonstrated because the municipality is presumed to have an interest. The court also considered that an action for cessation is not contingent on the condition of speed or urgency.[69] The circumstances under which residents can bring an action for cessation on behalf of the municipality if

---

61. *S v. Vzw KBVBV* SC 14 September 2004, *TMR* 2005, 105.
62. Lefranc, *supra* n. 60, 107.
63. I.e., to be constituted in the form of a non-profit association, to have the protection of the environment as its purpose, to have existed for at least three years, and to actually be active.
64. P. Bogaerts, 'Tien jaar stakingsvordering inzake leefmilieu. Kritisch aperçu van rechtspraak en rechtsleer (1993-2003)', *TMR* 2 (2003): 86-119.
65. SC 8 November 1996, *TMR* 1997, 30 with note by J. Van den Berghe.
66. SC 30 December 1993 *TMR* 2005, 192-193.
67. Bogaerts, *supra* n. 64, 105.
68. SC 14 February 2002 *RW* 2001-2002, 1504; Jadot, *supra* n. 58, 27-28.
69. SC 5 March 1998, *TMR* 1998, 161.

the latter fails to do so, actually gave rise to another problem. What if the municipality itself shares responsibility for the breach of environmental law by having issued an illegal license? This matter needed to be settled by the Constitutional Court, which ruled that by not allowing the action under such circumstances, would constitute an infringement of the principle of equality and non-discrimination.[70]

5.3.2   Council of State

The case law history of the Council of State has seen a somewhat different development on the matter of demonstrable interest. In the case that gave rise to the *Eikendael* judgment, the same environmental group had also appealed to the Council of State to secure the annulment of a planning scheme and a license which, in its view, were illegal. The Council of State, unlike the Supreme Court, allowed the environmental group's action.[71] According to Article 19 of the Coordinated Laws on the Council of State, actions for suspension and actions for annulment of administrative acts can be brought by any party that can demonstrate a 'prejudice or interest'. According to the case law, this interest must be personal and direct. Actions brought by natural persons against licenses for the execution of construction works or the operation of industries are not only admissible if they are instituted by owners or tenants (i.e. holders of a subjective right) who live in the immediate vicinity of the site in question. Since the early 1980s, a wider circle of interested parties is taken into consideration.[72] It is not necessary to live in the immediate vicinity of an industrial establishment to contest the environmental license that was granted to that establishment if it can be proven that the company in question causes a 'significant nuisance' which can be experienced many miles away.[73] In the area of town and country planning, the view became increasingly accepted that all residents of a neighbourhood have an interest in a proper planning of that neighbourhood. Zoning plans and traffic plans can therefore be challenged by anyone living in the area for which the plan is drawn up.[74] Since the mid-1980s, the Council of State also acknowledged that environmental groups could take action against government acts in order to protect collective environmental interests. The Council of State does require, however, that the organization be 'representative' of the group of people whose collective interests are threatened or damaged, and it will verify whether:

> the organization has such a level of support among the members of that group that it may be reasonably assumed that the positions adopted by the organization coincide with those of the interested parties themselves.[75]

70. *M Lenaerts cs v. Nv's Heerenbosch* CC 70/2007 26 April 2007; see in the same sense: A. *Heytens cs v. Nv Makro Zelfbedieningsgroothandel* CC 121/2007 19 September 2007.
71. *Vzw Werkgroep voor Milieubeheer Brasschaat* CS 21.384, 11 September 1981.
72. Lemmens & Verlinden, *supra* n. 58, 251; Jadot, *supra* n. 58, 11.
73. *Vzw Bond Beter Leefmilieu Tessenderlo and Pals* CS 27.042, 21 October 1986.
74. Lemmens & Verlinden, *supra* n. 58, 251.
75. See, for instance, *Vzw Bond Beter Leefmilieu-Interenvironnement* CS 20.882-20.885, 20 January 1981.

This approach is not without its problems, in particular for umbrella organizations. In a number of cases the Council, for example, ruled that an environmental umbrella organization did not have the authority to defend the specific interests of the constituent organizations, or even that a national environmental organization had no specific interest in taking action with regard to a local environmental issue. Local environmental groups, for their part, sometimes have difficulty proving that they have sufficient local support.[76]

All of this leads to inconsistent case law, with at times widely divergent views between different chambers of the Council of State. An example further illustrates this. Two licenses are required for the construction and operation of a silt processing plant and a dumping site for dredging spoil. Planning permission is required for the construction works and an environmental license for the operation of the plant. In connection with such a project on the territory of the City of Ghent bordering on the municipality of Merelbeke, a local environmental group from Merelbeke brought an action for annulment of both the environmental license and the planning permission. The Seventh Chamber of the Council of State, which had to rule on the action for annulment of the environmental license, accepted that the organization, whose purpose it is to '[a]chieve a genuine protection of the environment in all its forms' and to '[e]nsure that considerations of environmental protection are fully integrated in the town and country planning on the territory of the municipality of Merelbeke', has an interest in the annulment of a license for a large-scale silt dumping site just across the municipal boundary which is liable to have an impact on the territory of the municipality of Merelbeke.[77] The Tenth Chamber, however, which had to rule on the action for annulment of the planning permission, did not acknowledge this interest, saying that the town and country planning on the territory of the municipality of Merelbeke was not altered by the challenged planning permission.[78] There is a distinct impression that the Council of State has gradually become more restrictive in the assessment of the interest requirement, probably in view of the growing number of cases referred to it for consideration. The question that arises is whether this more restrictive approach is reconcilable with the requirements imposed in this respect by the Aarhus Convention, which is applicable in Belgium. The Aarhus Compliance Committee, which was requested to rule on a complaint lodged by the Flemish environmental umbrella organization *Bond Beter Leefmilieu Vlaanderen* regarding the restrictive case law of the Council of State in town and country planning matters, was at any rate of the opinion that this was not the case. The Committee considered that:

> The Convention does no prevent a Party from applying general criteria of the sort found in Belgian legislation. However, even though the wordings of the Belgian laws do not as such imply a lack of compliance, the jurisprudence of the Belgian courts, as reflected in the cases submitted by the Communicant,

---

76. Lemmens & Verlinden, *supra* n. 58, 254-255; Jadot, *supra* n. 58, 14-15.
77. *Vzw Aktiekomitee voor milieubescherming in Merelbeke* CS 170.173, 19 April 2007.
78. *Vzw Aktiekomitee voor milieubescherming in Merelbeke* CS 178.286, 7 January 2008.

implies a too restrictive access to justice for environmental organisations.
[...] Thus, if maintained by the Council of State, Belgium would fail to
provide for access to justice as set out in article 9, paragraph 3, of the Convention. By failing to provide for effective remedies, with respect to town
planning permits and decisions on area plans, Belgium would then also fail to
comply with article 9, paragraph 4.[79]

5.4   PENAL ENFORCEMENT

Breaches of most environmental laws are penalized in Belgium in the same manner
as criminal offences before the criminal courts. Although the victims of an offence
can bring such a case before a criminal court themselves by directly summoning
the suspected offender, it is very exceptional for this to happen because in such an
instance the burden of proof lies with the victim. Moreover, in environmental
offences it will not often happen that there is an identifiable victim, who must
also have the requisite interest. Another option is a complainant who can claim for
damages before the examining magistrate, who is then obliged to investigate the
case. If the investigation yields sufficient proof of guilt, the case can be brought
before the court by the public prosecution service. Although this procedure also is
quite exceptional for environmental offences, a number of serious cases have
already been prosecuted in this way in the past.

In the vast majority of cases, the decision to prosecute will rest with the public
prosecution service, which has discretionary power in this respect. Proceedings
usually begin with an official report by environmental inspectors or by the regular
police services who establish an infringement. The public prosecutor can order
these entities to gather additional information.[80] The public prosecution service
then has several options. It can decide not to prosecute if it turns out that the case
cannot be substantiated, for example, either because the perpetrator cannot
be identified or found, or because on closer inspection there is no offence because
force majeure is involved. The public prosecutor may also drop the case for reasons
of expediency. Although an offence has been committed and the necessary
evidence has been obtained, the public prosecution service may decide that the
case is not sufficiently serious to prosecute, or because it does not wish to put the
rehabilitation of the offender at risk. The public prosecution service may also
propose an amicable settlement on condition that the illegal situation is regularized

---

79. Aarhus Compliance Committee, *Findings and Recommendations with regard to compliance by
    Belgium with its obligations under the Aarhus Convention in the case of access to justice for
    environmental organizations to challenge decisions in court: Communication ACCC/C/2005/
    11* (Belgium: Bond Beter Leefmilieu Vlaanderen VZW, 2006).
80. If measures need to be taken that involve an infringement of the fundamental rights of suspects
    (house search, telephone tapping, seizure of documents or goods, pre-trial detention, etc.), a
    judicial investigation will be required, led by the examining magistrate. The examining
    magistrate must report regularly during the investigation to the Committals Division or the
    Indictment Division, composed of judges from the criminal court and the Court of Appeal
    respectively.

(for example, a license is obtained for an unlicensed activity) and the victims, if any exist, are offered compensation. The prosecution will be discontinued if the perpetrator agrees to the proposal to pay a particular sum of money in compensation. Finally, the public prosecution service may decide to bring the case before a criminal court. In practice, only a small number of environmental cases are prosecuted by the public prosecution service, with major differences discernible between judicial districts and different parts of the country.[81] Where on average around 60% of cases are dropped, and for 10% an amicable settlement is made and the remaining cases are actually prosecuted before the criminal courts,[82] the figures for the judicial district of Ghent show an entirely different picture in that only 15% of cases are dropped.[83] Despite efforts since the early 1990s to harmonize prosecution policy in environmental and town and country planning issues through agreements between the various actors involved (for example, in the context of the Committee on Prosecution Policy in the Flemish Region[84] which is a consultative body involving public prosecution services, police and environmental inspectors and where it is agreed which offences need to be prosecuted as a matter of priority), it has so far not been possible to remove these wide discrepancies.[85]

The environmental case law of the criminal courts has evolved considerably in recent decades. Not only is there a marked increase to be observed in the number of cases heard; the quality of the judgments has, generally speaking, also improved. This may be attributed to better training of judicial officers, greater sensitivity to environmental protection and an extension of the available legislative instruments. Whereas in the early 1980s criminal courts fairly readily accepted grounds for exemption from criminal liability such as 'necessity' and inevitable miscarriage of justice to conclude that an environmental offence should not give rise to penalties, this is no longer the case. The argument which was often accepted in the past, namely that there was a case of necessity because compliance with environmental law would be entirely impossible from a socio-economic point of view, and further that such compliance would lead to the immediate closure of the company with the resulting consequences in terms of job losses, is generally no longer accepted. There is only question of necessity if the perpetrator is faced with a choice between non-compliance with the law and committing an offence in order to prevent more serious damage. In this case, the question is: what takes precedence, environmental

---

81. See R. Mortier, 'De behandeling van leefmilieudossiers door het Openbaar ministerie. Analyse van de situatie in Nederlandstalig België', in *De handhaving van het Milieurecht/La répression des infractions en matière d'environnement*, ed. J. Van den Berghe (Mechelen: Kluwer, 2002), 1-42; and E. Staudt, 'Le rapport sur la politique des poursuites en Belgique francophone', in *id.*, 43-55.
82. Lavrysen, Van den Berghe & Van den Berghe, *supra* n. 29, 22.
83. *Ibid.*, 42.
84. A.-M. Gepts, 'De Commissie Vervolgingsbeleid; sleutel tot een betere handhaving?', in *De handhaving van het Milieurecht/La répression des infractions en matière d'environnement*, ed. J. Van den Berghe (Mechelen: Kluwer, 2002), 57-72.
85. *Ibid.*, 22.

interests or socio-economic interests? The case law has become established in such a way that such a weighing of interests is usually seen to have already taken place at two levels and that the court can only repeat this weighing of interests in very exceptional cases. In doing so, the court then has to bear in mind that, as a result of the incorporation of the right to the protection of a healthy environment in the Constitution, it can no longer be assumed that environmental interests are secondary to socio-economic interests. First, the legislator or regulator, in enacting environmental regulations, already weighed the various interests and considered it necessary to enact those regulations, despite the fact that certain environmental regulations may have major socio-economic consequences. Second, a licensing authority, which imposes special conditions in the issuing of a license, also performed such a weighing of interests and, within the limits of the law, was able to assess the socio-economic consequences of the conditions imposed. That is why a criminal court can only investigate the conditions for the existence of 'necessity' if it turns out that compliance with the Penal Code would have consequences that were not intended by the legislator or regulator and could not be anticipated by the administrative authority. If actual environmental damage occurs, it can rarely be argued that such damage is less serious than the socio-economic interests that need to be protected, or that the breach of the law was the only way to prevent that damage.[86] Inevitable miscarriage of justice as a result of complex legislation, and wrong advice or toleration by the authorities of an unlawful situation, is only very rarely accepted nowadays.[87]

The inspections carried out by the specialized environmental inspectorates are an important component in the chain of (criminal) enforcement of environmental laws.[88] In order to be able to conduct these inspections in an effective manner, the officials in question have fairly extensive rights of inspection. In principle, they can visit companies at any hour to carry out the necessary checks. Obstructing the performance of audits is a punishable offence under the majority of environmental laws. The importance of inspections is also recognized by the criminal courts. For example, the Criminal Court in Ghent considered that for the effective functioning of the inspection services and of the public service in general, it is essential that the supervisory officials carry out their duties without becoming the target of verbal or physical aggression.[89] Business managers who committed such aggression were

---

86. M. Faure, 'Strafrecht', in *Handboek Milieu- en Energierecht*, ed. K. Deketelaere (Brugge: Die Keure, 2006), 1250.
87. *Ibid.*, 1251-1257.
88. Research has shown that the recommendations, warnings and instructions which these officials can give when they report breaches of the law are fairly effective and that most of the companies that have received a warning usually manage to comply with environmental law within a fairly short time: C. Billiet & S. Rousseau, 'Zachte rechtshandhaving in het bestuurlijke handhavingsspoor: de inspectiebeslissing en het voortraject van bestuurlijke sancties. Een rechtseconomische analyse', *TMR* 14 (2005): 2-33.
89. Criminal Court, Ghent, 5 September 2000 *TMR* 2000, 522-523; see in the same sense: Court of Appeal, Ghent, 26 June 1988 *TMR* 1999, 150-152; Criminal Court, Ghent, 22 June 2001 *TMR* 2001, 333-335 and 414-416.

sentenced between three to eight months' imprisonment, half of which was effective.

Until 1999, criminal liability of juristic persons in Belgium was not accepted. Juristic persons could commit offences, but could not be punished for them. The criminal court had to enquire which natural persons within the juristic person could be held accountable for the offence due to their actions or negligence. Some controversial acquittals in environmental cases[90] served to inspire the introduction of criminal liability of juristic persons with the Act of 4 May 1999 *Amending the Penal Code*. This Act provides in a number of cases for an alternative liability of the juristic person and the natural person by whose action the offence was committed (in which case the person who committed the most serious offence can be convicted), and in a number of cases for a combination of liability of the juristic person and the natural person, namely when the latter committed the offence wittingly. It soon emerged from the case law that in environmental criminal law, combination of liability is possible in virtually all cases and that the public prosecution services and the criminal courts make ample use of this facility with a view to forcing company managers to be more responsible for their actions. The fact that a juristic person can be held responsible and be sentenced to appropriate penalties does not mean that senior company officers who share responsibility for the poor environmental performance of a company can simply hide behind the liability of the juristic person. A noteworthy example of this is a business manager who recently had been voted 'Manager of the Year' by a business journal and was sentenced to stiff penalties by the criminal court for an odour nuisance which had been dragging on for years and which was solved only with great difficulty. There were also substantial violations of the discharge limits for wastewater, late updating of the environmental license following the increased stockpiling of dangerous substances, and pumping of greater quantities of groundwater than permitted.[91] The company was sentenced to a fine of EUR 412,500 and the business manager to a fine of EUR 13,750.

The effectiveness of environmental criminal law was further increased with the introduction in 1990 of the concept of the special confiscation of financial benefits directly obtained as a result of the commission of the offence. Although this provision was specifically introduced to enable courts to take more effective action against illegal drug trafficking and to ensure that offenders do not remain in possession of the money which they unlawfully obtained, the usefulness of this instrument was soon acknowledged in environmental criminal law. Noncompliance with environmental regulations usually results in cost savings for

---

90. The Court of Appeal, Antwerp, acquitted various senior managers of a company of serious environmental offences because the offences were the result of no or insufficient expenditure on effluent treatment infrastructure, which in turn was the outcome of collective decisions of the Board of Directors, for which individual members could not be held responsible. See *OM v. LD, DDL & Nv F* Court of Appeal, Antwerp, 24 April 1992 *TMR* 1992, 17-20.

91. *OM v. HDL, AV, Ph.V & Nv UCO Sportswear* Criminal Court, Ghent, 5 February 2007 *NjW* 2007.

the company and in unfair competition in relation to legally compliant companies. In some judicial districts, the confiscation of financial benefits is demanded fairly systematically by the public prosecutor and granted by the judge.[92]

What is also significant is that a number of acts, decrees and ordinances allow the criminal court to impose remediation measures and, by way of safety precaution, to impose an operating ban when no assurance can be provided that the establishment concerned is able to operate in accordance with environmental regulations. The criminal case law shows an increasing use of these instruments. In order to enforce compliance with these measures, periodic penalty payments have been imposed in several cases.[93]

6   THE WAY FORWARD

Along with the expansion of environmental law in recent years, the Belgian courts are increasingly being confronted with environmental cases. Whereas in the early period the quality of judgments tended to be highly variable, either due to inadequate knowledge of environmental law or insufficient acknowledgement of the importance of the protection of a healthy environment, one gradually observes judges becoming better acquainted with environmental law. Partly under the influence of international,[94] European (the case law of the ECJ generally shows how much importance the court attaches to environmental protection),[95] and constitutional developments (the recognition of the right to the protection of a healthy environment as enshrined in Article 23 of the Constitution is an example of this), the courts are no longer inclined when faced with conflicting interests, to automatically sacrifice environmental interests in favour of economic interests. Recently appointed judges have increasingly been able during their basic training at university, judicial internships and/or environmental training courses for judicial officers which have been organized on a regular basis since 1995,[96] to become more thoroughly acquainted with the challenges posed to the judiciary by environmental issues and environmental law. Nevertheless, considerable differences remain from one court to another. In some of the larger judicial districts, special sections have been set up within the public prosecution services and chambers in the court which are able to focus exclusively on the enforcement of environmental

---

92. See e.g., *OM v. VF* Criminal Court, Ypres, 12 February 2007 *TMR* 2007, 562-563.
93. See, e.g., *OM v. EV & KG* Criminal Court, Ghent, 2 June 1998 *TMR* 1999, 152-153.
94. See South Africa DFA, 'The Johannesburg Principles on the Role of Law and Sustainable Development, adopted at the Global Judges Symposium held in Johannesburg, South Africa on 18-20 August 2002', <www.dfa.gov.za/docs/2002/ wssd0828a.htm>, 1 September 2008. See also, generally, the case law of the European Court of Human Rights in environmental matters.
95. L. Lavrysen, 'The European Court of Justice and the Implementation of Environmental law', in *The Role of the Judiciary in the Implementation and Enforcement of Environmental Law*, ed. A. Postiglione (Rome: ICEF, 2003), 43-100; *ibid.*, in *Reflections on 30 Years of EU Environmental Law. A High Level of Protection?*, ed. R. Macrory (Groningen: ELP, 2006), 417-448.
96. Lavrysen, Van den Berghe & Van den Berghe, *supra* n. 29, 14-19.

law. In the smaller districts, however, this has not happened, and it is unlikely to happen given the limited available human resources in the public prosecution service and the court.[97] In order to ensure that the efforts being made in terms of additional training of judicial officers in environmental law continue to pay off, it would seem essential to pursue a policy of forming larger judicial districts with larger courts (for example, merging the current twenty-seven courts to ten bigger courts – one for each province), so that within each Court of First Instance, one environmental chamber can be established. Within each public prosecution service, an adequately staffed and trained section specializing in environmental matters could further be established. Each Court of Appeal should also, following the example of the Court of Appeal in Ghent, have a specialized environmental chamber and a specialized section within the Attorney-General's office. Such environmental chambers would not only try environmental criminal cases, but also civil cases and actions for cessation. The establishment of adequately equipped specialized sections within the public prosecution services should make it possible to bring greater consistency to prosecution policy. In the Flemish Region, the planned establishment of the *Vlaamse Hoge Raad voor Milieuhandhaving* [Flemish High Council for Environmental Law Enforcement] offers a perfect opportunity to implement such reforms.[98]

The judiciary not only plays an important part in the enforcement of environmental law, but also offers legal protection against the government when, in enacting legislation or regulations or in taking individual decisions, in particular licensing decisions, government fails to observe higher legal standards to protect the environment or to guarantee the participation of citizens and interest groups in the decision-making process. Whereas access to the Constitutional Court can be considered fairly 'easy' and this Court succeeds in passing judgment within a reasonable time limit (the Court is obliged to render a decision within one year at the most), the same cannot be said of the Council of State. Some of the case law suggest an excessively restrictive interpretation of the 'interest' requirement, (thereby inordinately limiting the right to action of environmental organizations), and if this case law is not reviewed by the Court itself, legislative action will be needed to guarantee the application of the Aarhus Convention. An even greater challenge is the enormous backlog of work within the Council of State which results in undesirable delays. It now takes six months to one year for the Council of State to render a decision on an action for suspension (disputes which are assumed to involve extreme urgency), while for a hearing of a case on the merits there are waiting periods of five to ten years. Since instituting an action for suspension or an action for annulment does not suspend the challenged decision, it very often happens that the decision in question is already being implemented by the time a judgment is delivered on the action for suspension. If no suspension is ordered, it will be fairly certain that the judgment on the merits will have a purely

---

97. Mortier, *supra* n. 81, 22.
98. Lavrysen, Van den Berghe & Van den Berghe, *supra* n. 29, 43.

symbolic significance, since that judgment will only be delivered after the challenged decision has been fully implemented.

It is currently unclear whether the recent transfer of litigation involving immigration law to a separate court of law with only the possibility of appeal to the Council of State will serve to increase the Council's caseload capacity so as to ensure that decisions can be rendered within a reasonable time limit and in a manner that offers effective legal protection. More comprehensive reform will probably be necessary, and the establishment of administrative courts of first instance may need to be considered. This could be coupled with the expansion of the courts of first instance as suggested earlier, as well as the addition of a division to each provincial court which would act as administrative court of first instance. It will need to be examined whether the administrative environmental cases could not be entrusted to the specialized environmental chambers mentioned above, with the possibility of appeal to the Council of State; if not, there is a real risk that the specialization that already exists in the Council of State at first instance level may be undermined.

The proposed establishment in the Flemish Region of an Environmental Law Enforcement Council appears to be is a missed opportunity in the above respect. A fairly unwieldy specialized administrative court of law will be set up for a limited part of the enforcement policy, namely the imposition of administrative fines. Other administrative enforcement instruments, or even the guarantee of a broader legal protection against unlawful government action, will not fall within the remit of that Council. Apart from the constitutional objections that may arise with respect to the Council in question, we can ask ourselves whether this is really the best way to spend public money.

BIBLIOGRAPHY

Aarhus Compliance Committee. *Findings and Recommendations with regard to compliance by Belgium with its obligations under the Aarhus Convention in the case of access to justice for environmental organizations to challenge decisions in court: Communication ACCC/C/2005/11*. Belgium: Bond Beter Leefmilieu Vlaanderen VZW, 2006.

Alen, A. & R. Ergec. *Federal Belgium after the Fourth State Reform 1993*. 2nd ed. Brussels: Ministry of Foreign Affairs, External Trade and Cooperation for Development, 1998.

Alen, A. (ed.). *Treatise on Belgian Constitutional Law*. Deventer: Kluwer Law and Taxation Publishers, 1992.

Belgium Government Portal. 'Official Information and Services'. <www. fgov.be>, 4 August 2008.

Billiet, C. & S. Rousseau. 'Zachte rechtshandhaving in het bestuurlijke handhavingsspoor: de inspectiebeslissing en het voortraject van bestuurlijke sancties. Een rechtseconomische analyse'. *Tijdschrift voor Milieurecht* 14 (2005): 2-33.

Bocken, H. (ed.). *Vorderingsbevoegdheid voor milieuverenigingen/Le droit, pour les associations de défense de l'environnement, d'ester en justice*. Brussels: E. Story-Scientia, 1988.

Bogaerts, P. 'Tien jaar stakingsvordering inzake leefmilieu. Kritisch aperçu van rechtspraak en rechtsleer (1993-2003)'. *Tijdschrift voor Milieurecht* 2 (2003): 86-119.

Bossuyt, M. 'Constitutional Court'. <www.const-court.be>, 4 August 2008.

CEDRE. *Les juges et la protection de l'environnment*. Brussels: Bruylant, 1998.

CIBG. 'Living in Brussels'. <www.irisnet.be>, 4 August 2008.

Council of State, 'Welkom bij de Raad van State', <www.raadvst-consetat.be>, 4 August 2008.

De Pue, E., L. Lavrysen & P. Stryckers. *Milieuzakboekje 2007*. Mechelen: Wolters Kluwer, 2007.

De Sadeleer, N., G. Roller & M. Dross. *Access to Justice in Environmental Matters and the Role of NGO's: Empirical Findings and Legal Appraisal*. Groningen: Europa Law Publishing, 2005.

Deketelaere, K. (ed.). *Handboek Milieu- en Energierecht*. Brugge: Die Keure, 2006.

EPI. 'Environmental Performance Index'. <epi.yale.edu>, 10 September 2008.

Faure, M. 'Strafrecht'. In *Handboek Milieu- en Energierecht*, edited by K. Deketelaere. Brugge: Die Keure, 2006.

Flanders. 'The Official Portal Site'. <www.vlaanderen.be>, 4 August 2008.

Gepts, A.-M. 'De Commissie Vervolgingsbeleid; sleutel tot een betere handhaving?'. In *De handhaving van het Milieurecht/La répression des infractions en matière d'environnement*, edited by J. Van den Berghe. Mechelen: Kluwer, 2002.

Hachez, I. 'L'effet de *standstill*: Le pari des droits économiques, sociaux et culturels'. *Administration Publique Trimestriel* 24 (2000): 30-57.

Hazeur, T. 'L'intérêt à agir des associations de défense de l'environnement devant le Conseil d'Etat: quelle liberté pour le juge et quel rapport à la nature?'. *Aménagement, environnement et droit foncier* (2006): 105-114.

Jadot, B. 'Le droit à l'environnement'. In *Les droits économiques, sociaux et culturels dans la Constitution*, edited by R. Ergec. Brussels: Bruylant, 1995.

Jadot, B. 'L'interêt à agir en justice pour assurer la protection de l'environnement'. In *Les juges et la protection de l'environnement*, edited by Centre d'étude du droit de l'environnement. Brussels: Bruylant, 1998.

Jadot, B. 'Pour une meilleure prise en compte de l'environnement et les enjeux environnementaux dans la Constitution'. In *En hommage à Françis Delpérée: Itinéraires d'un constitutionnaliste*, edited by Bruylant. Brussels: Bruylant, 2007.

Jans, J.H. & H.H.B. Vedder. *European Environmental* Law. 3rd ed. Groningen: Europa Law Publishing, 2008.

Juridat. 'Le portail du Pouvoir judiciaire de Belgique'. <www.cass.be>, 4 August 2008.

Larssen, C. & M. Pallemaerts (eds). *L'accès à la justice en matière d'environnement – Toegang tot de rechter in milieuzaken*. Brussels: Bruylant, 2005.

Lavrysen, L. & J. Theunis. 'The Right to the Protection of a Healthy Environment in the Belgian Constitution: Retrospect and International Perspective'. In *Constitutional rights to an ecologically balanced environment*, edited by I. Larmuseau. Ghent: 2Mpact, 2007.

Lavrysen, L. (ed.). *Milieurechtspraak*. Mechelen: Kluwer, 2002.

Lavrysen, L. *De ontwikkeling van het Europese, Belgische en Vlaamse milieurecht in een wijzigende institutionele context*. Antwerp: Kluwer Rechtswetenschappen, 1998.

Lavrysen, L. 'European Environmental Law Principles in Belgian Jurisprudence'. In *Principles of European Environmental Law*, edited by R. Macrory. Groningen: Europa Law Publishing, 2004.

Lavrysen, L. *Handboek Milieurecht 2006*. Mechelen: Wolters Kluwer, 2006.

Lavrysen, L. 'The European Court of Justice and the Implementation of Environmental law'. In *The Role of the Judiciary in the Implementation and Enforcement of Environmental Law*, edited by A. Postiglione. Rome: International Court of the Environment Foundation, 2003.

Lavrysen, L. 'The European Court of Justice and the Implementation of Environmental law'. In *Reflections on 30 Years of EU Environmental Law. A High Level of Protection?*, edited by R. Macrory. Groningen: Europa Law Publishing, 2006.

Lavrysen, L., J. Van den Berghe & K. Van den Berghe. *Report to the European Union Forum of judges for the Environment (EUFJE) on the Belgian situation concerning Criminal Enforcement of Environmental Law*. <www.eufje.org>, 4 August 2008. Brussels: EUFJE, 2007.

Lefranc, P. 'Is het collectief belang een persoonlijk of eigen belang in het strafprocesrecht?'. *Tijdschrift voor Milieurecht* (2005): 105-107.

Lemmens, P. & J. Verlinden. 'Toegang tot de rechter in milieuzaken'. In *Rechtspraktijk en milieubescherming, referatenboek van het Antwerpse juristencongres 1991*, edited by Centrum voor Beroepsvervolmaking in de Rechten. Antwerp: Kluwer, 1991.

Lombaert, B. et al. *Mémento de l'environnement*. Waterloo: Kluwer, 2006.

Maes, G. 'Het standstillbeginsel in verdragsbepalingen en in art. 23 G.W.: progressieve (sociale) grondrechtenbescherming'. *Rechtskundig Weekblad* 69 (2005-2006): 1081-1094.

Martens, P. 'L'insertion des droits économiques, sociaux et culturels dans la Constitution'. *Revue Belge De droit Constitutionnel* 1 (1995): 3-20.

Mortier, R. 'De behandeling van leefmilieudossiers door het Openbaar ministerie. Analyse van de situatie in Nederlandstalig België'. In *De handhaving van het Milieurecht/La répression des infractions en matière d'environnement*, edited by J. Van den Berghe. Mechelen: Kluwer, 2002.

OECD. *Environmental Performance Reviews: Belgium*. Paris: OECD, 1998.

OECD. *Environmental Performance Reviews: Belgium*. Paris: OECD, 2007.

South Africa Department of Foreign Affairs. 'The Johannesburg Principles on the Role of Law and Sustainable Development, adopted at the Global Judges Symposium held in Johannesburg, South Africa on 18-20 August 2002'. <www.dfa.gov.za/docs/2002/wssd0828a.htm>, 1 September 2008.

Staudt, E. 'Le rapport sur la politique des poursuites en Belgique francophone'. In *De handhaving van het Milieurecht/La répression des infractions en matière d'environnement*, edited by J. Van den Berghe. Mechelen: Kluwer, 2002.

Tulkens, F. 'La cour d'arbitrage et la protection de l'environnement'. In *Les juges et la protection de l'environnement* edited by Centre d'étude du droit de l'environnement. Brussels: Bruylant, 1998.

UNDP. 'Human Development Report 2007/2008'. <hdr.undp.org/en>, 4 August 2008.

Van den Berghe, J. 'Het vorderingsrecht van burgers en milieuvereningen'. In *Rechtspraktijk en milieubescherming, referatenboek van het Antwerpse juristencongres 1991*, edited by Centrum voor Beroepsvervolmaking in de Rechten. Antwerp: Kluwer, 1991.

Wallonie. 'Le site du Gouvernement wallon'. <www.gov.wallonie.be>, 10 September 2008.

TABLE OF LEGISLATION

International Environmental Policy Cooperation Agreement 5 April 1995
Management of Polluted Soils Ordinance 13 May 2004
Management of the Risks of Major Accidents Involving Dangerous Substances
    Cooperation Agreement 21 June 1999
Nature Conservation Act 12 July 1973
Nature Conservation and Protection Ordinance 27 April 1995
Nature Conservation and the Natural Environment Decree 21 October 1997
Organization of Town and Country Planning Decree 18 May 1999
Prevention and Management of Packaging Waste Cooperation Agreement 30 May
    1996
Prevention and Management of Waste Decree 2 July 1981
Prevention and Management of Wastes Ordinance 7 March 1991
*Product Standards to promote Sustainable Production and Consumption Patterns
    and to Protect the Environment and Public Health Act* 21 December 1998
Protection of Surface Waters against Pollution Act 26 March 1971
*Protection of the Marine Environment in Maritime Areas under the Jurisdiction of
    Belgium Act* 20 January 1999
Protection of the Population and of the Environment Act 15 April 1994
Protection of Water against Pollution from Fertilizers Decree 22 December 2006
Protection of Wildlife and Hunting Ordinance 29 August 1991
Remediation of Polluted Soils and the Rehabilitation of Economic Sites Decree
    1 April 2004
Right of Action for the Protection of the Environment Act 12 January 1993
Soil Remediation and Soil Protection Decree 27 October 2006
Walloon Code on Town and Country Planning, Urban Development and Archi-
    tectural and Natural Heritage
Wastes Decree 27 June 1997
Water Intended for Human Use Decree 24 May 2002

TABLE OF CASES

European Court of Human Rights

A.M. Guerra v. Italian Republic ECHR 19 February 1998
Hatton v. United Kingdom ECHR 2 October 2001
Hatton v. United Kingdom ECHR (Grand Chamber) 9 June 2005
Lopez Ostra v. Kingdom of Spain ECHR 9 December 1994
Powell and Rayner v. United Kingdom ECHR 21 February 1990

Constitutional Court

A. Heytens cs v. Nv Makro Zelfbedieningsgroothandel CC 121/2007 19 September
    2007
Council of Ministers v. Walloon Government CC 47/88 25 February 1988

D Costanza cs v. J. Boton CC 29/96 15 May 1996
Inter-Environnement v. Walloon Government CC 11/2005 19 June 2005
Inter-Environnement v. Walloon Government CC 83/2005 27 April 2005
L Beckers and others and Vzw Net Sky and others v. Walloon Government CC 51/
    2003 30 April 2003
M Lenaerts cs v. Nv's Heerenbosch CC 70/2007 26 April 2007
Municipality of Kraainem v. Flemish Government CC 32/91 14 November 1991
Nv Hazegras cs v. Flemish Government CC 41/95 6 June 1995
Nv Obourg Cement cs v. Flemish Government CC 35/95 25 April 1995
P Thiry cs v. Walloon Government CC 101/2005 1 June 2005
Vzw BEMEFA cs v. Flemish Government CC 55/92 9 July 1992
Vzw Net Sky cs and R. Deneye cs v. Walloon Government CC 189/2005 14 December
    2005

Court of Cassation

Nv S. v. Vzw Werkgroep voor Milieubeheer Brasschaat SC 19 November 1982
SC 25 October 1985 *RW* 1985-1986, 2411
SC 30 December 1993 *TMR* 2005, 192-193
SC 8 November 1996, *TMR* 1997, 30
SC 5 March 1998 *TMR* 1998, 161
SC 14 February 2002 *RW* 2001-2002, 1504
S v. Vzw KBVBV SC 14 September 2004, *TMR* 2005, 105

Council of State

Dossogne CS 77.497, 9 December 1998
Schweren CS 75.557, 6 August 1998
Vzw Aktiekomitee voor milieubescherming in Merelbeke CS 170.173, 19 April
    2007
Vzw Aktiekomitee voor milieubescherming in Merelbeke CS 178.286, 7 January
    2008
Vzw Bond Beter Leefmilieu Tessenderlo and Pals CS 27.042, 21 October 1986
Vzw Bond Beter Leefmilieu-Interenvironnement CS 20.882-20.885, 20 January
    1981
Vzw Grez-Doiceau, Urbanisme et Environnement CS 135.408, 24 September 2004
Vzw Réserves naturelles CS 133.834, 13 July 2004
Vzw Werkgroep voor Milieubeheer Brasschaat CS 21.384, 11 September 1981

Other Cases

Criminal Court, Ghent, 5 September 2000 *TMR* 2000, 522-523
Criminal Court, Ghent, 22 June 2001 *TMR* 2001, 333-335
Criminal Court, Ghent, 22 June 2001 *TMR* 2001, 414-416

OM v. HDL, AV, Ph.V & Nv UCO Sportswear Criminal Court, Ghent, 5 February
2007 *NjW* 2007
Court of Appeal, Ghent, 26 June 1988, *TMR* 1999, 150-152
OM v. LD, DDL & Nv F Court of Appeal, Antwerp, 24 April 1992 *TMR* 1992, 17-20
OM v. EV & KG Criminal Court, Ghent, 2 June 1998 *TMR* 1999, 152-153
OM v. VF Criminal Court, Ypres, 12 February 2007 *TMR* 2007, 562-563

TABLE OF INTERNATIONAL INSTRUMENTS

Convention on Access to Information, Public Participation in Decision-Making
and Access to Justice in Environmental Matters 1998, 38 *ILM* 517 (1999)
European Convention on Human Rights 1950

ABBREVIATIONS

Amén	Aménagement du Territoire, Environnement et Droit Foncier
CC	Constitutional Court
CEDRE	Centre d'étude du droit de l'environnement
CIBG	Centrum voor informatica voor het Brusselse Gewest
CS	Council of State
CWATUP	Code wallon de l'aménagement du territoire, de l'urbanisme en du patrimoine
ECHR	European Court of Human Rights
EIA	Environmental Impact Assessment
EPI	Environmental Performance Index
EU	European Union
EUFJE	European Union Forum of Judges for the Environment
GDP	Gross Domestic Product
JLMB	Jurisprudence de Liège, de Mons et de Bruxelles
JT	Journal des Tribunaux
MER	Milieu-en energierecht
NGO	Non-governmental Organization
NJW	Nieuw Juridisch Weekblad
OECD	Organisation for Economic Co-operation and Development
RBDC	Revue belge de droit constitutionnel
SC	Supreme Court
TMR	Tijdschrift voor Milieurecht
TROS	Tijdschrift voor Ruimtelijke Ordening en Stedenbouw
UNDP	United Nations Development Programme
UNECE	United Nations Economic Commission for Europe (Geneva)
UNEP	United Nations Environmental Programme

Chapter 3
Germany

Eckard Rehbinder

1   INTRODUCTION

Germany is a densely populated country with a large number of agglomerations, a strong industrial, commercial and services sector, good infrastructure, but also an important agriculture and forestry sector. Such an economic structure is almost by necessity associated with major environmental burdens and challenges. As a response, since the beginning of the 1970s, Germany has pursued relatively stringent environmental policies and in this respect presently belongs to the leading nations in Europe. Many conventional environmental problems, especially high levels of air and water pollution, have been solved or at least mitigated. The most important challenges that Germany presently experience, stem from urban and long-distance motor vehicle traffic (air and noise pollution), the generation of electricity (air pollution and global warming), the chemical industry (toxic risks), abandoned waste and industrial facilities (soil and groundwater pollution), the permanent extension of infrastructure and urban settlements (conversion of land to non-natural uses) and agriculture (loss of biodiversity and soil degradation). It is, however, safe to say that with the exception of global warming and loss of biodiversity, most of these problems areas are under control.[1]

---

1. See Umweltbundesamt (ed.), *Daten zur Umwelt 2005* (Berlin: ESV, 2005).

Louis J. Kotzé and Alexander R. Paterson (eds), *The Role of the Judiciary in Environmental Governance: Comparative Perspectives*, pp. 123–150.
© 2009 Kluwer Law International BV, The Netherlands.

2   PRINCIPAL ENVIRONMENTAL LAWS

Germany has a rather fragmented body of environmental law. Apart from some horizontal laws such as the acts on environmental impact assessment (EIA), access to environmental information, environmental remedies, environmental damages and (private) environmental liability,[2] there is a large number of sectoral laws regulating air and noise pollution, water, soil, protection of nature, nuclear energy and radiation, toxic substances, genetically modified organisms, waste, and energy.[3] Moreover, various federal acts on spatial planning, infrastructure planning and building encompass important aspects of environmental protection and resource management.[4]

As the Federal Republic of Germany has a federal structure, State legislation also is of major importance, especially in the fields of nature protection, water resource management, and regional land-use planning. This is due to the fact that before the constitutional reform in 2006, the federal government only had a framework legislative competence in these areas. Under the new constitutional regime the federal government is vested with full (concurrent) legislative powers subject to a limited right of the States to deviate from federal water law and nature protection law. The new constitutional regime has led to a resumption of the project of codifying German environmental law which had been stalled in 1999 because of constitutional objections.

It should also be noted that German environmental law is to an ever-increasing extent influenced by the environmental law of the European Union (EU). Most legislative texts of the EU are directives that are addressed to the Member States

---

2.   *Gesetz über die Umweltverträglichkeitsprüfung* 2005 [Environmental Impact Assessment Act]; *Umweltinformationsgesetz* 2004 [Environmental Information Act]; *Gesetz zu ergänzenden Vorschriften zu Rechtsbehelfen in Umweltangelegenheiten* (*Umweltrechtsbehelfsgesetz*) 2006 [Environmental Remedies Act]; *Gesetz über die Vermeidung und Sanierung vom Umweltschäden* (*Umweltschadensgesetz*) 2007 [Environmental Damages Act]; *Umwelthaftungsgesetz* 1990 [Environmental Liability Act].

3.   *Gesetz zum Schutz vor schädlichen Umwelteinwirkungen durch Luftverunreinigungen, Geräusche, Erschütterungen und ähnliche Vorgänge* (*Bundes-Immissionsschutzgesetz*) 2002 [Federal Emission Control Act]; *Gesetz zur Ordnung des Wasserhaushalts* (*Wasserhaushaltsgesetz*) 2002 [Water Resources Management Act]; *Gesetz zum Schutz vor schädlichen Bodenveränderungen und zur Sanierung von Altlasten* (*Bundes-Bodenschutzgesetz*) 1998 [Federal Soil Protection Act]; *Gesetz über Naturschutz und Landschaftspflege* (*Bundesnaturschutzgesetz*) 2002 [Federal Nature Protection Act]; *Gesetz über die friedliche Verwendung der Kernenergie und den Schutz gegen ihre Gefahren* (*Atomgesetz*) 1985 [Nuclear Energy Act]; *Gesetz zum Schutz vor gefährlichen Stoffen* (*Chemikaliengesetz*) 2002 [Chemicals Act]; *Gesetz zur Regelung der Gentechnik* (*Gentechnikgesetz*) 1993 [Biotechnology Act]; *Gesetz zur Förderung der Kreislaufwirtschaft und Sicherung der umweltverträglichen Beseitigung von Abfällen* (*Kreislaufwirtschafts- und Abfallgesetz*) 1994 [Life Cycle Economy and Waste Act]; and *Gesetz für den Vorrang erneuerbarer Energien* (*Erneuerbare-Energien-Gesetz*) 2004 [Renewable Sources of Energy Act].

4.   *Raumordnungsgesetz* 1997 [Landuse Act]; *Allgemeines Eisenbahngesetz* 1993 [Railways Act]; *Bundesfernstraßengesetz* 2003 [Federal Highways Act]; *Luftverkehrsgesetz* 2007 [Air Traffic Act]; *Baugesetzbuch* 2004 [Federal Building Code].

and need to be transposed into national law, although in case of lack of, or insufficient or belated transposition, they may have a direct effect.

3   INSTITUTIONAL AND GOVERNANCE
            STRUCTURES

In all areas of environmental governance ranging from legislation to rule-making to execution on the ground, environmental governance in Germany is deeply influenced by constitutional principles. Article 20a Federal Constitution[5] obliges the State to protect the environment, and some fundamental rights such as the rights to health and property have also been construed to the extent that, beyond their traditional defensive function in the relationship between the State and individual, they confer upon the State an objective obligation to protect the factual basis for exercising these rights.[6] The objective State duties are mainly addressed to the legislature but also influence the interpretation, development and application of environmental laws by the executive and the judiciary. By contrast, the German Constitution does not recognize a separate fundamental right to a decent environment.

Besides the State obligation to protect the environment, the rule of law and the constitutional rights and principles concretising it are of paramount importance, often tending to limit the State's power effectively to protect the environment. This is particularly true for the fundamental rights of potential polluters such as the right to free exercise of a profession or business, the constitutional protection of property and the right to equal protection, the principle of proportionality of governmental action, the prohibition of infringements of fundamental rights without statutory empowerment, and the guarantee of judicial review of official action.

Due to the federal structure of Germany, the division of powers between the federal and State executives and administration plays an important role in the implementation of environmental laws. The constitutional position of the States is strong. Where the federal government has full legislative powers, it can also make regulations or administrative rules for implementing a federal statute, but only when the law so provides. In political practice, most environmental statutes contain such powers. However, the federal powers are limited by the fact that their exercise is conditional on the consent of the *Bundesrat*; the parliamentary representation of the States. The implementation and enforcement of federal laws on the ground lies in principle within the competence of the States. The States determine the competences, organizational structure, staff and budget of their environmental authorities. The more recent trend towards reduction of bureaucracy has also left its negative mark on the environmental administration. The influence the federal government can legally exercise on the implementation behaviour of the States is relatively slight. The independence the States enjoy is, however, mitigated by the concept of

---

5.   *Grundgesetz für die Bundesrepublik Deutschland* 1949.
6.   Recognized since 1978; BVerfGE 49, 89, 141.

'cooperative federalism'.[7] In all fields of environmental regulation there exist informal joint federal/State bodies where matters of common interest are discussed and, where possible, consensus positions on novel or controversial issues of interpretation of the relevant laws or their practical application are developed.

There are some exceptions to the rule of State execution of federal environmental laws, especially regarding major parts of the regulation of technical products, chemicals and genetically modified organisms, the licensing of nuclear power plants and the planning and construction of federal highways. In these areas, various federal agencies as well as the competent federal ministries have or may have executive powers. As a rule, the role of the Federal Ministry of the Environment and the Federal Environmental Agency is only a political or scientific/technical one.

4   OVERVIEW OVER THE JUDICIARY

The Constitution of the Federal Republic of Germany, in Article 19 (4), provides for comprehensive judicial control of official action where the rights of individuals have been violated. The competent tribunals and courts also have jurisdiction over matters relating to the implementation of EU law in Germany. The paramount principle is that of personal and material independence of the judiciary[8] and its obligation to decide according to statute and law.[9] The independence of the judiciary must also be respected by the executive including the judicial administration, especially the Ministry of Justice. However, certain subtle influences are exercised through the selection of holders of higher positions within the judiciary and the budget of the courts. In particular, recent endeavours to speed up court procedures have a potential adverse effect on judicial independence.

Under the *Administrative Court Procedure Act* (ACPA),[10] judicial protection against the State which extends to all official action, is mainly exercised by the administrative courts, which constitutes a separate branch of the judiciary. The administrative court system consists of three instances. The Administrative Court is a court of first instance. The Administrative Court of Appeal mainly is a court of appeal but also functions as a court of first instance for the review of zoning ordinances and decisions on some types of major projects potentially harmful to the environment. An appeal can only be lodged if it has been admitted by the Administrative Court or the Administrative Court of Appeal. The Federal

---

7. This concept has been developed in State practice; see W. Rudolf, 'Kooperation im Bundesstaat', in *Handbuch des Staatsrechts*, ed. J. Isensee & P. Kirchhof, 2nd ed. (Heidelberg: C.F. Müller, 1999), vol. IV, § 105, no. 20-23, 29-48.
8. Art. 97 Federal Constitution.
9. Art. 20 (3) Federal Constitution.
10. *Verwaltungsgerichtsordnung* 1991.

Administrative Court primarily is a court of appeal (upon admission) against decisions of the intermediate administrative courts. It acts as a court of first instance with respect to certain infrastructure projects of national importance. The two lower administrative tribunals are State courts but have jurisdiction over matters of State as well as federal law. The Federal Administrative Court is a federal court whose jurisdiction is limited to questions of federal law.

Judicial review of administrative action concentrates on individual decisions.[11] Such decisions can be annulled (action for annulment). Where the taking of an administrative decision applied for has been denied or the authority has not acted on the application in due course, the applicant can institute a mandamus action with the objective either to require the authority to take the decision applied for or, where the matter is not yet ripe for disposition or a discretionary decision is involved, to decide anew on the application considering the reasons given by the court.[12] In some instances, an action for a declaration is also admissible.[13]

Generic decisions are subject to judicial review for annulment only in some instances. This is particularly true of local plans.[14] By contrast, federal regulations can normally only be reviewed indirectly when the legality of a decision or imposition of a sanction based on the regulation is challenged and only under exceptional conditions directly through an action for a declaration. Finally, a required factual behaviour on the side of the administration (action or omission) can be enforced under federal common administrative law by an action for specific performance.

The 'ordinary' courts are competent courts for civil and criminal matters as well as the compensation of citizens for expropriation and breach of official duties by public officials.

The Federal Constitutional Court plays a certain role in environmental protection. This court is composed of jurists of high reputation coming from all professions, and which are selected by a joint committee of the two chambers of parliament. Therefore, party politics have a certain influence on the selection of the judges, although this influence is mitigated by rigorous requirements as to their qualifications. The Federal Constitutional Court is empowered to review the constitutionality of statutes and regulations, including environmental laws, on the request of the State organs and parties represented in parliament. Moreover, the Federal Constitution confers on everybody the right to lodge, after exhaustion of ordinary remedies, a constitutional complaint asserting the violation of fundamental rights by official action or inaction, including statutes and judicial decisions.[15]

---

11. See §§ 42(1), 113 ACPA.
12. §§ 42(1), 114 ACPA.
13. § 43 ACPA.
14. § 47 ACPA and State law.
15. Art. 93(1) no. 4a.

5   ACCESS TO THE JUDICIARY IN ENVIRONMENTAL
         MATTERS

5.1   STANDING OF INDIVIDUALS

5.1.1   The Basic Rights-Oriented Standing Concept

The traditional goal of judicial review of administrative action in Germany is the protection of individual rights, and particularized conflicts between an isolated individual and a public authority are the paradigm on which this notion of protection of rights rests. The standing criteria reflect this rights-oriented concept of judicial review of administrative action. These are designed to restrict access to administrative courts to cases where injury to an individual is involved and thus aim for excluding a public action by a plaintiff acting as a representative of the public interest. § 42 (2) ACPA provides with respect to individual decisions, that:

> unless otherwise provided by law, a suit is admissible only if the plaintiff asserts that he has been violated in his legal rights through the administrative act or its refusal or omission.

Mere injury in fact resulting from (objectively) illegal action on the part of the authority, is not in itself a sufficient ground on which to grant standing. Rather, the plaintiff must assert to have suffered injury to a legally protected individual interest. Moreover, there is no connection between standing to participate in administrative proceedings and for judicial review of administrative action. The violation of the right of a person to be heard and to raise objections in administrative proceedings as such, does not confer upon that person standing to challenge the legality of the ensuing administrative decision before an administrative court.

The test applied to determine whether the plaintiff can invoke a legally protected interest is the so-called 'protective law theory' (*Schutznormentheorie*).[16] The legal rule asserted to be violated, must be one designed to protect also the interests of individual persons rather than only the public at large, and the plaintiff must belong to the class of persons to be protected. The plaintiff cannot rest his or her claim on the protected interests of other persons also affected by the relevant decision. Therefore, the violation of rules enacted exclusively in the public interest, the mere effect of which may be to protect individuals, i.e. the mere factual benefit from such rules, is not sufficient to grant standing. Protective laws may be statutes or regulations. Fundamental rights can only serve under exceptional circumstances as a basis for the grant of standing before the administrative courts.[17] In particular, since Germany does not recognize a fundamental right to a decent environment,

---

16. F.O. Kopp & R. Schenke, *Verwaltungsgerichtsordnung*, 15th ed., (München: C.H. Beck, 2007), § 42 no. 39, 42, 43, 48 et seq.
17. BVerwGE 54, 211, 222; BVerwGE 66, 307, 309; H. Sendler, 'Die Bedeutung der Rechtsprechung des Bundesverwaltungsgerichts für den Umweltschutz', in *Umweltrecht im Wandel*, ed. K.-P. Dolde (Berlin: ESV, 2001), 975, 976-979.

in contrast to many other countries, fundamental rights do not serve to widen access to the judiciary.

In mandamus proceedings instituted with a view to requiring a public authority to issue an administrative decision (for example an application for a permit), the plaintiff must show that he or she may have a corresponding claim. This is also determined by the protective law theory.[18] Finally, § 47 ACPA requires that the plaintiff who challenges the legality of a local plan must show that his or her individual interests which had to be considered by the planning authority have been neglected.

5.1.2 Third Party Standing

The rules on standing raise problems where third parties (i.e. persons who assert to have suffered injury as a consequence for a permit addressed to another person or a plan that merely has repercussions on their interests), institute legal proceedings before an administrative court. In the absence of clear statutory language, the crucial question is to delimit individual and public protection by way of construing the relevant laws. In this respect, a highly developed and sometimes confusing body of case law has been established in the more than four decades since the enactment of the ACPA. No uniform construction of the relevant laws has yet emerged in this respect, especially with regard to building and planning law (including local plans). In the past, a major factor in the construction of the relevant legislation was the endeavour of the courts to keep the category of persons with standing as small as possible. More recently, however, there have been clear tendencies in the direction of a certain broadening of standing, especially in environmental and planning law.

In the field of environmental protection, the public interest in environmental protection in compliance with the law can always be vindicated 'indirectly' by the addressee of a decision or a directly aggrieved property owner. Beyond that, the application of the protective law theory renders quite varied results.[19]

5.1.3 Standing in Special Areas of Environmental Protection

Major environmental laws which protect the public at large as well as individuals against unacceptable risk such as the *Federal Emission Control Act* (air pollution and noise), the *Nuclear Energy Act* (nuclear radiation) and the *Biotechnology*

---

18. Kopp & Schenke, *supra* n. 16.
19. See E. Rehbinder, 'Germany', in *Access to Justice in Environmental Matters in the EU*, ed. J. Ebbeson (The Hague: KLI, 2002), 231, 237 et seq.; G. Winter, *German Environmental Law* (Dordrecht: Nijhoff, 1994), 49 et seq.; R. Steinberg, 'Judicial Review of Environmentally-Related Administrative Decision-Making', *Tel Aviv Studies in Law* 11 (1992): 61; H.D. Jarass, 'Der Rechtsschutz Dritter bei der Genehmigung von Anlagen', *NJW* (1993): 2844; as to general administrative law: M. Greve, 'The Non-Reformation of Administrative Law: Standing to Sue and Public Interest Litigation in West German Environmental Law', *Cornell ILJ* 22 (1989): 197.

Act,[20] are in principle protective laws, violation of which confers standing upon affected persons. However, two qualifications must be made:

As regards the *Federal Emission Control Act*, the prevailing opinion makes a distinction between protection against significant risk (danger) and mere precaution. While an alleged violation of the requirement to avoid dangers confers standing, non-compliance with the precautionary principle does in principle not. Precaution is considered to be a measure of general policy designed to reduce the 'population risk', i.e. the risk of the public at large, rather than that of specific individuals.[21] The plaintiff can always base an action on a violation of ambient quality requirements for the protection of health. By contrast, a violation of emission standards is in principle not actionable, subject to the exception that it is where no ambient quality standards exist, especially where the violation of emission standards for carcinogenic substances is invoked for which a threshold value of acceptable risk cannot be determined.[22] Secondly, in addition to the possible violation of a protective law, there must be injury in fact. This means that only 'neighbours' (in the broad sense) who live in the vicinity of the relevant facility and who are potentially exposed to its emissions for a certain time, will have standing.[23] Similar requirements apply to infrastructural projects such as roads, airports and waste deposits insofar as air pollution and noise are concerned.

In the fields of nuclear radiation and biotechnology, the standing criteria are somewhat broader in that a clear distinction between protection against dangers and precaution is not made. Moreover, the administrative courts are more generous with respect to the spatial element of standing; even people who live relatively far away from the source may have standing. However, this also depends on the kind of potential harm asserted (emissions versus accidents).[24] On the other hand, the substantiation burden is relatively heavy and demands a high degree of technical and scientific expertise.[25]

As regards water pollution, the rules of standing which are based on federal and State water law are more restrictive. In principle, only lawful (industrial, commercial and agricultural) water users as well as operators of water works, have standing to challenge agency action which illegally impairs the quantity or quality of water received.[26] To a limited extent, also (adjacent) landowners affected by abstraction of (ground) water and holders of fishing rights have standing.

---

20. § 5(1) no. 1, 2 Federal Emission Control Act; § 7(2) no. 3 Nuclear Energy Act; § 16(1) no. 3, (2) Biotechnology Act.
21. BVerwGE 61, 256, 262-68; BVerwGE 65, 313, 320.
22. BVerwGE 119, 329, 333; VGH Mannheim, NVwZ 1995, 292; see also BVerwGE 128, 278, no. 21-25.
23. BVerwG, NJW 1983, 1507; BVerwGE 61, 256, 268/69; OVG Lüneburg, NVwZ 1985, 357.
24. BVerwGE 72, 300, 315; BVerwG, NVwZ 1989, 1168; NVwZ 1997, 161 (nuclear radiation); OVG Hamburg, ZUR 1995, 53 (biotechnology).
25. BVerwGE 61, 256, 268; BVerwGE 70, 365, 368-70; more generous BVerwG, NVwZ 1997, 161.
26. BVerwGE 78, 40; BVerwGE 128, 358, no. 27/28; BGHZ 88, 34, 41-43.

Other normal uses of watercourses, for example, recreation and leisure, are not legally protected in the interest of individuals.

In the field of toxic substances, standing is normally denied because the public at large is affected and individualized harm to the plaintiff cannot be demonstrated.

Finally, protection of nature law is considered to exclusively protect the public at large. Hence, beyond addressees of a decision and property owners whose legal rights are taken or restricted by a decision made under the federal or State protection of nature laws, no individual is granted standing to invoke the illegality of State measures for nature protection or their omission.[27] In particular, the denial of standing extends to persons who regularly use a particular site for recreation and leisure. The same restrictive stance is applied to decisions taken under other laws, for example, regarding polluting facilities, and water uses or infrastructural projects insofar as the protection of nature is concerned.

5.2 STANDING OF ASSOCIATIONS AND MUNICIPALITIES

5.2.1 The Principle of Inadmissibility of Collective Suits

The rights-oriented concept of German law also has significant implications for suits instituted by groups, associations and municipalities. In principle, under common administrative law, informal groups (such as neighbourhood associations) as well as permanent associations, only have standing where they assert their own subjective rights, especially as owners of property (which, however, may not be acquired *ad hoc* for the sole purpose of barring a particular development).[28] Groups and associations are not allowed to vindicate the interests of their members even if the members, when instituting court action individually, would have standing. By the same token, they cannot vindicate the public interest only for the reason that, by virtue of their charter, their objective is the protection of the public interest.[29]

§ 42 (2) ACPA, however, expressly empowers the federal government (and in the absence of federal action also the States), to introduce public interest standing, especially by granting standing to associations. Since the early 1970s, there has been a (sometimes heated) debate on association suits.[30] Especially in the field of nature protection, it has been argued that environmental advocates are particularly needed

---

27. BVerwGE 54, 211, 224/25; BVerwGE 128, 358, no. 31.
28. BVerwGE 112, 135, 136-38; more liberal are the older decisions; see BVerwGE 67, 74, 76; BVerwGE 72, 15, 25/26.
29. BVerwGE 54, 211, 219/20; BVerwGE 101, 73, 81-83; BVerwG, NVwZ 2007, 1074.
30. See K. Balleis, *Mitwirkungs- und Klagerechte anerkannter Naturschutzverbände* (Frankfurt: PLV, 1996); E. Rehbinder, 'Verbandsklage', in *Handwörterbuch des Umweltrechts*, ed. O. Kimminich et al., 2nd ed. (Berlin: ESV, 1994), vol. 2, col. 2559; R. Wolf, 'Zur Entwicklung der Verbandsklage im Umweltrecht', *ZUR* 5 (1994): 1; T. Ormond, 'Environmental Group Actions in West Germany', in *Participation and Litigation Rights of Environmental Associations in Europe*, ed. M. Führ & G. Roller (Frankfurt: PLV, 1991), 77 et seq.

because, due to the narrow standing doctrine, pro-environment interest groups would not normally have access to administrative courts for ensuring the legality of the administration and protection of nature in conformity with the applicable laws. However, there has always been a widespread aversion against 'self-appointed guardians of the public interest'; arguably an unconscious relict of absolutism, but officially based on the lack of democratic legitimation of environmental associations. Moreover, there have been fears about a shift of the balance of power onto the judiciary, court congestion and prolongation of investment projects.

5.2.2   Statutory Association Standing

As a response to this situation, beginning in the early 1980s, gradually more States introduced association suits in the field of nature protection, although the scope of standing varied from State to State.[31] In 2002, the federal government finally followed the lead of the States and established association standing in the *Federal Protection of Nature Act*.[32] Standing is limited to 'recognized' associations, i.e. associations for the protection of nature and the environment which under § 59 or § 60 of the *Federal Protection of Nature Act* have been formally recognized by the federal government or the relevant State.[33] This requires fulfilment of certain prerequisites such as: a geographical scope extending at least to a State, proper performance in the field including financial responsibility, and openness to all persons who support the objectives of the association (which excludes foundations such as Greenpeace and the World Wildlife Foundation). Informal groups do not have access to judicial review. Standing is limited to the assertion of violations of legal rules that are designed to protect nature.[34] The association must have made use of its right to participate in the preceding administrative proceedings and substantiated its objections; otherwise it is precluded from raising a particular point. Instituting a court action shall be the *ultima ratio*. Moreover, under common federal administrative law, association standing is admitted insofar as a recognized environmental association asserts a violation of its participation rights granted by § 58 of the *Federal Protection of Nature Act*. Although this right is strictly procedural in character, the administrative courts allow an action for annulment of an administrative decision made in violation of this right in order to effect association participation.[35]

Apart from the specific association standing established under the *Federal Protection of Nature Act* and limited to protection of nature, the *Environmental Remedies Act* of 2006[36] introduced standing of recognized environmental

---

31. See Balleis, *supra* n. 30, Rehbinder, *supra* n. 30, Wolf, *supra* n. 30, and Ormond, *supra* n. 30.
32. §§ 59-61 Federal Protection of Nature Act.
33. § 61(1) Federal Protection of Nature Act.
34. BVerwGE 78, 347, 355; BVerwG, NVwZ 1998, 398; NVwZ 1999, 616.
35. BVerwGE 87, 62, 71-74; BVerwGE 104, 367, 372; BVerwGE 127, 208, 216-19. Under certain circumstances, the violation can be remedied pending court proceedings, especially with respect to federal highways and railways – the most frequent objects of association suits.
36. § 2 Environmental Remedies Act.

associations in the entire field of the environment with respect to major categories of decisions. This act implements the EC Directive 2003/35[37] which, in turn, transposes the Aarhus Convention[38] into EU law. Standing relates to decisions for which an EIA is required, facility permits subject to mandatory public partic-ipation under the *Federal Emission Control Act* and under the *Water Resources Management Act*, and permits for waste deposits under the *Life Cycle Economy and Waste Act*. The standing requirements are mostly shaped on the pattern of the association suit in the field of protection of nature. Standing is, however, limited to the invocation of environmental norms that 'establish rights of individuals',[39] and thereby inserts the protective law theory into the association suit. Arguably, this odd hybrid of an association suit is not in conformity with the EC Directive and the Aarhus Convention.[40]

5.2.3 Standing of Local Governments

Local governments such as municipalities and counties, have standing to defend their planning autonomy and the functioning of local institutions such as hospitals, kindergartens, and water supply facilities. The defence of the planning autonomy is limited to instances where the realization of existing plans is inhibited by State action. By contrast, these public bodies cannot assert the interests of their citizens, nor can they vindicate the public interest in the protection of he environment.[41]

5.3 GROUNDS, SCOPE AND DEPTH OF JUDICIAL REVIEW

5.3.1 Grounds for Judicial Review

Judicial review is limited to the legality of the challenged decision.[42] Under German law, legality in the first place means substantive legality. The primary objective of judicial review is to protect substantive individual rights and ensure the substantive correctness of the challenged decision. Procedural errors carry less weight. They do not lead to the annulment of the decision if it is evident that the

---

37. Directive of the European Parliament and the Council of 26 May 2003 providing for public participation in respect of drawing up certain plans and programmes relating the environment and amending with respect to public participation and access to justice Council Directives 85/337/EEC and 96/61/EC, 2003 OJ no. L 156, 17.
38. Convention on Access to Information, Public Participation in Decision-Making and Access to Justice in Environmental Matters 1998, 38 *ILM* 517 (1999).
39. § 2 no. 1 of the Act.
40. B. Dette, 'Access to Justice in Environmental Matters: the Aarhus Convention and legislative Initiatives for its Implementation', in *Environmental Law and Policy at the Turn to the 21st Century*, ed. T. Ormond et al. (Berlin: Lexxion, 2006), 63, 75-78.
41. BVerwGE 69, 256, 261; BVerwGE 81, 95, 108; BVerwGE 90, 96, 100; BVerwGE 100, 388, 391, 394/95; BVerwGE 125, 116, 291.
42. § 113(1), (5) ACPA.

violation has not influenced the decision.[43] Practically, procedural errors can only be relevant in discretionary decisions, planning decisions, and arguably also decisions applying broad statutory terms. However, under the *Environmental Remedies Act*[44] complete non-compliance with the obligation of carrying out an EIA or an EIA screening is deemed to always be relevant. Moreover, procedural errors can normally be remedied by the authority during the litigation.[45]

The court is not bound by the construction and application of law by the authority; it can substitute its opinion for that of the authority. However, there are exceptions. In instances of a discretionary decision, the decision or its denial or omission is reviewed only to the extent that the competent authority has exceeded the statutory limits of discretion or has used its discretion in a way inconsistent with the purpose of the empowerment.[46] The authority can supplement its reasoning also during pending court proceedings. Similar requirements are applied by the courts to planning decisions.[47]

5.3.2   Scope of Judicial Review: The Impact of the Protective Law Theory

Within this general framework, several rather complex issues arise. The first issue is the effect of the protective law theory on the scope of reviewing the merits of the case. § 113 (1) and (5) ACPA clearly set forth that in order to annul an administrative decision or to require the authority to take a decision denied or omitted, objective illegality is not sufficient; rather, the plaintiff must also be violated in his or her rights. This means that the grounds on which the grant of standing rests, also determine the scope of review.[48] The court can annul an illegal administrative decision only when and insofar as it infringes upon legally protected interests of the plaintiff on which he or she has or could have relied to be accorded standing. Likewise, an abuse of discretion is only relevant insofar as the purpose of the empowerment is to protect the interest of a class of persons to which the plaintiff belongs. Finally, the relevance of procedural errors is determined by the protective law theory. The practical effect of this position is that the addressee of an administrative decision or a property owner who is directly affected by it, has a right to comprehensive review of all kinds of (relevant) procedural and substantive violations of law. By contrast, third parties do not have such a right.[49]

Similar limitations apply to association suits. This seems evident with respect to the association suit under the *Environmental Remedies Act*[50] which is predicated

---

43. § 46 *Verwaltungsverfahrensgesetz* [Administrative Procedure Act].
44. § 4(1) Environmental Remedies Act.
45. § 45(2) Administrative Procedure Act.
46. § 114 ACPA.
47. BVerwGE 45, 309, 314/15; BVerwGE 56, 110, 122; BVerwGE 71, 166, 170; BVerwGE 87, 332, 341.
48. BVerwGE 48, 56, 60; BVerwGE 56, 110, 118; BVerwGE 67, 74; BVerwGE 87, 332, 334.
49. BVerwGE 61, 256, 275; BVerwGE 75, 285, 291/92; BVerwGE 85, 348, 368.
50. § 2 Environmental Remedies Act.

on the potential impairment of a subjective right of any individual. As regards association standing under the *Protection of Nature Act*,[51] since this is based on the asserted violation of protection of nature law, the courts have held that the grounds for granting standing also limit the scope of review. The association can request a review of the weighing process to the detriment of nature protection concerns, although such concerns normally do not enjoy a preference. By contrast, the need for the project as such, its systemic effects, as well as the entire weighing process, fall outside judicial scrutiny.

5.3.3 Depth of Judicial Review

The third issue relates to the depth of judicial review. In principle, judicial review in Germany is *de novo* both on questions of fact and of law. The Administrative Court is sovereign in construing the relevant statutory terms and applying them to the facts of the case. The interpretation and application of broad statutory terms contained in most environmental laws, such as 'danger', 'precaution', 'public interest', 'best available technology', 'economically tolerable' and the like, are in principle fully reviewable to the extent that the court can substitute its view for that of the authority. However, there is a certain trend towards deference to the authorities as regards complex scientific and technical issues. Since the famous 1985 decision by the Federal Administrative Court on the nuclear power plant Wyhl,[52] the administrative courts, in nuclear energy and biotechnology cases, tend to exert a considerable degree of deference to the authority's appreciation of the relevant risk, arguing that the authority disposes of a high degree of scientific and technical expertise, and is politically legitimized by the procedure set forth for arriving at the relevant decision. Moreover, since 1978 there has been an even more important general tendency to defer to the authority's risk assessment where the authority has concretized broad statutory terms by environmental standards.[53]

5.4 INTERIM JUDICIAL PROTECTION

The effectiveness of judicial review largely depends on the degree to which the administration is capable, by making a decision, omitting to act, or taking factual action in violation of law, to create a situation to the detriment of the environment which cannot be remedied after the fact. In contrast to many other countries, the normal rule of German administrative court procedure law is that an administrative or judicial remedy, especially an action before an administrative court, has an

---

51. § 61 Federal Protection of Nature Act.
52. BVerwGE 72, 300, 315-18; later decisions: BVerwGE 78, 177, 180; BVerwGE 81, 185, 190-92; BVerwG, NVwZ 1989, 1168; in the field of biotechnology: OVG Berlin, NVwZ 1995, 1023; NVwZ 1999, 96.
53. BVerwGE 55, 250, 259-61; BVerwGE 72, 300, 320; BVerwG, NVwZ 1988, 824; NVwZ 1995, 994, 995; NVwZ 1997, 161, 164/65.

automatic suspensory effect.[54] The authority can, however, order the immediate execution of the administrative decision if the public interest or paramount private interests warrant this.[55] Then the plaintiff can apply to the administrative court for the restoration of the suspensory effect.[56] The court decides in a summary procedure in which full proof of the facts need not be adduced and the merits are considered only summarily. If there are serious doubts as to the legality of the challenged decision, the suspensory effect will be restored. If it is evident that the decision is legal, the restoration will be refused. In all other cases, the court bases its decision on a balance of the conflicting interests.[57] There is, however, a fairly recent legislative tendency to limit the automatic suspensory effect in order to accelerate investments. In environmental law, this is particularly true of planning permits for certain infrastructure projects.[58] In such instances, the plaintiff must apply to the administrative tribunal for ordering the stay of the administrative decision.[59] The procedure is the same as in the case described above, but the 'negotiation position' of the affected citizen is worse because he or she has to take the initiative and adduce evidence in support of his or her position.

In all other cases, especially mandamus actions and actions for the review of local plans, the plaintiff can apply for an interim injunction if there is a danger that by changing the present situation, the realization of his or her rights may be frustrated or significantly impaired.[60] Once again, the administrative court decides in a summary procedure similar to that established by § 80 ACPA. The court can only take preliminary measures which do not exhaust the matter, such as a preliminary injunction or a temporary requirement not to apply a local plan to the detriment of the plaintiff.

6   THE WEALTH OF CASE LAW: SOME ILLUSTRATIVE
             JUDICIAL DECISIONS

Environmental law is a dynamic branch of administrative law which has greatly contributed also to innovations in general administrative law. Environmental litigation in Germany is increasing every year. Starting with a few decisions in the late 1970s, there are now a multitude of decisions of administrative courts of all instances every year that are published in specialized journals of environmental and general administrative law and later on partly in the official case collections.

---

54. §§ 80(1), 80a(1) ACPA.
55. §§ 80(2) no. 4, 80a(1) ACPA.
56. §§ 80(5), 80a(1) ACPA.
57. Kopp & Schenke, *supra* n. 16, § 80 no. 81-84.
58. E.g., § 17e(2) Federal Highways Act, § 18e(2) Railways Act.
59. § 80(5), 80a(1) ACPA.
60. §§ 123, 47(2) ACPA.

The majority of court cases are instituted by the addressees of administrative decisions or property owners directly affected. Third party litigation is less prevalent. In the field of nature protection, association suits are prevailing. This particularly concerns major infrastructure projects such as roads, railways, airports and navigation projects where the associations often attempt to use temporary uncertainties about the interpretation of EU nature protection law to prevent such projects or mitigate their adverse effects.[61] The following section limits itself to analyse three illustrative decisions.

Various judgments by the Federal Administrative Court relate to the contents and limits of the precautionary principle which is a permit prerequisite under various sectoral environmental laws. One court case concerning the nuclear power plant Whyl, in the southwest of Germany, aroused strong public attention. Here, following demonstrations against the project, third parties challenged the legality of a siting permit for the plant. In its judgment rendered in 1985, the Federal Administrative Court[62] first had to decide whether the competent agency had erred in making the requisite preliminary positive determination that the facility would meet the permit requirements under the *Nuclear Energy Act*.[63] In contrast to general legislative practice, the *Nuclear Energy Act* does not distinguish between protection from significant risk and precaution, but requires that precaution against damage caused by the facility be taken according to the state of science and technology. The court held that under the Act, also such possible harm must be considered which cannot be positively ruled out because according to the present state of knowledge, particular causal relationships can neither be affirmed nor denied. This means that a mere suspicion of a significant risk or a 'potential of concern' is sufficient. In the opinion of the court, a potential of concern need not necessarily be based on empirical knowledge. Plausible theoretical considerations and calculations are also relevant. Moreover, in response to the widespread and potentially deleterious effects of nuclear radiation, the court deviated from common practice that denies third party standing in the area of precaution. It recognized standing based on an alleged non-compliance with the applicable dose limit values, which in Germany are considered to be precautionary rather than addressing significant risk. Finally, a major contribution of the decision to develop environmental law, lies in the recognition of the primary responsibility of the executive for the assessment and evaluation of risk and therefore, contrary to general practice, in a quite extensive deference to agency expertise. This is particularly true where the agency has used its empowerment to adopt, on the basis of scientific knowledge and the results of public participation, administrative rules for concretising the broad statutory terms of the Act.

---

61. W. Vallendar, 'Europäisches Naturschutzrecht: Die Verbandsklage – Risiken und Nebenwirkungen für Infrastrukturvorhaben', *UPR* 28 (2008): 1.
62. BVerwGE 72, 300.
63. § 7 Nuclear Energy Act.

Standing was also the subject of a decision of the Federal Administrative Court rendered in 1990 which involved an association suit against the planning permit for a marina at the Lake of Constance.[64] The association asserted that its participation rights under the *Federal Protection of Nature Act* of 1976[65] had been violated. In contrast to the general theory of irrelevance of participation for standing, the court granted the association standing on the grounds that the Act establishes recognized associations as guardians of the public interest and therefore the special participation right was a subjective right that could be enforced. In the opinion of the court, the enforcement could also be effected indirectly by bringing an action for annulment of the administrative decision rendered in the improper procedure. This decision and other decisions following it,[66] have had a major impact on public views on association suits and paved the way for the subsequent introduction of association standing at federal level.

Finally, a fairly recent decision of the Federal Administrative Court handed down in September 2007[67] is remarkable. It concerns a non-attainment area where an action plan for meeting the ambient quality standard for particulates as required by EU air quality directives and the implementing *Federal Emission Control Act*[68] was missing. The Act provides that all authorities shall take the necessary measures for meeting the ambient quality standards, in particular by setting forth action plans. It could have been concluded from the wording of the law and would also have better reflected the complexity of securing compliance, that the action plan should in principle have priority and affected citizens could normally only require the determination of such plans. However, in a move to strengthening citizen rights for the protection of health, the court held that an affected neighbour had a direct claim against all relevant authorities for taking appropriate measures, although the agency retains some margin of discretion. For the solution of practical difficulties in distributing the emission reduction burden of multiple sources, the court simply referred to the principle of proportionality.

Civil litigation plays a minor role in the field of environmental protection. A certain exception is litigation based on public law regarding compensation for State interventions into property in land which is entrusted to the civil courts. Civil litigation in the strict sense, i.e. litigation arising under private law, mainly concerns local conflicts, such as noise nuisances. There have also been some cases on liability under the *Environmental Liability Act* and § 22 *Water Resources Management Act*. Mostly, the impact of civil litigation on the enforcement of existing environmental law and its development has been slight.

---

64. BVerwGE 87, 69. The standing issue arose in the framework of a controversy between the parties as to whether the case had become moot or was initially unfounded.
65. § 29 *Bundesnaturschutzgesetz* of 1976 [Federal Protection of Nature Act], the predecessor of the present act.
66. *Supra* n. 35.
67. BVerwGE 128, 278; see the decisions of another chamber of the court which afforded the action plan priority in planning proceedings; BVerwGE 121, 57; BVerwGE 123, 23.
68. § 47 Federal Emission Control Act.

7   JUDICIAL CONTRIBUTION TO ENVIRONMENTAL
         GOVERNANCE

7.1   INTRODUCTION

As already stated, the traditional paradigm of judicial review of administrative
action is constituted by particularized conflicts between the State and an isolated
and abstract individual. The standing criteria and the grounds and scope of review
reflect this rights-oriented concept of judicial review. Although there is a certain
development towards broadening the grounds for granting standing in environmental matters, the administrative courts in principle continue to adhere to tradition. The
protective law theory is not being challenged, it is only refined in certain respects.

7.1.1   Shortcomings of the Rights-Based Approach

This stance has several shortcomings. The role of the plaintiff as either user of the
environment (polluter) or victim of environmental pollution or other degradation,
is not sufficiently reflected. The systematic distinction between the addressee of
an administrative decision or property owner directly aggrieved, including third
parties, amounts to a discrimination of a particular role in environmental conflicts.
Third parties are plaintiffs of second order, with respect to both standing and
grounds and scope of judicial review. This is not a necessary result of a rights-
based approach in judicial review. The example of other jurisdictions which also
adhere to a subjective concept of judicial review shows that a broader standing
concept is possible, for instance, standing based on illegality in addition to injury in
fact or on sufficient interest.

 Moreover, the collective nature of environmental conflicts is systematically
ignored. Normally in environmental conflicts, not a single person but rather a
multitude of persons are affected. Instead of isolated conflicts involving individual
rights, the courts often have to deal with politicized conflicts between economy,
technological progress and ecology, societal disagreement on the assessment of
risks and, at least in fact, a multitude of aggrieved persons that surpass the traditional protection-of-rights concept. 'Diffuse' interests of this kind are not considered to be relevant – neither in granting standing nor in delineating the grounds and
scope of review. Rather, the administrative courts take the view that a plaintiff
cannot improve his situation by the mere fact that other persons are affected in the
same way. An extreme expression of this narrow stance is the somewhat artificial
view, that regarding planning decisions, only that segment of the weighing process
can be scrutinized that concerns the plaintiff[69] (as if a unitary weighing process
could realistically be divided into several segments). Also, the denial of standing of
informal or formal groups who bunch diffuse interests, even if their members when
suing individually would have standing, belongs to this category of thought.

---

69. See the cases cited *supra* n. 48 and 49.

Finally, systemic effects are not normally considered in judicial review of decisions on the environment instituted by third parties.[70] This is particularly true of complex causation chains and latent cause-effect relationships, long-distance transportation of pollutants, the summation of small doses of pollutants and combined effects of different pollutants. Systemic environmental challenges such as climate change, depletion of the ozone layer, long-term soil degradation, or persistence of chemicals, do not reach the judiciary at the demand of third parties. In addition, in spite of the more recent enrichment of German environmental law with sustainability clauses, issues of sustainability have only marginally occupied the German administrative courts. This is even true in the field of traditional management of natural resources. For example, neither the need for generating electricity from nuclear energy, nor the long-term effects presented by the necessity to manage nuclear waste over generations, enters into judicial scrutiny of a pertinent administrative decision at the request of third parties.

Apart from the rejection of diffuse effects, the interest of an individual, or an association as a citizen or a group of citizens, or of a municipality in controlling the proper functioning of the executive in environmental matters or exercising democratic participation rights for improving environmental protection, is in principle considered to fall outside the scope of judicial review. Although the traditional distinction between State and society seems to be obsolete, the German administrative courts maintain the position that only the infringement of personal rather than political rights legitimizes judicial review. Neither individuals nor organizations shall act as self-nominated guardians of the public interest. The violation of the democratic right to participate in administrative procedures as such does not in principle confer standing to go against the resulting decision. The rejection of the functional and democratic rationales of judicial review[71] explains the aversion against association suits for vindicating the public interest in environmental matters, with the result that the legislature had to intervene with the aim to partially introduce a full-fledged association suit.

7.1.2   Broadening the Judicial Perspective

At second glance, however, the German rights-based approach is not as monolithic as it may appear. First, the self-interest of enterprises whose standing is rather comprehensive may bring to the forum environmental issues that are precluded to third parties. Thus, it has been held in litigation instituted by a polluter, that the precautionary principle also legitimizes action against long-distance transportation of air pollutants.[72] In a special area of sustainability, namely waste management, the interest of enterprises in avoiding expensive waste disposal by carrying out cheaper

---

70. See G. Winter, 'Wahrnehmungsfilter des Bundesverwaltungsgerichts – Der Fall Ökologie', in *Festgabe 50 Jahre Bundesverwaltungsgericht*, ed. E. Schmidt-Aßmann et al. (Köln: CHV, 2003), 1029, 1032 et seq.
71. J. Ebbeson, 'Comparative Introduction', in *Access to Justice in Environmental Matters in the EU*, ed. *id.* (The Hague: KLI, 2002), 3-7.
72. BVerwGE 69, 37, 44; BVerwG, NVwZ 1995, 994, 995.

recycling, prompted a number of court decisions regarding the question as to when recycling is environmentally acceptable despite possible adverse effects associated with it.[73] Generally speaking, insofar as the relevant substantive environmental law pursues a wider regulatory perspective, for example, in spatial planning, EIA, water resources management and sustainability, the administrative courts, when addressees of a decision or property owners directly affected bring a case to the forum, would not ignore the regulatory framework in exercising their review functions.

Second, returning to advocates of environmental protection, there is a certain tendency towards granting standing also in the field of precaution for human health, both in the fields of nuclear radiation and toxic air pollutants, thus acknowledging that public health is no greater than the sum of individual health of all persons affected.[74] Moreover, in contrast to the general theory of dissociation of participation and standing, the Federal Administrative Court has recognized association standing for asserting the violation of specific participation rights conferred on environmental associations by the *Federal Protection of Nature Act*.[75] The action which now has lost much of its importance due to the statutory introduction of association standing, goes beyond simple enforcement of the right to participation. Rather, the relevant association can demand the annulment of the administrative decision rendered in the improper procedure. Finally, in appropriate cases, the administrative courts may practically overcome the particularization of environmental conflicts through the limits placed on standing and review of the merits by joining suits brought by several categories of plaintiffs. Accordingly, in recent litigation on the planning and construction of a new central airport for Berlin, the Federal Administrative Court[76] simultaneously dealt with suits instituted by a multitude of private plaintiffs including: property owners who would be expropriated as a consequence of the project and who could demand a comprehensive review of the merits and third parties who were limited to invoking noise nuisances; municipalities who could rely on an encroachment of their planning autonomy; and environmental associations who challenged the legality of the planning permit for alleged violation of protection of nature law.

7.2   CONTRIBUTION TO THE INTERPRETATION AND DEVELOPMENT OF ENVIRONMENTAL LAW

7.2.1   Law Making Role of the Courts

A core function of German courts – in line with their traditional role – has been to clarify open questions of environmental law, especially by construing broad

---

73. E.g., BVerwGE 111, 136, 139-43; BVerwG, NVwZ 2000, 1356; NVwZ 2005, 954.
74. BVerwGE 72, 300, 318/19; BVerwGE 119, 329, 333/34; VGH München, NVwZ-RR 2006, 456, 461.
75. See cases cited *supra* n. 35.
76. BVerwGE 125, 116.

statutory terms. German law does not recognize the principle of *stare decisis*. A court decision has legal force beyond the individual case only because of its reasoning. Although the judge only decides on the pending individual case, and thereby the concrete conflict or controversy, it is the German understanding of the role of the judiciary that it has to ensure the unity of law and secure legal certainty in the relations between those who are subject to, and have to apply, existing law. Especially decisions by the courts of last instance are often meant to address general legal questions. Under this perspective, the courts do not only decide cases, but also create judicial norms.

In environmental law, the interpretive function of the judiciary is even more important than in other areas. The dynamics of democratic legislation in this field with its ever-increasing number of new laws and amendments of existing ones, often are the source of vague, ill-defined or even inconsistent rules, and overlaps and gaps in regulation which, if they are not remedied by executive rule-making, would require court intervention. Moreover, positive law does not constitute an absolute, insurmountable frame for the judiciary. German law does not only recognize the power and obligation of the judge to interpret the law, but also to develop it. Article 20(3) Federal Constitution expresses this judicial task by stating that the judge is bound by statute and law. A clear delimitation between interpretation and development of the law is not possible.

Some examples of this *de facto* 'law-making' role of the judiciary in environmental matters, are presented by judicial pronouncements regarding the interpretation of the precautionary principle, the expansion of standing (normally denied) to precautionary action in the absence of protective ambient standards, the judicial self-restraint in case of scientifically complex administrative decisions and environmental standards, and the recognition of an individual right to protective measures for complying with ambient air quality standards.

7.2.2   Controlling National Implementation of EU Directives

A particular role is exercised by German courts in serving as a first filter for the control of national implementation of EU environmental directives. As was stated above, German environmental law is to an ever-increasing extent influenced by EU environmental legislation. Regulations are directly applicable to every citizen in the EU, while directives which are far more frequent, are addressed to the Member States and need to be transposed into national law. The regulatory concepts and the systematic structure of EU environmental directives often differ from those of German law. Moreover, as a result of compromises in the political bargaining process, key provisions of the directives are often formulated in a rather vague form, leaving room for divergent interpretations. When a new directive has to be implemented, it is not always clear which legislative steps it exactly requires to be taken. This may lead to implementation deficits already at the stage of transposition of the relevant directive into national law.

The German judiciary originally took a rather reserved position towards EU law, tending to mitigate the resulting conflicts by fitting the relevant directives into the German system rather than adjusting it to European law. Good examples are presented by various decisions that render EIA a rather toothless device. The Federal Administrative Court denies the EIA any substantive legal effect and, in line with § 46 *Administrative Procedure Act*, normally excludes the judicial review of administrative decisions for procedural errors in instances of non-compliance with the EIA requirements on the grounds that the error was irrelevant.[77] In construing the notion of waste under the EC Framework Waste Directive,[78] the German administrative courts tended to simply apply earlier case law based on the *German Waste Act*.[79] The notion of intentional impairment of protected species under the Habitats Directive[80] was interpreted to the extent that an impairment that was legal under national law, for example, under a zoning ordinance, could never be intentional because the ultimate purpose was not the impairment but rather the realization of the zoning ordinance.[81] There are a number of cases in which German court decisions on implementation issues have been annulled by the European Court of Justice (ECJ) or could no longer be maintained as a result of decisions of that court involving other parties. The ECJ is the ultimate authority in this field, as open questions of interpretation of EU directives must be referred to it by national courts of last instance and can be referred to it by all other courts.[82]

However, especially in the more recent past, the German administrative courts are taking a more open stance toward EU environmental law. There is a growing awareness that European law is – like the national Constitution – a source of law that is paramount to national law and that its notions and regulatory concepts need not necessarily be similar to those that judges are familiar with under national law. Some examples of an increased 'opening' towards EU law are the various administrative court decisions which attempt to prevent a frustration of habitat protection under the European Habitats Directive by infrastructure projects before formal determination of protected areas.[83] Another example in this respect is a decision of the Federal Administrative Court that recognized a subjective right of citizens affected by traffic-borne air pollution to concrete measures for ensuring compliance with the ambient air quality standards established by the EU.[84]

---

77. BVerwGE 100, 370, 377/78, 380; BVerwGE 104, 337, 346/47; BVerwGE 127, 95, 100.
78. Council Directive 75/442/EEC on Waste, 1975 O.J. no. L 194, 47, as amended.
79. See the decisions cited *supra* note 74; furthermore OVG Lüneburg, NVwZ 1998, 1202, 1204.
80. Council Directive 92/43/EEC on the conservation of natural habitats and of wild fauna and flora, 1992 O.J. no. L 206, 7.
81. BVerwGE 112, 321, 329-31; BVerwG, NVwZ 2005, 943, 947; but see now BVerwG, NuR 2006, 779, 782.
82. Art. 234 EC Treaty.
83. E.g. BVerwGE 107, 1, 21/22; BVerwGE 110, 302, 308/09; BVerwGE 112, 140, 155/56.
84. *Supra* n. 68.

7.2.3   Controlling the Functioning of the Administration and Beyond

As stated, the rationale underlying judicial review of administrative action in Germany is the vindication of subjective rights. Nevertheless, although the functional rationale of judicial review is not recognized, the rights-based approach at least indirectly also serves to control the proper functioning of the administration in environmental matters and thereby promote the public interest. The control function of administrative courts in Germany does not only consist in cassation, namely merely quashing administrative decisions that are illegal (and violate individual rights). Based on a broader understanding of the division of powers between the judiciary and the executive, and with a view to provide effective judicial protection, German courts can also address orders to the administration. This is especially true of mandamus actions and proceedings for interim relief.

Regarding the contents of judicial review, the borderline between the judiciary and the executive is not clearly delineated. To a certain extent, the administrative courts can substitute their opinion for that of the administration, although they may not practically assume the role of the administration. The determination of the facts of the case, as well as the interpretation and application of the law, including the interpretation and application of broad statutory terms frequently used in environmental law, are entrusted to the courts, subject to some exceptions of judicial self-restraint in cases of scientifically and technically complex issues and administrative rule-making. Moreover, while administrative planning and resource management and enforcement discretion in the field of the environment must be respected, the exercise of this discretion can be reviewed. This review is quite extensive and goes well beyond the scrutiny of arbitrary and capricious action. In particular, the full development of the principle of proportionality has led to a stricter review of the merits. German administrative courts even recognize that administrative discretion can shrink to zero when under the circumstances of the case, only a single decision is deemed to be in conformity with law. This is particularly true when there exist serious threats to life and health.[85]

It should be noted that the legislature enjoys a much wider political discretion. In cases where the objective State duty to protect human health is invoked, the Federal Constitutional Court limits intervention to cases of complete inaction or manifestly insufficient action. Environmental issues that have been litigated include forest damage due to air pollution, ozone pollution, exposure to smoking, and electromagnetic radiation.[86] There is not a single environmental case where the court has ever held the legislature to be in violation of its duty to protect.

---

85. BVerwGE 128, 278 no. 21-25; BVerwGE 74, 234, 236, 239-40.
86. BVerfG, NJW 1989, 3264; NJW 1996, 651; NJW 1998, 2961; NVwZ 2007, 1638.

7.2.4   Fast-Tracking Court Proceedings and Judicial Protection

Apart from the narrow standing doctrine and the connected limitation of the grounds of judicial review, the structure of German administrative court procedure law is generally beneficial to environmental plaintiffs. This is true for the existence of three court instances, the power of the court of appeal to review questions of fact and law *de novo*, and of the Federal Administrative Court to review at least questions of law *de novo*, the non-adversarial character of the court procedure, the automatic suspensory effect of actions for annulment, and the availability of interim relief in all other cases.

Some more recent changes that aim for fast-tracking court procedures, however, have the potential of shifting the balance to the detriment of environmental plaintiffs, or at least to counteract innovative decisions. The system of judicial review in three instances has been substantially modified by elevating litigation on major projects to the appeal courts, and in other instances, even to the Federal Administrative Court deciding as first instance. The suspensory effect of actions for annulment has been curtailed. Appeal to the Administrative Court of Appeal currently is only by admission. In many cases, it is no longer a chamber of the administrative court of first instance, but rather a single judge of the chamber who decides a case. The reduction of the system of instances and the high substantiation requirements to reach the second instance, arguably impair the capacity of the judiciary to decide on novel legal issues by 'trial and error', and thereby encourage conservative court decisions. This is exacerbated by the (limited) conversion of the Federal Administrative Court into a court of first instance which deprives it of the experience of trial courts, it conflicts with the very function of a high court, and is amenable to deflect its function as guardian of the unity of law. The abolishment of the automatic suspensory effect of the action in important categories of environmental cases, compels the plaintiff to take the initiative for demanding interim relief if he or she seeks to halt the project. It leads to an early summary review of the merits of the administrative decision based on incomplete facts and legal reasoning which will often end the entire litigation process. This does not only improve the strategic position of the administration and the beneficiary of the administrative decision, but also promotes a tendency of the administrative courts simply to follow the prevailing view on controversial legal issues. This said, society pays a relatively high price for moderate savings of time.

8   FUTURE PERSPECTIVES

Germany has a well-functioning and powerful judiciary which, however, has its shortcomings in the field of environmental protection.[87] The judicial system has

---

87. See Winter, *supra* n. 70.

been characterized as a system of limited access to the courts, but broad review of the merits of administrative decisions.[88] Access to the courts is based on a narrow rights-oriented approach which no longer responds adequately to the structure of environmental problems. Although it appears that the scrutiny German administrative courts exercise over the merits of administrative decisions is much more extensive than in many other countries, it must be noted that even the grounds and scope of review are limited by the protective law theory. This considerably reduces the problem-solving capacity of the judiciary in environmental matters. Following some recent trends inspired by EU law, an 'opening' of the concept of subjective rights to include the recognition of procedural rights, would be a minimal reform that remains 'within the system'. Moreover, the traditional aversion against self-nominated advocates of the public interest that is reflected by the narrow implementation of the Aarhus model of association suit, should be overcome. Recent complaints about abuses of the association suit have to do with uncertainties about the interpretation of EU law which must be solved at EU level. The German variant of the association suit (outside protection of nature law), arguably will not withstand scrutiny by the ECJ and the Aarhus Compliance Committee. Finally, one might consider introducing a complete action for direct review of generic decisions including all regulations and qualified administrative rules. Such modernizations appear necessary in order to improve environmental governance by controlling the functioning of the administration, comprehensively protecting citizens' environmental rights, and enforcing effective democratic participation in decision-making.

BIBLIOGRAPHY

Balleis, K. *Mitwirkungs- und Klagerechte anerkannter Naturschutzverbände*. Frankfurt am Main: Peter Lang Verlag, 1996.

Dette, B. 'Access to Justice in Environmental Matters: the Aarhus Convention and legislative Initiatives for its Implementation'. In *Environmental Law and Policy at the Turn to the 21st Century*, edited by T. Ormond, M. Führ & R. Barth. Berlin: Lexxion, 2006.

Ebbeson, J. 'Comparative Introduction'. In *Access to Justice in Environmental Matters in the EU*, edited by J. Ebbeson. The Hague: Kluwer Law International, 2002.

Epiney, A. & K. Sollberger. *Zugang zu Gerichten und gerichtliche Kontrolle im Umweltrecht*. Berlin: Erich Schmidt Verlag, 2002.

Greve, M. 'The Non-Reformation of Administrative Law: Standing to Sue and Public Interest Litigation in West German Environmental Law'. *Cornell International Law Journal* 22 (1989): 197-244.

---

88. A. Epiney & K. Sollberger, *Zugang zu Gerichten und gerichtliche Kontrolle im Umweltrecht* (Berlin: ESV, 2002), 84-88; R. Sparwasser, 'Gerichtlicher Rechtsschutz im Umweltrecht', in *Umweltrecht im Wandel*, ed. K.P. Dolde (Berlin: ES, 2001), 1017, 1035-1036.

Jarass, H.D. 'Der Rechtsschutz Dritter bei der Genehmigung von Anlagen'. *Neue Juristische Wochenschrift* (1993): 2844-2849.

Kopp, F.O. & R. Schenke. *Verwaltungsgerichtsordnung*, 15th ed. München: C.H. Beck, 2007.

Ormond, T. 'Environmental Group Actions in West Germany'. In *Participation and Litigation Rights of Environmental Associations in Europe*, edited by M. Führ & G. Roller. Frankfurt am Main: Peter Lang Verlag, 1991.

Rehbinder, E. 'Germany'. In *Access to Justice in Environmental Matters in the EU*, edited by J. Ebbeson. The Hague: Kluwer Law International, 2002.

Rehbinder, E. 'Verbandsklage'. In *Handwörterbuch des Umweltrechts*, edited by O. Kimminich, H. von Lersner & P.C. Storm. 2nd ed. Berlin: Erich Schmidt-Verlag, 1994.

Rudolf, W. 'Kooperation im Bundesstaat'. In *Handbuch des Staatsrechts*, edited by J. Isensee & P. Kirchhof. 2nd ed. Heidelberg: C.F. Müller, 1999.

Steinberg, R. 'Judicial Review of Environmentally-Related Administrative Decision-Making', *Tel Aviv Studies in Law* 11 (1992): 61-64.

Sendler, H. 'Die Bedeutung der Rechtsprechung des Bundesverwaltungsgerichts für den Umweltschutz'. In *Umweltrecht im Wandel*, edited by K.-P. Dolde. Berlin: Erich Schmidt Verlag, 2001.

Sparwasser, R. 'Gerichtlicher Rechtsschutz im Umweltrecht'. In *Umweltrecht im Wandel*, edited by K.P. Dolde. Berlin: Erich Schmidt Verlag, 2001.

Umweltbundesamt (ed.). *Daten zur Umwelt 2005*. Berlin: Erich Schmidt Verlag, 2005.

Vallendar, W. 'Europäisches Naturschutzrecht: Die Verbandsklage – Risiken und Nebenwirkungen für Infrastrukturvorhaben'. *Umwelt- und Planungsrecht* 28 (2008): 1-7.

Winter, G. *German Environmental Law*. Dordrecht: Nijhoff, 1994.

Winter, G. 'Wahrnehmungsfilter des Bundesverwaltungsgerichts – Der Fall Ökologie'. In *Festgabe 50 Jahre Bundesverwaltungsgericht*, edited by E. Schmidt-Aßmann et al. Köln: Carl Heymanns Verlag, 2003.

Wolf, R. 'Zur Entwicklung der Verbandsklage im Umweltrecht' *Zeitschrift für Umweltrecht* 5 (1994): 1-12.

TABLE OF LEGISLATION

Allgemeines Eisenbahngesetz 23 December 1993 (BGBl. I), 8 November 2007 (BGBl. I)

Baugesetzbuch 23 September 2004 (BGBl. I), 5 September 2006 (BGBl. I)

Bundesfernstraßengesetz 20 February 2003 (BGBl. I), 28 June 2007 (BGBl. I)

Gesetz für den Vorrang erneuerbarer Energien 21 July 2004 (BGBl. I), 7 December 2006 (BGBl. I)

Gesetz über die friedliche Verwendung der Kernenergie und den Schutz gegen ihre Gefahren 15 June 1985 (BGBl. I), 31 October 2006 (BGBl. I; BGBl. 2007 I)

Gesetz über die Umweltverträglichkeitsprüfung 25 June 2005 (BGBl. I 1757), 23 October 2007 (BGBl. I 2470)

Gesetz über die Vermeidung und Sanierung vom Umweltschäden 19 May 2007
(BGBl. I)

Gesetz über Naturschutz und Landschaftspflege 25 March 2002 (BGBl. I 1193),
10 May 2007 (BGBl. I)

Gesetz zum Schutz vor gefährlichen Stoffen 20 June 2002 (BGBl. I), 20 May 2008
(BGBl. I)

*Gesetz zum Schutz vor schädlichen Bodenveränderungen und zur Sanierung von
Altlasten* 17 March 1998 (BGBl. I), 9 December 2004 (BGBl. I)

*Gesetz zum Schutz vor schädlichen Umwelteinwirkungen durch Luftverunreini-
gungen, Geräusche, Erschütterungen und ähnliche Vorgänge* 26 September
2002 (BGBl. I), 23 October 2007 (BGBl. I)

Gesetz zu ergänzenden Vorschriften zu Rechtsbehelfen in Umweltangelegenheiten
(EG-Richtlinie 2003/35/EG) 7 December 2006 (BGBl. I)

*Gesetz zur Förderung der Kreislaufwirtschaft und Sicherung der umweltverträgli-
chen Beseitigung von Abfällen* 27 Sepember 1994 (BGBl. I S), 19 July 2007
(BGBl. I S)

Gesetz zur Ordnung des Wasserhaushalts 19 August 2002 (BGBl. I), 10 May 2007
(BGBl. I)

Gesetz zur Regelung der Gentechnik 16 December of 1993 (BGBl. I) 1 April 2008
(BGBl. I)

Grundgesetz für die Bundesrepublik Deutschland 23 May 1949 (BGBl. I),
28 August 2006 (BGBl. I)

Luftverkehrsgesetz 20 May 2007 (BGBl. I), 23 November 2007 (BGBl. I)

Raumordnungsgesetz 18 August 1997 [BGBl. I), 9 October 2006 (BGBl. I)

Umwelthaftungsgesetz 10 December 1990 (BGBl. I)

Umweltinformationsgesetz 22 December 2004 (BGBl. I)

Verwaltungsgerichtsordnung 19 March 1991 (BGBl. I), 21 December 2006 (BGBl. I)

Verwaltungsverfahrensgesetz 23 January 2003 (BGBl. I), 5 May 2004 (BGBl. I)

TABLE OF CASES

BVerfGE 49, 89   BVerwGE 72, 15
BVerwGE 45, 309   BVerwGE 72, 300
BVerwGE 48, 56   BVerwGE 74, 234
BVerwGE 54, 211   BVerwGE 78, 177
BVerwGE 55, 250   BVerwGE 78, 347
BVerwGE 56, 110   BVerwGE 78, 40
BVerwGE 61, 256   BVerwGE 81, 185
BVerwGE 65, 313   BVerwGE 85, 348
BVerwGE 66, 307   BVerwGE 87, 332
BVerwGE 67, 74   BVerwGE 87, 62
BVerwGE 69, 256   BVerwGE 90, 96
BVerwGE 70, 365   BVerwGE 100, 370
BVerwGE 71, 166   BVerwGE 100, 388

TABLE OF INTERNATIONAL INSTRUMENTS

Convention on Access to Information, Public Participation in Decision-Making and Access to Justice in Environmental Matters 1998, 38 *ILM* 517 (1999)

Treaty for Establishing the European Community 1992, consolidated version of 2006, 2006 OJ No. C 321/E

ABBREVIATIONS

ACPA	Administrative Court Procedure Act
BGBl	Bundesgesetzblatt (Official Journal)
BGH	Bundesgerichtshof (Federal Supreme Court)
BGHZ	Decisions of the Federal Supreme Court in Civil Matters
BVerfG	Bundesverfassungsgericht (Federal Constitutional Court)
BVerfGE	Decisions of the Federal Constitutional Court
BVerwG	Bundesverwaltungsgericht (Federal Administrative Court)
BVerwGE	Decisions of the Federal Administrative Court
EU	European Union

EIA	Environmental Impact Assessment
ILM	International Legal Materials
NJW	Neue Juristische Wochenschrift
NuR	Natur und Recht
NVwZ	Neue Zeitschrift für Verwaltungsrecht
NVwZ-RR	Neue Zeitschrift für Verwaltungsrecht - Rechtsprechungs-Report
OJ	Official Journal of the European Union
OVG	Oberverwaltungsgericht (Administrative Court of Appeal)
UPR	Umwelt- und Planungsrecht
VGH	Verwaltungsgerichtshof (Administrative Court of Appeal)
ZUR	Zeitschrift für Umweltrecht

Chapter 4

United Kingdom

Karen Morrow

1   INTRODUCTION

1.1   ENVIRONMENTAL ISSUES

As well as being the first nation to enjoy the fruits of the industrial revolution and its attendant urbanization, the United Kingdom (UK) was also at the forefront in experiencing the environmental problems that accompanied it. As a relatively small but also comparatively densely populated nation, the UK environment is under considerable stress. The complex and fragmented arrangements that characterize environmental governance internally within the UK, together with the fact that many environmental issues are regional or even global in their implications, ensure that the challenges facing government and the judiciary in this area remain considerable.

The most recently published Government Survey of Public Attitudes and Behaviours toward the Environment[1] reveals that the environment remains an important area of public concern being ranked fourth by respondents (after crime, health and education) among those areas that the government should

---

1. Published on 2 November 2007. See DEFRA, 'Government Survey of Public Attitudes and Behaviours toward the Environment 2007', <www.defra.gov.uk/environment/statistics/pubatt/download/pas2007report.pdf>, 11 August 2008.

Louis J. Kotzé and Alexander R. Paterson (eds), *The Role of the Judiciary in Environmental Governance: Comparative Perspectives*, pp. 151–179.
© 2009 Kluwer Law International BV, The Netherlands.

deal with. Key areas of concern identified in the survey include climate change, transport, waste and recycling, resource use and biodiversity.

This chapter focuses primarily on mainstream pollution control regimes but readers should be aware that a variety of other areas and in particular those related to broader questions of resource management are also highly relevant to the operation of environmental governance in the UK. Chief among these are land-use planning and species and habitat conservation, with other areas such as health and safety law also playing a supporting role.

1.2   PRINCIPAL ENVIRONMENTAL LAWS

1.2.1   Pollution Control[2]

Given the constraints imposed by the need for brevity, this section concentrates on the law as it applies in England, though it should be noted that, in part as a consequence of devolution, provisions that broadly mirror those discussed often exist within other constituent nations of the UK.

The UK has a long history of laws that can broadly be defined as 'environmental'. Originating in the last half of the nineteenth century they continued to develop sporadically during the first three quarters of the twentieth century, with initiatives such as the *Clean Air Act* 1956 and *Clean Air Act* 1968,[3] in response to the most obvious social and environmental impacts of the industrial revolution.[4] In common with most of the developed world, the advent of modern environmental regulation in this jurisdiction can, for the most part, be traced to the last three decades. The bold (but flawed and therefore only partially effective) *Control of Pollution Act* 1974 (COPA), however, represented something of a false start to modernising environmental regulation and it is arguably only in the current wave of environmental legislation, marked by the passing of the *Environmental Protection Act* (EPA) in 1990, that regulation in this area has begun to mature. The EPA is a highly ambitious statute, overhauling COPA and extending beyond it to cover a wide range of areas of environmental concern. Much of it has subsequently been replaced, often in response to developments in European Community (EC) law. Nonetheless, it is instructive to examine the key areas that it covers, notably: Part I, which introduced integrated pollution control (IPC, not to be confused with integrated pollution prevention and control (IPPC)) and local air pollution control; Part II, which radically overhauled waste law and made provision for contaminated land (subsequently substantially amended); Part III, which updated the law on statutory nuisance and clean air; Part VI, which introduced a regime for genetically

---

2. There is also copious legislation relating to radioactivity, though space precludes a discussion of this in the present context.
3. Subsequently consolidated and updated in the *Clean Air Act* 1993.
4. Examples include the *Alkali Act* 1863 and the *Rivers Pollution Prevention Act* 1876.

modified organisms; and Part VII, which introduced new institutional arrangements for nature conservation.

The next landmark law was the *Environment Act* 1995 which, in addition to overhauling the contaminated land regime,[5] unites[6] the regulatory functions exercised by Her Majesty's Inspectorate of Pollution (HMIP) in respect of IPC, with those of the National Rivers Authority (NRA) for water and the waste regulation activities that had originally been allocated by the EPA to local authorities. In terms of the *Environment Act*, these functions are placed within the remit of a new Environment Agency (EA) in England and Wales and the Scottish Environmental Protection Agency (SEPA) for Scotland. It also makes provision for a variety of other pollution and resource issues including air pollution and national parks.

The *Pollution Prevention and Control Act* (PPCA) was passed in 1999 in order to give effect to the UK's obligation to introduce IPPC under Directive 96/61/EC on Integrated Pollution Prevention and Control and a number of other provisions relating to pollution, especially those relevant to offshore installations. The PPCA applies to all activities falling under the Directive, and also to those activities that had been regulated under Part I of the EPA, but were not covered by the Directive.

Although the *Water Act* 1989 (WA) pre-dates the EPA, it was passed with the primary aim of privatising the water industry, and running to some 194 sections and 27 schedules, it unsurprisingly soon proved to be so unwieldy that it was swiftly subsequently divided into five separate laws and simultaneously amended to give effect to recommendations of the Law Commission. The WA did contain some provisions that would ultimately prove to be significant in terms of environmental governance, not least those creating new regulatory machinery in the form of the NRA (which subsequently provided the template for the Environment Agency) and the Director General for Water Services (DGWS). The most significant of the new legislative instruments that replaced the WA in terms of environmental regulation, are: the *Water Resources Act* 1991 (WRA), which consolidates provision for the NRA; and the *Water Industry Act* 1991 (WIA) which deals with water and sewerage undertakers and the powers of the DGWS to regulate them.

1.2.2 Nature, Habitat and Landscape Conservation

In addition to the important area of pollution control, the UK also enjoys a body of law governing natural resource management, notably nature, species and habitat conservation.[7] A comprehensive conservation designation was introduced on the

---

5. The EPA provisions on contaminated land had proved highly controversial and ultimately unworkable, though the 1995 amendments scarcely fared better and have in their turn been replaced by Contaminated Land (England) Regulations 2000 SI 2000/227 (as amended).
6. This process has in itself proved problematic, see e.g., House of Commons, 'The Environment Agency', Seventh Report of Session 2005-06, <www.publications.parliament.uk/pa/cm200506/cmselect/cmenvfru/780/780i.pdf>, 12 September 2008.
7. There is obviously some overlap between these spheres, e.g., particularly in relation to the aquatic environment and waste management issues, though, for reasons of convenience, they will be dealt with separately here.

UK mainland by the *National Parks and Access to the Countryside Act* (NPACA) 1949 which contains provisions to protect the beauty, wildlife and culture of designated sites in the national interest and to foster public understanding of, and facilitate recreational opportunities in, these areas. Each is administered by its own National Parks Authority. The NPACA also introduced the Area of Outstanding Natural Beauty (AONB) designation to protect sites of exceptional landscape value. The latter are primarily administered by local authorities, often in collaboration with non-governmental organizations (NGOs). The *Countryside Act* 1968 (CA) expanded the conservation agenda to the countryside more generally.

The *Wildlife and Countryside Act* 1981 (WCA) introduced a fairly rudimentary form of habitat and species protection through the Sites of Special Scientific Interest (SSSI) system. The protection offered under the WCA proved extremely weak and it has only been through the promulgation of the *Countryside and Rights of Way Act* 2000 (covering a range of countryside issues and in particular the provision of enhanced public access to the countryside) that the system has become more fully realized.

The *Natural Environment and Rural Communities Act* 2006 (NERCA) is designed, amongst other things, to implement the Government's Rural Strategy.[8] It accordingly amends aspects of the CA, the EPA, the NPACA, and the WCA; and ties up a number of loose ends in respect of the law relating to resource issues concerning biodiversity in general and SSSIs in particular.

1.2.3   Contextual Provisions

While not strictly environmental laws, there are certain contextual provisions that intimately affect the operation of pollution control and other aspects of environmental law. Chief amongst these is the town and country planning regime currently prescribed in the *Town and Country Planning Act* 1990 (as amended) and related legislation. The relationship between planning and other aspects of environmental law, notably pollution control, has long been recognized as problematic[9] and attempts to address this, currently encapsulated in the government's Planning Policy Statement 23 (PPS 23),[10] have proven neither entirely convincing nor successful. Other more general legislation, such as the *Sustainable Communities Act* 2007, also has the potential to affect environmental governance to a degree.

The level of detail varies significantly across the primary environmental laws discussed above. All are, however, considerably expanded upon through secondary legislation which provides detailed coverage that cannot be included in the parent

8. Published in July 2004, see DEFRA, 'Foreword by the Secretary of State', <www.defra.gov.uk/rural/strategy/foreword.htm>, 28 August 2008.
9. The necessity of arriving at a *modus vivendi* between the planning and pollution control regimes was a prominent theme in the twenty-third report of the RCEP, 'Environmental Planning', <www.rcep.org/uk/epreport/>, 16 August 2008.
10. ODPM, 'Planning Policy Statement 23: Planning and Pollution Control', <www.communities.gov.uk/documents/planningandbuilding/pdf/planningpolicystatement23.pdf>, 12 September 2008.

enactments. Secondary legislation also provides the main coverage for a number of EC law areas of environmental activity, not least environmental impact assessment (EIA) and agricultural pollution. The use of diverse forms of legislation in the sphere of environmental law is also increasing as a consequence of devolution in those areas where competence has been transferred from Westminster.

1.3   INSTITUTIONS AND GOVERNANCE STRUCTURES

Following the Next Steps Initiative of the 1990s,[11] environmental governance at a central government level has been split between responsibility for policy and operational competence. The institutions and governance structures responsible for fulfilling these two broad functions are discussed in turn below.

1.3.1   Policy Matters

The responsibility for policy matters falls largely within the purview of government departments. The principal department in this regard within the UK is the Department for Environment, Food and Rural Affairs (DEFRA). The Secretary of State for Environment, Food and Rural Affairs sits in the Cabinet and is responsible for both UK policy matters and for environmental policy in England. The minister is accountable to parliament for policy matters pertaining to his or her department. There is, however, a major component of environmental governance that does not fall within the remit of DEFRA. Town and country planning falls under the control of the Department for Communities and Local Government. Other departments of State also have considerable influence in environmental governance in the UK in several areas such as business, enterprise and regulatory reform, and transport. Cross cutting issues fall to be examined by the Ministerial Committee on Economic Development: Sub Committee on Environment and Energy, which exercises authority over 'international and domestic policy on environment and energy issues'. This Sub Committee also reports to other Ministerial Committees where necessary.[12]

Since the advent of devolution in the UK, the devolved authorities in Scotland, Wales and Northern Ireland play a role in environmental policy in their jurisdictions insofar as they are authorized to do so by relevant legislation, namely: the *Scotland Act* 1998, the *Government of Wales Act* 2006,[13] the *Northern Ireland Act* 1998, and the *Northern Ireland Act* 2000. The devolved ministries with prime responsibility for the environment are the Rural Affairs and Environment

---

11. For a discussion of broader British practice in this area, see, R. Sandberg, 'A Whitehall farce? Defining and conceptualising the British Civil Service', *PL* (2006): 653.
12. For details see, Cabinet Office, 'Ministerial Committee on Economic Development: Sub-Committee on Environment and Energy Composition', <www.cabinetoffice.gov.uk/secretariats/committees/edee.aspx>, 28 August 2008.
13. This has been replaced by the *Government of Wales Act* 1998.

(Scotland); Environment, Sustainability and Housing (Wales); and the Department of the Environment (DoENI) (Northern Island). Each of these ministries is represented by a cabinet minister in their respective administrations.

An additional and rather unusual body that is worth discussing in the context of environment governance in the UK is the British-Irish Council (BIC) which was established by the 1999 British-Irish Agreement.[14] The BIC's membership is broader than its name might suggest, as it is made up of representatives of not only the British and Irish governments, but also the devolved administrations in Northern Ireland, Scotland and Wales and representatives from the other smaller jurisdictions in the British Isles – the Isle of Man, Guernsey and Jersey. The BIC aims to provide a forum for developing common policies and agreeing shared actions on matters of mutual interest for the benefit of all of its members. The environment has been one of the areas in which it has been most active to date.[15]

Finally, it is worth noting that, in addition to central government and the devolved administrations' competencies in the development of environmental policy, local government also has a role to play in some, albeit limited, aspects of policy in this sphere, most notably in respect of town and country planning and Local Agenda 21.

1.3.2   Operational Matters

One result of Margaret Thatcher's avowed intention to minimize the role of the State was a move, through the 'Next Steps' initiative, to slim down the machinery of central government by splitting the policy-making aspects of executive activity from day to day operational activities. While the former remained the province of scaled down government departments, the latter became the responsibility of Non-Departmental Public Bodies (NDPBs). In the environmental sphere, competence for many operational aspects of pollution control rest primarily in the hands of the EA in England and Wales, and SEPA in Scotland. In Northern Ireland the situation differs in form (if not greatly in substance) from that in England and Wales and Scotland. As of 1 July 2008, the reorganized and renamed Northern Ireland Environment Agency (NIEA) replaced the Environment and Heritage Service[16] of the DoENI, though it remains an agency of the Northern Ireland Executive.[17]

---

14. Established by the British-Irish Agreement which entered into force on 2 December 1999 – see British-Irish Council, 'Agreement between the Government of the United Kingdom of Great Britain and Northern Ireland and the Government of Ireland', <www1.british-irishcouncil.org/documents/text.asp>, 12 September 2008.

15. See British-Irish Council, 'Environment', <www1.british-irishcouncil.org/work/environment.asp>, 28 August 2008.

16. See Northern Ireland Assembly, 'Ministerial Statement on Environmental Governance of 27 May 2008', <www.niassembly.gov.uk/record/reports2007/080527.htm#4>, 28 August 2008.

17. This goes against the recommendation of The Review of Environmental Governance Final Report that the EHS be reconstituted as a NDPB along the lines of the EA and SEPA, see Review of Environmental Governance Northern Ireland, 'Foundations for the Future, May 2007', <www.regni.info/final_report-3.pdf>, 28 August 2008.

The NIEA carries out operational functions in the same way as its counterparts on the mainland.

In respect of water, the privatization of water resources has meant that some regulatory powers with environmental implications in respect of water supply and sewerage services rest with the Director-General of Water Services. Other aspects of environmental governance, notably those concerned with biodiversity and landscape preservation, fall within the sphere of influence of other agencies such as Natural England, Scottish Natural Heritage and the Countryside Council for Wales. In Northern Ireland, these issues fall within the remit of the NIEA. Issues of national and common concern fall under the remit of the Joint Nature Conservation Committee.

In some areas of pollution control, notably air pollution and now some aspects of pollution prevention and control (PPC), operational competence is also enjoyed by local government and indeed in certain contexts, for example noise pollution, the latter has primary competence. Local government also enjoys some responsibilities for habitat, species and landscape conservation issues on a purely local scale.

In addition to these arrangements, a number of expert appointed bodies exist which are charged with advising the government on broader aspects of environmental issues. Most significant among these are the Royal Commission on Environmental Pollution (RCEP) and the Sustainable Development Commission.

2   OVERVIEW OF THE COURT SYSTEM

2.1   HISTORICAL DEVELOPMENT OF THE JUDICIARY

Historically, the UK judiciary has deferred to parliament in its role, holding the doctrine of parliamentary supremacy as the core value in the Constitution. Under this doctrine, briefly put, an act of parliament is deemed the highest form of law in the British Isles and primary legislation is not to be questioned in the courts. This nineteenth century orthodoxy, best summed up in the works of Dicey,[18] underwent what initially appeared to be fairly innocuous but may ultimately prove to be revolutionary change, beginning in the latter part of the twentieth century with the *European Communities Act* 1972 (ECA) (as amended). Section 2(4) of the ECA placed UK courts under a duty to construe domestic law in such a way as to give effect to Community law as defined in the Act. This provision allowed the judiciary to place UK legislation, including acts of parliament, under greater scrutiny than ever before. The effect of the ECA was to place limits on parliamentary supremacy, at least insofar as it falls within the sphere of Community law, a fact clearly illustrated by the *Factortame* litigation.[19]

---

18. A.V. Dicey, 'Introduction to the Study of the Law of the Constitution 1885', <www.constitution.org/cmt/avd/law_con.htm>, 28 August 2008.
19. Beginning with *R v. Secretary of State for Transport, ex p Factortame Ltd* Case C-213/89 (No. 2) [1991] 1 AC 603.

The power of the judiciary to subject primary legislation to scrutiny was further enhanced by the *Human Rights Act* 1998 (HRA) which incorporated the European Convention on Human Rights 1950[20] (ECHR) into UK law. While the HRA does not allow judges to hold an act of parliament invalid, under section 4 it does allow courts to issue a declaration of incompatibility in respect of legislation that is not ECHR compliant. A ruling to this effect does not render the statute in question invalid, but it does place considerable pressure on the government to change the law in order to bring it in line with the Convention. As a result, the operation of the HRA is arguably altering the dynamics of the relationship between the executive and the judiciary in relevant areas.[21]

It is debatable that the possibility of questioning UK primary legislation in European Union (EU) and Convention law, has initiated a shift in the balance of power within the British Constitution, placing the rule of law rather than parliamentary supremacy centre stage.[22] This has arguably already resulted in significant changes in attitude and certainly has the potential to generate significant further effects, an observation that appears to be borne out by the recent extra judicially expressed view of Lord Phillips, the current Lord Chief Justice, that:

> The rule of law will not fully prevail unless the domestic law of a country permits judges to review the legitimacy of executive action. This is increasingly becoming the single most important function of the judge in the field of civil law, at least in my jurisdiction.[23]

Further fundamental changes altering the status of the judiciary have been set in motion by the *Constitutional Reform Act* 2005 (CRA). The implementation of Part II of this act has already seen the Lord Chancellor replaced as head of the judiciary in England and Wales by the Lord Chief Justice, introducing a greater separation of powers than had previously been the case in the UK. The position of Lord Chancellor was subsequently replaced by that of Minister of Justice when the new Department of Justice was set up in May 2007. Further significant developments rooted in the CRA will take place in the near future with the most important undoubtedly being the creation of a new Supreme Court for the UK under Part III of the Act, which is set to replace the House of Lords as the UK's final court of appeal from October 2009.

---

20. Council of Europe, 'The European Convention on Human Rights', <www.hri.org/docs/ ECHR50.html>, 11 August 2008.
21. See House of Lords, Relations between the Executive, the Judiciary and Parliament, HL Paper 151, 6th Report of Session 2006-07 (London: TSO, 2007) Appendix 3 by K. Malleson, 'The Effect of the Constitutional Reform Act 2005 on the Relationship between the Judiciary, the Executive and Parliament'.
22. Lord Steyn, 'Democracy, the rule of law and the role of judges', *EHRLR* 3 (2006): 243.
23. J. Phillips LCJ, 'Judicial independence', speech delivered at the Commonwealth Law Conference on 12 September 2007, (Nairobi, 2007), <www.judiciary.gov.uk/docs/speeches/lcj_ kenya_clc_120907.pdf>, 28 August 2008, 2.

2.2   COURT STRUCTURE AND HIERARCHY

In addition to the usual considerations of judicial hierarchy, the court structure in the UK reflects the fact that there are three main legal jurisdictions in operation in the country, the largest encompassing England and Wales, with broadly similar but smaller scale arrangements applicable in Northern Ireland,[24] and Scotland enjoying its own distinctive institutions[25] reflecting its unique legal heritage.

What follows is a simplified summary of the UK court structure,[26] tailored to focus upon those aspects of the system that are most likely to be concerned with environmental cases. The explanation provided, for reasons to space, centres on the Courts Service as it operates in England and Wales.

Magistrates Courts deal with summary offences and are accordingly often the first courts, and in the majority of routine case situations the only courts, to deal with many environmental cases, notably those resulting from the application of command and control regulation.

Crown Courts, through their competence over indictable offences may also be the point of origin for more serious environmental cases rooted in the application of command and control systems. In addition, Crown Courts hear appeals from Magistrates Courts in respect of summary offences. At this level, civil cases involving the environment will be handled by County Courts.

The High Court may also (sitting as the Divisional Court) hear appeals from Magistrates Courts and will hear appeals from County Courts and other public bodies, notably local authorities and NDPBs. The High Court may also be the point of origin for environmental cases in a number of its specialist divisions, notably the Administrative Court (in respect of claims for judicial review) and, to a lesser extent, the Queen's Bench Division (in particular in respect of tort cases).

The Criminal Division of the Court of Appeal hears appeals from Crown Courts in respect of criminal matters and its Civil Division hears appeals from the High Court, and, in some cases the County Courts, in respect of civil matters.

The House of Lords (soon to become the Supreme Court) is the highest court in both civil and criminal cases and normally hears appeals from the Court of Appeal, and in rare cases from the High Court. It is also the final destination for contested appeals originating in Scotland and Northern Ireland.

Tribunals may also have a role to play in environmental cases with rights of appeal to the High Court or Court of Appeal, as per the relevant statutory provisions.

---

24. For more details see, Northern Ireland Court Service, 'Serving the Community through the Administration of Justice', <www.courtsni.gov.uk/>, 28 August 2008.
25. Sheriffs Courts carry out similar functions to Magistrates Courts, the High Court of Justiciary is the supreme criminal court in Scotland and the Court of Session, with its Inner and Outer Houses functions in a manner which is broadly analogous to the Court of Appeal. For further details see, Scottish Courts, 'Scottish Courts Services', <www.scotcourts.gov.uk/>, 28 August 2008.
26. For more detail see, HMCS, 'The Court Structure of Her Majesty's Courts Service', <www.hmcourts-service.gov.uk/aboutus/structure/index.htm>, 28 August 2008.

3   ANALYSIS OF SIGNIFICANT ENVIRONMENTAL
           JUDGMENTS

3.1   PRIVATE LAW (LAW OF TORTS)

The common law has an inherent flexibility which, at least in principle, makes it
well equipped to effectively respond to evolving societal priorities. In the nineteenth century the UK courts showed themselves, on the whole, to be very willing
to mold the common law, in particular the law of torts, to deal with the new
challenges posed by the industrial revolution.[27] Examples in this respect are
St Helen's Smelting Co. v. Tipping (1865) 11 HLC 642 (which applied the law
of nuisance to industrial air pollution) and *Rylands v. Fletcher* [1868] LR 3 HL 330
(which imposed liability in respect of damage caused to neighbouring property by
the escape of materials that were likely to do mischief that had been accumulated
by a defendant through the non-natural use of his or her land).[28] Having said this,
even at that time, the role of the common law was becoming secondary to the
burgeoning base of legislation that had begun to swiftly emerge to regulate environmental concerns.[29] The main role of the common law rapidly became to fill the
interstices in the legislative regime. This remains the case today and it is arguable
that the courts in recent years have shown themselves to be much more averse to
giving free reign to the common law than their predecessors.

     This is very clearly demonstrated in the hugely significant House of Lords'
decision in *Cambridge Water Co. Ltd v. Eastern Counties Leather* [1994] 2 AC
264. Cambridge Water (CW) supplied potable water and owned land with a borehole from which it was licensed to extract water for sale. Unbeknownst to CW,
percholoroethylene (PCE) leaching from Easter Counties Leather's (ECL) nearby
tannery had contaminated the aquifer that fed their borehole. This became
problematic when Directive 80/778 (Drinking Water Directive) came into force,
as it prohibited PCE in water for human consumption at the levels present in CW's
supply. As a result, CW had to find an alternative source of water. It did so at
considerable expense and then initiated proceedings against ECL in negligence,
nuisance and under the rule in the *Rylands* case seeking redress for its losses. CW's
claims failed comprehensively at first instance, but the company succeeded in its
claim in nuisance in the Court of Appeal, which applied the ruling in *Ballard v.
Tomlinson* (1885) 29 Ch D 115 in support of a natural right to abstract uncontaminated groundwater. This judgment created an extra-judicial furore in the banking and insurance sectors and, in this context, it was perhaps unsurprising that the

---

27. See, generally, S. Coyle & K. Morrow, *The Philosophical Foundations of Environmental Law*
    (Oxford: Hart, 2004).
28. Note that in some jurisdictions, notably in the United States, liability under the rule in Rylands v.
    Fletcher has evolved into a general principle of liability for dangerous things. This has not,
    however, been the case in the UK.
29. See, B. Pontin, 'Tort Law and Victorian Government Growth: The Historiographical Signifi-
    cance of Tort in the Shadow of Chemical Pollution and Factory Safety Regulation', *OJLS* 18
    (1998): 661.

House of Lords allowed ECL's appeal. At this level, the case was determined principally in nuisance. The Law Lords refused to impose liability on ECL for damage that was not reasonably foreseeable at the time when the PCE spillages that caused the contamination occurred. The key role accorded to foreseeability in this case, borrowing both terminology and fault-based values from the ideology of the dominant law of negligence, and adding a new dimension to the supposed strict liability approach applicable in nuisance, seriously curtails the ability of the common law to engage with issues of historic pollution. It is very telling that the court was unwilling to apply strict liability in this context, although the common law would have allowed it to do so. Lord Goff explicitly stated that the application of strict liability in this area should be the province of parliament: '...as a general rule, it is more appropriate for strict liability in respect of operations of high risk to be imposed by Parliament, than by the courts.'[30]

The re-examination of established law on the right to bring an action in nuisance in the 1990s also provides interesting insights into the judicial role in mediating between doctrine and social *mores*. The debate opened with the Court of Appeal decision in *Khorasandjian v. Bush* [1993] 3 All ER 668, which saw the adoption of a more generous approach to access to the courts under this head, with the removal of the requirement that a claimant have a legal interest in the affected property. In this case the claimant who had been harassed by an ex-boyfriend, making repeated phone calls to her at her parents' and grandmother's homes, was granted an injunction, despite lacking a proprietary interest in either home.[31] This followed the approach in the Canadian case of *Motherwell v. Motherwell* (1976) 73 DLR (3d) 62.

This expansive approach was again evident in the Court of Appeal decision in *Hunter v. Canary Wharf Ltd London Docklands Development Corporation* [1996] 1 All ER 482 which allowed actions by several hundred local residents whose television reception had been adversely affected over a period of years by the Canary Wharf Tower in London and actions against the London Docklands Corporation in respect of nuisance during construction activities. Many of the plaintiffs were the spouses or children of those with proprietary interests in properties in the area, but lacking such interests themselves. However, a majority in the House of Lords in *Hunter v. Canary Wharf Ltd London Docklands Development Corporation* [1997] 2 All ER 426 returned to the orthodox position on this issue, as expressed in *Malone v. Laskey* [1907] 2 KB 141, requiring a proprietary interest in the property affected in order to establish a right to bring an action in nuisance. Several arguments underpin the majority decision, including an unwillingness to expand a tort against land in such a way as to transform it into tort against the person, although Lord Cooke, in an erudite and persuasive dissenting speech, favoured an expansionist approach.

Having noted that in many cases involving pure common law, modern judges tend perhaps to be more cautious than their predecessors in developing the law, it is

---

30. At 305.
31. The matter would now be dealt with under the *Protection from Harassment Act* 1997.

interesting to look at the House of Lords' decision in *TransCo Plc. v. Stockport Metropolitan Borough Council* [2004] 2 AC 1. The case involved the first opportunity that the Law Lords had had to rule on the continued viability of the rule in the *Rylands* case following the *Cambridge Water* decision. Many thought that the Lords would use the opportunity to extinguish the rule[32] but this did not in fact happen. The case concerned a claim under the rule by *TransCo* in respect of works that had been necessary to shore up one of its gas mains which had been undermined by a water leak from a block of flats owned and supplied with water by the council. The council had not been negligent. The Lords took the view that the rule in the *Rylands* case is simply a subspecies of nuisance and that, while it is to be retained, it is to be applied narrowly. The rule as it now stands was stated by Lord Bingham:

> An occupier of land who can show that another occupier of land has brought or kept on his land an exceptionally dangerous or mischievous thing in extraordinary or unusual circumstances is in my opinion entitled to recover compensation from that occupier for any damage caused to his property interest by the escape of that thing, subject to defences of act of God or of a stranger, without the need to prove negligence.[33]

It would therefore appear that the courts are not willing to entirely cede their role relating to strict liability to the legislature and statute.

3.2   JUDICIAL REVIEW

A further significant area in which the UK courts have influenced the development of environmental governance in the UK is in the specialist field of public law judicial review. The courts are very much in the driving seat in this area, both in terms of procedure and the development of the substantive law. On a procedural level, the courts have shown a willingness to use their discretion[34] on standing to allow broad access to review proceedings, as evidenced in *R v. HMIP and the Minister of Agriculture, Fisheries and Food, ex parte Greenpeace* [1994] 2 CMLR 548. This case concerned an application to review a permit granted to the Thermal Oxide Reprocessing Plant situated at the Sellafield nuclear plant. Greenpeace was accorded standing on a number of grounds: it had members in the local area; it was a recognized expert in the area; and, granting it access to the courts would ensure that the issues were examined in a judicial forum. This liberal approach to standing continued in *R v. Secretary of State for Foreign and Commonwealth Affairs, ex parte World Development Movement* [1995] 1 WLR 386, in which an NGO was granted access to the court on the basis that had it been barred

---

32. This had already happened in Australia in the case of *Burnie Port Authority v. General Jones Pty Ltd* [2004] 68 ALJ 331.
33. At 11.
34. S. 42(1), 1A *Supreme Court Act* 1981, as amended. Civil Procedure Rule r. 3.4.

from proceeding, a serious allegation of potential illegality would have been excluded from judicial scrutiny. It should, however, also be noted that the courts can also use their discretion on standing to bar access to judicial review, as in the case of vexatious litigants.[35]

Judicial review proceedings also frequently raise significant procedural issues concerning the administration as illustrated, for example, in *R (Edwards and others) v. Environment Agency and Others* [2006] EWCA Civ. 877. This matter concerned an appeal against a refusal by the court *a quo* to set aside a PPC permit. Rugby's cement plant had originally been subject to an EIA and an IPC authorization under the EPA 1990, but subsequently required a permit under the PPCA 2000. At the same time, Rugby wished to partially alter the fuel for its kiln to waste tyres. During the consultation period for the new permit, concerns arose about the public health implications of the proposed change. As a result, the EA sought further information from Rugby and commissioned reports on the issue by one of its specialist research divisions. The latter concluded that there were concerns about dust emissions, but not about the proposed tyre burning. Only some of this material was made available to the public. The EA considered the information before it but refused to make the details public, on the basis that the information was 'integral' to a decision that had not yet been taken and which would be prejudiced were it to be revealed. The PPC permit was issued in August 2003, with conditions requiring a trial of the tyre burning and imposing limits for dust emissions from low-level sources. The claim for judicial review, with Edwards as the nominal claimant, was instituted in October 2003. The application focused on the tyre burning issue and the non-disclosure of information. The specialist reports were partially revealed in March 2005, but only made wholly public a day or two before the case was heard. In response, the claimants changed the emphasis of their case and Lindsay J allowed them to reformulate their grounds. He took the view that the non-disclosure of the reports infringed the 'common law duty of fairness to provide fully informed consultation before making its decision'.[36] However, he went on to conclude that this non-disclosure had not in the end proved significant and exercised his discretion to refuse relief. The claimants' appeal was unsuccessful. The Court of Appeal was of the opinion that fairness did not generally necessitate that decision-makers reveal aspects of their internal decision-making processes.[37] However, the court went on to conclude that, in this case, the specialist reports were material and that the public should have been given the opportunity to comment. Having said this, the court agreed that Lindsay J had been entitled to exercise his discretion to refuse relief. The court based its decision on a number of grounds, some more convincing than others. The decisive factor appears to have

---

35. See in this respect *Ewing v. Office of the Deputy Prime Minister* [2005] EWCA Civ. 1583.
36. Para. 22 (CA).
37. *Bushell & Anor v. Secretary of State for Environment* [1981] AC 75, *R (Alconbury Developments Ltd) v. Secretary of State for the Environment, Transport and the Regions* [2003] AC 295.

been there was no unexpected environmental damage in the three years that the plant had been operating under the disputed permit.[38]

The recent case of *R (on the application of Greenpeace Ltd) v. Secretary of State for Trade and Industry* [2007] EWHC 311 (Admin) illustrates an expansive judicial approach on the substance of a claim for judicial review in a particularly sensitive and controversial environmental context. Greenpeace sought a quashing order in respect of the government's decision to support new developments in nuclear energy as part of the UK's energy mix. The government had stated in a White Paper published in 2003[39] that it would not support newly built nuclear plants and would instead promote renewable energy. It added an explicit promise that if nuclear new build were to be considered, it would require 'the fullest public consultation'.[40] The government decided to review the White Paper in 2005 and published a revised consultation paper on 23 January 2006. The public were granted until 14 April 2006 to comment on it. The consultation paper stated that due to changes in the circumstances of energy supply, nuclear new build would be reconsidered, though it added that the government was not making policy proposals on the issue at that stage.[41] The coverage of the nuclear new build issue in the consultation paper was fairly cursory. When the government subsequently published its report on 11 July 2006, it stated it proposed to facilitate nuclear new build and that a further consultation exercise and White Paper on this issue would follow before the end of 2006.

Greenpeace's claim centred on an alleged breach of legitimate expectation. It argued that the government had broken its promise that there would only be a change of policy on nuclear new build after 'the fullest public consultation'. The NGO argued that the 'consultation paper' released in 2006 was in fact only an 'issues paper' as its content was deficient, vague, inadequate and incomplete, and accordingly failed to open the substantive issue of nuclear new build for public consultation.

Even though the claim involved matters of high policy, in which the courts are often reluctant to intervene, Sullivan J deemed it justiciable[42] as the promise under consideration had been made at the highest level. Significantly, and showing high awareness of wider developments in environmental law, he alluded[43] to the limits imposed on the executive's freedom of action in the formulation of policy in this area by the UNECE Convention on Access to Environmental Information, Public Participation in Decision-Making and Access to Justice in Environmental Matters 1998 (Aarhus Convention).[44] The case was ultimately determined,

---

38. Para. 126.
39. Secretary of State for Transport and Industry, 'Our Energy Future: Creating a Low Carbon Economy', <www.berr.gov.uk/files/file10719.pdf>, 28 August 2008.
40. *Ibid.*, para. 4.68.
41. Executive Summary to the Consultation Document.
42. Applying *R (Nadarajah and Abdi) v. Secretary of State for the Home Department* [2005] EWCA Civ. 1363.
43. Para. 49 and 51.
44. 38 *ILM* 517 (1999). See also UNECE, 'Convention on Access to Information, Public Participation in Decision-Making and Access to Justice in Environmental Matters', <www.unece.org/env/pp/documents/cep43e.pdf>, 12 September 2008.

however, through the application of domestic law relating to legitimate expectation[45] and fairness.[46] Sullivan J held that given the broad discretion accorded to decision-makers in respect of consultation, the courts would only intervene where it was found that ' . . . something went "clearly and radically" wrong'.[47] Reading the 2006 consultation paper as a whole and in context, he agreed with Greenpeace that it was in fact an issues paper and that the consultation process had been seriously flawed.[48] The judge accordingly granted a declaration to this effect but did not go as far as granting the quashing order sought by Greenpeace. The case ultimately proved to be a hollow victory for Greenpeace as the government simply initiated a new consultation exercise that did not ultimately affect the policy outcome in the subsequent energy White Paper 'Meeting the Energy Challenge'.[49]

3.3   STATUTORY INTERPRETATION

In addition to developing purely judge-made law, the common law is increasingly used to elucidate the application of legislation through the process of statutory interpretation. It has long been clear that where statutory regimes are in place, they are the starting point for considering questions of legal liability.[50] This principle remains the case, as demonstrated in the House of Lords' decision in *X (Minors) v. Bedfordshire County Council* [1995] 2 AC 633, and applies not only to positive acts but also to omissions as held in *East Suffolk Rivers Catchment Board v. Kent* [1941] AC 74.

The interpretative capacity of the courts naturally comes to the fore in cases where the effect of legislation is unclear. One area where the courts have attempted to bring clarity is in identifying the boundary between planning and pollution control. In *Gateshead MBC v. Secretary of State for the Environment and Northumbrian Water* [1994] 71 P&CR 350 the applicant sought to build a chemical waste incinerator. The council refused planning permission owing to the fact that pollution impacts associated with the proposed incinerator had not been adequately dealt with in the planning application. It was of the view that if planning permission was granted an IPC license would simply follow as a matter of course, and it was not convinced that the local environment would be adequately protected as a result.

The Court of Appeal acknowledged the overlap between planning and pollution control, together with the appropriateness of considering such issues in the planning process. The court even went so far as to hold that in some cases, where it

---

45. *R v. Brent London Borough Council, ex parte Gunning* (1985) LGR 168 and *R v. North & East Devon Health Authority, ex parte Coughlan* [2001] QB 213.
46. *R (Edwards and others) v. Environment Agency and Others* [2006] EWCA Civ. 877.
47. Para. 63.
48. Para. 120.
49. DTI, CM 7124, London, 23 May 2007. See BERR, 'Energy white paper: meeting the energy challenge', <www.berr.gov.uk/energy/whitepaper/page39534.html>, 1 September 2008.
50. See *East Suffolk Rivers Catchment Board v. Kent* [1941] AC 74.

was clear that the failure to deal with pollution issues would lead to the refusal of an IPC license, it would be appropriate to refuse planning permission. However, the court also stated that where issues were less cut and dried, they should be left to the expertise of the appropriate pollution control body. The *Gateshead* decision accordingly sheds some light on the relationship between planning and pollution control authorities and authorization processes. This issue does, however, require more thoroughly consideration by government.

Judging from recent jurisprudence, there is evidence that the courts are increasingly willing to adopt a purposive approach when interpreting environmental law. In *Environment Agency (Formerly NRA) v. Empress Car Co. (Abertillery) Ltd* [1998] 1 All ER 481, for example, the House of Lords reversed a long line of authority (including *Wychavon DC v. National Rivers Authority* [1993] 1 WLR 125,[51] and the House of Lords decision in *National Rivers Authority v. Yorkshire Water Services Ltd* [1995] 1 AC 444) which had made it much easier for defendants to escape liability for water pollution offences. Empress owned an industrial site adjacent to a river on which was situated a diesel tank. The tank had originally been fitted with the requisite pollution control devices but Empress had overridden them in order to get easier access to it. The outlet pipe had a tap but no lock. The site had been vandalized in the past and the incident in question involved the tap being opened at night by a trespasser, resulting in the diesel polluting the river. The EA successfully prosecuted Empress for 'causing' pollution under section 85 of the WRA. The appeal was ultimately heard in the House of Lords where Empress argued that owing to the fact that the pollution had been caused by the positive act of the trespasser and not itself, it had not caused the pollution. The House of Lords took a much broader view of the matter and having considered the purpose of the statute and the company's conduct, held that the company had caused the pollution. This followed the Court of Appeal decision in *Attorney General's Reference (No. 1 of 1994)* [1995] EnvLR 227 which determined that more than one party could cause pollution in a given case.

This type of purposive approach toward statutory interpretation has also been recently demonstrated in the context of legislation rooted in EC law obligations. *United Utilities Water Plc. v. Environment Agency* [2007] UKHL 41 concerned the application of permits for sewage treatment plants under the PPC (England and Wales) Regulations 2000 (SI 2000/1973). United Utilities ran a complex network of facilities for sewage treatment and sought declarations for a number of test sites to the effect that PPC permits were not required where only partial and preliminary treatment was undertaken before the sludge was transferred to a central facility for further treatment prior to disposal. The case was only partially successful (in respect of sludge that was ultimately recovered, rather than disposed of, as provided for by an exception in the applicable regulations) in the lower courts. United Utilities' appeal to the House of Lords in respect of three of its preliminary treatment plants failed. Lord Hoffman clearly stated in his judgment that

---

51. On the interpretation of 'causing' pollution under s. 107(1)(c) of the WRA.

'the purpose of the legislation was, amongst other things, to protect the environment against potential damage from the operations involved...'.[52]

The question of liability for historic pollution referred to above arose again, this time in a statutory context, in *R (National Grid) v. Environment Agency* [2007] 1 WLR 1780. In this case, however, the Law Lords took what may be considered a less purposive approach than that demonstrated above. The court was called to rule on the question of liability under section 78F of the EPA (as inserted by section 57 of the *Environment Act* 1995) for cleanup of contaminated land. In this case, coal tar had been deposited by the owners' predecessor in title. The site in question had originally been run as a gas works by a private business, then a public authority from the early twentieth century until 1965, after which it was sold for the purpose of a small housing development. National Grid inherited the assets and liabilities of the relevant part of the nationalized gas undertaking as a result of a series of complex transactions following privatization in the 1980s. In 2005 the EA designated the site as contaminated and undertook expensive remediation work. It identified National Grid as an 'appropriate person' to bear the costs of this under section 78F and sought to recover the monies from them. National Grid challenged this decision in a claim for judicial review, which failed at first instance. The subsequent appeal to the House of Lords succeeded. The Lords took the view that the term 'appropriate person' in section 78F referred to someone who had caused or knowingly permitted the contamination. The court further found that the statutory provisions transferring pre-existing liability to National Grid did not extend to cover liability imposed under statutes prescribed after the original polluting event. According to Lord Hoffman:

> It is true that the ... legislation was retrospective in the sense that it created a potential present liability for acts done in the past. But that is not the same as creating a deemed past liability for those acts. There is nothing in the Act to create retrospectivity in this sense.[53]

The House of Lords accordingly issued a quashing order. The approach adopted by the Lords in the *National Grid* case is comparatively narrow and exhibits extreme caution in respect of imposing liability for the remediation of historic pollution even in a statutory context. The contamination in question was certainly present on site before privatization, although it only became legally problematic thereafter. Lord Scott laid great store on the fact that the deposit of coal tar would not have been considered problematic at the time when it occurred.[54] There were three possible candidates who could be liable under section 78 – the polluter (no longer extant in this case); the current owners (ordinary householders, whom the EA had elected not to pursue); and the public purse. The crux of the EA's argument was that National Grid, as a statutory successor in title, should fall into the first category. Lord Neuberger in particular was sympathetic to the notion of the application

---

52. Para. 5.
53. Para. 4.
54. Para. 12.

of the polluter pays principle to successors in title,[55] especially in respect of the contaminated land regime. He ultimately took the view, however, that such an expansive approach should be determined by parliament, and not the courts.[56] Given the outcry from the powerful and influential property sector that has accompanied similar prior legislation relating to contaminated land, this would seem to be an unlikely prospect. In similar future situations it would therefore appear that loss of this nature will lie where it falls, or upon the public purse. It is also arguable that the approach adopted in the *National Grid* case may discourage the EA from taking a proactive approach to contaminated sites in future, unless section 78 can be interpreted and applied in a broader manner. This would appear unlikely, however, given the confusing wording of the statutory framework. Although the court's approach arguably defeats the very purpose of the protection for human health and the environment envisaged in the legislation, it may be argued that the Law Lords took a necessarily restrictive view given the definition of a 'responsible person' under section 78. Parliament would accordingly be well advised to legislate again on this point.

3.4   HUMAN RIGHTS ACT CASES

The HRA, as noted above, has given the UK courts new opportunities and indeed a new perspective[57] from which to adjudicate on some very contentious issues. A number of these have arisen in significant environmental cases.[58] Notable amongst these is *Marcic v. Thames Water Utilities Ltd* [2002] QB 929 which involved an action based on damage consequent upon the claimant's property being inundated by sewage. The HRA made it incumbent on the courts to reconsider the application of the law in this area, which had been thought largely settled from the late nineteenth century.

Marcic's house and garden had since 1992 been subject to repeated flooding from sewers which fell under the responsibility of Thames Water Utilities Ltd (TWU). These sewers had overtime become inadequate for dealing with the quantity of sewage and surface waters draining into them. Marcic eventually took action himself to protect his house from inundation, but his garden remained subject to repeated flooding. TWU was under a statutory duty to provide and improve the sewers and to secure effective drainage. The company, however, had more flooding problems to address than its finite resources would accommodate and so it put in place a points system in order to set priorities. Areas where houses were subject

---

55. Para. 29.
56. Para. 33.
57. See, e.g., *McKenna v. British Aluminium* [2002] EnvLR 30.
58. See, e.g., C. Rodgers, 'Protection of Sites of Special Scientific Interest: The Human Rights Act dimension', *JPEL* (2005): 997; and K. Morrow, 'The Rights Question: The Initial Impact of The Human Rights Act on Domestic Law relating to the Environment', *JPEL* (2005): 1010.

to inundation were ranked highest and these were so numerous that there was no realistic prospect of Marcic's situation being remedied.

Marcic had a right of complaint to the DGWS under section 18 of the WIA 1991. However, he choose to institute civil proceedings in negligence, nuisance and under the rule in the *Rylands* case. These were dismissed. He also unsuccessfully invoked breach of statutory duty. Marcic further alleged a breach of section 6(1) of the HRA and succeeded on this ground in the High Court (with reference to Article 8 and Article 1 to the First Protocol of the ECHR). As a result he was awarded damages, but only from the date on which the HRA came into force (2 October 2002).

TWU appealed and Marcic cross-appealed. The Court of Appeal upheld the decision of the court *a quo* regarding the application of the HRA. Furthermore, it held TWU liable in nuisance, thus entitling Marcic to damages for the full duration of the interference. In addition, the court also took the view that the statutory remedy under section 18 of the WIA was unsuitable for Marcic's needs. This was extremely controversial in that it allowed common law and Convention rights to circumvent an established statutory regime, thereby imposing potentially crippling financial burdens on sewerage undertakers.

The case inevitably came before the House of Lords in *Marcic v. Thames Water Utilities* [2003] UKHL 66 which upheld TWU's appeal. The House of Lords took the view that the detailed regulatory regime under the WIA, together with the supervisory jurisdiction of the courts in judicial review, were sufficient to protect Convention rights and deal with complaints. The Court refused to allow a parallel common law right to sue, as the effect of this would be to displace the applicable statutory regime.[59] The Law Lords thought that the DGWS was in a better position than the courts to adjudicate on the appropriate balance between someone in Marcic's position and TWU's other customers. The House of Lords accordingly followed the approach adopted by the European Court of Human Rights Grand Chamber in *Hatton v. United Kingdom* [2003] 37 EHRR 28, recognising that the ECHR was 'fundamentally subsidiary' to the role of national authorities in evaluating domestic needs and conditions.[60]

A further case involving the interplay between nuisance and the HRA arose in *Dennis v. Ministry of Defence* [2003] (EWHC) 793. In this matter the claimants sought damages and a declaration in respect of noise nuisance emanating from a Royal Air Force (RAF) base situated near their country estate. At first instance, Buckley J held that there was indeed a serious nuisance, aggravated by its persistence and unpredictability. A key issue for consideration was whether the interference experienced by the claimants was justified by the public interest. Buckley J, applying the Marcic decision, held that only reasonably necessary interference could be warranted, adding that a public interest defence would only be valid in nuisance if it could also succeed in a human rights claim on the same facts. He took the view here that while the public interest required the RAF to continue operations

---

59. Para. 35.
60. Para. 97.

at the base, the claimants should not be expected to carry the cost of the public benefit. As a result, he decided that justice would be served by refusing the declaration sought, but by granting damages to cover the claimants' loss of capital value and past and future loss of use and amenity. Buckley J added, *obiter*, that had the law of nuisance not been adequate to dispose of the case, human rights provisions would have achieved the same result.

4   CRITICAL SURVEY

Although the UK courts have been engaging with environmental law and governance issues for a considerable period of time, their record in this area has been, at best, chequered. During the nineteenth century the judiciary showed an outstanding ability to apply the judicial function in a creative and innovative fashion in order to respond to the societal pressures and environmental pressures associated with the industrial revolution.[61] However, the same cannot be said for their role during the course of most of the twentieth century, during which time the judiciary has been subject to intense criticism.[62] While a reduction in pure common law activity in the environmental sphere was to be expected owing to the emerging statutory framework, other factors have contributed to reducing its role as a tool of environmental governance.

The courts appear to have become ever more reluctant to act in controversial areas, notably in the application of strict liability, preferring instead to abdicate responsibility for developing the law in this fashion to parliament. This was clearly illustrated in the *Cambridge Water*[63] and *United Utilities*[64] cases. There are many reasons for this trend, a significant one being the rise of the law of negligence, predicated on fault, following the landmark ruling in *Donaghue v. Stevenson* [1932] AC 562. The twentieth century furthermore saw the law of negligence permeating many areas of the common law. Chief among these are liability in nuisance and under the rule in the *Rylands* case which, on paper at least, had so much to offer in terms of environmental governance. However, it is significant that when the Lords were presented with the opportunity to extinguish the latter in the *TransCo*[65] case, they opted not to do so, supporting, if weakly, the view that while it may not be in good health, reports of the death of the common law in the sphere

---

61. See Coyle & Morrow, *supra* n. 27.
62. See, e.g., J. Lowry & R. Edmunds (eds), *Environmental Protection and the Common Law* (Oxford: Hart, 2000); Sir R. Macrory & M. Woods, 'Modernising environmental justice: Regulation and the Role of an Environmental Tribunal', <www.ucl.ac.uk/laws/environment/ tribunals/docs/full_report.pdf>, 28 August 2008; M. Adebowale, 'Using the Law: Access to Environmental Justice – Barriers and Opportunities', <www.defra.gov.uk/environment/ enforcement/pdf/ejureport.pdf>, 28 August 2008, (Capacity Global, a report for DEFRA); and Coyle & Morrow, *supra* n. 27.
63. *Supra* 3.1.
64. *Supra* 3.3.
65. *Supra* 3.1.

of the environment are overstated.[66] The very nature of the common law, as has been repeatedly illustrated through its long history, is that it springs back to life in unexpected ways when the need arises. The common law appears to have been able to draw renewed vitality from contemporary and often surprising sources such as the HRA[67] and the Aarhus Convention.[68]

As a final observation on the influence of the common law on the judiciary, it is interesting to note the extent to which fault-based notions of liability within the common law have influenced the judicial interpretation statutory strict liability provisions. As is evident in a long line of water pollution cases, including the *Wychavon* and *NRA* cases,[69] the judiciary applied something akin to a fault based-approach to liability, requiring defendants to have performed a positive action causing pollution even where the relevant statute provided for strict liability. However, the judiciary appears to have returned to a purposive approach to statutory interpretation in the context of strict liability, as evidenced in the *Empress*[70] case. Having appeared for many years to have, to all intents and purposes, lost confidence in the viability of non-fault based approaches to environmental law, the courts seem to be gaining new vigour in their approach from both societal support for environmental priorities[71] and from more specialized debate surrounding optimising the judicial function in relation to the environment.[72]

5 THE WAY FORWARD

5.1 KEY CHALLENGES

The overarching consideration for the judiciary contributing to the development of environmental governance in the UK is perhaps to be found in the extremely challenging task of attempting to satisfy increased and increasing public expectation that the law deal effectively with environmental problems.

Among the most significant of the specific challenges faced by the courts in developing environmental governance, lies the fact that one of the areas most fully within their control, the civil law, has been pushed ever further into the background by the attempt to put in place all encompassing environmental meta-statutes. Having said this, be it ever so well drafted, statute law can never tackle all eventualities and there remains a role for the common law in responding to legislative gaps and vagaries. The fact that the role accorded to the common law is increasingly a residual one, should not negate its significance as it often comes into play where individuals stand to bear damage sustained in pursuit of the public good.

---

66. P.R. Ghandi, 'Requiem for Rylands v. Fletcher', *Con&PL* (1994): 309.
67. *Supra* 3.4.
68. *Supra* 3.2.
69. *Supra* 3.3.
70. *Ibid*.
71. *Supra* 1.1.
72. *Infra* 5.

However, the contemporary hesitancy of the judiciary to recognize non-fault based approaches to common law liability may have serious implications for the individual, law and the environment. In other areas, however, notably judicial review, the courts have been very prepared to engage with environmental issues although pragmatism would appear to occasionally triumph over principle. One of the greatest challenges facing the judiciary in this regard is how to effectively and efficiently deal with rising case loads.[73]

As the function of purely judge-made private law diminishes, the role of the courts in shaping environmental governance through statutory interpretation is growing steadily. This is notwithstanding the burden that this places on the legal system both in respect of applying individual enactments and distilling the complex interactions between them.[74] At the same time, legislation in the environmental sphere is often extremely technical and the nature of the material under consideration can pose considerable, though by no means unique[75] or insurmountable, problems for the judiciary. To minimize these problems, training has been provided to magistrates[76] and judges in higher court structures. It appears that judges are increasingly willing and able to grapple with fairly complex technical issues which arise in environmental disputes, as illustrated in the *Edwards* and *United Utilities* cases. While the learning curve has been steep, this training appears to have proven extremely valuable in raising the capacity of judicial officers to deal with environmental matters. Ongoing training is nonetheless required given: the constant flux of environmental legislation and policy, often fuelled by international and EU law obligations; emerging new facets of domestic law, such as under the HRA; and shifting national, regional and local priorities and competences.

5.2   KEY OPPORTUNITIES

Having outlined some of the challenges posed to the role of the judiciary in environmental governance, it is also important to consider some future opportunities for extending the role of the courts in this sphere.

In principle, the common law tradition sees the courts well equipped to deal with complex societal challenges of the type exhibited in environmental governance. The judicial process is an art rather than a mechanical enterprise and it therefore theoretically allows considerable space for judicial creativity. This having been said, as amply demonstrated in the case law, much depends on the willingness of individual judges to exploit the latitude. Sir Robert Carnwath has remarked that ' . . . judges are, or should be, one of the most informed and stable

---

73. Sir H. Woolf, 'Are the Judiciary Environmentally Myopic?', *JEL* 4 (1992): 1-14.
74. Sir R. Carnwath, 'Environmental litigation – A Way through the Maze', *JEL* 11 (1999): 3.
75. Many areas display comparable levels of complexity, e.g., medical negligence.
76. Adebowale, *supra* n. 62.

sections of their society'.[77] Many members of the UK judiciary are making it their business to be well informed about, and to engage effectively with, environmental law issues. This is particularly evident in the realm of judicial review and the application of the HRA, as demonstrated, for example, in the *Greenpeace*[78] and *Dennis*[79] cases.

However, as is apparent from several of the cases discussed in this chapter, much can be gained through developing the debate on environmental law and governance though litigation. This has been demonstrated in various cases (such as *Marcic*,[80] *Cambridge Water*,[81] and *Hunter*[82]) where it appears that the lower courts are often more activist in their approach than the House of Lords. This is perhaps in tacit acknowledgement that there remains the prospect of a final reckoning before the latter. At its best, this makes for a full and often very stimulating airing of the issues, allowing consideration of both radical and conservative approaches. High quality dissenting judgments also add to the richness and texture of the common law.[83] A fine example of this is Lord Cooke's speech in Hunter[84] in which he drew on a wealth of legal authority including (as has become much more mainstream following the promulgation of the HRA) ECHR jurisprudence to construct a very thought provoking and modern treatment of nuisance. Cooke's speech also drew heavily upon another resource that often serves to enrich domestic judicial engagement with environmental issues – jurisprudence from other common law jurisdictions. The opportunity to engage with authority from fellow commonwealth jurisdictions, with their shared legal heritage but distinctive jurisprudential approaches, can provide a useful lens through which to re-examine problematic cases, as demonstrated in the *Hunter*[85] and *TransCo*[86] cases.

A final and potentially hugely significant opportunity to enhance the contribution of the judiciary to environmental governance in the UK is to create specialist environmental courts or tribunals. There is broad consensus that the scale and nature of modern environmental law places the courts under a heavy burden and that change is required in order to optimize their performance in this area. As a result, initiatives promoting more specialized forms of adjudication (in the form of an environmental court or tribunal) have gained wide support from leading members of the judiciary, the RCEP,[87] academics, NGOs

---

77. See, e.g., Sir R. Carnwath, 'Judicial Protection of the Environment: At Home and Abroad', *JEL* 16 (2004): 315, 316.
78. *Supra* 3.2.
79. *Supra* 3.4.
80. *Ibid.*
81. *Supra* 3.1.
82. *Ibid.*
83. M. Kirby, 'Judicial dissent – Common Law and Civil Law Traditions', *LQR* 123 (2007): 379.
84. *Supra* 3.1.
85. *Ibid.*
86. *Ibid.*
87. RCEP, *supra* n. 9.

and even within the executive itself.[88] The government has in principle shown that it is willing to entertain the idea of creating separate judicial structures to hear environmental matters.[89] However, the practical realization thereof appears a long way from becoming a reality. In England and Wales, current initiatives appear to concentrate on making the current system function more effectively.[90] In fairness, in the context of the ongoing reforms to the judicial system under the *Constitutional Reform Act*,[91] it has perhaps not been the most opportune time to consider additional radical change to judicial structures. In Scotland, however, the previous administration went so far as to consult on the creation of a specialist environmental court, although it was of the view that the case for such a development was not made out in its jurisdiction.[92] Despite current unwillingness on the part of government to act in this regard, the depth and breadth of discussion relating to the role of the judiciary generally, and its particular role in environment governance, should ensure that these issues remain topical for the foreseeable future.

BIBLIOGRAPHY

Adebowale, M. 'Using the Law: Access to Environmental Justice – Barriers and Opportunities'. <www.defra.gov.uk/environment/enforcement/pdf/ejureport.pdf>, 28 August 2008.
BERR. 'Energy white paper: meeting the energy challenge'. <www.berr.gov.uk/energy/whitepaper/page39534.html>, 1 September 2008.
British-Irish Council. 'Agreement between the Government of the United Kingdom of Great Britain and Northern Ireland and the Government of Ireland'. <www1.british-irishcouncil.org/documents/text.asp>, 12 September 2008.
British-Irish Council. 'Environment'. <www1.british-irishcouncil.org/work/environment.asp>, 28 August 2008.
Cabinet Office. 'Ministerial Committee on Economic Development: Sub-Committee on Environment and Energy Composition'. <www.cabinetoffice.gov.uk/secretariats/committees/edee.aspx>, 28 August 2008.
Carnwath, R., Sir. 'Environmental litigation – A Way through the Maze'. *Journal of Environmental Law* 11 (1999): 3-14.

---

88. Ministry of Agriculture Fisheries and Food and the National Assembly for Wales, 'Salmon and Freshwater Fisheries Review 2004', <www.defra.gov.uk/fish/freshwater/pdf/sffrev.pdf>, 28 August 2008.
89. Government Response to the Review, *supra* n. 91, see Ministry of Agriculture Fisheries and Food, 'Review of Salmon and Freshwater Fisheries: Government Response', <www.defra.gov.uk/fish/freshwater/pdf/salmon.pdf>, 28 August 2008.
90. DEFRA, 'Review of Enforcement in Environmental Regulation: Report of Conclusions 2006', <www.defra.gov.uk/environment/enforcement/pdf/enforcereview-report.pdf>, 28 August 2008.
91. See *supra* 2.1.
92. Scottish Executive Environment Group, 'Strengthening and Streamlining: The Way Forward for the Enforcement of Environmental Law in Scotland', <www.scotland.gov.uk/Resource/Doc/155498/0041750.pdf>, 28 August 2008.

Carnwath, R., Sir. 'Judicial Protection of the Environment: At Home and Abroad'. *Journal of Environmental Law* 16 (2004): 315-328.

Council of Europe. 'The European Convention on Human Rights'. <www.hri.org/docs/ECHR50.html>, 11 August 2008.

Coyle, S. & K. Morrow. *The Philosophical Foundations of Environmental Law.* Oxford: Hart, 2004.

DEFRA. 'Foreword by the Secretary of State'. <www.defra.gov.uk/rural/strategy/foreword.htm>, 28 August 2008.

DEFRA. 'Government Survey of Public Attitudes and Behaviours toward the Environment 2007'. <www.defra.gov.uk/environment/statistics/pubatt/download/pas2007report.pdf>, 11 August 2008.

DEFRA. 'Review of Enforcement in Environmental Regulation: Report of Conclusions 2006'. <www.defra.gov.uk/environment/enforcement/pdf/enforcereview-report.pdf>, 28 August 2008.

Dicey, A.V. 'Introduction to the Study of the Law of the Constitution 1885'. <www.constitution.org/cmt/avd/law_con.htm>, 28 August 2008.

Ghandi, P.R. 'Requiem for Rylands v. Fletcher'. *Conveyancer and Property Lawyer* (1994): 309-321.

HMCS. 'The Court Structure of Her Majesty's Courts Service'. <www.hmcourts-service.gov.uk/aboutus/structure/index.htm>, 28 August 2008.

House of Commons, Environment Food and Rural Affairs Committee. 'The Environment Agency', Seventh Report of Session 2005-06. Vol. 1. <www.publications.parliament.uk/pa/cm200506/cmselect/cmenvfru/780/780i.pdf>, 12 September 2008.

House of Lords, Select Committee on the Constitution. Relations between the Executive, the Judiciary and Parliament, HL Paper 151, 6th Report of Session 2006-07 Report with Evidence. London: The Stationery Office, 2007.

Kirby, M. 'Judicial dissent – Common Law and Civil Law Traditions'. *Law Quarterly Review* 123 (2007): 379-395.

Lowry, J. & R. Edmunds (eds). *Environmental Protection and the Common Law.* Oxford: Hart, 2000.

Macrory, R., Sir & M. Woods. 'Modernising environmental justice: Regulation and the Role of an Environmental Tribunal'. <www.ucl.ac.uk/laws/environment/tribunals/docs/full_report.pdf>, 28 August 2008.

Ministry of Agriculture Fisheries and Food and the National Assembly for Wales. 'Salmon and Freshwater Fisheries Review 2004'. <www.defra.gov.uk/fish/freshwater/pdf/sffrev.pdf>, 28 August 2008.

Ministry of Agriculture Fisheries and Food. 'Review of Salmon and Freshwater Fisheries: Government Response'. <www.defra.gov.uk/fish/freshwater/pdf/salmon.pdf>, 28 August 2008.

Morrow, K. 'The Rights Question: The Initial Impact of The Human Rights Act on Domestic Law relating to the Environment'. *Journal of Planning and Environmental Law* (2005): 1010-1021.

Northern Ireland Assembly. 'Ministerial Statement on Environmental Governance of 27 May 2008'. <www.niassembly.gov.uk/record/reports2007/080527.htm#4>, 28 August 2008.

Northern Ireland Court Service. 'Serving the Community through the Administration of Justice'. <www.courtsni.gov.uk/>, 28 August 2008.

ODPM. 'Planning Policy Statement 23: Planning and Pollution Control'. <www.communities.gov.uk/documents/planningandbuilding/pdf/planning policystatement23.pdf>, 12 September 2008.

Phillips, J. LCJ. 'Judicial independence', speech delivered at the Commonwealth Law Conference on 12 September 2007. Nairobi, 2007. <www.judiciary. gov.uk/ docs/speeches/lcj_kenya_clc_120907.pdf>, 28 August 2008.

Pontin, B. 'Tort Law and Victorian Government Growth: The Historiographical Significance of Tort in the Shadow of Chemical Pollution and Factory Safety Regulation'. *Oxford Journal of Legal Studies* 18 (1998): 661-680.

RCEP. 'Environmental Planning'. <www.rcep.org/uk/epreport/>, 16 August 2008.

Review of Environmental Governance Northern Ireland, 'Foundations for the Future, May 2007', <www.regni.info/final_report-3.pdf>, 28 August 2008.

Rodgers, C. 'Protection of Sites of Special Scientific Interest: The Human Rights Act dimension'. *Journal of Planning and Environmental Law* (2005): 997-1009.

Sandberg, R. 'A Whitehall farce? Defining and conceptualising the British Civil Service'. *Public Law* (2006): 653-663.

Scottish Courts. 'Scottish Courts Services'. <www.scotcourts.gov.uk/>, 28 August 2008.

Scottish Executive Environment Group. 'Strengthening and Streamlining: The Way Forward for the Enforcement of Environmental Law in Scotland'. <www.scotland.gov.uk/Resource/Doc/155498/0041750.pdf>, 28 August 2008.

Secretary of State for Transport and Industry. 'Our Energy Future: Creating a Low Carbon Economy'. <www.berr.gov.uk/files/file10719.pdf>, 28 August 2008.

Steyn, Lord. 'Democracy, the rule of law and the role of judges'. *European Human Rights Law Review* 3 (2006): 243-253.

UNECE. 'Convention on Access to Information, Public Participation in Decision-Making and Access to Justice in Environmental Matters'. <www.unece.org/ env/pp/docu ments/cep43e.pdf>, 12 September 2008.

Woolf, H., Sir. 'Are the Judiciary Environmentally Myopic?'. *Journal of Environmental Law* 4 (1992): 1-14.

TABLE OF LEGISLATION

Alkali Act 1863
Clean Air Act 1956
Clean Air Act 1968
Clean Air Act 1993
Constitutional Reform Act 2005

TABLE OF CASES

TABLE OF INTERATIONAL INSTRUMENTS

ABBREVIATIONS

AONB	Area of Oustanding Natural Beauty
BIC	British-Irish Council
CA	Countryside Act
COPA	Control of Pollution Act
CRA	Constitutional Reform Act
DEFRA	Department of Environment, Food and Rural Affairs
DoENI	Department of Environment for Northern Ireland
EA	Environment Agency (England)
ECHR	European Convention on Human Rights
EIA	Environmental Impact Assessment
EPA	Environmental Protection Act
HMIP	Her Majesty's Inspectorate of Pollution
HRA	Human Rights Act
IPC	Integrated Pollution Control
IPPC	Integrated Pollution Prevention and Control
JNCC	Joint Nature Conservation Committee
LCJ	Lord Chief Justice
NDPBs	Non-Departmental Public Bodies
NERCA	Natural Environment and Rural Communities Act
NIEA	Northern Island Environment Agency
NGO	Non-governmental Organization
NIEA	Northern Ireland Environment Agency
NPACA	National Parks and Access to the Countryside Act
NRA	National Rivers Authority
ODPM	Office of the Deputy Prime Minister
PPC	Pollution Prevention and Control
RAF	Royal Air Force
RCEP	Royal Commission on Environmental Pollution
SEPA	Scottish Environmental Protection Agency
SSSI	Sites of Special Scientific Interest
UNECE	United Nations Economic Commission for Europe
WCA	Wildlife and Countryside Act
WIA	Water Industry Act
WRA	Water Resources Act

Chapter 5

United States of America

Nicholas Robinson

1   INTRODUCTION

In the federal system constituting the United States of America (USA), the judicial authority is divided between a system of federal courts including territorial courts, the fifty independent State court systems, and the independent tribal courts of the several sovereign indigenous nations, plus the judicial courts of the Commonwealth of Puerto Rico. Several jurisdictions also have special environmental tribunals, such as the Vermont Environmental Court[1] or the administrative environmental tribunals within the New York's Department of Environmental Conservation.[2] The exercise of environmental decision-making in the courts involves governmental and non-governmental civil enforcement of the extensive environmental laws, judicial review of the promulgation by administrative agencies of rules and regulations required by environmental statutes, and the criminal prosecution of individuals or companies for violations of the environmental laws.

Judicial decisions during the decade from the late 1960s through the 1970s were instrumental in ensuring that the first generation of environmental statutes would be rigorously implemented. Public interest environmental law was born in

---

1. See Vermont Judiciary, 'Vermont Environmental Court', <www.vermontjudiciary.org/courts/environmental/index.htm>, 12 September 2008.
2. NYSDEC, 'Conserving, Improving, and Protecting New York's Natural Resources and Environment', <www.dec.ny.gov>, 12 September 2008.

Louis J. Kotzé and Alexander R. Paterson (eds), *The Role of the Judiciary in Environmental Governance: Comparative Perspectives*, pp. 181–208.
© 2009 Kluwer Law International BV, The Netherlands.

the USA at this time, with the creation of the Natural Resources Defense Council (NRDC), the Environmental Defense Fund (EDF) or the Sierra Club Legal Defense Fund (SCLDF),[3] plus regional organizations such as the Chesapeake Bay Foundation and the Isaac Walton League. These public interest law organizations sought to emulate the success of the earlier Civil Rights Movement in America, in order to protect nature and the public health. However, since judicial enforcement of the environmental legislation of the 1970s required companies and government agencies to change many of their time-honored practices, a backlash emerged. Those opposed to environmental reforms also sought to call upon the judiciary to defend their past practices. Trade associations, such as the Chlorine Chemistry Council or the Engine Manufacturers Association, and individual companies, such as American Electric Power, Inc. or Chevron USA, commenced litigation to overturn newly promulgated environmental rules and to permit established business practices to continue.

Perhaps because there is no environmental 'Bill of Rights' in the USA Constitution, the traditionally conservative USA Supreme Court has been hostile to expanding the environmental rights of citizens. The Supreme Court's guidance to lower federal courts, coinciding with the appointment of a large number of conservative new federal judges by Republican presidents, stimulated a somewhat negative judicial attitude toward public interest environmental litigation,[4] together with a mild receptivity to the environmental claims of the business sector. At the appellate levels of federal judicial decision-making, courts have relied upon narrow administrative procedural rules and legal presumptions (such as which party has the burden of proof) to issue rulings that frequently resulted in forestalling needed judicial elaboration or strengthening of environmental norms.

The judicial attitude towards environmental law issues in federal courts does not extend to the State court systems, or to the administrative environmental tribunals, which often carry a heavy docket of environmental law enforcement cases. Throughout much of he USA, ready access to the judicial system is the norm, and environmental laws are widely observed, in part because there are strong administrative and judicial sanctions for non-compliance. For the most part, access to environmental information is widely available throughout the States, although roughly half the States have not enacted State laws for environmental impact assessment (EIA) or freedom of information. In contrast to federal courts, many of the highest State courts, such as the Supreme Courts of California and Minnesota

---

3. The SCLDF is now named EarthJustice, and EDF is now simply Environmental Defense. The NRDC continues. They all commenced many environmental protection legal actions, which bare their names as plaintiffs. Federal tax laws allow individuals to make contributions exempt from income taxation to qualifying NGOs, such as these. S. 501(c)(3), Internal Revenue Code. Such NGOs are incorporated under the laws of the State where they are founded, and then can operate throughout all States.

4. See, e.g., the empirical analysis of how federal judges responded to citizen suits involving review of environmental impact assessments under the National Environmental Policy Act (NEPA), in J.E. Austin et al., *Judging NEPA: A 'Hard Look' at Judicial Decision Making Under the National Environmental Policy Act* (Washington, DC: ELI, 2005).

or the Court of Appeals of New York, have consistently advanced a more sophis-ticated and effective concept for environmental law than has the USA Supreme Court.

2   MAIN ENVIRONMENTAL ISSUES AND LAWS

The principal issues affecting the environment in the USA reflect the varied con-ditions throughout the geography of the nation. Weak economic support for older cities and rapid spread of suburban municipalities produce many environmental challenges, which mix with problems of pollution and the other economic 'exter-nalities' of the agricultural and manufacturing sectors. To understand how the courts deal with these issues, it is necessary to understand the allocation of governmental authority provided in the federal Constitution.

The USA Constitution assigns congress responsibility to make laws governing the property of the USA federal government, including the public lands. One-third of the lands in the western States and in Alaska are still 'federal public lands'. Some State laws, such as fish and game laws, may apply in these areas. Since the late 1800s, congress has enacted an extensive body of statutes and created large num-bers of agencies to govern the natural resources, under the Department of the Interior, or in the case of forest lands, under the Department of Agriculture. Pro-tection for endangered species and conservation of national parks and monuments are subject to federal laws. The Constitution also authorizes congress to regulate uses of the navigable rivers of the nation.

In contrast, riparian and coastal uses of lands and water, and most land devel-opment and uses of human settlements and stewardship of cultural or historic heritage properties, are the responsibility of State and local governments. States authorize local zoning and land use laws, which in turn, are subject to review by the federal courts when they implicate the federal Constitution's guarantee that prop-erty may not be taken without just compensation; the USA Supreme Court has ruled that if a regulation greatly diminishes the value of property, it may constitute a 'taking' of property requiring 'just' compensation, just as would the use of eminent domain to confiscate private property for a public use. Finally, since 1970, congress has enacted many federal statutes to control pollution of air and water and soil, regulate use and disposal of hazardous chemicals and nuclear power, statutes which require States to manage solid waste, and statutes to regulate pesticides.

Notwithstanding congressional enactment of broad environmental policies in section 101 of the *National Environmental Policy Act* 1969 (NEPA),[5] the courts have declined to read this law to provide a framework environmental law for the federal government. Some States have enacted framework laws, for example, the

---

5.   42 US Code s. 4321.

codification of the Environmental Conservation Law of the State of New York.[6] However, environmental law throughout the federal and State systems in the USA is piecemeal, adopted in an ad hoc response to perceived environmental problems.[7] The environmental problems of the nation are surveyed in the some twenty annual reports of the President's Council on Environmental Quality (CEQ), but in the Clinton Administration the CEQ stopped preparing these 'environmental state of the nation reports'. CEQ has a statutory duty to do so, but neither congress and the courts nor the president have required observance of this duty. The deteriorating national environmental trends 'officially' are unnoticed. The World Watch Institute's 'State of the World' report indicates that the impact of economic activity in the USA grew by 21% from 1992 to 2002.[8] Environmental quality has declined in proportion.

Despite recurrent environmental problems, environmental law in the USA has been a measurable success. For example, most of the hazardous waste sites produced since the Industrial Revolution have been remediated, and now 'brown field' rules encapsulate and reuse such remaining sites. Urban smog is abated or controlled in most cities, but not entirely as asthma rates are increasing; regulations to restrict emission of fine particulate matter now require stricter controls for protecting the public health. States and cities control indoor air pollution, and have greatly reduced tobacco smoking. Surface water pollution is largely abated, and municipal sewage controlled. Vast areas of wilderness are protected, and extensive systems of national, State and local parklands are well established and continue to expand. Substances that deplete the stratospheric ozone layer are strictly regulated. Criminal enforcement of environmental law is a reality, with investigators and prosecutors assigned to these tasks.

Although federal and State environmental law is voluminous, it is not holistic. Enforcement of laws in effect is fairly reliable, but not adequate to reverse many patterns of environmental degradation. Acid rain was reduced in volume, but is still an insidious pollutant; melting bridges and reducing biological productivity and species extinction rates continue to climb. Short-term economic demand for carbon fuels prompts repeated calls to remove protection of off-shore habitats where oil and gas are located, and have allowed a most egregious pattern of strip mining of coal in West Virginia. Moreover, the incremental accumulation of nitrogen where most river catchment systems meet the sea, causes dead zones. By 2008, the dead zone at the mouth of the Mississippi was as large as the State of Connecticut, and growing. Bioaccumulation of chemicals in humans is more extensive than ever,

---

6. See Vol. 17 ½ McKinney's Consolidated Laws of New York, codified between 1970-1972, New York (State), *McKinney's Consolidated Laws of New York annotated with Annotations from State and Federal Courts and State Agencies* (St. Paul, Minn.: West Group, 1939). This is one of the few examples of comprehensive environmental codification of environmental laws, and it is found, improbably perhaps, in a common law jurisdiction.
7. See R.J. Lazarus, *The Making of Environmental Law* (Chicago: UCP, 2004).
8. WWI, 'State of the World 2006: A Worldwatch Institute report on progress toward a sustainable society', (New York: Norton, 2006), 18.

and the toxicity of most of the more than 65,000 chemicals in active use, has not yet been tested. There remains a long list of contemporary environmental issues that require the remedial treatment of yet further new environmental statutes.

The role of the judiciary in the architecture of America's environmental protection systems is a limited one. Statutes have supplanted, or vastly reduced, the role that the courts could serve through application of common law remedies. The courts are essential for providing the foundations of the rule of law, without which, environmental laws cannot be effective. However, unless congress or the State legislatures revise the statutory constraints on what judges can do in addressing environmental problems, courts in the USA necessarily will have a markedly limited role in the governance of environmental decision-making. In the States, the lack of a federal constitutional environmental mandate forecloses opportunities for the courts to frame new remedies for increasingly problematic environmental issues. This is underscored by the emergence of environmental justice remedies, provided in instances of environmental decisions that invidiously impact on minorities or the poor,[9] since the civil rights laws grow out of a constitutional mandate. Judicial attention to environmental justice suggests how much stronger environmental law could be in the USA if the federal Constitution similarly provided for environmental rights.[10]

When enacting the many environmental statutes in the 1970s, congress creatively invoked the nation's federal framework to provide nation-wide norms while requiring each State to enact implementation legislation tailored appropriately to the legal traditions, economic, geographic and other conditions of each State. Thus, the *Clean Air Act*[11] requires each State to adopt a State Implementation Plan to attain the national primary ambient air quality standards adequate to protect the public health.[12] States are mandated to enact regional solid waste plans to manage refuse. States must further establish water quality standards for all the surface waters in their borders[13] and must establish a State-wide permit system for waste water discharge[14] if they wish to assume regulatory authority over discharges to their waters (otherwise the USA Environment Protection Agency (EPA) governs these). States were given grants to plan and prepare coastal zone management (CZM) land use systems,[15] and once approved, all federal agencies

---

9. See President Executive Order 12,898, 59 Federal Register 7,629 (1994). Regulations of the EPA based on the Civil Rights Act are at 40 Code of Federal Regulations s. 7.35. Typical environmental justice issues are well described in R. Bullar, *Highway Robbery: Transportation Racism and New Routes to Equity* (London: South End Press, 2004).

10. In 1968, congress considered, but failed to act on a proposed environmental amendment to the USA Constitution. See HR Res. 1321, 90th Congress, 2d Session (1968), and R.L. Ottinger, 'Legislation and the Environment: Individual Rights and Government Accountability', *Cornell LR* 55 (1970): 672.

11. 42 US Code s. 7401, et seq.

12. *Ibid.*, s. 110.

13. *Clean Water Act*, 33 US Code s. 1251, at s. 1313.

14. *Ibid.*, s. 1342.

15. *Coastal Zone Management Act*, 15 US Code s. 1451.

must follow the State CZM rules.[16] In order to implement the federal environmental legislation, most States have enacted a parallel set of State environmental statutes.[17] This means that the terminology and normative system for much environmental laws is nation-wide, and when either federal or State courts interpret the laws, they share common concepts and definitional frameworks. This fosters a more consistent national approach to understanding environmental laws, even as they are applied differently in State to State.

While congress and the State legislatures enact the environmental statutes, it is the administrative agencies at the federal and State levels that promulgate the vast sets of highly technical environmental regulations. Rule-making is generically governed by the *Administrative Procedure Act*.[18] All agencies at the federal level, and in those States with comparable laws such as the *New York State Administrative Procedure Act*, must give public notice of the intent to issue a new rule, publish the draft rule, invite public comment, respond to the public comment, and do so all before enacting the new regulation and publishing it. Courts are authorized to oversee compliance with this system. It is also the agencies that issue licenses or permits, and they must do so based on the submission of a public record that demonstrates that the applicant is entitled to the permit sought and with which specific conditions sufficient to protect the environment and the public. When the application is contested, or when the proposed action is such that an EIA is required before the permit may be granted, the agency must receive public comment and consider the comments. The issuance of a permit follows completion of any EIAs, and is accompanied by public notice. In all instances, agencies are legally obligated to provide copies of the documents for rule-making or permit decisions, and most other government documents must be provided to any person who requests them.[19] Because of the complexity of environmental regulations, often agencies are authorized to convene advisory committees of experts. The scheduled meetings of these committees are open to the public, and notice must be given.[20]

All these procedures must be adhered to as fundamental elements of due process of law, and if the courts determine that they have not been followed, agency actions can be remanded to the agency to be taken anew, with sanctions to ensure adherence to due process of law. Often, judicial decisions guide new agency rule-making. For example, federal courts were essential to interpreting the requirements of the *National Environmental Policy Act* 1969,[21] and in 1978, the President's CEQ restated these judicial decisions in drafting the national generic regulations governing the procedures that all federal agencies must follow when

---

16. *Ibid.*, at s. 1456 (enacted and known as the s. 307 'federal consistency clause' under the Coastal Zone Management Act).
17. See the evaluation in K. Engle, 'State Environmental Standard Setting: Is There a "Race" and is it "To the Bottom?"', *Hastings LJ* 48 (1997): 271.
18. 5 US Code, Ch. 5, s. 551 et seq.
19. *Freedom of Information Act* (FOIA), 5 US Code s. 552. Comparable laws exist in many States, e.g. the Freedom of Information Law (FOIL) of the State of New York.
20. Open Meetings are provided for in 5 US Code s. 552(b).
21. 42 US Code s. 4321, et seq.

conducting EIAs.[22] Comparable patterns exist under the independent State laws, with significant variations. These perspectives illustrate that the judicial power is essential to ensuring the integrity of all administrative decision-making, and to helping agencies understand a shared and consistent, definitive understanding of an environmental law.

The chapter further expands on other environmental laws, including the common law, in section 3.3 below, and does so also by specifically indicating how the courts have dealt with some of these laws.

3 OVERVIEW OF THE USA JUDICIARY

3.1 INTRODUCTION

The courts of the States initially were part of, or patterned upon, the courts of the several European nations that colonized North America.[23] The common law system of English jurisprudence prevailed in most of the States along the Atlantic seaboard. New York reflected some of its original Dutch Civil law traditions even after the English regimes took hold. In California, and parts of the south-west, the traditions of Spanish civil law have continued, as have some French civil law traditions in the State of Louisiana. Following the revolution, as each colony became an independent State, it established its own written constitution and, following the accepted wisdom of the Enlightenment Era, these States separated the judiciary from the executive powers and legislature. Imbued with democratic thinking, and opposed to a judiciary of aristocrats, most States provided for the direct election of judges, along with the governors and legislators. In the late twentieth century, election of judges has been criticized, and some States have provided for gubernatorial appointment of judges with legislative confirmation, as is the norm for the federal judiciary. State judges usually serve for specific terms in office, and can be reappointed or re-elected. States elected to continue the rules of the common law until such time as the newly elected State legislature could enact new laws. These State judicial systems continue throughout the nation, and predate the practice of the federal courts. A few States, like New York, have established a Judicial Institute, to provide for continuing judicial education.

When the States negotiated the Constitution for their United States in 1789, in Article III, the States provided for an independent Supreme Court and authorized the legislature, by statute, to establish all subsidiary systems of federal courts. States may bring suits against other States directly in the Supreme Court, and

---

22. 40 Code of Federal Regulations, Part 1500; see commentary at 43 Federal Register 55,990 (28 November 1978). See also the report of the US President's Council on Environmental Quality, CEQ, 'The National Environmental Policy Act: A Study of its Effectiveness After 25 Years, 1997', <www.whitehouse.gov/ceq>, 12 September 2008.

23. See, generally, L. Friedman, *A History of American Law* (New York: Simon & Schuster, 1973) and M. Horowitz, *The Transformation of American Law, 1780-1860* (Harvard: HUP, 1977).

have done so regarding environmental matters.[24] Through adopting the *Judiciary Act*, Congress established the federal court system. All federal judges are appointed by the president, and confirmed by vote of the senate upon recommendation of the Judiciary Committee. They serve for life, and may only be removed by formal impeachment proceedings.

The federal courts are divided into circuits, and within each circuit, into districts. The court of first instance is the Federal District Court, which hears civil cases and criminal trials. To cope with the growing volume of litigation in federal courts, congress has established federal magistrates, serving under the District Court Judges. Magistrates hear many criminal and civil procedural matters, freeing up the District Court judges to preside over trials. The Federal Rules of Civil Procedure and the Federal Rules of Criminal Procedure apply to all these deliberations nation-wide. For example, when sufficient numbers of urban dwellers retreat to popular parks, such as Yosemite National Park, there is a USA Magistrate's Court to hear criminal matters arising in the park.

Federal appeals from the District Courts are heard by a panel of three appellate judges for the Circuit Court of Appeals where the district is situated. The circuit can elect to have selected appeals reheard by the full complement of all circuit judges, sitting *en banc*. Appeals from the Circuit Court then may be taken up by the USA Supreme Court if the court grants a *Writ of Certiorari* to hear the appeal. The court grants such appeals selectively, for instance, in order to clarify the law when different circuit courts arrive at inconsistent interpretations of the same federal statute, or to hear matters interpreting the Constitution, or to review a decision otherwise raising questions deemed important by the court. To handle the volume of appeals of national importance, without burdening the Supreme Court, congress created an Appeals Circuit for the District of Columbia, which handles a large number of appeals involving federal statutes, including environmental legislation. Congress also has established specialized courts, for instance, the Court of International Trade located in New York City. Congress further has authorized major federal agencies to establish their own administrative court systems, such as those for the one third of USA territory governed as federal public lands under the cabinet-level Department of the Interior, or for the environmental quality laws under the non-cabinet-level USA EPA, or for the licensing of nuclear electrical generating facilities by the Nuclear Regulatory Commission's licensing and appeals boards, established under the *Atomic Energy Act* 1954.

In addition, land use and natural resources matters involving the sovereign Indian Tribes, are heard in Tribal Courts where the nations have established such courts. Within the lands reserved for these nations, their courts are independent of the State or federal systems. The federal environmental laws often provide that Tribal Courts can apply environmental law statutes.[25] In the Caribbean, there is a

---

24. See, e.g., *New York v. New Jersey*, 256 US 296 (1921), regarding equitably apportionment of the waters of the Delaware River, or *Wisconsin v. Illinois*, 281 US 179 and 690 (1930) ordering abatement of water pollution from one State into another.
25. See, e.g., under the Clean Water Act, s. 518.

federal court for Puerto Rico and the Virgin Islands, but there is also an independent court system established under the independent authority of Puerto Rico, applying its civil law and other commonwealth laws.

3.2   THE COURTS AND ENVIRONMENTAL ISSUES (GENERAL
            OBSERVATIONS)

The roots of modern environmental law in the USA can be found in important judicial decisions such as *Scenic Hudson Preservation Conference v. Federal Power Commission* (1966).[26] This ruling was a factor in congress' enactment of the *National Environmental Policy Act* 1969, and in the subsequent enactment of several federal statutes authorizing 'citizen suits' to seek judicial orders compelling implementation of environmental legislation. In contrast to the early success of public interest environmental litigation, much of the ensuing four decades of extensive environmental judicial decision-making in the federal (and some State) courts across the USA have actually retarded attaining statutory objectives for restoring environmental quality. This is because most environmental lawsuits have been commenced by industry, in order to secure judicial review of administrative regulations in order to nullify their promulgation and secure their remand back to agencies for redrafting. Moreover, since the federal Constitution makes no provision for environmental rights, the property-rights orientation of the USA Supreme Court precludes it from examining the remedial and progressive interpretations of environmental statutes. On the other hand, when the government prosecutes persons for violations of these same statutes, the courts treat the criminal environmental laws carefully and not unlike prosecution for other sectors.[27] Criminal environmental law has become an important aspect of law enforcement.[28]

It is remarkable how the federal courts respond to the nature of each environmental case, and the legal presumptions applicable in each. In government prosecutions, courts follow their customary rules. In judicial review, the economic plaintiff has a strategic advantage and most often prevails over the administrative agency. In citizen suits, the fact of commencing the lawsuit produced salutary political responses, and while private parties often settle rather than contest the suits, the courts are less disposed to consider the environmentalists' claims.

---

26. 354 F. 2d 608 (2nd Cir., 1965).
27. Environmental statutes make companies and the corporate officers and employees who make decisions, each criminally liable. See, e.g., *US v. Northeastern Pharmaceutical & Chemical Co.*, 810 F. 2d 726 (8th Cir. 1986), or *US v. Weitzenhoff*, 35 F. 3d 1275 (9th Cir., 1994), or *US v. Hopkins*, 53 F. 3d 533 (2d Cir., 1995). Many environmental crimes are classified as felonies and convicted individuals are regularly sentenced to serve time in jail.
28. R.J. Lazarus, 'Meeting the Demands of Integration in the Evolution of Environmental Law: Reforming Environmental Criminal Law', *GLJ* 83 (1995): 2407; see the response in L.J. Schiffer & J.F. Simon, 'The Reality of Prosecuting Environmental Criminals: A Response to Professor Lazarus', *GLJ* 83 (1995): 2531.

While pubic interest litigation rarely induces courts to expand the substantive scope of environmental laws, it does sustain the procedural rights that environmental statutes provide. Access to the courts throughout the USA affords environmentalists their most important environmental opportunities. By submitting to courts' legal claims questioning governmental decisions affecting nature conservation, public health or resource management, citizen plaintiffs shine light on how environmental quality is sustained or compromised. Since freedom of information laws and EIA laws afford citizens access to most environmental data in government files, the environmental plaintiff can evaluate when claims of environmental rights can be asserted. When such claims are combined with other rights, such as those posed by the environmental justice movement, the courts become an important factor in environmental governance.

The role that the judiciary serves in the environmental governance at federal and State levels within the USA can be illustrated with reference to: (a) the common law and statutory foundations for judicially cognizable rights, and (b) the courts' responsibilities in judicial review of administrative decisions. These aspects are explored below.

3.3   LEGAL FOUNDATIONS FOR JUDICIAL DECISIONS

The common law provides several rights that courts traditionally have recognized and applied. These rights are founded on State law, as received from the practice in England.[29] Both federal and State courts in the USA rely upon the restatements, prepared by the American Law Institute,[30] to frame the judicial recognition of the laws governing the doctrines of public nuisance, private nuisance, negligence, trespass, and riparian property rights. In addition, the public trust doctrine arises in the common law, and ensures the public access to the foreshores and navigable waters of the several States. Any person whose actual and demonstrative injury or aggrievement, by virtue of a violation of a common law duty, is deemed to have standing (*locus standi*) to file a claim with a State court to enforce such a right. When a common law claim is alleged on the same facts that give rise to a claim arising under a federal statute, the individual plaintiff can raise that claim in federal court under the doctrine of pendant jurisdiction. In deciding the common law claims, the federal judge must apply the law of the State where the claim arises.

Environmental claims, especially where widespread pollution is caused by a number of actors, are difficult for common law courts to consider. The courts cannot often simply assess evidence to find a wrong and then determine a concomitant financial penalty. Judicial process has proven ill equipped to cope with complex evidentiary challenges, for instance, in establishing causation in claims of negligence, or to cope with difficulties in framing and overseeing an equitable remedy to abate pollution or to restore a natural area. In one classic

---

29. See W.L. Prosser, *Handbook on the Law of Torts*, 4th ed. (St. Paul, Minn.: West Group, 1971).
30. See, e.g., The Restatement of Torts Second (1978).

decision, *Boomer v. Atlantic Cement Company*,[31] New York's highest court refused to enjoin pollution from a cement works on the grounds that the remedy should be part of a comprehensive solution to pollution, which required statutory reforms from the legislation or administrative regulations from an environmental agency. That court would only assess money damages for past pollution, making clear its expectation that it was the legislature's duty to solve the pollution problems of the entire cement industry, not the court's. In contrast, where there have been instances of threats to the broader and traditional public rights of access to navigable waters guaranteed in the public trust doctrine, courts have issued injunctions to guarantee continued public access to areas where the trust applied.[32] Examples of such enforcement include instances where parties sought to deny navigation access by fill placed in lakes in Massachusetts or estuarine mud flats in California, or across access to Chicago's waterfront, in *Illinois Central Railroad v. Illinois*.[33] However, in matters where local governmental land use decisions allowed real estate development, as in a housing subdivision encroaching on agricultural lands, the Supreme Court of Arizona in *Spur Industries, Inc. v. Del E. Webb Development Co.*,[34] refused to allow continued uninterrupted animal husbandry practices when residents complained of a nuisance, even through the residents 'came to the nuisance'.

Federal and State courts have most often applied common law rights in traditionally well accepted settings, for instance, when courts affirm a common law right by assessing money damages. Since the 1960s, throughout courts in the USA, the common law has rarely afforded a significant basis for courts to be a significant factor in environmental decision-making. Extensive environmental legislation substantially precludes the courts from expanding common law remedies and causes of action.

Most environmental quality laws at the federal level apply to all States through the Constitution's provision that congress regulates commerce among the States, with the Indian nations in North America, and internationally. In 2007, the USA Supreme Court affirmed this constitutional foundation implicitly in its decision that the EPA must regulate carbon dioxide emissions as greenhouse gas 'pollutants,' in *Massachusetts v. EPA*.[35] Since air and water pollution, or the trade in chemicals and movements of hazardous wastes affect commerce, congress has adopted systems for uniform national environmental laws through the *Clean Air Act* (1970),[36] the *Clean Water Act* (1972),[37] the *Toxic Substances Control Act*,[38] the *Comprehensive Environmental Response, Compensation and Liability Act*

---

31. 26 NY 219 (1970).
32. J.L. Sax, 'The Public Trust Doctrine in Natural Resources Law: Effective Judicial Intervention', *Mich. LR* 68 (1970): 471.
33. 146 US 387 (1892).
34. 108 Ariz. 178 (1972).
35. 127 SC 1438, 167 L. Ed. 2d 248 (2007).
36. 42 US Code 7401, et seq.
37. 33 US Code 1251, et seq.
38. 15 US 2601, et seq.

(CERCLA, or Superfund) (1980),[39] the *Oil Pollution Act* (1990),[40] and other laws. The EPA administers these environmental quality laws.

Most federal natural resource laws arise from congressional duties to manage the public lands of the USA, under the property clause of the Constitution. Only the *Surface Mining Control and Reclamation Act* 1977 has been grounded on the commerce clause- a situation similar to the environmental quality statutes. The *Multiple-Use Sustained-Yield Act* 1960,[41] along with the *Forest and Rangeland Renewable Resources Planning Act*,[42] and other legislation for national forests, are administered through the Department of Agriculture. The *Federal Land Policy and Management Act* 1976,[43] along with a large body of statutes governing lease or sale of minerals found on public lands, and the administration of national parks and most wilderness areas, through the Department of the Interior. The natural resources regime for the marine environment falls under the National Oceanographic and Atmospheric Administration; federal marine jurisdiction is for the first twelve miles, and then governs the exclusive economic zone for 200 miles off shore. Beyond the federal lands in the western States and Alaska, it is the State governments that regulate most natural resources.

State natural resource laws govern forests, fish and game and other wildlife, soil conservation, mining and mined land reclamation, water allocation and use, urban tree conservation, watershed management, and a host of issues specific to each State. States govern coastal land uses and have jurisdiction three miles into the ocean. All States have well established State park systems. State regimes vary; for instance, Nebraska regulates land use on the scale of watershed catchment areas. New York had established the largest wilderness area outside of Alaska; the Adirondack and Catskill Forest Preserve encompasses parklands larger than Yellowstone, Yosemite and the Grand Canyon combined. Illinois has a State-wide inventory of all biological resources. The States embracing the Great Lakes have adopted a Great Lakes Compact to coordinate their water and coastal management with the adjacent provinces of Canada. States have long maintained extensive departments of public health and agriculture, and set standards of environmental education in school curricula. The full description of such varied State environmental statutes is beyond the scope of this analysis, but all such State administrative programs are subject to judicial oversight.

Under the Fifth Amendment of the USA Constitution, applicable also to the State governments by virtue of the Fourteenth Amendment, the USA Supreme Court has ruled that State governments may regulate private property through rules and regulations in order to prevent conduct that would cause a public nuisance. For instance, laws that restrict real estate development to preserve the environmental quality of Lake Tahoe, shared by California and Nevada,

---

39. 42 US Code 9601, et seq.
40. 33 US 2701, et seq.
41. 16 US Code ss 528 to 531.
42. 16 US Code 1600, et seq.
43. 43 US Code 1701, et seq.

are deemed not to be a 'taking' of a property right (*Tahoe-Sierra Preservation Council v. Tahoe Regional Planning Agency*),[44] nor are laws for land use and zoning (town and country planning) laws, (*Village of Euclid v. Amber Realty Co.*),[45] nor those that protect historically important cultural heritage, (*Penn Central Transportation Co. v. City of New York*).[46] The Supreme Court has found that these State environmental controls are not regulatory takings.

Each of the major federal environmental statues makes a provision for citizens to enforce their provisions. For instance, section 505 of the *Clean Water Act* provides that 'any citizen' may commence a civil action on his own behalf against any person (including the USA and any other governmental instrumentalities) who is alleged to be in violation of the Act or a standard adopted under its authority. State legislatures have followed the federal statutes in providing similar remedies for citizens to enforce the environmental quality laws.[47] Each year, throughout the USA, environmental non-governmental organizations (NGOs) (such as the Sierra Club, EarthJustice and the Natural Resources Defense Council, or regional groups such as the Riverkeeper for the Hudson River or for the Delaware River), sue to enforce the laws against water polluters. The citizen plaintiffs bring the same sort of enforcement action that the federal or State agencies could bring, but often do not because they lack personnel, technical or other resources, or the political will to act. The courts handle such cases as routine enforcement actions, with the polluters often electing to settle the suit rather than be found to have violated the law.[48] Under environmental aspects of the USA securities and corporate laws, if a company is found liable by a court, it must report the fact to its shareholders and cannot deduct the fines for tax purposes as an expense. When a company settles a citizen suit, for instance by agreeing to an order confirming that it has ended its polluting activities, and by making a payment to restore environmental damage or provide a new environmental amenity (such as a riverside park), these payments can be deducted as business expenses before profits are computed for income tax purposes, and are not a direct reduction on the profits. Most citizen suit matters do not reach the appellate courts, because the parties settle or do not appeal. However, when the Supreme Court had considered such matters, it has been hostile to expanding citizen suits.

Defendants have fought against expanding the role of citizen suits, and the USA Supreme Court has accommodated them. In *Gwaltney of Smithfield Ltd v. Chesapeake Bay Foundation* (1987),[49] the court ruled that a citizen suit under the

---

44. 535 US 302 (2002).
45. 272 US 365 (1926).
46. 438 US 104 (1978).
47. See, generally, S. Novick, *Law of Environmental Protection*, vol. 2 (Deerfield, IL: Clark Boardman Callaghan, 1987), s. 12.02[8].
48. Settlements have generated some backlash. See D. Mann, 'Polluter-Financed Environmentally Beneficial Expenditures: Effective Use or Improper Abuse of Citizen Suits Under the Clean Water Act', *EL* 21 (1991): 175 (commentary).
49. 484 US 49 (1987). On remand, the lower courts allowed the plaintiffs to show 'a good faith allegation of ongoing violation' so that the defendant could not evade the suit. *Chesapeake Bay*

Clean Water Act could not continue once the polluter ceased discharges, since section 505 conferred authority to sue against persons 'in violation,' meaning a continuous and on-going act. Once the polluter stopped discharging waste, citizen enforcement is no longer authorized. Congress corrected this interpretation in amendments to the *Clean Air Act*, allowing suits for past air violations to be continued to a point of closure even if the air discharge ceased. Congress has not yet enacted similar provisions for the *Clean Water Act* or the other laws, since President Bush and the Republican majority prevented the amendments from moving forward. The Supreme Court has also sought to limit the scope of standing to sue in citizen suit matters.[50]

Across all the environmental statutes, congress has thus provided a procedural basis for citizen to seek observance of environmental law. The substantive norms for environmental protection are strong, if incomplete in their scope. Unfortunately, the administrative law procedures to ensuring that administrative agencies comply with these statutes has delayed or diminished the efficacy of environmental laws.

3.4   ADMINISTRATIVE LAW AND JUDICIAL REVIEW

While citizen suits often receive widespread attention, alleging (as they do) a violation of the law, less attention is given to the many, complex law suits filed by economic interests seeking judicial review of proposed agency regulations designed to implement statutes. The number of citizen suits is relatively few compared to the number of cases filed by companies and trade associations and property owners seeking judicial review of governmental administrative rules that would restrict their activities. While citizen environmental plaintiffs brought some judicial review cases to stall attempts by the administration of President George W. Bush to repeal or reinterpret regulations based on the major environmental statutes, the greatest use of judicial review has been by corporate economic interests.

Through the many environmental statutes, congress mandates that the EPA study environmental problems and issue rules to abate them. If a company or trade association can secure a court ruling that invalidates a regulation issued by the EPA on some procedural ground, it invariably wins a ruling remanding the matter for new rule-making. The company has avoided complying with the new regulation pending the litigation (one to three years), and again pending the remand (one to three years of renewed rule-making, with public comment). The company or trade association has won anywhere from three to six or more years of continuing

———
Foundation v. Gwaltney of Smithfield Ltd 844 F. 2d 170 (4th Cir.), and the trial court found a likelihood of continuing violation. *Id.*, at 688 F. Supp. 1078 (E.D. Va, 1988), *aff'd* 890 F. 2d 690. A penalty of USD 289,822 for nitrogen discharges was affirmed. See generally the note by L.R. Okster, 'Smithfield Foods: A Case for Federal Action', *Wm & Mary Envr'l L. & Pol. Rev.* 23 (1999): 381-390.
50.   See, e.g., *Friends of the Earth v. Laidlaw Environmental Services*, 528 US 167 (2000).

business as usual, and environmentalists have seen the environmental problem in question persist much longer than when congress mandated it be abated.

This pattern, whereby vested economic interests employ judicial review to avert or avoid the impact of environmental regulation, is based on sound administrative law concepts. In 1946, congress enacted the *Administrative Procedure Act* (APA) to allow the judiciary to have oversight of how the growing numbers of administrative agencies used or misused the authority that congress had conferred upon them. Under section 10 of the APA:

> A person suffering legal wrong because of agency action, or adversely affected or aggrieved by agency action, within the meaning of the relevant statute, is entitled to judicial review thereof.[51]

The scope of judicial review includes whether the agency acted in an arbitrary or capricious way or an abuse of discretion, or in excess of statutory authority, or without observance of proper procedures, or in a way unsupported by substantial evidence.[52] In enacting environmental laws, congress elaborated on this basic allocation of judicial review to provide detailed rules for how national clean water[53] or clean air[54] regulations should be reviewed. The courts have had to devote substantial time to interpreting the procedures for how environmental judicial review should take place, and this has further delayed implementation of the environmental statutes.

For example, *Lead Industries v. EPA*[55] challenged the EPA's evidence in establishing the exposure standards in the National Ambient Air Quality Standards to protect the public health from exposure to lead. The standard was upheld, ruling that the *Clean Air Act* did not allow economic factors to limit the establishment of health based standards. The empirical evidence on lead is clear, and the 1990 amendments to the *Clean Air Act* set the stage for the EPA to study and to strengthen protection of the public against lead poisoning.[56] Notwithstanding the clear statutory language, and this prior decision confirming the statute, when President Bush's first EPA administrator strengthened the lead exposure rules, a trade association sued to forestall the new rules on the grounds that the economic factors should have been considered. In *Whitman v. American Trucking Association*,[57] the Supreme Court rejected this argument, but found grounds to remand some aspects of the rulemaking back to the EPA. The plaintiffs lost on the merits, but their litigation won them time, delaying the impact of new rules. On the other hand, the public health was denied the statutory promise of new protection.

---

51. 5 US Code s. 702.
52. 5 US Code s. 706.
53. S. 509, 33 US Code s. 509.
54. S. 307, 42 US Code s. 7607.
55. 478 F. 2d 1130 (DC Cir., 1980).
56. L. Johannes, 'New Study Shows Need for Tougher Air Rules', *WSJ* 2 (2000): B10.
57. 531 US 457 (2001).

In like vein, many regulations to implement the *Clean Water Act* were delayed. The EPA provided every industrial sector in the nation with technology-based effluent limitations. The Supreme Court upheld the legislation's mandate in *EPA v. National Crushed Stone Association*.[58] Nonetheless, in the next decade, economic interests challenged the validity of twenty-seven sets of effluent guidelines. The EPA process had legitimate problems, but judicial review did little to help solve them.[59]

Beyond the problems that have emerged for judicial review of environmental regulations under the APA, the hostility to environmental regulation by President George W. Bush and his congressional allies has resulted in the promulgation of new administrative rules, making it even more difficult for the EPA to promulgate any rule. In 2000, vested economic interests secured enactment by Congress of the *Information Quality Act*,[60] without the benefit of hearings. The Act required the Office of Management and Budget (OMB) in the President's Executive Office to issue guidelines ensuring and maximizing the quality, objectivity, utility and integrity of information (including statistical information) disseminated by Federal Agencies. The OMB issued its rules in 2002,[61] and these made it both more cumbersome and difficult for agencies to issue rules, and also provided an enormous new set of issues that could be subject to judicial review. These developments have created opportunities for abuse of administrative procedures that make implementation of new or revised environmental standards very difficult. Use of judicial review, in turn, makes the judicial process complicit in the executive branch's efforts to avert or avoid strengthening of environmental law. Leading environmental law commentators have branded this abuse of administrative law as 'sophisticated sabotage'.[62]

4   ANALYSIS OF SIGNIFICANT ENVIRONMENTAL
           JUDGMENTS

4.1   INTRODUCTION

Any thorough evaluation of federal and State environmental case law is well beyond the scope of this analysis; the volume of decided cases is overwhelming, and the cases often technical and lengthy, many with lengthy written decisions of fifty pages or longer. Many of the 'leading' cases have been evaluated historically.[63]

---

58. 449 US 64 (1980).
59. See the analysis in W. Pederson, 'Turning the Tide on Water Quality' *Ecology LQ* 15 (1988): 69.
60. S. 515 of Title V or Public Law 106-554, contained within the Fiscal Year 2001 Treasury and General Government Appropriations Act.
61. 67 Federal Register 8452.
62. T.O. McGarity, S. Shapiro & D. Bollier, *Sophisticated Sabotage: The Intellectual Games used to Subvert Responsible Regulation* (Washington, DC: ELI, 2004).
63. R.J. Lazarus & O.A. Houck (eds), *Environmental Law Stories* (New York: Thomson West, 2005).

Most cases are technical and limited to their facts, and have contributed little to strengthen the canon of environmental judicial interpretation.

Many rulings, in fact, have limited the scope of environmental law. One pattern of USA Supreme Court cases illustrates this phenomenon. The Supreme Court gradually limited the scope of EIA under the *National Environmental Policy Act*.[64] These cases illustrate a larger opposition by vested 'business as usual' interests to environmental analysis.[65] The court's decisions do require agencies to adhere to rigorous environmental assessments, but then permit the federal agency to use its discretion to ignore the environmental mitigation measures that the assessments have revealed. Beyond being illogical, this body of case law is inconsistent with the language of section 102(2)(c) NEPA and runs counter to comparable international EIA practice in the European Union, Canada, and elsewhere. The State Supreme Court of California and the New York Court of Appeals have not followed the USA Supreme Court's line of decisions. These States require that agencies substantively mitigate any adverse environmental impacts that the EIA process reveals is reasonably possible.[66]

From the perspective of understanding how judicial rulings can strengthen environmental law, comparative study may most usefully focus on those select court decisions that point to ways whereby courts may strengthen and enhance human stewardship of the environment, and advance sustainable development. Three important cases reflect some of the most insightful environmental deliberations by courts in the USA.

4.2   Burdens of Proof: Observing the Land Ethic

State courts have undertaken procedural reforms that place the burden of proof on the party who is alleged to be harming the environment, to show that the threatened harm is or will be avoided. The 'land ethic' advocated by Aldo Leopold, provides a normative basis for courts to apply such a burden of proof rule. As environmental quality deteriorates, society requires observance of environmental laws; when a person, including a governmental agency, proposes to act to harm the environment, the land ethic assigns to that person the obligation of establishing that the proposed act in fact will not harm the environment in violation of the law. The plaintiff need only ask the court to review the intended action, with the burden of proof at the

---

64. This began with a divided court deciding *Vermont Yankee Nuclear Power Corp v. NRDC*, 435 US 519 (1978), reversing consistent interpretations by the circuit courts in the District of Columbia Circuit, (2d Cir.), and elsewhere. See the unanimous decision in *Marsh v. Oregon Natural Resources Council*, 490 US 360 (1989).
65. R.G. Dreher, 'NEPA Under Siege: The Political Assault on the National Environmental Policy Act', *Geo. Envtl. L. & Pol'y Inst.* (2005), <www.law.georgetown.edu/gelpi/news/ documents/ NEPAUnderSiegeFinal.pdf>, 12 September 2008.
66. M.B. Gerrard, D.A. Ruzow & P. Weinstein, Environmental Impact Review in New York (New York: Matthew Bender, 1990).

outset shifting to the defendant to prove his conduct is not harmful to the environment. The State of Minnesota has adopted legislation in this respect.[67]

Minnesota's statute has caused the State's governmental authorities to be more careful in their environmental decision-making. The courts have implemented the procedure. For instance, in the case of a road that would have bisected a freshwater wetland that was shared by two adjacent farms, the highway department had not examined alternative routes that might protect the wetland. One farmer allowed the siting of the road in his real property, but the neighboring farmer feared for the harm to the entire wetland itself, which was one ecological system crossing both farms. The Supreme Court of Minnesota, in an opinion by Mr Justice Yetka, cited the land ethic as a rule of law as follows:

> A generation ago, the conservationist Aldo Leopold espoused a 'land ethic' which he described as follows: 'All ethics so far evolved rest upon a single premise: that the individual is a member of a community of interdependent parts. His instincts prompt him to compete for his place in the community, but his ethics prompt him also to co-operate (perhaps in order that there may be a place to compete for). The land ethic simply enlarges the boundaries of the community to include solids, waters plants and animals, or collectively: the land. In short, a land ethic changes the role of Homo Sapiens from conqueror of the land-community to plain member and citizen of it. It implies respect for his fellow-members, and also respect for the community as such' . . . In the Environmental Rights Act, our state legislature has given this ethic the force of law.[68]

The Minnesota Supreme Court sustained the ecological unit of the wetland, and required the highway department to show that it considered alternative routes that would have protected the wetlands. The court wrote:

> To some of our citizens, a swamp or marshland is physically unattractive, an inconvenience to cross by foot and an obstacle to road construction or improvement. However, to an increasing number of our citizens who have become concerned enough about the vanishing wetlands to seek legislative relief, a swamp or marsh is a thing of beauty. To one who is willing to risk wet feet to walk though it, a marsh frequently contains a springy soft moss, vegetation of many varieties, and wildlife not normally seen on higher ground. It is quiet and peaceful – the most ancient of cathedrals – antedating the oldest of manmade structures. More than that, it acts as nature's sponge, holding heavy moisture to prevent flooding during heavy rainfalls and slowly releasing the moisture and maintaining the water tables during dry cycles. In short, marshes and swamps are something to protect and preserve.[69]

---

67. 'Environmental Rights Act' Min. St. 116B.01. The shifting of the burden of proof is at Min. St. 116B.04.
68. *County of Bryson v. Freeborn* 309 Minn. 178, 243 NW 2d 316 (1976), quoting from A Sand County Almanac, 203.
69. *Ibid.*, 189.

Minnesota has continued to apply the land ethic as a rule of law since this decision in 1976.[70] The Supreme Court of Wisconsin has taken up the land ethic as a rule of law under hazardous waste land remediation laws.[71] In considering whether the legislature intended an owner of property containing contaminated soil to take remedial action, this court stated:

> Aldo Leopold, the great Wisconsin conservationist in his well-known work, A Sand County Almanac, (1948) at p. 203 said: 'Individual thinkers since the days of Ezekiel and Isaiah have asserted that the despoliation of land is not only inexpedient but wrong.' The statutes under consideration are a legislative recognition that the discharge of hazardous substances is one form of despoliation. The legislature has enacted this law to correct that wrong.[72]

While courts in Minnesota, Michigan and Wisconsin have recognized the land ethic, it remains for other States to study and emulate these cases.

4.3   'TECHNOLOGY FORCING': REVERSING DEGRADING PRACTICES

One of the innovations in the 1970 *Clean Air Act* is that it establishes a clear duty to protect the public health from air pollution. Simply because conduct was authorized and useful, as in burning oil or coal to produce needed electricity, did not sanction poisoning the air that everyone must breathe. Congress required the EPA to study and promulgate a national ambient air quality standard, requisite to protect the public health 'allowing an adequate margin of safety'.[73] Each State implementation plan is to assure that all the air within the State meets this standard.[74] In St. Louis, Missouri, the Union Electric Company argued that it was economically and technologically unfeasible for it to meet this standard. In *Union Electric Company v. EPA*,[75] the USA Supreme Court held that the statute establishes a clear public health standard that had to be met, by finding new technology or closing down the polluting activities. The court allowed Missouri, in its implementation plan, to force the company to find or invent the needed new technology. This inducement process has been termed, 'technology forcing'.

---

70. See, e.g., *In The Matter of the Application of Allard Christenson* 417 NW 2d 607, 18 *ELR* 20,947 (1987): 'We reaffirm our statement that the state's environmental legislation had given this land ethic the force of law, and imposed on the courts a duty to support the legislative goal of protecting the state's environmental resources.' See also *McLeod County Bd of Commissioners v. State* 549 NW 2d 630 (1996).
71. Wis. State s. 144.76(3).
72. *Grube v. Daun*, 210 Wis. 2d 681, 593 N.W. 2d 523 (1997), citing *State v Mauthe*, 123 Wisc. 2d 288, 366 N.W. 2d 871 (1985).
73. S. 109, Clean Air Act, 42 US Code 7409.
74. S. 110, Clean Air Act, 42 US Code 7410.
75. 427 US 246 (1976).

In his decision for the court, Mr Justice Marshall explained technology forcing as follows:

> The 1970 Amendments to the Clean Air Act were a drastic remedy to what was perceived as a serious and otherwise unchecked problem of air pollution. The Amendments place the primary responsibility for formulating pollution control strategies on the States, but nonetheless subject the States to strict minimum compliance requirements. These requirements are of a 'technology-forcing character,' Train v. NRDC [421 US 60 (1975)], and are expressly designed to force regulated sources to develop pollution control devises that might at the same time appear to be economically or technologically infeasible.... The State has virtually absolute power in allocating emission limitations so long as the national standards are met ... Congress plainly left with the States, so long as the national standards were met, the power to determine which sources would be burdened by regulation and to what extent. Technology forcing is a concept somewhat new to our national experience and it necessarily entails certain risks. But Congress considered those risks in passing the 1970 Amendment and decided that the dangers posed by uncontrolled air pollution made them worth taking.

Technology forcing has been used for the rapid elimination of the use of chlorofluorocarbons and other substances that deplete the stratospheric ozone layer.[76] Opponents to using technology forcing laws have been able to promote the use of economic incentives, or emission trading schemes, or voluntary codes, as alternatives. Very little use has been made of the legal procedures for technology forcing. Unfortunately, there is little evidence these have induced the development of much needed innovative technological practices.[77]

4.4   SAFEGUARDING THE NATURAL INTEGRITY OF WILD FORESTS

Since 1894, New York State's Constitution provides that the forest preserve in the Adirondack and Catskill mountains 'shall be kept as forever wild forest land'.[78] In the 1880s and into the 1890s, unprincipled timbering activities were clear-cutting the Adirondacks and causing vast flooding and forest fires. The loss of biodiversity was acute, and flooding, erosion and siltation were widespread. Legislative attempts to license and regulate the conduct had been corrupted by bribery, incompetence, and a lack of enforcement resources. The forest preserve provided much of the freshwater resources of the State, and to safeguard the forests and their

---

76. Congress made releases of CFCs illegal in 1990 in the Clean Air Act Amendments of that year, in response to the agreements in London under the Vienna Convention to Protect the Stratospheric Ozone. Public Law 101-549, at 42 US Code 7671, et seq.
77. See D. Dudeck & J. Palmisano, 'Emissions Trading: Why is This Thoroughbred Hobbled?', *Colum. J. Envt'l L.* 13 (1988): 217-256.
78. Article XIV, Constitution of the State of New York.

hydrologic resources, the voters adopted a Constitution to bar all economic activity in the preserve. Sustainable development was allowed on adjacent lands. To ensure that the 'forever wild' protection was observed, the constitutional amendment allowed any one to bring a law suit to the courts to enforce this constitutional provision. This may be the first 'citizen suit' authority enacted in law, just as this is the first legislative mandate for maintaining wilderness.

A NGO, the Association for the Protection of the Adirondacks,[79] commenced judicial enforcement of the 'forever wild' provisions, against some of New York's most powerful political and economic forces, securing the Court of Appeal's landmark decision in *Association for the Protection of the Adirondacks v. MacDonald*. In order to develop a Bobsled run for the 1932 Winter Olympics, the Olympic Organizing Committee arranged for legislation to be enacted, and signed by Governor Franklin Roosevelt, authorizing the new sports facility at Lake Placid 'on lands in which any necessary easement may be provided'.[80] The Olympic Committee sought to encroach on 'forever wild' forest lands by securing an easement for their new facility. The State's Conservation Department cooperated with the Committee rather than defend the 'forever wild' mandate. The encroachment seemed small to everyone, except the defenders of the wilderness. The nationally renowned constitutional law expert, Louis Marshall, a leader of the association, observed: 'My experience tells me that a latitudinarian interpretation, on the theory that the violation is unimportant and trivial, invariably leads to an effective neutralization of the constitutional provision so treated'.[81] The association invoked its right under the Constitution to sue to compel observance of the 'forever wild' mandate.

The Appellate Division of the Supreme Court held against the Conservation Department's decision to allow the bobsled run, holding that under the State's Constitution, the forest preserve 'must always retain the character of a wilderness'.[82] Rather than accept this ruling, the Attorney General appealed to the Court of Appeals. In 1930, New York's highest court, writing through Judge Frederick C. Craine, closed the door on the 'latitudinarian' thinking that characterized the government's response to the 'forever wild' mandate between 1894 and 1929. The court held, plainly, that the 'Adirondack Park was to be preserved, not destroyed'.[83] The court rejected the attempt of the legislature, abetted by the governor and his Conservation Department, in effect to amend the Constitution by a statute. The forest preserve trees 'cannot be cut or removed to construct a toboggan slide simply and solely for the reason that . . . [the 'forever wild' mandate

---

79. The Association's legal work is reported at APA, 'The Association for Protection of the Adirondacks', <www.protectadks.org>, 12 September 2008.
80. L. 1929, L. 417.
81. Cited in F. Graham Jr, *The Adirondack Park: A Political History* (New York: Knopf, 1978), 187, taken from personal correspondence of Louis Marshall, in C. Reznikoff (ed.), *Louis Marshall: Champion of Liberty*, vol. II (Philadelphia: JPSA, 1957), 1063.
82. *Association for the Protection of the Adirondacks v. MacDonald*, 278 App. Div. 73 at 81 (1929).
83. *Association for the Protection of the Adirondacks v. MacDonald*, 253 NY 234, 170 N.E. 902 (1930).

in] the Constitution says it cannot be done'.[84] The court explained the duty that
governmental authorities have toward the forest preserve under Article XIV:

> The forests were to be preserved as wild forest lands, and the trees were not to
> be sold or removed or destroyed.[85] . . . A very considerable use may be made
> by campers and others without in any way interfering with this purpose of
> preserving as wild forest lands.[86]

It proceeded to state that:

> Therefore all things necessary [for preservation of the forest preserve] were
> permitted, such as measures to prevent forest fires, the repair to roads and
> proper inspection, or the erection and maintenance of proper facilities for the
> use by the public which did not call for the removal of the timber in any
> material degree. The Forest Preserve is preserved for the public; its benefits
> are for the people of the State as a whole. Whatever the advantages may be of
> having wild forest lands preserved in their natural state, the advantages are for
> everyone within the State and for the use of the people of the State. Unless
> prohibited by the constitutional provision, this use and preservation are subject
> to the reasonable regulations of the Legislature.[87]

The Court of Appeals in the *MacDonald* ruling invited the legislature to further
clarify how the State is to sustain 'forever wild forests' so that the people may
derive the myriad benefits simply of spending time amidst wild nature. It is clear
that wild forest lands cannot include new roads, or many other uses that occasionally in the past have been allowed to encroach on the forest preserve. The legislature eventually did enact reasonable further land use regulations, established an
Adirondack Park Agency to ensure that private lands are used only in ways that
protect the forest preserve, and provided authority for the Department of Environmental Conservation to promulgate the Adirondack State Land Master Plan.[88]

4.5   CRITICAL SURVEY

The three cases discussed above indicate how the courts are always essential to
reaffirming the rule of law, but can also provide great value by examining and
sustaining the underlying environmental values that the Constitution or statute
singles out. The environmental values cannot exist apart from the natural world
that produced them. When a democracy protects nature for the benefit of all, its

---

84. *Id.*, 253 NY 240.
85. *Id.*, 253 NY 240.
86. *Id.*, 253 NY 241.
87. *Id.*, 253 NY 238-239.
88. McKinney's, *supra* n. 6, Title 8, Forest Resources Planning, Art. 9, Lands and Forests, NYS.
     Environmental Conservation Law of the State of New York.

legislative decision carries a superior ranking, above laws that afford economic opportunities that may be secured and enforced for the benefit of an individual. When a judge treats these two types of laws as co-equal, that court is perpetuating the depletion and degradation of shared, long-term environmental values in nature, in order to provide that economic vested interests can continue to reap the short-term benefits of their exploitation of natural resources. Carried to its logical end, scarce natural resources are depleted and destroyed, while the benefits are monetized and treated as private 'wealth' by the economy. This dichotomy of judicial approach is apparent in court decisions across the USA.

5   THE WAY FORWARD

Given the precedents in decisions of the USA Supreme Court to treat economic rights as superior to environmental community rights, it will be necessary to amend the USA Constitution to provide for a clear 'right to the environment'. Alternatively, congress could enact new legislation that has the effect of reversing the Supreme Court's crabbed interpretation of the NEPA and its tolerance for dilatory acceptance of the federal environmental regulations. Public interest litigation to protect the environment in the federal and State courts makes these arguments. When citizens sue, their suits shine light on government or vested economic behavior, and *ipso facto* uphold the rule of law. At their best, courts recognize and advance the fundamental environmental norms inherent in the land ethic, securing rights to breathe clean air or drink fresh water, and sustaining biodiversity in wild lands. At their worst, the courts disregard any living or ecological relationship that humans have with nature, and perpetuate a narrow economic exploitation of nature. The anthropogenic hubris of the latter is what environmental law has sought to redress.

To be sure, business and economic enterprises also have a need for courts to protect the rule of law and their *legitimate* interests. Environmental laws reconceived what is legitimate, as the *Union Electric* decision illustrates. Unfortunately, traditionally conservative courts too often blindly follow precedent and do not recognize or embrace the new definitions of legitimacy. Grounded in the science of ecology, environmental law is not like other fields of legislation guiding social preferences. Society's dependency on ecosystem services is a factual reality; for instance, once the natural resource values of wetlands are identified and protected by a statute, these ecosystems must be sustained. They provide shared benefits to the entire socio-economic setting, and their legal status requires judicial recognition even if they are constraints on previously unfettered economic behavior. Many federal and State environmental statutes in the USA arguably are about identifying and planning ways to sustain ecosystem services. Most judges have never studied environmental law, or the environmental sciences; many judgments in courts across the USA appear at best to be merely ecologically illiterate, and at worst blinkered or blinded by uncritical obedience to the assumed economic paradigm of the day.

Environmental cases throughout the USA are likely to continue to reflect the sort of inconsistency and imbalance that reflected judicial decisions regarding slavery before the Civil War. Aldo Leopold believed society treated nature as if enslaved,[89] denying the community of life any of its inherent rights. However, the land ethic is implied in the legal concept of 'be kept' as 'forever wild lands' in Article XIV of the New York Constitution, and it inheres in the public health standard for clean air. It is expressly enacted as a rule of law in some States. Aldo Leopold elaborated the idea, along with his ideas for the value of wilderness,[90] in his essay, 'The Land Ethic'.[91] Much of the land ethic has been endorsed in the World Charter for Nature[92] and in the subsequent Earth Charter,[93] and was promoted in Agenda 21, the blue print for action agreed by the USA at the Rio Earth Summit in 1992.[94] Many local authorities have adopted the Earth Charter to guide their local decision-making.

While the land ethic is not yet widely considered a rule of law in the USA, the land ethic could become more widely effective through the enactment of a simple judicial procedure proposed by Prof. Joseph Sax in 1971.[95] Under his proposed rule, a citizen could 'make a *prima facie* showing that the conduct of the defendant has, or is likely to pollute, impair, or destroy the air, water or other natural resources or the public trust therein,' and then a defendant 'may rebut the *prima facie* showing by the submission of evidence to the contrary'.[96] The genius of this simple procedure is that the government is held accountable whenever in a specific situation it fails to observe its legal obligation to protect the environment. If courts are to play a more positive role in environmental governance in the USA, it will come with adoption of such reforms.

BIBLIOGRAPHY

APA. 'The Association for Protection of the Adirondacks'. <www.protectadks. org>, 12 September 2008.

---

89. A. Leopold, *A Sand County Almanac* (Oxford: OUP, 1949), in his essay 'The Upshot'. Cf. with the dissenting opinion in *Sierra Club v. Morton*, 405 US 727 (1972), in which Mr Justice Blackmun and Mr Justice Douglas articulate the interrelationship of people and nature, and explain how law must come to recognize the distinct legal interests within this web of life.
90. Leopold, *supra*, 188-200.
91. *Ibid.*, 201-226.
92. UN General Assembly Resolution 37/7. The USA was the only nation to vote against adoption of this charter in the UN General Assembly.
93. See ECI, 'The Earth Charter', <www.earthcharter.org>, 28 August 2008. It is a normative statement, adopted as guidance by many local authorities across the USA. It is not yet a statutory text.
94. See N.A. Robinson, *Agenda 21: Earth's Action Plan* (Dobbs Ferry: Oceana Publication, 1993).
95. J.L. Sax, *Defending the Environment: A Strategy for Citizen Action* (New York: Knopf, 1971).
96. *Ibid.*, 250, setting forth the text of s. 3, enrolled Bill No. 3055, State of Michigan, 75th Legislature, Regular Session of 1970.

Austin, J.E., et al. *Judging NEPA: A 'Hard Look' at Judicial Decision Making Under the National Environmental Policy Act*. Washington, DC: Environmental Law Institute, 2005.

Bullar, R. *Highway Robbery: Transportation Racism and New Routes to Equity*. London: South End Press, 2004.

CEQ. 'The National Environmental Policy Act: A Study of its Effectiveness After 25 Years, 1997'. <www.whitehouse.gov/ceq>, 12 September 2008.

Craig, R. *The Clean Water Act and the Constitution: Legal Structure and the Public's Right to a Clean and Healthy Environment*. Washington, DC: Environmental Law Institute, 2005.

Dreher, R.G. 'NEPA Under Siege: The Political Assault on the National Environmental Policy Act'. *Georgetown Environmental Law & Policy Institute* (2005). <www.law.georgetown.edu/gelpi/news/documents/NEPAUnderSiegeFinal.pdf>, 12 September 2008.

Dudeck, D. & J. Palmisano. 'Emissions Trading: Why is This Thoroughbred Hobbled?'. *Columbia Journal of Environmental Law* 13 (1988): 217-256.

ECI. 'The Earth Charter'. <www.earthcharter.org>, 28 August 2008.

ELI. 'Environmental Law Reporter'. <www.eli.org>, 28 August 2008.

ELI. 'Environmental Statutes Outline: A Guide to Federal Laws'. <www.eli.org>, 28 August 2008.

Engle, K. 'State Environmental Standard Setting: Is There a "Race" and is it "To the Bottom?"'. *Hastings Law Journal* 48 (1997): 271-376.

Friedman, L. *A History of American Law*. New York: Simon & Schuster, 1973.

Gerrard, M.B., D.A. Ruzow & P. Weinstein. *Environmental Impact Review in New York*. New York: Matthew Bender, 1990.

Grad, F. *Treatise on Environmental Law*. New York: Mathew Bender, 1972.

Graham, F., Jr. *The Adirondack Park: A Political* History. New York: Knopf, 1978.

Hays, S.P. 'Three Decades of Environmental Politics: The Historical Context'. In *Government and Environmental Politics*, edited by M.J. Lacey. Maryland: Johns Hopkins University Press, 1991.

Horowitz, M. *The Transformation of American Law, 1780-1860*. Harvard: Harvard University Press, 1977.

Johannes, L. 'New Study Shows Need for Tougher Air Rules', *Wall Street Journal*, 2 (2000): B10.

Kendall, D. (ed.). *Redefining Federalism: Listening to the States in Shaping Our Federalism*. Washington, DC: Environmental Law Institute, 2004.

Lazarus, R.J. & Houck, O.A. (eds). *Environmental Law Stories*. New York: Thomson West, 2005.

Lazarus, R.J. 'Meeting the Demands of Integration in the Evolution of Environmental Law: Reforming Environmental Criminal Law'. *Georgetown Law Journal* 83 (1995): 2407-2484.

Lazarus, R.J. *The Making of Environmental Law*. Chicago: University of Chicago Press, 2004.

Leopold, A. *A Sand County Almanac*. Oxford: Oxford University Press, 1949.

Mann, D. 'Polluter-Financed Environmentally Beneficial Expenditures: Effective Use or Improper Abuse of Citizen Suits Under the Clean Water Act'. *Environmental Law* 21 (1991): 175.

McGarity, T.O., S. Shapiro & D. Bollier. *Sophisticated Sabotage: The Intellectual Games used to Subvert Responsible Regulation*. Washington, DC: Environmental Law Institute, 2004.

Nash, R. *Wilderness and the American Mind*. Connecticut: Yale University Press, 1967.

New York (State). *McKinney's Consolidated Laws of New York annotated with Annotations from State and Federal Courts and State Agencies*. St. Paul, Minn.: West Group, 1939.

Novick, S. *The Law of Environmental Protection*. Washington, DC: Environmental Law Institute, 1980.

Novick, S. *Law of Environmental Protection*. Vol. 2. Deerfield, IL: Clark Boardman Callaghan, 1987.

NYSDEC. 'Conserving, Improving, and Protecting New York's Natural Resources and Environment'. <www.dec.ny.gov>, 12 September 2008.

Okster, L.R. 'Smithfield Foods: A Case for Federal Action'. *William and Mary Environmental Law and Policy Review* 23 (1999): 381-390.

Ottinger, R.L. 'Legislation and the Environment: Individual Rights and Government Accountability'. *Cornell Law Review* 55 (1970): 666-672.

Pederson, W. 'Turning the Tide on Water Quality' *Ecology Law Quarterly* 15 (1988): 69-102.

Prosser, W.L. *Handbook on the Law of Torts*, 4th ed. St. Paul, Minn.: West Group, 1971.

Reznikoff, C. (ed.). *Louis Marshall: Champion of Liberty; Selected Papers and Addresses*. Vol. II. Philadelphia: Jewish Publication Society of America, 1957.

Robbins, R.M. *Our Landed Heritage: The Public Domain, 1776-1970*. Princeton: Princeton University Press, 1976.

Robinson, N.A. *Agenda 21: Earth's Action Plan*. Dobbs Ferry: Oceana Publication, 1993.

Sax, J.L. *Defending the Environment: A Strategy for Citizen Action*. New York: Knopf, 1971.

Sax, J.L. 'The Public Trust Doctrine in Natural Resources Law: Effective Judicial Intervention'. *Michigan Law Review* 68 (1970): 471-570.

Schiffer, L.J. & J.F. Simon, 'The Reality of Prosecuting Environmental Criminals: A Response to Professor Lazarus'. *Georgetown Law Journal* 83 (1995): 2531-2539.

Shabecoff, P. *A Fierce Green Fire: The American Environmental Movement*. New York: Hill & Wang, 1993.

Vermont Judiciary. 'Vermont Environmental Court'. <www.vermontjudiciary. org/courts/ environmental/index.htm>, 12 September 2008.

WWI. 'State of the World 2006: A Worldwatch Institute report on progress toward a sustainable society'. New York: Norton, 2006.

TABLE OF LEGISLATION

TABLE OF CASES

Scenic Hudson Preservation Conference v. Federal Power Commission (1966) 354
    F. 2d 608 (2nd Cir., 1965)
Spur Industries, Inc. v. Del E. Webb Development Co. 108 Ariz. 178 (1972)
Tahoe-Sierra Preservation Council v. Tahoe Regional Planning Agency 535 US
    302 (2002)
Union Electric Company v. EPA 427 US 246 (1976)
Village of Euclid v. Amber Realty Co. 272 US 365 (1926)
Whitman v. American Trucking Association 531 US 457 (2001)

TABLE OF INTERNATIONAL INSTRUMENTS

UN General Assembly Resolution 37/7 1982
Vienna Convention for the protection of the Ozone Layer (1987) 26 *ILM* 1516

ABBREVIATIONS

CERCLA	Comprehensive Environmental Response, Compensation and Liability Act
CEQ	Council on Environmental Quality
CFC	chlorofluorocarbons
CZM	coastal zone management
ECI	Earth Charter Initiative
EDF	Environmental Defense Fund
EIA	environmental impact assessment
ELI	Environmental Law Institute
EPA	Environment Protection Agency
FOIA	Freedom of Information Act
FOIL	Freedom of Information Law
NEPA	National Environmental Policy Act
NGO	Non-governmental Organization
NRDC	Natural Resources Defense Council
NYSDEC	New York State Department of Environmental Conservation
OMB	Office of Management and Budget
SCLDF	Sierra Club Legal Defense Fund
WWI	Worldwatch Institute

Chapter 6
Canada

Jamie Benidickson and
Heather McLeod-Kilmurray

1 INTRODUCTION

1.1 ENVIRONMENTAL ISSUES

As the twenty-first century gets underway, major environmental issues confront Canadian society in its global context. Scientists have projected further pronounced deterioration in the availability of fish stocks following several decades of population decline and accompanying economic hardship.[1] Forests are under threat from largely unreformed patterns of human exploitation and in some regions from invasive species, notably the mountain pine beetle that has devastated woodlands in British Columbia and now threatens neighboring Alberta. Water quality and availability are of growing concern across the country, with continuing anxiety associated with: the drinking water crises in the recent past;[2] widespread apprehension about the effects of blue green algae in Quebec; and resource depletion in

---

1. R.A. Myers & B. Worm, 'Rapid worldwide depletion of predatory fish communities', *Nature* 423 (2003): 280.
2. Hon. D.R. O'Connor, Report of the Walkerton Inquiry (Ontario: Queen's Printer for Ontario, 2002); Hon. R.D. Laing, Report of the Commission of Inquiry into matters relating to the safety of the public drinking water in the City of North Battleford, Saskatchewan (Saskatoon: CoI, 2002).

Louis J. Kotzé and Alexander R. Paterson (eds), *The Role of the Judiciary in Environmental Governance: Comparative Perspectives*, pp. 209–248.
© 2009 Kluwer Law International BV, The Netherlands.

western Canada.[3] Urban residents have been alerted to the adverse consequences of smog and other forms of air contamination that may have particularly harmful implications for children.[4]

Overlaying this array of sectoral concerns is the inescapable public policy challenge of climate change. Although Canadian provincial and territorial governments were initially slow to respond, the scope of official intervention is now expanding owing to increased public pressure calling for actions that are more consistent with the extent of the impacts that lie ahead.[5] Indeed, the extraordinary pace of climate change in the arctic region of northern Canada can almost be evidenced daily.

1.2   ROLE OF COURTS

There is a variety of actual and potential roles for the judiciary in environmental governance. In Canada, courts are powerful, independent and well-respected public institutions. From very early days, courts have put teeth into common law causes of action in the protection of the environment, and more recently have overseen the enforcement of environmental legislation. The courts have also played a more general role in the sense of helping to reflect aspirational societal attitudes toward environmental protection, pronouncing on general environmental values as well as more recently adding a Canadian perspective to emerging environmental law principles.

Any discussion of the judicial role in resolving particular problems must address practical and philosophical considerations. There are many practical advantages and limitations to using litigation as a tool for achieving protection and change.[6] The structural disadvantages often cited by those who oppose judicial involvement in environmental issues include the lack of environmental specialization of judges, the institutional limitations of common law courts where independent advice is generally lacking, and the anti-democratic effect of placing complex polycentric issues into the hands of unelected decision-makers. Costs, delays and other barriers to litigation represent further limitations. Other less obvious barriers emerge from values and priorities embedded within the law itself or within traditional

---

3. K. Bakker (ed.), *Eau Canada: The Future of Canada's Water* (Vancouver, BC: UBC Press, 2007); D.W. Schindler & W.F. Donahue, 'An impending water crisis in Canada's western prairie provinces', <www.pnas.org/cgi/doi/10.1073/pnas.0601568103>, 31 July 2008.
4. D. Wigle, *Child Health and the Environment* (Oxford: OUP, 2003); Commission for Environmental Co-operation, *Children's Health and the Environment in North America* (Montréal, Québec: CEC, 2006).
5. G. Simpson, M. Jaccard & N. Rivers, *Hot Air: Meeting Canada's Climate Change Challenge* (Toronto: McClelland & Stewart, 2007); National Round Table on the Environment and the Economy, *Getting to 2050: Canada's Transition to a Low-emission Future* (Ottawa: The Round Table, 2007).
6. H. McLeod-Kilmurray, 'Lowering Barriers to Judicial Enforcement: Civil Procedure and Environmental Ethics', proceedings of 4th Annual Colloquium of the IUCN Academy of Environmental Law (forthcoming).

judicial attitudes. Judges have often felt themselves institutionally unsuited to resolving complex scientific problems, and a significant deferential attitude toward professional and governmental expertise has been documented. Some argue that squeezing environmental problems into the framework of legal rules, principles and procedures created for very different situations, can distort or impede understanding. In addition, within the predominant judicial paradigm in Canadian common law, courts have tended to focus on liberal individualism, rights discourse and resolution of individual disputes. This may cause judges to overlook parts of environmental issues that do not fall squarely within these ways of thinking.[7]

However, the advantages of judicial involvement in environmental decision-making are important, unique and powerful. Canadian courts present neutral forums where all sides are given a fair hearing. Judges must ultimately provide a clear set of reasons as to why the dispute has been resolved in a particular way. Judges themselves, in issuing the Johannesburg Declaration, have emphasized that it is an essential function of the judiciary to 'promot[e] the goals of sustainable development through the application of the rule of law and the democratic process', including by playing a role in enforcement, interpretation of law, and by helping to 'integrat[e] Human Values . . . into contemporary global civilization by translating these shared values into action through strengthening the respect for the Role of Law both internationally and nationally'.[8] In this vein, some Canadian judges have reflected societal aspirations in terms of environmental protection. As Justice Charles Gonthier, formerly of the Supreme Court of Canada, has observed, judicial pronouncements can allow courts to go beyond the letter of the law to impact environmental governance on a broader scale:

> Thus, as a complement to the rule of law, there is the spirit of the law. The spirit of the law is not concerned so much with setting down rules. Rather, it reflects the values which a society draws upon in its development of legal rules. Sharing the logic of sustainable development, these values of the spirit of the law must include cooperation, commitment, responsibility, community, trust, fairness, security and empathy. These are constituent elements of solidarity or fraternity. These values like liberty and equality, are fundamentally moral values, values to which we aspire though seldom attain. They interact with liberty and equality while also interacting with each other and together they weave the cloth of fraternity.[9]

---

7. See e.g., L.M. Wenner, 'Environmental Policy in the Court' in *Environmental Policy in the 1990s*, ed. N.J. Vig & M.E. Kraft, 2nd ed. (Washington DC: CQ Press, 1994); E. Swanson & E. Hughes, *The Price of Pollution: Environmental Litigation in Canada* (Edmonton AB: Environmental Law Centre, 1990); B.L. Strayer, *The Canadian Constitution and the Courts*, 2nd ed. (Toronto: Butterworths, 1983).

8. Preamble. See UNEP, 'Johannesburg Principles on the Role of Law and Sustainable Development', adopted at the Global Judges Symposium, Johannesburg, South Africa, 18-20 August 2002, <www.pnuma.org/deramb_ing/JohannesburgPrinciples.pdf>, 12 September 2008.

9. Justice C. Gonthier, 'Sustainable Development and the Law', *McGill Int'l J. on Sustainable Development Law and Policy* 1 (2005): 13.

As we will see in detail below, Canadian judges have made inspirational observations in many environmental cases, leading to changes in environmental law that reflect evolving attitudes toward the challenges of sustainability.

This chapter addresses the significant contributions of Canadian courts in environmental governance, including those involving common law, administrative, criminal and procedural aspects of environmental litigation. Before addressing the substantive contributions of the Canadian judiciary, however, it is important to provide some contextual background.

1.3   PRINCIPAL ENVIRONMENTAL LAWS

Canada is a federal State comprised of ten provinces and three territories. In this regard, it is important to note the division of constitutional responsibility for environmental matters between the federal government and provincial governments.[10] With reference to areas of constitutional authority such as fisheries, criminal law, or Indian lands, as well as a general residual power, the federal government has enacted a wide range of environmental legislation. The provinces have enacted environmental legislation on the basis of their constitutional authority respecting public lands, municipal affairs, or property and civil rights within their jurisdictions.

Although elements of the legislative framework governing environmental protection may be traced through the twentieth century, and indeed to earlier times, the primary statutes at both the federal and provincial levels date from approximately 1970 when departments of the environment were formally established in most jurisdictions. At the federal level, environmental protection and environmental assessment (EA) legislation is most prominent. The *Canadian Environmental Protection Act, 1999*[11] (CEPA, 1999) and the *Canadian Environmental Assessment Act*[12] (CEAA) undergo mandatory parliamentary review at regular intervals and are almost constantly under re-examination. As discussed below, judicial interpretation of the legal foundations of early EA initiatives was instrumental in promoting the implementation of the current federal statutory framework. Other important federal environmental legislation includes the *Fisheries Act*,[13] *Pest Products Control Act*[14] and *Species at Risk Act*.[15]

In keeping with the constitutional sharing of environmental responsibility in Canada between the federal government and the provinces, each of the latter has

---

10. See generally: P. Hogg, *Constitutional Law of Canada* (Scarborough, Ont.: Carswell, 2007); and P. Monahan, *Constitutional Law* (Toronto: Irwin Law, 2006).
11. SC 1999, c. 33.
12. SC 1992, c. 37.
13. RSC 1985, c. F-14.
14. SC 2002, c. 28.
15. SC 2002, c. 29.

enacted environmental protection legislation with corresponding institutions for administration and enforcement.[16]

Non-Canadian readers will also be interested to learn of section 35 of the *Constitution Act*, 1982[17] which provides that the 'existing aboriginal and treaty rights of the aboriginal peoples of Canada are hereby recognized and affirmed'. This provision has had particular significance in the environmental context where, again, judicial interpretation has been extremely influential.

1.4   INSTITUTIONS AND GOVERNANCE STRUCTURES

At the federal and State level, a Department of the Environment or equivalent, along with ministries devoted to natural resources, agriculture and health, exercise environmental authority as conferred under the relevant statutory framework.[18] Despite intermittent consideration of entrenching 'central agency' status for the department with primary responsibility for the environment, authority over environmental matters is generally widely dispersed amongst numerous agencies and departments with 'line' responsibilities for particular environmental issues.[19] Administrative agencies with specific responsibilities for matters such as EA, the review of environmental licensing and permit decisions, pesticide use and approvals or water use authorizations, operate in association with such departments and ministries.

An inter-governmental body, the Canadian Council of Ministers of the Environment (CCME), works on an ongoing basis to promote collaborative or harmonized policy initiatives throughout the country. It has been instrumental, for example, in promoting common approaches to matters such as principles of liability for contaminated lands. Other inter-governmental organizations include the Prairie Provinces Water Board, a long-standing institution whose responsibilities may be augmented by the growing pressures that climate change places on water availability in the waterways crossing Alberta, Saskatchewan and Manitoba.

In conjunction with the North American Free Trade Agreement[20] involving Canada, the United States and Mexico, the North American Agreement on

---

16. See, e.g.: *Environmental Management Act* SBC 2003, c. 53; *Environmental Protection and Enhancement Act* RS.A. 2000, c. E-12; *Environmental Management and Protection Act* 2002, c. E-10.1; *Environment Act* CCSM c. E-125; *Environmental Protection Act* RSO 1990, c. E.19; *Ontario Water Resources Act* RSO 1990, c. O.40; *Environmental Quality Act* RSQ c. Q-2; *Clean Air Act* C-5.2; *Clean Water Act* C-6.1; *Environment Act* SNS 1994-1995, c. 1; *Environmental Protection Act* SNL 2002, c. E-14.2; *Environmental Protection Act* c. E-9; *Environmental Protection Act* RSNWT 1988, c. E-7; and *Environment Act* RSY 2002, c. 76.

17. *Constitution Act, 1982*, being Sch. B to the *Canada Act 1982* (UK), 1982, c. 11.

18. See, e.g.: *Department of the Environment Act* RSC 1985, c. M-8.

19. Recently, however, Manitoba took the unusual step of consolidating responsibility for all water-related matters in the province under the authority of the Ministry of Water Stewardship.

20. *North American Free Trade Agreement Between the Government of Canada, the Government of Mexico and the Government of the United States*, 17 December 1992, Can. T.S. 1994 No. 2, 32 I.L.M. 289 (entered into force 1 January 1994).

Environmental Co-operation[21] established procedures for inter-governmental and citizen-initiated complaints under the auspices of the Commission for Environmental Co-operation. This new international body joins the International Joint Commission as one of a small number of inter-governmental institutions playing distinctive roles in Canadian environmental management.

On the institutional front, it is also important to note the important role played by Canadian royal commissions and public inquiries. These independent investigative and policy-making initiatives have often been headed up by members of the judiciary and have been occasionally responsible for providing valuable direction to environmental policy. The Mackenzie Valley Pipeline under the leadership of Justice Thomas Berger, then of the British Columbia Supreme Court, is a particularly noteworthy example. The inquiry is associated with developments in EA, public participation and aboriginal interests in resources management. More recent inquiries into the malfunctioning of water supply systems in Ontario and Saskatchewan under the chairmanship of Justices Dennis R. O'Connor and Robert D. Laing, respectively, have significantly influenced water quality protection and drinking water supply systems across Canada.[22]

2   OVERVIEW OF THE COURT SYSTEM

2.1   Historical Development of the Judiciary

Hundreds of judges currently serve across Canada's courts which range from provincial courts with specifically circumscribed jurisdiction, to senior courts of appeal and the Supreme Court of Canada, whose authority encompasses 'an appellate, civil and criminal jurisdiction within and throughout Canada'.[23]

Many of Canada's courts trace their origins to corresponding British institutions adopted in the colonies.[24] Described for convenience as 'Section 96' courts, a reference to the constitutional source of authority for the appointment of their members, these bodies are understood to exercise inherent general jurisdiction in relation to 'all civil and criminal, provincial, federal, and constitutional matters'.[25] Since Canadian Confederation in 1867, new courts have been statutorily-created, including some whose existence is traceable to section 101 of the *Constitution Act*

---

21. *Ibid.*
22. Hon. T.R. Berger (Commissioner), *Northern Frontier, Northern Homeland: Report of the Mackenzie Valley Pipeline Inquiry*, Vol. 1 & 2, (Ottawa: Minister of Supply and Services, 1977).
23. *Supreme Court of Canada Act* RSC 1985, c. S-26, s. 35.
24. See, generally, G. Gall, *The Canadian Legal System*, 5th ed. (Toronto: Carswell, 2004); P. Russell, *Canada's Trial Courts: Two Tiers or One?* (Toronto: University of Toronto Press, 2007); Canadian Abridgement, *Canadian Court System* (Toronto: Thomson/Carswell, 2006).
25. See *Canada (Human Rights Commission) v. Canadian Liberty Net* [1998] 1 SCR 626 at 653.

(1867),[26] namely: the Supreme Court of Canada; the Federal Court; and Federal Court of Appeal. These courts have been established pursuant to provincial authority for the administration of justice.[27] The prosecution of environmental offences would ordinarily be initiated in a provincial court exercising criminal jurisdiction.

The principle of judicial independence, elaborated in Canada on the basis of evolving British tradition,[28] has been vigorously defended and enhanced in the modern era, notably with reference to section 11(d) of the Charter of Rights and Freedoms[29] which provides that: 'Any person charged with an offence has the right . . . to be presumed innocent until proven guilty according to law in a fair and public hearing by an independent and impartial tribunal.'[30] Security of tenure is a foundational element of independence, for both federally and provincially-appointed judges. It is achieved generally in Canada on the basis of appointments 'during good behaviour' or removability from office 'only for cause', with procedural safeguards in the form of a judicial inquiry as a precondition for dismissal.[31] Beyond security of tenure, elements of judicial independence include administrative control in relation to matters affecting the exercise of the judicial function, such as the assignment of judges and court lists, and a large measure of financial security.[32] As a result, courts are independent, powerful and well-respected institutions of governance in Canada.

2.2   COURT STRUCTURE AND HIERARCHY OF COURTS

At the top of the judicial pyramid in Canada stands the Supreme Court of Canada, whose nine members hear appeals from the provinces and from the Federal Court of Appeal. The Supreme Court of Canada may also hear constitutional references submitted from either the federal or provincial governments and has, on occasion in the past, considered such requests in relation to natural resource and environmental matters.[33]

---

26. S. 101 of the *Constitution Act, 1867* provides that: 'The Parliament of Canada may . . . provide for . . . a General Court of Appeal for Canada, and for the Establishment of any additional Courts for the better Administration of the Laws of Canada.'
27. S. 92(14) of the *Constitution Act, 1867* confers upon each provincial legislature responsibility for: '[T]he Administration of Justice in the Province, including the Constitution, Maintenance, and Organization of Provincial Courts, both of Civil and Criminal Jurisdiction, and including Procedure in Civil Matters in those Courts.'
28. W.R. Lederman, 'The Independence of the Judiciary', *CBR* 34 (1956): 1139.
29. *Canadian Charter of Rights and Freedoms*, Part I of the *Constitution Act, 1982,* being Sch. B to the *Canada Act 1982* (UK), 1982, c. 11.
30. See: *R v. Valente* [1985] 2 SCR 673; and M.L. Friedland, *A Place Apart: Judicial Independence and Accountability in Canada* (Ottawa: Canadian Judicial Council, 1995).
31. For a full discussion of these issues see Hogg, *supra* n. 10, Ch. 7 'Courts'; C. Forcese & A. Freeman, *The Laws of Government: The Legal Foundations of Canadian Democracy* (Toronto: Irwin Law, 2005), 291-294.
32. *Re Remuneration of Judges (1997)* [1997] 3 SCR 3.
33. See, e.g.: *A.G. Canada v. A.G. Ontario, Quebec, and Nova Scotia* [1898] AC 700; and *Reference re Waters and Water Powers* [1929] SCR 19.

The Federal Court of Canada, pursuant to its statutory mandate, exercises jurisdiction regarding the decisions of any 'federal board, commission or other tribunal'. Subject to a circumscribed class of exceptions, this authority extends to 'any body or person or persons having, exercising or purporting to exercise jurisdiction or powers conferred by or under an Act of Parliament'.[34] In relation to environmental matters, this has involved the court in judicial review of an important series of decisions concerning the scope and operation of the *Canadian Environmental Assessment Act*.[35]

The Section 96 courts, the superior court of the provinces, include: courts of appeal; district and county courts; and other institutions variously styled as high courts or divisional courts. These courts adjudicate constitutional and common law claims, applications for judicial review from the decisions of environmental agencies as well as criminal prosecutions, many of which will have been initiated in provincial courts possessing criminal jurisdiction.

Although modest indications of judicial specialization are apparent in parts of the Canadian court system relating to taxation, commercial matters, and family law, this direction has not been pursued in relation to the environment. The absence of a specialized environmental court is sometimes considered a shortcoming in the Canadian context as environmental matters may involve significant technical elements and an increasing range of new and distinctive principles. However, this trend is entirely consistent with the overall nature of judicial appointments in Canada and the challenges of assessing technical evidence are certainly not confined to environmental matters.[36]

Members of the judiciary are appointed from the ranks of experienced members of the profession and serve generally with reference to whatever cases come before them. It is therefore possible that a judge adjudicating an environmental dispute will have no prior familiarity with the subject matter or any distinctive principles. It is accordingly the case that the values, principles and perceptions brought by members of the Canadian judiciary to their deliberations in environmental matters are broadly derived from the varied and diverse legal backgrounds of participating judges.

However, arrangements are in place under the auspices of the National Judicial Institute (NJI) to offer members of the judiciary opportunities for professional development. On occasion, these have included conferences, workshops or training programmes addressing environmental issues. The NJI, for example, as one component of its Science and the Law course package, offered an on-line course on Sustainable Development Law and Climate Change. A previous initiative addressed genetically modified organisms (GMOs) in the context of controversial

---

34. *Federal Court Act* RSC c. F-7, s. 2(1).
35. For a recent example, see *Miningwatch Canada v. Canada (Minister of Fisheries and Oceans)* (2008), 33 CELR (3d) 1 (FC.).
36. S.N. Lederman, 'Judges as Gatekeepers: The Admissibility of Scientific Evidence Bases on Novel Theories', in *Special Lectures 2003: The Law of Evidence*, ed. Law Society of Upper Canada (Toronto: Irwin Law, 2004), 475-506.

litigation. For its part, the Federal Court has also conducted workshops on science and the law.[37]

2.3   APPLICABLE LAW

The role of the Canadian judiciary in environmental governance has historically revolved around the application and interpretation of Canada's federal and provincial environmental laws. Adjudicative proceedings in the environmental context have, however, called for judicial application of common law principles relating, for example, to causes of action in tort, property or contract law. In the province of Quebec, analogous disputes are considered with reference to the Code Civil.[38]

Limited indications of judicial recognition of elements of aboriginal law and practice have begun to appear in Canadian environmental policy,[39] although the most prominent example of distinctive principles may be sentencing principles found in the Criminal Code[40] of Canada.

Principles of international law, including the precautionary principle, have been judicially considered in Canada. To the extent that claims of customary status might attach to principles of international environmental law, they might be received into Canadian law through a process of adoption. In the case of international treaty law, however, it is ordinarily understood that applicability in Canada depends upon domestic statutory implementation. This approach is consistent with the federal nature of the Constitution in that it forestalls the exercise of treaty-making authority by the federal government in a manner that would alter the internal allocation of powers between the two levels of government.[41]

The *Constitution Act* (1982)[42] introduced profound changes in the relationship of the judiciary to the legislature in Canada. In particular, section 52(1) specifically provides that: 'The Constitution of Canada is the supreme law of Canada, and any law that is inconsistent with the provisions of the Constitution is, to the extent of the inconsistency, of no force or effect.' In consequence of this provision, constitutional adjudication in Canada extends beyond a determination of jurisdictional authority as between the federal and provincial governments. Now, Canadian courts engage in an assessment of legislation against the standard of substantive rights such as equality rights and the civil liberties set out in the Canadian Charter of Rights and Freedoms.[43] Statutory provisions, including environmental legislation, may now be

---

37. I. Binnie, 'Science in the Courtroom: the Mouse that Roared', *UNBLJ* 56 (2007): 307.
38. L. Giroux, 'Environmental Law in Quebec', in *Environmental Law and Policy*, ed. E. Hughes, A.R. Lucas & W.A. Tilleman, 3rd ed. (Toronto: Emond Montgomery, 2003).
39. J. Borrows, 'Living between Water and Rocks: The Environment, First Nations and Democracy' (Toronto:University of Toronto Press, 2002), Ch. 2, *Recovering Canada: The Resurgence of Indigenous Law*.
40. RSC 1985, c. C-46.
41. J. Currie, *Public International Law* (Toronto: Irwin Law, 2001), 201-215.
42. *Supra*, n. 17.
43. *Canadian Charter of Rights and Freedoms*, *supra* n. 29, ss 7-14, 15.

tested in relation to constitutionally recognized safeguards such as: vagueness; proportionality; respect for life, liberty and security of the person; and security against unreasonable search and seizure.[44]

In addition to prominent environmental laws noted above, significant elements of the Canadian legal framework have been elaborated in subordinate legislation or regulations where more detailed standards and requirements are often set out.[45] Much of the institutional specialization that exists in Canadian environmental law is associated with administrative tribunals and other agencies created in connection with this regulatory framework and charged specifically with environmental decision-making.[46]

3   ANALYSIS OF SIGNIFICANT ENVIRONMENTAL
         JUDGMENTS

In the absence of legislation, early Canadian environmental cases drew upon common law principles, demonstrating firmly on occasion the willingness of the judiciary to safeguard property interests from environmental harm. In the 1929 case of *Groat v. Edmonton*,[47] for example, the City was sued by a downstream riparian owner for polluting a stream with municipal storm sewer discharge. The Supreme Court recognized a riparian proprietor's right to drain his or her land but emphatically asserted that such a right 'may not be exercised to the injury and damage of the riparian proprietor below, and it can afford no defence to an action for polluting the water in the stream'. Boldly, the court proclaimed that 'pollution is always unlawful and, in itself, constitutes a nuisance'.[48] The City was required to abate the nuisance within two years. This kind of analysis allowed the court to add force to common law actions, such as nuisance, as tools of environmental protection.

Another early water pollution case, *K.V.P. Co. v. McKie*,[49] is indicative of the important role of courts in environmental protection. In this case, riparian owners successfully sued a pulp and paper mill whose effluent was polluting the Spanish River. The trial court judge used very strong language to reject a defense associated with the economic importance of the mill to the local community:

> . . . if I were to consider and give effect to an argument based on the defendant's economic position in the community, or its financial interests, I would

---

44. See, e.g.: *R v. Canadian Pacific Railway* [1995] 2 SCR 1028.
45. See generally: J.M. Keyes, *Executive Legislation* (Toronto: Butterworths, 1992); and J.P. Salembier, *Regulatory Law and Practice in Canada* (Toronto: Butterworths, 2004).
46. J. Swaigen & A.D. Levy, 'The Expert's Duty to the Tribunal: A Tool for Reducing Contradictions Between Scientific Process and Legal Process', *CJELP* 11 (1997): 277; J. Swaigen, 'The Role of the Civil Courts in Resolving Risk and Uncertainty in Environmental Law', *JELP* 1 (1990): 199.
47. *Groat v. Edmonton [City]* [1928] SCR 522.
48. *Ibid.*, at 532.
49. [1949] SCR 698; [1949] 1 DLR 39 (Ont. C.A.); [1948] 3 DLR 201 at 206 (Ont. HC). See E. Brubaker, *Property Rights in the Defence of Nature* (Toronto: Earthscan Publications, 1995), Ch. 4.

in effect be giving to it a veritable power of expropriation of the common law rights of the riparian owners, without compensation.[50]

In upholding lower court decisions granting damages and an injunction, the Supreme Court agreed that since '[p]ollution has been shown to exist, damages would not be a complete and adequate remedy'.[51]

It is clear, therefore, that Canadian courts have played a role in limiting the powers of both public actors and private actors to pollute with impunity. The two decisions above further illustrate the judiciary's opposition to companies effectively being allowed to buy the right to pollute by paying damages in lieu of an injunction. However, the *KVP* case also demonstrates the ease with which judicial power can be undermined by a legislature determined to put other interests such as job security ahead of environmental protection. Although all three levels of court had in this matter agreed that the pollution should be prevented, the provincial government passed legislation specifically to overturn this injunction and ensure that the mill could not only continue to operate, but continue to pollute.[52] The legacy of the *KVP* case resonated for some time in the province of Ontario.[53]

Despite such important historical decisions, this chapter focuses primarily on the environmental decisions of the Supreme Court following the widespread introduction of modern environmental legislation from the 1970s onwards.[54] In one ground-breaking decision, *R v. Sault St. Marie*,[55] the Supreme Court removed some of the barriers to using the criminal law model as a tool of environmental enforcement. The court created a new category – the regulatory offence – as a type of offence that was most appropriate to environmental harms. These regulatory offences are distinct from the one extreme of full *mens rea* crimes and the other

---

50. *Ibid.*, 214.
51. *Ibid.*, 703.
52. The province of Ontario amended its *Lakes and Rivers Improvement Act* RSO 1937, c. 45 by means of *An Act to Amend the Lakes and Rivers Improvement Act* SO 1949, c. 8, to make it more difficult to get an injunction against water polluting companies generally. This was done between the time of the Court of Appeal decision and the Supreme Court of Canada's hearing of the matter, although the Supreme Court refused to allow this change to cause it to revoke the injunction. The province then passed the more specific *Act respecting The KVP Company Limited*, SO 1950, c. 33 to override the injunction.
53. Both the environmentally good and bad outcomes in the KVP case were seen in two cases in the 1950s. In *Stephens v. The Village of Richmond Hill* [1955] OR 806 (HC), aff'd [1956] OR 88 (CA) and *Burgess v. The City of Woodstock* [1955] OR 814 (HC) the courts relied on the KVP case to restrain municipalities from dumping raw sewage into Ontario rivers. Despite the courts' refusal to sacrifice private property rights to economic necessity, '[o]n March 20, 1956, the government introduced *An Act to Amend The Public Health Act*. The Act dissolved the injunctions against Woodstock and Richmond Hill. It went even further, deeming any sewage project approved by the Department of Health to be operated by statutory authority. Brubaker, *supra* n. 49, Ch. 5. See also J. Benidickson, 'Water Supply and Sewage Infrastructure in Ontario, 1880-1990s: Legal and Institutional Aspects of Public Health and Environmental History', in *The Walkerton Inquiry: Commissioner Paper 1,* ed. S. Protti (Toronto: Ontario Ministry of the Attorney General, 2002).
54. E.g., *Canadian Environmental Protection Act* RSC 1985, (4th Supp.), c-16; *Canadian Environmental Assessment Act* SC 1992, c. 37.
55. [1978] 2 SCR 1299.

extreme of absolute liability offences. They create strict liability, meaning that the defendant's liability will be assumed once the plaintiff has proven the defendant's *actus reus*; but the defendant can avoid liability if it can succeed in proving that it conducted its operations with due diligence or reasonable care.

A strong incentive to implement due diligence was provided by *R v. Bata Industries Ltd.*[56] Although not decided by the Supreme Court, the case bears mentioning in the context of criminal liability as it considered the personal liability of corporate directors or officers in the context of environmental harm arising from corporate activities. The *Bata* case dealt with liability for leaking storage drums that were discharging chemical waste. The corporation was convicted under the *Ontario Water Resources Act,*[57] with the offences of discharging material that impaired the quality of groundwater. In a wake-up call for corporations, later unfortunately weakened on appeal, the trial court held that a director and an officer were also convicted for the resulting contamination.[58]

With public concern over the state of the environment increasing, the Supreme Court of Canada made another significant decision in *Friends of the Oldman River Society v. Canada (Minister of Transport).*[59] A local citizen's group sought to review an approval to build a dam on the Oldman River in Alberta because it was granted without complying with the requirements of the federal Environmental Assessment Review Process Guidelines Order.[60] Since the title of this instrument included the term 'guidelines', it had been assumed that this instrument was not binding on government. The Supreme Court held that on the contrary, 'parliament has elected to adopt a regulatory scheme that is "law", and thus amenable to enforcement through prerogative relief'.[61] This decision invigorated the law of EA in Canada, and also strengthened the role of interest groups in the enforcement of environmental law, a subject to which we return shortly.

The Supreme Court has also been frequently called upon to address the ever-vexing challenge of regulating environmental protection in a federal State. Indeed, the decision in the *Oldman* case had federal-provincial dimensions, and this is an area of environmental governance where the court has made unique contributions. In *R v. Hydro Québec,*[62] a constitutional challenge was raised by the defendant, a regulated industrial concern, to an interim order made under the toxic substances provisions of the *Canadian Environmental Protection Act.*[63]

---

56. (1992), 9 OR (3d) 329 (Prov Ct).
57. RSO 1980, c. 361. Charges under the Ontario *Environmental Protection Act* RSO 1980, c. 141, s. 147a were stayed.
58. Although the directors and officers of the company were convicted, the court ruled that the Chairman of the Board was not liable as there was an adequate environmental management system in place, it was therefore reasonable for him to rely on his delegates to adequately perform their tasks (*supra* n. 56 at 140-145).
59. *Friends of the Oldman River Society v. Canada (Minister of Transport)* [1992] 1 SCR 3.
60. SOR/84-467.
61. *Supra* n. 59 at para. 37.
62. [1997] 3 SCR 213.
63. *Supra* n. 54.

The defendant argued that the order was *ultra vires* the federal level of government and, therefore, the company could not be held liable in terms of the order for the spill of polychlorinated biphenyls. Despite a sharp internal division, the Supreme Court found that the order was valid as the federal government had jurisdiction to regulate these toxic substances as part of its criminal statutory competence.[64] At the same time, the court took the opportunity to speak more generally about the nature of environmental problems and the scope of various jurisdictional powers to deal with them.[65]

The Supreme Court has also enhanced the environmental authority of municipal governments to deal with environmental issues and underscored the relevance of international environmental law principles in the Canadian context. In the case of *114957 Canada Ltée (Spraytech, Société d'arrosage) v. Hudson (Town)*,[66] a landscaping company was found liable for breaching a municipal by-law passed by the Town of Hudson, Quebec, which restricted the use of pesticides for cosmetic purposes. The company argued that pesticide regulation, already subject to federal and provincial intervention, was not within the jurisdiction of the municipal government. The court further clarified the law relating to inter-jurisdictional conflict in a federal system and upheld that validity of the by-law.[67] By invoking the precautionary principle and the principle of subsidiarity in inter-preting environmental laws in Canada, the judgment encouraged extensive further deliberation about the general significance of these and other environmental principles in the domestic context.[68]

At about the same time as the *Spraytech* case, the court first addressed the class action procedure in environmental cases. In *Hollick v. Metro Toronto (Municipality)*,[69] a group of local residents sought compensation and an injunction against the defendant which operated a municipal landfill in their neighbourhood. The court indicated that while the class action procedure could be useful in environmental cases,[70] it was not found to be the 'preferable procedure' for resolving the common

---

64. *Supra* n. 62 at paras 118-160.
65. *Ibid.*, paras 112-117.
66. [2001] 2 SCR 241.
67. The Supreme Court held that although there was 'a tri-level regulatory regime' in the sense that laws governing pesticides exist at the federal, provincial and municipal levels, since each dealt with a different aspect of pesticide regulation, it was possible to comply with all three and there was accordingly no invalidity. *Ibid.*, paras 39-43.
68. The Supreme Court noted that: '... reading s. 410(1) to permit the Town to regulate pesticide use is consistent with principles of international law and policy ... The interpretation of By-law 270 contained in these reasons respects international law's "precautionary principle" ... In the context of the precautionary principle's tenets, the Town's concerns about pesticides fit well under their rubric of preventive action.' *Ibid.*, paras 30-32.
69. (1999), 32 CELR (NS) 1 (Ont CA), 2001 SCC 68.
70. The court referred to its own precedent in *Western Canadian Shopping Centres v. Dutton* [2001] 2 SCR 534 where it held that '[t]he class action plays an important role in today's world. The rise of mass production, the diversification of corporate ownership, the advent of the mega-corporation, and the recognition of environmental wrongs have all contributed to its growth. A faulty product may be sold to numerous consumers ... Environmental pollution may have consequences for

issues in this case. This was due to the particular facts of the matter, including the court's view that alternative avenues for achieving access to justice were adequate, and that there was no need for litigation to promote behaviour modification on the part of the landfill operators. However, the heart of the court's reservation was its apparent reluctance to allow private, common law actions to play an expanded role in environmental protection.

Another groundbreaking decision took place in 2004, on two very complex and current issues: how to economically value environmental services and harm; and whether the government can sue for environmental harm not only as a property owner, but also based on its *parens patriae* jurisdiction as guardian of the public interest in the environment. In *British Columbia v. Canadian Forest Products Ltd,*[71] a private forestry company was responsible for a fire that also damaged public forests. While the court limited the provincial government's recovery under tort law to the loss of the commercial value of the trees, it declared that this result was solely due to the lack of evidence of broader types of harm. The decision strongly suggested that damages for harm to the forest ecosystem, above and beyond the commercial value of the trees, would be appropriate where ecological loss was clearly made out. It also held that the 'notion of the Crown as holder of inalienable "public rights" in the environment and certain common resources', accompanied by the Attorney General's right 'to sue for their protection representing the Crown as parens patriae' was an important jurisdiction that 'should not be attenuated by a narrow judicial construction'.[72]

Shifting from these historic principles to new environmental frontiers, the court was recently asked to turn its mind to the issue of genetic modification. In *Schmeiser v. Monsanto,*[73] the Supreme Court of Canada held that Monsanto was entitled to the full protection of its patent on genetically modified canola, and that Schmeiser, a conventional farmer, was liable for breach of that patent when he saved seeds from his previous year's harvest and later planted them. Schmeiser's crop was found to contain Monsanto's seeds, although Schmeiser never purchased or planted these seeds. The court was, however, of the view that Schmeiser knew or should have known these seeds had drifted onto his property;[74] presumably creating some obligation on him to destroy that part of the crop where they were located in order to avoid infringing Monsanto's patent on seeds (seeds which it was admitted, drift uncontrollably into other farmers' fields). In a strongly worded dissent, Madame Justice Arbour held that since it is illegal to patent a plant, Monsanto's patent could only extend to the gene and cell, not the seeds and plants

---

citizens all over the country. Conflicts like these pit a large group of complainants against the alleged wrongdoer . . . The class action offers a means of efficiently resolving such disputes in a manner that is fair to all parties' at para. 26, and also ended its reasons, having refused certification in this case, by stating '(w)hile the appellant has not met the certification requirements here, it does not follow that those requirements could never be met in an environmental tort case', at para. 37.

71. 2004 SCC 38.
72. *Ibid.,* paras 74-80.
73. [2004] 1 SCR 902.
74. *Ibid.,* paras 59-68, and paras 92 and 95.

themselves.[75] Her analysis indicates that the court had the option of leading the law on genetically modified plants in a different direction, and of striking a very different balance between the interests of patent holders and the protection of the environment.

This brief overview of significant environmental judgments indicates that the Supreme Court of Canada has contributed to environmental governance in all areas of law including private, administrative, and criminal law, and in areas where there is overlap with competing fields, such as patent and municipal law.

4   CRITICAL SURVEY

The preceding overview of leading environmental decisions, largely drawn from the jurisprudence of the Supreme Court of Canada, provides a basis for a critical thematic survey of the judiciary's contribution to environmental governance.

4.1   FUNDAMENTAL ENVIRONMENTAL VALUES

It has been widely recognized that in the last two decades, the Supreme Court of Canada has made significant contributions to environmental governance by means of its explicit and consistent 'recognition of fundamental environmental values'.[76] This evolution was traced by the court itself in *British Columbia v. Canadian Forest Products Ltd*,[77] where the court started its reasoning with this important contextual statement:

> As the Court observed in *Canada (Attorney General) v. Hydro-Québec*, [1997] 3 SCR 213, at para. 85, legal measures to protect the environment 'relate to a public purpose of superordinate importance'. In *Friends of the Oldman River Society v. Canada (Minister of Transport)*, [1992] 1 SCR 3, the Court declared, at p. 16, that '[t]he protection of the environment has become one of the major challenges of our time. In *R v. Canadian Pacific Ltd*, [1995] 2 SCR 1031, 'stewardship of the natural environment' was described as a fundamental value (para. 55)... Still more recently, in *114957 Canada Ltée (Spray-tech, Société d'arrosage) v. Hudson (Town)*, [2001] 2 SCR 241, 2001 SCC 40, the Court reiterated, at para. 1: ' ... our common future, that of every Canadian community, depends on a healthy environment ... This Court has recognized that '(e)veryone is aware that individually and collectively, we are

---

75. *Ibid.*, para. 108 onward.
76. J.V. DeMarco, 'The Supreme Court of Canada's Recognition of Fundamental Environmental Values: What Could be Next in Canadian Environmental Law?'. *JELP* 17 (2007): 159.
77. *Supra* n. 71.

responsible for preserving the natural environment ... environmental protection [has] emerged as a fundamental value in Canadian society (...).[78]

Commentators have observed that these 'fundamental environmental values' recognized by the Supreme Court of Canada include: environmental rights;[79] the polluter-pays principle;[80] the precautionary principle;[81] the principle of intergenerational equity;[82] the principle of sustainability;[83] and the public trust doctrine.[84]

The Supreme Court's recognition of the fundamental value of environmental protection is important for several reasons. First, when a court perceives a case to be 'environmental', and places the dispute into this specific context, the environmental aspects of the case take an important place in the resolution of the dispute. Indeed, part of the problem in the majority decision in the *Schmeiser*[85] case was that the court approached the dispute as a patent case which happened to involve plants, rather than an environmental conflict which happened to involve patent law.[86] In addition, the fact that it is the Supreme Court that is making these important pronouncements on the value of environmental protection also indicates that the judiciary in Canada does perceive itself as one of the important institutions in resolving environmental problems, rejecting the often-raised arguments that due to their complexity and polycentricity, environmental issues should be resolved by the other branches of government.

Second, this broad-based and repeated emphasis by the Supreme Court on the importance of environmental protection and its nature as a fundamental and shared right can have significant impacts on lawmakers, litigants and lower courts; in terms of future approaches to drafting legislation, framing arguments and crafting reasons for judgments respectively.[87]

---

78. *Ibid.*, para. 8, as cited in DeMarco, *supra* n. 76, 161-62.
79. DeMarco, *supra* n. 76, 165, reports that there are three cases in which the court 'has referred to environmental rights ... Notably, this has occurred regardless of whether the Court has been interpreting statutes in a jurisdiction that explicitly recognizes environmental rights ... or in one that does not.' *R v. Canadian Pacific Ltd* [1995] 2 SCR 1031; *Imperial Oil v. Quebec (Administrative Tribunal)* [2003] 2 SCR 624; *R v. Hydro-Québec, supra* n. 61.
80. Imperial Oil case, *supra* n. 79 as cited in DeMarco, *supra* n. 76, 180.
81. *Supra* n. 66.
82. Imperial Oil case, *supra* n. 79.
83. Friends of the Oldman River Society case, *supra* n. 59; Imperial Oil case, *supra* n. 79.
84. British Columbia case, *supra* n. 71.
85. Schmeiser case, *supra* n. 73.
86. For similar comments in relation to putting procedural rules in context, see H. McLeod-Kilmurray, '*Hollick* and Environmental Class Actions: Putting the Substance into Class Action Procedure', *Ottawa L. R.* 34 (2002-2003): 263.
87. DeMarco, *supra* n. 76. See also M. Campbell, 'Re-inventing Intervention in the Public Interest: Breaking Down Barriers to Access', *Journal of Environmental Law and Practice* 15 (2005): 187 who argues that one of the most significant barriers to interveners is their calculation of the odds that they will be denied leave (in other words any discouraging message the courts send may pre-empt sincere attempts to intervene even in meritorious cases).

4.2   FEDERALISM AND THE ENVIRONMENT

As noted above, the Constitution of Canada[88] divides jurisdiction over environmental management between the federal and provincial governments, with any residual authority falling to the federal government. This situation invariably gives rise to conflicts, overlaps, or omissions.

Perhaps the clearest indication of the contribution of the courts to the challenges of federalism and the environment is the notable evolution in judicial attitudes over the years. This is embodied in two starkly contrasting judgments of Mr Justice La Forest: first, in dissent in *R v. Crown Zellerbach Canada Ltd*;[89] and second, writing for the majority in the *Hydro Quebec* case[90] nine years later. In *Crown Zellerbach*, the majority upheld federal legislation on ocean dumping against claims that it properly fell within provincial jurisdiction under the 'national concern' branch of the residual Peace, Order and Good Government power.[91] The majority was satisfied that protecting the marine environment from pollution has the 'singleness, distinctiveness and indivisibility that clearly distinguishes it from matters of provincial concern and scale of impact on provincial jurisdiction that is reconcilable with the fundamental distribution of legislative power under the Constitution'.[92] However, LaForest J's dissenting reasons, resulting in a 5-4 split on the court, are typical of a more traditional approach to federalism in environmental cases:

> Regulation to control pollution, which is incidentally only part of the even larger global problem of managing the environment . . . has profound implications for the federal-provincial balance mandated by the Constitution. The challenge for the courts, as in the past, will be to allow the federal Parliament sufficient scope to acquit itself of its duties to deal with national and international problems while respecting the scheme of federalism provided by the Constitution. . . . To allocate environmental pollution exclusively to the federal Parliament would, it seems to me, involve sacrificing the principles of federalism enshrined in the Constitution.[93]

Whatever importance the environment might have had, is clearly subordinated to the judicial preoccupation with maintaining the constitutional division of legislative power. It is revealing to contrast LaForest's change of heart when writing for the majority in the *Hydro Quebec* case, discussed above. In that case, the court was no longer asking which level of government *can* legislate for environmental protection; it spoke instead of '[t]he all-important *duty* of Parliament *and* the provincial legislatures to make full use of the legislative powers

---

88. *Constitution Act, 1982*, being Sch. B to the *Canada Act 1982* (UK), 1982, c. 11.
89. [1988] 1 SCR 401.
90. *Supra* n. 62.
91. *Supra* n. 89.
92. *Ibid.*, para. 33.
93. *Ibid.*, paras 62 and 71.

respectively assigned to them in protecting the environment'.[94] The role of the courts is to 'progressively defin[e] the extent to which these powers may be used to that end':[95]

> In performing this task, it is incumbent on the courts to secure the basic balance between the two levels of government envisioned by the Constitution. However, in doing so, they must be mindful that the Constitution must be interpreted in a manner that is fully responsive to emerging realities and to the nature of the subject matter sought to be regulated. Given the pervasive and diffuse nature of the environment, this reality poses particular difficulties in this context.[96]

The priority in the latter judgment was clearly on protecting the environment, with the division of powers interpreted to that end. As noted, the *Hydro Quebec* case broadened the reach of the federal criminal law power. The court held that to trigger the criminal law power, it was not necessary to assimilate environmental considerations within the traditional 'health and security' protection aspect of Canadian criminal law. It held that 'the protection of a clean environment is a public purpose . . . sufficient to support a criminal prohibition'[97] in its own right.

The Canadian experience shows that the federal structure can be used both as a sword and as a shield by government regulators. Thus, the evolution of the thinking of the Supreme Court of Canada, namely that federalism must work to solve environmental problems, not that environmental issues must always be squeezed or distorted to fit into our constitutional structure, sends a judicial message to legislators and executive decision-makers alike that using federalism issues as an excuse not to protect the environment will not be upheld by the courts.

---

94. *Supra* n. 62 at para. 86 (emphasis added).
95. *Ibid.*
96. It is important to note that the dissenting reasons merely held that this particular attempt by the federal government to make a criminal provision relating to toxic substances failed because of the way it was written; the dissent agreed with the majority that the federal government could create such a criminal provision: ' . . . none of this should be read as foredooming future attempts by Parliament to create an effective national – or, indeed, international – strategy for the protection of the environment. We agree with La Forest J. that achieving such a strategy is a public purpose of extreme importance and one of the major challenges of our time. There are, in this regard, many measures open to Parliament which will not offend the division of powers set out by the Constitution, notably the creation of environmental crimes. Nothing, in our view, prevents Parliament from outlawing certain kinds of behaviour on the basis that they are harmful to the environment. But such legislation must actually seek to outlaw this behaviour, not merely regulate it.' *Ibid.*, para. 61.
97. He went on to justify his reversal from his earlier reasons: 'In *Crown Zellerbach*, I expressed concern with the possibility of allocating legislative power respecting environmental pollution exclusively to Parliament. I would be equally concerned with an interpretation of the Constitution that effectively allocated to the provinces, under general powers such as property and civil rights, control over the environment in a manner that prevented Parliament from exercising the leadership role expected of it by the international community and its role in protecting the basic values of Canadians regarding the environment through the instrumentality of the criminal law power.' *Ibid.*, para. 154.

Similarly, it can also be read as encouraging, or at least permitting, bold and innovative legislative strategies aimed at protecting the environment while respecting the division of powers.[98]

4.3   STRENGTHENING ENVIRONMENTAL LEGISLATION

Another often-cited example of the impact of courts on environmental protection in Canada is the significant role played by the judiciary in strengthening early approaches to EA. These decisions, including that in the *Oldman River* case, eventually resulted in a statutory scheme governing this area of environmental protection. In this case, an instrument that the government had understood to be merely a guideline or policy document, was held to be binding law: federal departments were under an enforceable legal duty to comply with it.

Litigation to compel federal EAs has often been initiated by environmental protection advocates or local residents who were dissatisfied with the provincial assessment process. They sought to involve the federal government in order to obtain a more thorough or effective assessment; and ultimately to have the development in question, or at least its environmentally harmful impacts, stopped. In many of these cases, despite delays in the judicial review proceedings, the federal ministers were held to have a duty to comply with EA requirements.[99]

Unfortunately, the courts in Canada have in more recent times been considerably more reluctant to add to the effectiveness of the legislative scheme now in place. For example, the environmentally disastrous Alberta Oil Sands projects[100] have not only passed through the EA process, but also through judicial challenges to this process. In the case of *Prairie Acid Rain Coalition v. Canada (Minister of Fisheries & Oceans)*,[101] the Fort Hills Oil Sands Project was subject to both a provincial and a federal EA. The Coalition objected to the federal Minister of

---

98. *Species at Risk Act* SC 2002, c. 29.
99. See e.g.: *Friends of the Island Inc. v. Canada*, [1993] 2 FC 229 (TD), reversed only as to costs (1995), 131 DLR (4th) 285 (FCA), appeal to SCC refused (1996), 138 DLR (4th) vii (SCC); *Alberta Wilderness Association v. Cardinal River Coals Ltd* [1993] 3 FC 425 (TD); and other cases cited in H. McLeod-Kilmurray, '*Stichting Greenpeace* and Environmental Public Interest Standing before the [European] Community Judicature: Some Lessons from the Federal Court of Canada', *CYELS* 1 (1998): 269-306.
100. The Alberta Oil sands projects involve extracting bitumen from the earth to create oil in a process that is environmentally devastating and whose resulting oil is more polluting in terms of greenhouse gas emissions than more conventionally sourced oil. For two contrasting views, see Sierra Club of Canada, 'Tar Sands Time Out Newest Press Release', <www.tarsandstimeout.ca/index.php?option=com_content&task=view&id=13 &Itemid=34>, 12 September 2008, and the Government of Alberta, 'What is Oil Sands', <www.energy.gov.ab.ca/OilSands/793.asp>, 12 September 2008. An example of judicial review being granted in relation to environmental assessment of one such project, particularly on the issue of greenhouse gas emissions, is *Pembina Institute for Appropriate Development v. Canada (Attorney General)* 2008 FC 302 (TD).
101. 2006 FCA 31.

Fisheries and Oceans exercising his discretion to delimit the scope of the federal assessment required, determining this to be 'the destruction of Fort Creek and ancillary or subsidiary works and activities',[102] a very small piece of the overall oil sand project. The court here determined that the standard of review was 'reasonableness' because, '[a]s long as the responsible authority takes into account relevant considerations and does not take into account irrelevant considerations, the Court should not engage in a re-weighing process'.[103] The court dismissed the application, finding that the narrow scope for the EA, as determined by the minister, was not unreasonable. This decision has been criticized by environmental groups, who not only call for individual oil sands projects to be assessed in their entirety, but claim that the only adequate EA would be a regional assessment to evaluate the cumulative impacts of all the oil sands projects in the Athabascan region.[104]

The *Prairie Acid Rain* decision seems to be premised on the argument that courts merely apply the law, and reveals a strongly deferential stance by the judiciary. Whether this deference is justified by the presumed expertise of the executive branch, or some notion that courts are ill equipped to deal with complex scientific assessments, it certainly marks a shift away from the judicial approach to EA legislation in its earlier days in Canada. Given the government's stated support for EA generally, and Canada's international obligations in terms of EA, including climate change which the oil sands clearly affect, this turn toward judicial deference causes one to ask whether Canadian courts are continuing their historic role of contributing to, and strengthening, environmental protection legislation.

4.4   PROCEDURAL INNOVATIONS TO FACILITATE ENVIRONMENTAL
               LITIGATION

Some of the most significant impediments to allowing courts to play a more effective role in environmental protection involve issues of procedure and not substance. Most environmental harms are imposed on large groups of people, and therefore they do not fit comfortably within the traditional two-party, private law, and adversarial model of litigation. Many of the innovations which have

---

102. *Ibid.*, at para. 6.
103. *Ibid.*, at para. 11.
104. Sierra Legal Defence Fund news release of 6 October 2003 reads: 'over 20 oil sands developments are proposed for the Athabasca region. Alarmingly, says the Sierra Club, this onslaught of development is being evaluated on a project by project basis, despite the probability of unforeseen and undesirable cumulative effects from this proliferation of development.' See SLDF, 'Regional Environmental Assessment Needed for Oil Sand Region', <www.sierraclub.ca/national/media/oil-sands-03-10-06.html>, 12 September 2008. See also declaration by Canada's Environmental Community on 'Managing Tar Sands for the Long Term' in the Sierra Club of Canada, 'Tar Sands Action Guide: A Guide to Environmental Advocacy during, and after, the Oil Sands Public Consultations', <www.sierraclub.ca/prairie/files/TarSandsActionGuide.pdf>, 12 September 2008.

alleviated procedural barriers such as standing, intervention, group litigation and costs, were created by the courts themselves.[105]

Barriers such as standing and costs are not only relevant from a procedural perspective. They impact on whether an environmental case gets brought to court, who brings it and how; and accordingly also significantly impact on the evolution of substantive environmental law.[106] If it were not for judicial innovations in relation to standing and interveners, Canadian courts would not have: played such an important role in strengthening EA in Canada;[107] had the benefit of a variety of viewpoints when addressing the novel issue of genetic modification;[108] incorporated international environmental principles into Canadian law;[109] or helped to focus attention on the broad economic and intrinsic value of environmental resources and services.[110]

The barrier of standing prevented those who did not have a direct, personal interest in a dispute from litigating it.[111] The Supreme Court of Canada developed the public interest standing rule,[112] which now provides that anyone can bring an issue to court if: (1) there is a serious issue to be tried; (2) the applicant has a genuine interest in the issue; and (3) there is no 'other reasonable and effective way to bring the issue before the Court'.[113] Interested individuals or groups may also participate in environmental cases if they obtain leave to act as interveners.[114]

---

105. In some cases, these changes were later included in legislation.
106. On various aspects of the importance of procedural rules in environmental litigation, see McLeod-Kilmurray, *'Stichting Greenpeace'*, *supra* n. 99; McLeod-Kilmurray, *'Hollick'*, *supra* n. 86, 301-305; H. McLeod-Kilmurray, *'Hoffman v. Monsanto*: Courts, Class Actions, and Perceptions of the Problem of GM Drift', *Bulletin of Science, Technology and Society* 27, no. 3 (2007): 188, and McLeod-Kilmurray, 'Lowering Barriers', *supra* n. 6.
107. See cases discussed above, many of which were brought by citizen or public interest groups benefitting from public interest standing rules.
108. *Harvard College v. Canada (Commissioner of Patents)* [2002] 4 SCR 45; Schmeiser case, *supra* n. 73.
109. Spraytech case, *supra* n. 66.
110. British Columbia case, *supra* n. 71.
111. The traditional public nuisance rule provided that where harm was imposed on the public generally, the Attorney General must bring the case to court on behalf of the public, unless any individual could show special damage. A classic case is *Hickey v. Electric Reduction Co. of Canada Ltd* (1970), 21 DLR (3d) 368 (Nfld TD).
112. The test was developed in a trilogy of cases involving challenges to the constitutionality of legislation: *Thorson v. Attorney General of Canada* [1975] 1 SCR 138, *Nova Scotia Board of Censors v. McNeil* [1976] 2 SCR 265, and *Minister of Justice of Canada v. Borowski* [1981] 2 SCR 575; and expanded to the administrative law sphere in *Minister of Finance v. Finlay* [1986] 2 SCR 607. Although not dealing expressly with environmental issues, the rules developed by the courts above are of direct relevance to the environmental context.
113. Borowski case, *supra* n. 112, 598, as cited in the Finlay case, *supra* n. 112, para. 26.
114. Ontario *Rules of Civil Procedure*, RRO 1990, Reg. 194, (amended to O. Reg. 260/05); *Supreme Court of Canada Rules*, SOR/2002-1456; see also J.V. DeMarco, 'Assessing the Impact of Public Interest Interventions on the Environmental Law Jurisprudence of the Supreme Court of Canada: A Quantitative and Qualitative Analysis', *Supreme Court Law Review* (2d) 30 (2005): 299; J. Koshan, 'Dialogue or Conversation? The Impact of Public Interest Interveners on Judicial Decision Making', in *Canadian Institute for the Administration*

Scholars have found that public interest interveners have strongly impacted on the development of important precedents in environmental law, in particular by: making new, or fuller, arguments on points of law; suggesting 'novel interpretive approaches' to legislative interpretation; bringing inter-disciplinary research findings to the attention of the court; enlarging the context to include 'social, cultural or economic circumstances'; and presenting comparative jurisprudence.[115]

Despite these advances, procedural barriers remain. One is the issue of liability for legal costs. The Ontario Law Reform Commission has called for immunity from costs for public interest interveners,[116] which becomes more important when government funding for public interest litigation is not available.[117] An even more promising judicial innovation is the awarding of interim costs. *B.C. (Minister of Forests) v. Okanagan Indian Band*,[118] involved a logging dispute on land to which the Band claimed it had aboriginal title. The court granted interim costs to the impecunious aboriginal respondents.[119] The court held that access to justice should outweigh the goal of indemnification in public interest cases.[120] However, interim costs have not been widely awarded.

Not all environmental public interest cases which have reached the courts as a result of generous rules of standing, intervention or costs, are won on the merits.[121]

---

of Justice, Participatory Justice in a Global Economy: The New Rule of Law, ed. P. Hughes & P. Molnari (Montreal: Les Editions Themis, 2004), 246.

115. Mr Justice J.C. Major, 'Interveners and the Supreme Court of Canada', *National (A.B.C.)* 8, no. 3 (1999): 27, as summarized by DeMarco, *supra* n. 114, 301.

116. Recommendation 17 of the Ontario Law Reform Commission suggested the following approach: 'An intervenor will be immune from costs where all of the following conditions have been met: where the proceeding involves issues the importance of which extends beyond the immediate interests of the parties involved; where the intervenor has no personal, proprietary or pecuniary interest in the outcome of the proceeding or, if he or she has such an interest, it clearly does not justify the intervention economically; and where the intervenor has contributed significantly to the resolution of the issues.... an intervenor generally may recover costs from another party.' OLRC, Report on the Law of Standing (Toronto: Ontario Ministry of the Attorney General, 1989).

117. Adequate funding is an important factor not only in determining whether to intervene at all, but in limiting how effective an intervener can be if leave is granted. Michael Jeffery has argued that those seeking to protect the environment often lack the resources to make their participation effective, frustrating decision-makers who know that the case for one is more fully presented than the opposing view. See M. Jeffery, 'Intervenor Funding as the Key to Effective Citizen Participation in Environmental Decision-Making: Putting the People Back into the Picture', *Ariz. JICL* 19 (2002): 643.

118. [2003] 3 SCR 371, aff'g (2001), 95 BCLR (3d) 273 (BCCA), varying 2000 BCSC 1135.

119. See further C. Tollefson, D. Gilliland & J.V. DeMarco, 'Towards a Public Interest Costs Jurisprudence', *CBR* 83 (2004): 477, <www.law.uvic.ca/ctollef/documents/costsinpublic interestlitigation.pdf>, 6 August 2008.

120. *Ibid.* See also C. Tollefson, 'The Implications of Okanagan Indian Band for Public Interest Litigants: A Strategic Discussion Paper', AGM: Court Challenges Program of Canada (Winnipeg, 19 November 2005), </www.law.uvic.ca/ctollef/documents/Okanagan-paper-myNov17final_000.doc>, 6 August 2008.

121. A good example is where the Sierra Club of Canada sought to challenge the Canadian governments' decision to approve the building of two CANDU reactors (see generally Canadian

The courts must balance competing interests in each individual case brought before them. Two things are however clear: first, an approach to procedure which limits access without fairly balancing the competing interests means that there is no possibility of the environment winning on the merits. Second, without these procedural innovations, many important environmental issues would not have received judicial attention and analysis, and many perspectives – judicial as well as public – would not have evolved to their current state. These procedural innovations, which allowed greater access to justice, greater diversity of representation and increased participation, are necessary prerequisites for an effective judicial role in environmental protection.[122]

4.5   RECONCILING ENVIRONMENTAL AND ABORIGINAL RIGHTS

Aboriginal rights to lands and resources figure prominently in Canadian environmental litigation, occasionally in a manner that is consistent with environmental protection legislation, and sometimes in conflict with it. As previously noted, section 35 of the Canadian Charter of Rights and Freedoms[123] provides that the 'existing aboriginal and treaty rights of the aboriginal peoples of Canada are hereby recognized and affirmed'. In several cases,[124] aboriginal peoples engaging in fishing or other traditional resource use were charged with violating environmental protection laws. This permitted the judicial consideration and legal evolution of aboriginal, constitutional and fiduciary law within the environmental context. Recent cases such as *Delgamuukw v. British Columbia*[125] confirmed the importance of aboriginal rights, yet also affirmed that these constitutionally protected aboriginal rights can be limited by environmental laws. In *Marshall v. Canada*,[126] the Supreme Court affirmed that this also applied to aboriginal rights derived from treaties, although it clarified the basis on which infringements will be permissible. To be permissible, legislation that infringes aboriginal rights must be based on a valid legislative objective. It must involve appropriate consultation with the affected aboriginal peoples,[127] and constitute a minimal infringement of their rights.

Nuclear Association, 'Nuclear Facts: What is the Qinshan Project?', <www.cna.ca/english/pdf/NuclearFacts/NulcearFacts-Qinshan-july2003.pdf>, 6 August 2008.) The case was never heard on the merits as Sierra agreed to drop the case in return for the respondents agreeing to forego thousands of dollars in court costs awarded against Sierra. Elizabeth May, then of Sierra, argued that this had the effect of removing 'a political scandal [. . .] from any possibility of exposure in the courts'. In this regard see E. May, 'Why the CANDU case was dropped', <www.sierraclub.ca/national/programs/atmosphere-energy/nuclear-free/candu-case/candu-case-2003.html>, 6 August 2008.

122. See McLeod-Kilmurray, 'Lowering Barriers', *supra* n. 6.
123. *Supra* n. 29, s. 35.
124. See, e.g.: *R v. Sparrow* [1990] 1 SCR 1075; and *R v. Gladstone* [1996] 2 SCR 723.
125. [1997] 3 SCR 1010.
126. [1999] 3 SCR 533 (Marshall No. 2).
127. The duty to consult outlined in *Delgamuukw* was confirmed in *Haida Nation v. British Columbia* [2004] 3 SCR 511 to apply to developments in relation to land which is the subject of ongoing land claims negotiations but to which title has not been finally confirmed.

The special fiduciary duty of the federal government toward aboriginal peoples must be respected. Cases to date demonstrate the difficult challenges courts face in balancing environmental concerns against competing fundamental interests and values, even constitutionally protected ones.

However, the potential of aboriginal constitutional and treaty rights may not yet have been fully explored. Scholars have argued that protecting aboriginal rights, where these are dependent on use of natural resources and intimate cultural connection to land and place, may necessarily entail the right to environmental protection.[128] An even more ambitious argument is that the right to use these resources necessarily implies the right to their use in an uncontaminated state.[129] Conversely, interference with environments, ecosystems and habitats may constitute indirect infringement of aboriginal rights, or a breach of the government's fiduciary duty.

> The greater the success of [arguments for including habitat protection or general ecosystem management as part of the nature or content of an Aboriginal or treaty right], the more constitutionally entrenched ecosystem conservation will be and the more opportunities that will exist for habitat protection.[130]

These are arguments Canadian courts may face in the near future.

More fundamentally, the intersection between aboriginal and environmental issues presents opportunities for greater judicial roles in environmental governance. It also provides an opportunity for changing judicial approaches to these questions, which may in turn influence attitudes among lawmakers, policy-makers and the public. These include issues of environmental justice and environmental racism, and the insights of some aboriginal perspectives on environmental philosophy or ethics. While the environmental justice literature is still developing in Canada, it is clear that aboriginal peoples enjoy far fewer of the benefits and suffer far more of the costs of activities resulting in environmental harm. Mercury poisoning,[131] higher concentrations of toxics in breast-milk[132] and changes to the gender

---

128. M. Valiante, 'Legal Foundations of Canadian Environmental Policy', in *Canadian Environmental Policy: Context and Cases*, ed. D. Van Nijnatten & R. Boardman, 2nd ed. (Oxford: OUP, 2002), 9-12, and as excerpted in Hughes, et al., *supra* n. 38, 457.

129. See L.M. Collins, 'Indigenous Environmental Rights in Canada: the Right to Conservation Implicit in Treaty and Aboriginal Rights to Hunt, Fish, and Trap', Unpublished paper on file with authors.

130. J. Woodward & T. Syed, 'The Importance of Aboriginal Rights and Perspectives for Species Protection and Habitat Conservation', paper presented at the National Conference on Aboriginal Law and Governance, Pacific Business and Law Institute, (Vancouver, BC, 21 June 2000), 4-14 to 4-23, and as excerpted in Hughes, Lucas and Tilleman, *supra* n. 128, 460.

131. *Grassy Narrows and Islington Indian Bands Mercury Pollution Claims Settlement Act* SC 1986, c. 23.

132. E. Dewailly et al., 'High Levels of PCBs in Breast Milk of Inuit Women from Arctic Quebec', *BECT* 43 (1989): 641, as cited in E. Dewailly & C. Furgal, 'POPs, the Environment and Public Health', in *Northern Lights Against POPs: Combating Toxic Threats in the Arctic*, ed. D.L. Downie & T. Fenge (Montreal: McGill-Queens UP, 2003), 3.

distribution in birth rates among aboriginal communities,[133] are some of the most extreme effects of environmental injustice in Canada, and are inequities which the courts could play a role in rectifying.

4.6   CREATIVE ENVIRONMENTAL SENTENCING

Canadian courts have often sought to indicate that environmental harm is illegal and offensive and should be treated as such so as to achieve the criminal law goals of punishment and deterrence. More recent and creative approaches to sentencing have also attempted to emphasize its potential preventative and remediatory role, which is even more important in the context of environmental law.

    One of the most comprehensive analyses of the underlying philosophy, purposes and relevant factors in environmental sentencing, particularly in situations with a corporate defendant, was the 1980 case of *R v. United Keno Hill Mines Ltd,*[134] written by Mr Justice Stuart of the Yukon Territorial Court. The offending corporation was charged with discharging mining effluent into a creek in excess of its water license. The court provided a detailed inventory of the kinds of harm done by pollution to human health and the environment, and the problem of overlooking cumulative impacts.[135] While it conceded that there is a 'range of inherent criminality in pollution offences', the court emphasized that 'pollution offences must be approached as crimes, not as morally blameless technical breaches of a regulatory standard'.[136] Key factors which the court highlighted as requiring consideration during sentencing included the 'nature of the environment affected, . . . [and the] extent of injury'.[137] The court stated that the fact that the offender is a corporation, adds additional sentencing factors such as the 'criminality of conduct, . . . extent of attempts to comply, . . . remorse, . . . size of corporation, . . . profits realized by the offence . . . [and] criminal record'.[138] The court further noted that '[i]n most cases restitution is a better means of attacking illegal gains than a fine. Restitution might embrace losses to corporate competitors, damage to public and private property, and the cost of prosecution'.[139]

    The court went on to consider a range of 'sentencing tools' beyond the traditional monetary fine, including: personal liability of corporate directors;[140]

---

133. C.A. Mackenzie, A. Lockridge & M. Keith, 'Declining Sex Ratio in a First Nation Community', *Environmental Health Perspectives* 113 (2005): 1295, <ehp.niehs.nih.gov/docs/2005/8479/abstract.html>, 6 August 2008.
134. (1980) 10 CELR 43 (Yukon Terr. Crt.).
135. *Ibid.*, para. 9.
136. *Ibid.*, para. 10.
137. *Ibid.*, paras 11-16, (including not only the actual damage caused but the potential damage that might have emanated from the polluter's activities as well as 'the consequential or peripheral adverse impacts, the prospects and cost of repairing the damage, the duration of the damage', at para. 14).
138. *Ibid.*, paras 17-37.
139. *Ibid.*, para. 35.
140. *Ibid.*, paras 38-48.

continuing judicial orders to prevent continued violations by repeat corporate offenders;[141] and the possible involvement of victims, or at least public interest environmental groups to personify them, in devising appropriate penalties.[142] These principles and factors are very much in keeping with the non-mandatory sentencing criteria later incorporated in section 287 of the *Canadian Environmental Protection Act*, 1999.

The court also made reference to creative environmental sentencing, though limiting itself to a fine in that case. Subsequent legislative amendments have permitted the courts to be more creative and varied in their sentencing options, such as: ordering defendants to publish details of the offence; imposing continuing monitoring and reporting obligations; or ordering defendants to implement pollution prevention plans, environmental audits or 'an environmental management system that meets a recognized Canadian or international standard'.[143] *R v. Prospec Chemicals Ltd*[144] was the first case in which a corporate defendant was sentenced to have its environmental management system come into compliance with the international standard of ISO 14000.[145] Other interesting orders have included: paying part of a fine to the Environmental Damages Fund,[146] educational funds, research funds, environmental groups or projects; and other preventive approaches to ensure the defendant does not repeat its actions.[147]

4.7   MISSED OPPORTUNITIES: TOXIC TORTS

Some commentators argue that the common law – despite its prominent contribution in early decisions such as *Groat v. Edmonton* and *KVP v. McKie* – is now underutilized. It has even been suggested that 'tort's unique characteristics enable it to supplement, and in some cases even outperform, statutory environmental law'.[148]

---

141. *Ibid.*, para. 53, proposal 9.
142. *Ibid.*, at para. 53, proposal 10. On the facts of this case, the contrition and cooperation of the corporation, as well as lack of significant environmental harm, led to a moderate penalty. However, the clear and detailed analysis of underlying principles regarding the role of criminal law in environmental protection, and the special considerations applying to corporations, was a breakthrough.
143. CEPA, *supra* n. 11, c. 33, s. 291(e).
144. (2000), 75 Alta LR (3d) 267.
145. ISO, 'ISO 14000 Essentials', <www.iso.org/iso/iso_14000_essentials>, 10 September 2008.
146. The Environmental Damages Fund (EDF) serves as a special purpose account to manage funds received as compensation for environmental damage. Environment Canada is the custodian and administers the EDF on behalf of the government of Canada. For further information on the Fund see generally: Environment Canada, 'Environment Canada Damages Fund', <www.ec.gc.ca/edf-fde>, 12 September 2008.
147. See, e.g.: *R v. Gemtec* 2007 NBQB 199; and the news release on 6 November 2006 by Environment Canada, 'Saint John Company Found Guilty of Illegal Sale of Ozone-Depleting Substances', <atlantic-web1.ns.ec.gc.ca/newsreleases/Default.asp?lang=En&n=80A2D6D4-1>, 12 September 2008.
148. L.M. Collins, 'Strange Bedfellows? The Precautionary Principle and Toxic Tort: A Tort Paradigm for the 21st Century', *ELR* 7 (2005): 10362.

Indeed, some regard the common law as the best tool for challenging the *status quo* of inadequate regulatory standards or enforcement.[149]

However, Canadian courts have not embraced the potential of common law actions to respond to the evolving challenges of modern environmental problems, at least in the context of class action litigation.[150] Despite recent class action legislation in many provinces,[151] and indications by the Supreme Court itself that environmental cases with their complexity and diffuse effects, are ideally suited to class litigation,[152] there have been very few environmental class actions certified.[153] This seems to have much to do with judicial attitudes toward allowing private law to play an important role in resolving mass torts.

In three recent cases, *Hollick*, *Pearson*, and *Hoffman*,[154] class actions were brought based on private common law actions such as negligence, private nuisance, public nuisance, trespass and under the strict liability principle in *Rylands v. Fletcher*.[155] In each case, the applicants sought both compensatory damages and injunctions to prevent continuation of the harm. The courts generally held that the class action was not the preferable procedure for resolving these particular disputes. The courts' analysis of the tort claims is, however, significant.

A recurring theme inherent in each of these cases was the courts' finding that the alleged harm had to be assessed on an individual rather than collective basis. While it is possible that the request for damages caused the courts to become unduly focused on individual recovery, as opposed to the first stage of the inquiry, namely where legal liability lay,[156] it is interesting to note that the courts seemed to

---

149. See, e.g.: J. Lowry & R. Edmunds (eds), *Environmental Protection and the Common Law* (Oxford: Hart Publishing, 2000); and M.D. Faieta et al., (eds), *Environmental Harm: Civil Actions and Compensation* (Toronto: Butterworths, 1996).

150. See: McLeod-Kilmurray, '*Hollick*', *supra* n. 86; and McLeod-Kilmurray, '*Hoffman*', *supra* n. 106.

151. See, e.g.: Ontario *Class Proceedings Act* 1992, SO 1992, c. 6; and Saskatchewan *Class Actions Act* SS 2001, c. C-12.01.

152. See *Western Canadian Shopping Centres Inc. v. Dutton* 2001 SCC 46, para. 26.

153. See *Comité d'environnement de la Baie Inc. v. Société d'electrolyse et de chimie Alcan Ltée* (1990), 6 CELR (NS) 150, and R. Cotton, A.P. Brebner & C.L. Clairman, 'Environmental Class Actions: The Revenge of the Neighbourhoods', paper given at the Mass Tort Litigation Insight Conference (Toronto, 9 November 1998), 95, as cited in McLeod-Kilmurray, '*Hoffman*', *supra* n. 106.

154. Hollick case, *supra* n. 69, involved neighbours challenging pollution from a landfill. In *Pearson v. Inco Ltd* (2005), 18 CPC (6th) 77, inhabitants sued a local factory for nickel contamination. *Hoffman v. Monsanto Canada Inc.* [2007] 6 WWR 387, involved organic canola farmers suing the marketers of genetically modified canola. Certification was refused in the Hollick and Hoffman cases, and was granted in the Pearson case only after the claims were greatly reduced from environmental and health claims to mere claims for reduction in property values.

155. *Rylands v. Fletcher* (1868) LR 3 HL 330 (HL).

156. See McLeod-Kilmurray, '*Hoffman*', *supra* n. 106, referring to D. Rosenberg, 'Class Actions for Mass Torts: Doing Individual Justice by Collective Means', *Ind. L. J.* 62 (1986-87): 561, and D. Rosenberg, 'Decoupling Deterrence and Compensation Functions in Mass Tort Class Actions for Future Loss', *Virg. L. R.* 88 (2002): 1871.

adopt excessively technical readings of the tort requirements; to require that the proof of common law actions themselves were individual rather than collective issues. In the *Hollick* case, for example, the court held, in relation to the claim of private nuisance for the drift of odour and debris from the landfill site, that:

> liability for nuisance in the present case in favour of any individual property owner or resident, can only be established by evidence that the particular individual personally suffered sensible discomfort or evidence that emissions from the defendant's premises have interfered with the reasonable enjoyment of their properties. . . . Every incident complained of would have to be separately examined together with its impact upon every household and a conclusion reached as to whether each owner or occupier had been impacted sufficiently that a finding of nuisance is justified.[157]

However, an analysis of the elements of private nuisance – namely assessing the severity of harm, duration of interference, sensitivity of the plaintiff, character of the neighbourhood, utility of the defendant's conduct and the reasonableness of the use of property – all require an assessment of the experience of affected parties living in the area where the nuisance occurred. Accordingly, any judicial analysis of these elements would be significantly enhanced, rather than hindered, by considering evidence of the collective experience, as opposed to just that of individuals.[158]

In the *Hoffman* case,[159] the court could not say with certainty that the organic farmers would fail in their claim based on the fact that the drifting genetically modified seeds amounted to an interference with enjoyment of their land, and significantly stated that: 'anyone who actively creates a nuisance whether or not in occupation of the land from which it emanates can be liable and this liability continues so long as the offensive condition remains regardless of his ability to abate it and stop the harm'.[160] However, the judge did go on to say that:

> The implications of holding a manufacturer, or even inventor, liable in nuisance for damage caused by the use of its product or invention by another would be very sweeping indeed. It is my conclusion that where the activity complained of is the activity of one who is not in occupation or control of adjoining land, and no independent malfeasance is alleged, then, at the very least, direct causation of the damage alleged must be alleged. This is not the case. I conclude that there are no facts alleged in this case that could support a finding that the defendants substantially caused the nuisance alleged.[161]

It is apparent from this statement that the Canadian judiciary is resistant to expanding tort liability in environmental cases of this nature. While this may be due to a

---

157. *Supra* n. 69 at para. 20-22.
158. See McLeod-Kilmurray, '*Hollick*', *supra* n. 86, 301-305.
159. *Supra* n. 154.
160. *Ibid.*, at para. 113.
161. *Ibid.*, at para. 122.

perception that these issues have been adequately addressed in legislation, it has been argued that government approval alone should not preclude private law actions, especially where this legislation and the government agencies responsible for its implementation, are failing to protect the environment.[162]

A restrictive approach to private law causes of action in the environmental context undermines both the role of the courts and the utility of the common law in environmental protection. As long ago as 1972, a leading Canadian commentator said that the very strength of common law actions is their ability to evolve with changing social problems and priorities, such as those associated with environmental protection, and that: 'indeed, if it is the genius of the common law to extend existing principle to accommodate new social reality, the challenge here is irresistible'.[163] As evidenced by the recent jurisprudence discussed above, the Canadian judiciary at this time does unfortunately not appear to view the challenge in a similar light.

5   CONCLUSION: NEXT STEPS, KEY CHALLENGES AND
           KEY OPPORTUNITIES

Although Canadians continue to await a vigorous national response to climate change, environmental protection statutes, EA legislation and basic biodiversity programmes have been in place for some time. Legal reform in the past few decades has led to the development of comprehensive federal and provincial legislative frameworks to safeguard the environment and to promote sustainable development in Canada. These new legal frameworks now require effective implementation.

Mechanisms to promote compliance are varied and include voluntary codes, economic incentives, information-based strategies, novel administrative monetary penalties, and formal enforcement action in the form of criminal prosecution. Many past opportunities for Canadian judicial innovation in the environmental sphere have been directly associated with the exercise of prosecutorial authority. In this regard, we have noted various significant Canadian decisions such as *Sault St. Marie*, *Crown Zellerbach*, *Sparrow*, *Bata* and *United Keno Mines*. These cases gave rise to new insights with, on occasion, distinct environmental features. They did, however, largely engage the courts on traditional grounds such as the liberty of citizens in relation to government action and interrelation between the authority of different spheres of government.

---

162. McLeod-Kilmurray, '*Hollick*', *supra* n. 86, 299; McLeod-Kilmurray, '*Hoffman*', *supra* n. 106, 196; J. Chandler, 'Manufacturer Liability for the drift of GM plants and the Effect of Prior Government Approval', paper presented at The Fields of Law panel discussion, University of Ottawa Faculty of Law (Ottawa, 30 March 2006).
163. J.P.S. McLaren, 'The Common Law Nuisance Actions and the Environmental Battle – Well-Tempered Swords or Broken Reeds?', *Osgoode Hall L. J.* 10 (1972): 510.

The substantial contribution of public interest litigants to the courts' environmental docket should not, however, be forgotten as EA decisions, such as that in the *Oldman River* case, so clearly illustrate. This is an area, especially at the federal level, where determined and persistent environmental advocates have closely monitored the exercise of statutory authority by government.[164] There is every reason to believe that such scrutiny will continue.[165]

These judicial review cases may be distinguished from the previous cluster of prosecutorial cases because they focus on public authority with respect to the environment. While many have dealt with issues of statutory interpretation or the standard of judicial review of administrative action, they have at least served to introduce the courts to the purposes, goals, aspirations and values of environmental law, albeit in sometimes rudimentary ways.

Although conflicts of this nature will continue to arise, there is a range of factors which may alter the nature of the future role of the Canadian judiciary in environmental governance. Policy shifts in the direction of voluntary measures or towards economic incentives as key tools for influencing behaviour, have been noted above. The virtues of voluntary instruments in particular, have received recent attention.[166] There is also evidence in Canada, however, of a greater willingness to explore the utility of economic incentives as supplements or alternatives to the traditional command and control approach to regulation.[167] Should these types of regulatory measures gain favour, there is some possibility that more traditional forms of environmental enforcement will correspondingly decline in prominence. In addition, human and financial resource constraints experienced by enforcement authorities could systematically reduce the frequency with which legal controversies emerge from prosecutorial action in the environmental field. Indeed, while observers are hesitant to advance explanations for the trend, there are already indications that prosecutorial activity has declined in some Canadian jurisdictions.[168] On the civil front, the costs of litigation and the continuing possibility of an adverse cost award against unsuccessful public interest litigants constitute significant deterrents to approaching the courts for relief. Recent indications from the bench suggest a modest alleviation of these concerns. However, the situation

---

164. See, e.g.: *Friends of the West Country Assn. v. Canada (Minister of Fisheries and Oceans)* (1999), 31 CELR (NS) 239 (FCA); and *Canadian Parks and Wilderness Society v. Canada (Minister of Canadian Heritage)* (2003), 1 CELR (3d) 20 (FCA).
165. See, e.g.: *Miningwatch Canada v. Canada (Minister of Fisheries and Oceans)* (2008) FCA 209.
166. See, e.g.: R.B. Gibson (ed.), *Voluntary Initiatives: the new politics of corporate greening* (Peterborough: Broadview Press, 1999); and K. Webb (ed.), *Voluntary Codes: Private Governance, the Public Interest and Innovation* (Ottawa: Carleton Research Unit for Innovation, Science and Environment, 2004).
167. See, e.g.: National Round Table on the Environment and the Economy, *Economic Instruments for Long-term Reductions in Energy-based Carbon Emissions* (Ottawa: The Round Table, 2005).
168. West Coast Environmental Law Association, *No Response: A Survey of Environmental Law Enforcement and Compliance in British Columbia* (Vancouver: WCELA, 2007).

remains uncertain and as we have noted above, threatens to restrict the future development of private law principles in the environmental context.

We are not alone in speculating about general forces that may shape the field of environmental law in Canada. There are, writes one well-respected colleague, 'increasing pressures for greater openness and accountability, for more democratic processes, and for justice, all of which require accommodation in the design and implementation of environmental law'.[169] In addition to these underlying political considerations, the author notes the following future influences: '[T]he economy (and particularly the process of globalization), the developments in information technology, and the shift to a service economy will have a significant impact; legal developments at the international level will increasingly affect Canadian environmental law.'[170]

International developments have already exerted a considerable influence on Canadian environmental law. It was in the aftermath of Our Common Future,[171] the report of the World Commission on Environment and Development, that the concept of sustainable development found its way into the preambles and purpose clauses of numerous federal and provincial environmental statutes. The precautionary principle followed a similar trajectory and it was with explicit reference to international experience that the Supreme Court of Canada speculated as to its possible relevance in determining the validity of municipal by-law decisions.[172]

The statutory entrenchment of these international environmental law principles, alongside environmental science-based principles (such as adaptive management or ecological integrity) and ethical principles (such as inter-generational equity), represent a future source of challenge and opportunity for the judiciary.[173]

Several of these concepts have already played central roles in Canadian environmental litigation, with mixed results. Judicial application of sustainability in the context of Ontario forest management legislation strongly re-enforced the underlying principle.[174] Ecological integrity as a decision-making standard was to a significant degree undermined by judicial interpretation.[175] The polluter pays principle has been vigorously endorsed at the highest level of Canadian

---

169. M. Valiante, 'The Future of Environmental Law', in Hughes, et al., *supra* n. 38, 658.
170. *Ibid.*
171. World Commission on Environment and Development, *Our Common Future* (Oxford: OUP, 1987).
172. *114957 Canada Ltée (Spraytech) v. Hudson (Town)* 2001 SCC 40.
173. J. Benidickson et al., *Practicing Precaution and Adaptive Management: Legal, Institutional and Procedural Dimensions of Scientific Uncertainty* (Ottawa: UOIE, 2005).
174. See, e.g.: *Algonquin Wildlands League v. Ontario (Minister of Natural Resources)* (1998), 26 CELR (NS) 163 (Ont Div Ct); (2000), 32 CELR (NS) 233 (Ont. CA).
175. See, e.g.: *Canadian Parks and Wilderness Society v. Canada (Minister of Canadian Heritage)* (2003), 1 CELR 3d 20 (FCA). See further S. Fluker, 'Maintaining Ecological Integrity is Our First Priority – Policy Rhetoric or Practical Reality in Canada's National Parks?', *JELP* 13 (2003): 131.

jurisprudence.[176] However, the value of environmental loss for which such payment might be expected remains less certain.[177]

Across the country, significant statutory advances are in evidence. For example, new endangered species legislation from the province of Ontario takes biological diversity as its point of departure. The preamble of this Act states:

> Biological diversity is among the great treasures of our planet. It has ecological, social, economic, cultural and intrinsic value. Biological diversity makes many essential contributions to human life, including foods, clothing and medicines, and is an important part of sustainable social and economic development.[178]

As disputes and uncertainties arise concerning the application of this and similar legislation, such language provides a strong signal concerning the expectations of law-makers and offers a wide range of levers for environmentally-supportive interpretations.

Effective implementation of environmental values throughout the Canadian legal system will entail more widespread acceptance of sustainability as a fundamental norm taking its rightful place alongside fairness within the constellation of overarching judicial principles. That process may be underway in Canada, but it has not enjoyed the encouragement of constitutional recognition that has been observed in some other jurisdictions.

The Canadian judiciary has shown that it can, and does, play a role in allowing the law to evolve to meet the needs of modern problems, and can influence societal attitudes toward these issues, while remaining within its limited role as only one branch in the process of environmental governance. Judges in Canada have assured its populace that the environment is important, as is the role of the judiciary in its protection and governance. The Supreme Court of Canada has stated, for example, that 'individually and collectively, we are responsible for preserving the natural environment', and that environmental protection is 'a public purpose of superordinate importance'.[179] The next few years will offer opportunities to determine if Canadian courts really mean it.

BIBLIOGRAPHY

Bakker, K. (ed.). *Eau Canada: The Future of Canada's Water*. Vancouver, BC: UBC Press, 2007.

Benidickson, J. et al. *Practicing Precaution and Adaptive Management: Legal, Institutional and Procedural Dimensions of Scientific Uncertainty*. Ottawa: University of Ottawa Institute of the Environment, 2005.

---

176. *Imperial Oil Ltd v. Quebec (Minister of the Environment)* [2003] 2 SCR 264.
177. *British Columbia v. Canadian Forest Products Ltd* 2004 SCC 38.
178. See, e.g.: *Endangered Species Act 2007*, SO 2007. c. 6.
179. See, e.g.: *R. v. Canadian Pacific Ltd* [1995] 2 SCR 1028 at p.1075.

Benidickson, 'Water Supply and Sewage Infrastructure in Ontario, 1880-1990s: Legal and Institutional Aspects of Public Health and Environmental History' <ozone.scholarsportal.info/bitstream/1873/7663/1/10294043.pdf>, 1 August 2008. In *The Walkerton Inquiry: Commissioned Paper 1* edited by S. Protti. Toronto: Ontario Ministry of the Attorney General, 2002.

Berger, Hon. T.R. *Northern Frontier, Northern Homeland: Report of the Mackenzie Valley Pipeline Inquiry.* Vol. 1 & 2. Ottawa: Minister of Supply and Services, 1977.

Binnie, I. 'Science in the Courtroom: the Mouse that Roared' *University of New Brunswick Law Journal* 56 (2007): 307-327.

Borrows, J. 'Living between Water and Rocks: The Environment, First Nations and Democracy' (Toronto, University of Toronto Press, 2002).

Brubaker, E. *Property Rights in the Defence of Nature.* <www.environmentprobe.org/enviroprobe/pridon/index.html>, 1 August 2008. Toronto: Earthscan Publications, 1995.

Campbell, M. 'Re-inventing Intervention in the Public Interest: Breaking Down Barriers to Access'. *Journal of Environmental Law and Practice* 15 (2005): 187-218.

Canada Environmental Community. 'Managing Tar Sands for the Long Term'. <www.sierraclub.ca/prairie/files/TarSandsAction Guide.pdf>, 12 September 2008.

Canadian Abridgement. *Canadian Court System.* Toronto: Thomson/Carswell, 2006.

Canadian Nuclear Association. 'Nuclear Facts: What is the Qinshan Project?'. <www.cna.ca/english/pdf/NuclearFacts/NulcearFacts-Qinshan-july2003.pdf>, 6 August 2008.

Canadian Nuclear Association. 'Qinshan Nuclear Facts'. <www.cna.ca/english/pdf/NuclearFacts/NulcearFacts-Qinshan-july2003.pdf#search='qinshan'>, 17 November 2008.

Chandler, J. 'Manufacturer Liability for the drift of GM plants and the Effect of Prior Government Approval'. Paper presented at The Fields of Law panel discussion, University of Ottawa Faculty of Law. Ottawa, 30 March 2006.

Collins, L.M. 'Indigenous Environmental Rights in Canada: the Right to Conservation Implicit in Treaty and Aboriginal Rights to Hunt, Fish, and Trap'. Unpublished paper on file with authors.

Collins, L.M. 'Strange Bedfellows? The Precautionary Principle and Toxic Tort: A Tort Paradigm for the 21st Century'. *Environmental Law Reports* 7 (2005): 10361-10371.

Commission for Environmental Co-operation. *Children's Health and the Environment in North America.* Montréal, Québec: Commission for Environmental Cooperation, 2006.

Cotton, R., A.P. Brebner & C.L. Clairman. 'Environmental Class Actions: The Revenge of the Neighbourhoods', paper given at the Mass Tort Litigation Insight Conference. Toronto, 9 November 1998.

Currie, J. *Public International Law.* Toronto: Irwin Law, 2001.

DeMarco, J.V. 'Assessing the Impact of Public Interest Interventions on the Environmental Law Jurisprudence of the Supreme Court of Canada: A Quantitative and Qualitative Analysis'. *Supreme Court Law Review* (2d) 30 (2005): 299-332.

DeMarco, J.V. 'The Supreme Court of Canada's Recognition of Fundamental Environmental Values: What Could be Next in Canadian Environmental Law?'. *Journal of Environmental Law and Practice* 17 (2007): 159-204.

Dewailly, E. & C. Furgal. 'POPs, the Environment and Public Health'. In *Northern Lights Against POPs: Combating Toxic Threats in the Arctic*, edited by D.L. Downie & T. Fenge. Montreal: McGill-Queens UP, 2003.

Dewailly, E. et al. 'High Levels of PCBs in Breast Milk of Inuit Women from Arctic Quebec'. *Bulletin of Environmental Contamination and Toxicology* 43 (1989): 641-646.

Environment Canada. 'Environment Canada Damages Fund'. <www.ec.gc.ca/edf-fde>, 12 September 2008.

Environment Canada. 'Saint John Company Found Guilty of Illegal Sale of Ozone-Depleting Substances'. <atlantic-web1.ns.ec.gc.ca/newsreleases/Default.asp?lang=En&n=80A2D6D4-1>, 12 September 2008.

Faieta, M.D. et al. (eds). *Environmental Harm: Civil Actions and Compensation*. Toronto: Butterworths, 1996.

Fluker, S. 'Maintaining Ecological Integrity is Our First Priority – Policy Rhetoric or Practical Reality in Canada's National Parks?'. *Journal of Environmental Law and Practice* 13 (2003): 131-135.

Forcese, C. & A. Freeman. *The Laws of Government: The Legal Foundations of Canadian Democracy*. Toronto: Irwin Law, 2005.

Friedland, M.L. *A Place Apart: Judicial Independence and Accountability in Canada*. Ottawa: Canadian Judicial Council, 1995.

Gall, G. *The Canadian Legal System*. 5th ed. Toronto: Carswell, 2004.

Gibson, R.B. (ed.). *Voluntary Initiatives: the new politics of corporate greening*. Peterborough: Broadview Press, 1999.

Giroux, L. 'Environmental Law in Quebec'. In *Environmental Law and Policy*, edited by E. Hughes, A.R. Lucas & W.A. Tilleman, 3rd ed. Toronto: Emond Montgomery, 2003.

Gonthier, C. Justice. 'Sustainable Development and the Law'. *McGill International Journal on Sustainable Development Law and Policy* 1 (2005): 11-18.

Government of Alberta. 'What is Oil Sands'. <www.energy.gov.ab.ca/OilSands/793.asp>, 12 September 2008.

Hogg, P. *Constitutional Law of Canada*. Scarborough, Ont.: Carswell, 2007.

Hughes, E., Lucas, A., and Tilleman, W. (eds), *Environmental Law and Policy*. 3rd ed. Toronto: Emond Montgomery, 2003.

International Organization for Standardization, online: <www.iso.org/iso/iso_14000_essentials>.

ISO. 'ISO 14000 Essentials'. <www.iso.org/iso/iso_14000_essentials>, 10 September 2008.

Jeffery, M. 'Intervenor Funding as the Key to Effective Citizen Participation in Environmental Decision-Making: Putting the People Back into the

Picture'. *Arizona Journal of International and Comparative* Law 19 (2002): 643-677.

Keyes, J.M. *Executive Legislation*. Toronto: Butterworths, 1992.

Koshan, J. 'Dialogue or Conversation? The Impact of Public Interest Interveners on Judicial Decision Making'. In *Canadian Institute for the Administration of Justice, Participatory Justice in a Global Economy: The New Rule of Law*, edited by P. Hughes & P. Molnari. Montreal: Les Editions Themis, 2004.

Laing, Hon. R.D. Report of the Commission of Inquiry into matters relating to the safety of the public drinking water in the City of North Battleford, Saskatchewan. Saskatoon: Commission of Inquiry, 2002.

Lederman, S.N. 'Judges as Gatekeepers: The Admissibility of Scientific Evidence Bases on Novel Theories'. In *Special Lectures 2003: The Law of Evidence*, edited by Law Society of Upper Canada. Toronto: Irwin Law, 2004.

Lederman, W.R. 'The Independence of the Judiciary'. *Canadian Bar Review* 34 (1956): 1139-1179.

Lowry, J. & R. Edmunds (eds). *Environmental Protection and the Common Law*. Oxford: Hart Publishing, 2000.

Mackenzie, C.A., A. Lockridge & M. Keith. 'Declining Sex Ratio in a First Nation Community'. *Environmental Health Perspectives* 113 (2005): 1295-1298. <ehp.niehs.nih.gov/docs/2005/8479/abstract.html>, 6 August 2008.

Major, Mr Justice J.C. 'Interveners and the Supreme Court of Canada', *National (A.B.C.)* 8, no. 3 (1999): 27.

May, E. 'Why the CANDU case was dropped'. <www.sierraclub.ca/national/programs/atmosphere-energy/nuclear-free/candu-case/candu-case-2003.html>, 6 August 2008.

McLaren, J.P.S. 'The Common Law Nuisance Actions and the Environmental Battle – Well-Tempered Swords or Broken Reeds?'. *Osgoode Hall Law Journal* 10 (1972): 505-562.

McLeod-Kilmurray, H. '*Hoffman v. Monsanto*: Courts, Class Actions, and Perceptions of the Problem of GM Drift'. *Bulletin of Science, Technology and Society* 27, no. 3 (2007): 188-201.

McLeod-Kilmurray, H. '*Hollick* and Environmental Class Actions: Putting the Substance into Class Action Procedure'. *Ottawa Law Review* 34 (2002-2003): 263-306.

McLeod-Kilmurray, H. 'Lowering Barriers to Judicial Enforcement: Civil Procedure and Environmental Ethics'. Proceedings of 4th Annual Colloquium of the IUCN Academy of Environmental Law, (forthcoming).

McLeod-Kilmurray, H. '*Stichting Greenpeace* and Environmental Public Interest Standing before the Community Judicature: Some Lessons from the Federal Court of Canada'. *Cambridge Year Book of European Legal Studies* 1 (1998): 269-306.

Monahan, P. *Constitutional Law*. Toronto: Irwin Law, 2006.

Myers, R.A. & B. Worm. 'Rapid worldwide depletion of predatory fish communities'. *Nature* 423 (2003): 280-283.

National Round Table on the Environment and the Economy. *Economic Instruments for Long-term Reductions in Energy-based Carbon Emissions*. Ottawa: The Round Table, 2005.

National Round Table on the Environment and the Economy. *Getting to 2050: Canada's Transition to a Low-emission Future*. Ottawa: The Round Table, 2007.

O'Connor, Hon. D.R. Report of the Walkerton Inquiry. Ontario: Queen's Printer for Ontario, 2002.

OLRC. Report on the Law of Standing. Toronto: Ontario Ministry of the Attorney General, 1989.

Rosenberg, D. 'Class Actions for Mass Torts: Doing Individual Justice by Collective Means'. *Indiana Law Journal* 62 (1986-87): 565-566.

Rosenberg, D. 'Decoupling Deterrence and Compensation Functions in Mass Tort Class Actions for Future Loss'. *Virginia Law Review* 88 (2002): 1871-1919.

Russell, R. *Canada's Trial Courts: Two Tiers or One?* Toronto: University of Toronto Press, 2007.

Salembier, J.P. *Regulatory Law and Practice in Canada*. Toronto: Butterworths, 2004.

Schindler, D.W. & W.F. Donahue. 'An impending water crisis in Canada's western prairie provinces'. <www.pnas.org/cgi/doi/10.1073/pnas.0601568103>, 31 July 2008.

Sierra Club of Canada. 'Tar Sands Action Guide: A Guide to Environmental Advocacy during, and after, the Oil Sands Public Consultations'. <www.sierraclub.ca/prairie/files/TarSandsActionGuide.pdf>, 12 September 2008.

Sierra Club of Canada. 'Tar Sands Time Out Newest Press Release'. <www.tarsandstimeout.ca/index.php?option=com_content&task=view&id=13&Itemid=34>, 12 September 2008.

Simpson, G., M. Jaccard & N. Rivers. *Hot Air: Meeting Canada's Climate Change Challenge*. Toronto: McClelland & Stewart, 2007.

SLDF. 'Regional Environmental Assessment Needed for Oil Sand Region'. <www.sierraclub.ca/national/media/oil-sands-03-10-06.html>, 12 September 2008.

Strayer, B.L. *The Canadian Constitution and the Courts*. 2nd ed. Toronto: Butterworths, 1983.

Swaigen, J. & A.D. Levy. 'The Expert's Duty to the Tribunal: A Tool for Reducing Contradictions Between Scientific Process and Legal Process'. *Canadian Journal of Environmental Law and Practice* 11 (1997): 277-302.

Swaigen, J. 'The Role of the Civil Courts in Resolving Risk and Uncertainty in Environmental Law' *Journal of Environmental Law and Practice* 1 (1990): 199-217.

Swanson, E. & E. Hughes. *The Price of Pollution: Environmental Litigation in Canada*. Edmonton AB: Environmental Law Centre, 1990.

Tollefson, C. 'The Implications of Okanagan Indian Band for Public Interest Litigants: A Strategic Discussion Paper', AGM: Court Challenges Program of

Canada (Winnipeg, 19 November 2005). </www.law.uvic.ca/ctollef/documents/Okanagan-paper-myNov17final_000.doc>, 6 August 2008.

Tollefson, C., D. Gilliland & J.V. DeMarco, 'Towards a Public Interest Costs Jurisprudence', *Canada Bar Review* 83 (2004): 473-514. <www.law.uvic.ca/ctollef/documents/costsinpublicinterestlitigation.pdf>, 6 August 2008.

UNEP. 'Johannesburg Principles on the Role of Law and Sustainable Development'. Adopted at the Global Judges Symposium, Johannesburg, South Africa, 18-20 August 2002. <www.pnuma.org/deramb_ing/JohannesburgPrinciples.pdf>, 12 September 2008.

Valiante, M. 'Legal Foundations of Canadian Environmental Policy'. In *Canadian Environmental Policy: Context and Cases*, edited by D. Van Nijnatten & R. Boardman, 2nd ed. Oxford: Oxford University Press, 2002.

Valiante, M. 'The Future of Environmental Law'. In *Environmental Law and Policy*, edited by E. Hughes, A.R. Lucas & W.A. Tilleman, 3rd ed. Toronto: Emond Montgomery, 2003.

Webb, K. (ed.). *Voluntary Codes: Private Governance, the Public Interest and Innovation*. Ottawa: Carleton Research Unit for Innovation, Science and Environment, 2004.

Wenner, L.M. 'Environmental Policy in the Court'. In *Environmental Policy in the 1990s*, edited by N.J. Vig & M.E. Kraft. 2nd ed. Washington DC: CQ Press, 1994.

West Coast Environmental Law Association. *No Response: A Survey of Environmental Law Enforcement and Compliance in British Columbia*. Vancouver: WCELA, 2007.

Wigle, D. *Child Health and the Environment*. Oxford: Oxford University Press, 2003.

Woodward, J. & T. Syed. 'The Importance of Aboriginal Rights and Perspectives for Species Protection and Habitat Conservation'. Paper presented at the National Conference on Aboriginal Law and Governance. Pacific Business and Law Institute, Vancouver, BC, 21 June 2000.

World Commission on Environment and Development. *Our Common Future*. Oxford: Oxford University Press, 1987.

TABLE OF LEGISLATION

Act respecting The KVP Company Limited SO 1950, c. 33
Canada Act 1982 (UK), 1982, c. 11
Canadian Charter of Rights and Freedoms 1982
Canadian Environmental Assessment Act SC 1992, c. 37
Canadian Environmental Protection Act RSC 1985, (4th Supp.), c-16
Canadian Environmental Protection Act SC 1999, c. 33
Class Actions Act SS 2001, c. C-12.01
Class Proceedings Act 1992, SO 1992, c. 6
Clean Air Act C-5.2

TABLE OF CASES

Burgess v. The City of Woodstock [1955] OR 814 (HC)

Canada (Human Rights Commission) v. Canadian Liberty Net [1998] 1 SCR 626

Canadian Parks and Wilderness Society v. Canada (Minister of Canadian Heritage) (2003), 1 CELR (3d) 20 (FCA)

Comité d'environnement de la Baie Inc. v. Société d'electrolyse et de chimie Alcan Ltée (1990), 6 CELR (NS) 150

Delgamuukw v. British Columbia [1997] 3 SCR 1010

Friends of the Island Inc. v. Canada (1995), 131 DLR (4th) 285 (FCA)

Friends of the Island Inc. v. Canada (1996) 138 DLR (4th) vii (SCC)

Friends of the Island Inc. v. Canada [1993] 2 FC 229 (TD)

Friends of the Oldman River Society v. Canada (Minister of Transport) [1992] 1 SCR 3

Friends of the West Country Assn. v. Canada (Minister of Fisheries and Oceans) (1999), 31 CELR (NS) 239 (FCA)

Groat v. Edmonton [City] [1928] SCR 522

Haida Nation v. British Columbia [2004] 3 SCR 511

Harvard College v. Canada (Commissioner of Patents) [2002] 4 SCR 45

Hickey v. Electric Reduction Co. of Canada Ltd (1970), 21 DLR (3d) 368 (Nfld TD)

Hoffman v. Monsanto Canada Inc. [2007] 6 WWR 387

Hollick v. Metro Toronto (Municipality) (1999), 32 CELR (NS) 1 (Ont CA), 2001 SCC 68

Imperial Oil v. Quebec (Administrative Tribunal) [2003] 2 SCR 624

K.V.P. Co. v. McKie [1949] SCR 698; [1949] 1 DLR 39 (Ont CA); [1948] 3 DLR 201 (Ont. HC)

Marshall v. Canada [1999] 3 SCR 533 (Marshall No. 2)

Miningwatch Canada v. Canada (Minister of Fisheries and Oceans) (2008), 33 CELR (3d) 1 (FC)

Minister of Finance v. Finlay [1986] 2 SCR 607

Minister of Justice of Canada v. Borowski [1981] 2 SCR 575

Nova Scotia Board of Censors v. McNeil [1976] 2 SCR 265

Pearson v. Inco Ltd (2005), 18 CPC (6th) 77

Prairie Acid Rain Coalition v. Canada (Minister of Fisheries & Oceans) 2006 FCA 31

R v. United Keno Hill Mines Ltd (1980), 10 CELR 43 (Yukon Terr. Crt.)

R v. Bata Industries Ltd (1992), 9 OR (3d) 329 (Prov. Ct.)

R v. Canadian Pacific Ltd [1995] 2 SCR 1031

R v. Canadian Pacific Railway [1995] 2 SCR 1028

R v. Crown Zellerbach Canada Ltd [1988] 1 SCR 401

R v. Gemtec 2007 NBQB 199

R v. Gladstone [1996] 2 SCR 723

R v. Hydro Québec [1997] 3 SCR 213

R v. Prospec Chemicals Ltd (2000), 75 Alta LR (3d) 267

R v. Sault St. Marie [1978] 2 SCR 1299

R v. Sparrow [1990] 1 SCR 1075

R v. Valente [1985] 2 SCR 673
Re Remuneration of Judges (1997) [1997] 3 SCR 3
Reference re Waters and Water Powers [1929] SCR 19
Rylands v. Fletcher (1868) LR 3 HL 330 (HL)
Schmeiser v. Monsanto [2004] 1 SCR 902
Stephens v. The Village of Richmond Hill [1955] OR 806 (HC), [1956] OR 88 (CA)
Thorson v. Attorney General of Canada [1975] 1 SCR 138
Western Canadian Shopping Centres v. Dutton [2001] 2 SCR 534

ABBREVIATIONS

CEPA   Canadian Environmental Protection Act
CEAA   Canadian Environmental Assessment Act
CCME   Canadian Council of Ministers of the Environment
NJI   National Judicial Institute
EA   Environmental Assessment
EDF   Environmental Damages Fund
GM   Genetically Modified
GMOs   Genetically modified Organisms
ISO   International Organization for Standardization
OLRC   Ontario Law Reform Commission
SLDF   Sierra Legal Defence Fund
WCELA   West Coast Environmental Law Association

Chapter 7
Brazil

Ingo Sarlet and Tiago Fensterseifer*

1   INTRODUCTION

A State's primary reason for existing is based on the duty to respect, protect and promote its citizens' dignity (individually or collectively). This goal must therefore be continuously accomplished by the State – and by society itself, if one were to afford the duty a wide interpretation and application. The contemporary State's protection duties are based on its constitutional commitment to generally promote the achievement of fundamental rights and to remove possible obstacles to their fulfilment. The implementation of fundamental liberties and guarantees accordingly requires purposeful and positive action (not only negative action in the sense that rights should be protected) by the public authorities, aimed at removing relevant economic, social and cultural obstacles.

The *Constitution of the Federal Republic of Brazil* (BFC) of 1988 contains various fundamental rights and duties, including an environmental right. Any deterrence or obstacle that interferes with the fulfilment of the environmental right (such as the conduct or omission of an individual or organ of State) must accordingly be dealt with and eradicated by the State.

---

*   Our sincere thanks go to Ivar Hartmann, Pontifical Catholic University of Porto Alegre for his efforts in translating this chapter. We also thank Professor Carlos Molinaro for his useful comments.

Louis J. Kotzé and Alexander R. Paterson (eds), *The Role of the Judiciary in Environmental Governance: Comparative Perspectives*, pp. 249–267.
© 2009 Kluwer Law International BV, The Netherlands.

The current constitutional profile of the Democratic State of Brazil (as envisaged by the BFC) constructs the State as both a 'guardian' and a 'friend' of all fundamental rights,[1] including the environmental right. All organs of State are therefore bound by the duty to realize fundamental rights, especially insofar as this duty relates to the improvement and safeguarding of human dignity. Fundamental rights in general, and specifically the environmental right, accordingly impose a positive obligation on the State to realize the objectives of these rights. Thus, to a greater or lesser extent, all State organs are constitutionally obliged to act as effectively as possible, within their constitutional mandates, to promote the fulfilment of citizens' fundamental rights.

One of the key organs of State is the judiciary, which plays an important role in fulfilling the constitutional dictate imposed on the State. This chapter considers the role that the Brazilian judiciary plays in safeguarding and realizing environmental rights and entitlements. The principal hypothesis is that the judiciary must direct and mould its actions by always taking into account its constitutional duty as a guardian of the environmental right, fending off actions or omissions (private or public) which violate this right. Moreover, the judiciary is constitutionally mandated to exercise judicial control over actions which may damage or threaten any constitutional right.[2] The present enquiry is therefore firmly based on an environmental rights-based approach and contemporary constitutional theory.

Within the above context, this chapter: identifies the main environmental challenges facing Brazil; overviews the environmental legal framework which seeks to regulate these challenges; describes the structure of the Brazilian judicial system; critically analyses relevant jurisprudence which illustrates the role of the Brazilian judiciary in environmental governance, particularly pertaining to omissions by the State (the legislative and executive authorities) to realize environmental rights; and finally, critically evaluates the judiciary's performance to date.

2   MAIN ENVIRONMENTAL ISSUES

Owing to the size of country, the complexity of ecosystems falling within its territory and the different socio-economic realities confronting the nation, Brazil faces a diverse array of environmental problems. Among the most salient ecological issues are the deforestation of the Amazon Jungle and other prime ecological sites such as the world's largest area of wetlands (*Pantanal*) and the Atlantic Forest (Mata Atlântica). This deforestation is for the most part the result of expanding agricultural activity (chiefly of cattle farms) generating a cycle of devastation, habitat destruction, biodiversity depletion and species extinction.

---

1. On the affirmation of the contemporary State of Law model as a State that is a 'guardian or friend' of fundamental rights, see J.C. Vieira De Andrade, *Os Direitos Fundamentais na Constituição Portuguesa de 1976* [The Fundamental Rights on the Portuguese 1976 Constitution], 2nd ed. (Coimbra: Almedina, 2001), 143.
2. Art. 5(XXXV) of the BFC.

In addition to the above challenges facing Brazil's natural environment, there are many problems facing those situated in its urban environments. A significant proportion of the Brazilian population does not have access to clean drinking water, especially those residing in the north-eastern region of the country. Waste management and basic sanitation services are inadequate. Issues of environmental justice are also prevalent as workers and low-income families are frequently compelled to live adjacent to industrial areas, exposing them to high levels of pollution, especially air pollution.

3   PRINCIPAL ENVIRONMENTAL LAWS

The Brazilian legal system has endorsed a commitment to the protection of the environment, especially since the 1980s, with the promulgation of the *National Environmental Protection Policy Statute* 6.938 of 1981 and the *Public Civil Action Statute* 7.347 of 1985. It must be acknowledged, however, that even prior to the prescription of these two laws, several others had shaped the initial normative scheme for environmental protection in Brazil. These included the *Popular Action Statute* 4.717 of 1965, the *Forest Act* 4.717 of 1965, the *Wildlife Protection Act* 5.197 of 1967 and the *Civil and Criminal Liability Act for Nuclear Activities* 6.453 of 1977. Other important environmental laws emanating from the period preceding the promulgation of the BFC in 1988 include the *Whale Hunting Prohibition Act* 7.643 of 1987, the *National Coastal Zone Management Act* 7.661 of 1988 and the *National Environment Fund Act* 7.661 of 1988.

Following the entrance of the BFC, a number of new environmental laws were promulgated in order to give effect to the environmental right enshrined therein. These include the *Toxic Substance Control Act* 7.802 of 1989, the *National Water Act* 9.433 of 1997, the *Environmental Crime Act* 9.605 of 1998, the *National Environmental Education Policy Act* 9.795 of 1999, the *National Park System Mining Regulation Act, the City Act* 10.257 of 2001, the *Bio Safety Act* 11.105 of 2005 and the *Water and Sewage Act* 11.445 of 2007.

4   CONSTITUTIONALIZATION OF ENVIRONMENTAL
           PROTECTION IN BRAZIL

The BFC was enacted in 1988. Under the strong influence of the international legal order[3] and the emergence of domestic environmental and ecological values, the right to an ecologically balanced environment was enshrined as a fundamental

---

3. Particularly the sentiments reflected in the UN Stockholm Declaration on the Human Environment (1972), the Rio de Janeiro Declaration on Environment and Development (1992), the UN Framework Convention on Climate Change (1992), the Convention on Biodiversity (1992), and the Vienna Declaration and Programme of Action, enacted during the Second World Conference on Human Rights (1993).

right in the BFC. It further establishes a set of principles and rules related to environmental protection,[4] thereby acknowledging the vital influence of environmental quality on human development (especially in so far as it influences human dignity) in the sense of warranting and promoting universal welfare.

Besides constitutionalizing environmental protection in the Brazilian legal system in the chapter 'Social Order of the Constitution,' the BFC contains several other provisions relating to environmental protection, thereby linking environmental protection with several other constitutional themes.[5] Article 225 read with Article 5(2) confers on the environmental right the status of a fundamental right attributed to individuals and the community, and also renders environmental protection one of the fundamental objectives of the Brazilian democratic State. There is accordingly constitutional recognition of the dual nature of environmental protection in the Brazilian legal system; a duty on the State and the community to give effect to

---

4. Ch. VI – Environment – Art. 225. According to this provision: 'All have the right to an ecologically balanced environment, which is an asset of common use and essential to a healthy quality of life, and both the Government and the community shall have the duty to defend and preserve it for present and future generations. Paragraph 1 – In order to ensure the effectiveness of this right, it is incumbent upon the Government to: I – preserve and restore the essential ecological processes and provide for the ecological treatment of species and ecosystems; II – preserve the diversity and integrity of the genetic patrimony of the country and to control entities engaged in research and manipulation of genetic heritage; III – define, in all units of the Federation, territorial spaces and their components which are to receive special protection, any alterations and suppressions being allowed only by means of law, and any use which may harm the integrity of the attributes which justify their protection being forbidden; IV – require, in the manner prescribed by law, for the installation of works and activities which may potentially cause significant degradation of the environment, a prior environmental impact study, which shall be made public; V – control the production, sale and use of techniques, methods or substances which represent a risk to life, the quality of life and the environment; VI – promote environmental education in all school levels and public awareness of the need to preserve the environment; VII – protect the fauna and the flora, with prohibition, in the manner prescribed by law, of all practices which represent a risk to their ecological function, cause the extinction of species or subject animals to cruelty. Paragraph 2 – Those who exploit mineral resources shall be required to restore the degraded environment, in accordance with the technical solutions demanded by the competent public agency, as provided by law. Paragraph 3 – Procedures and activities considered as harmful to the environment shall subject the *infractors*, be they individuals or legal entities, to penal and administrative sanctions, without prejudice to the obligation to repair the damages caused. Paragraph 4 – The Brazilian Amazonian Forest, the Atlantic Forest, the *Serra do Mar*, the *Pantanal Mato-Grossense* and the coastal zone are part of the national patrimony, and they shall be used, as provided by law, under conditions which ensure the preservation of the environment, therein included the use of mineral resources. Paragraph 5 – The unoccupied lands or lands seized by the states through discriminatory actions which are necessary to protect the natural ecosystems are inalienable. Paragraph 6 – Power plants operated by nuclear reactor shall have their location defined in federal law and may not otherwise be installed.'
5. As for the constitutional provisions that relate environmental matters with other themes and fundamental rights, the following can be cited as examples: Art. 7(XXII) and Art. 200(VIII) (the right to labour); Art. 170(VI) (the economic order and free initiative); Art. 186(II) (the right to property); Art. 200(VIII) (the right to health); Art. 216(V) (cultural rights); Art. 220(3)(II) (social communication); Art. 225(1)(VI) (the right to education); and Art. 231(1) (indigenous rights).

the right, and the right of individuals ' . . . to an ecologically balanced environment, which is an asset of common use and essential to a healthy quality of life.'

The 'fundamental right and duty' model of environmental protection enshrined in the BFC modifies the traditional approach whereby the State is the sole guardian of the environment. According to the BFC, the whole of Brazilian society (individuals and the community) share this role with the State. This enables citizens to approach a court to require adjudication on environmental matters, either through an associative citizens' suit (that is through civil environmental associations) or individually. This interpretation can be derived from the normative content of Article 225 of the BFC. Moreover, the collective nature of the environmental right was illustrated in a recent decision where the Brazilian Supreme Court stressed the *duty of solidarity* that emanates from the environmental right and from which flows the obligation of environmental protection; an obligation shared by the community and the State.[6]

In tune with similar developments in other countries, the constitutionalization of environmental protection was preceded by a long struggle, starting with an increase in awareness in political and social circles. Environmental activism, which began to flourish in the 1970s, later resulted in the adoption of legislative measures that introduced a significant number of claims and new environmental values within judicial and political domains in Brazil. The most important statute dedicated exclusively to environmental protection is the *National Environmental Protection Policy Statute* 6.938 of 1981 (NEPPS), which establishes the regulatory framework for environmental protection in the Brazil. The statute also provides a thorough and systematic approach to the subject of environmental protection. Amongst its most important aspects are the liability regime, which imposes strict liability on polluters,[7] and procedures for environmental impact assessment (EIA).[8] The NEPPS must be read with the *Public Civil Action Statute* 7.347 of 1985, which prescribes civil liability for environmental damage.[9] It allows for both individuals and groups of individuals (acting through civil associations) to protect the environmental rights enshrined in the BFC,[10] thereby assuring higher levels of social control and, as a result, greater public participation in environmental governance.

In terms of the BFC, the object of environmental protection may exist in four different dimensions, which may be partially or wholly integrated. These are: a) the

---

6. It is noteworthy that (as expressed in the decision itself) the constitutional demand for environmental protection implies the existence of a: 'special obligation – which is up to the State and collectivity itself – of defending and preserving it for the benefit of the present and future generations, so as to avoid, in this manner, the outburst, in the bosom of social communion, of the grave intergenerational conflicts marked by the disrespect to the solidarity duty in the protection of the integrity of this essential asset, which is of common use to all those who compose the social group'. SFC, Full Bench, Direct Action of Unconstitutionality no. 3.540-1 (Federal District), Court opinion delivered by Min. Celso de Mello, 1 September 2005.
7. Art. 14(1).
8. Art. 10.
9. Art. 1(I).
10. Art. 5.

natural or physical environment, which includes natural resources generally, and which consists of land, water, the atmosphere, flora and fauna; b) the cultural environment, which includes the historical, artistic, landscape, archaeological and tourist heritage; c) the artificial or man-made environment, which includes constructed urban space, ranging from buildings to public utilities; and d) the working environment, which concerns the environment where work is performed.[11] Brazilian legal doctrine[12] and jurisprudence[13] are mutually supportive when it comes to acknowledging the right to a healthy environment as one of the fundamental rights. In addition to Title II of the BFC (the central provision listing fundamental rights and guarantees), Article 5(2)[14] specifically enshrines the environmental right.

The majority of commentators are of the opinion that the environmental right has, in terms of Article 5(1) of the BFC, direct application to other norms outlining fundamental rights and warranties. The environmental right is protected from possible constitutional amendment by Article 60(4)(IV) of the BFC. The right is also shielded from any measure diminishing its scope or its power to provide legal protection as it is subject to the provision prohibiting social retreat.[15] In the

---

11. Art. 7(XXII, XXIII and XXXIII); and Art. 200 (II and VIII) of the BFC.
12. On this subject see, among others, A.H. Benjamin, 'Meio Ambiente e Constituição: Uma Primeira Abordagem' [Environment and Constitution: A First Approach], paper given at Anais do 6° Congresso Internacional de Direito Ambiental (São Paulo: IMESP, 2002), 89-101; J.R. Morato Leite, *Dano Ambiental: do Individual ao Coletivo Extrapatrimonial* [Environmental Damage: from Individual Damage to Immaterial Collective Damage] (São Paulo: Revista dos Tribunais, 2000), 15-96; F.L.F. Medeiros, *Meio ambiente: Direito e Dever Fundamental* [Environment: Fundamental Right and Duty] (Porto Alegre: LdA, 2004); A.P. Gavião Filho, *Direito Fundamental ao Ambiente* [Fundamental Right to the Environment] (Porto Alegre: LdA, 2005); O.P.B. Teixeira, *O Direito ao meio Ambiente Ecologicamente Equilibrado como Direito Fundamental* [The Right to an Ecologically-Balanced Environment as a Fundamental Right] (Porto Alegre: LdA, 2006); J.A. da Silva, *Direito Ambiental Constitucional* [Environmental Constitutional Law], 4th ed. (São Paulo: Malheiros, 2003); P.A.L. Machado, *Direito Ambiental Brasileiro* [Brazilian Environmental Law], 13th ed. (São Paulo: Malheiros, 2005), especially Title II of Ch. I: *Constituição Federal e Meio Ambiente* [Federal Constitution and Environment], 102-144. More recent works include J.J.G. Canotilho & J.R. Morato Leite (eds), *Direito Constitucional Ambiental Brasileiro* [Brazilian Constitutional Environmental Law] (São Paulo: Saraiva, 2007); and T. Fensterseifer, *Direitos Fundamentais e Proteção do Ambiente* [Fundamental Rights and Environmental Protection] (Porto Alegre: LdA, 2008).
13. SFC, Full Bench, Direct Action of Unconstitutionality no. 3.540-1 (Federal District), opinion by Min. Celso de Mello, decided on 1 September 2005. In this matter, the court duly noted the expansion of the scope of this fundamental right. It particularly highlighted the diffuse and collective entitlement of all members of, and groups in, Brazilian society to third dimension fundamental rights (side by side with fourth dimension rights, i.e. the right to peace) and the entrenchment of the principle of solidarity.
14. Art. 5(2) of the BFC: The rights and guarantees expressed in the BFC do not exclude others deriving from the regime and from the principles adopted by it, or from the international treaties of which the Federal Republic of Brazil is a party.
15. I.W. Sarlet, *A Eficácia dos Direitos Fundamentais* [The Efficacy of Fundamental Rights], 8th ed. (Porto Alegre: LdA, 2007), 442-470.

environmental context, this operates as a ban on ecological retreat.[16] The idea that constitutional environmental rules have total efficacy is highly significant for the purpose of the present enquiry. This is so because in Brazil's case, the relevant environmental rights enshrined in the BFC have direct application and can accordingly be enforced in the courts. Whilst one still would rely on, for example, the 'public civil action' and the 'popular action' to enforce environmental rights through the courts,[17] it is generally accepted that successful enforcement of these rights does not depend on the support of secondary or other environmental laws.

5	STRUCTURE AND MAIN FUNCTIONS OF BRAZILIAN COURTS

In brief, the Supreme Federal Court is the highest court in Brazil. The role of 'guardian' of the BFC is assigned to this court as prescribed by Article 102 of the BFC. The Superior Court of Justice, on the other hand, functions as the supreme court in all non-constitutional matters, with its jurisdiction outlined in Article 104 of the BFC. Its decisions, especially those in the constitutional domain, are subject to review by the Supreme Federal Court.

The Federal Justice hears general federal matters and acts as an appeal forum for cases from the regional federal courts, whose jurisdiction is determined by Articles 106 and 108 of the BFC. There is also a regular State Court of Justice for each Brazilian State, as set out by Article 125 of the BFC. The State Courts of Justice and State judges have jurisdiction on all issues that are not settled by the federal courts, with the exception of labour and military disputes. The latter are resolved by a special federal justice.

There is no exclusive competence to settle environmental issues. Environmental issues can accordingly be directed to any State or federal judge, depending on the wish of the plaintiff and the defendant and on the legal asset in dispute. The Brazilian judicial system also does not provide for a specialized environmental court. The only judicial forums which to an extent specialize in environmental matters are the federal courts, some of which have individual judges with specialized knowledge of environmental issues.

When an act of the State violates a constitutional principle or rule concerning the environment, it can be judicially reviewed. The courts' decision is binding (having *erga omnes* effect) and should accordingly be followed by everyone. This is done by way of a 'direct action of unconstitutionality' which seeks to annul (completely or in part) a legislative provision or act. The 'direct action of unconstitutionality' can be filed in the federal States' Courts of Justice (in the event that it

---

16. On the prohibition of environmental retreat see C.A. Molinaro, *Direito Ambiental: Proibição de Retrocesso* [Environmental Law: Retreat Prohibition] (Porto Alegre: LdA, 2007).
17. P. de B. Antunes, *Direito Ambiental* [Environmental Law], 7th ed. (Rio de Janeiro: Lúmen Júris, 2005), 72.

is a State or city norm that offends the State Constitution),[18] or in the Supreme Federal Court (in the event that it is a State or federal norm that conflicts with the BFC).[19] It is worth noting that in terms of Article 103 of the BFC, all Brazilian judges and courts competent in the domain of concrete and diffuse constitutional review can: incidentally pronounce on the constitutionality of normative acts during a regular trial; refrain from applying unconstitutional normative acts; and annul acts performed in accordance with the unconstitutional norm. The effect of such a pronouncement is, however, limited to the specific case in question, unless there is a decision by the Supreme Federal Court attributing general binding effect to the ruling.

Article 127(III)(1) of the BFC empowers various environmental authorities (such as the Public Ministry, the Public Institute for Environmental Protection, the Brazilian Institute for the Environment and Renewable Natural Resources (IBAMA), and the Ministry of Public Defense)[20] to institute civil action against citizens whose actions damage natural heritage. These authorities may be assisted by non-governmental organizations (NGOs) and other private actors. Another important procedural instrument is the so-called 'popular action',[21] which empowers citizens to institute claims against the State where its procedures, actions or omissions cause environmental damage. In the case of criminal liability for environmental damage, the legal standing for filing suits rests solely with the Public Ministry.[22]

Among other fundamental rights and guarantees, the BFC expressly enshrines the guarantee of the 'unavoidability of judicial control over any injury or threat thereof to rights'.[23] This ensures a wide and seamless right to intervention by the judiciary, and renders illegitimate any legislative or administrative measure aimed at diverting the possibility of judicial control over potential violations of the rights secured by the BFC.

---

18. Art. 125(2) of the BFC.
19. Art. 102(I)(a) of the BFC.
20. In terms of Art. 5 of the *Public Civil Action Statute* 7.347 of 1985, the Public Ministry, as the State entity charged with the safekeeping of society's interests (in consumer protection or environmental protection, for example), is the main State agent to which the task of collective procedural environmental protection is assigned (Art. 129(III) of the BFC). The Public Defender, on the other hand, is the public institution charged with promoting poor people's access to justice (Art. 134 of the BFC), and which also has legal standing to act in defense of the environment, especially in situations when environmental protection is tied to entrenched social rights (like health or housing). Both the Public Ministry and the Public Defender are considered to perform functions essential to justice in the Brazilian constitutional order (Ch. IV). IBAMA is a public entity which answers to the federal administration. Its primary function is to implement governmental environmental policy (Art. 6(IV) of NEPPS).
21. Art. 5(LXXIII) of the BFC.
22. There are both a federal and a State Public Ministry, who act independently of one another and whose standings and attributions vary according to the matter at hand. The federal ministry is usually appointed to work on cases that belong to the federal justice's jurisdiction.
23. Art. 5(XXXV).

6 ANALYSIS OF SIGNIFICANT ENVIRONMENTAL JUDGMENTS

6.1 Property Right Limitations and Private Agents' Environmental Protection Duty

The protection of the environment impinges on economic activity to such an extent that the environmental right frequently causes limitations to other rights such as the right to property or the right to exercise personal freedom. There is specifically often a conflict between environmental protection and the right to property. In Brazil, the acknowledgement of a *social purpose* or an *ecological purpose of private property*, as prescribed by the BFC,[24] creates a legal and economic order informed by the notion of sustainable development, in which the execution of the constitutional dictate of environmental protection demands limitations being placed on the right to property. This is also apparent in Article 225 of the BFC, which imposes a duty to defend the environment on not only the public sector but also citizens (private sector). The environmental duties imposed on the private sector and the State are complimentary, but not entirely similar. Through its duty, the State imposes limitations on the use of property to achieve various environmental imperatives. Private citizens will be subject to these restrictions. They may also, however, be subject to restrictions stemming from their own duty owed to the environment.

The Brazilian judiciary[25] has held that a property owner has the obligation (of a *propter rem* nature) to repair environmental damage evident on his or her land, regardless of his or her fault in causing it (strict liability). Moreover, no right exists to claim compensation for the cost of such repair. An example of such a statutory duty imposed on a property owner to restore the environment is the duty to recompose and re-plant forests in degraded land areas where a conservation unit,[26] permanent preservation area,[27] or legal reserve[28] is to be established. As far as the environmental purpose of the property is concerned, the Superior Court of Justice has held that it would not be fit to pay an indemnification to the land owner whose property rights are restricted because of the establishment of a conservation unit, permanent preservation area, or legal reserve. The Superior Court of Justice has

---

24. Arts 5(XXIII); 170(III); (VI); and 186 (II).
25. SCJ Civil Appeal no. 4026465/7 (São Paulo), Public Law Section, Special Chamber for the Environment, opinion by Renato Nalini J, decided on 29 June 2006.
26. *National Park System Mining Regulation Act* 9.985 of 2000, which regulates Art. 225(1)(I),(II),(III) and (VII) of the BFC.
27. *Forest Act* 4.771 of 1965 designates as a 'permanent preservation area' the 'area, covered or not by native vegetation, with environmental purpose of preserving the water resources, the landscape, the geological stability, the biodiversity, the fauna and flora's genetic flux, protecting the soil and securing human populations' welfare' (Art. 1(2)(II)).
28. *Ibid.* The Act designates as a 'legal reserve' the 'area found on the inside of a countryside property or possession, except for those of permanent preservation, needed for the sustainable use of natural resources, the conservation and rehabilitation of ecological procedures, the conservation of biodiversity and the shelter of native flora and fauna' (Art. 1(2)(III)).

found that a legal reserve and a permanent preservation area 'cannot be the object of economic entrepreneurship.' Even where the property owner has acquired degraded property on which a conservation area is situated, there exists a liability on him or her, regardless of fault (again, strict liability), to remedy the degradation.[29]

The decision of the Superior Court of Justice described above suggests that the court favours imposing positive obligations on property owners to rectify environmental damage on their land. In the context of legal reserves and permanent preservation areas it is interesting to note that the court inferred such an obligation (*propter rem* in nature) from the property right, as opposed to the right to an ecologically balanced environment, entrenched in the BFC. The court also considered imposing positive obligations on property owners holding land in legal reserves and permanent preservation areas. Accordingly, property owners in such areas may labour under both a 'negative' obligation not to pollute or degrade the area, and a 'positive' obligation to take action to protect it. In weighing up the interests at stake, the Superior Court of Justice clearly prioritized environmental protection over property rights in key conservation areas, so as to give effect to the constitutional goal of sustainable development.

6.2   CRUELTY TO ANIMALS

The Brazilian judiciary (specifically the Supreme Federal Court) has banned cruelty to animals by declaring unconstitutional the practices of *farra do boi*[30] in the State of Santa Catarina and *briga do galo*[31] in Rio de Janeiro, in terms of Article

---

29. SCJ, Appeal no. 343.741 (Paraná), 2nd Group, Court opinion by Min. Franciulli Netto, made public on 7 October 2002. There are other decisions along the same lines by the SCJ: Appeal no. 263.383 (Paraná), 2nd Group, opinion by Min. João Otávio de Noronha, decided on 16 June 2005; Appeal no. 237.690 (Mato Grosso do Sul), 2nd Group, opinion by Min. Paulo Almeida, decided on 12 March 2002; Appeal no. 282781 (Paraná), opinion by Min. Eliana Calmon, 2nd Group, decided on 16 April 2002.

30. The *farra do boi*, or bullock antics, originated in the Azores islands. A bullock is released in the city streets and is chased by people until finally being sacrificed. The Supreme Federal Court was called upon to consider the constitutionality of this tradition in the Santa Catarina State. Having applied the proportionality principle and weighed the local communities' right to cultural manifestations against animal cruelty inherent in the tradition, the court banned the practice so as to protect the animals' physical integrity and welfare. The court held that the tradition was openly violent and cruel to animals and accordingly contravened the BFC. It stated further that cultural practices undertaken in other parts of the country which subjected bullocks to human antics (consisting of fabric, wood and papier-mâché) but which did not harm the living beings, were endowed with sensibility and accordingly preserved under the BFC. SFC, Appeal no. 153.531-8 (Santa Catarina), opinion by Min. Francisco Resek, decided on 3 June 1997.

31. SFC, Full Bench, Direct Action of Unconstitutionality no. 1.856-6 (Rio de Janeiro), preliminary court order, opinion by Min. Carlos Veloso, unanimous decision, Justice Diary, Section I, 09.22.2000, 69. The Supreme Federal Court has again faced the matter in the trials of Direct Actions of Unconstitutionality numbers 2.514-7 (Santa Catarina) and 3776 (Rio Grande do Norte).

225(1)(VII) of the BFC. This constitutional provision imposes a duty on the State to 'protect fauna and flora by prohibiting, in the manner prescribed by law, behaviour that endangers their ecological function, causes the extinction of species, or subjects animals to cruelty'. Inherent in this provision is an acknowledgement that all forms of life (including animals) hold value and require protection. It would accordingly appear that the environmental provisions contained in the BFC are not exclusively aimed at protecting the instrumental value of the environment, and the natural species occurring therein, for human use and consumption.

This eco-centric approach is somewhat limited as the Supreme Federal Court has not expressly attributed rights to animals or other non-human life forms. The court has, however, recognized animal life as an end in itself and that non-human life forms also have a sense of dignity and intrinsic value.[32] All decisions impinging on animal rights are accordingly mediated through the norms contained in the BFC, which prefer to describe the relationship between human beings and animals as a form of guardianship, particularly in the context of activities which are not essential to the satisfaction of human needs.[33] The theory appears to be that human interests should be truly essential (such as those relating to the right to health) to justify the instrumental use of animals. Where this threshold is not satisfied, any such use or practice will be deemed unconstitutional.

6.3   ENVIRONMENTAL SANITATION: THE CONSTITUTIONAL WARRANTY OF A MINIMUM STANDARD OF ENVIRONMENTAL QUALITY AND THE STATE'S PROTECTIVE DUTY

The approach of the Superior Court of Justice relating to the provision of basic sanitation services clearly reflects the interplay between environmental rights and socio-economic rights (such as the provision of basic sanitation and amenities). It further clearly highlights the important, albeit controversial, role that the judiciary

---

32. I.W. Sarlet, *Dignidade da Pessoa Humana e Direitos Fundamentais na Constituição Federal de 1988* [Human Dignity and Fundamental Rights in the Brazilian Federal Constitution of 1988], 5th ed. (Porto Alegre: LdA, 2007), 34-35; I.W. Sarlet & T. Fensterseifer, 'Algumas notas sobre a dimensão ecológica da dignidade da pessoa humana e sobre a dignidade da vida em geral' [Brief Notes about the Ecological Dimension of the Human Dignity and the Dignity of Life in General Terms], in *A Dignidade da Vida e os Direitos Fundamentais para além dos Humanos: Uma Discussão Necessária* [The Dignity of Life and the Fundamental Rights Beyond Humans: a Necessary Discussion], ed. C.A. Molinaro et al. (Belo Horizonte: Editora Fórum, 2008), 175-205.

33. Brazilian commentary and jurisprudence regarding the link between the BFC and animal rights is growing. Examples include: the ban on amateur hunting in the Rio Grande do Sul State (Proceeding no. 2004.71.00.021481-2, within the Federal Environmental Court Subdivision of the Porto Alegre Judicial Circumscription); and the confirmation of the right of a biology student of the Rio Grande do Sul Federal University to refuse to participate in practical classes involving the use of animals, forcing the institution to offer the student alternative practical classes (Proceeding no. 2007.71.00.019882-0, within the same Court Subdivision).

plays in attempting to pronounce on the validity of, or absence of, executive action aimed at giving practical effect to these rights.

With regard to the provision of basic sanitation services for instance, the approach of the Brazilian judiciary has been to allow the review of administrative action where the executive has not fulfilled its obligation to provide the requisite services. Altering its historic restrictive approach to the judicial review of environment-related administrative acts,[34] the Superior Court of Justice has emphasized its prerogative to enquire into administrative actions of the executive. The Superior Court of Justice has concluded in a public civil action filed by the Public Ministry, that it is possible for the court to impose an obligation on the executive to carry out soil recuperation works which are indispensable to environmental protection. In making this order, the court affirmed the role of the judiciary to review the suitability of discretionary executive acts, where these acts were required to conform to the criteria of morality and proportionality, and the rights and principles contained in the BFC.[35]

In the context of environmental sanitation, the Superior Court of Justice has also shown its willingness to review administrative action, such as the discontinuation of garbage collection (an essential sanitation service provided by public authorities).[36] The court held that discontinuing the service prejudiced citizens' fundamental rights enshrined in the BFC such as the rights to health, the environment and human dignity. It held further that the authorities had no discretion when it came to executing administrative action (such as the collection of garbage), which gave effect to such constitutionally enshrined rights. It would accordingly appear that where the exercise of administrative discretion contravenes a duty imposed on the State under the BFC, the judiciary will be willing to review it. The judgment further suggests that the State is under a duty to take positive action to practically realize the rights and duties contained in the BFC. Therefore, where the practical realization of a constitutional right or duty is at stake, the jurisprudence appears to lean toward acknowledging the right of citizens to approach the court to compel the State to fulfil its constitutional mandate. This is evidenced in another decision of the Superior Court of Justice in which the court compelled the State to provide sanitation and water treatment services to a significantly polluted area.[37]

---

34. SCJ Appeal no. 138.901 (Goiânia), Justice Diary of 17 November 1997, 59456, 1st Group, opinion by Min. José Delgado, decided on 15 September 1997; and Appeal no. 169.876 (São Paulo), 1st Group, opinion by Min. José Delgado, decided on 16 June 1998.
35. SCJ Appeal no. 429.570 (Goiânia), opinion by Min. Eliana Calmon, 2nd Group, decided on 11 November 2003.
36. SCJ Appeal No. 575.998 (Minas Gerais). In this decision, it was duly noted that garbage removal constituted an essential service indispensable to the maintenance of public health, and that its interruption or discontinuation challenged the entrenched clause of respect for human dignity. The decision also reinforced the value of civil public action as a legitimate means for safekeeping trans-individual rights.
37. SCJ Appeal no. 70011759842 (Rio Grande do Sul), opinion by Nelson Antônio Monteiro Pacheco J, decided on 1 December 2005. In this matter the SCJ (Rio Grande do Sul) compelled the city of Santa Maria to install a local system of sewers, as its failure to do so undermined the

In the matters discussed above, the Brazilian judiciary has not gone as far as creating public policy; it has merely sought to ensure that the executive complies with its duties entrenched in the BFC and associated legislation.[38] Therefore, where the executive abstains from fulfilling such duties, the judiciary appears prepared to review the executive's failure to do so in compliance with its constitutional imperative to pronounce on the validity of any violation or threat to the rights enshrined in the BFC. The duties imposed on the executive include guaranteeing minimum levels of environmental quality.[39] It is therefore conceivable that where the environment is concerned, a positive duty rests on the executive to preserve, protect and secure a core of environmental services (an ecological or environmental existential minimum). Citizens would appear to have a corresponding right to ensure that the executive fulfils this duty and can seek recourse to the courts where the executive fails to do so. This approach corresponds generally with that proposed by Alexy who argues for the existence of a definitive right to service (fulfilling the existential minimum) in the context of socio-economic rights.[40] One of the additional important principles to arise from the above jurisprudence relating to the provision of basic socio-economic services, is that budgetary constraints do not provide the public authorities with a valid defense for not providing core environmental services.[41]

environment, compromised public health and violated human dignity. Furthermore, in SCJ Appeal no. 70012091278 (Rio Grande do Sul), opinion by Arno Werlang J, decided on 25 January 2006, the court granted a preliminary order against the Public Health Department, regardless of previous budget projections, compelling it to implement a sanitation project in the light of residents' constitutional rights to the environment and public health.

38. A.J. Krell, *Discricionariedade Administrativa e Proteção Ambiental* [Administrative Discretion and Environmental Protection] (Porto Alegre: LdA, 2004), 85; L.G. Marinoni, *Tutela Inibitória: Individual e Coletiva* [Inhibitive Processual Protection: Individual and Collective], 3rd ed. (São Paulo: Revista dos Tribunais, 2003), 108.

39. Marinoni, *supra*, 103.

40. R. Alexy, *Teoría de los Derechos Fundamentales* [Theory of Fundamental Rights] (Madrid: Centro de Estudios Políticos e Constitucionales, 2001), 499; A.P. de Barcellos, *A Eficácia Jurídica dos Princípios Constitucionais: O Princípio da Dignidade da Pessoa Humana* [The Legal Efficacy of Constitutional Principles: the Human Being Dignity Principle], 2nd ed. (Rio de Janeiro: Renovar, 2008); R.L. Torres, 'A Metamorfose dos Direitos Sociais em Mínimo Existencial', in *Direitos Fundamentais Sociais: Estudos de Direito Constitucional, Internacional e Comparado* [Fundamental Social Rights: Studies on Constitutional, International and Comparative Law], ed. I.W. Sarlet (Rio de Janeiro: Renovar, 2003), 11-46; Sarlet, *supra* n. 15, 317-387.

41. On the issue of the relationship between budgetary constraints and the preservation of fundamental human rights, see: SFC Appeal no. 393175 (Rio Grande do Sul), opinion by Min. Celso de Mello, decided on 12 December 2006 (right to health); SFC Appeal no. 410715 (São Paulo), opinion by Min. Celso de Mello, decided on 22 November 2005 (right to education); SFC Appeal no. 45 (Federal District), opinion by Min. Celso de Mello, decided on 29 April 2004, SFC News Bulletin no. 345 (right to education); SCJ Appeal no. 861.262 (Rio Grande do Sul) opinion by Min. Eliana Calmon, decided on 5 September 2006 (right to health); SCJ Appeal no. 811.608 (Rio Grande do Sul), opinion by Min. Luiz Fux, decided on 15 May 2007 (right to health).

The above discussion has focused on the situation where socio-economic rights complement environmental rights. However, these rights on occasion conflict with one another and where this occurs, it would be prudent for the Brazilian judiciary to employ the proportionality principle to resolve any discord. Where any action poses a significant risk to the general constitutional 'umbrella' enshrined to protect human dignity and the environment, the latter should prevail. The proportionality principle, and the related notion of reasonability, should accordingly only be considered when it is necessary: to halt or prohibit excessive State intervention as far as fundamental environmental assets are concerned; and to prohibit grossly insufficient protective measures invoked by the State. In both instances, the judiciary should be guided by the objective of optimizing environmental protection in the realm of fundamental rights.[42] Employed in this manner, proportionality and reasonability could be used in a manner which gives effect to the interests of future generations, as postulated by the concept of sustainability.[43]

7   CRITICAL EVALUATION

The above critical survey of the judiciary's performance in reviewing the environmental service functions of the executive clearly illustrates that whilst certain strides have been made by the judiciary to hold the executive to account, there is significant scope for extending its current role.

The Brazilian judiciary has been called upon to pronounce on the manner in which the State gives effect to the positive and negative components of the socio-economic and environmental rights enshrined in the BFC. The judiciary appears to have adopted a fairly activist role in this regard. Whilst not going as far as prescribing policy, the judiciary has sought to ensure that the executive complies with its statutory and constitutional duties, particularly those relating to the provision of environmental services. The balance between judicial activism and unwarranted judicial interference in the executive realm is a fine line and the judiciary would be well advised to retain respect for the separation of powers doctrine enshrined in

---

42. On the importance of the proportionality principle in the consideration of surplus prohibition and insufficient or defective protection prohibition, see particularly: I.W. Sarlet, 'Constituição e Proporcionalidade: O Direito Penal e os Direitos Fundamentais Entre Proibição de Excesso e Proibição de Insuficiência' [Constitution and Proportionality: Criminal Law and Fundamental Rights-Prohibition of Excess and Insufficiency], *RBCC* 47 (2004): 60-122; L.L. Streck, 'A Dupla Face do Princípio da Proporcionalidade e o Cabimento de Mandado de Segurança em Matéria Criminal: Superando o Ideário Liberal-individualista-clássico' [The Double Face of Proportionality in Criminal Matters: Overcoming the Liberal-Individualistic-Classical Paradigm], *RMPERGS* 53 (2004): 223-251; and L. Feldens, *A Constituição Penal: A Dupla Face da Proporcionalidade no Controle de Normas Penais* [The Penal Constitution: the Double Face of the Proportionality on the Control of Criminal Legal Standard) (Porto Alegre: LdA, 2005). On the environmental field, see J. Freitas, 'Princípio da Precaução: Vedação de Excesso e de Inoperância' [The Precautionary Principle: Excess Prohibition and Insufficiency Prohibition], *Separata Especial de DARIP* 35 (2006): 33-48.
43. Canotilho & Morato Leite, *supra* n. 12, 2.

the BFC. The principal duty to execute environmental governance lies with the executive and to a lesser extent with the legislature. The judiciary has the power and duty to intervene in their governance realm, but this power should only be exercised in exceptional circumstances and in strict accordance with the provisions contained in the BFC. The judiciary should not, however, show such a degree of deference that it ultimately reneges on its duty to protect socio-economic and environmental rights, and scrutinize the undue or absent exercise of executive and legislative authority.[44]

The judiciary, which always acts on the intervention of some public or private actor, has in the past been strongly attached to the tradition of protecting individual rights. Taking greater heed of the international trend to acknowledge collective rights and diffuse guardianship would significantly increase access to the judiciary and promote its role in environmental governance. The judgments discussed in this chapter highlight the importance of promoting public interest or civil litigation.[45] Broadening legal standing, especially in matters related to diffuse and collective rights (through public civil actions and direct actions of unconstitutionality), will not only expand the role of the judiciary in environmental governance but simultaneously promote democratic ideals. According to human rights theory, ensuring access to justice is an essential component of democracy.[46] Allowing broad legal standing intensifies citizens' participation, even when the citizen is represented by entities such as non-governmental or civic organizations,[47] and provides a key 'instrument through which the individual exercises his or her right to take part in the governance of public affairs'.[48]

An additional way to promote the role of the Brazilian judiciary in environmental governance and citizens' access to environmental justice, would be to establish more specialist environmental courts, particularly within federal State judicial structures. The success of such an initiative would, however, depend on the provision of proper infrastructure and resources to such courts and to promote their decentralization to State capitals and regional cities. A further prerequisite would be long-term investment in the training of members of the judiciary and State prosecutors, to ensure that they are well versed in the requisite legal frameworks and complexities frequently associated with environmental issues. Finally, establishing an integrated and cooperative system for gathering and disseminating accurate and current information relating to environmental policy and governance, especially in the context of federal regimes, would further enhance the functioning of both the judiciary and executive.

---

44. On how judges and courts are bound by fundamental rights see: Sarlet, *supra* n. 15, 396-399.
45. L.G. Marinoni, *Teoria Geral do Processo* [General Theory of Process] (São Paulo: Revista dos Tribunais, 2006), 196.
46. *Ibid.*, 198.
47. *Ibid.*, 199.
48. *Ibid.*, 198.

BIBLIOGRAPHY

Alexy, R. *Teoría de los Derechos Fundamentales.* Madrid: Centro de Estudios Políticos e Constitucionales, 2001.

Antunes, P. de B. *Direito Ambiental,* 7th ed. Rio de Janeiro: Lúmen Júris, 2005.

Barcellos, A.P. de. *A Eficácia Jurídica dos Princípios Constitucionais: O Princípio da Dignidade da Pessoa Humana.* 2nd ed. Rio de Janeiro: Renovar, 2008.

Benjamin, A.H. 'Meio Ambiente e Constituição: uma primeira abordagem'. Paper given at Anais do 6° Congresso Internacional de Direito Ambiental. São Paulo: IMESP, 2002.

Canotilho, J.J.G. & J.R. Morato Leite (eds). *Direito Constitucional Ambiental Brasileiro.* São Paulo: Saraiva, 2007.

Feldens, L. *A Constituição Penal: A Dupla Face da Proporcionalidade no Controle de Normas Penais.* Porto Alegre: Livraria do Advogado, 2005.

Fensterseifer, T. *Direitos Fundamentais e Proteção do Ambiente.* Porto Alegre: Livraria do Advogado, 2008.

Freitas, J. 'Princípio da Precaução: Vedação de Excesso e de Inoperância'. *Separata Especial de Direito Ambiental da Revista Interesse Público* 35 (2006): 33-48.

Gavião Filho, A.P. *Direito Fundamental ao Ambiente.* Porto Alegre: Livraria do Advogado, 2005.

Krell, A.J. *Discricionariedade Administrativa e Proteção Ambiental.* Porto Alegre: Livraria do Advogado, 2004.

Machado, P.A.L. *Direito ambiental Brasileiro.* 13th ed. São Paulo: Malheiros, 2005.

Marinoni, L.G. *Teoria Geral do Processo.* São Paulo: Revista dos Tribunais, 2006.

Marinoni, L.G. *Tutela Inibitória: Individual e Coletiva.* 3rd ed. São Paulo: Revista dos Tribunais, 2003.

Medeiros, F.L.F. *Meio ambiente: Direito e dever fundamental.* Porto Alegre: Livraria do Advogado, 2004.

Mirra, Á.V. *Ação Civil Pública e a Reparação do Dano ao Meio Ambiente.* São Paulo: Editora Juarez de Oliveira, 2002.

Molinaro, C.A. *Direito Ambiental: Proibição de Retrocesso.* Porto Alegre: Livraria do Advogado, 2007.

Morato Leite, J.R. *Dano ambiental: do individual ao coletivo extrapatrimonial.* São Paulo: Revista dos Tribunais, 2000.

Perez Luño, A.E. *Los derechos fundamentales,* 8th ed. Madrid: Editorial Tecnos, 2005.

Sarlet, I.W. & T. Fensterseifer. 'Algumas notas sobre a dimensão ecológica da dignidade da pessoa humana e sobre a dignidade da vida em geral'. In *A Dignidade da Vida e os Direitos Fundamentais para além dos Humanos: Uma Discussão Necessária,* edited by C.A. Molinaro et al. Belo Horizonte: Editora Fórum, 2008.

Sarlet, I.W. *A eficácia dos direitos fundamentais,* 8th ed. Porto Alegre: Livraria do Advogado, 2007.

Sarlet, I.W. 'Constituição e Proporcionalidade: O Direito Penal e os Direitos Fundamentais Entre Proibição de Excesso e Proibição de Insuficiência'. *Revista Brasileira de Ciências Criminais* 47 (2004): 60-122.

Sarlet, I.W. *Dignidade da Pessoa Humana e Direitos Fundamentais na Constituição Federal de 1988*, 5th ed. Porto Alegre: Livraria do Advogado Editora, 2007.

Silva, J.A. da *Direito Ambiental Constitucional.* 4th ed. São Paulo: Malheiros, 2003.

STF. 'Página Principal: Supremo Tribunal Federal'. <www.stf.gov.br>, 14 September 2008.

STJ. 'Superior Tribunal de Justiça – O Tribunal da Cidadania'. <www.stj.gov.br>, 14 September 2008.

Streck, L.L. 'A Dupla Face do Princípio da Proporcionalidade e o Cabimento de Mandado de Segurança em Matéria Criminal: Superando o Ideário Liberal-individualista-clássico'. *Revista do Ministério Público do Estado do Rio Grande do Sul* 53 (2004): 223-251.

Teixeira, O.P.B. *O direito ao meio ambiente ecologicamente equilibrado como direito fundamental.* Porto Alegre: Livraria do Advogado, 2006.

Torres, R.L. 'A Metamorfose dos Direitos Sociais em Mínimo Existencial'. In *Direitos Fundamentais Sociais: Estudos de Direito Constitucional, Internacional e Comparado*, edited by I.W. Sarlet (Rio de Janeiro: Renovar, 2003.

Tribunal de Justiça. 'Tribunal de Justiça do Estado do Rio Grande do Sul'. <www.tj.rs.gov.br>, 14 September 2008.

Vieira De Andrade, J.S. *Os direitos fundamentais na Constituição portuguesa de 1976*, 2nd ed. Coimbra: Almedina, 2001.

TABLE OF LEGISLATION

Bio Safety Act 11.105 of 2005
Cetacean Fishing or Whale Hunting Prohibition Act 7.643 of 1987
City Act 10.257 of 2001
Civil and Criminal Responsibility Act for Nuclear Activities N 6.453 of 1977
Environmental Crime Act 9.605 of 1998
Forest Act 4.771 of 1965
National Coast Zone Management Act 7.661 of 1988
National Environmental Education Policy Act 9.795 of 1999
National Environmental Fund Act 7.661 of 1988
National Environmental Protection Policy Statute 6.938 of 1981
National Park System Mining Regulation Act 9.985 of 2000
Public Civil Action Statute 7.347 of 1985
Popular Action Statute 4.717 of 1965
Toxic Substance Control Act 7.802 of 1989
Water Act 9.433 of 1997
Water and Sewage Act 11.445 of 2007
Wildlife Protection Act 5.197 of 1967

TABLE OF CASES

SCJ 2nd Civil Group Appeal no. 70012091278 (Rio Grande do Sul)
SCJ Appeal no. 138.901 (Goiânia)
SCJ Appeal no. 169.876 (São Paulo)
SCJ Appeal no. 237.690 (Mato Grosso do Sul)
SCJ Appeal no. 263.383 (Paraná)
SCJ Appeal no. 282.781 (Paraná)
SCJ Appeal no. 343.741 (Paraná)
SCJ Appeal no. 429.570 (Goiânia)
SCJ Appeal no. 429.570 (Goiânia)
SCJ Appeal no. 575.998 (Minas Gerais)
SCJ Appeal no. 70011759842 (Rio Grande do Sul)
SCJ Appeal no. 811.608 (Rio Grande do Sul)
SCJ Appeal no. 861.262 (Rio Grande do Sul)
SCJ Civil Appeal no. 4026465/7 (São Paulo)
SFC Appeal no. 153.531-8 (Santa Catarina)
SFC Appeal no. 393175 (Rio Grande do Sul)
SFC Appeal no. 410715 (São Paulo)
SFC Appeal no. 45 (Federal District)
SFC Direct Actions of Unconstitutionality no. 2.514-7 (Santa Catarina)
SFC Direct Actions of Unconstitutionality no. 3776 (Rio Grande do Norte)
SFC Full Bench, Direct Action of Unconstitutionality no. 1.856-6 (Rio de Janeiro)
SFC Full Bench, Direct Action of Unconstitutionality no. 3.540-1 (Federal District)
SFC News Bulletin no. 345

TABLE OF INTERNATIONAL INSTRUMENTS

Convention on Biological Diversity (1992) 31 *ILM* 818
Declaration on Environment and Development (1992) 31 *ILM* 874
United Nations Framework Convention on Climate Change (1992) 31 *ILM* 849
United Nations Stockholm Declaration on the Human Environment (1972) 11 *ILM* 1416

ABBREVIATIONS

BFC	Brazilian Federal Constitution
EIA	Environmental Impact Assessment
IBAMA	Brazilian Institute for the Environment and Renewable Natural Resources
LdA	Livraria do Advogado
NEPPA	National Environmental Protection Policy Act

NEPPS	National Environmental Protection Policy Statute
NGO(s)	Non-governmental organization(s)
RBCC	Revista Brasileira de Ciências Criminais
DARIP	Direito Ambiental da Revista Interesse Público
RMPERGS	Revista do Ministério Público do Estado do Rio Grande do Sul
SCJ	Superior Court of Justice
SFC	Supreme Federal Court

Chapter 8
Argentina

Juan Carballo

1   INTRODUCTION

This chapter analyzes the role of the Argentinean judiciary in achieving sustainable environmental governance at domestic level. It commences by describing the most prevalent environmental issues in Argentina. The chapter then briefly discusses relevant environmental institutions that play a protagonist role in environmental governance, concluding with a brief description of the main environmental laws. It then proceeds to describe the judicial system in Argentina which is characterized by two parallel structures: the federal and the provincial branches, both of which are subject to the Argentinean Supreme Court. This part of the contribution also explains the main relationships between these two branches of the judiciary, highlighting the importance of the Supreme Court as the head of both structures. The chapter then proceeds to analyze significant environmental judgments that influence, or may influence, environmental governance in Argentina.

The structure outlined above must be understood within the context of constitutional provisions relating to environmental protection. It was not until the most recent constitutional reform, in 1994, that the Constitution recognized the right to a healthy environment in section 41, which reads as follows:

> All inhabitants are entitled to the right to a healthy and balanced environment fit for human development in order that productive activities shall meet present needs without endangering those of future generations; and shall have the

Louis J. Kotzé and Alexander R. Paterson (eds), *The Role of the Judiciary in Environmental Governance: Comparative Perspectives*, pp. 269–294.
© 2009 Kluwer Law International BV, The Netherlands.

duty to preserve it. As a first priority, environmental damage shall bring about the obligation to repair it according to law. The authorities shall provide for the protection of this right, the rational use of natural resources, the preservation of the natural and cultural heritage and of the biological diversity, and shall also provide for environmental information and education. The Nation shall regulate the minimum protection standards and the provinces those necessary to reinforce them, without altering their local jurisdictions. The entry into the national territory of present or potential dangerous wastes, and of radioactive ones, is forbidden.

This constitutional provision has had a significant impact on environmental governance, considering that it not only guarantees this right for the first time, but also establishes minimum protection standards. Much of the Argentinean environmental governance regime is built on the premise of this right, which continues to influence the judiciary's approach to environmental governance, as is illustrated during the course of this chapter.

2   MAIN ENVIRONMENTAL ISSUES

Argentina is faced by several environmental challenges ranging in magnitude and severity, and these challenges significantly differ from rural to urban areas. In rural areas these challenges are usually connected with agricultural activities (mainly deforestation[1] and pollution due to increased use of pesticides and herbicides)[2] and mining activities (water and air pollution).[3] In the urban regions, environmental challenges include: lack of access to clean water; improper waste management; water and air pollution; inadequate sewage systems; and overcrowded housing developments.[4]

In addition to the above general challenges, several specific environmental challenges can also be discerned. Biodiversity resources are increasingly threatened by the clearing of forests for agriculture (almost all of the cleared land is dedicated to transgenic soya).[5] This phenomenon has already resulted in the

---

1. Unidad de Manejo del Sistema de Evaluación Forestal, 'Informe sobre deforestación en Argentina, 2007' [Deforestation in Argentina Report, 2007], <www.ambiente.gov.ar/archivos/web/UMSEF/File/deforestacin_argentina_v2.pdf>, 14 September 2008.
2. J.L. Costa, 'Impacto de los agroquímicos en el ambiente' [The impact of agrochemicals on the environment],   <www.inta.gov.ar/balcarce/noticias/inta_expone/AuditorioGuillermoCovas/ImpactoAgroqAmbiente.pdf>, 14 September 2008.
3. See for an example of pollution due to mining activities: J. Avila et al., 'Análisis del impacto ambiental de la explotación minera del yacimiento El Timbó, Tucumán, Argentina', paper delivered at the 13th Congreso Geológico Argentino (Buenos Aires, 1996).
4. N. Clichevsky, *Pobreza y políticas urbano-ambientales en Argentina* (Santiago de Chile: CEPAL, 2002).
5. ESDS, 'Perspectivas del medio ambiente en la Argentina' [Environmental prospects in Argentina], (Buenos Aires: Informe Geo Argentina, 2004), <www.ambiente.gov.ar>, 8 June 2008.

destruction of 70% of the *bosque chaqueño* [Chaco Forest] and 50% of the *selva tucumana* [Tucuman Jungle]. Moreover, loss of native forests also leads to erosion and desertification.

The country further struggles with various forms of pollution. Both surface and subterranean waters are polluted by the industrial, agricultural and mining sectors (especially in the northwestern region of the country, near the Andean Mountains). Water pollution further impacts on access to clean drinking water, especially in urban regions.[6] Industrial waste is a major concern in the larger cities such as Buenos Aires, Córdoba and Rosario; and causes serious public health risks including the increased prevalence of cancer and respiratory diseases.

Improper domestic waste management is of great concern. Almost all Argentinean cities, regardless of their size, geographic area or population, are experiencing a decline in environmental quality due to improper waste disposal methods and low recycling rates. Waste management is usually dealt with by the informal sector in an effort to create employment. As these activities are informal, they are not properly regulated, with dire consequences to people living in cities.

Notwithstanding the prolonged existence of these environmental challenges, the Argentinean population appears to be somewhat desensitized regarding the gravity of environmental concerns affecting their quality of life and the broader environment. As Reboratti[7] explains:

> in a long list of problems, we could include deforestation, water pollution, erosion, indiscriminate fishing, over-grazing, mining impacts and urban flooding as the most pressing issues. However, until relatively recently, this list has not been sufficient to cause a reaction by society.

It was not until the paper mills conflict between Argentina and Uruguay in 2002, that Argentinean society displayed some constructive interest in environmental challenges. In this conflict, currently before the International Court of Justice (ICJ), the population of the Argentinean city of Gualeguaychú opposed the construction of two paper mills on the Uruguayan side of a river because of the potential severe environmental impacts they posed. The government of Argentina also opposed the project. The government of Uruguay, on the other hand, defended these industries as a legitimate source of job creation and economic growth, considering that they would use the best available technology (BAT) to minimize environmental impacts. Currently, only one of the two mills has been built, and at the time of writing, both governments were still awaiting the final response from the ICJ.

---

6. The right to water was recently addressed by the courts in *Marchicio José Bautista y otros c/ Superior gobierno de la provincia de Córdoba y otros – recuso de amparo* (19 Octubre 2004) Primera instancia, Córdoba.
7. C. Reboratti, Environmental conflicts and environmental justice in Argentina', in *Environmental Justice en Latin America: Problems, promise and practice*, ed. D. Carrouthers (London: MIT Press, 2008), 103.

The growth of environmental awareness (as is evidenced from the above example), the rise of environmental movements, and some crucial judicial decisions (discussed below), should increasingly shape the environmental governance effort in Argentina.

3   ENVIRONMENTAL INSTITUTIONS AND
             GOVERNANCE STRUCTURES

Argentina is a republican, democratic and federal State which, in its constitutional design, provides for significant government power at the provincial level.[8] Constitutionally speaking,[9] the powers and functions that are not reserved for the federal government, can be exercised by the provincial governments. The Constitution provides for another level of governance, namely that of municipalities, which include all cities with a minimum of 10,000 inhabitants. The Constitution recognizes the autonomy of these cities and affords a special status to Buenos Aires, the capital of Argentina.[10] In this sense, the Constitution provides for a four-tiered governance structure, namely: federal government, provincial government, the City of Buenos Aires, and local government.

Several norms distribute institutional power among these different levels.[11] These norms also create new institutions and establish procedures to deal with different challenges whilst respecting the legal institutional structure. These norms are of special importance to environmental issues, as is illustrated further below. The president of Argentina is the head of the executive branch while a congress with two chambers is in charge of the legislative branch.

At national level, the most important environmental authority in the executive branch[12] is the Environmental and Sustainable Development Secretary (ESDS), which directly reports to the Chief of Ministers. Within the governments of provinces and municipalities, there usually are environmental agencies which have

---

8. Argentina has twenty-three provinces.
9. Constitution, s. 121 states that: The provinces reserve to themselves all the powers not delegated to the Federal Government by this Constitution, as well as those powers expressly reserved to them by special pacts at the time of their incorporation.
10. Constitution, s. 123 states that: Each province enacts its own Constitution as stated in s. 5, ensuring municipal autonomy and ruling its scope and content regarding the institutional, political, administrative, economic and financial aspects.
11. There are various norms which determine the current political structure, including, inter alia: the Constitution, s. 75, pt 12, which states that 'the National Congress is empowered to enact the Civil, Commercial, Criminal, Mining, Labour and Social Security Codes, in unified or separate bodies'. This means that provinces cannot regulate on these subjects which are exclusively reserved for the national congress.
12. See further on the executive branch with its different ministries and secretariats, PNA, 'Presidencia de la Nación Argentina' [Presidency of the Argentinean Nation], <www.presidencia. gov.ar>, 14 September 2008.

different positions in the respective hierarchies according to the priority given to the environment in each context.

As regards the legislative branch,[13] there is a commission within the Deputies Chamber dealing specifically with environmental matters, namely, the Natural Resources and Human Environment Conservation Commission (*Recursos naturales y conservación del ambiente humano*). Other commissions which may also impact on environmental governance include: Agriculture and Cattle (*Agricultura y ganadería*) and Energy and Fuels (*Energía y combustibles*). In the senate, the Commissions on Environment and Sustainable Development (*Ambiente y desarrollo sustentable*); Agriculture, Cattle and Fishing (*Agricultura, ganadería y pesca*); and Mining, Energy and Fuels (*Minería, energía y combustibles*) also deal with environmental matters either directly or indirectly.

The Environmental Federal Council (*Consejo federal de medio ambiente* (CoFeMa)) is a mixed institution with representatives from the federal, the twenty-three provinces and the City of Buenos Aires. This council was created by the *General Environmental Law* (Number 25.675) and its main objective is to generate an integral environmental public policy which should consider local, regional, national and international factors. Even though the Constitution affords considerable power to the provinces regarding natural resource regulation, this combined institution does not have great influence on environmental governance.

The most significant and influential environmental regulation occurs at national level (through the Commission on Environment and Sustainable Development), mostly because the distribution of financial resources is significantly biased towards the national government.[14] Environmental regulation at the provincial and local spheres is further highly dependent on financial and technical support from the national government, and in some instances the provinces and municipalities are not adequately funded to affect sufficient environmental regulation.[15]

---

13. See further on the legislative branch with its different chambers, Congreso, 'Bienvenidos al Congreso de la Nación Argentina' [Congress of the Argentinean Nation], <www.congreso. gov.ar>, 14 September 2008.
14. According to a study in 2001, all the provinces together enjoyed only a 35.7% share of the public expenditure, while the national government had been allocated the remaining 64.3%. A. Porto, 'Disparidades regionales y federalismo fiscal' [Regional inequalities and fiscal federalism] (La Plata: UNLP, 2004), <www.depeco.econo.unlp. edu.ar/federalismo/pdfs/libro_ federalismo.pdf>, 14 September 2008. See also A. Porto, 'Finanzas Públicas Subnacionales: La Experiencia Argentina' [Public sub-national finance: the Argentinean experience] (La Plata: UNLP, 2004), <www.depeco.econo.unlp.edu.ar/federalismo/pdfs/docfed12.pdf>, 28 August 2008, and A. Porto, 'Etapas de la coparticipación federal de impuestos' [Stages in the federal tax distribution among provinces] (La Plata: UNLP, 2003), <www.depeco.econo.unlp.edu.ar/ federalismo/pdfs/docfed2.pdf>, 28 August 2008.
15. The National ESDS also, e.g., collaborates with various small, medium and large municipalities through the Sustainable Municipalities Plan by providing financial and technical support if the local governments comply with certain objectives. See further, ESDS, *supra* n. 5.

4   PRINCIPAL ENVIRONMENTAL LAWS

As has been stated above, section 41 of the Constitution guarantees everyone the
right to a healthy environment, and this provision constitutes the main principle
around which environmental law and governance in Argentina revolves. The formulation of the rights contained in the Constitution was significantly influenced
by international law. The Convention on the Rights of the Child (CRC),[16] for
example, has been incorporated into Argentinean law and it affords environmental
entitlements to children in addition to those they enjoy under the environmental
right. Moreover, the judiciary in *Giroldi, Horacio y otro* (1995)[17] ruled that
decisions of international human rights courts should guide judicial decisions in
Argentina. Therefore, some decisions of the Inter-American Court of Human
Rights,[18] especially those relating to the environment, impact on how the right
to a healthy environment is understood at domestic level.

Argentina has also signed several multilateral environmental agreements
(MEAs)[19] and, since international treaties take precedence over national laws in
Argentina,[20] measures of environmental protection derived from the international
legal order are both comprehensive and quite influential.

---

16. The Convention states in s. 2c: 'States Parties shall pursue full implementation of this right and,
    in particular, shall take appropriate measures:... (c) To combat disease and malnutrition,
    including within the framework of primary health care, through, inter alia, the application of
    readily available technology and through the provision of adequate nutritious foods and clean
    drinking-water, taking into consideration the dangers and risks of environmental pollution.'
17. *Giroldi, Horacio y otro* (7 Abril, 1995) SC de Justicia de la Nación.
18. Environment-related decisions of the Inter American Court of Human Rights include, inter alia, the
    following: *Claude-Reyes et al. v. Chile. Merits, Reparations and Costs* (19 September 2006) Series
    C, 151; *Raxcacó-Reyes v. Guatemala. Merits, Reparations and Costs* (15 September 2005) Series
    C, 133; *Myrna Mack-Chang v. Guatemala. Merits, Reparations and Costs* (25 November 2003)
    Series C, 101; *Fermín Ramírez v. Guatemala. Merits, Reparations and Costs* (20 June 2005) Series
    C, 126; and *Bámaca-Velásquez v. Guatemala. Merits* (15 November 2000) Series C, 70.
19. Some of the MEAs signed by Argentina include the following: Basel Convention on the Control
    of Transboundary Movements of Hazardous Wastes and Their Disposal, 1991; Bonn Conven-
    tion on Migratory Species, 1991; Convention on Biological Diversity, 1994; Convention on
    International Trade in Endangered Species of Wild Fauna and Flora, 1980; Kyoto Protocol,
    2001; Montreal Protocol on Substances that Deplete the Ozone Layer, 1990; Rotterdam
    Convention on the Prior Informed Consent Procedure for Certain Hazardous Chemicals and
    Pesticides in International Trade, 2000; Stockholm Convention on Persistent Organic Pollu-
    tants, 2004; UN Framework Convention on Climate Change, 1993; and Vienna Convention for
    the Protection of the Ozone Layer, 1989.
20. Constitution s. 31 provides that: '[T]his Constitution, the laws of the Nation enacted by Con-
    gress in pursuance thereof, and treaties with foreign powers, are the supreme law of the Nation;
    and the authorities of each province are bound thereby, notwithstanding any provision to the
    contrary included in the provincial laws or constitutions, except for the province of Buenos
    Aires, the treaties ratified after the Pact of 11 November 1859' (translated). This provision
    should be read with Art. 27 of the Vienna Convention on the Law of Treaties which states that 'a
    party may not invoke the provisions of its internal law as justification for its failure to perform a
    treaty'. This was confirmed by the Supreme Court in *Ekmekdjian, Miguel A. c. Sofovich,
    Gerardo y otros* (7 Julio 1992) SC de la Nación, where the court found that the Vienna
    Convention gives priority to international treaties over internal law.

Congress is mandated to create environmental laws in terms of section 41 of the Constitution. These laws should contain minimum environmental requirements and standards,[21] and are to be followed by the provinces. The latter provision is a clear exception to the rule established by section 124 of the Constitution, which states that provinces have the original domain over natural resources in their territories.[22] Accordingly, even though the provinces have the original domain over natural resources, they are compelled to follow federal laws and the minimum environmental requirements and standards provided by these laws.

The broader constitutional framework has significantly been enriched by several national laws containing minimum environmental requirements that seek to regulate certain framework and sectoral issues. By way of summary, these include:[23] the *General Environmental Law* (Number 25.675); the *Integral Management of Industrial and Service Activities Law* (Number 25.612); the *Management and Eradication of Polychlorinated Biphenyls Law* (Number 26.670); the *Water Management Law* (Number 25.688); the *Domestic Waste Management Law* (Number 25916); and the *Protection of Native Forests Law* (Number 26.331).

The General Environmental Law arguably is the most significant amongst these environmental laws since it establishes framework principles and objectives for the more general Argentinean environment policy. The objectives of the national environmental policy include: protection of environmental resources (both natural and cultural); improvement of the quality of life of future generations; promotion of civil participation in environmental issues; maintenance of the equilibrium and dynamics of ecological systems; conservation of biological diversity; and promotion of rational and sustainable use of natural resources.[24]

This framework environmental law also establishes general principles which guide the implementation of all environmental laws in Argentina, including the: congruence principle (provincial and local legislation should follow the General Environment Law); preventive principle; precautionary principle; principle of inter-generational equity; principle of progressivism (the objectives of environmental policies should be accomplished in stages in order to progressively attain a better environment); responsibility principle (the generator of present or future negative impacts on the environment is responsible for preventive and corrective measures); subsidiarity principle (the federal government has the duty to cooperate

---

21. 'Minimum protection standards/environmental requirement' provided in s. 41, described above, requires that every environmental law must provide a common environmental protection standard for the entire national territory, and that laws should further seek to impose the necessary measures to ensure environmental protection. These measures are to be determined according to ecological system dynamics, environmental load capacity, and taking into account the imperative of sustainable development. See General Environment Law (25.675), s. 6.
22. Constitution, s. 124 states that the provinces have original dominion over the natural resources existing in their territory.
23. For copies of these laws, see CDI, 'Centro de Documentación e Información del Ministerio de Economía – Argentina' [Centre of Documentation and Information of the Economy Ministry – Argentinean Presidency], <infoleg.mecon.gov.ar/>, 28 August 2008.
24. General Environment Law (25.675), s. 2.

or participate in a complementary way in private activities to protect the environment); sustainability principle; solidarity principle (both the federal government
and the provinces will be responsible for the prevention and mitigation of the trans-
borders effects of their actions); and cooperation principle (the shared natural
resources and ecological systems will be used with equity and rationality).[25]

Section 5 of the General Environmental Law provides that the different levels
of government should integrate all these principles in their governance activities.[26]
Finally, section 8 prescribes the principal mechanisms for achieving sustainable
environmental governance.[27] These include: the environmental order of the territory (a political and technical process that seeks to ensure sustainable use of land
and resources within a certain territory); environmental impact assessment (EIA);
a control system for entropic activities; environmental education; environmental
diagnosis and information systems; and an economic regime for the promotion of
sustainability.

5   THE JUDICIAL SYSTEM IN ARGENTINA[28]

The Constitution establishes the judiciary as the authority for ensuring that the
other branches of government exercise their functions in accordance with their
constitutional mandate.[29] The judiciary therefore plays a specific protagonist

---

25. *Ibid.*, s. 4.
26. *Ibid.*, s. 5.
27. *Ibid.*, s. 8.
28. See further on the judiciary, PJNA, 'Poder Judicial de la Nación: República Argentina'
    [Judiciary of the Nation: Republic of Argentina], <www.pjn.gov.ar>, 14 September 2008.
29. In the original 1883 National Constitution there is no express reference in this regard but
    the Supreme Court in 1888 understood that 'it is basic in our constitutional organization, the
    judicial capacity and duty to compare laws in order to check whether they are or they are not
    in accordance to the text of the National Constitution . . . This is one of the supreme and
    fundamental objectives of the national judicial power and one of the biggest guarantors for
    the constitutional rights' – *Municipalidad de la Capital v. Elortondo* (14 Abril 1888) SC de la
    Nación. In the 1994 constitutional reform there is a new section where this capacity is recog-
    nized even in a prompt and summary proceeding. S. 43 states: 'Any person shall file a prompt
    and summary proceeding regarding constitutional guarantees, provided there is no other legal
    remedy, against any act or omission of the public authorities or individuals which currently or
    imminently may damage, limit, modify or threaten rights and guarantees recognized by this
    Constitution, treaties or laws, with open arbitrariness or illegality. In such case, the judge may
    declare that the act or omission is based on an unconstitutional rule.' These facts are considered
    to imply that 'without fear of being wrong, the Argentinean Supreme Court is one of the eldest
    (sic) judicial courts with capacity to declare unconstitutional any law or administrative decision
    of the other branches', see R.G. Ferreyra, 'Corte Suprema de Justicia argentina y control de
    constitucionalidad: Vicisitudes y retos del papel institucional del Tribunal' [Argentinean
    Supreme Court and constitutional control: vicissitudes and challenges of the institutional
    role of the tribunal], in *Derecho Constitucional. Memoria del Congreso Internacional de
    Culturas y Sistemas Jurídicos Comparados* [Constitutional Direction: Memorial of the
    International Congress on the Culture of Comparative Judicial Systems], ed. M. Carbonell
    (México: UNAM, 2004).

political role that has been increasing in recent times.[30] Argentina does not have a specialized constitutional court to exclusively adjudicate on constitutional matters (also including matters where administrative State action may potentially encroach on constitutional entitlements). This competency lies with federal and provincial courts which can pronounce on the constitutionality of laws and administrative acts in cases under their jurisdiction.

The judiciary consists of a three-tiered system namely, the federal court, twenty-three provincial courts, and a special court for Buenos Aires City. These three divisions are subject to the overriding authority of the Supreme Court and the Magistrate Council (responsible for the administration of the courts and selection of judges). The judicial system also comprises of the Public Ministry, which includes the Attorney General's Office, the Public Prosecutor's Office and the Public Defender's Office. Other relevant federal justice system institutions include the National Ministry of Justice and Human Rights, the Federal Penitentiary Service and the Federal Police.

The distribution of federal courts within the Argentinean territory is decided by the national congress in accordance with section 108 of Constitution.[31] According to 2005 data, there are 883 judges in the national judicial system who have had to deal with 1,002,296 cases.[32]

Argentina's provinces have a similar judicial structure, with some local variations. For example, the Province of Buenos Aires justice system is formed by different courts with supreme authority resting in the Superior Justice Tribunal. This system also includes the provincial judicial branch, which is composed of the Public Ministry (with both prosecutors and public defenders), the provincial Judicial Council, the provincial Ministry of Justice, and the Buenos Aires Provincial Police.[33] The Superior Justice Tribunal is the highest provincial court and there are

---

30. In the last few decades, courts – especially supreme and constitutional courts – have become more important political actors, in the sense that they are contributing to define some public policies. This fact contradicts the traditional idea of judges rendering decisions only for particular cases. When courts play a significant role in the definition of a specific public policy, they are certainly making decisions that affect more people than just those participating in a judicial case. R. Sieder, L. Schjolden & A. Angell (eds), *The Judicialization of Politics in Latin America* (New York: Palgrave Macmillan, 2006), 3, state that 'with respect to the judicialization of politics, clearly one important dimension is the way in which judges who carry out constitutional judicial review end up making, or substantially contributing to the making of public policy, thus broadening the scope of "judge-made law" '. These facts were marked in 1995 by N. Tate & T. Vallinder, *The Global Expansion of Judicial Power* (New York: NYUP, 1995), and it is possible to also observe these trends in Europe, cf. A. Stone Sweet, *Governing with Judges: Constitutional Politics in Europe* (Oxford: OUP, 2000), Latin America (cf. Sieder, Schjolden & Angell, *supra*), and several other countries such as Israel, New Zealand, South Africa and Canada, cf. R. Hirschl, *The Origins and Consequences of the New Constitutionalism* (Cambridge: HUP, 2004).
31. Constitution, s. 108: 'The Judicial Power of the Nation shall be vested in a Supreme Court and in other lower courts which Congress may constitute in the territory of the Nation.'
32. CEJAS, 'Report on Judicial Systems in the Americas 2006-2007', <www.cejamericas. org>, 9 June 2008.
33. Cordoba Province has a similar structure.

several first and second instance tribunals distributed throughout the provincial territory.

The Supreme Court manages its own resources and has the power to determine its own internal organization as well as that of the federal courts. These duties and powers are exercised through Supreme Court regulatory decrees *(acordadas)* and resolutions, through which the court has established regulations both for its own operation and that of the federal courts. It also has ordered the modification, creation and reorganization of offices, departments and administrative and judicial areas in response to changing jurisdictional structures.

The Supreme Court is the head of both the federal and provincial judicial systems and the court of last instance for national issues. Therefore, even when its decisions have no formal consequences for the inferior courts and judges, the Supreme Court has an important impact on other judges as the main guidance for constitutional interpretation.[34] Members of the Supreme Court are appointed by the president of Argentina and confirmed by the senate. One of the members of the Supreme Court is elected as president by fellow members.

Given Argentina's complex federal system, determining which court has jurisdiction to hear a matter can be difficult. The general trend is that the majority of cases are decided by provincial courts and only exceptional cases by federal courts.[35]

At the federal and provincial levels, courts and judges are specialized in different matters such as civil law, penal law or administrative law. No specialized environmental courts or judges with specialist training to hear environmental matters exist. There is, however, a penal prosecutor specialized in environmental matters and crimes.

6   ANALYSIS OF SIGNIFICANT ENVIRONMENTAL
         JUDGMENTS

The main focus of the following analysis is on environmental judgments delivered by the Supreme Court. There are, however, a significant number of other judgments by inferior courts which have also contributed to shaping the interpretation of environmental laws and procedural rules in order to ensure environmental

---

34. See for a discussion on the role of the law of precedent and the influence of the Supreme Court on other jurisdictions, A. Morello & E. Quevedo Mendoza. *Efectos generales de determinadas sentencias de la Corte Suprema* (Buenos Aires: LexisNexis, 2003).

35. Constitution, s. 116 states: The Supreme Court and the lower courts of the Nation are empowered to hear and decide all cases arising under the Constitution and the laws of the Nation, with the exception made in s. 75, subs. 12, and under the treaties made with foreign nations; all cases concerning ambassadors, public ministers and foreign consuls; cases related to admiralty and maritime jurisdiction; matters in which the Nation shall be a party; actions arising between two or more provinces, between one province and the inhabitants of another province, between the inhabitants of different provinces, and between one province or the inhabitants thereof against a foreign state or citizen (translated).

sustainability. The analysis therefore also reflects on a selection of these judgments insofar as they illustrate the contribution of inferior courts to environmental governance in Argentina.

6.1 INFERIOR COURTS

Even prior to the constitutional reform of 1994, which entrenched the right to a healthy and balanced environment, there were several inferior court decisions related to the promotion of environmental governance in Argentina. One example is the case of *Kattan v. Poder ejecutivo* (1983),[36] where the plaintiffs challenged the grant of an authorization to fish fourteen special dolphins in Argentinean coastal waters. The plaintiffs were of the opinion that the authorization undermined the Convention on International Trade in Endangered Species of Wild Fauna and Flora (ratified by the national law number 22.344 in 1981). The court accepted the plaintiffs' standing to protect the environment and suspended the resolutions of the National Fishing Agency which had issued the fishing authorization.

Following the 1994 constitutional reform, the Supreme Court of Buenos Aires Province, in the case of *Copetro v. Almada* (1998),[37] confirmed an earlier judgment which ordered Copetro SA, a petroleum company, to pay compensation to the plaintiff and to adapt its production process to stop air pollution. The Supreme Court of Buenos Aires determined, in an ancillary order, that if Copetro SA failed to make these adaptations, the factory would be closed. The tribunal affirmed that:

> it is imperative to transform the judicial conceptions to protect the real aspects of the collective life, typical of the modern society, that affect impersonal and diffused interests that deserve the most energetic and anticipated defense and, in this context, the right to a healthy environment can be understood as an extension of the sphere of human personality.[38]

This decision underlines the importance for the judiciary to adapt its rules and institutions and conceptions of current societal (environmental) issues, in order to protect 'impersonal and diffused interests' and, consequently, the right to a healthy environment.

The case of *Barragan v. Gobierno de la Ciudad de Buenos Aires* (2003)[39] concerned noise pollution caused by traffic on a highway in Buenos Aires City. In this case, the second instance tribunal affirmed that the right to a healthy environment includes the right not to be affected by noise pollution. It further held that the government has the duty to develop public policies while every person and institution has the duty to respect the environment.[40] In this decision, the tribunal

---

36. *Kattan v. Poder ejecutivo* (10 Mayo 1983) 1 Instancia, Cont. Adm. Fed. Juzg. 2, Bs As.
37. *Copetro v. Almada* (19 Mayo 1998) SC Just. Bs As.
38. *Copetro v. Almada* (19 Mayo 1998) SC Just. Bs As, III b.
39. *Barragan v. Gobierno de la Ciudad de Buenos Aires* (2 Octubre 2003) Juzg. Cont. Adm. y Trib. Ciudad Bs As.
40. *Ibid.*, XXVIII b.

ordered both the Buenos Aires Government and a private firm that was in charge of highway maintenance, to take measures to decrease the sound level in order to respect the right of the people living near the road to a healthy environment. An interesting contribution to environmental governance in this decision is the affirmation that even when there is not an express regulation regarding noise pollution, both public and private actors have the duty to respect the environment and take measures to mitigate environmental impacts such as noise pollution.

The highest court of the Province of Buenos Aires has furthermore applied the preventive principle entrenched in the General Environmental Law.[41] In the case of *Asociación Civil Ambiente Sur v. Municipalidad de Avellaneda* (2003),[42] the court imposed a cautionary measure to stop the construction of a new market in an ecological reserve in Avellaneda City. The court held that the potential damage caused by constructing the new market, particularly that associated with deforestation, would be impossible to repair in the future. The court ordered the suspension of all construction pending the preparation and presentation of a report detailing the possible environmental impacts associated with the project.

The Superior Tribunal of Rio Negro Province, in the case of *Consejo de Desarrollo de las Comunidades Indígenas v. Provincia de Rio Negro* (2005),[43] had the opportunity to pronounce on the strong link between the environment and indigenous people. In this matter, a mining plant (*Proyecto Calcatreu*) sought to mine gold and silver deposits located on indigenous land. The indigenous people claimed that the mining plant and operations affected their right to self-determination by endangering their cultural customs, and their right to a healthy environment owing to water and air pollution. The claim was brought by the *Consejo de Desarrollo de las Comunidades Indígenas* (CODECI) (Indigenous Communities Development Council) through an *amparo*.[44] The claim was principally based on the need to protect biological and cultural diversity (section 41 of the Constitution); and the need to ensure participation of indigenous communities in decisions that might affect their lands and ways of living (section 75(17) of the Constitution).[45]

---

41. General Environment Law (25.675), s. 4.
42. *Asociación Civil Ambiente Sur v. Municipalidad de Avellaneda* (19 Marzo 2003) SC Just. Bs As.
43. *Consejo de Desarrollo de las Comunidades Indígenas v. Provincia de Rio Negro* (16 Agosto 2005) Sup. Trib. Just. Río Negro.
44. The *amparo* is a prompt and summary legal proceeding first recognized by the Argentinean Supreme Court in: *Kot, Samuel SRL s/ Acción de amparo* (5 Septiembre 1958) SC de la Nación and *Siri, Angel, s./interpone recurso de hábeas corpus* (27 Diciembre 1957) SC de la Nación. S. 43 of the Constitution provides in this respect that: Any person shall file a prompt and summary proceeding regarding constitutional guarantees, provided there is no other legal remedy, against any act or omission of the public authorities or individuals which currently or imminently may damage, limit, modify or threaten rights and guarantees recognized by this Constitution, treaties or laws, with open arbitrariness or illegality.
45. Constitution, s. 75, pt 17 states that: 'Congress is empowered . . . to recognize the ethnic and cultural pre-existence of indigenous peoples of Argentina. To guarantee respect for the identity

The above constitutional provisions were echoed in the principles of biological and cultural diversity and participation in environmental matters, prescribed in the General Environmental Law.[46] The tribunal accepted the *amparo* and ordered different agencies[47] of the executive branch of government to ensure respect for the environmental right, including respect for the cultural and social rights of indigenous people such as the Peñi Mapu, Npung Curra and Putren Trulli. The tribunal also recognized the right of these communities to participate in decision-making procedures related to the land.

More recently, a court in Corrientes Province delivered a decision with some interesting considerations as regards *locus standi* in environmental matters. In *Crignoli v. Aguerre'* (2006),[48] the applicant filed an *amparo* against, among others, the *Instituto Correntino del Agua* (ICA) [Corrientes Water Institute] in order to stop the use of fertilizers that were polluting the environment in the Iberá Park. In accepting the *amparo*, the court held that when collective or diffuse rights are threatened, any person has standing to present an *amparo* to stop the environmentally damaging activity. Following the General Environmental Law,[49] there is no need to be directly affected by the action in question, as long as the claim seeks to stop environmentally deleterious action. This is a position decidedly conducive to promoting access to justice in environmental matters. This decision also strengthens the idea of 'minimum environmental requirements'[50] discussed above, and further is evidence of an emerging practice where inferior (provincial) courts apply national environmental law in order to induce more effective environmental protection.

Despite the fact that all the above decision are those of inferior courts,[51] they have had significant practical impacts and create important precedents to strengthen environmental protection.

---

and the right to bilingual and intercultural education; to recognize the legal capacity of their communities, and the community possession and ownership of the lands they traditionally occupy; and to regulate the granting of other lands adequate and sufficient for human development; none of them shall be sold, transmitted or subject to liens or attachments. To guarantee their participation in issues related to their natural resources and in other interests affecting them. The provinces may jointly exercise these powers' (translated).

46. General Environment Law (25.675), s. 4.
47. *Consejo de Ecología y Medio Ambiente* (CODEMA) [Ecology and Environment Council], *Dirección General de Minería* [Mining General Direction], *la Dirección de Tierras y Colonización* [Lands and Colonization Direction], *Departamento Provincial de Aguas* (DPA) [Provincial Water Department].
48. *Crignoli v. Aguerre* (13 Octubre 2006) C. Civ. y Com. Corrientes.
49. General Environment Law (25.675), s. 30.
50. *Ibid.*, s. 6.
51. The inferior courts (as opposed to the supreme courts) are increasingly considered the ideal *fora* to develop environmental jurisprudence. See E. Faggi, *El medio ambiente en la justicia* (Buenos Aires: LexisNexis, 2005).

6.2   Supreme Court

The Supreme Court had the opportunity to pronounce on several environmental matters during the past few years. The following discussion focuses on some of the more prominent decisions.

The case of *Almada v. Copetro* (2001),[52] having worked its way through several provincial tribunals, eventually came before the Supreme Court. The initial injunction application, granted by the Supreme Court of Buenos Aires, was lodged by an individual seeking the reparation of environmental damage (and resultant compensation) caused by a factory operated by Copetro SA. Copetro SA sought to appeal the decision of the court of first instance to the Supreme Court of Argentina, as it believed it was fatally flawed. The Supreme Court of Argentina, however, affirmed the decision of the inferior court and Copetro SA were accordingly ordered to cease polluting the area and pay compensation. The court, however, chose to amend an ancillary order compelling the closure of the factory consequent on the company's failure to abide by the principal order. Even though the Supreme Court rejected the ancillary order, the judgment has been upheld as an important precedent regarding compensation for environmental damage resulting from industrial pollution.

In *Comunidad indígena del pueblo Wichi Hoktek T'Oi v. Secretaría de medio ambiente y desarrollo sustentable* (2002),[53] the Supreme Court had to decide whether an *amparo* was the appropriate remedy to order the cessation of deforestation activities in some areas of Salta Province inhabited by an indigenous community (*Wichi Hoktek T'Oi*). An authorization had been issued by the Provincial Environmental and Sustainable Development Secretary (an organ of State) to deforest the area. The court *a quo* (Supreme Court of Salta) considered that an *amparo* was not the appropriate mechanism and remedy as it was a *prompt* and *summary* proceeding applicable in those circumstances where there were certain limitations regarding proof and debate.[54] The Supreme Court, however, disagreed with the court *a quo*. It held that the environmental risk in question was current and could have irreversible consequences including: loss of biodiversity, climate change, desertification, and may further negatively impact on socio-economic rights such as access to water, education, and preservation of cultural diversity. The Supreme Court accordingly ordered the inferior court to accept the *amparo* as an appropriate remedy in this instance. The court also affirmed that it would be an excessive respect for procedural rules to deny this injunction on the basis that there

---

52. *Almada v. Copetro* (27 Febrero 2001) SC de la Nación.
53. *Comunidad indígena del pueblo Wichi Hoktek T'Oi v. Secretaría de medio ambiente y desarrollo sustentable* (11 Julio 2002) SC de la Nación.
54. In the Argentinean legal system, the *amparo* is usually considered an exceptional proceeding with some limits regarding proof (for instance the number of witnesses any party is able to call), and debate (discussion terms in every stage of the process). This is the reason why some tribunals consider that when the discussions are complex within a case, the *amparo* is not the appropriate mechanism to solve them.

was not sufficient room for 'debate and proof'.[55] It ruled that it was necessary to make procedural rules slightly more flexible, especially in light of the possible serious environmental consequences of deforestation. The judiciary, as a consequence of this judgment, has sent a clear message to other branches of government and organs of State that: there are environmental considerations which may override rigid procedural constraints; and that environmental protection is not only important for safeguarding the natural environment, but also for protecting social and cultural interests. Moreover, the judgment reflects how environmental, social and cultural considerations may impact on the manner in which the judiciary understand and implement their procedures and functions.

In *Asociación de Superficiarios de la Patagonia v. YPF SA* (2004),[56] a civil association sought an *amparo* against a group of enterprises[57] that were carrying out petroleum activities in the *cuenca neuquina* region, an area formed by the Colorado and Negro rivers. The plaintiff sought reparation for environmental damage caused by the defendant's activities, which it alleged were not employing BAT. The environmental damage included: soil, air and water pollution; deforestation; and desertification of large areas. The plaintiff further sought the following orders: that adequate measures be taken by the defendant to prevent future negative impacts on the environment; that the defendant cease all industrial activity; and that the defendant establish insurance for possible environmental damage in accordance with the General Environmental Law.[58] In its petition, the applicant also requested the participation of the ombudsman as a third party because of the collective rights that were involved in a decision of this nature. Considering that the rivers in the region were also part of other provinces, the applicant further requested the participation, as interested parties, of the provincial governments of Buenos Aires, La Pampa, Mendoza, Neuquén and Rio Negro; and the *Consejo Federal de Medio Ambiente* (CoFeMA) [Environmental Federal Council]. The claim was based on the principles of prevention, responsibility and sustainability entrenched in the General Environmental Law.[59]

The Supreme Court denied the relief owing to defects in the plaintiff's case. The court agreed that the provinces and the CoFeMA should participate in the proceedings. It, however, held that the participation of the ombudsman should be left to his/her discretion. In a dissenting judgment, three justices (Vazquez,

---

55. *Comunidad indígena del pueblo Wichi Hoktek T'Oi v. Secretaría de medio ambiente y desarrollo sustentable* (11 Julio 2002) SC de la Nación, pt 5.
56. *Asociación de Superficiarios de la Patagonia v. YPF SA* (13 Julio 2004) SC de la Nación.
57. The enterprises included: YPF SA, Petrobras Argentina SA, Pluspetrol Exploración y Producción SA, Chevron San Jorge SRL, Gas Medanito SA, Hidenesa Hidrocarburos del Neuquén SA, Pioneer Natural Resource SA, Capex SA, and Petrolera Santa Fe SRL y Astra CAPSA.
58. The General Environmental Law (25.675), prescribes in s. 22 the duty to establish an environmental insurance for all the activities that might negatively impact on the environment. However, as insurance has many technical variables that need to be established in order to be able to set a regular cost and its limits, the application of this section was postponed until further details could be given by the national executive branch on its implementation.
59. General Environment Law (25.675), s. 4.

Zaffaroni and Maqueda) ruled that there was indeed an obligation on the company to provide for insurance.[60] They also considered it necessary to request information from government to establish the causes of pollution and to identify the actual polluters.[61] The dissent also held that it would be crucial for the ombudsman to participate in the proceedings owing to the diffuse array of rights involved.[62] The dissenting judgment evidences a 'deeper' and more thorough interpretation of the General Environment Law and a greater understanding and appreciation of the relevant environmental institutions involved.[63]

In *Mendoza, Beatriz S. y otros c. Estado Nacional y otros* (2004),[64] the Supreme Court displayed a greater commitment to contribute to environmental governance, by affirming that judges should play an active role in endeavours to protect the right to a healthy environment. The case (the final decision of which was still pending at the time of writing) was initiated by several residents of Buenos Aires, claiming compensation for damage to individual rights (health and property) caused by environmental pollution stemming from industrial activities along the Riachuelo River. The plaintiffs argued that the activities had been condoned by certain government agencies and sought a court order preventing the pollution, restituting the damaged environment and compensating them for environmental damage. The plaintiffs based their petition on the General Environmental Law, which establishes environmental standards for industries and provides for standing in these types of environmental cases.[65] It was common cause that the river and its surrounding area, currently home to some 3,5 million inhabitants,[66] (almost 10% of the total Argentinean population),[67] was one of the most polluted areas in the country. In its first resolution, the Supreme Court accepted the direct standing of the plaintiffs.[68] The court ordered the executive branches of the different jurisdictions[69] to develop and apply an integrated environmental management plan for the area.

---

60. *Asociación de Superficiarios de la Patagonia v. YPF SA* (13 Julio 2004) SC de la Nación. Dissenting, pt 5.
61. *Ibid.*, pt 7.
62. *Ibid.*, pt 8.
63. M. Valls de Rossi, 'El daño ambiental en la Corte Suprema Argentina. Recomposición. Obligación de contratar un seguro, 2004' [Environmental damage in the Argentinean Supreme Court. Recomposition. Duty to provide an insurance], <www.prodiversitas.bioetica.org>, 9 June 2008.
64. *Mendoza, Beatriz S. y otros c. Estado Nacional y otros* (20 Junio 2006) SC de la Nación.
65. General Environment Law (25.675), ss 2, 4 and 30.
66. Auditoría General de la Nación. 'Cuenca Matanza-Riachuelo: Documento de difusión' [Matanza – Riachuelo Basin: Discussion Document], April 2006, <www.farn.org.ar/participacion/riachuelo/documentos/informe_AGN_resumen.pdf>, 14 September 2008, 13.
67. According to the last census, in 2001, the total population of Argentina consisted of 36 million inhabitants. See INDEC, 'Instituto Nacional de Estadísticas y Censos de la República Argentina' [National Statistics and Census: Institute for the Republic of Argentina], <www.indec.mecon.ar>, 28 August 2008.
68. *Mendoza, Beatriz S. y otros c. Estado Nacional y otros* (20 Junio 2006) SC de la Nación. pts 6, 10 and 14.
69. The National Environmental Secretary, the provincial government of Buenos Aires, and the governments of the cities.

As a result of this particular order, government agencies proceeded to establish the *Autoridad de Cuenca Matanza Riachuelo* (ACUMAR) [Matanza-Riachuelo Basin Authority], which is a mixed institution formed by representatives from the national government, the Province of Buenos Aires government, and other local governments.[70] Considering that the final decision of the process would directly impact on thousands of people in the area, the Supreme Court chose to call a public hearing in order to ensure broad-based community participation which should inform the court's final findings. The judicial and legal process was accordingly adjusted by the court to more adequately cater for diffuse interests and collective rights.[71] Five public hearings have been held during which the federal governments, non-governmental organizations (NGOs), corporations and members of the public have been offered the opportunity to air their views, and in so doing, clarify various issues for the insight (and benefit) of the court. This ground-breaking alteration of traditional judicial proceedings provided the impetus for the Supreme Court in *Acordada* (30/2007) (a subsequent decision), to declare public hearings a useful mechanism to evaluate the quality of justice and to promote public participation judicial activities.[72] Another significant result of the judgment in *Mendoza, Beatriz S. y otros c. Estado Nacional y otros* (2004),[73] is that the court made it clear that extraordinary measures may be required on the side of judges where environmental issues and interests are at stake. The court stated in this respect that:

> the improvement or degradation of the environment benefits or affects the whole society, because it is a good that belongs to the social and trans-individual sphere and that is the reason why judges may use a particular power to assure the effectiveness of these constitutional mandates.[74]

The judgment has further significantly impacted on public environmental policies for the region, especially insofar as the integrated environmental management plan could influence these policies. In a later resolution, the Supreme Court ordered the federal government, the government of the Province of Buenos Aires, the local government of the City of Buenos Aires, and CoFeMA to establish an integrated environmental management plan for the Matanza-Riachuelo River. In drafting the plan, the authorities were ordered to consider the following principles enshrined in the General Environmental Law: the environmental order of the territory;[75]

---

70. These include: Lanús, Avellaneda, Lomas de Zamora, Esteban Echeverría, La Matanza, Ezeiza, Cañuelas, Almirante Brown, Morón, Merlo, Marcos Paz, Presidente Perón, San Vicente y General Las Heras, within Buenos Aires Province. ACUMAR was created by national law number 26.168, which was ratified by the governments of Buenos Aires Province and Buenos Aires City. See ACUMAR, 'Autoridad de Cuenca Matanza Riachuelo' [Matanza-Riachuelo Basin Authority], <www.acumar.gov.ar/>, 14 September 2008.
71. A. Gil Domínguez, *El caso 'Mendoza': Hacia la construcción pretoriana de una teoría de los derechos colectivos*, (Buenos Aires: Editorial La Ley, 2006).
72. CSJN, Acordada 30/2007.
73. Mendoza case, *supra* n. 68.
74. *Ibid.*, pt 18.
75. General Environment Law (25.675), ss 8, 9 and 10.

scope of control over human activities;[76] EIA;[77] environmental education;[78] and public access to environmental information (especially as regards the affected communities).[79] The Supreme Court allowed considerable room for discretion on the part of those public authorities tasked with drafting the integrated environmental management plan in the sense that the plan only had to conform to certain basic principles and not explicit prescriptions imposed by the court. During its evaluation of the plan, the court conceded it did not have the appropriate technical expertise necessary to adequately pronounce on the suitability of the plan. The court accordingly, and commendably so, approached the National University of Buenos Aires to assist in the evaluation process, thereby further expanding the already comprehensive public participation and information process.

7   CRITICAL EVALUATION AND WAY FORWARD

The analysis above suggests that judges should play an increasingly active and innovative role where the environment is at stake. This would make it possible to overcome various strict, rigorous and often inhibitive procedural rules and judicial traditions. A flexible approach is conducive to the concept of sustainable environmental governance, especially when considering the diverse interests usually at stake in environmental matters. Moreover, sometimes courts do not have sufficient knowledge to adjudicate intricate and highly technical environmental issues. Co-opting expertise and allowing broad-based public participation to inform the courts' reasoning, are in keeping with international norms and practices and comprehensively answer to sustainability imperatives.

The Argentinean judiciary has also significantly contributed, and continues to contribute to, the development of environmental law. Generally speaking, environmental law in Argentina is a relative young legal discipline which only really started to spread its roots from 1994 (the time of the constitutional reform) onwards. The environmental regime is based on the environmental right and it is evident that the courts are willing to extend this rights-based approach to environmental governance to safeguard not only environmental, but also social and cultural values, interests and rights.

It is encouraging that the Argentinean judiciary is increasingly willing to rely on the principles of sustainability to assess the effects of activities which may be detrimental to the environment, especially insofar as the determination of possible future harm to the environment is concerned. The principles of sustainability (including, among others, the polluter pays, preventive, precautionary and intergenerational equity principles), arguably are meant to guide behaviour and

---

76. *Ibid.*, s. 10.
77. *Ibid.*, s. 11.
78. *Ibid.*, s. 14.
79. *Ibid.*, ss 16 and 18.

decisions which may affect the environment. By employing these principles to also guide its decisions, and by imposing obligations resulting from these principles on both the private and public sectors, the courts are evidently endorsing the validity of these principles as a means to facilitating sustainability.

An analysis of the case law above also suggests that the courts would, despite the restrictions imposed on them by the *trias politica* doctrine, not hesitate to direct government environmental authorities and other organs of State, to heed their legal obligations to safeguard interests flowing from, inter alia, the environmental right, even if this means establishing new institutions and ensuring sustainability through innovative mechanisms such as the integrated environmental management plan used in the *Mendoza* case.

A more direct result of the judgments in *Asociación de Superficiarios de la Patagonia v. YPF SA* (2004) and the *Mendoza* case, is the possible creation of a financial insurance regime for environmental damage. This surely would add to contingency measures catering for those instances where compensation for environmental damage is not readily recoverable.

The courts also recognize the importance of public participation in environmental governance. The *Mendoza* decision to hold mandatory public hearings and provide information to all interested and affected parties is commendable, not only because it facilitates 'management by outsiders', but also because it provides an opportunity to control the quality of the judicial process.

There, of course, also remain various challenges as regards judicial involvement in environmental governance. First, the concept of 'environment' necessitates a very broad consideration of all factors which may impact on the environment *per se*. Although the courts seem willing to consider cultural and social issues alongside environmental concerns, it remains to be seen how far the courts will go to further expand the conceptual parameters of the 'environment'. As has been illustrated above, it is not common practice for the judiciary to integrate natural variables with social and cultural considerations, but this integration is essential in order to protect the wide conception of 'environment'.[80]

Second, a significant constitutional challenge facing the judiciary is to address environmental challenges without unduly encroaching on the limits imposed by the *trias politica* doctrine; an encroachment which could negatively impact on the fine equilibrium of power between the branches of government. What are the limits of judicial intervention in this respect? Should the quantity, urgency, depth and complexity of environmental problems be considered to delimit the degree of encroachment? In Argentina, the importance and urgency of environmental challenges are evident, but this arguably should not override constitutional models of State governance and associated institutional risks which may disturb the fine balance of State power among the judiciary, the executive and the legislature.

Third, courts should adjust procedural rules to cater more adequately for diverse issues in environmental protection. This could be complicated because such adjustment must always respect substantive (usually traditional) principles

---

80. In accordance with the Constitution, national laws and international conventions.

and rules of the judicial process. In the words of the Supreme Court, it is possible to adjust the judicial process to make it more flexible as long as the essential procedures are respected.[81] This, however, is easier said than done. Moreover, which elements are essential for due judicial process? The courts arguably should apply great care in a determination of these elements, while simultaneously considering what would be best for ensuring the protection of the environment.

Fourth, it is important to correctly control non-legal knowledge that may affect judicial decisions. The courts are willing to consult with interested and affected parties (including expert institutions such as universities), which consultation should inform judicial decisions. However, due to the complexity of environmental matters, this consultation process should be carefully managed by the courts and innovative approaches should be considered to adequately connect legal and non-legal information and expertise.

Fifth, environmental challenges know no boundaries. The highly formalized and rigid jurisdictional boundaries may result in environmental challenges not being holistically addressed by the courts as conflict between jurisdictions may arise. It would accordingly be prudent for the judiciary to establish clear interpretation rules regarding the most appropriate court to decide on specific environmental issues, especially in those instances where trans-jurisdictional environmental issues arise. This would facilitate greater legal certainty, save time, and prevent environmental damages occurring and continuing while jurisdictional issues are being clarified.

BIBLIOGRAPHY

ACUMAR. 'Autoridad de Cuenca Matanza Riachuelo'. <www.acumar.gov.ar/>, 14 September 2008.

Allende Rubino, H. *Presupuestos mínimos del derecho procesal ambiental.* Buenos Aires: Editorial La Ley, Suplemento de Derecho Ambiental 2005.

Auditoría General de la Nación. 'Cuenca Matanza-Riachuelo: Documento de difusión', April 2006, <www.farn.org.ar/participacion/riachuelo/documentos/informe_AGN_resumen.pdf>, 14 September 2008.

Avila, J. et al. 'Análisis del impacto ambiental de la explotación minera del yacimiento El Timbó, Tucumán, Argentina'. Paper delivered at the 13th Congreso Geológico Argentino. Buenos Aires, 1996.

Badino, J. *Minería aurífera en Esquel. La Corte Suprema de Justicia de la Nación reafirma el buen camino hacia la preservación ambiental.* Buenos Aires: LexisNexis, 2008.

Basterra, M. *El amparo ambiental, ¿acción popular o acción colectiva? El caso 'Crignoli'.* Buenos Aires: Editorial La Ley, Suplemento de Derecho Ambiental, 2006.

Bibiloni, H. *El proceso ambiental* Buenos Aires: LexisNexis, 2005.

---

81. Mendoza case, *supra* n. 68, pt 4.

Bidart Campos, G. *Manual de la Constitución Reformada*. Buenos Aires: Editorial Ediar, 1997.

Cafferata, N. *El tiempo de las 'cortes verdes'*. Buenos Aires: Editorial La Ley, Suplemento de Derecho Ambiental, 2007.

Carballo, J. 'Courts, environment and public policies'. Paper presented at New Haven Conference on Environmental Governance and Democracy, 2008. Yale University: UNITAR, 2008. <www.yale.edu/envirocenter/envdem>, 9 June 2008.

CDI. 'Centro de Documentación e Información del Ministerio de Economía – Argentina'. <infoleg.mecon.gov.ar/>, 28 August 2008.

CEJAS. 'Report on Judicial Systems in the Americas 2006-2007'. <www.cejamericas.org>, 9 June 2008.

Clichevsky, N. *Pobreza y políticas urbano-ambientales en Argentina*. Santiago de Chile: Comisión Económica para Latino América y el Caribe, División de Medio Ambientey Asentamientos Humanos, UN, 2002.

Congreso. 'Bienvenidos al Congreso de la Nación Argentina'. <www.congreso.gov.ar>, 14 September 2008.

Costa, J.L. 'Impacto de los agroquímicos en el ambiente'. <www.inta.gov.ar/balcarce/noticias/inta_expone/AuditorioGuillermoCovas/ImpactoAgroqAmbiente.pdf>, 14 September 2008.

Devia, L., P. Noseda & A. Sibileau. *Estado vs. ciudadanos: Cómo hacer realidad la protección común del ambiente*. Rosario: La Ley Litoral, 2006.

Duverges, D. *Novedades en Jurisprudencia Ambiental*. Buenos Aires: Editorial La Ley, Suplemento de Derecho Ambiental. 2007.

ESDS. 'Perspectivas del medio ambiente en la Argentina', Buenos Aires: Informe Geo Argentina, 2004. <www.ambiente.gov.ar>, 8 June August 2008.

Etchichury, H. *Tres enfoques sobre el derecho al medio ambiente*. Córdoba: Lerner Editora, 2006.

Faggi, E. *El medio ambiente en la justicia*. Buenos Aires: LexisNexis, 2005.

Ferreyra, R.G. 'Corte Suprema de Justicia argentina y control de constitucionalidad: Vicisitudes y retos del papel institucional del Tribunal'. In *Derecho Constitucional. Memoria del Congreso Internacional de Culturas y Sistemas Jurídicos Comparados*, edited by M. Carbonell. México: Universidad Nacional Autónoma de México, 2004.

Fleitas Ortiz de Rozas, A. 'Gestión ambiental y Justicia'. *Revista de Derecho Ambiental* 1 (2005): 126-135.

Gil Domínguez, A. *El caso 'Mendoza': Hacia la construcción pretoriana de una teoría de los derechos colectivos*. Buenos Aires: Editorial La Ley, Suplemento de Derecho Ambiental, 2006.

Hirschl, R. *The Origins and Consequences of the New Constitutionalism*. Cambridge: Harvard University Press, 2004.

Hoban, T. & R. Brooks. *Green Justice: The Environment and the Courts*. Colorado: Westview Press, 1987.

INDEC. 'Instituto Nacional de Estadísticas y Censos de la República Argentina'. <www.indec.mecon.ar>, 28 August 2008.

Kagan, R. 'Adversarial Legalism and American Government'. In *The New Politics of Public Policy*, edited by M. Landy & M. Levin. Baltimore: John Hopkins University, 1995.

Kemelmajer de Carlucci, A. 'Estado de la jurisprudencia nacional en el ámbito relativo al daño ambiental colectivo después de la sanción de la ley 25.675, ley general del ambiente (LGA), 2006'. <www.acaderc.org.ar>, 9 June 2008.

Kraft, M. *Environmental Policy and Politics*. Green Bay, University of Wisconsin, 2004.

Maqueda, J. 'Derecho Constitucional Ambiental'. *Revista de Derecho Ambiental* 11 (2007): 1-25.

Morag-Levine, N. 'Partners no more: Relational Transformation and the Turn to litigation in two Conservationist Organizations'. *Law and Society Review* 37, no. 3 (2003): 457-509.

Morello, A. & C. Sbdar. *Teoría y realidad de la tutela jurídica del ambiente*. Buenos Aires: Editorial La Ley, Suplemento de Derecho Ambiental, 2007.

Morello, A. & E. Quevedo Mendoza. *Efectos generales de determinadas sentencias de la Corte Suprema*. Buenos Aires: LexisNexis, 2003.

Morello, A. & N. Cafferata. *Las industrias, la tutela del ambiente y la Corte Suprema*. Buenos Aires: LexisNexis, 2001.

Paruelo, J., J. Guerschmanand & S. Veron. 'Expansión agrícola y cambios en el uso del suelo'. *Revista Ciencia hoy en línea* 15, no. 87 (2005): 14-23.

PJNA. 'Poder Judicial de la Nación: República Argentina'. <www.pjn.gov.ar>, 14 September 2008.

PNA. 'Presidencia de la Nación Argentina'. <www.presidencia.gov.ar>, 14 September 2008.

Porto, A. 'Disparidades regionales y federalismo fiscal'. La Plata: Universidad Nacional de La Plata, 2004. <www.depeco.econo.unlp.edu.ar/federalismo/pdfs/libro_federalismo.pdf>, 14 September 2008.

Porto, A. 'Etapas de la coparticipación federal de impuestos'. La Plata: Universidad Nacional de La Plata, 2003. <www.depeco.econo.unlp.edu.ar/federalismo/pdfs/docfed2.pdf>, 28 August 2008.

Porto, A. 'Finanzas Públicas Subnacionales: La Experiencia Argentina'. La Plata: Universidad Nacional de La Plata, 2004. <www.depeco.econo.unlp.edu.ar/federalismo/pdfs/docfed12.pdf>, 28 August 2008.

Reboratti, C. 'Environmental conflicts and environmental justice in Argentina'. In *Environmental Justice en Latin America: Problems, promise and practice*, edited by D. Carrouthers. London: MIT Press, 2008.

Rodríguez, C. 'El papel del Juez Ambiental en la protección del ambiente'. *Revista de Derecho Ambiental* 9 (2007): 145-155.

Rodríguez, C. *Ley General del Ambiente de la Republica Argentina*. Buenos Aires: LexisNexis, 2007.

Sabsay, D. *Derecho ambiental. Una nueva etapa en la defensa de los bienes públicos ambientales*. Buenos Aires: Editorial La Ley, Suplemento de Derecho Ambiental, 2007.

Sabsay, D. *La Corte Suprema de Justicia de la Nación y la sustentabilidad de la Cuenca Matanza*-Riachuelo. Buenos Aires: Editorial La Ley, Suplemento de Derecho Ambiental, 2006.

Sagüés, N. *Elementos de Derecho Constitucional*. Buenos Aires: Editorial Astrea, 1999.

Sieder, R., L. Schjolden & A. Angell (eds). The Judicialization of Politics in Latin America. New York: Palgrave Macmillan, 2006.

Stone Sweet, A. *Governing with Judges: Constitutional Politics in Europe*. Oxford: Oxford University Press, 2000.

Tate, N. & T. Vallinder. *The Global Expansion of Judicial Power*. New York: New York University Press, 1995.

Unidad de Manejo del Sistema de Evaluación Forestal. 'Informe sobre deforestación en Argentina, 2007'. <www.ambiente.gov.ar/archivos/web/UMSEF/File/deforestacin_argentina_v2.pdf>, 14 September 2008.

Valls de Rossi, M. & R. Bril. *Prevención y compensación frente al daño ambiental: El seguro ambiental*. Buenos Aires, LexisNexis, 1998.

Valls de Rossi, M. 'El daño ambiental en la Corte Suprema Argentina. Recomposición. Obligación de contratar un seguro, 2004'. <www.prodiversitas.bioetica.org>, 9 June 2008.

TABLE OF LEGISLATION

TABLE OF CASES

TABLE OF TREATIES AND INTERNATIONAL INSTRUMENTS

Montreal Protocol on Substances that Deplete the Ozone Layer (1987) 26 *ILM* 1541
Rotterdam Convention on the Prior Informed Consent Procedure for Certain Hazardous Chemicals and Pesticides in International Trade (1999) 38 *ILM* 1
Stockholm Convention on Persistent Organic Pollutants (2001) 40 *ILM* 532
United Nations Framework Convention on Climate Change (1992) 31 *ILM* 849
Vienna Convention for the Protection of the Ozone Layer (1987) 26 *ILM* 1516
Vienna Convention on the Law of Treaties (No. 19865) 7 January 1967

ABBREVIATIONS

ACUMAR	*Autoridad de Cuenca Matanza Riachuelo* [Matanza-Riachuelo Basin Authority]
BAT	Best Available Technology
Bs As	Buenos Aires
CDI	Centre of Documentation and Information
CEJAS	*Centro de Estudios de Justicia de las Américas* [Center of Studies on Justice for the Americas]
CEPAL	*Comisión Económica para América Latina y el Caribe* [Economic Commission for Latin America and the Caribbean]
CODECI	*Consejo de Desarrollo de las Comunidades Indígenas* [Indigenous Communities Development Council]
CODEMA	*Consejo de Ecología y Medio Ambiente* [Ecology and Environment Council]
CoFeMa	*ConsejoFfederal de Medio Ambiente* [Environmental Federal Council]
CRC	Convention on the Rights of the Child
CSJN	Corte Suprema de Justicia de la Nación [National Supreme Court of Justice]
DPA	*Departamento Provincial de Aguas* [Provincial Water Department]
ECLAC	Economic Commission for Latin America and the Caribbean
EIA	Environmental Impact Assessment
ESDS	Environmental and Sustainable Development Secretary (*Secretaría de Ambiente y Desarrollo Sustentable*)
I/A Court HR	Inter American Court of Human Rights
ICA	*Instituto correntino del agua* [Corrientes water institute]
ICJ	International Court of Justice
INDEC	*Instituto Nacional de Estadísticas y Censos de la República Argentina* [National Statistics and Census Institute for the Republic of Argentina]
INTA	*Instituto Nacional de Tecnología Agropecuaria* [National Agricultural and Cattle Technology Institute]
MEA(s)	Multilateral Environmental Agreement(s)

NGO	Non-governmental Organization
PCB(s)	Polychlorinated biphenyl(s)
PNA	*Presidencia de la Nación Argentina* [Presidency of the Argentinean Nation]
SA	*Sociedad Anónima* [Anonimous Society]
SC	*Suprema Corte* [Supreme Court]
UNLP	*Universidad Nacional de La Plata*

Chapter 9

Paraguay

Sheila Abed*

1   INTRODUCTION

The Republic of Paraguay is experiencing its first fifteen years of continued democracy since its independence from Spain, in May 1811. The three branches that form the Republic's government are going through the uneasy but necessary trail towards a consolidated democratic culture. Although the ties with the past are still strong, there have been many changes in the institutional demographics of the country. The country has likewise seen its fair share of changes on the environmental governance front.

    The emergence of environmental law in Paraguay coincided with the enactment and promulgation of the Constitution of 1992. Prior to 1992, environmental norms were part of laws that had as their objectives the regulation of natural resources and protection of public health. Unfortunately, these legal provisions were less than effective, particularly because of their limited or nonexistent enforcement.

    Since 1992, intensive legislative developments on environmental matters have occurred, although they remain incomplete, dispersed and rather disorganized. At the same time, serious enforcement initiatives concerning environmental

*   The author greatly acknowledges the contribution of Ezequiel Santagada (IDEA's Legal Department coordinator and Professor of Law, Universidad Católica Ntra. Sra. de la Asunción), to this chapter.

Louis J. Kotzé and Alexander R. Paterson (eds), *The Role of the Judiciary in Environmental Governance: Comparative Perspectives*, pp. 295–319.
© 2009 Kluwer Law International BV, The Netherlands.

legal norms have only begun four to five years ago. Within the sphere of the judicial branch of government, the Attorney General's Office – through its Specialized Unit on Environmental Crimes – has been the main governmental body responsible for this positive change. Thus, one of the most visible character-istics of environmental governance in Paraguay is the preponderance of criminal environmental law, and the judiciary has played and continues to play a key role in this respect.

Against the above general background, this chapter critically reflects on the strengths and weaknesses of Paraguayan environmental governance, and par-ticularly analyses the important role the Paraguayan judiciary plays in devel-oping environmental governance. The chapter concludes that the current extensive role played by environmental criminal law needs to be matched with increased activism, by both citizens and judges, in the field of administra-tive and civil law.

2   ENVIRONMENTAL ISSUES

2.1   LOCATION AND SIZE

Paraguay is located at the centre of the southern half of South America, northeast of Argentina. It is also bordered by Bolivia to the northwest and Brazil to the east. With an area of 406,750 square kilometres (157,046 square miles), Paraguay almost equals the State of California in size. Asunción, the nation's capital, is situated at the easternmost point of the Argentinean border, just south of the centre of Paraguay.[1] The nation is landlocked, which sets it apart from virtually all of Latin America. Its geographical location could be considered a detriment to the nation's economy. Major cities that provide river ports, such as Asunción, Villeta, and Encarnación (the latter lying to the south of Asunción), help alleviate the economic side effects of the nation's lack of access to ocean ports. Ciudad del Este, a commercial centre on the Paraná River, is the second largest city of the country.

In environmental terms, the country's landlocked situation and its relative poverty makes it very difficult to submit diplomatic claims to the neighbouring countries over transboundary pollution originating in those territories. It often happens that before a claim, these countries, particularly Brazil and Argentina, retaliate with economic measures.[2]

---

1. Paraguay's border to Argentina to the southwest measures 1,880 km (1,168 miles), its Bolivian border is 750 km (466 miles), and the Brazilian border is 1,290 km (802 miles).
2. This happened, for instance, in 2006, in a Paraguayan claim to Argentina for the irregular operation of three paper mills, located in Argentinean territory, which polluted the shared zone of the Parana River. Immediately after formulating the claim, Paraguayan trucks carrying meat to the Chilean market – which necessarily must cross Argentinean territory – were delayed for several days at the Paraguayan-Argentinean border.

2.2   POPULATION

Recent estimates place the population of Paraguay at six million people. Due to its Spanish colonization and heritage, at least 90% of the population is Roman Catholic and 95% of the population is *mestizos* (a racial mix of Spanish and Amerindian people). This renders the population surprisingly homogenous in comparison to most of Latin America. The *mestizo* population has strong pride in their *Guaraní* heritage and traditions (the primary indigenous group and culture of Paraguay). Spanish was the only official language until 1992 when *Guaraní* also became an official language. *Guaraní* is spoken by approximately 90% of the population. Spanish is used predominantly in business and government matters, but both languages are utilized in education. At least half of the population is bilingual.

People between the ages of 0 and fourteen years constitute 39% of the population, while those between the ages of fifteen and sixty-four constitute 56%. At least half of the latter age group is below thirty years of age, rendering two-thirds of the population younger than thirty. The population of Paraguay grew from 2,4 million to 4,3 million between 1970 and 1990 (80%), and grew 30% from 1990 to 2000. With an annual population growth rate of 2.6% as of 2001, the population is estimated to reach 6,98 million by 2010. The average life expectancy of the population is 73.92 years.

Migration to the urban areas of Paraguay is common, but more than half of the nation's population still lives in rural areas, mostly in the east. Only about 5% of the population lives to the west of the Paraguay River. High rates of emigration from 1950 to 2000 have contributed to a large percentage (40%) of Paraguayans living outside their country which aids in alleviating the high population growth rate. Many Paraguayans have historically immigrated to Argentina, particularly during and after the Chaco War of 1936 and the Civil War of 1947, and also during the 1950s and 1970s. Paraguay has one of the world's lowest population densities. The nation's most densely populated area is Asunción and its surroundings, where also the largest number of Paraguay's few industries are situated. This population-industry concentration, together with a lack of infrastructure and planning, has made the country's capital and surrounding areas one of the most polluted in Paraguay.

2.3   ECONOMY

Agriculture and cattle-raising are the two most important economic activities. Recent studies show that these sectors are responsible for approximately 90% of all exports trade.[3] These sectors also constitute almost 26% of the Gross Domestic Product (GDP).[4]

---

3. A. Nervi & R. Dietze, *Negociaciones Internacionales en Agricultura* (Asunción: Ministerio de Industria y Comercio & Ministerio de Relaciones Exteriores BID, 2002).
4. Banco Central del Paraguay, Gerencia de Estudios Económicos, *Cuentas Nacionales 1991-2001* (Asunción: Departamento de Cuentas Nacionales y Mercado Interno, 2002).

Paraguay lacks significant mineral and petroleum resources, but possesses vast hydroelectric resources, including the world's largest hydroelectric generation facility, the Itaipú Dam, built and operated jointly with Brazil. Remittances from Paraguayans living abroad have significantly contributed to sustained economic growth. According to the Inter-American Development Bank, remittances totalled some USD 650 million in 2006.

Paraguay's industrial sector is still largely underdeveloped, with much of the population still employed in subsistence agriculture. Economic growth tends to be limited by Paraguay's reliance on imports of manufactured goods. Capital goods are further necessary to supply the investment and industrial imperatives necessary to develop the industrial sector of the economy. This has led to a widening of the country's trade deficit, estimated at USD 1.1 billion in 2006.

2.4   Main Environmental Issues

For many years, the Upper Paraná Atlantic Forest in Paraguay had one of the highest rates of deforestation in Latin America. The forests continue to be trans-formed into agricultural land without adequate planning. Ranching and agriculture have already invaded extremely fragile forestland, which, due to the property of the soil, is only suitable for forest re-growth. Although significantly degraded and fragmented, these forests remain important for conservation purposes, particularly in the context of efforts to restore green corridors.

According to a recent analysis by the Global Land Cover Facility of the University of Maryland, the National Aeronautics and Space Administration (NASA), and the organization Guyrá Paraguay, 35% of the Atlantic Forest was lost in Paraguay between 1989 and 2003.[5] Although the government has controlled deforestation to a certain extent, more efforts are required to ensure responsible soy cultivation and sustainable forest management. A stronger commitment is also needed to restore priority forest areas. Moreover, while there are a number of protected areas in the Atlantic Forest, the majority exist merely as reserves in theory. In practice, there are not sufficient financial resources to facilitate adequate protection of these forests. Large-scale agriculture, as well as the severe deforestation problem, has also led to soil and water contamination because of the use of forbidden agrochemicals, or improper use of allowed substances.

With regard to the environmental problems caused by hydroelectric dams, a distinction must be made between Itaipu and Yacyreta (the Paraguayan dam shared with Argentina). The main environmental challenge posed by Itaipu is the loss of soil that occurs as a consequence of the lack of implementation of adequate protection measures around the reservoir of the dam. The main environmental problem caused by Yacyreta, is the periodic flooding of large areas of the city of Encarnacion when the reservoir level is increased, especially in those times

---

5. Guyra Paraguay, 'Conservando la Biodiversidad' [Conserving Biodiversity], <www.guyra. org.py>, 14 September 2008.

when Argentina requires more energy. This happens mainly because the mitigation works have not yet been finalized.

3   PRINCIPAL ENVIRONMENTAL LAWS

3.1   CONSTITUTIONAL PROVISIONS

Various provisions directly or indirectly relating to the environment can be found in the Constitution. For example, every person has a right to live in a healthy and ecologically equilibrated environment;[6] activities that may result in environmental alterations will be regulated by law; and law will define and establish sanctions for environmental crimes. Any damage to the environment will entail the obligation to restore and pay for damages.[7] Every person has the right, either individually or collectively, to demand from public officials to adopt measures to defend the environment, the integrity of their natural habitat, public health, national cultural heritage, consumers' interests and any other areas that, because of their juridical essence, pertain to the community and are related to the quality of life and to property belonging to the community.[8] The Constitution also provides that anyone who considers him or herself seriously affected by a clearly illegitimate act or omission, either by governmental authorities or individuals, or anyone whose rights may be in imminent danger, and who in light of the urgency of the matter cannot seek a remedy through regular legal channels, may file a petition for *amparo*[9] before a competent judge. Proceedings will be brief, summarized, and free of charge, and will entail an *actio popularis* in some instances as determined by the relevant law.[10]

    The Constitution establishes that treaties, conventions and international agreements approved and ratified by congress, laws dictated by congress, and other related legal provisions of lesser rank, constitute the national legal system, in descending order of pre-eminence.[11] Paraguay has approved and ratified most of the United Nations environmental agreements and international conventions, including, inter alia: the Convention on International Trade in Endangered Species;[12] the UNESCO World Heritage Convention;[13] the Framework Convention on Climate Change[14] and its Kyoto Protocol;[15] the Convention on Biological

---

6. Art. 7, Constitution.
7. Art. 8, Constitution.
8. Art. 38, Constitution.
9. This remedy's parallel in the common law system would be a 'writ of injunction' and the *mandamus* combined.
10. Art. 134, Constitution.
11. Arts 137 and 141, Constitution.
12. CITES, ratified by the Paraguayan Congress as Law 583/76.
13. Signed in Paris in 1972 and adopted as national law by Law 1231/96.
14. Signed in 1992 in Rio de Janeiro, subscribed by Paraguay at the same year and adopted as national law by Law 251/93.
15. Signed in Kyoto on December 11, 1997, subscribed by Paraguay in 1998 and adopted as national law by Law 1447/99.

Diversity[16] and its Cartagena Protocol;[17] the Vienna Convention for the Protection of the Ozone Layer[18] and its Montreal Protocol;[19] the Ramsar Convention on Wetlands;[20] the Convention to Combat Desertification;[21] the Basel Convention on the Control of Transboundary Movements of Hazardous Wastes and their Disposal;[22] the Stockholm Convention on Persistent Organic Pollutants;[23] and the Rotterdam Convention on the Prior Informed Consent (PIC) Procedure for Certain Hazardous Chemicals and Pesticides in International Trade.[24]

The Constitution also establishes that Paraguay, on an equal footing with other States, accepts the possibility of entering into a supranational legal system that guarantees the enforcement of human rights, peace, justice, and cooperation, as well as political, socio-economic, and cultural development.[25]

3.2   REGIONAL COOPERATION AND INSTRUMENTS

Along with Argentina, Brazil and Uruguay, Paraguay is a founding member of the Common Market of the South, or MERCOSUR, as it is commonly referred to. To date, MERCOSUR has not been able to advance beyond an incomplete customs union. The possibility of establishing a common market is still far away. Members, however, maintain the political will to remain united to this supranational structure. In the environmental field, members had only been able to negotiate and approve the Framework Agreement on the Environment[26] (which contains mere soft law provisions), and the Environmental Emergencies Protocol signed in July 2004 and which has not yet entered into force. The current dispute resolution mechanism is regulated in the Olivos' Protocol,[27] which has led to the creation of the Permanent Court of Review (TPR), according to its Spanish acronym) in the City of Asunción. This is an appeals court that revises the *ad hoc* arbitration awards that solve disputes among the Member States. It is also entitled to provide consultative opinions. In 2006, it solved two cases between Argentina and Uruguay regarding environmental issues related to the free circulation of goods and services. However, this starting point is not sufficient for the TPR to have a significant influence on Paraguayan environmental law.

---

16. Signed in 1992 in Rio de Janeiro, subscribed by Paraguay in the same year and adopted as national law by Law 253/93.
17. Adopted in 2000 in Montreal, Canada, subscribed by Paraguay in 2001 and adopted as national law by Law 2309/03.
18. Signed in Vienna on March 22, 1985 and adopted as national law in 1992, by Law 61/92.
19. Signed in Montreal on September 16, 1987 and adopted as national law in 1992, by Law 61/92.
20. Signed in Ramsar in 1971 and adopted as national law by Law 350/94.
21. Signed in Paris in 1996 and adopted as national law by Law 970/96.
22. Signed in Basel on March 22, 1989, and adopted as national law in 1995, by Law 567/95.
23. Signed in Stockholm on May 22, 2001 and adopted as national law in 2004 by Law 2333/04.
24. Signed on September 11, 1998 and adopted as national law in 2003 by Law 2135/03.
25. Art. 145, Constitution.
26. Signed in Asunción on June 22, 2001 and adopted as national law by Law 2068/03.
27. Signed in Buenos Aires on February 18, 2002 and adopted as national law by Law 2070/03.

Paraguay has also signed the American Convention on Human Rights[28] (also known as the Pact of San José) and ratified its San Salvador Protocol[29] dealing with economic, social and cultural rights. The Pact of San José, according to Article 33, has two competent bodies with respect to matters relating to the fulfilment of the commitments made by Member States: the Inter-American Commission on Human Rights and the Inter-American Court of Human Rights. The latter provides binding decisions on cases submitted to the court. According to the renowned *opinio juris* and some court decisions in Argentina and Paraguay,[30] its precedents are also mandatory for all countries that are part of the Inter-American system of human rights protection.

The Inter-American Court of Human Rights has not yet adjudicated a case in which environmental issues have been at stake.[31] However, its fruitful precedents regarding the protection of the rights to life and health have already been invoked in the Paraguayan courts in order to reach a jurisdictional declaration recognising the right to live in a healthy and ecologically equilibrated environment as a human right.[32] Although this is a positive development,[33] there remains room for improvement around this declaration. Environmental litigation, before it reaches the Inter-American Court of Human Rights, has various possibilities to enhance environmental governance, not only in Paraguay, but also in other countries belonging to the Inter-American system.

3.3   ENVIRONMENTAL IMPACT ASSESSMENT

The *Environmental Impact Assessment Act* 294 of 1993 (EIAA) is Paraguay's most important environmental legal norm. Its scope embraces the majority of economic activities, both public and private. It also includes activities that had been developed prior to when this law entered into force, as well as all future projects or

---

28. Signed in San José on 22 November 1969 and adopted as national law in 1989 by Law 1/89.
29. Signed in San Salvador on 17 November 1988, and adopted as national law in 1997 by Law 1040/97.
30. Argentina: CSJ de la Nación, 24 August 2004, Fallos: 327:3294. Paraguay: Agreement and Sentence No. 306, 25 May 2005, CSJ and Final Judgment No. 40, 21 July 2007, Juzgado de Liquidación y Sentencia 1, Asunción.
31. In September 2007, the Inter-American Court of Human Rights requested provisional measures in the *La Oroya* (Perú) case. This decision was still pending at the time of writing.
32. In the cases *Mayagna Awas Tigni v. the Republic of Nicaragua and Yakye Axa* and *Sawhoya-maxa v. the Republic of Paraguay*, (and particularly the latter case), the Inter-American Court of Human Rights arguably has already begun to establish ties which, regarding the problem of indigenous communities and State violations against their right to community property which affects their traditional lands, would inevitably open the path to an Inter-American instance for the protection of environmental rights.
33. Agreement and Sentence No. 78, 18 August 2003, Tribunal de Apelaciones de la Niñez y la Adolescencia de Asunción. See S. Abed (ed.), *Régimen Jurídico Ambiental de la República del Paraguay. Análisis crítico. Normas legales y reglamentarias actualizadas y concordadas* (Asunción: IDEA, 2007).

activities that may cause environmental impacts of any kind.[34] This wide scope of application allows officials to apply enforcement in areas that lack regulation, such as transportation and disposal of hazardous wastes.

The Environmental Impact Declaration (EID or Environmental License) is the administrative act that ends the environmental impact assessment (EIA) procedure. The EID is an unavoidable legal requirement necessary to obtain access to bank credit, to be granted with tax exemptions and to obtain other public authorizations, including those required under the framework of other environmental laws, such as the *Wildlife Act* 96 of 1992, or the recent *Water Resources Act* 3239 of 2007.

3.4   AGRICULTURE

The importance of the EIAA is amplified by Law 1863/01 or 'Agrarian Statute', as it is widely known. This law specifically regulates the acquisition and maintenance of rural land. The Constitution establishes the fundamentals for agrarian reform and rural development in Articles 115 and 116. These include rationalization and regularization of land use and cultivation practices in order to avoid its degradation, as well as the defence and preservation of the environment.

The Agrarian Statute develops these constitutional provisions by establishing that rural property achieves its social and economic functions (also required by the Constitution in Article 109) when it is adjusted to parameters of environmental sustainability. The latter is only considered achieved when there is compliance with the procedures of the EIAA. Consequently, when a rural landowner does not comply with the EIAA, his or her property may be considered a non-productive estate because it does not comply with the social and economic function required by the Constitution. The consequences of this situation are as follows:

The Constitution establishes two types of expropriation: a) one that guarantees that expropriation will occur in every instance following a specific law, and that the government will not take the property before paying a fair compensation[35] (a provision applicable, in principle, to all private property, which is considered inviolable); and b) another that is applicable to non-productive estates, whose owners do not possess the rights included in Article 109 (in this instance the State first takes possession of the estate and then (it can take many years) pays a price, that is not necessarily a fair compensation).[36]

---

34. Art. 1 defines 'environmental impact' as: 'all environmental modifications which are provoked by human activities or constructions which have positive or negative, direct or indirect consequences which affect life in general, biodiversity, the quality or a significant quantity of natural or environmental resources and their use, the well-being, health and personal security, customs and habits, cultural heritage or legitimate ways of life'.
35. Art. 109, Constitution.
36. Art. 116, Constitution.

3.5   GENERAL PROVISIONS

Along with the obligation to comply with the environmental management plan that accompanies every environmental license, individuals must also comply with the following provisions: refrain from dumping harmful substances into streams or rivers in quantities which exceed the maximum concentration of harmful substances allowed by the competent administrative authority;[37] refrain from discarding or depositing garbage or waste in unauthorized places;[38] refrain from using unauthorized agrochemicals or from violating the maximum quantities or concentrations allowed by the competent administrative authority;[39] refrain from emitting gases in quantities which exceed the maximum concentration of noxious substances allowed by the competent administrative authority;[40] refrain from producing noise which exceeds the maximum levels allowed by the competent administrative authority;[41] refrain from conducting any deforestation activities without the prior authorization of the competent administrative authority;[42] preserve or conduct reforestation in forests necessary for the protection of soils and streams and rivers; refrain from hunting or fishing without prior authorization of the competent administrative authority;[43] and maintain a reserve of 25% of the natural forests existent in rural estates in 1974.[44]

The *Protected Areas Act* 352 of 1992 deals with public protected areas and private protected areas on properties where owners benefit from tax exemptions, and provides for a rapid eviction procedure and further guarantee that the land will not be expropriated during its declaration as a protected area.

The *Valuation and Payment of Environmental Services Act* 3001 of 2006 seeks to provide incentives for environmental protection and restoration by means of a market mechanism that compensate those who conserve ecosystems for the public benefit.

4   INSTITUTIONS AND GOVERNANCE STRUCTURES

4.1   INSTITUTIONAL FRAMEWORK ESTABLISHED BY THE CONSTITUTION

According to the Constitution, the Paraguayan State is a centralized, democratic and representative republic whose government is exercised by three independent branches: the executive, legislative and judicial branches. Every branch is

---

37. Sanitary Code 836 of 1981 and the *Water Resources Act* 3239 of 2007.
38. Sanitary Code, *supra* n. 37.
39. Law 123/91 and Law 2459/04.
40. Sanitary Code, *supra* n. 37.
41. *Noise Pollution Act* 1100 of 1997 and Art. 2000 of the Civil Code 1183 of 1985.
42. *Forestry Act* 422 of 1973 and Law 536/95.
43. *Wildlife Act* 96 of 1992 and the *Fishing Act* 799 of 1995.
44. *Forestry Act* 422 of 1973.

independent from the other and it is not permitted to encroach on the domain of or exercise the powers of another branch as per the *trias politica* doctrine. The president is elected in general elections for a five-year term of office, and there are no possibilities for re-election.

The National Congress consists of two chambers: the House of Representatives (*Diputados*) and the Senate. Legislators are elected in the same general elections during which the president is elected. There are no mid-term elections and all legislators can be re-elected.

The Supreme Court is composed of nine members. The power to nominate candidates is vested in the Council for Magistrates and appointments are made by the Senate with the consent of the president. Candidates for the first instance division and appellate courts are also nominated by the Council for Magistrates from a list of three candidates and in this instance, appointments are made by the Supreme Court. Every judge, both from the Supreme and inferior courts, is appointed for a five year period and, if he or she is confirmed two consecutives times after the first appointment, will hold office while maintaining good behaviour, or until the age of 75.

The Attorney General's Office represents society before the State's jurisdictional organizations. It is an autonomous entity that is part of the judicial branch. It composes of the Attorney General and State attorneys as determined by law. The Attorney General holds office for five years and he or she may be re-elected. He or she is appointed by the executive branch with the concurrence of the Senate from a list of three candidates proposed by the Council of Magistrates.

State attorneys are appointed following the procedures established for the appointment of judges in the Constitution, described above. Their term in office, as well as procedures for their removal, are similar to those applicable to judges.

Apart from the Central Bank, the Constitution establishes two other autonomous public organizations, namely the Ombudsman and the Office of the Comptroller General of the Republic. The Ombudsman is a congressional commissioner charged with defending human rights, channelling popular complaints, and protecting community interests. Despite the fact that all these rights are related to the protection of the environment, there has unfortunately not been a specific exercise of the rights in the area of environmental protection as far as the Ombudsman is concerned. The Office of the Comptroller General of the Republic is charged with supervising State, departmental, and municipal economic and financial activities in the manner established by the Constitution and the law.

Constitutions preceding the Constitution of 1992 also ruled the unitarian form of government, although the centralism espoused by these was much more notorious than currently is the case. Together with the statement that Paraguay is a unitarian State in terms of the 1992 Constitution, the latter also proclaims in Article 1 that 'it is decentralized according to this Constitution and the law'. Decentralization of governmental functions has been channelled through traditional institutions responsible for the country's political and administrative organization, namely, departmental[45] and municipal governments. The 1992 Constitution has rearranged their functions and attributes, affording them their own economic resources and establishing elections to access governmental positions.

Paraguay's territory is divided into seventeen departments, 242 municipalities and the City of Asunción. Although local governments are autonomous, this autonomy is rather limited. Departmental governments are responsible for the coordination of activities with the different municipalities within the department, the formulation of a departmental development plan (which must be coordinated with the national development plan), and the coordination of activities with central government, particularly in areas such as health and education.

Subject to the Constitution and the law, municipal governments have the powers to regulate urbanism, transportation, environmental issues, cultural issues, marketplaces, social and sanitary assistance, sports, and tourism. They are also entitled to create their own inspection and police departments.

4.2   ENVIRONMENTAL GOVERNANCE INSTITUTIONS

In accordance with the *National Environmental System, the National Environmental Council and the Ministry of the Environment Act* 1561 of 2000, the National Environmental Council (or CONAM) is responsible for defining, supervising and evaluating national environmental policies. This council comprises of representatives from central governmental institutions, local governments, production associations, academia, and environmental non-governmental organizations (NGOs).

The Paraguayan National Environmental Policy was approved in 2005 by the National Environmental Council. The Ministry of Environment is responsible for applying legal environmental norms and accompanying regulations in accordance with the National Environmental Policy. It is important to note that this policy is not above any law sanctioned by congress and promulgated by the executive branch. It is simply an interpretational guide to enable authorities in charge of enforcing environmental norms to exercise their power, as well as to ensure that these authorities' rights and obligations are in fact fulfilled. In a sense, the Paraguayan National Environmental Policy is therefore meta-juridical.

The Ministry of Environment is the administrative authority responsible for the enforcement of environmental law, as well as for the coordination of the enforcement of environmental norms found within other laws with their respective enforcement authorities, particularly the Ministry of Public Health, the Ministry of Agriculture and Cattle Raising, and the Ministry of Industry and Trade.

The Ministry of Environment is entitled to promote the decentralization of his or her attributions and functions among local governments. Although this decentralization sounds positive, in practice, it has only recently been done to some

---

45. 'Department' is not to be confused with the normal use of the word, which usually denotes an organ of State in a government regime. Departments in Paraguay rather are similar to provinces or States in a traditional federation.

extent and then only in some departmental governments. In contrast, municipal governments are already in charge of their territorial co-ordination, recollecting, and disposing of household waste and controlling unacceptable noise levels including emission of car fumes.

Regarding the legislative branch, Law 40/90 created the National Commission for the Defence of Natural Resources (CONADERNA), whose function it is to coordinate the actions of organizations that are carrying out activities to defend ecosystems. This commission comprises of representatives from both chambers of congress, institutions from the executive branch, the manufacturing and commerce sectors, academia and environmental NGOs. Although its role overlaps with that of CONAM, CONADERNA has served as a forum for discussion and consensus on some environment-related legislative proposals.

With regard to the judicial branch, the Attorney General's Office relies on a Specialized Unit on Environmental Crimes. District attorneys who are members of this unit work exclusively on investigating and conducting criminal prosecution against those who commit environmental crimes. This is further elaborated below.

5   OVERVIEW OF THE COURT SYSTEM

All environmental issues related to proceedings carried out to obtain permits or licenses fall within the sphere of administrative law. There is no legal norm in Paraguay that regulates these proceedings before organizations within the executive or local governments. In practice, these proceedings are included in the regulatory norms promulgated by the president, or the ministers responsible for law enforcement. Once administrative remedies have been exhausted, interested parties have the contentious administrative action at their disposal, which essentially is an 'action against the administration' or a jurisdictional claim or appeal to reconsider the decision made by administrative officials within the Court of Accounts (also known as the Court of Auditors). The latter institution is a jurisdictional organ of the judicial branch in charge of resolving administrative law disputes while controlling the legality of actions in a broad sense. The Criminal Division of the Supreme Court of Justice can revise, through appeal procedures, all decisions made by the Court of Accounts.

Besides permits, the majority of environmental legal norms include administrative sanctions directed at violators and applied by authorities involved in the enforcement of these laws. Interested parties also have the contentious administrative action available to them against these resolutions.

There are no precedents for environmental cases brought in terms of civil proceedings in order to repair environmental damage or to pay for it. The few cases to prevent or to stop environmental damage have been filed by means of *amparo*. Any first instance or district judge, according to territorial criteria, has jurisdiction to resolve these cases. Assignments are carried out randomly in Asunción by district or first instance judges. The pronouncements of these judges can be appealed to the Court of Appeals corresponding to the District Court.

Many of the *amparo* cases have been filed as an *actio popularis*. The courts have accepted this broad standing based on Article 38 of the Constitution, and, since *actio popularis* is not regulated by the law, also in terms of Article 45 *in fine* of the Constitution, which states that the lack (or absence) of regulatory laws cannot be invoked to deny any right established in the Constitution.

Since practically all unlawful environmental conduct is included in criminal law provisions, most cases regarding environmental damage fall within the sphere of criminal law. This is the reason why there are no precedents filed before the courts in relation to civil issues that seek to repair environmental damage. The Criminal Code 1160 of 1997 establishes that repair, in addition to sanctions, can be demanded from criminal courts. It is possible to appeal to the Criminal Court of Appeals and, eventually, through an extraordinary remedy (the cassation), to the Criminal Division of the Supreme Court of Justice. It is also possible to file a claim for unconstitutionality before the Constitutional Division of the Supreme Court of Justice. Only this division of the Supreme Court is capable of declaring the unconstitutionality of a sentence or a legal norm or regulation. The majority of the most significant environmental precedents[46] is derived from decisions taken within the framework of these unconstitutionality actions.

6   PROCEDURES GIVING RISE TO FREQUENT LITIGATION

The most important administrative procedures in Paraguay relating to environmental matters, are those relating to EIA. The administrative authority in charge of EIA is the Ministry of Environment. The EIA procedure is regulated by *Decree* 14.281 of 31 July 1996.[47] The proponent of the project to be evaluated takes part in the procedure. According to the regulative decree, any interested party that becomes aware of the development and procedure, after the public information process has taken place, may also become involved. This is a rather strict interpretation of the relevant law because, according to Article 38 of the Constitution, any person has the right to take part in this procedure, whether he or she has an interest or not. Such a person should be able to act in defence of the environment and of the habitat's integrity and public health; all of which are matters that concern the entire community.

Before commencing the EIA procedure within the Ministry of Environment, the project's proponent should obtain a non-objection certificate from the departmental government in whose territory the project is proposed to take place. For this certificate to be issued, the departmental authorities also evaluate whether the project falls within the department's development plan. A municipal certificate

---

46. Although non-binding in Paraguay, precedent helps pave the way for determining future cases involving similar facts or issues and they accordingly constitute one of the most important sources of law.
47. For an extensive overview of the EIA procedure, see Abed, *supra* n. 33.

must also be obtained. To this end, the authorities assess whether the proposed location for the project is in line with territorial planning requirements. During a claim for unconstitutionality, in which it was argued that departmental officers had no environmental authority (either constitutional or legal), because this would militate against municipal autonomy, the Supreme Court ruled that departmental authorities, together with municipal authorities, are in charge of the control tasks prior to the EIA. This is so because of the importance of the environment for the community and in order to avoid possible negative consequences to the ecosystem and to health in the event that precautionary measures are not taken.[48]

In another case, in which Asuncion's Municipality claimed the EIA law to be unconstitutional by arguing that it violated municipal autonomy on environmental matters, the Supreme Court ruled that the law is enforceable at the national level, that it does not undermine municipal autonomy because environmental matters are not circumscribed to the limits of the municipal territory, and that the EIA law has also reasonably been regulated in terms of Articles 7, 8 and 38 of the Constitution. The court, in other words, found that environmental authority or jurisdiction should be shared between national, departmental and municipal governments according to the law, and that Congress can exercise its discretion in environmental matters to determine to what extent each government has a portion of that jurisdiction. Regarding Article 38, although *obiter*, the court averred that the EIA procedure is one of the procedures in which every person has the right to request measures in defence of the environment.[49]

A contentious administrative action can be filed against the decision of the Ministry of Environment, when the minister issues, denies or cancels an environmental license. According to information provided by the Ministry of Environment, only about ten cases of denial have been appealed under this course of action,[50] and in those cases where a final decision had been taken, the petitioner's pretensions were overruled.

Some cases have reached the Court of Accounts in which fines related to non-compliance with the EIA law were questioned. It is noteworthy that the EIAA does not contemplate fines among its penalties. This penalty has been established by a ministerial resolution.[51] This possibly is a flagrant case of unconstitutionality, as it contradicts the legality principle provided by the Constitution.[52] Nevertheless,

---

48. Agreement and Sentence No. 333, 12 July 2000, CSJ. Unpublished.
49. Agreement and Sentence No. 28, 20 May 1995, CSJ, Revista Jurídica La Ley Paraguaya – LLP, 1995, 256.
50. Internal information provided by the Director of the Juridical Affairs' Direction of the Office of the Ministry of the Environment, Alba Villalba de Llanes.
51. Resolution 363/04.
52. Art. 9, para. 2 reads: 'No one may be forced to do anything that is not mandated by law, and no one may be prevented from doing something that is not prohibited by law' and Art. 17: 'In a criminal process or in any other process which could result in punishment or sanction, everyone has the right: (. . .) To be sentenced only at the end of a trial based on a law that was already in force when the unlawful fact was committed, and not to be tried by special tribunals.'

the Court of Accounts has declared the validity of this kind of penalty.[53] Although the author does not agree with this position, the Court of Accounts was not competent to declare the unconstitutionality of the penalty (only the constitutional division of the Supreme Court is entitled to take such a decision), and the interested parties did not argue this point. The procedure for the enforcement of penalties is determined by the Ministry of Environment's Resolution 1881 of 8 November 2005. Since the promulgation of this resolution, more than 4,500 files have been opened for infractions under environmental legislation.[54] Before this resolution, the Ministry of Environment had only commenced investigations, but had never imposed penalties, as it lacked a procedure that would guarantee the right of defence. In order to avoid constitutional challenges, the Ministry of Environment in practice imposes low penalties. In addition, it negotiates with the offender to promote compliance with the environmental legislation, under warning of cancellation of the relevant environmental license and with subsequent notice to the municipal authority to close the facility. Nevertheless, there is already a draft modification of the EIA law, which contemplates fines among the penalties, and grants the Ministry of Environment the power to close non-compliant facilities.

Finally, the Court of Accounts did get the opportunity to pass sentence in a case in which a company challenged the competence of a municipality to enforce penalties under its own environmental regulations. The court ruled that municipalities, exercising the authority vested upon them by the central government, have the competence to dictate regulations and enforce penalties.[55]

7 CRIMINAL PROSECUTION

As mentioned above, practically all forms of unlawful environmental conduct are included, in principle, in criminal law provisions. Environmental criminal law provisions are included in *Sanctioning of Crimes against the Environment Act* 716 of 1996 and in the Criminal Code 1160 of 1997.[56] Act 716 of 96 is a special criminal norm (written at the time to fulfil the mandate in Article 8 in the Constitution), that sanctions some insignificant criminal conduct, such as burning of waste in public spaces, which would actually be more suitable for administrative law provisions. The Criminal Code, on the other hand, prioritizes punishment of more serious types of behaviour, such as pollution of water, air, or soil, or damage to protected areas.

---

53. Agreement and Sentence No. 10, 8 March 2006, Tribunal de Cuentas, Primera Sala, LLP 2006, 486.
54. See *supra* n. 50.
55. Agreement and Sentence No. 158, 27 September 2000, Tribunal de Cuentas, Primera Sala, LLP 2001, 351.
56. Arts 197 to 202.

The main characteristic of the Paraguayan environmental criminal framework is the abundance of incomplete criminal law provisions, which can only be completed or complimented by resorting to other laws and regulations, particularly administrative regulations. Without considering traditional criticism against this sort of criminal provisions, there are two further issues that need to be highlighted, namely, lack of certain administrative regulations which complete the environmental criminal provisions (such as those which are related to noxious gases), and lack of publication of these norms. In Paraguay, general administrative regulations are rarely published and some of these unpublished norms are used to complete criminal provisions.[57]

All environmental crimes in Paraguay are subject to public criminal action, which is carried out exclusively by the Attorney General's Office and District Attorneys. The Criminal Procedure Code grants victims the possibility to conduct an 'adhesive accusation', meaning that they have standing to participate in the investigative and prosecutorial stages, during the trail and, in some cases, for appealing the sentence on procedures initiated by the Attorney General's Office. Plaintiffs seldom participate in environmental cases and as far as could be established, there has been only one such a case in which an NGO attempted to intervene as a plaintiff. The Court of Appeals rejected this intervention arguing that, as regards environmental cases, NGO interests mix with the interests of the entire society which, within the criminal framework, can only be represented by the Attorney General's Office in accordance with Article 28 of the Criminal Procedures Code 1286 of 1998.[58]

Most criminal environmental cases that are not dismissed during the investigative or prosecutorial stages, do not reach the trial stage.[59] Instead of a conviction that does not imply to serve time in prison (up to two years), or the dismissal of the criminal prosecution because of the insignificance of the action, or because it fails to gain public interest, an agreement is instead concluded between the Attorney General's Office and the defendants in which they promise to accomplish certain measures, including, but not limited to, repairing the damage caused. This is the reason why there are no precedents of civil actions for repairing environmental damage. Interested parties may file their denouncements against environmental damages at the Attorney General's Office. Should they have a particular interest in the case, defendants' recognition before a criminal judge of having caused the damage to the environment *per se* (in order not to serve time in prison), will facilitate the proof of the individual damages caused *par ricochet*, within the

---

57. E.g., with regard to water contamination, SEAM Resolution 222/02 is used. The Resolution has never been published in the Official Gazette.

58. Interlocutory Order No. 111, 8 October 2003, Tribunal de Apelaciones en lo Civil, Comercial, Laboral, Criminal, Tutelar y Correccional del Menor de San Juan Bautista, Misiones, LLP, 2004, 127.

59. According to the information provided by the Specialized Unit on Environmental Crimes Coordinator, Ricardo Merlo Faella, in Asunción, there is an average of one or two oral trials regarding environmental matters annually. In order to place this number in context, in 2007 alone, 500 files were opened.

framework of civil actions seeking compensation. These civil actions may be carried out before both criminal and civil courts.

It is the author's belief that the proliferation of criminal environmental cases within the framework of the current criminal procedure framework, minimizes the possibility of allocating more resources towards investigating and prosecuting serious environmental damages which are rather frequent in Paraguay. In addition, it hampers the development of civil environmental law that could allow improvement of the methodology utilized to measure environmental damages by allowing specialized NGOs to participate in the process. Environmental district attorneys furthermore lack appropriate skills to deal with civil matters and do not have the time or the means necessary to reasonably measure environmental damages. In practice, compensation for environmental damage is merely symbolic in relation to the damage caused.

Another problem caused by criminalising environmental conduct is the inability to file *amparo* actions to request a cessation of environmental damage. When dealing with these petitions, judges dismissed them, arguing that the criminal process is the regular or appropriate legal channel to obtain a remedy against environmental damage.[60] The problem lies in the fact that due to their legal background (that prioritizes criminal law), the judiciary is more interested in the sanction than repairing damage or stopping damage-causing conduct. Moreover, there are not sufficient lawyers or judges trained to effectively deal with environmental cases. In practice, this renders *amparo* actions the only effective remedy through which to prevent environmental damage. This situation also impedes more active civil society participation given that, in practice, citizens can only denounce to the Attorney General's Office when they have evidence of environmental damage, but then they have to wait inordinate periods of time for this authority to act (given that the Attorney General's Office is the only competent authority to initiate a public criminal action). Citizens do not have the opportunity to exercise effective control over the criminal process (they only adhere, with strict limitations, to the public criminal action initiated by a district attorney), and in most instances their role is limited to aiding the efforts of the district attorneys.

In conclusion, although the efforts of most district attorneys within the Specialized Unit on Environmental Crimes is admirable, given that they are the face of the State's response to environmental degradation, it is the author's belief that the juridical configuration of the Paraguayan environmental judicial system is dysfunctional with regard to the objective of guaranteeing the right to live in a healthy and ecologically equilibrated environment. This is because the process lacks two of the ideal tools mostly used to deal with environmental matters, namely, access to participation and environmental justice as espoused by Principle 10 of the Río Declaration of 1992.

---

60. For instance, Interlocutory Order No. 69, 12 May 2006, Juzgado de la Niñez y la Adolescencia del Quinto Turno, Asunción. Unpublished.

8   SIGNIFICANT COURT JUDGMENTS OF
         ENVIRONMENTAL RELEVANCE

Generally, the judiciary is reluctant to make a finding against government, and environmental issues are not an exception. Thus, relevant judicial decisions do not cause any significant changes in society, which should be to compel government to adopt positive environmental measures or policies. Currently, decisions rather confirm and highlight some existing positive aspects within the environmental judicial system, since there is little room for innovative reforms in this respect.

This section proceeds to analyze two jurisprudential lines that, in the author's opinion, are part of the backbone of the development of Paraguayan environmental law. These include the characterization of the right to live in a healthy and ecologically equilibrated environment as a human right; and access to environmental justice by means of the *actio popularis*.

In a 1996 decision, Agreement and Sentence Number 180, 28 May 1996,[61] in which the enforceability and scope of the right of assembly were discussed (notably not specifically involving environmental issues), the Supreme Court stated that: 'the State is constituted for the purpose to apply and facilitate human rights'.[62] With this declaration, the Supreme Court sought to highlight the conceptual break between a history of authoritarianism in which it was considered that the '[S]tate (was) the granter of rights, which is the reason why one had to acquire permission to use them',[63] and the new reality of constructive democratic values where there currently is an obligation on government to positively realize human rights.

In two different cases heard in 1999, which involved environmental rights, the Supreme Court stated that: first, based on the fact that the right to property is not absolute and allows limitations, limitations placed on the right to harmonize it with the environmental right, are based on the primacy of general interest over individual interests;[64] and second, that that general interest is based on the fact that human life depends on the preservation of the environment.[65] In the Agreement and Sentence Number 426, 8 July 1999, the Supreme Court stated:

> [D]espite the fact that certain factories are installed in a fixed zone and dedicated to a particular activity, this cannot result in an absolute limitation in which state policy can be modified in relation to this activity. If governmental authorities thought that the activity (. . .) could be carried out without

---

61. In 1987, shortly before the end of the dictatorial regime of Alfredo Stroessner, the police forbid the entrance to participants of a television program organized by the journalist Humberto Rubin. Mr Rubin started an *amparo* action, which was dismissed in the first and second instances. Against those, he started an unconstitutionality action. Making clear that after such a long time, the decision would have a strong symbolic significance, the court accepted the unconstitutionality action and overturned the decisions dictated in the *amparo* trial.
62. Agreement and Sentence No. 180, 18 May 1996, CSJ. See J. Sapena (ed.), *Jurisprudencia constitucional* (Asunción: Intercontinental, 2000).
63. See *supra* at 44.
64. Art. 128, Constitution.
65. Agreement and Sentence No. 98, 5 April 199, SCJ. LLP 2000, 177.

limitations regarding geographical areas, that is, they thought that it was not necessary to prohibit this activity in certain areas within the national territory, and factories continued operations under these conditions, this does not mean that the State cannot adopt any measures regarding factories which have already been installed. Maintaining this posture implies giving certain factories unlimited rights. Although it will be impossible to affect what has been done permanently for them, this does not imply that future activities will not be able to be changed.

In the Agreement and Sentence Number 98, 5 April 1999, the Supreme Court stated:

> [T]he right to live in a healthy and balanced environment is a fundamental attribute of the people which is recognized at a constitutional and international level. (. . .) As one can conclude after having read all of the aforementioned, environmental affairs are a global problem and not a circumstantial historical whim. Human life depends on environmental conservation. This is where its importance comes from and the reason why private property does not have an absolute character and is subordinate to a social order.[66]

In both these judgments, the Supreme Court decided on actions of unconstitutionality filed by individuals against environmental laws which limited forestry activities. After this declaration, there remained only a single step before clearly expressing that the right to live in a healthy and ecologically equilibrated environment is a human right. In 2003, within the framework of an *amparo* action promoted by an NGO against a private company and a State bank to prevent damage in the core zone of a protected area, a Court of Appeals of Asunción stated that:

> [In this case] the protection of diffused interests is threatened, as it is undoubtedly constituted in the preservation of the environment which constitutionally corresponds to all citizens (Art. 7 of the Constitution) and which . . . is a human right.[67]

This decision fused the two elements of access to environmental justice by means of the *actio popularis* and the consideration of the right to a healthy environment as a human right. With regard to the *actio popularis*, the Supreme Court of Justice stated in 1997, in Agreement and Sentence Number 323, 8 July 1997, that: '[T]he defence of a diffuse interest, as is the environment, deserves special considerations, especially in a country such as ours, in which citizen participation is urgently claimed in the quest for the common good'.[68] In 2002, a Court of Appeals in Asunción found that:

> [T]he constitutional protection of the environment included in Arts. 7 and 8 and protected by an *actio popularis* in Art. 38 is granted, considering the rights

---

66. *Ibid.*
67. See n. 33.
68. Agreement and Sentence No. 323, 8 July 1997, CSJ.

of the person, the human being, notwithstanding the very elements of the environment, whether they be alive or inert.[69]

Here, besides displaying a decidedly anthropocentric view of the environment, the *actio popularis* is included in Article 38 of the Constitution and not in Article 134 as was the case in other judgments. This is quite significant, since it opens the path to public claims (in principle to all sorts of processes), not only *amparos*. This criteria for active broad standing when dealing with claims for defending the environment, was adopted by the Supreme Court in 2005, when it stated that despite the rejection of an *amparo* action brought by an NGO, the object of claim could be satisfied by ordinary procedural means.[70]

Therefore, despite the absence of constitutional regulations that establish the right to a healthy environment and the ability to enforce such a right through the courts, the judiciary, particularly the Supreme Court, have concluded that the right to a healthy environment is a fundamental human right, and that it is possible for individuals and civil society organisations to exercise this right in any judicial process.

It is important to point out that these conclusions would also apply to the legal standing of civil society organizations in the framework of criminal trials; despite the fact that criminal courts still have not accepted this form of legal standing. In the author's opinion, it is merely a matter of time before a case in which a civil society organization attempts to intervene by means of an 'adhesive accusation' in a criminal trial, reaches the Supreme Court.

9   CRITICAL SURVEY

Measured in terms of efficiency, Paraguayan environmental governance is far from functioning optimally, and the judiciary has done little to ameliorate this situation. For example, despite the fact that Paraguay has outstanding constitutional environmental provisions, has ratified most of the existing multilateral environmental agreements, and has seen remarkable environmental law-making, the country has lost most of its forests (only less than 5% of the original forest cover remains in the Interior Atlantic Forest Area).[71]

As the analysis in this chapter suggests, environmental and criminal legislation tend to concentrate competence and powers in the governmental structure, but the Paraguayan Constitution is generous in terms of public participation in the decision-making process and control over governmental performance. Moreover, most of the judges have been extremely traditional and have been reluctant to explore novel judicial assets and innovative approaches when deciding environmental issues.

---

69. Agreement and Sentence No. 86, 14 August 2002, Tribunal de Apelaciones en lo Civil y Comercial de Asunción, Sala 3, LLP 2002, 1117.
70. Agreement and Sentence No. 89, 14 March 2005, CSJ.
71. WWF, 'World Wildlife Fund Paraguay', <www.wwf.org.py>, 14 September 2008.

The Paraguayan judiciary requires a more democratic culture, and a more intense environmental conscience. Although most of the environmental decisions reviewed here indicate important progress towards further developing environmental governance, dangerous vestiges of the past remain. For example, in 2005, the Constitutional Division of the Supreme Court reversed a sentence of the Court of Appeals of the city of Encarnación,[72] in a case that was to become the genesis of a firm environmental judicial doctrine, in tune with the constitutional environmental provisions. Although the arguments of the majority to reverse that decision were strictly procedural, one of the members of the Constitutional Division stated that '[T]he legislation mentioned in the sentence, about protection of diffuse interests and protection of the environment are programmatic, not operative',[73] thereby ignoring not only the spirit, but also the letter of the 1992 Constitution. It has been pointed out above that every right and guarantee established in the Constitution is in fact 'operative', as it is clearly expressed in its Article 45 *in fine*.

There is another argument that supports the above conclusions. For the sake of argument, let us pretend for an instant that the right to live in a healthy environment is a programmatic right. This would mean that the State commits to develop in a progressive manner the validity of a certain right, until (sometime in the future) it is able to guarantee its full enjoyment. This would imply that the government may under no circumstances worsen or diminish the extent to which this right is presently enjoyed or exercised, as this would constitute a failure to give effect to its constitutional mandate to progressively develop this right. The San Jose de Costa Rica Pact[74] establishes the obligation of the signatory countries to progressively develop the human rights established in the Pact and in the constitutional and legal regulations of the signatory countries in Article 29. Therefore, to argue that the validity of any right (in this case, to live in a healthy environment) cannot be petitioned in trial because it is programmatic and not operative, is to ignore the validity of the San Jose de Costa Rica Pact which has a supra-legal hierarchy, as established by Article 137 of the Paraguayan Constitution. Fortunately, this position was never invoked after the judgment, but it is an example of the latent threats and the need to develop judicial structures that contribute to good environmental governance.

10   THE WAY FORWARD

The duty and need to achieve good environmental governance in Paraguay does not stand isolated from the process of building and ensuring good democratic

---

72. Agreement and Sentence No. 121/04/01, 10 June 2004, Tribunal de Apelación, Primera Sala, Encarnación, Revista Electrónica de Derecho Ambiental, see, IDEA, 'Instituto de Derecho y Economía Ambiental' [Environmental Law and Economics Institute], <www.idea.org.py>, 14 September 2008.
73. Agreement and Sentence No. 301, 25 May 2005, CSJ, LLP 2005, 1306.
74. See *supra* n. 28.

governance. Both necessarily imply broad-based participation and citizen control over governmental structures and processes, as well as an emphasis on the training of governmental officers, including judges, particularly at the local level.

As for the judiciary and environmental governance, it is proposed that a legal reform of the criminal justice system is necessary, as well as reform of the mechanisms to facilitate access to justice. This would involve applying criminal environmental legislation to those cases where the environment is severely damaged, facilitating citizen participation to activate the juridical mechanisms of prevention, and ceasing and repairing environmental damage. With regard to this last point, the author is moderately optimistic, as there is a draft Environmental General Code[75] that has been submitted to the Ministry of Environment for consideration. This code establishes uniform principles for interpreting all valid environmental legal norms. It further regulates the restoration of environmental damage and provides procedures for access to justice in environmental matters.

Until the reforms envisaged by the code are implemented, the judiciary, and particularly the Supreme Court, can play a leading role in bringing forward and moulding this change, thereby deepening the lines already explored in some of their decisions, and using as a valid tool the experience of the Inter-American system of protection of human rights, particularly regarding its development of an approach aimed at effective protection of rights, including environmental rights.

BIBLIOGRAPHY

Abed, S. (ed.). *Régimen Jurídico Ambiental de la República del Paraguay. Análisis crítico. Normas legales y reglamentarias actualizadas y concordadas.* IDEA: Asunción, 2007.

Banco Central del Paraguay, Gerencia de Estudios Económicos. *Cuentas Nacionales 1991-2001.* Asunción: Departamento de Cuentas Nacionales y Mercado Interno, 2002.

Guyra Paraguay. 'Conservando la Biodiversidad'. <www.guyra.org.py>, 14 September 2008.

IDEA. 'Instituto de Derecho y Economía Ambiental'. <www.idea.org.py>, 14 September 2008.

Nervi, A. & R. Dietze. *Negociaciones Internacionales en Agricultura.* Working Document series: Comercio Internacional publications ATN/SF-5888-PR. Asunción: Ministerio de Industria y Comercio & Ministerio de Relaciones Exteriores BID, 2002.

Sapena, J. (ed.). *Jurisprudencia constitucional.* Asunción: Intercontinental, 2000.

WWF. 'World Wildlife Fund Paraguay'. <www.wwf.org.py>, 14 September 2008.

---

75. LLP 2007, Environmental Law Supplement, Number 1 (May).

TABLE OF LEGISLATION

TABLE OF CASES

Agreement and Sentence No. 89, 14 March 2005, CSJ
Agreement and Sentence No. 301, 25 May 2005, CSJ, LLP 2005, 1306
Agreement and Sentence No. 306, 25 May 2005, CSJ
Agreement and Sentence No. 10, 8 March 2006, Tribunal de Cuentas, Primera
    Sala, LLP 2006, 486
Interlocutory Order No. 69, 12 May 2006, Juzgado de la Niñez y la Adolescencia
    del Quinto Turno, Asunción
Final Judgment No. 40, 21 July 2007, Juzgado de Liquidación y Sentencia 1,
    Asunción
Mayagna Awas Tigni v. the Republic of Nicaragua and Yakye Axa
Sawhoyamaxa v. the Republic of Paraguay

TABLE OF REGIONAL AND INTERNATIONAL INSTRUMENTS

American Convention on Human Rights (1969)
Basel Convention on the Control of Transboundary Movements of Hazardous
    Wastes and their Disposal (1989) 28 *ILM* 567
Cartagena Protocol (2000) 39 *ILM* 1027
Convention on Biological Diversity (1992) 31 *ILM* 818
United Nations Framework Convention on Climate Change (1992) 31 *ILM* 849
Convention on International Trade in Endangered Species of Wild Fauna and Flora
    (1973) 46 *ILM* 1178
Convention for the Protection of World Cultural and Natural Heritage (1972)
Kyoto Protocol (1997) 37 *ILM* 22
MERCOSUR Environmental Emergencies Protocol
MERCOSUR Framework Agreement on the Environment
MERCOSUR Olivos' Protocol
Montreal Protocol on Substances that Deplete the Ozone Layer (1987) 26 *ILM* 1550
Rotterdam Convention on the Prior Informed Consent Procedure for Certain
    Hazardous Chemicals and Pesticides in International Trade (1999) 38 *ILM* 1
San Salvador Protocol (1999) 28 *ILM* 156
Stockholm Convention on Persistent Organic Pollutants (2001) 40 *ILM* 532
United Nations Convention to Combat Desertification in Countries Experiencing
    Serious Drought and/or Desertification (1994) 33 *ILM* 1328
Vienna Convention on the Protection of the Ozone Layer (1987) 26 *ILM* 1516

ABBREVIATIONS

CITES   Convention on International Trade in Endangered Species
CONADERNA *Comisión Nacional de Defensa de los Recursos Naturales*
                    [National Commission for the Defence of Natural Resources]
CONAM   *Comisión Nacional del Ambiente* [National Environmental
                    Council]

CSJ	Corte Suprema de Justicia
EIA	*Evaluación de Impacto Ambiental* [Environmental Impact Assessment]
EIAA	Environmental Impact Assessment Act
EID	Environmental Impact Declaration
GDP	Gross Domestic Product
MERCOSUR	*Mercado Común del Sur* [Common Market of the South]
NASA	National Aeronautics and Space Administration
NGO	Non-govermental Organization
PIC	Prior Informed Consent
SCJ	Supreme Court of Justice
TPR	*Tribunal Permanente de Revision* [Permanent Court of Review]
UNESCO	United Nations Educational, Scientific and Cultural Organization
WWF	World Wildlife Fund

Chapter 10

Australia

*Linda Pearson**

1   INTRODUCTION

1.1   ENVIRONMENTAL ISSUES

Australia is an island continent with an area of 7.6 million km^2 and a population of 20 million. Australia has maritime boundaries with Indonesia, Papua New Guinea, New Zealand, New Caledonia, Solomon Islands and East Timor. Australia's geographic location and its size mean that it includes a wide range of climate zones such as: temperate climates in coastal areas, particularly in the south east; tropical climates in the north; and a small region of alpine climate. Australia is a geologically stable continent with weathered and fragile soils. More than one-third of Australia is arid and receives an average annual rainfall of less than 250 mm. Another third is semi-arid with an annual average rainfall between 250 and 500 mm. Low rainfall means that there are few sizeable rivers and about 60% of the country by area is entirely dependent on groundwater. Human settlement goes back at least 50,000 years and the first European settlement was established in 1788. More than 80% of the Australian

* My thanks to Kate Purcell for research assistance, and to Rosemary Lyster for her helpful comments.

Louis J. Kotzé and Alexander R. Paterson (eds), *The Role of the Judiciary in Environmental Governance: Comparative Perspectives*, pp. 321–353.
© 2009 Kluwer Law International BV, The Netherlands.

population live on just 1% of the land surface, concentrated in the south east part of the country.[1]

The key environmental issues facing Australia relate in part to the pattern of human settlement, which is concentrated along the coastline and where rapid population growth has increased demand for water, energy and other resources. Inland water systems and catchments are subject to stress. Almost 70% of the water used in Australia is used for agriculture. Water allocation and use in the Murray Darling Basin is particularly complex. The Murray Darling Basin covers an area of just over a million square kilometres and is divided between the States of New South Wales, Victoria, Queensland and South Australia and the Australian Capital Territory. The Basin generates 40% of Australia's agriculture and pastoral production and supplies much of the water used in South Australia.[2] Irrigated agriculture accounts for 96% of the water taken from the Basin's river systems. Environmental consequences include degradation of river and groundwater bodies and salinity.[3]

Australia is one of the twelve most biologically diverse countries in the world.[4] Loss of biodiversity is a major environmental issue. Bates[5] notes:

> In just two centuries since Europeans arrived in Australia, half the forests have been cleared, more than half our arid and semi-arid lands degraded, and half (that is, 20) of all the mammal species which have become extinct worldwide in the last 200 years have been in Australia. Currently some 800 species of plants and 111 species of animals are considered endangered or vulnerable in Australia. Ecological communities such as temperate grasslands have also dwindled to near extinction.

Threats to biodiversity include grazing pressure, weeds and feral animals, changed fire regimes, habitat fragmentation, vegetation clearing (particularly in eastern Australia), changed hydrology, salinity and pollution.[6]

Climate change has already impacted on water, natural ecosystems, agriculture and horticulture. Many species of flora and fauna are at risk from rapid climate change because of restricted geographical and climatic ranges. The Intergovernmental Panel on Climate Change Fourth Assessment Report predicts a significant loss of biodiversity by 2020 in ecologically rich sites including the Great Barrier Reef and the Queensland Wet Tropics.[7] Water security in southern and eastern Australia is expected to be a significant issue. Ongoing coastal development and

---

1. DEWHA, 'Australia: SoE 1996', <www.environment.gov.au/soe/1996/index.html>, 17 December 2007.
2. D. Connell, *Water Politics in the Murray-Darling Basin* (Sydney: Federation Press, 2007), 8.
3. *Ibid.*
4. DEWHA *supra* n. 1 at p.2-12.
5. G. Bates, *Environmental Law in Australia*, 6th ed. (Sydney: LexisNexis Butterworths, 2006), 430.
6. S. Cork et al., 'Biodiversity: Theme commentary', <www.environment.gov.au/soe/2006/publications/commentaries/biodiversity/pressures.html>, 19 December 2007.
7. M.L. Parry et al. (eds), *Climate Change 2007: Impacts, Adaptation and Vulnerability, Working Group II Contribution to Intergovernmental Panel on Climate Change Fourth Assessment Report* (Cambridge: Cambridge University Press, 2008), 9 et seq., Summary for Policymakers.

population growth are projected to exacerbate risks from rising sea levels and increased storm events.[8] Australia's contribution to global warming, in particular through its extraction of coal, much of which is exported for use in foreign power stations, poses significant policy and legal challenges.

1.2   Principal Environmental Laws

The limitations of the common law for environmental protection have meant that most Australian environmental law is contained in legislation. Writing in 1984, Fowler[9] characterized Australian environmental law as manifested in a positive or protective component, and a negative or exploitative component:

> The positive component may be divided into two broad sections: rules for the protection of the environment from undue degradation by human activity, and rules for the conservation of natural, built and cultural items within the environment. The negative component also constitutes two groups: rules for the disposition of natural resources and rules which promote or facilitate development activity.

Fowler includes in the protective component legislation relating to land use planning, assessment of environmental impacts, pollution control and waste disposal. It is significant to note the extent to which environmental factors have increasingly been integrated into the legislation falling within the 'negative' component since this classification over two decades ago.

Australia is a federation and accordingly there are two sources of environmental legislation: the Commonwealth Parliament, and the parliaments of the six States and two Territories.[10] The legislative powers of the Commonwealth Parliament are set out in the *Commonwealth of Australia Constitution Act* 1900 (Constitution). Some of these powers are vested exclusively in the Commonwealth and the remainder can be exercised concurrently with the States. Where there is an inconsistency between a Commonwealth law and a law of a State, the former prevails to the extent of the inconsistency.[11] The States retain legislative power in areas not specifically conferred on the Commonwealth.

There is no specific reference to 'environment' in the list of legislative powers of the Commonwealth in section 51 of the Constitution. The extent, and limits, of the power of the Commonwealth Parliament to legislate over environmental matters, has been defined in a number of decisions of the High Court of Australia.

---

8. K. Hennessy et al., 'Australia and New Zealand', in Parry et al. (eds), *supra* n. 7, 507-540.
9. R.J. Fowler, 'Environmental Law and its Administration in Australia', *EPLJ* 1 (1984): 18.
10. The States are New South Wales, Queensland, South Australia, Tasmania, Victoria and Western Australia. The Territories are the Australian Capital Territory and the Northern Territory. A useful starting point for accessing Australian legislation and decisions of the courts, including the specialist environmental courts and tribunals, is AUSTLII, 'Australasian Legal Information Institute', <www.austlii.edu.au>, 21 July 2008.
11. *Commonwealth of Australia Constitution Act* 1900, s. 109.

The key steps in defining the extent of the Commonwealth's powers are traced in section 3.2 below.

The earliest legislation addressing matters now regarded as falling within the ambit of environmental law was State legislation concerned with the allocation and development of natural resources. Consistent with the common law rights of ownership of land vested in the Crown, legislation in each State enables the Crown to create interests in land, ranging from grants of fee simple through to leases, licenses and permits, and to impose restrictions on these interests.[12] State legislation governs public and private forestry activities,[13] mining,[14] water allocation[15] and access to fisheries within State waters.[16] Recognition of common law native title by the High Court in *Mabo v. Queensland (No 2)* (1992) 175 CLR 1, and the subsequent enactment of the *Native Title Act* 1993 (Cth), has led to complex issues of reconciliation of statutory schemes establishing rights of access to resources with native title rights; both common law and conferred by legislation.[17] For the most part, State resource allocation legislation was drafted to promote extraction and utilization of the resource. More recently, this legislation has come to incorporate environmental objectives, including the promotion of sustainable development.

The States have primary responsibility for land use legislation. Until the mid-twentieth century, the focus was on public health and safety. After the end of the Second World War, the States were encouraged to introduce planning controls

12. The current legislation is *Crown Lands Act* 1989 (NSW), *Land Act* 1958 (Vic), *Crown Lands Act* 1929 (SA), *Land Administration Act* 1997 (WA), *Crown Lands Act* 1976 (Tas), and *Land Act* 1994 (Qld). The severance of mineral rights from the rest of land, by providing that future land grants should contain a reservation of all minerals, began in New South Wales in 1884 and was adopted by all jurisdictions: C.W. O'Hare, 'A History of Mining in Australia', *ALJ* 45 (1971): 285-287.

13. *Forestry Act* 1916 (NSW), *Forestry Act* 1959 (Qld), *Forestry Act* 1950 (SA), *Forest Property Act* 2000 (SA), *Conservation, Forests and Lands Act* 1987 (Vic), *Conservation and Land Management Act* 1984 (WA), *Forest Practices Act* 1985 (Tas).

14. *Mining Act* 1992 (NSW), *Mineral Resources Act* 1989 (Qld), Mining Act 1971 (SA), *Mineral Resources Development Act* 1990 (Vic), *Mineral Resources Development Act* 1995 (Tas), *Mining Act* 1978 (WA).

15. *Water Management Act* 2000 (NSW), *Water Act* 1989 (Vic), *Water Act* 2000 (Qld), *Rights in Water and Irrigation Act* 1914 (WA), *Water Resources Act* 1997 (SA), *Water Management Act* 1999 (Tas).

16. *Fisheries Management Act* 1994 (NSW), *Fisheries Act* 1994 (Qld), *Fisheries Management Act* 2007 (SA), *Fisheries Act 1959* (Tas), *Fisheries Act* 1995 (Vic), *Fish Resources Management Act* 1994 (WA).

17. In *Yanner v. Eaton* (1999) 201 CLR 351 the High Court considered the conflict between the right of members of the Aboriginal community to take fauna in the exercise of their common law native title rights, and the statutory conferral on the Crown of property in fauna. In *Western Australia v. Ward* (2002) 213 CLR 1 the High Court gave detailed consideration to the relationship between native title and the grant of mining leases. In *Northern Territory of Australia v. Arnhem Land Aboriginal Land Trust* [2008] HCA 29 the High Court held that the grant in fee simple of land including tidal areas under the Aboriginal Land Rights (Northern Territory) Act 1976 (Cth) conferred the right to exclude people wishing to fish in those waters, including those holding fishing licences granted under Northern Territory legislation.

through the 1945 Commonwealth-State Housing Agreement under which the Commonwealth government agreed to provide funds to the States for public housing, on condition that the States ensured that there was adequate town planning legislation. This early legislation tended to follow the model adopted in the United Kingdom under the *Town and Country Planning Act* 1932, of providing binding controls on development through different zones, and reserving land for various public purposes. By the 1970s, planning legislation in most jurisdictions began to incorporate assessment of environmental impacts in development decision-making.[18] At the same time, the States were introducing pollution control legislation in response to increasing public awareness of the effects of industrialization and development. The early pollution control legislation tended to focus on the environmental media polluted (air, water and land) and to regulate the discharge of waste and pollution from activities identified as sources of pollution.[19] More recent legislation takes a broader view of pollution control and incorporates market-based incentives in addition to command and control regulatory strategies.[20] In some jurisdictions pollution control and planning law have been integrated in legislation, while in others, assessment processes mandated under different legislation have been integrated at an administrative level.[21]

Commonwealth environmental legislation has a relatively narrow coverage. Under the *Environment Protection and Biodiversity Conservation Act* 1999 (Cth) (EPBC Act) the trigger for Commonwealth involvement in assessment and approval of an activity depends on whether a 'matter of national environmental significance' is involved. There are seven matters of national environmental significance: properties included in the World Heritage list;[22] places included in the National Heritage list;[23] wetlands included in the Ramsar Convention;[24] nationally listed

18. The umbrella planning, development control and environmental impact assessment (EIA) legislation is now the *Environmental Planning and Assessment Act* 1979 (NSW), *Integrated Planning Act* 1997 (Qld), *Development Act* 1993 (SA), *Land Use Planning and Approvals Act* 1993 (Tas), *Planning and Environment Act* 1987 (Vic), *Town Planning and Development Act* 1928 (WA) and *Environment Protection Act* 1986 (WA).
19. Victoria was an exception to this approach, enacting in 1970 a comprehensive *Environment Protection Act*: Bates, *supra* n. 5, 389.
20. The key pieces of legislation are the *Protection of the Environment Operations Act* 1997 (NSW), *Environmental Protection Act* 1994 (Qld), *Environment Protection Act* 1993 (SA), *Environmental Management and Pollution Control Act* 1994 (Tas), *Environment Protection Act* 1970 (Vic) and *Environmental Protection Act* 1986 (WA).
21. Queensland is an example of the former, having brought mining activities under the *Environmental Protection Act* 1994 (Qld). New South Wales is an example of the latter: proposed development that requires development consent from a local government authority and also approval under a range of specified legislation (including pollution and heritage) is referred to as 'integrated development', and consideration under all other relevant legislation occurs at the same time as the development consent process: *Environmental Planning and Assessment Act* 1979 (NSW) Part 4, Div. 5.
22. *Environment Protection and Biodiversity Conservation Act* 1999, ss 12-15A.
23. *Ibid.*, ss 15B, 15C.
24. *Ibid.*, ss 16-17B.

threatened species or endangered ecological communities;[25] listed migratory species included in the Bonn Convention, bilateral agreements with Japan and China, or any other international agreement;[26] certain nuclear actions;[27] and Commonwealth marine areas.[28] Under the EPBC Act it is an offence (subject to some exceptions identified in Part 4 of the Act) to take an action that has or will have a significant impact on a matter of national environmental significance without the approval of the Commonwealth Minister. The EPBC Act establishes a process for the referral of proposals, the determination by the minister as to the form of assessment required, and the approval. Approval may not be required if the Commonwealth Minister has accredited a State or Territory assessment process or outcome. The EPBC Act also requires approval for actions likely to have a significant impact on Commonwealth land, and for actions undertaken by Commonwealth agencies likely to have a significant impact on the environment, whether inside or outside Australian jurisdiction.[29] Other significant areas of recent Commonwealth legislation include encouraging renewable energy[30] and regulating water management in the Murray Darling Basin.[31]

The approach adopted in the EPBC Act can be explained in part by the piecemeal conferral of legislative power on the Commonwealth in the Constitution (see the discussion at section 3.2 below). However, the political dimensions of policy-making in a federal system are also responsible. Following a sustained period of litigation in the High Court during the 1970s and 1980s, which reached its high point in the dispute between the Commonwealth and Tasmanian governments over the construction of the Franklin Dam,[32] the Commonwealth government adopted an approach described as 'co-operative federalism'. The 1990s saw work on developing a number of national strategies, including an Oceans Policy, National Forests Policy, National Greenhouse Strategy, National Strategy for Ecologically Sustainable Development, National Wetlands Program, National Strategy for the Conservation of Australia's Biological Diversity and the National Action Plan for Salinity and Water Quality.[33] The central policy document that emerged from this process was the Intergovernmental Agreement on the Environment (IGAE), signed in 1992 by the Commonwealth, States and Territories, and the

---

25. *Ibid.*, ss 18-19.
26. *Ibid.*, ss 20-20B.
27. *Ibid.*, ss 21-22A.
28. *Ibid.*, ss 23-24A. There has been considerable debate as to whether climate change should be included as a trigger to Commonwealth involvement: see A. Macintosh, 'The Greenhouse Trigger: Where did it go and What is its Future?', in *Climate Law in Australia 2007*, ed. T. Bonyhady & P. Christoff (Sydney: Federation Press, 2008), 46-66.
29. C. McGrath, 'Key Concepts of the Environment Protection and Biodiversity Conservation Act 1999 (Cth)', *EPLJ* 22 (2005): 20.
30. See R. Lyster et al., *Environmental and Planning Law in New South Wales*, (Sydney: Federation Press, 2007), Ch. 5; R. Lyster, 'Chasing Down the Climate Change Footprint of the Private and Public Sectors: Forces Converge', *EPLJ* 24 (2007): 281-321.
31. *Water Act* 2007 (Cth).
32. *Commonwealth v. Tasmania* (1983) 158 CLR 1.
33. See Bates, *supra* n. 5, 76-78.

Australian Local Government Association as the representative of local government.[34] The IGAE provides that the States have primary responsibility for environmental management within their jurisdiction, and the Commonwealth has a role in respect of national environmental issues. Under the IGAE, the parties agreed to accredit other jurisdictions' environmental impact assessment (EIA) processes. A significant feature of the IGAE is its inclusion of definitions of principles of ecologically sustainable development (ESD). The reference to '*ecologically* sustainable development' in the IGAE reflects the approach adopted by the Australian government in developing policy following the report of the World Commission on Environment and Development and the United Nations Conference on Environment and Development, in emphasizing the integration of economy and environment:

> Ecologically sustainable development means using, conserving and enhancing the community's resources so that ecological resources, on which life depends, are maintained and the total quality of life, now and in the future can be increased.[35]

The principles of ESD identified and defined in the IGAE are the precautionary principle, intergenerational equity, conservation of biological diversity and ecological integrity, and improved valuation, pricing and incentive mechanisms.

1.3   INSTITUTIONS AND GOVERNANCE STRUCTURES

Australia is a constitutional monarchy. The Head of State is Queen Elizabeth II, represented by the Governor General at the Commonwealth level, and by Governors in the States. There are three levels of government in Australia: Commonwealth, State and Territory, and local. The Commonwealth Constitution is based on a tripartite separation of powers and establishes legislative (Chapter I), executive (Chapter II) and judicial (Chapter III) branches of government. The Commonwealth Parliament is bicameral and consists of the House of Representatives (one member representing each electorate) and the Senate (twelve senators from each State and two from each Territory). Legislation must pass both Houses and receive assent from the Governor-General as the Queen's representative. Legislation appropriating revenue or imposing taxation must originate in the House of Representatives.[36]

The parliaments of all States (with the exception of Queensland) are also bicameral. Representation and electoral laws vary between jurisdictions. Legislation must

---

34. The IGAE can be located as a schedule to the *National Environment Protection Council Act* 1994 (Cth), and at DEWHA, 'IGAE', <www.environment.gov.au/esd/national/igae/index.html>, 22 July 2008.
35. Commonwealth Government, *Ecologically Sustainable Development* Discussion Paper, (Canberra: AGPS, 1990). See discussion in Bates, *supra* n. 5, 123-125.
36. Constitution s. 53.

pass both (if bicameral) Houses and receive assent from the Governor (or Administrator in the case of the Northern Territory) as the Queen's representative.

Executive government follows a similar pattern in the Commonwealth, States and Territories. Ministers chosen usually by the Prime Minister (for the Commonwealth), the Premier (for the States) and the Chief Minister (for the two Territories) head portfolio departments and are responsible for the administration of legislation as specified in Administrative Arrangements Orders from time to time. Responsibility for the administration of environmental legislation varies between jurisdictions. The arrangement at the Commonwealth level following the 2007 change in government is that the Department of the Environment, Water, Heritage and the Arts administers most Commonwealth environmental legislation (including the EPBC Act) and the Department of Climate Change deals with national and international climate change matters.[37] There are separate Departments of Agriculture, Fisheries and Forestry, and Resources, Energy and Tourism. In the States and Territories the planning, environment protection and natural resource management portfolios are generally separated.

The Commonwealth Constitution was drafted on the assumption of the continued existence of the former colonies as States after federation in 1901. Local government has no independent recognition in the Commonwealth Constitution but is afforded some recognition in each State Constitution.[38] The powers and responsibilities of local government authorities are specified in State legislation.[39] In Queensland, Tasmania, Victoria and Western Australia, local government authorities have a limited law-making capacity, generally limited to making laws relating to fees and charges.[40]

Local government plays a significant role in land use planning and development control decision-making, and in enforcement of pollution control legislation. The responsibilities are generally shared between State and local government agencies. Planning occurs at State, regional and local levels. In New South Wales, for example, planning instruments are made by the Governor or Minister as an exercise of delegated legislative power. Local environmental plans are drafted by the relevant local government authority, following a standard instrument formulated at the State level, or other agencies as the Minister directs. State environmental planning policies are made at the State level.[41] In other jurisdictions

---

37. See DEWHA, 'Environment Home', <www.environment.gov.au>, 22 July 2008.
38. *Constitution Act* 1902 (NSW) s. 51; *Constitution of Queensland* 2001 (Qld) Ch. 7; *Constitution Act* 1934 (SA) Part 2A; *Constitution Act* 1934 (Tas) Part IVA; *Constitution Act* 1975 (Vic) Part IIA; *Constitution Act* 1889 (WA) ss 52 and 53.
39. *Local Government Act* 1993 (NSW); *Local Government Act* 1993 (Qld); *Local Government Act* 1999 (SA); *Local Government Act* 1993 (Tas); *Local Government Act* 1989 (Vic); *Local Government Act* 1995 (WA).
40. *Local Government Act* 1993 (Qld) s. 26 (local laws); *Local Government Act* 1993 (Tas) Part 11 (by-laws); *Local Government Act* 1989 (Vic) (local laws); *Local Government Act* 1995 (WA) 3.5 (local laws).
41. *Environmental Planning and Assessment Act* 1979 (NSW) Part 3. The *Environmental Planning and Assessment Amendment Act* 2008 has made significant changes to planning and development

(for example, Victoria and Queensland) the framework for State or regional planning policies is included in each local planning scheme.[42] Responsibility for enforcing pollution laws may fall on either the relevant local government authority or a State agency (often called an Environment Protection Authority) as the 'appropriate regulatory authority', depending on whether the premises fall within prescribed categories identified as likely to emit pollution.[43]

2 THE COURT SYSTEM

2.1 HISTORICAL DEVELOPMENT OF THE JUDICIARY

European settlement in Australia in 1788 took the form of a convict settlement, and the first legal institutions were limited to a criminal court and a civil court, both with summary procedure. The colonies were regarded as settled colonies, rather than conquered or ceded colonies, and accordingly received the English common law insofar as it was appropriate to local conditions, and the rules of equity, and continued to attract common law rules when conditions became appropriate.[44] Statute law appropriate to each new colony was received into it.[45] Other British legislation that expressly or by necessary implication applied to the colony did so as well, whether passed before or after the date of settlement.[46]

The pre-existing rights of indigenous Australians were not recognized until the High Court decision in *Mabo v. Queensland (No 2)* (1992) 175 CLR 1, which held that the common law of Australia recognized continuing rights to land in the form of native title, and rejected the application of the doctrine of *terra nullius* in Australian law. While continuing native title rights are recognized, the courts have refused to recognize any form of Aboriginal sovereignty.[47]

The first courts in the colonies of New South Wales and Tasmania (then called Van Dieman's Land) were essentially military courts, consisting of a Judge-Advocate and military officers. The first formal establishment of a superior court, known as the Supreme Court, came in 1823 in the colonies of New South Wales and Tasmania. The Supreme Court had the jurisdiction of the superior courts of justice at Westminster.[48] Other colonies were subsequently established, and

---

control, in particular by abolishing regional environment plans, and through changes to assessment of development proposals.

42. Bates, *supra* n. 5, 269.
43. *Protection of the Environment Operations Act* 1997 (NSW) s. 6.
44. *Cooper v. Stuart* (1889) 14 App Cas 286 (PC).
45. The date of reception has been fixed by statute: 25 July 1828 for the four eastern colonies, and 1 June 1829 for Western Australia and 28 December 1836 for South Australia: J. Crawford & B Opeskin, *Australian Courts of Law*, 4th ed., (Oxford: OUP, 2004), 17.
46. Crawford & Opeskin, *supra* n. 45, 18.
47. *Ibid.*, 16, citing *Coe v. Commonwealth* (1978) 18 ALR 592, (1979) 24 ALR 118; *Coe v. Commonwealth (No 2)* (1993) 118 ALR 193.
48. *New South Wales Act* 1823 (4 Geo IV c 96), s. 11.

with them, a Supreme Court and later, inferior courts.[49] Colonial judges were appointed at pleasure and could be removed by the Crown. The development of representative and then responsible government was a gradual process, receiving impetus in 1850 with the passage of the *Australian Constitutions Act*.[50] The basic framework for transfer of effective legislative control over the executive to local legislatures was established in each of the colonies during the 1850s.[51] With the arrival of responsible government came a degree of judicial independence, culminating in the current position where judges are appointed by the Governor or Governor-General (acting on the advice of the Executive Council), holding their commissions during their good behavior until they reach a statutorily imposed retirement age (usually 70 years).[52] Most judges are senior practicing barristers.

2.2	COURT STRUCTURE AND HIERARCHY OF COURTS

2.2.1   Federal Courts and Tribunals

The High Court of Australia was created by section 71 of the Constitution, and exercises both original jurisdiction and appellate jurisdiction. The High Court is the final appellate court and determines appeals from both the State and Territory Supreme Courts, and from the Federal Court of Australia.[53] Since 1984, special leave to appeal is required and the criteria for the granting of such leave are set out in section 35A of the *Judiciary Act* 1903 (Cth).[54] In determining whether or not to grant special leave, the Court is required to have regard to whether the proceedings involve a question of law that is of public importance, because of its general application or otherwise, or where there is a need to resolve differences of opinion between courts or within one court; and whether the interests of the administration of justice require consideration by the High Court of the judgment to which the application relates. Factors which the court has taken into account include whether the proceedings raise a legal issue of relevance beyond the parties, or involve an

---

49. Crawford & Opeskin, *supra* n. 45, 22-23.
50. *Australian Constitutions Act* 1850 (13 & 14 Vict c 59).
51. D. Clark, *Principles of Australian Public Law*, 2nd ed. (Sydney: LexisNexis Butterworths, 2007), 42-44.
52. *Ibid.*, 242-253.
53. Constitution, s. 73. Appeals from the High Court to the Privy Council were limited to matters of non-federal jurisdiction by the *Privy Council (Limitation of Appeals) Act* 1968 (Cth) and abolished under the *Privy Council (Appeals from the High Court) Act* 1975 (Cth). Appeals from the State Supreme Courts to the Privy Council were abolished by the *Australia Acts* 1986 (Cth) and (UK): see discussion by Sir A. Mason, 'The Evolving Role and Function of the High Court', in *The Australian Federal Judicial System*, ed. B. Opeskin & F. Wheeler (Melbourne: Melbourne University Press, 2000), 99-102.
54. The abolition of rights of appeal as of right, and the requirement for special leave, was enacted through amendments to the *Judiciary Act* 1903 (Cth) and the *Federal Court of Australia Act* 1976 by the *Judiciary Amendment Act (No 2)* 1984 (Cth) and the *Federal Court of Australia Amendment Act* 1984 (Cth): see Sir A. Mason, *supra* n. 53, 112.

essentially discretionary judgment.[55] The court has confirmed the constitutional validity of the amendments introducing the requirement for special leave, and stated that it gives 'greater emphasis to the public role in the evolution of the law than to the private rights or interests of the parties to the litigation'.[56]

The original jurisdiction of the High Court is conferred by sections 75 and 76 of the Constitution, and section 30 of the *Judiciary Act* 1903 (Cth). Section 75 of the Constitution confers original jurisdiction in matters: arising under any treaty; in which the Commonwealth (or a person suing or being sued on behalf of the Commonwealth) is a party; between States or residents of different States; or in which a writ of mandamus, prohibition or an injunction is sought against an officer of the Commonwealth. Section 30 of the *Judiciary Act* 1903 (Cth) confers original jurisdiction in all matters arising under, or involving the interpretation of, the Constitution.

Chapter III of the Constitution enables the creation of other federal courts. The Federal Court of Australia, established under the *Federal Court of Australia Act* 1976 (Cth), is a superior court of law and equity, and has an extensive original jurisdiction. The most significant conferral of jurisdiction relevant in environmental matters is under section 39B of the *Judiciary Act* 1903 (Cth). Since 1983, the Federal Court has had jurisdiction in matters in which a writ of mandamus, prohibition or an injunction is sought against an officer of the Commonwealth.[57] The court's jurisdiction was extended in 1984 by enabling the High Court to transfer matters commenced in that court's original jurisdiction,[58] and again in 1997 to enable the court to hear matters arising under Commonwealth legislation.[59] An alternative pathway for challenging government decisions is provided under the *Administrative Decisions (Judicial Review) Act* 1977 (Cth), which enables review of decisions of an administrative character made under Commonwealth legislation.[60] The jurisdiction of the Federal Court extends to matters arising under the *Trade Practices Act* 1974 (Cth) and under the Corporations Law.

The Federal Magistrates Court was established in 1999. Its jurisdiction includes review of administrative decisions under the *Administrative Decisions (Judicial Review) Act* 1977 (Cth), and any matters transferred to it by the Federal Court.[61] Appeals from the Federal Magistrates Court are heard in the Federal

---

55. Crawford & Opeskin, *supra* n. 45, 183.
56. *Ibid.*, 183, citing *SmithKline & French Laboratories (Australia) Ltd v. Commonwealth* (1991) 173 CLR 194 at 218.
57. *Judiciary Act* 1903 (Cth), s. 39B(1).
58. *Ibid.*, s. 44(2A).
59. *Ibid.*, s. 38B(1A)(c). An example of a challenge bought under s. 39B of the *Judiciary Act* is *The Wilderness Society Inc v. Minister for the Environment and Water Resources* (2007) 96 ALD 655, a challenge to a decision of the minister concerning the assessment process for a proposed pulp mill.
60. See, e.g., *Anvil Hill Project Watch Association Inc v. Minister for the Environment and Water Resources* [2007] FCA 1480.
61. *Federal Court of Australia Act* 1976 (Cth), s. 32AB(8A).

Court. Federal jurisdiction is conditioned by the requirement that there be a 'matter' and federal courts cannot therefore give advisory opinions.[62]

Environmental issues are also adjudicated in Australia's well-developed system of tribunals. At the federal level, administrative tribunals are limited to the exercise of executive power and cannot exercise judicial power.[63] This restriction does not apply to tribunals established by the States, however, which are in turn subject to some limitations regarding issues of federal law.[64] The Administrative Appeals Tribunal (AAT) was established in 1976 and has jurisdiction to review decisions made under over 400 Commonwealth enactments. While the largest part of the AAT's workload comes from its jurisdiction in veterans' entitlement and social security matters, review of decisions made under Commonwealth environmental legislation is a significant part of its workload.[65] In general, the AAT has the power to review administrative decisions afresh on the material available at the time of the review, and to affirm, vary, or set aside a decision and substitute a new decision.[66]

2.2.2   State Courts and Tribunals

Each State and Territory has a Supreme Court, exercising all the powers inherent in a superior court of record. The relationship between the Supreme Court and lower courts varies across the jurisdictions. In general terms, however, the Supreme Court exercises original civil and criminal jurisdiction, and determines appeals from the lower courts. The State courts can exercise federal jurisdiction and this conferral of jurisdiction provides a degree of protection from interference by State legislatures.[67]

New South Wales and South Australia have established specialist environment courts: the Land and Environment Court and the Environment Resources and

---

62. *Re Judiciary and Navigation Acts 1903-1920* (1921) 29 CLR 257; *Re McBain; ex parte Australian Catholic Bishops Conference* (2002) 209 CLR 372.

63. *R v. Kirby; ex parte Boilermakers' Society of Australia* (1956) 94 CLR 254; *Drake v. Minister for Immigration and Ethnic Affairs* (1979) 2 ALD 60.

64. *Trust Company of Australia Limited (trading as Stockland Property Management) v. Skiwing Pty Ltd (trading as Café Tiffany's)* [2006] NSWCA 185, 66 NSWLR 77; *Attorney General v. 2UE Sydney Pty Ltd & Ors* [2006] NSWCA 349; *Commonwealth v. Anti-Discrimination Tribunal (Tasmania)* [2008] FCAFC 104.

65. Examples include: *Re The International Fund for Animal Welfare (Aust) Pty Ltd and Minister for Environment and Heritage* (2005) 93 ALD 594, a review of a decision of the minister to approve the import of Asian elephants included in the Convention on International Trade in Endangered Species of Wildlife, Fauna and Flora; and *Re Humane Society International and Minister for the Environment* (2006) 93 ALD 640, a review of a decision approving fishing operations in the Southern Bluefin Tuna fishery.

66. *Administrative Appeals Tribunal Act* 1975 (Cth) s. 43.

67. *Judiciary Act* 1903 (Cth) s. 77(iii); see *Northern Australian Aboriginal Legal Aid Service Inc v. Bradley* (2004) 218 CLR 146, and *Fardon v. Attorney-General for the State of Queensland* (2004) 210 ALR 50, and G. Carney, *The Constitutional Systems of the Australian States and Territories*, (Cambridge: Cambridge University Press, 2006), Ch. 10.

Development Court respectively. Victoria, Western Australia, Tasmania and the Northern Territory have gone down the path of establishing a tribunal to deal with environmental matters: respectively the Victorian Civil and Administrative Tribunal, the State Administrative Tribunal, the Resource Management and Planning Appeal Tribunal, and the Lands and Mining Tribunal. Queensland has a Planning and Environment Court which hears primarily land use appeals from decisions of local government authorities, and a Land Court hearing other matters, including cultural heritage and resource development issues.

The constitution of each of these bodies varies between jurisdictions. The Land and Environment Court of New South Wales and the Environment, Resources and Development Court of South Australia, are constituted by judges and commissioners who have qualifications and experience relevant to the work of the courts.[68] The Resource Management and Planning Appeal Tribunal of Tasmania has a legally qualified chairperson and deputy chairperson, and other members with qualifications relevant to the Tribunal's work.[69] The Planning and Development Court of Queensland is constituted by a District Court judge appointed to sit in the Planning and Environment Court.[70] The Western Australian State Administrative Tribunal is headed by a judge of the Supreme Court and its membership includes magistrates, legally qualified persons and persons with other qualifications relevant to the Tribunal's jurisdiction.[71] Similarly, the Victorian Civil and Administrative Tribunal is headed by a Supreme Court judge and members may be qualified legal practitioners or persons with other relevant qualifications and experience.[72]

The functions and powers of each of these courts and tribunals also varies between jurisdictions, but in general terms include a merits review function, where the rules of evidence do not apply and the court or tribunal exercises the power and discretion of the initial decision-maker (usually a local government authority or State government agency). Some exercise a judicial review function, scrutinizing the legality of decisions, and a civil enforcement function; and some exercise criminal jurisdiction.[73] In those jurisdictions where the specialist environmental court or tribunal does not exercise judicial review or criminal jurisdiction, those matters will be heard and determined in the Supreme Court or other courts.

---

68. *Land and Environment Court Act* 1979 (NSW), *Environment, Resources and Development Court Act* 1993 (SA).
69. *Resource Management and Planning Appeal Tribunal Act* 1993 (Tas).
70. *Integrated Planning Act* 1997 (Qld).
71. *State Administrative Tribunal Act* 2004 (WA).
72. *Victorian Civil and Administrative Tribunal Act* 1988 (Vic).
73. The most comprehensive jurisdiction is that of the Land and Environment Court of New South Wales, which exercises merits review (Classes 1, 2 and 3), judicial review and civil enforcement (Class 4), and criminal jurisdiction, original (Class 5) and appellate (Classes 6 and 7).

3   SIGNIFICANT COURT JUDGMENTS OF
               ENVIRONMENTAL RELEVANCE

The significant court judgments of environmental relevance fall within four main
categories:

- Establishing the limits of the common law;
- Establishing the extent of national responsibility for environmental
  governance;
- Interpretation of environmental and other legislation; and
- Public participation and enforcement.

3.1   ESTABLISHING THE LIMITS OF THE COMMON LAW

Australia inherited the common law of England, including the torts of nuisance,
trespass and negligence.[74] The High Court has stated that there is only one
common law for Australia and not any separate body of State common law or
separate common law for each State.[75] The limited scope of the common law
for environmental protection arises from its focus on harm to individuals' property or personal rights and interests, rather than harm to the environment
per se.[76] An example of this limitation arose in the case of *Ball v. Consolidated
Rutile Ltd* [1991] 1 Qd R 524, an action brought by commercial fishermen
against a mining company in relation to slippage of a sand dune into water
causing damage to the plaintiffs' prawn nets. The claim in public nuisance
failed, as the Supreme Court held that the statutory license to take fish did
not confer any special right over and above the rights of the public generally,
nor did it confer any right to have the waters kept clear of deposits such as the
dune slippage. Further, the deposit of material making it more difficult to catch
fish did not constitute a public nuisance.

Much of the civil litigation in negligence has concerned attempts to impose
liability on government agencies for their negligent exercise of statutory powers or
duties, or their failure to prevent harm through a non-exercise of statutory powers
or duties. Some claims have succeeded.[77] Others have failed, particularly where
the argument is that a failure to exercise a statutory power has caused harm that

---

74. The cause of action in *Rylands v. Fletcher* (1866) LR 1 Ex 265 was held by the High Court to
    have been subsumed into the general principles of negligence: *Burnie Port Authority v. General
    Jones Pty Ltd* (1994) 179 CLR 520.
75. *Lipohar v. R* (1999) 200 CLR 485.
76. Bates, *supra* n. 5, 171.
77. *L Shaddock & Associates Pty Ltd v. Parramatta City Council* (1981) 150 CLR 225, concerning
    failure to provide correct information; *Sutherland Shire Council v. Heyman* (1985) 157 CLR
    424; *Armidale City Council v. Alec Finlayson Pty Ltd* (1999) 104 LGERA 9, concerning
    rezoning of contaminated land; *Punterio v. Water Administration Ministerial Corp* (1999)
    104 LGERA 419, concerning failure of a water supply authority to warn of chemical additives,
    resulting in damage to crops.

could have been avoided.[78] The difficulty arises in establishing that the government agency owed a duty of care to the plaintiff. A further limitation on the usefulness of the common law has come through legislation in most jurisdictions significantly restricting the circumstances in which a public authority can be held liable.[79]

3.2   Establishing the Extent of National Responsibility for Environmental Governance

The national government established under the Constitution in 1901 was given specific legislative responsibilities, most of which can be exercised concurrently with the States. The States were left with the residual responsibility for matters not specifically conferred on the new Commonwealth government. That meant that the States retained their legislative and administrative responsibilities for land use controls and resource management. While there is no express conferral of power to legislate in relation to environmental matters, the High Court has confirmed through a number of cases that the federal government can legislate to achieve environmental outcomes.

Several heads of legislative power have been the subject of litigation in the High Court, most often through a challenge by a State or States to the enactment of legislation, or a challenge by an individual or corporation to the enforcement of Commonwealth legislation. The heads of power most relevant to environmental matters include section 51(i): 'trade and commerce with other countries and among the states'; section 51(xx): 'foreign corporations, and trading or financial corporations formed within the limits of the Commonwealth'; and section 51(xxvi): 'external affairs'. The Commonwealth's financial powers include a power under section 96 to 'grant financial assistance to any State on such terms and conditions as the Parliament thinks fit', and its power to make laws with respect to taxation, including income tax, customs and excise. The Commonwealth's power 'to impose duties of customs and of excise, and to grant bounties on the production or export of goods' is exclusive.[80]

The trade and commerce power has been interpreted by the High Court so as to enable the Commonwealth to impose conditions on the export or import approval on environmental grounds. In *Murphyores Inc Pty Ltd v. Commonwealth* (1976) 136 CLR 1, the High Court upheld a decision by the Commonwealth government to refuse approval for the export of mineral sands on environmental grounds.

---

78. *Graham Barclay Oysters Pty Ltd v. Ryan* (2002) 125 LGERA 1, holding that neither the local council nor the State agency was liable for injury caused by consumption of contaminated oysters.
79. *Civil Liability Act* 2002 (NSW), *Civil Liability Act* 2003 (Qld), *Civil Liability Act* 1936 (SA), *Civil Liability Act* 2002 (Tas), *Wrongs Act* 1958 (Vic), *Civil Liability Act* 2002 (WA). For a discussion of some of the issues see J. McDonald, 'A Risky Climate for Decision-making: The Liability of Development Authorities for Climate Change Impacts', *EPLJ* 24 (2007): 405.
80. Constitution s. 90.

This power has been used to support legislation imposing environmental controls on the export of woodchips.[81]

Legislative powers of both the Commonwealth and States are restricted to some degree by section 92 of the Constitution, which requires that 'trade, commerce, and intercourse among the States...shall be absolutely free'. The key is whether the relevant legislation is discriminatory or protectionist. For example, Tasmanian regulations restricting the sale of undersize crayfish were held to be valid on the basis that while they did protect the Tasmanian crayfish industry (by assisting in the protection and conservation of the natural resource), they did not give Tasmanian crayfish production or intrastate trade and commerce a competitive or market advantage over imported crayfish.[82] Other legislation, ostensibly based on environmental factors, has not fared so well. South Australian legislation imposing a higher level of deposit on beer sold in non-refillable bottles, and requiring retailers selling beer in non-refillable bottles to accept empty returns and refund the deposit whether or not they sold the original item, was held to be invalid, as the High Court concluded that the primary aim of the legislation was to protect local beer producers from competition from a Western Australian producer.[83]

The Commonwealth's power has received an increasingly broad interpretation. The power enables the Commonwealth to legislate with respect to 'trading corporations', which includes State government agencies whose trading activities are a substantial part of their activities.[84] The legislative power is not limited to the trading activities of the corporation. In the *Tasmanian Dam* case,[85] the High Court held that the Commonwealth could legislate to prohibit the construction of a dam and its associated works, which were proposed to be undertaken in order to engage in a trading activity, namely the sale of electricity. In *New South Wales v. Commonwealth* [2006] HCA 52, the High Court held that section 51(xx) enabled the Commonwealth to legislate with respect to workplace relations for foreign, trading or financial corporations, opening the way for legislation concerned with the internal management of corporations.

The most significant head of Commonwealth legislative power is the external affairs power in section 51(xxvi). Under this head of power, the Commonwealth can legislate if the subject matter of the legislation is of 'international concern', or to implement any treaty obligation.[86] The rapid growth of international environmental law since the early 1970s has meant a significant expansion in Commonwealth legislative power. Such legislation includes the *Environment Protection and Biodiversity Conservation Act* 1999 (Cth), implementing the Convention on

---

81. Export Control (Unprocessed Wood) Regulations 1986, made pursuant to the *Export Act* 1983 (Cth).
82. *Cole v. Whitfield* (1988) 165 CLR 360.
83. *Castlemaine Tooheys Ltd v. South Australia* (1990) 169 CLR 436.
84. *Commonwealth v. Tasmania* (1983) 158 CLR 1 (usually referred to as the *Tasmanian Dam* case), concerning the Tasmanian Hydro-Electric Commission.
85. *Ibid.*
86. *Commonwealth v. Tasmania* (1983) 158 CLR 1.

World Cultural and Natural Heritage (11 ILM 1358 (1972)), the Convention of the Conservation of Migratory Species of Wild Animals (19 ILM 15 (1980)), the Ramsar Convention on Wetlands of International Importance (11 ILM 97 (1972)), and the Convention on International Trade in Endangered Species of Wild Flora and Fauna (12 ILM 1085 (1973)).[87]

3.3   Interpretation of Environmental and other Legislation

The High Court, Federal Court, Supreme Courts and some of the specialist environmental courts have the power to review administrative decision-making to ensure legality, and to set aside decisions found to fall short of the required standard. A central obligation imposed on administrative decision-makers is that they have regard to all relevant factors and disregard irrelevant factors in exercising discretionary powers, and act for the purpose for which the power was conferred.[88] Contemporary laws increasingly include objectives and principles of ecologically sustainable development. Their form varies and includes: a simple statement of objects;[89] a direction that decision-makers take into account certain prescribed objects or other specified matters;[90] and, in some instances, a direction that they exercise their discretionary powers so as to achieve these objectives.[91]

Where legislation does not include a list of factors to be taken into account, the relevant factors are implied from the subject matter, scope and purpose of the legislation.[92] There is a growing line of authority on the extent to which decision-makers may, or are required to, take into account principles of ecologically sustainable development. Much of this analysis has been undertaken in the context of merits challenges to land use and resource decision-making.[93]

---

87. Other significant legislation relying on the external affairs power includes the *Environment Protection (Sea Dumping) Act* 1981, implementing the London Dumping Convention; the *Protection of the Sea (Prevention of Pollution from Ships) Act* 1983 (Cth) implementing the MARPOL Convention; and the *Ozone Protection Act* 1989 (Cth) implementing the Vienna Convention and Montreal Protocol. See D. Rothwell & B. Boer, 'From the Franklin to Berlin: The Internationalisation of Australian Environmental Law and Policy', *Sydney Law Review* 17 (1995): 242.
88. M. Aronson, B. Dyer & M. Groves, *Judicial Review of Administrative Action*, 3rd ed. (Sydney: Lawbook Co, 2004), 254-263.
89. E.g., *Environmental Planning and Assessment Act* 1979 (NSW) s. 5.
90. *Environment Protection and Biodiversity Conservation Act* 1999 (Cth) s. 391 (circumstances when the minister must have regard to precautionary principle); *Environmental Protection Act* 1994 (Qld) s. 7 and Sch. 3 (providing 'standard criteria').
91. *Fisheries Management Act* 1991 (Cth): s. 3(1) objectives to be pursued, and s. 3(2) objectives to which decision-makers must have regard; *Water Management Act* 2000 (NSW): s. 9(1) imposing a duty on persons exercising functions under the act to take reasonable steps to promote the water management principles of the act (see *Murrumbidgee Groundwater Preservation Association v. Minister for Natural Resources* [2004] NSWLEC 122).
92. *Minister for Aboriginal Affairs v. Peko Wallsend Ltd* (1986) 162 CLR 24.
93. A comprehensive summary of the key cases is provided by Biscoe J. in *Walker v. Minister for Planning* [2007] NSWLEC 741.

The first case to consider the precautionary principle was *Leatch v. National Parks and Wildlife Service* (1993) 81 LGERA 270. This was a challenge, on the merits, to a decision to issue a license permitting a council to take and kill endangered fauna from an area of bushland where a road was to be constructed. At the time of this decision, the relevant legislation did not make any reference to principles of ecologically sustainable development. Stein J (then in the Land and Environment Court) described the precautionary principle as 'a statement of commonsense', and held:

> While there is no express provision requiring consideration of the 'precautionary principle', consideration of the state of knowledge or uncertainty regarding a species, the potential for serious or irreversible harm to an endangered fauna and the adoption of a cautious approach in protection of endangered fauna is clearly consistent with the subject matter, scope and purpose of the Act.[94]

Stein J held that there had been inadequate assessment of the need for the road, and that a 'cautious approach' should be taken in respect of the endangered fauna. He accordingly set aside the decision to grant the license. Subsequent cases in the Land and Environment Court did not go so far,[95] and other courts were less willing to consider principles of sustainability in the absence of a legislative direction.[96] In 1998, the *Environmental Planning and Assessment Act* 1979 (NSW) was amended to include in its objects the object 'to encourage . . . ecologically sustainable development'. As a consequence, the Land and Environment Court has held that decision-makers are required to have regard to the principles of ecologically sustainable development; and in particular, in having regard to 'the public interest' as a mandated consideration in determining development applications to give effect to the objects of the Act.[97]

Merits challenges in other jurisdictions have raised the application of the precautionary principle. In *Conservation Council of South Australia v. Development Assessment Commission and Tuna Boat Owners Association (No 2)* [1999] SAERDC 86, the South Australian Environment Resources and Development Court assessed a development application for tuna farms and held that it should be refused on the grounds that it undermined the precautionary principle.[98] Other decisions where approvals have been refused on this basis include *Skye*

---

94. (1993) 81 LGERA 270 at 282-283.
95. *Nicholls v. Director-General of National Parks and Wildlife* (1994) 84 LGERA 397; *Greenpeace Australia Ltd v. Redbank Power Company Ltd* (1994) 86 LGERA 143.
96. See e.g., *Friends of Hinchinbrook Society Inc v. Minister for the Environment* (1997) 93 LGERA 23.
97. *Carstens v. Pittwater Council* (1999) 111 LGERA 1; *Hutchinson Telecommunications (Australia) Pty Ltd v. Baulkham Hills Shire Council* [2004] NSWLEC 104; *BGP Properties Pty Ltd v. Lake Macquarie City Council* (2004) 138 LGERA 237.
98. On appeal the Full Court of the Supreme Court agreed that the ERD Court was required to determine whether the proposed development would be ecologically sustainable: *Tuna Boat Owners Association of SA Inc v. Development Assessment Commission* (2000) 110 LGERA 1.

Environmental Services Pty Ltd v. Frankston City Council [2004] VCAT 682, and decisions of the AAT regarding the allocation of fishing quotas.[99] In contrast, in a recent challenge to a decision to approve a wind farm, the Land and Environment Court drew upon principles of sustainability and intergenerational equity and the scheme of relevant legislation, to support an argument that energy sources resulting in less greenhouse gas emission be substituted for those that result in more greenhouse gas emission. The court approved the construction of sixty-nine turbines, instead of the fifty-four approved by the minister.[100]

The most detailed analyses of the concept of ESD have occurred in decisions of the Land and Environment Court. In *Telstra Corporation Ltd v. Hornsby Shire Council* (2006) 146 LGERA 10, Preston J (Chief Judge of the Land and Environment Court) analyzed the application of the precautionary principle as usually defined in Australian legislation.[101] The context was an appeal on the merits against the council's refusal to approve the construction of a mobile phone tower owing to objections raised by nearby residents. Preston J found that the first requirement, that there be 'threats of serious or irreversible environmental damage', was not established and so there was no basis on which the precautionary principle could be applied. Several decisions have applied the principle of conservation of biological diversity and ecological integrity,[102] while the polluter-pays principle has been applied in sentencing for environmental offences.[103]

Principles of ESD have also been applied in judicial review proceedings challenging the legality of environmental decisions. In *Gray v. Minister for Planning* (2006) 152 LGERA 258, the Land and Environment Court held that the principles of ESD were impliedly relevant matters which decision-makers exercising powers under Part 3A of the *Environmental Planning and Assessment Act 1979* (NSW) had to take into account. The case concerned an environmental assessment for a proposed coal mine, for which the inclusion of a 'detailed greenhouse gas assessment' was required. Pain J held that the principles of

---

99. Starting with *Re Dixon and Australian Fisheries Management Authority* [2000] AATA 442: see discussion in J. Peel, *The Precautionary Principle in Practice: Environmental Decision-Making and Scientific Uncertainty*, (Sydney: Federation Press, 2005), Ch. 5 – Taking a 'Precautionary Approach' to Fisheries Management.
100. *Taralga Landscape Guardians Inc v. Minister for Planning and RES Southern Cross Pty Ltd* [2007] NSWLEC 59.
101. The formulation relevant in this case was that in s. 6(2) of the *Protection of the Environment Administration Act* 1991 (NSW): '... If there are threats of serious or irreversible environmental damage, lack of full scientific certainty should not be used as a reason for postponing measures to prevent environmental degradation. In the application of the precautionary principle, public and private decisions should be guided by: (i) careful evaluation to avoid, wherever practicable, serious or irreversible damage to the environment, and (ii) an assessment of the risk-weighted consequence of various options.'
102. *BGP Properties Pty Ltd v. Lake Macquarie City Council* [2004] NSWLEC 399; *Bentley v. BGP Properties Pty Ltd* [2006] NSWLEC 34.
103. See detailed analysis in *Environment Protection Authority v. Waste Recycling and Processing Corporation* [2006] NSWLEC 419.

intergenerational equity and the precautionary principle required that the assessment include an assessment of greenhouse gas emissions arising from the end use of the coal. In *Walker v. Minister for Planning* [2007] NSWLEC 741, Biscoe J held in the Land and Environment Court, that there was a requirement that the Director-General form an opinion as to which aspects of ESD were relevant to a project in determining what had to be included in a report to the minister. In the circumstances of this project (a proposed residential subdivision on a flood constrained coastal plain) the court held that the minister was required to have regard to climate change flood risk. The Court of Appeal disagreed, holding on appeal that while the minister was required to have regard to the public interest, that did not of itself make it mandatory that the minister have regard to one or more of the principles of ESD. This approach is consistent with that taken in other judicial review proceedings, particularly in the federal courts.[104]

3.4   PUBLIC PARTICIPATION AND ENFORCEMENT

Access to the courts and tribunals is an essential requirement for public participation in decision-making and enforcement of environmental laws. In the absence of legislation, the courts apply the common law test for standing to determine which applicants are entitled to initiate judicial review challenges. In 1980, the High Court reformulated the test for standing for a declaration and injunction, holding that the applicant was required to establish a 'special interest' in the subject matter of the action.[105] While the applicant in that case, the Australian Conservation Foundation, failed to convince the court that its interests went beyond what the court described as a mere intellectual or emotional concern, the test as reformulated was not limited to pecuniary or other rights or interests. Subsequent cases have applied the test, while distinguishing the case on its facts. Environmental organizations with a record of involvement in a particular issue or area, and recognition of some kind from government (in particular, inclusion in the decision-making process), have been held to have a special interest sufficient to found standing.[106] The 'special interest' test is similar to the legislative test for standing to challenge Commonwealth decisions provided in the *Administrative Decisions (Judicial*

---

104. *Minister for Planning v. Walker* [2008] NSWCA 224. See *Drake-Brockman v. Minister for Planning* [2007] NSWLEC 490; *Wildlife Preservation Society of Queensland/Proserpine/ Whitsunday Branch Inc v. Minister for the Environment and Heritage* [2006] FCA 736.
105. *Australian Conservation Foundation v. Commonwealth* (1980) 146 CLR 493.
106. *Australian Conservation Foundation v. Minister for Resources and Harris-Daishowa (Australia) Pty Ltd* (1989) 76 LGRA 200; *North Coast Environment Council v. Minister for Resources* (1994) 85 LGERA 270. However, the concern to exclude those with limited interests remains: *OneSteel Manufacturing Pty Ltd v. Whyalla Red Dust Action Group* [2006] SASC 114; *Friends of Elliston v. South Australia & Australian Bight Infrastructure Pty Ltd* [2007] SASC 19.

Review) Act 1977 (Cth), which requires an applicant to show that they are a 'person aggrieved', defined to mean that their interests have been adversely affected.[107]

Increasingly, contemporary laws prescribe standing requirements. Some laws include open standing provisions. Most New South Wales environmental laws, for example, allow 'any person' to initiate proceedings to enforce the law, whether or not any right has been infringed.[108] The EPBC Act applies a modified test, allowing an 'interested person' to initiate proceedings for an injunction to enforce the Act.[109]

The High Court took a significant step in enabling public interest environmental litigation when it endorsed the approach adopted by the Land and Environment Court relating to costs. The usual rule in judicial review and civil enforcement proceedings is that the unsuccessful party pays the costs of the successful party. In *Oshlack v. Richmond River Council* (1994) 82 LGERA 236, Stein J in the Land and Environment Court, considered the authorities and outlined the principles relevant to justify a departure from the normal rule. These principles included: whether the matter was one of public interest; whether the challenge was arguable; whether an important aspect of public law had been determined; whether the matter raised novel and significant issues or provided insights into the operation of the legislation; and what the objectives of the applicant were, namely whether to protect the environment or simply to secure personal profit or gain. The High Court endorsed that approach.[110]

In general, the courts limit their scrutiny of decision-making in judicial review challenges to issues of law. Judicial review of government decision-making at common law focuses on jurisdictional error, and unless the common law writ of *certiorari* is available for error of law on the face of the record, non-jurisdictional errors will not be subject to review. A judicial review court will not examine the merits of a decision: its role is 'to set the limits on the exercise of that discretion, and a decision made within those boundaries cannot be impugned'.[111] An important exception to the courts' unwillingness to review findings of fact is where the court characterizes a particular fact or circumstance as a 'jurisdictional fact'. In such instances, the courts have held that the existence or non-existence of that fact or circumstance is a precondition for the valid exercise of power of the decision-maker, and a reviewing court has the power to determine (on evidence which may

---

107. S. 3(4).
108. The first such legislation was the *Environmental Planning and Assessment Act* 1979 (NSW) s. 123. The most generous provision is s. 252 of the *Protection of the Environment Operations Act* 1997 (NSW) under which any person may bring an action to restrain not just a breach or threatened breach of that act, but a breach or threatened breach of any other act if the breach is likely to cause harm to the environment.
109. An 'interested person' is defined as a person whose interests are affected, or who has engaged in a series of activities for protection or conservation of, or research into, the environment within the previous two years, or, if an organization has objects or purposes which include the protection or conservation of, or research into, the environment: s. 475.
110. *Oshlack v. Richmond River Council* (1998) 193 CLR 72.
111. *Minister for Aboriginal Affairs v. Peko-Wallsend Ltd* (1986) 162 CLR 24 at 40-41, per Mason J.

not have been available to the original decision-maker) whether or not that fact or circumstance exists.[112] Jurisdictional fact review has been a feature of environmental litigation since the late 1990s, and has provided a useful avenue for public interest challenges to decision-making processes. Some of the factual circumstances held to be jurisdictional facts include: whether or not a particular area fell within the statutory definition of a 'place' for the purposes of registration on the national heritage register;[113] whether an application for approval of a proposed mine was 'in respect of development . . . that is likely to significantly affect threatened species';[114] and whether a proposed expansion of a waste treatment plant would produce conditions (in this case, odor emissions) that were 'offensive or repugnant to the occupiers or users of land in the locality'.[115] A conclusion that a particular fact or circumstance is a jurisdictional fact, has resulted in a requirement for more rigorous assessment of environmental impacts, and in some instances has led to a conclusion that a proposed development cannot proceed at all.[116] The process of determining whether a particular fact or circumstance is a jurisdictional fact can raise complex issues of statutory interpretation.[117]

4   CRITICAL SURVEY

The task of determining the extent of the Commonwealth's power to legislate in relation to environmental issues has been complex, and has depended significantly on prevailing views within the High Court as to the scope of the enumerated heads of power in the Constitution. Most significantly, the adoption of a broad reading of the power to legislate with respect to 'external affairs' has enabled the expansion of the ambit of the Commonwealth's legislative power in the context of the dramatic expansion of the range of international environmental law since the early 1970s. The issue, as it has emerged since the 1980s, has not necessarily been defining the limits of the power, but the willingness of the executive government to exercise its powers. There are, however, signs that this may change, as evidenced by the

---

112. Aronson, Dyer & Groves, *supra* n. 88, 227-228.
113. *Australian Heritage Commission v. Mt Isa Mines Ltd* (1997) 187 CLR 297. S. 4(1) of the *Australian Heritage Commission Act* 1975 (Cth) defined eligible places by reference to 'aesthetic, historic, scientific or social significance or other special value for future generations as well as for the present community'.
114. *Timbarra Protection Coalition Inc v. Ross Mining NL* (1999) 46 NSWLR 55: if so, the development application had to be accompanied by a species impact statement under s. 77(3)(d1) of the *Environmental Planning and Assessment Act* 1979.
115. *Corporation of the City of Enfield v. Development Assessment Commission* (2000) 199 CLR 135.
116. *Woolworths Ltd v. Pallas Newco Pty Ltd* [2004] NSWCA 422.
117. A jurisdictional fact argument was rejected in *Anvil Hill Project Watch Association Inc v. Minister for the Environment and Water Resources* [2007] FCA 1480, affirmed on appeal: [2008] FCAFC 3.

decision of the Commonwealth government to take control of managing water allocation and other issues in the Murray Darling Basin.[118]

The courts have also been engaged, through the implementation of principles of judicial review of administrative action, in identifying the limits of judicial scrutiny of administrative decision-making. In this context, much depends on the drafting of the relevant legislation. Where legislation provides, or is read to provide, that the principles of ESD are but one of the considerations to be taken into account, the courts have applied the general principle that the weight to be given to any one consideration is a matter for the decision-maker, subject to the over-riding requirement that the decision not be so unreasonable that no reasonable decision-maker could have so decided. Consideration of principles of ESD does not dictate one course of action to the exclusion of others.[119] In this context, there has been criticism of some of the judicial analysis, particularly in relation to the application of the precautionary principle.[120] However, legislation drafted in such a way as to include ESD as one of a number of objectives to which decision-makers must have regard, places an obstacle in the path of the courts wishing to recognize ESD as the primary objective, not merely one of many often competing considerations.[121]

There has been some reluctance to extend principles facilitating environment litigation. While in *Oshlack v. Richmond River Council* the High Court endorsed the proposition that in appropriate public interest cases, a court could properly decline to order an unsuccessful party to pay the successful party's costs, it has been difficult to persuade subsequent courts to follow this precedent. The absence of an open standing provision in the relevant legislation was held to be sufficient to distinguish the *Oshlack* precedent in *South-West Forest Defence Foundation Inc v. Executive Director, Department of Conservation and Land Management (No 2)* (1998) 101 LGERA 114; and the complexity and novelty of the legal issues raised may in some instances be critical.[122] In *The Wilderness Society Inc v. Minister for the Environment and Water Resources* [2007] FCA 1863, there is a suggestion that the increasingly frequent recourse to the courts, facilitated by open or generous standing provisions, may in fact work against an applicant. There the court held that the following factors were insufficient to displace the respondents' expectations that having successfully opposed the application they would be awarded their costs: the protection of the environment; the proper administration of the legislation; the applicant's altruistic motives; and the importance of not discouraging

---

118. *Water Act* 2007 (Cth).

119. *Bridgetown/Greenbushes Friends of the Forest Inc v. Executive Director of the Department of Conservation and Land Management* (1997) 94 LGERA 380 (Supreme Court of Western Australia).

120. Peel, *supra* n. 99; J. Peel, 'When (Scientific) Rationality Rules: (Mis) Application of the Precautionary Principle in Australian Mobile Phone Tower Cases', *J. Env. L.* 19, no. 1 (2007): 103-120.

121. Bates, *supra* n. 5, 128.

122. *Save the Ridge Inc v. Commonwealth* [2006] FCAFC 51.

access to the courts 'could be common to many other proceedings challenging matters of public administration or matters concerning the protection of the environment'.[123] Reluctance to decline to order costs is consistent with a willingness to order security for costs, even in a context of legislative encouragement of public interest environmental litigation.[124]

5   THE WAY FORWARD

5.1   KEY CHALLENGES

The most significant challenge to any judicial contribution to development of principles of environmental governance is the inability of the courts and tribunals to initiate cases, and their dependence on the parties both to present opportunities and to continue matters until judicial resolution. The High Court has some control over its workload through the requirement that it grant special leave to appeal, and its capacity to transfer matters commenced in its original jurisdiction to the Federal Court for determination. However, this is a negative control and does not ensure that that court, or any other, is presented with appropriate cases to develop principles of sustainability. The Australian Network of Environmental Defenders Offices Inc (ANEDO), which consists of nine independently constituted and managed community environmental law centers located in each State and Territory of Australia, plays a vital role in this regard. Each Environmental Defenders Office (EDO) provides legal representation and advice, and to the extent that resources are available, ensures that appropriate cases are brought to the courts and tribunals.[125]

Courts and tribunals must apply the law as enacted. While there is always room for interpretation, legislation which clearly identifies the need to consider or promote sustainable development will be implemented by the courts. Tribunals and courts engaged in merits review of decisions of local government authorities or other agencies will generally apply the policies formulated by those agencies. If those policies are comprehensive, their application can promote good environmental outcomes.[126]

A restraint on judicial activism comes in the awareness of the courts of the fine line between enforcement of legality and limits on executive power, and what the executive might perceive as an unwarranted judicial interference. It is not unknown

---

123. [2007] FCA 1863 at [31].
124. *Melville v. Craig Nolan & Associates Pty Ltd* [2002] NSWCA 32.
125. Links to each EDO is at ANEDO, 'EDO Home', <www.edo.org.au>, 22 July 2008.
126. See, e.g., *Northcape Properties Pty Ltd v. District Council of Yorke Peninsula* [2008] SASC 57, upholding the application of a policy requiring an erosion buffer for coastal development, and *Charles & Howard Pty Ltd v. Redland Shire Council* [2007] QCA 200, upholding a requirement to consider the impact of climate change on sea levels when considering where to locate a proposed development.

for legislation to be passed to override unwelcome judicial decisions.[127] Self-imposed judicial restraint may be equally significant in limiting the potential judicial contribution, and some have argued that consequently, it is not realistic to rely on the judiciary to bring about environmental change, particularly in emerging areas such as climate change.[128]

A further constraint comes in the form of legislative attempts to limit or preclude judicial review in the form of privative, or ouster clauses. Some provisions are intended to deny judicial review, while others are drafted to limit judicial review to challenges brought within three months.[129] The Australian courts generally adopt a strict construction of such clauses, reading them subject to a presumption that they will not generally exclude review, in particular where there is jurisdictional error or breach of natural justice.[130]

5.2   KEY OPPORTUNITIES

The major developments in environmental legislation which have taken place since the 1970s, starting with the imposition of EIA, licensing requirements and enhanced opportunities for public participation both in the assessment process and in enforcement, were accompanied by a recognition in some jurisdictions that environmental litigation differs from other types of litigation. In 1985, the then Chief Justice of New South Wales held that the open standing provision in the *Environmental Planning and Assessment Act* 1979 (NSW), combined with the objects of the legislation, made 'it apparent that the task of the court is to administer social justice in the enforcement of the legislative scheme of the Act . . . a task that

---

127. Some examples include legislation to overcome the decisions in *Parramatta City Council v. Hale* (1982) 47 LGRA 319; *Drake & Ors; Auburn Council v. Minister for Planning and Anor; Collex Pty Ltd* [2003] NSWLEC 270. See discussion in Hon. J. P. McClellan, 'The Executive and the Judiciary: A Potential for Conflict', <www.lawlink.nsw.gov.au/lawlink/lec/ll_lec.nsf/pages/LEC_speeches_and_papers#mcclellan>, 13 May 2005. The Queensland government legislated to approve the proposed mining lease following the successful appeal in *Queensland Conservation Council Inc v. Xstrata Coal Queensland Pty Ltd* [2007] QCA 338: see C. McGrath, 'The Xstrata Case', in *Climate Law in Australia 2007*, ed. T. Bonyhady & P. Christoff (Sydney: Federation Press, 2008), 227. As McGrath notes, this was the second occasion on which Xstrata has had the benefit of legislative intervention following an adverse judicial ruling: *Lansen & Ors v. Northern Territory Minister for Mines and Energy & Ors* [2007] NTSC 28.
128. J. Peel, 'The Role of Climate Change Litigation in Australia's Response to Global Warming', *EPLJ* 24 (2007): 101.
129. Some examples of the latter are in planning legislation, *Environmental Planning and Assessment Act* 1979 (NSW) ss 35 and 101, and in water legislation, *Water Management Act* 2000 (NSW) s. 47, imposing a time limit of three months.
130. *Plaintiff S157/2002 v. Commonwealth* (2003) 211 CLR 476. Provisions which purport to impose a time limit on seeking judicial review will usually be read to as to allow a challenge on any basis within the time period, and as not precluding challenge where there is jurisdictional error after that period: *Woolworths Ltd v. Pallas Newco Pty Ltd* [2004] NSWCA 422; *Bodruddaza v. Minister for Immigration and Multicultural Affairs* [2007] HCA 14.

travels far beyond administering justice inter partes'.[131] McClellan J, former Chief Judge of the Land and Environment Court, has argued that legislative moves to broaden standing to challenge the lawfulness of decision-making have created a greater expectation that there could be interference by a court, and:

> ... the fact that having accepted a role for judges in administrative review of environmental decisions, the granting of authority to judges to intervene and declare a decision by the executive invalid has not been seen as such a significant intrusion into the role of the executive government.[132]

The increasing incorporation into environmental legislation of the principles of ESD, whether as objects or as objectives, provides further opportunity for the courts and tribunals, both in providing a model for good decision-making in merits review, and in setting the boundaries and expectations for decision-makers in judicial review.[133]

BIBLIOGRAPHY

Aronson, M., B. Dyer & M. Groves. *Judicial Review of Administrative Action.* 3rd ed. Sydney: Lawbook Co, 2004.

AUSTLII. 'Australasian Legal Information Institute'. <www.austlii.edu.au>, 21 July 2008.

Australian Network of Environmental Defenders Offices. 'EDO Home'. <www.edo.org.au>, 22 July 2008.

Bartlett, R. *Native Title in Australia.* 2nd ed. Sydney: LexisNexis Butterworths, 2004.

Bates, G. *Environmental Law in Australia.* 6th ed. Sydney: LexisNexis Butterworths, 2006.

Bonyhady, T. & P. Christoff (eds). *Climate Law in Australia 2007.* Sydney: Federation Press 2008.

Carney, G. *The Constitutional Systems of the Australian States and Territories.* Cambridge: Cambridge University Press, 2006.

Clark, D. *Principles of Australian Public Law.* 2nd ed. Sydney: LexisNexis Butterworths, 2007.

Commonwealth Government. *Ecologically Sustainable Development* Discussion Paper. Canberra: AGPS, 1990.

---

131. *F. Hannan Pty Ltd v. Electricity Commission (NSW) (No. 3)* (1985) 66 LGRA 306 at 313, per Street CJ.
132. McClellan J *supra* n. 127, 9.
133. See in particular papers by Hon. B. Preston SC, Chief Judge of the Land and Environment Court, including 'Judicial Implementation of the Principles of Ecologically Sustainable Development' and 'Administrative Law in an Environmental Context: An Update', available at LawLink, 'Speeches and Papers', <www.lawlink.nsw.gov.au/law link/lec/ll_lec.nsf/pages/LEC_speeches_and_papers#preston>, 22 July 2008.

Connell, D. *Water Politics in the Murray-Darling Basin*. Sydney: Federation Press, 2007.

Cork, S. et al. 'Biodiversity: Theme commentary'. <www.environment. gov.au/soe/2006/publications/commentaries/biodiversity/pressures.html>, 19 December 2007.

Crawford, J. & B. Opeskin. *Australian Courts of Law*. 4th ed. Oxford: Oxford University Press, 2004.

Department of the Environment, Water, Heritage and the Arts. 'Australia: State of the Environment 1996'. <www.environment.gov.au/soe/1996/index.html>, 17 December 2007.

Department of the Environment, Water, Heritage and the Arts. 'Environment Home'. <www.environment.gov.au>, 22 July 2008.

Department of the Environment, Water, Heritage and the Arts. 'Intergovernmental Agreement on the Environment'. <www.environment.gov.au/esd/national/ igae/index.html>, 22 July 2008.

Fisher, D.E. *Australian Environmental Law*. Sydney: Thomson Lawbook Co, 2003.

Fowler, R.J. 'Environmental Law and its Administration in Australia'. *Environmental and Planning Law Journal* 1 (1984): 10-49.

Hennessy, K. et al. 'Australia and New Zealand'. In *Climate Change 2007: Impacts, Adaptation and Vulnerability. Contribution of Working Group II to the Fourth Assessment Report of the Intergovernmental Panel on Climate Change*, edited by M.L. Parry et al. Cambridge: Cambridge University Press, 2008.

LawLink. 'Speeches and Papers'. <www.lawlink.nsw.gov.au/lawlink/lec/ ll_lec.nsf/pages/LEC_speeches_and_papers#preston>, 22 July 2008.

Lipman, Z. & G. Bates. *Pollution Law in Australia*. Sydney: LexisNexis Butterworths, 2002.

Lyster, R. 'Chasing Down the Climate Change Footprint of the Private and Public Sectors: Forces Converge'. *Environmental and Planning Law Journal* 24 (2007): 281-321.

Lyster, R., et al. *Environmental and Planning Law in New South Wales*. Sydney: Federation Press, 2007.

Macintosh, A. 'The Greenhouse Trigger: Where did it go and What is its Future?'. In *Climate Law in Australia 2007*, edited by T. Bonyhady & P. Christoff. Sydney: Federation Press, 2008.

Mason, Sir A. 'The Evolving Role and Function of the High Court'. In *The Australian Federal Judicial System*, edited by B. Opeskin & F. Wheeler. Melbourne: Melbourne University Press, 2000.

McClellan, P. Hon. J. 'The Executive and the Judiciary: A Potential for Conflict'. <www.lawlink.nsw.gov.au/lawlink/lec/ll_lec.nsf/pages/LEC_speeches_and_ papers#mcclellan>, 13 May 2005.

McDonald, J. 'A Risky Climate for Decision-making: The Liability of Development Authorities for Climate Change Impacts'. *Environmental and Planning Law Journal* 24 (2007): 405-416.

McGrath, C. 'Key Concepts of the Environment Protection and Biodiversity Conservation Act 1999 (Cth)'. *Environmental and Planning Law Journal* 22 (2005): 20-38.

McGrath, C. 'The Xstrata Case'. In *Climate Law in Australia 2007*. In *Climate Law in Australia 2007*, edited by T. Bonyhady & P. Christoff. Sydney: Federation Press, 2008.

O'Hare, C.W. 'A History of Mining in Australia'. *Australian Law Journal* 45 (1971): 281-287.

Opeskin, B. & F. Wheeler (eds). *The Australian Federal Judicial System*. Melbourne: Melbourne University Press, 2000.

Parry, M.L. et al. (eds). *Climate Change 2007: Impacts, Adaptation and Vulnerability, Working Group II Contribution to Intergovernmental Panel on Climate Change Fourth Assessment Report*. Cambridge: Cambridge University Press, 2008.

Peel, J. *The Precautionary Principle in Practice: Environmental Decision-Making and Scientific Uncertainty*. Sydney: Federation Press, 2005.

Peel, J. 'The Role of Climate Change Litigation in Australia's Response to Global Warming'. *Environmental and Planning Law Journal* 24 (2007): 90-105.

Peel, J. 'When (Scientific) Rationality Rules: (Mis) Application of the Precautionary Principle in Australian Mobile Phone Tower Cases'. *Journal of Environmental Law* 19, no. 1 (2007): 103-120.

Preston, B. Hon. J. 'Judicial Implementation of the Principles of Ecologically Sustainable Development'. <www.lawlink.nsw.gov.au/lawlink/lec/ll_lec.nsf/pages/LEC_speeches_and_papers#preston>, 22 July 2008.

Preston, B. Hon. J. 'Administrative Law in an Environmental Context: An Update'. <www.lawlink.nsw.gov.au/lawlink/lec/ll_lec.nsf/pages/LEC_speeches_and_papers#preston>, 22 July 2008.

Rothwell, D. & B. Boer. 'From the Franklin to Berlin: The Internationalisation of Australian Environmental Law and Policy'. *Sydney Law Review* 17 (1995): 242-277.

TABLE OF LEGISLATION

Commonwealth

Administrative Appeals Tribunal Act 1975
Administrative Decisions (Judicial Review) Act 1977
Australia Act 1986
Environment Protection and Biodiversity Conservation Act 1999
Environment Protection (Sea Dumping) Act 1981
Export Act 1983
Federal Court of Australia Act 1976
Fisheries Management Act 1991
Judiciary Act 1903

Native Title Act 1993
Ozone Protection Act 1989
Privy Council (Limitations of Appeals) Act 1968
Privy Council (Appeals from the High Court) Act 1975
Protection of the Sea (Prevention of Pollution from Ships) Act 1983
Water Act 2007
Export Control (Unprocessed Wood) Regulations 1986

New South Wales

Civil Liability Act 2002
Constitution Act 1902
Crown Lands Act 1989
Environmental Planning and Assessment Act 1979
Fisheries Management Act 1994
Forestry Act 1916
Land and Environment Court Act 1979
Local Government Act 1993
Mining Act 1992
Protection of the Environment Administration Act 1991
Protection of the Environment Operations Act 1997
Water Management Act 2000

Queensland

Civil Liability Act 2003
Constitution of Queensland 2001
Environmental Protection Act 1994
Fisheries Act 1994
Forestry Act 1959
Integrated Planning Act 1997
Land Act 1994
Local Government Act 1993
Mineral Resources Act 1989
Water Act 2000

South Australia

Civil Liability Act 1936
Constitution Act 1934
Crown Lands Act 1929
Development Act 1993
Environment Protection Act 1993
Environment, Resources and Development Court Act 1993
Fisheries Management Act 2007

Forestry Act 1950
Local Government Act 1999
Mining Act 1971
Water Resources Act 1997

Tasmania

Civil Liability Act 2002
Constitution Act 1934
Crown Lands Act 1976
Environmental Management and Pollution Control Act 1994
Fisheries Act 1959
Forest Practices Act 1985
Land Use Planning and Approvals Act 1993
Local Government Act 1993
Mineral Resources Development Act 1995
Resource Management and Planning Appeal Tribunal Act 1993
Water Management Act 1999

Victoria

Conservation, Forests and Lands Act 1987
Constitution Act 1975
Environment Protection Act 1970
Fisheries Act 1995
Land Act 1958
Local Government Act 1995
Mineral Resources Development Act 1990
Planning and Environment Act 1987
Victorian Civil and Administrative Tribunal Act 1988
Water Act 1989
Wrongs Act 1958

Western Australia

Civil Liability Act 2002
Constitution Act 1889
Conservation and Land Management Act 1984
Environmental Protection Act 1986
Fish Resources Management Act 1994
Land Administration Act 1997
Mining Act 1978
Rights in Water and Irrigation Act 1914
State Administrative Tribunal Act 2004
Town Planning and Development Act 1928

United Kingdom

Australia Act 1986
Australian Constitutions Act 1850
Commonwealth of Australia Constitution Act 1900
New South Wales Act 1823
Town and Country Planning Act 1932

TABLE OF CASES

Environment Protection Authority v. Waste Recycling and Processing Corporation [2006] NSWLEC 419

Friends of Elliston v. South Australia & Australian Bight Infrastructure Pty Ltd [2007] SASC 19

Friends of Hinchinbrook Society Inc v. Minister for the Environment (1997) 93 LGERA 23

Graham Barclay Oysters Pty Ltd v. Ryan (2002) 125 LGERA 1

Gray v. Minister for Planning (2006) 152 LGERA 258

Greenpeace Australia Ltd v. Redbank Power Company Ltd (1994) 86 LGERA 143

F. Hannan Pty Ltd v. Electricity Commission (NSW) (No. 3) (1985) 66 LGRA 306

Re Humane Society International and Minister for the Environment (2006) 93 ALD 640

Hutchinson Telecommunications (Australia) Pty Ltd v. Baulkham Hills Shire Council [2004] NSWLEC 104

Re The International Fund for Animal Welfare (Aust) Pty Ltd and Minister for Environment and Heritage (2005) 93 ALD 594

Lansen & Ors v. Northern Territory Minister for Mines and Energy & Ors [2007] NTSC 28

Leatch v. National Parks and Wildlife Service (1993) 81 LGERA 270

Lipohar v. R (1999) 200 CLR 485

Mabo v. Queensland (No. 2) (1992) 175 CLR 1

Melville v. Craig Nolan & Associates Pty Ltd [2002] NSWCA

Minister for Aboriginal Affairs v. Peko-Wallsend Ltd (1986) 162 CLR 24

Minister for Planning v. Walker [2008] NSWCA 224

Murphyores Ltd v. Commonwealth (1976) 136 CLR 1

Murrumbidgee Groundwater Preservation Association v. Minister for Natural Resources [2004] NSWLEC 122

New South Wales v. Commonwealth [2006] HCA 52

Nicholls v. Director-General of National Parks and Wildlife (1994) 84 LGERA 397

North Coast Environment Council v. Minister for Resources (1994) 85 LGERA 270

Northcape Properties Pty Ltd v. District Council of Yorke Peninsula [2008] SASC 57

Northern Australian Aboriginal Legal Aid Service Inc v. Bradley (2004) 218 CLR 416

Northern Territory of Australia v. Arnhem Land Aboriginal Land Trust [2008] HCA 29

OneSteel Manufacturing Pty Ltd v. Whyalla Red Dust Action Group [2006] SASC 114

Oshlack v. Richmond River Council (1994) 82 LGERA 236

Oshlack v. Richmond River Council (1998) 193 CLR 72

Parramatta City Council v. Hale (1982) 47 LGRA 319

Punterio v. Water Administration Ministerial Corp (1999) 104 LGERA 419

R v. Kirby; ex parte Boilermakers' Society of Australia (1956) 94 CLR 254

Re Dixon and Australian Fisheries Management Authority [2000] AATA 442
Re Judiciary and Navigation Acts 1903-1920 (1921) 29 CLR 257
Re McBain; ex parte Australian Catholic Bishops Conference (2002) 209 CLR 372
Rylands v. Fletcher (1866) LR 1 Ex 265
Save the Ridge Inc v. Commonwealth [2006] FCAFC 51
L Shaddock & Associates Pty Ltd v. Parramatta City Council (1981) 150 CLR 225
Skye Environmental Services Pty Ltd v. Frankston City Council [2004] VCAT 682
SmithKline & French Laboratories (Australia) Ltd v. Commonwealth (1991) 173
    CLR 194
*South West Forest Defence Foundation v. Department of Conservation and Land
    Management (No. 2)* (1998) 101 LGERA 114
Sutherland Shire Council v. Heyman (1985) 157 CLR 424
*Taralga Landscape Guardians Inc v. Minister for Planning and RES Southern
    Cross Pty Ltd* [2007] NSWLEC 59
Telstra Corporation Ltd v. Hornsby Shire Council (2006) 146 LGERA 10, [2006]
    NSWLEC 133
The Wilderness Society Inc v. Minister for the Environment and Water Resources
    [2007] FCA 1863
Timbarra Protection Coalition Inc v. Ross Mining NL (1999) 46 NSWLR 55
*Trust Company of Australia Ltd (trading as Stockland Property Management) v.
    Skiwing Pty Ltd (trading as Café Tiffany's)* [2006] NSWCA 184
Walker v. Minister for Planning [2007] NSWLEC 741
Western Australia v. Ward (2002) 213 CLR 1
The Wilderness Society Inc v. Minister for the Environment and Water Resources
    (2007) 96 ALD 655
*Wildlife Preservation Society of Queensland/Proserpine/Whitsunday Branch Inc v.
    Minister for the Environment and Heritage* [2006] FCA 736
Woolworths Ltd v. Pallas Newco Pty Ltd [2004] NSWCA 422
Yanner v. Eaton (1999) 201 CLR 351

ABBREVIATIONS

AAT	Administrative Appeals Tribunal
ANEDO	Australian Network of Environmental Defenders Office Inc
AUSTLII	Australasian Legal Information Institute
DEWHA	Department of the Environment, Water, Heritage and the Arts
EDO	Environmental Defenders Office
EIA	Environmental Impact Assessment
EPBC Act	Environment Protection and Biodiversity Act 1999 (Cth)
ESD	Ecologically Sustainable Development
IGAE	Intergovernmental Agreement on the Environment

Chapter 11

New Zealand

*Klaus Bosselmann**

1   INTRODUCTION

New Zealand is an island nation situated in the South-West Pacific comprising two main islands, the North Island (Te Ika-a-Maui) and the South Island (Te Wai Pounamu) and an array of smaller islands.[1] New Zealand's relatively small population of just over 4.2 million people[2] is fairly multicultural, 15% being Maori who are the Tangata Whenua, or indigenous people, of New Zealand.[3] With 270,500 km[2] of territory stretching 1,500 km in length, New Zealand is a long, narrow country defined by its outstanding geographical features and diverse range of landscapes. The North Island is characterized by its rolling hill farmland and active volcanoes; while the mountainous South Island is divided by the Southern Alps which rise to 3000 m and continue most of the island's length, creating rainforests to the west and farmlands to the east.

---

*   I am indebted to Mia Koning for her manifold assistance.

1.   These smaller islands include Great Barrier Island, Stewart Island/Rakiura, Kermadec Islands, Auckland Islands and the Chatham Islands. New Zealand also has jurisdiction in Tokelau, Cook Islands and Ross Dependencies in Antarctica.
2.   To view an updated population projection, see Statistics New Zealand, 'Estimated resident population of New Zealand', <www.stats.govt.nz/populationclock.htm>, 17 September 2008.
3.   For latest Census data, see Statistics New Zealand, '2006 Cencus', <www.stats.govt.nz/census/census-outputs/default.htm>, 12 December 2007.

Louis J. Kotzé and Alexander R. Paterson (eds), *The Role of the Judiciary in Environmental Governance: Comparative Perspectives*, pp. 355–380.
© 2009 Kluwer Law International BV, The Netherlands.

A further defining aspect of New Zealand's geography is its lengthy coastline, estimated between 15,000 km and 18,000 km, and its claim to the world's fourth largest Exclusive Economic Zone (EEZ) at 4,000,000 km^2.[4] New Zealand's distinctive geographical features form an integral part of its environment and the determination of its immediate environmental concerns. The changing environment across the country presents New Zealand with the benefit of using, and the challenge of sustaining and preserving, the range of available natural resources.

2   ENVIRONMENTAL ISSUES

New Zealand's environmental issues tend to be less about remedying existing environmental problems and more about the preservation and sustainable use of natural and physical resources. Its fortunate geographic and demographic make-up has meant that many common environmental issues that plague other countries have not been felt as severely. The major concerns for New Zealand revolve around the use and management of its natural resources and, as an agricultural nation, lessening this industry's impact on land. Still, as a growing, evolving country, New Zealand's environmental advantages may begin to shift, giving rise to concerns over air and water pollution, the cost of urbanization and global warming.

New Zealand's physical remoteness from other countries, low population density and immediate proximity to the sea means that any problems of air pollution are typically confined to specific urban areas, where traffic pollution and wood burning fires contribute significantly to the degradation of air quality.[5] The cause of this pollution has been identified as being generally residential, and as the population increases and urban areas continue to expand, air quality will come under increasing pressure.[6] Recognising that air pollution does not necessarily manifest visually and that it is not enough to be content with pollution simply being blown elsewhere, the recent introduction of a national environmental standard for air quality demonstrates an attempt to lessen New Zealand's atmospheric impact.[7]

The abundance and importance of New Zealand's water resources require a high level of protection and management. The ability to sustain its marine resources will be a crucial part of New Zealand's future. With such an accessible coastline and large EEZ, the obvious economic opportunities must be understood within a wider context that recognizes the incredible biodiversity of plants and animals, and the delicate balance that maintains that wealth of life. The challenge

---

4. B. Mansfield, 'Law of the sea', in *Te Ara: The Encyclopedia of New Zealand*, ed. MCH (Wellington: MCH, 2003), <www.TeAra.govt.nz/EarthSeaAndSky/OceanStudyAndConservation/LawOfTheSea/en>, 12 December 2007.
5. ME, *Proposed National Environmental Standards for Air Quality: Resource Management Act Section 32 Analysis of Costs and Benefits* (Wellington: ME, 2004).
6. *Ibid.*
7. Resource Management (National Environmental Standards Relating to Certain Air Pollutants, Dioxins, and Other Toxics) Regulations 2004 (SR 2004/309).

to sustain the potential for fishing, aquaculture, tourism, mining and biotechnology as facilitated by marine resources, will continue to be an important environmental consideration in New Zealand.

The future production, consumption and management of energy are acknowledged environmental concerns for New Zealand, as for all countries. The implementation of new legislative regimes and the development of a national environmental standard for electrical transmission reflect the government's recognition of the growing need to regulate and balance energy consumption.

New Zealand has a large agricultural sector which exports its products all over the world. The cost to the environment to support this farming lifestyle has already been considerable. The problems of farm waste, pests and weeds, contribute significantly to the slow deterioration of the New Zealand environment, and the mass clearance of native forests, loss of biodiversity and soil degradation, continue to be pressing environmental concerns.

New Zealand produces 0.2% of the world's carbon emissions.[8] Regardless of its relatively small contribution, the global nature of climate change will touch and affect New Zealand as a small trading nation which is dependent on other markets for survival. Even more importantly, the consequences for its natural environment demand that climate change be recognized as a long-term, strategic issue. As an example of its willingness to mitigate emissions, New Zealand has signed and ratified the Kyoto Protocol,[9] but its impending failure to meet its commitments highlights the need for a more serious understanding of what this entails.[10]

3   PRINCIPAL ENVIRONMENTAL LAWS

The primary source of environmental law in New Zealand is legislation. Over the past twenty years, New Zealand has dramatically reformed its environmental and resource management laws. The fundamental environmental laws can now be found in comprehensive statutes that outline what responsibilities exist and who is accountable for undertaking them.[11] Before this reform, resource-use laws were scattered and developed in reaction to environmental issues as they arose.[12] The result of these uncoordinated regimes was an immense collection of laws that dealt with individual aspects of resource-use in isolation from one another.

---

8. *Per capita* New Zealand's carbon emissions are among the highest in the world.
9. Kyoto Protocol (1997) 37 *ILM* 22. The *Climate Change Response Act* 2004 had the effect of ratifying the Kyoto Protocol.
10. Castalia, *Greenhouse Gas Emission Policies: Is there a way forward? Report to greenhouse policy coalition* (Castalia Strategic Advisors, September 2005). K. Bosselmann, 'Achieving the Goal and Missing the Target: New Zealand's Implementation of the Kyoto Protocol', *MJICEL* 2 (2006): 75-106.
11. D. Nolan (ed.), *Environmental and Resource Management Law*, 3rd ed. (Wellington: LexisNexis, 2005), 37.
12. G.W.R. Palmer, *Environment – The International Challenge: Essays* (Wellington: VUP, 1995), 150.

The staggered development of environmental laws meant the absence of any underlying principle or approach and inconsistencies in the general standards applied.[13] The spectrum of institutional structures that evolved, along with their various mechanisms for dispute settlement, contributed to the creation of a body of environmental law that lacked any real cohesion and which ineffectively dealt with environmental issues as a whole. Government review of these statutes in the late eighties and the emergence of international influences such as the Brundtland Report,[14] led to a shift from a primarily reactive, protective approach, towards integrated resource management and sustainability.[15]

3.1   RESOURCE MANAGEMENT ACT 1991

In July 1988, the Resource Management Law Reform project began and the eventual result was the *Resource Management Act* 1991 (RMA) which now exists as the primary source of New Zealand's resource-use law.[16] It had the effect of consolidating most of the laws relating to management of natural and physical resources into one statute and establishing a common purpose and process for resource management.[17] The RMA governs planning and development of resources on private and public land, requiring parties to obtain a resource consent for any activity that would otherwise violate provisions in the Act.[18]

One of the most distinctive features of the RMA is that it establishes the promotion of sustainable management as its overarching purpose. Although this signals a new approach to environmental law by making it a legal imperative that the management of all physical and natural resources be sustainable, one possible drawback of the RMA is its use of the term 'management'. Sustainable management, as used in the RMA, is narrower in focus than the broader, and preferable concept of 'sustainable development' as described in the Brundtland Report. The narrower concept of sustainable management focuses only on the environmental effects of activities.[19]

Since the RMA, subsequent environmental legislation has been drafted to ensure a level of consistency with the overall purpose encompassed in the Act. Section 5 sets out the purpose of the Act and it provides as follows:

> (1) The purpose of this Act is to promote the sustainable management of natural and physical resources.

---

13. *Ibid.*
14. Report of the World Commission on Environment and Development 1987 (Brundtland Report).
15. Nolan, *supra* n. 11, 85-87.
16. Palmer, *supra* n. 12, 150-161; see also D. Young, *Values as Law: The History and Efficacy of the Resource Management Act* (Wellington: Milne, 2001).
17. Nolan, *supra* n. 11, 94-95.
18. For more information on resource consents, see R. Harris, *Handbook of Environmental Law* (Wellington: RNZ, 2004), 87-97.
19. ME, *Environment Update Series, Information Sheet No. 6* (Wellington: ME, 1991) cited in Nolan, *supra* n. 11, 93-94.

(2) In this Act, 'sustainable management' means managing the use, development, and protection of natural and physical resources in a way, or at a rate, which enables people and communities to provide for their social, economic, and cultural well-being and for their health and safety while –

(a) Sustaining the potential of natural and physical resources (excluding minerals) to meet the reasonably foreseeable needs of future generations; and

(b) Safeguarding the life-supporting capacity of air, water, soil and ecosystems; and

(c) Avoiding, remedying, or mitigating any adverse effects of activities on the environment.

This section has become the subject of extensive debate and the different interpretations of section 5 affect the strength of the Act's purpose of promoting 'sustainable management'. The application of section 5 of the RMA by the courts (particularly the Environment Court) has played, and will continue to play, a decisive role in the successful development of New Zealand's environmental law. This is further explored below.

Section 5 is supported by the guiding principles in sections 6, 7 and 8 which have effectively created a hierarchy of considerations to be contemplated by decision makers. Section 6 sets out matters of national importance to be recognized and provided for; covering the preservation and protection of outstanding natural features, indigenous flora and fauna, and coastal environments; and making special provision for recognising the relationship between the Maori and their ancestral lands. Section 7 provides a list of 'other matters' that must be given particular regard to, including: *kaitiakitanga*;[20] the intrinsic value of ecosystems;[21] and the efficient use and development of physical resources.[22] Section 8 is considered a special provision aiming to incorporate the principles of the Treaty of Waitangi which is New Zealand's founding document. The Treaty is a broad statement of principles on which the British and Maori made a political compact to found a nation State and build a government in New Zealand. The principles, such as good faith, partnership and active protection, are held to be defining characteristics of the relationship between the Maori people and the Crown (the Treaty partners). Section 8 requires all persons exercising functions and powers under the Act to take into account the principles of the Treaty.[23]

---

20. See the RMA 1991, s. 7(a). Kaitiakitanga, a Maori concept, has been translated to mean 'guardianship' or 'stewardship' for the purposes of the RMA. For more information on Maori concepts see S.M. Mead, *Tikanga Maori: Living by Maori Values* (Wellington: Huia, 2003).
21. See the RMA 1991, s. 7(d).
22. *Ibid.*, s. 7(aa).
23. The principles of the Treaty are the key characteristics imputed into the relationship between the Maori people and the Crown as Treaty partners. For more information see, J. Hayward, 'The Principles of the Treaty of Waitangi' (appendix), in *Rangahaua Whanui National Overview Report*, ed. A. Ward, vol. 3 (Wellington: Waitangi Tribunal, 1997).

The RMA made other important changes. The Act reformed the old rules of *locus standi* making, at least theoretically, the new processes more inclusive and contestable by allowing open access to the planning process and the courts.[24] The Act divides responsibility between central government, regional councils and territorial authorities aiming for integration through the use of national, regional and district policy statements and plans.[25] Compatibility of local plans with national policies and consistency across local governments is an important aspect of the kind of integrated management the RMA seeks to promote. The Act provides for the issuing of National Environmental Statements (NES), allowing the prescription of national standards relating to certain discharges but, despite their potential to be enormously useful, to date, only one NES has been issued.[26]

Later amendments to the RMA established a specialist Environment Court with jurisdiction to hear appeals in respect of resource consent applications, requirements and policy statements and plans. The court is more flexible in its consideration of evidence and has the ability to enforce compliance with the Act through enforcement orders.[27]

3.2   ENERGY EFFICIENCY AND CONSERVATION ACT 2000

The purpose of this act is to promote energy efficiency, energy conservation and the use of renewable sources of energy.[28] Following from the RMA, there is some provision in section 6 to take into account the reasonably foreseeable needs of future generations. It establishes the Energy Efficiency and Conservation Authority and legislates for a National Energy Efficiency and Conservation Strategy which is essentially a statement of the government's policies, objectives and means of achieving targets in relation to energy.[29]

3.3   HAZARDOUS SUBSTANCES AND NEW ORGANISMS ACT 1996

A legislative regime for the introduction of new species and the control of hazardous substances was implemented in 1996. Its purpose is: 'to protect the

24. For a critical analysis of access to environmental justice see D. Grinlinton, 'Contemporary Environmental Law in New Zealand', in *Environmental Law for a Sustainable Society*, ed. K. Bosselmann & D. Grinlinton, vol. 1 (Auckland: NZCEL, 2002), 19 *et seq.*
25. For more information about National Policy Statement, National Environmental Standards, Regional and District Plans, see Nolan, *supra* n. 11, 161-178.
26. In September 2004, a NES dealing with air pollutants was issued, creating fourteen national standards (*supra* n. 7); NES relating to human drinking water, water measuring devices, telecommunications facilities and electricity transmission are currently being developed. For more information see ME, 'National Environmental Standards', <www.mfe.govt.nz/laws/standards/index.html>, 12 December 2007.
27. See the RMA 1991, Parts XI-XII.
28. See the *Energy Efficiency and Conservation Act* 2000, s. 5.
29. See the *Energy Efficiency and Conservation Act* 2000, ss 8-12.

environment, and the health and safety of people and communities, by preventing or managing the adverse effects of hazardous substances and new organisms'.[30] Section 5 expresses sustainable management principles similar to those in the RMA, and account for the sustainability of flora and fauna and the intrinsic value of ecosystems is contained in section 6. The *Biosecurity Act* 1993 provides further protection and regulation of unwanted pests in New Zealand.

3.4   Fisheries Act 1996

Fishing in New Zealand is regulated by a Quota Management System (QMS) which dictates the total allowable catch for a given species which is allocated in the form of catch permits. This process is guided by sustainable management principles similar to those present in the RMA, with the 'utilization of fisheries resources' being balanced against 'ensuring sustainability'.[31] Certain environmental principles and sustainability measures are prescribed and consistency with international obligations and Treaty settlements is mandated.[32]

3.5   Crown Minerals Act 1991

The RMA, quite significantly, excludes governance of mineral resources.[33] The allocation of mineral permits and access rights fall under the *Crown Minerals Act* 1991. It allows for the extraction of Crown minerals in return for the payment of royalties but does not directly address environmental issues or provide for public processes in relation to mining activities. There is no mention of any guiding sustainable principles as in most other environmental legislation. However, the RMA still governs the 'environmental externalities'[34] of mining activities, allowing room for sustainable management, if not in the depletion of the resource, then at least in respect of managing its environmental impacts.

3.6   Forests Act 1949

The *Forests Act* was amended in 1993 to promote the 'sustainable forest management of indigenous forest' situated on private land using sustainable management plans set up under Part III of the Act.[35] Indigenous forests located on

---

30. See the *Hazardous Substances and New Organisms Act* 1996, s. 4.
31. See the *Fisheries Act* 1987, s. 8.
32. *Ibid.*, ss 5, 9 and 11.
33. See the RMA 1991, s. 5(2)(a). The depletion of mineral resources is excluded from intergenerational considerations.
34. K. Bosselmann & D. Grinlinton (eds), *Environmental Law for a Sustainable Society*, vol. 1 (Auckland: NZCEL, 2002), 32.
35. See the *Forests Act* 1949, Part 3A.

public land typically fall under the management mandate of the Department of Conservation.

3.7   Environment Act 1986

Under this act, the Ministry for the Environment (ME) and the Office of the Parliamentary Commissioner for the Environment (PCE) are established.

3.8   Conservation Act 1987

This act creates the Department of Conservation, New Zealand Conservation Authority, and Conservation Boards. It further prescribes broad principles for managing and protecting conservation areas which can be established by the Minister of Conservation, according the special legal status of the land.[36]

4   INSTITUTIONS AND GOVERNANCE STRUCTURES

New Zealand is a sovereign, independent, unitary State with a constitutional monarchy, responsible government and a unicameral legislature.[37] As a former colony, New Zealand's legal system and constitutional make-up has largely been taken directly from the Westminster system of the United Kingdom (UK). Accordingly, law derives from two main sources, statute law and common law. Government policy will generally be implemented through legislation and the courts are given the task of interpreting and applying those laws. The courts are bound by the precedent of higher courts in a specific hierarchical structure. New Zealand takes after the UK again in that its Constitution is not contained in one clearly identifiable, written document and the statutes and conventions which do seem to form part of the New Zealand Constitution are not entrenched as higher law. One commentator describes it as comparable to a breeze, felt but not seen.[38] Generally, the Constitution is recognized as being contained in several key pieces of legislation,[39] conventions, letters patent of the Governor General, the Treaty of Waitangi, certain imperial enactments from England,[40] and principles of rule of law as developed through the common law courts. One of the defining aspects of the New Zealand constitutional system is parliamentary sovereignty. Parliament

---

36. Any land acquired for conservation purposes is held as Crown land. See *Conservation Act* 1987, s. 7.
37. R. Mulholland, *Introduction to the New Zealand Legal System*, 10th ed. (Wellington: Butterworths, 2001), 30.
38. *Ibid.*, 27.
39. For instance, the *Constitution Act* 1986, *New Zealand Bill of Rights Act* 1990, *Electoral Act* 1993, *Judicature Act* 1908 and the *District Courts Act* 1947. See Mulholland, *supra* n. 37, 30.
40. The *Imperial Laws Act* 1988 preserves, e.g., the Magna Carta and Habeas Corpus.

is the supreme law making body and it is important to note that legislation cannot be struck down in courts as is possible in other jurisdictions.[41]

With respect to the institutions and administrative structures of environmental governance, the different roles of central and local government are a key feature. These are explored hereafter.

4.1   CENTRAL GOVERNMENT

The two main agencies responsible for the management, protection and preservation of the environment are the ME and the Department of Conservation. The ME was established in 1986 under the *Environment Act* and took over the responsibilities of other former ministries. It administers key environmental legislation including the *Environment Act*, the *Ozone Layer Protection Act* 1996, the *Resource Management Act* 1991, the *Hazardous Substances and New Organisms Act* 1996 and the *Soil Conservation and Rivers Control Act* 1941.[42] The primary function of the Ministry is codified in section 31 of the *Environment Act* as being an advisory body to the Minister for the Environment 'on all aspects of environmental administration' including management policies for resources, significant environmental impacts, with particular emphasis on those inadequately legislated for, and effective provision for public participation in planning and policy processes. The Ministry also gathers and distributes information, advises other governmental agencies and has the primary responsibility for any reform or amendment to the RMA.[43] The Ministry also has specific functions under other acts, for instance, recommending national policy statements and national environmental standards under the RMA.[44]

The PCE has an important role of monitoring the efficiency of environmental governance. It reports directly to parliament. When set up in 1987 under the *Environment Act*, the PCE was the first independent environmental watchdog of its kind in the world. The PCE has wide powers to investigate complaints or carry out self-initiated investigations, but can only make formal recommendations and has no power to regulate.[45]

The Department of Conservation, established under the *Conservation Act* 1987, is distinct from the ME, with its purpose being to advocate and promote the conservation of natural and physical resources.[46] The Department is responsible for natural and historic resources including national parks, marine and wildlife reserves, sanctuaries, national reserves and conservation land. It also controls the introduction of new species, the granting of leases, licenses, permits, easements

---

41. For a comprehensive discussion of the Constitution of New Zealand see Mulholland, *supra* n. 37, 25-75.
42. Nolan, *supra* n. 11, 65-67.
43. *Ibid.*, 67.
44. See the RMA 1991, s. 24.
45. Harris, *supra* n. 18, 72.
46. See the *Conservation Act* 1987, s. 6.

for activities in conservation areas, and is responsible under the RMA for the compulsory preparation of a New Zealand Coastal Policy Statement.[47]

Other ministries such as the Ministry of Agriculture and Forestry, the Ministry of Fisheries and the Ministry of Transport, also have important roles in the governance of the New Zealand environment but require only a brief mention for present purposes.[48]

4.2	LOCAL GOVERNMENT

Under the RMA, the role of local government has been significantly enlarged. Although the central government can issue national guidelines to direct the formulation of regional and district plans, the RMA system allows a greater level of autonomy for regional councils.[49] At the local government level, management is distributed between regional and territorial authorities (which include district and city councils) as empowered by the *Local Government Act* 1974 and the *Local Government Act* 2002.[50] In practice, the RMA is administered by local authorities. They issue consents to businesses, developers and individuals whose activities will impact on the physical environment of the area. These include activities like building, mining, and constructing manufacturing plants.

There are currently sixteen different Regional Councils and section 30 of the RMA outlines their purpose and functions which include: the integrated management of physical and natural resources;[51] formulating objectives and policies related to land of regional significance;[52] and maintaining biodiversity.[53] Regional Councils must prepare a regional policy statement, which is subject to review every ten years, consistent with any existing national standards.[54] Regional Councils may also choose to develop a regional plan which serves as a guide for the development of consistent district plans.[55] Such plans may deal with issues separately, or may address issues encompassing a variety of environmental concerns.

Territorial authorities manage smaller areas within a given region and are responsible for the preparation of compulsory district plans.[56] Plans must give effect to the relevant regional policy statement, any national policy statements,

---

47. See the RMA 1991, s. 28. See further Nolan, *supra* n. 11, 67-70.
48. For more information relating to other ministries, see Nolan, *supra* n. 11, 70-83.
49. Nolan, *supra* n. 11, 159.
50. For current information on the different levels of local government, see J. Wilson, 'Government and nation', in *Te Ara: The Encyclopedia of New Zealand*, ed. MCH (Wellington: MCH, 2003), <www.TeAra.govt.nz/EarthSeaAndSky/OceanStudyAndConservation/LawOfTheSea/en>, 12 December 2007.
51. See the RMA 1991, s. 30(a).
52. *Ibid.*, s. 30(b).
53. *Ibid.*, s. 30(ga).
54. *Ibid.*, s. 59-62.
55. *Ibid.*, s. 63-70.
56. *Ibid.*, s. 72-77.

and regional coastal statements. Any disputes that arise with regard to any policy or plans can be referred to the Environment Court.

5   THE COURTS

5.1   HISTORY OF THE COURTS

The historical development of the New Zealand court system is inextricably tied to that of the UK's. However, fortunately, by the time New Zealand was colonized in the mid-nineteenth century, the complications that had accompanied the establishment of modern English courts had largely been resolved. New Zealand inherited the common law system and traditionally possessed only one court that had general jurisdiction. Before the signing of the Treaty of Waitangi[57] in 1840, there was no official legal system in place. Maori regulated themselves according to *tikanga* (their customary law) and control over European settlers was difficult. Initially treated as an extension of the Australian State of New South Wales, officials there made attempts to preserve order in New Zealand and hear criminal and civil cases. This was largely ineffective because of the distance involved. Cessation of sovereignty to the British paved the way for the adoption of British law into New Zealand and the establishment of the first court of New Zealand, namely the Supreme Court, in December 1841.[58]

From its creation, the Supreme Court has had dual jurisdiction, administering both common law and equity and initially had only one judge, the Chief Justice. As a new colony, there were not enough judges to set up an appeal court until 1862, and the Governor and members of the executive council acted as a temporary appellate body during that period. After 1840, the Legislative Council also created a series of lower-level courts such as the Court of Requests, the Courts of Petty Sessions and in 1846, the Resident Magistrates' Courts. Resident Magistrates had limited jurisdiction to hear criminal cases and civil claims and these courts eventually evolved into the modern Districts Courts. The original District Courts were set up as a middle court in 1858 upon the abolition of the Court of Request and the Courts of Petty Sessions, but overlap between the District Courts and both the Resident Magistrates' Court and Supreme Court, led to its own abolition in 1909. During this time, the Resident Magistrates' Courts assumed more responsibility and gained extended authority.

The *Judicature Amendment Act* 1957 established a separate court of appeal. Further major restructuring of the court system occurred in 1980 following recommendations by the Royal Commission on the Courts, which was specifically set up

---

57. The Treaty of Waitangi purportedly ceded sovereignty over New Zealand to the British Crown.
58. Mulholland, *supra* n. 37, 77-79. See further, Courts of New Zealand, 'The History of the Court System', <www.courtsofnz.govt.nz/about/system/history/overview.html>, 12 December 2007. For a comprehensive overview of New Zealand history see M. King, *The Penguin History of New Zealand* (Auckland: Penguin, 2003).

in 1976 to examine the court system.[59] The *District Courts Amendment Act* 1979 changed the *Magistrates' Courts Act* 1947 to the *District Courts Act*, and in 1980, the Magistrates' Courts became the modern District Courts. The Supreme Court was also renamed the High Court and the jurisdiction for the new Districts Courts and High Court was extended.

From the inception of the first New Zealand court, the highest court had been the Judicial Committee of the Privy Council- an English court that heard appeals from New Zealand (and other colonies). From 2004, the *Supreme Court Act* 2003 replaced the Privy Council with the Supreme Court, thereby rendering New Zealand's court system entirely self sufficient and independent of the historical regulation from English courts.

5.2   HIERARCHY OF THE COURTS

The area of jurisdiction for each court is prescribed by statute[60] and they operate within a specific hierarchy, with each lower court bound to follow the decisions of the higher court. A system of inferior and superior courts facilitates a right of appeal and also allows courts with a higher status to exercise jurisdiction over more significant issues.[61] In New Zealand, the hierarchy of the courts is as follows: the District Courts, the High Court, the Court of Appeal and finally the Supreme Court.

The District Courts, provided for in the *District Courts Act* 1947, are at the base of the hierarchy and are, along with the High Court, originating courts where claims are initially heard. The bulk of civil and criminal cases are heard in approximately eighty District Courts throughout New Zealand.[62] There are limitations placed on the amounts claimable in a District Court but parties may, by agreement or by abandoning part of their claim, bring the case under its jurisdiction where it would normally fall to the High Court. In some circumstances, the District Courts can hold a trial by jury, and the continued extension of its jurisdiction has resulted in the High Court assuming more of a supervisory role, as it deals with appeals from this level.[63]

The High Court (formerly the Supreme Court) is established under the *Judicature Act* 1908 and has unlimited jurisdiction. As well as having the power to hear originating claims, it hears appeals from the District Courts and other bodies. Appeals from the High Court go to the Court of Appeal which does not have original jurisdiction. The Court of Appeal, set up under the *Judicature Amendment Act* 1957, operates as the first appellate court with the last right of appeal falling to the new Supreme Court.

---

59. Mulholland, *supra* n. 37, 84.
60. See the *Judicature Act* 1908 and the *District Courts Act* 1947.
61. Mulholland, *supra* n. 37, 81.
62. *Ibid.*, 83-84.
63. *Ibid.*, 85-86.

While the court structure is fairly standard, there are other specialized courts that must be taken into account, namely the existence of a separate Family Court, Employment Court and Environmental Court. Each of these courts was established to fill a specific legal niche and their procedures and jurisdiction reflect this. The Environment Court is of special importance in relation to the development of environmental law in New Zealand, as it has the role of practically applying the concepts and words of statutes. Its success or failure in doing so is formative for domestic environmental law.

5.3   ENVIRONMENT COURT

Formerly the Planning Tribunal, the Environment Court is a central institution in resource management. Established under the *Resource Management Amendment Act* 1996, the court has specifically been created to hear matters concerning the environment and now deals with a multitude of statutes.[64] The court is granted jurisdiction under the RMA to hear appeals relating to, among others, the content of regional and district statements and plans, resource consents, subdivisions, environmental effects from mining, and non-notification of resource consents.[65] It has other declaratory powers and wide jurisdiction to enforce the provisions of the RMA. Because of the broad nature of the latter act, the Environment Court has a pivotal role in clarifying how generalized concepts and purposes will actually apply.[66] In this sense, it has a very real impact on the development and success of environmental law. One criticism of this court, and the RMA system itself, is that it operates in a purely reactive manner with no originating power to inquire or investigate.[67] Regardless, the decisions of the court give an important indication of the state of New Zealand's environmental law and provide important examples of environmental jurisprudence.

6   JUDGMENTS OF ENVIRONMENTAL RELEVANCE

The RMA placed the concept of 'sustainable management' at the heart of New Zealand's system of environmental law. This concept and its varying interpretations have been the subject of many decisions in the Environment Court and debates outside the court. This resulted in differing opinions on what 'sustainable management', as stipulated in section 5(1) entails, and further, what standard must be met to comply with the safeguards in sections 5(2)(a), (b) and (c) of the RMA

64. The laws include: the RMA, *Historic Places Act* 1993; *Forests Act* 1949; *Local Government Act* 1974; *Transit New Zealand Act* 1989; *Electricity Act* 1992; *Crown Minerals Act* 1991; *Biosecurity Act* 1993; and *Public Works Act* 1981.
65. See the RMA 1991, ss 269-298.
66. Nolan, *supra* n. 11, 54-59.
67. *Ibid.*, 55.

(see discussion above). The Environment Court has, through its jurisprudence, developed two different approaches to interpreting section 5 of the RMA – the so-called 'environmental bottom line approach' and 'overall judgment approach'.

The bottom line approach requires that all the safeguards set out in section 5 of the RMA be satisfied before the purpose of the Act can be said to have been fulfilled. This approach holds the view that section 5(2) and its safeguards do not contain competing interests to be weighed and balanced against each other; but rather that all the safeguards must be ensured in order for the Act's purpose, i.e., 'sustainable management', to be achieved. This approach hinges on the interpretation of the word 'while'. If it can be read to mean 'so long as', then the bottom line approach will be the natural consequence of that interpretation and the promotion of sustainable management is only achieved if sections 5(2)(a),(b) and (c) are observed. This approach finds its origins in a ME working paper[68] and gathered support from the speech of Simon Upton, the then Minister for the Environment, who explained at the third reading of the Bill that:

> The Bill provides us with a framework to establish objectives with a biophysical bottom line that must not be compromised. Provided that those objectives are met, what people get up to is their affair. As such, the Bill provides a more liberal regime for developers. On the other hand, activities will have to be compatible with hard environmental standards and society will set those standards.[69]

Two cases, *Foxley Engineering Ltd v. Wellington City Council*,[70] and *Campbell v. Southland DC*,[71] cite the use of the environmental bottom line approach. In *Foxley Engineering Ltd*, there was an appeal from a decision of the Wellington City Council granting resource consent to establish a service station and car park. At the time, the court was still known as the Planning Tribunal and in its decision referred to section 5, explaining:

> The provisions of s. (5)(2)(a)(b)(c) may be considered cumulative safeguards … They are safeguards which must be met before the Act's purpose is fulfilled. The promotion of sustainable management has to be determined therefore in the context of these qualifications which may be accorded the same legal weight.[72]

The Tribunal revoked the resource consent based on the potential adverse effects the authorized activities would have had on the inner city amenities and heritage values.

---

68. ME, *Working Paper No. 24: Sustainability, Intrinsic Values and the Needs of Future Generations* (Wellington: ME, 1989).
69. Hansard 51b, Resource Management Bill Third Reading (July 1991), 3018-3020.
70. *Foxley Engineering Ltd v. Wellington City Council* (Planning Tribunal, W12/94, 16 March 1994).
71. *Campbell v. Southland District Council* (Planning Tribunal, W114/94, 14 December 1994).
72. *Foxley Engineering Ltd. v. Wellington City Council* (Planning Tribunal W 12/94, 16 March 1994), 40.

In the *Campbell* case, there was an appeal against the granting of resource consent by the Southland District Council to allow an international airport in Southland. The Tribunal repeated the view expressed above in the quote from *Foxley Engineering Ltd* and also cancelled the consent. The Tribunal rejected an approach that would require a balancing exercise, holding that '[S]ection 5 is not about achieving a balance between benefits occurring from an activity and its adverse effects . . .',[73] thus favoring a fundamental sustainability approach.

The High Court decision of *New Zealand Rail Ltd v. Marlborough DC*,[74] made some similar observations about the RMA in stating: '[T]here is a deliberate openness about the language, its meanings and its connotations which I think is intended to allow the application of policy in a general and broad way'.[75] This observation is meant to convey that the purposefull definition in section 5 needs to be understood as an overarching commitment to achieving sustainability.[76]

This 'environmental bottom line' approach proposes a strong model for the concept of sustainable management. Compliance with the safeguards involves anticipating the reasonably foreseeable needs of future generations, safeguarding the life-supporting capacity of resources and avoiding, remedying or mitigating adverse affects on the environment. If compliance to such concepts is given uncompromised priority, then resource management will take on the sustainable characteristics envisaged in the RMA.

Another approach has, however, developed through the Environment Court jurisprudence. The 'overall judgment approach' employs a method of weighing up all the relevant factors and deciding generally whether a proposal promotes sustainable management or not. It was explained in *McGuire v. Hastings District Council*,[77] that '[T]he Act has a single broad purpose' and in achieving that purpose, authorities are bound by particular considerations, most importantly those contained in sections 5, 6, 7 and 8 of Part II of the Act. Adopting an overall, broad judgment approach, authorities are responsible for measuring up relevant considerations against each other and then reaching a balanced decision. The case *Trio Holdings v. Marlborough DC*,[78] involved a marine farming application to grow sponges from which anti-cancer compounds were to be extracted. The court concluded that the adverse effects were not so serious as to be inconsistent with the requirement for sustainable management. Here, the court performed a balancing test, weighing the benefits of the proposed venture against the possibility of environmental harm, and noted that, ' . . . the proposal has the potential to provide for the social and economic wellbeing of the communities . . .' and had difficulty

---

73. S. Upton, H. Atkins & G. Willis, 'Section 5 Re-visited: A Critique of Skelton and Memon's analysis', *RMJ* 10, no. 3 (2002): 16.

74. *New Zealand Rail Ltd v. Marlborough District Council* [1994] NZRMA 70.

75. Upton, et al., *supra* n. 73, 17.

76. S. Curran, 'Sustainable Development v. Sustainable Management: The Interface between the Local Government Act and the Resource Management Act', *NZJEL* 8 (2004): 279.

77. *McGuire v. Hastings District Council* [2002] 2 NZLR 577; (2001) 8 ELRNZ 14; [2001] NZRMA 557.

78. *Trio Holdings v. Marlborough District Council* [1997] NZRMA 97.

'...accepting that the visual impairment from the buoys of the sponge farm-...should prevail over an issue of the national health and welfare which stems from the implications of this proposal'.[79]

This 'overall judgment approach' was clearly articulated in *North Shore CC v. Auckland Regional City*,[80] which involved the exclusion of the Okura catchment from the urban limits of North Shore City. In this judgment, the court found that although the urbanization proposal met the first part of the definition of sustainable management, it did not meet the three safeguards prescribed in the subparagraphs of section 5(2). In reaching this conclusion, the court contemplated that the parts of section 5(2) required:

> an overall broad judgment of whether a proposal would promote the sustainable management of natural and physical resources . . . Such judgment allows for comparison of conflicting considerations and the scale and degree of them, and their relative significance or proportion in the final outcome.[81]

A similar approach was taken in *Genesis Power Ltd v. Franklin District Council*,[82] where the court found that the benefits of a wind farm proposal, when viewed in a national context, outweighed the adverse effects on the immediate area. The court further held that to reflect the Act's purpose, it was sufficient that overall, there was the promotion of sustainable management as per section 5.

This refinement of the balancing and weighing approach was supported by Skelton and Memon[83] and since the role of the Act is essentially a 'conflict resolving statute' it follows that there will be an element of weighing. Other commentators, however, maintain that a strict reading of section 5 compels resource managers to secure the outcomes detailed in subparagraphs (a), (b) and (c), which effectively operate as high-level constraints.[84] If the overall judgment approach of weighing socio-economic merits and environmental affects of a proposal is used, they perceive an undermining of the sustainability principle.

Apart from the question of how to apply the concept of sustainable management, the Environment Court has also dealt with cases relating to climate change and the complicated interaction between New Zealand policy and the RMA. In the case *Environmental Defence Society v. Auckland Regional Council*,[85] the Environment Court had the opportunity to decide on the applicability of the RMA to greenhouse gases. The Environmental Defence Society appealed against a consent granted to a gas-powered power generation plant, known as 'Otahuhu C', allowing it to discharge 1,2 million tons of CO_2 per year. The appeal was dismissed by Whiting J, on the grounds that the national and international consequences could

---

79. Upton, et al., *supra* n. 73, 17.
80. *North Shore City Council v. Auckland Regional City* [1997] NZRMA 59.
81. *Ibid.*, at 94.
82. *Genesis Power Ltd v. Franklin District Council* (EC, A 148/2005, 7 September 2005).
83. P. Skelton & A. Memon, 'Adopting Sustainability as an Overarching Environmental Policy: A Review of Section 5 of the RMA', *RMJ* 10, no. 1 (2002): 6.
84. Upton, et al., *supra* n. 73, 13.
85. *Environmental Defence Society v. Auckland Regional Council* [2002] NZRMA 492.

not be adequately assessed and that the New Zealand government preferred to address greenhouse gases in a different way.[86] To further quote Whiting J:

> The government has already signalled that it does not see RMA controls and the mechanisms as being cost effective for managing greenhouse emissions. Climate change is an international issue and should therefore be dealt with consistently on a national level. The RMA consenting and planning process means that there will always be a risk of inconsistent treatment and costs of implementing and managing requirements for different regions.[87]

These comments only reinforce the need for national environmental standards or a national policy statement for climate change. Since this case, through an amendment to the RMA in 2004, the government deliberately exempted greenhouse gases from consideration under the Act.[88] This cleared the way for a carbon charge as a national economic instrument and centrepiece of the government's 2002 proposed climate change package.[89] No such scheme ever manifested and in 2005, the government specifically dropped its proposal for a carbon tax.

It is strange that New Zealand's most advanced environmental law, the RMA, cannot be used for reducing greenhouse gas emissions. A recent decision appealed from the Environment Court to the High Court, addressed the limited scope of the RMA in this respect. Section 104E of the RMA states that a consent authority must not have regard to the effects of discharge of greenhouse gases on climate change, except to the extent that the use and development of renewable energy enables a reduction in the discharge into air of greenhouse gases. The case of *Greenpeace New Zealand v. Northland RC*,[90] was an appeal against the Environment Court's decision[91] to grant Might River Power Ltd a resource consent to operate Marsden B, a coal-fired electricity generating station. Greenpeace argued that the decision failed to pay regard to sections 7(i) and (j)[92] of the RMA which deal with the effects of climate change and the benefits of renewable energy; and further, that section 104E could be interpreted to require that the benefits of renewable energy be taken into account in all resource consent applications, not just those dealing immediately with renewable energy projects.[93] The Environment Court had held that section 104E only allowed consideration of the effects of discharge on climate change in the case of applications to use or develop renewable energy. This decision ultimately precluded the consideration of any effects that non-renewable

---

86. *Ibid.*, para. 88.
87. *Ibid.*, para. 18.
88. See the *Resource Management (Energy and Climate Change) Amendment Act* 2004.
89. For history and details of the government's 2002 'Preferred Policy Package on Climate Change' see J. Bosselmann, J. Fuller & J. Salinger, *Climate Change in New Zealand: Scientific and Legal Assessments*, NZCEL Monograph Series 2 (Auckland: NZCEL, 2002), 51-109.
90. *Greenpeace New Zealand v. Northland Regional Council* [2007] NZRMA 87.
91. *Greenpeace New Zealand v. Northland Regional Council* (EnvC A094/06).
92. These sections were inserted as part of the *Resource Management (Energy and Climate Change) Amendment Act* 2004.
93. S. Christensen, *Intensive: Resource Management* (Wellington: NZLS, 2000), 10-11.

energy sources might have on climate change from the resource application process. On appeal, the High Court reversed this finding, holding:

> If the application for a discharge permit which otherwise qualifies under s 104E includes no proposal which, if consented to and built, would enable a 'reduction in the discharge into air of greenhouse gases' by the 'use and development of renewable energy' then that, too, is a factor the consent authority is entitled to take into account in deciding whether to exercise its discretion and grant resource consent.[94]

The court determined that section 104E also applies to a non-renewable energy project insofar as it may be beneficial to greenhouse gas reduction, and that consent authorities should be able to balance the benefits of hypothetical renewable energy projects against applications concerning non-renewable energy projects.

The wider implications of the High Court's ruling are not yet clear. On the one hand, the objective of the 2004 Amendment was to deal with climate change on a nationally uniform basis. The court's interpretation of section 104E would meet this objective.[95] On the other hand, in removing the ability of local authorities to control greenhouse gases, the government is effectively keeping all its policy options open.[96] Clearly, the court's interpretation is at odds with the government's complete reliance on market-based economic instruments. This case has been appealed by a state owned enterprise, Genesis Energy, to the Court of Appeal and judgment is pending.

The courts (especially the Environment Court) have also had to grapple with determining what level of environmental risk is acceptable when considered against the purpose of the RMA.[97] The constitution of the Environment Court ensures that it possesses a wide range of expertise that equips it to deal with environmental issues in a more considered manner than 'normal' courts.[98] The assessment of potential environmental risks involves the consideration of policies, educated predications, experiments and simulations; and the court must use the expertise of its members, bearing in mind public and environmental interests, in reaching its decision.[99] When faced with the task of assessing the risk of future environmental impacts, common reference is made to the precautionary principle[100] and the precautionary approach. Statutory expressions of the precautionary approach[101] have led to its discussion and application in the courts. The case of *Golden Bay Marine Farmers v. Tasman DC*,[102] which outlined the

---

94. *Greenpeace New Zealand v. Northland Regional Council* [2007] NZRMA 87, para. 50.
95. C. Warnock, 'Greenhouse Gases and Climate Change', *RMB* (2006): 193.
96. K. Palmer, 'Origins and Guiding Ideas of Environmental Law', in *Environmental Law for a Sustainable Society*, ed. K. Bosselmann & D. Grinlinton, vol. 1 (Auckland: NZCEL, 2002).
97. R. Somerville, QC, *Intensive: The Courts and the Environment – Serious Issues: Environmental and Resource Management Law* (Wellington: NZLS, 2003), 55.
98. *Ibid.*, 56.
99. *Ibid.*, 56.
100. Rio Declaration on Environment and Development, June 1992, Principle 15.
101. See, e.g.: RMA 1991, s. 3; and *Hazardous Substances and New Organisms Act* 1996, s. 7.
102. *Golden Bay Marine Farmers v. Tasman District Council* (EC, W42/01, 27 April 2001), 76.

application of the precautionary approach in appeals and proposed plan changes, is a good example.[103] In this case, the precautionary approach to risk management was considered by reference to section 3(f) of the RMA, which relates to 'potential effects of low probability but high potential impact'. The court held that the precautionary approach could be built into the objectives, methods and policies of any plans or implemented through enforcement orders from the Environment Court.[104]

The Environment Court has also accepted that the precautionary principle may, in circumstances where severe and irreversible damage might occur, be generally considered.[105] In *McIntyre v. Christchurch City Council*,[106] the potential effects of a telecommunications transmitter were at issue and the court deliberated on the application of the precautionary principle. The court was careful to distinguish between the precautionary approach as specifically provided for in the RMA, and the more general precautionary principle that has been developing in international environmental jurisprudence. The court held that although it was not relevant in evaluating potential effects on the environment, it was a matter that the court could take into account under section 105 of the RMA as part of its discretionary judgment. This potential inclusion of the principle into decision-making would facilitate the incorporation of values and elements beyond those set out in legislation, but disagreement over the precautionary principle's applicability makes it difficult to identify any common approach to the matter.[107] McIntyre has found support in cases like *Telecom NZ v. Christchurch CC*,[108] and *Ngaati Kahu*.[109] The courts, however, have restricted the application of the principle in other matters. In *Wratten v. Tasman DC*,[110] the court expressed significant doubt as to the principle's relevance and reaffirmed that its application should be strictly confined to cases dealing with irreversible harm and scientific uncertainty. These doubts are echoed in *Shirley Primary School v. Telecom Mobile Communications Ltd*,[111] which concerned an application for consent to establish, operate and maintain a cellular radio base station adjacent to a primary school; and in which concerns were raised about the potential for the station to cause the school pupils ill health. The court thought it inappropriate to apply the principle, finding that it was already implicit in the RMA[112] and that its specific application would create

---

103. Nolan, *supra* n. 11, 1020.
104. *Ibid.*
105. *McIntyre v. Christchurch City Council* [1996] NZRMA 289; *Ngaati Kahu Ki Whangaroa Co-operative Society v. The Northland Regional Council* EC, A95/00, 4 August 2000, paras 155-163.
106. *McIntyre v. Christchurch City Council* [1996] NZRMA 289.
107. Nolan, *supra* n, 11, 1017.
108. *Telecom New Zealand Limited v. Christchurch City Council* EC, Q 165/96, 15 November 1996.
109. *Ngaati Kahu Ki Whangaroa Co-operative Society v. The Northland Regional Council* [2001] NZRMA 299, paras 155-163.
110. *Wratten v. Tasman District Council* EC, W 8/98, 17 March 1998.
111. *Shirley Primary School v. Telecom Mobile Communications Ltd* [1999] NZRMA 66.
112. See the RMA 1991, s. 3(f).

complications and a 'double-counting' of the need for caution.[113] The court proceeded to outline a decision-making process for resource consent cases involving environmental risk assessment:

> It is important to recognise that when deciding whether natural and physical resources will be sustainably managed, decision makers under the Act are usually making decisions about future events. The decision-maker has:
>
> (a) under section 104(1): to decide what the primary facts are; and to evaluate those facts as propositions about the future ('risks if adverse effects, 'chances' if beneficial) – usually those propositions are given as the opinions of experts; and
>
> (b) to carry out a further evaluation when undertaking the weighing and balancing . . . exercise required under section 105(1) to decide the ultimate question.[114]

Despite the strong comments in the *Shirley* case recommending that the precautionary principle remains outside the realm of judicial consideration, in *Ngaati Kahu*, the court, having considered the decisions in *McIntyre*, *Shirley* and *Wratten*, found them to be consistent in their consideration of the precautionary principle in relation to resource consents, and stated that:

> The Court makes a judgment on such an application after finding facts based on evidence of probative value. The precautionary principle may be applied . . . where, on the totality of evidence, it finds that due to scientific uncertainty, exercise of the consent would be likely to cause serious or irreversible harm to the environment.[115]

Most recently, the Environment Court acknowledged in *Golden Bay Marine Farmers v. Tasman District Council*[116] that 'the precautionary principle (described as a precautionary approach beyond what is implicit in the Act itself) appears to continue to have a role in determining resource consent applications'.

7   CRITICAL SURVEY AND FUTURE PERSPECTIVES

The RMA is central to New Zealand's system of environmental governance, although it provides very few rules regarding the management of natural and physical resources. It functions more as a framework, relying heavily on subordinate legislation and administration through the courts.[117] Its administration

---

113. *Shirley Primary School v. Telecom Mobile Communications Ltd* [1999] NZRMA 66, 135 para. 223.
114. *Ibid.*, 100, para. 116.
115. *Ngaati Kahu Ki Whangaroa Co-operative Society v. The Northland Regional Council* [2001] NZRMA 299, para. 161.
116. *Golden Bay Marine Farmers v. Tasman District Council* EC, W42/01, 27 April 2001, 76.
117. Somerville, *supra* n. 97, 51-52.

through local government and review through the courts, have largely determined the success and/or failure of environmental governance in New Zealand.

Fundamentally, the RMA had been enacted to pursue two goals: integrated resource management and sustainability.[118] The explanatory note to the RMA stated that issues of development must not be considered in isolation from environmental issues. In 1993, the ME provided further guidance by explaining essential components of integrated environmental management including: integration across media (water, land and air); integration across agencies (local, regional and territorial authorities); and integration across time (accumulation of activities and effects over time).[119] This last component may be the most complex to achieve as cumulative effects[120] may extend across boundaries and only be felt over a long period of time.

Measuring and controlling these effects are the key objectives of environmental governance. Although addressed by the goal of integrated management, they are essentially a concern of sustainability; the second goal of the RMA. It is here where most of the problems of environmental governance present themselves. New Zealand's courts have struggled with the complexities of sustainability in much the same way as courts in other jurisdictions have. To date, no clear definition exists that would allow the judiciary to clearly separate sustainable activities from unsustainable activities. The RMA process has certainly not provided the legal solution to achieving sustainability in New Zealand, but the jurisprudence which has stemmed from the courts having to grapple with its provisions, may be helpful to other jurisdictions in some important ways.

By enacting the RMA with its focus on sustainability and, at the same time, establishing a specialized environment court, the government has created a much improved framework.

Obviously, reasoning around sustainability has had some impact on the way judges approach environmental cases. Justice Peter Salmon has stressed the fundamental importance of the sustainability principle 'as the only meaningful cure to the problems that face the world'.[121] The fact that there is little consistency in the reasoning of the courts could in part be attributed to a slow learning process. When one of the RMA's main initiators, the former Prime Minister Sir Geoffrey Palmer, reviewed the making of the RMA, he expressed regret 'that Parliament did not abolish the Planning Tribunal when the new legislation was framed. (...) The need to change the judicial culture was overlooked'.[122] In a similar vein, the PCE has criticized authorities and courts for not sufficiently focusing on the RMA's 'core thrust' with its recognition of 'intrinsic values' and ecological 'bottom

---

118. Nolan, *supra* n. 11, 88.
119. ME, 'Not Just an Add On', *PQ* March (1993): 18.
120. The RMA 1991 (s. 3) defines the term 'effect' to include 'any cumulative effect arises over time or in combination with other effects'.
121. P. Salmon, 'Sustainable Development in New Zealand', unpublished paper presented to the Auckland Branch Resource Management Law Association, (November 2002), 3.
122. G.W.R. Palmer, 'The Making of the Resource Management Act', in *Environment – The International Challenge: Essays*, ed. G.W.R. Palmer (Wellington: VUP, 1995), 145, 170.

lines'.[123] The PCE has repeatedly reminded the people of New Zealand that sustainability is a foundational principle for society and its economy (otherwise referred to as strong sustainability), requiring a profound shift of values and policies.[124]

Commentators on the RMA and its interpretation by the courts have often stressed that the principle of sustainability[125] has been incorporated in the RMA to give environmental law an 'ecological orientation'.[126] While the Act's conception of sustainable management is narrower than that of sustainable development, it shares its core idea of ecological sustainability. Thus, the yardstick for environmental governance is not balancing environmental, economic and social concerns, but the protection of ecological integrity which can never be compromised.

Ultimately, the design of laws and composition of courts is not the central issue. More important is the ethical orientation of all those involved in environmental decision-making. Perhaps the traditional concept of environmental governance should be advanced to governance for sustainability.[127]

BIBLIOGRAPHY

Bosselmann, J., J. Fuller & J. Salinger. *Climate Change in New Zealand: Scientific and Legal Assessments*. NZCEL Monograph Series 2. Auckland: New Zealand Centre for Environmental Law, 2002.

Bosselmann, K. & D. Grinlinton (eds). *Environmental Law for a Sustainable Society*, vol. 1. Auckland: New Zealand Centre for Environmental Law, 2002.

Bosselmann, K. 'Achieving the Goal and Missing the Target: New Zealand's Implementation of the Kyoto Protocol'. *Macquarie Journal for International and Comparative Environmental Law* 2 (2006): 75-106.

Bosselmann, K. *The Principle of Sustainability: Transforming Law and Governance*. Aldershot: Ashgate, 2008.

Bosselmann, K., R. Engel & P. Taylor. *Governance for Sustainability: Issues, Challenges and Successes*. The World Conservation Union Environmental Law and Policy Series. Bonn: IUCN, 2008.

Castalia. *Greenhouse Gas Emission Policies: Is there a way forward? Report to greenhouse policy coalition* (Castalia Strategic Advisors, September 2005).

---

123. PCE, *Towards Sustainable Development: The Role of the Resource Management Act 1991* (Wellington: OPCE, 1998), 7; and PCE, *Sustainability Review 2007: New Zealand's Progress towards Sustainable Development* (Wellington: OPCE, 2007).
124. PCE, *Creating Our Future: Sustainable Development for New Zealand* (Wellington: OPCE, 2002), 35.
125. K. Bosselmann, *The Principle of Sustainability: Transforming Law and Governance* (Aldershot: Ashgate, 2008).
126. Nolan, *supra* n. 11, 92.
127. K. Bosselmann, R. Engel & P. Taylor, *A Guide to Governance for Sustainability: Issues, Challenges and Successes*, The World Conservation Union Environmental Law and Policy Series (Bonn: IUCN, 2008).

Christensen, S. *Intensive: Resource Management*. Wellington: New Zealand Law Society, 2000.

Courts of New Zealand. 'The History of the Court System'. <www.courtsofnz. govt.nz/about/system/history/overview.html>, 12 December 2007.

Curran, S. 'Sustainable Development v. Sustainable Management: The interface between the Local Government Act and the Resource Management Act'. *New Zealand Journal of Environmental Law* 8 (2004): 264-294.

Grinlinton, D. 'Contemporary Environmental Law in New Zealand'. In *Environmental Law for a Sustainable Society*, edited by K. Bosselmann & D. Grinlinton, vol. 1. Auckland: New Zealand Centre for Environmental Law, 2002.

Hansard 51b. Resource Management Bill Third Reading. July 1991.

Harris, R. *Handbook of Environmental Law*. Wellington: Royal Forest and Bird Protection Society of New Zealand Inc, 2004.

Hayward, J. 'The Principles of the Treaty of Waitangi'. In *Rangahaua Whanui National Overview Report*, edited by A. Ward, vol. 3. Wellington: Waitangi Tribunal, 1997.

King, M. *The Penguin History of New Zealand*. Auckland: Penguin, 2003.

Mansfield, B. 'Law of the sea'. In *Te Ara: The Encyclopedia of New Zealand*, edited by MCH. Wellington: Ministry for Culture and Heritage, 2003. <www.TeAra.govt.nz/EarthSeaAndSky/OceanStudyAndConservation/Law OfTheSea/en>, 12 December 2007.

ME. 'National Environmental Standards'. <www.mfe.govt.nz/laws/standards/ index.html>, 12 December 2007.

Mead, S.M. *Tikanga Maori: Living by Maori Values*. Wellington: Huia, 2003.

Ministry for the Environment. *Environment Update Series, Information Sheet No. 6* Wellington: ME, 1991.

Ministry for the Environment. 'Not Just an Add On'. *Planning Quarterly* March (1993): 18.

Ministry for the Environment. *Proposed National Environmental Standards for Air Quality: Resource Management Act Section 32 Analysis of Costs and Benefits*. Wellington: ME, 2004.

Ministry for the Environment. *Working Paper No. 24: Sustainability, Intrinsic Values and the Needs of Future Generations*. Wellington: ME, 1989.

Mulholland, R. *Introduction to the New Zealand Legal System*, 10th ed. Wellington: Butterworths, 2001.

Nolan, D., ed. *Environmental and Resource Management Law*. 3rd ed. Wellington: LexisNexis, 2005.

Palmer, G.W.R. *Environment – The International Challenge: Essays*. Wellington: Victoria University Press, 1995.

Palmer, G.W.R. 'The Making of the Resource Management Act'. In *Environment – The International Challenge: Essays*, edited by G.W.R. Palmer. Wellington: Victoria University Press, 1995.

Palmer, K. 'Origins and Guiding Ideas of Environmental Law'. In *Environmental Law for a Sustainable Society*, edited by K. Bosselmann & D. Grinlinton, vol. 1. Auckland: New Zealand Centre for Environmental Law, 2002.

Parliamentary Commissioner for the Environment. *Creating Our Future: Sustainable Development for New Zealand*. Wellington: Office of the Parliamentary Commissioner for the Environment, 2002.

Parliamentary Commissioner for the Environment. *Sustainability Review 2007: New Zealand's Progress towards Sustainable Development*. Wellington: Office of the Parliamentary Commissioner for the Environment, 2007.

Parliamentary Commissioner for the Environment. *Towards Sustainable Development: The Role of the Resource Management Act 1991*. Wellington: Office of the Parliamentary Commissioner for the Environment, 1998.

Salmon, P. 'Sustainable Development in New Zealand'. Unpublished paper presented to the Auckland Branch Resource Management Law Association. November 2002.

Skelton, P. & A. Memon. 'Adopting Sustainability as an Overarching Environmental Policy: A Review of Section 5 of the RMA'. *Resource Management Journal* 10, no. 1 (2002): 1-10.

Somerville, R., QC. *Intensive*: *The Courts and the Environment – Serious Issues: Environmental and Resource Management Law*. Wellington: New Zealand Law Society, 2003.

Statistics New Zealand. '2006 Cencus'. <www.stats.govt.nz/census/census-outputs/default.htm>, 12 December 2007.

Statistics New Zealand. 'Estimated resident population of New Zealand'. <www.stats.govt.nz/populationclock.htm>, 17 September 2008.

Upton, S., H. Atkins & G. Willis. 'Section 5 Re-visited: A Critique of Skelton and Memon's analysis'. *Resource Management Journal* 10, no. 3 (2002): 10-22.

Warnock, C. 'Greenhouse Gases and Climate Change'. *Resource Management Bulletin* (2006): 191-193.

Wilson, J. 'Government and nation'. In *Te Ara: The Encyclopedia of New Zealand*, edited by MCH. Wellington: Ministry for Culture and Heritage, 2003. <www.TeAra.govt.nz/EarthSeaAndSky/OceanStudyAndConservation/Law OfTheSea/en>, 12 December 2007.

Young, D. *Values as Law: The History and Efficacy of the Resource Management Act*. Wellington: Milne Print Ltd, 2001.

TABLE OF LEGISLATION

Biosecurity Act 1993
Climate Change Response Act 2004
Conservation Act 1987
Constitution Act 1986
Crown Minerals Act 1991
District Courts Act 1947

TABLE OF CASES

New Zealand Rail Ltd v. Marlborough District Council [1994] NZRMA 70
Ngaati Kahu Ki Whangaroa Co-operative Society v. The Northland Regional Council EC, A95/00, 4 August 2000
Ngaati Kahu Ki Whangaroa Co-operative Society v. The Northland Regional Council [2001] NZRMA 299
North Shore City Council v. Auckland Regional City [1997] NZRMA 59
Shirley Primary School v. Telecom Mobile Communications Ltd [1999] NZRMA 66
Telecom New Zealand Limited v. Christchurch City Council EC, Q 165/96, 15 November 1996
Trio Holdings v. Marlborough District Council [1997] NZRMA 97
Wratten v. Tasman District Council EC, W 8/98, 17 March 1998

TABLE OF INTERNATIONAL INSTRUMENTS

Kyoto Protocol (1997) 37 *ILM* 22
Report of the World Commission on Environment and Development (1987)
Rio Declaration on Environment and Development (1992) 31 *ILM* 874

ABBREVIATIONS

EC	Environment Court
EEZ	Exclusive Economic Zone
ME	Ministry for the Environment
NES	National Environmental Statements
PCE	Parliamentary Commissioner for the Environment
QMS	Quota Management System
RMA	Resource Management Act 1991
Treaty	Treaty of Waitangi
UK	United Kingdom

Chapter 12

Pakistan

Parvez Hassan and Jawad Hassan*

1   INTRODUCTION

This chapter addresses the environmental issues facing Pakistan and the role of the judiciary in developing environmental governance in the country. Various laws, rules and regulations have been enacted with the aim of curtailing and controlling environmental pollution. These have been interpreted and implemented by the courts of Pakistan in several cases. Notwithstanding the foregoing, there still exists a gap between government policies and legislative objectives and their implementation. The environmental issues that are currently faced in Pakistan are discussed below. Principal environmental laws of Pakistan are also outlined, along with the governance structure and a brief overview of the courts of Pakistan. Further, the landmark judgments on environmental issues are discussed, followed by a consideration of the challenges that are presently confronting the judiciary in implementing environmental laws in Pakistan and improving the country's overall environmental governance effort.

* The authors gratefully acknowledge the valuable assistance of Ms Maryam Mamdot, Barrister-at-Law, Hassan & Hassan (Advocates), Lahore (Pakistan), in the preparation of this chapter.

Louis J. Kotzé and Alexander R. Paterson (eds), *The Role of the Judiciary in Environmental Governance: Comparative Perspectives*, pp. 381–409.
© 2009 Kluwer Law International BV, The Netherlands.

2   ENVIRONMENTAL ISSUES

Pakistan is a federal republic comprising of: the Islamabad Capital Territory; the four Provinces of Balochistan, North West Frontier, Punjab and Sindh; and the Federally Administered Tribal Areas. It has a population of about 160 million people. The country adopted a Constitution in 1973, which has survived repeated amendments by military governments.

Pakistan was one of the earlier countries in the Asia Pacific Region to promulgate, in 1983, a national framework law on environmental protection.[1] Population pressures, misallocation of national resources, and the lack of enforcement of the framework environmental law have, however, led to a situation where the overwhelming majority of the population continues to be without access to the basic amenities of life, specifically clean water and clean air. Pakistan's cities, burdened with an ever-increasing exodus from rural areas, are bursting at the seams and faced with the challenge of providing satisfactory access to housing, public transportation, health care and waste disposal facilities. Forest cover, a crucial guardian of the climate and soil, is at about 4%, one of the lowest global percentages. The Indus river system, which provided the backbone to the granary of British India, continues to be threatened with salinity and water logging. The rivers and public waterways have become repositories for untreated chemicals, and industrial and domestic waste which threatens the food chain. The country's mangroves, one of the largest eco-systems of its type in the world, are threatened by land development and pollution. The menace of increasing desertification also continues to overwhelm the country. Notwithstanding some gains in several areas as a result of trophy hunting schemes supported by local communities, the wildlife heritage is under serious threat. Growing energy needs also are not adequately met and cultural heritage is the victim of neglect and inattention.[2]

3   PRINCIPAL ENVIRONMENTAL LAWS

3.1   GENERAL LAWS

There is no specific reference to environmental protection either as a fundamental right or as a principle of policy in the Constitution of Pakistan, 1973 (Constitution). In fact, the only reference to the environment is found in the Concurrent List, Item 24 of the Constitution, which provides for 'environment pollution and ecology' as a concurrent legislative competence of the federal and provincial governments.

---

1. *Pakistan Environmental Protection Ordinance*, 1983.
2. The Pakistan Environmental Protection Agency (PEPA) catalogues the important publications of the government of Pakistan on environmental matters which acknowledges the challenges before Pakistan, see Pakistan Environmental Protection Agency, 'Publications', <www.environment. gov.pk/Publications.htm>, 21 September 2008. An earlier exposition of environmental problems of Pakistan can be found in M.A. Khan, *Government of Pakistan, Environment and Urban Affairs Division, Environmental Profile of Pakistan* (Islamabad: Government of Pakistan, Environment and Urban Affairs Division, 1986).

The general federal and provincial laws that include some environmental provisions include: the Pakistan Penal Code 1860; the Code of Criminal Procedure 1868; the *Canal and Drainage Act* 1873; the *Explosives Act* 1884; the *Forest Act* 1927; the *Factories Act* 1934; the *West Pakistan Fisheries Ordinance* 1961; the *West Pakistan Regulation and Control of Loudspeakers and Sound Amplifiers Ordinance* 1965; the *Agricultural Pest Ordinance* 1971; the *Territorial Waters and Maritime Zones Act* 1976; the *Motor Vehicles Ordinance* 1965; the *Provincial Wildlife Protection Ordinances*; and the *Provincial Local Government Ordinances*, 2001 (PLGO). The *Pakistan Environmental Protection Ordinance, 1983*, constitutes the first attempt to create a framework environmental law for the country.

3.2   PAKISTAN ENVIRONMENTAL PROTECTION ORDINANCE, 1983

The main object of the 1983 Ordinance was to 'provide for the control of pollution and preservation of living environment and for matters connected therewith or ancillary thereto' (preamble). At the federal level, the 1983 Ordinance established the Pakistan Environmental Protection Council (PEPC) as the supreme policy-making body supported by the Pakistan Environmental Protection Agency (PEPA). The PEPA was, in a way, the implementation arm of the PEPC. Four Environmental Protection Agencies (provincial EPAs) were also established at the provincial level and each of these is mandated to work under the policies prescribed by the PEPC and implemented by the PEPA.

Section 8 of the 1983 Ordinance, being the main substantive provision, broke new ground by requiring an environmental impact assessment (EIA) for development projects. In terms of the Ordinance, an EIA was required for any project the construction or completion of which was likely to adversely affect the environment. The EIA had to be filed with the PEPA at the time of planning the project and had to include information on: the environmental impacts associated with the project, the treatment works related to the proposed project, the unavoidable adverse environmental effects of the proposed project, and the steps to be taken by the project proponent to minimize these effects. However, although an EIA theoretically was a statutory requirement for commencing a range of activities, the regulations which were to give practical effect to the implementation of the above requirements were never prescribed. Therefore, the only substantive provision of the 1983 Ordinance was stillborn.

3.3   PAKISTAN ENVIRONMENTAL PROTECTION ACT, 1997

The 1997 Act, which replaced the 1983 Ordinance, provides for the protection, conservation, rehabilitation and improvement of the environment, prevention and control of pollution, and promotion of sustainable development. It expands on the environmental matters covered in the 1983 Ordinance and is unique in the sense that its enactment was preceded and informed by extensive public debate so as to enhance public ownership of the law.

The 1997 Act retains the institutional framework created under the 1983 Ordinance. The PEPC continues to be the supreme policy-making body, supported by the PEPA, and provincial EPAs. The PEPC is mandated to approve national environmental policies within the framework of a national conservation strategy as may be approved by the federal government from time to time.[3] Provincial Sustainable Development Funds have been established to provide financial assistance to suitable projects.[4] Discharges or emissions exceeding the National Environmental Quality Standards (NEQS) established by the PEPC or other standards established by the PEPA, are prohibited. The federal government has also been empowered to levy a pollution charge on persons not complying with the NEQS.[5] A two-stage environmental screening process has been introduced for proposed projects involving the filing of either an initial environmental examination (IEE) or, for projects likely to cause an adverse environmental effect, a comprehensive EIA.

Importing hazardous waste[6] and the handling of hazardous substances have been prohibited except under license.[7] To ensure compliance with the NEQS, the PEPA and provincial EPAs are empowered to direct that motor vehicles install prescribed pollution control devices, use prescribed fuels, or undergo prescribed maintenance or testing. The PEPA and provincial EPAs can issue environmental protection orders (EPOs) to deal with an actual or potential adverse environmental effect in violation of the provisions of the 1997 Act. Environmental Tribunals have been established with exclusive jurisdiction to try serious offences under the 1997 Act. Minor offences relating to pollution by motor vehicles, littering, waste disposal and the violation of rules and regulations, can be tried by Environmental Magistrates. An aggrieved person can file a complaint with the Environmental Tribunal after giving thirty days notice to the relevant PEPA or provincial EPA.

3.4   RULES AND REGULATIONS

Section 31 of the 1997 Act enables the federal government to make rules for carrying out the objectives of the Act, including rules for implementing the provisions of international environmental agreements specified in the schedule to the 1997 Act.[8]

---

3. S. 4.
4. S. 9.
5. S. 11(2).
6. S. 13.
7. S. 14.
8. Some of the international agreements included in the schedule to the Act are: International Plant Protection Convention 1951; Plant Protection Agreement for South-East Asia and Pacific Region 1956; Agreement for the Establishment of a Commission for Controlling the Desert Locust in the Eastern Region of its Distribution Area in South-West Asia 1963; Convention on Wetlands of International Importance Especially as Waterfowl Habitat 1971; Convention Concerning the Protection of World Culture and Natural Heritage (World Heritage Convention) 1972; Convention on International Trade in Endangered Species of Wild Fauna and Flora 1973; Convention on Biological Diversity 1992; and United Nations Framework Convention on Climate Change 1992.

The 1997 Act also grants powers to the PEPA to make regulations, with the approval of the federal government, that are consistent with the provisions of the 1997 Act and the rules made under it.[9] Section 33(2) of the 1997 Act sets out that these regulations may provide for the: submission of periodical reports, data or information by any government agency, local authority or local council in respect of environmental matters; preparation of emergency contingency plans for coping with environmental hazards and pollution caused by accidents, natural disasters and calamities; appointment of officers, advisors, experts, consultants and employees; levy of fees, rates and charges in respect of services rendered, actions taken and schemes implemented; monitoring and measurement of discharges and emissions; categorization of projects to which, and the manner in which, the provisions of the 1997 Act relating to EIA apply; prescription of guidelines for preparing initial environmental examinations, EIAs and developing procedures for their filing, review and approval; establishment of procedures for handling hazardous substances; and the installation of devices in, and use of fuels by, and maintenance and testing of motor vehicles for the control of air and noise pollution.

Several rules and regulations have been issued to date. The rules include: the National Environmental Quality Standards (Self-Monitoring and Reporting by Industries) Rules 2001; the Provincial Sustainable Development Fund (Procedure) Rules 2002; the Provincial Sustainable Development Fund (Utilization) Rules 2002; the Industrial Pollution Charge (Calculation and Collection) Rules 2002; the Environmental Samples Rules 2001; the Hospital Waste Management Rules 2005; the Environmental Tribunal Rules 1999; and the Pakistan Bio-safety Rules 2005. Regulations issued thus far include: the Review of IEE/EIA Regulations, 2000;[10] and the Environmental Laboratories Certification Regulations, 2001.[11]

4 INSTITUTIONS AND GOVERNANCE STRUCTURES

4.1 THE FEDERAL MINISTRY

A Federal Minister of Environment was first appointed in the Federal Cabinet in March 1989. The Federal Minister is supported by the Ministry of Environment headed by a federal secretary.

4.2 PAKISTAN ENVIRONMENTAL PROTECTION COUNCIL

The PEPC was established in 1983 as the supreme environmental policy-making body in the country. The president of Pakistan was to act as chairman, the Federal

---

9. S. 33.
10. See The Gazette of Pakistan, Statutory Notification SRO No. 339(I)/2000 of 13 June 2000.
11. See The Gazette of Pakistan, Statutory Notification SRO No. 258(I)/2000 of 10 February 2000.

Minister for Environment as vice chairman, the governors of the four provinces as members, any other persons as appointed by the federal government as members, and the secretary to the government as the secretary of the PEPC.

The form and structure of the PEPC was largely retained following the enactment of the 1997 Act. Under section 3 of the 1997 Act, the prime minister or his/her nominee shall be the chairperson of the PEPC and the Federal Minister for Environment shall be its vice chairperson. Chief ministers of the four provinces and provincial ministers for environment are also included. Further, the federal government may appoint up to thirty-five persons as members of the PEPC, out of whom at least twenty are required to be non-government officials. The non-official members are to be drawn from civil society including five representatives of the Chambers of Commerce and Industry and industrial associations, and one or more representatives of: the Chambers of Agriculture; the medical and legal professions; trade unions and non-governmental organizations (NGOs) concerned with the environment and development; and scientists, technical experts and educationists. The federal secretary for Environment is the secretary of the PEPC.

The powers and functions of the PEPC are set out in section 4 of the 1997 Act. The PEPC is tasked with: coordinating and supervising the enforcement of the 1997 Act; approving comprehensive national environmental policies and ensuring their implementation within the framework of a national conservation strategy as may be approved by the federal government from time to time; approving the NEQS; providing guidelines for the protection and conservation of species, habitats, and biodiversity in general, and for conserving renewable and non-renewable resources; coordinating and integrating the principles and concerns of sustainable development into national development plans and policies; and considering the National Environmental Report and giving appropriate directions thereon.

4.3   PAKISTAN ENVIRONMENTAL PROTECTION AGENCY

The PEPA, established under the 1983 Ordinance and similarly retained under the 1997 Act, is headed by a Director-General appointed by the federal government, who exercises and performs the powers and functions of the PEPA. The Director-General may delegate any of the powers and functions to the administrative, technical and legal staff of the PEPA. The primary responsibility for administering and implementing the provisions of the 1997 Act lies with the Director-General of the EPAs in terms of sections 6 and 7 of the 1997 Act. However, section 26 of the 1997 Act specifically deals with the issue of delegation of functions and powers and enables the federal government to delegate any of its or the federal EPA's functions and powers to the provincial EPAs.

Section 5(6) provides that, in order to assist the PEPA, the federal government shall establish advisory committees for various sectors, and appoint as members thereof eminent representatives of the relevant sector, educational institutions, research institutes and NGOs.

The functions and powers of the PEPA are set out in section 6 and section 7 of the 1997 Act respectively. The functions of the PEPA include: administering and implementing the provisions of the 1997 Act and the rules and regulations made under it; preparing, in coordination with the appropriate government agency, national environmental policies for approval by the PEPC; taking all necessary measures for implementing national environmental policies approved by the Council; preparing and publishing an Annual National Environment Report on the State of the Environment; preparing or revising and establishing the NEQS with approval of the PEPC; ensuring enforcement of the NEQS; and establishing standards for the quality of the ambient air, water and land, in consultation with the appropriate provincial agency.

4.4 THE PROVINCIAL MINISTRY

At the provincial level, all four provinces have environment ministries headed by a provincial minister and environmental departments headed by a provincial secretary. Regarding enforcement at the provincial level, section 8 of the 1997 Act directs the provincial Secretary of Environment to establish provincial EPAs.

4.5 PROVINCIAL EPAS

Provincial EPAs are established under section 8 of the 1997 Act to exercise and perform such powers and functions as are delegated to them by the provincial government under section 26(2) of the Act.

The Provincial EPA is headed by a Director-General appointed by the provincial government. The Director-General may delegate any of his/her powers and functions to any of the administrative, technical and legal staff appointed by the provincial government. Section 8(6) of the 1997 Act compels the provincial government to establish advisory committees for various environmental sectors to assist the provincial EPA in the discharge of its functions. The members of these committees comprise of eminent representatives of the relevant sector, educational institutions, research institutes and NGOs.

4.6 OTHER RELEVANT FEDERAL MINISTRIES AND PROVINCIAL DEPARTMENTS

In addition to the above federal ministries, provincial ministries, departments and agencies, there are other ministries at the federal level and departments at the provincial level that deal with environmental issues. At the federal level, these include the Ministry of Food, Agriculture and Livestock (MINFAL); the Ministry of Health; and the National Environmental Co-ordination Committee (NECC) (previously known as the Marine Pollution Control Board (MPCB)). The Department of Local Government and Department of Forests and Wildlife also play an important role in environmental governance at the provincial level.

4.7   MARINE POLLUTION CONTROL BOARD

In 1994, the Government of Pakistan set up the MPCB to supervise and implement pollution control and prevention measures along Pakistan's coastline. The cabinet entrusted the functions of the MPCB to the NECC in September 2001, as envisaged by section 7(k) of the 1997 Act. The NECC accordingly suggests measures for prevention and elimination of marine pollution.

4.8   LOCAL GOVERNMENTS

After the promulgation of the Provincial Local Government Ordinance (PLGO) in 2001, district governments were established consisting of Zilla Nazim and district administrative departments. The Zilla Nazim is the head of the district government who performs such functions and exercises such powers as have been assigned to him/her under the PLGO. These can include maintaining administrative and financial discipline, ensuring district-wide development, exercising leadership; facilitating efficient functioning, developing strategies and determining time frames for accomplishing relevant goals. The new system of local governance has been designed to more efficiently address specific needs and challenges, including environmental challenges, within each district. The district government is responsible to the people and the provincial government for improving governance and service delivery.

The PLGO has specifically enhanced the implementation and enforcement of environmental regulation at the local level. The federal Secretary of the Environment has further delegated such powers and functions to the provincial EPA. However, to ensure environmental compliance at the local level, it is suggested that some powers under the 1997 Act need to be delegated to local government.

5   OVERVIEW OF THE COURT SYSTEM

5.1   HISTORICAL DEVELOPMENT

The momentous United Nations Conference on the Human Environment, held in Stockholm in 1972 (from which the Stockholm Declaration emerged), pioneered international concern for resource management and environmental protection. The Stockholm Declaration eloquently proclaimed that the natural resources of the earth, including the air, water, land, flora and fauna, and especially representative samples of natural ecosystems, must be safeguarded for the benefit of present and future generations. Some countries' constitutions include the right to a healthy environment as a fundamental right, while others impose a duty on citizens and States to protect the environment and promote the quality of life of all. Although the Constitution of Pakistan was adopted in 1973, one year after Stockholm,[12] and despite providing specific provisions on fundamental rights relating to equality, religion, association and property, there is no specific reference to environmental protection in the Constitution.

In 1959, in *Province of East Pakistan v. MD Mehdi Ali Khan*,[13] the Pakistani Supreme Court held that:

> Any one who challenges the constitutionality of a law must raise a case in the decision of [sic] which has real and personal interest, in the sense that as an individual he would be adversely affected if the law which operates against him is not found and declared to be unconstitutional. He cannot move the Court *pro bono publico* or merely as a 'tax payer'.

However, the Pakistani courts have never shown an unerring devotion to procedural limitations. In *Imtiaz Ahmed v. Ghulam Ali*,[14] which was also a decision by the Supreme Court, it was observed that:

> [t]he proper place for procedure in any system of the administration of justice is to help and not thwart the grant to the people of their rights. All technicalities have to be avoided unless it is essential to comply with on grounds of public policy. Any system which by giving effect to the form and not to the substance defeats substantive rights [and] is defective to that extent.

This lowering of the threshold of entry (*locus standi*) took time and it was only after the Indian courts had developed the methodology of public interest litigation that the doctrine took root in Pakistan. This happened in 1988 when, in *Benazir Bhutto v. Federation of Pakistan*,[15] (*Benazir Bhutto* case), the full bench of the Supreme Court of Pakistan paved the way for future public interest litigation in Pakistan. The co-chairperson of one of Pakistan's leading political parties, Ms Benazir Bhutto, filed a direct petition in the Supreme Court of Pakistan under Article 184 of the Constitution, which allows the Supreme Court to make an order if a question of public importance has arisen regarding the enforcement of fundamental rights included in the Constitution. The martial law government in power at the time had passed an amendment to the *Political Parties Act* (III of 1962) which compelled political parties to register themselves with the Election

---

12. Although Pakistan was to play a leading role in the Rio Earth Summit in 1992, it was barely visible in the UN Stockholm Conference on the Human Environment in 1972 for it had just emerged from the trauma and shame of the war of secession that led to the creation of Bangladesh in 1971. This may also explain the absence of environmental provisions in the 1973 Constitution.
13. 1959 PLD SC 387, 408.
14. 1963 PLD SC 382, 400.
15. 1988 PLD SC 416.

Commission of Pakistan prior to contesting in the elections. Ms Bhutto, in her petition, contended that the amendment constituted a violation of Article 17 of the Constitution which guaranteed the right of association. The Supreme Court declared that the amendment was *ultra vires* Article 17 and held further that the right to form an association was a continuing right and therefore any enactment which violated it could be struck down.

In this case, the State had argued that Ms Bhutto had no *locus standi*, as the political party was not the aggrieved party. Responding to the contention of the State, the court declared that the exercise of the power of the Supreme Court under Article 184 is not only available to the 'aggrieved party'. It shared the concern of the Indian courts that a constitutional right should not be a 'dead letter'. The court accordingly held that where the fundamental rights of a class or a group of persons who are unable to seek redress from a court have been violated, the traditional rule of *locus standi* can be dispensed with and procedures available in public interest litigation can be employed if it is brought to the Court by a person with *bona fide* intentions. Placing reliance on the Indian Supreme Court decision in *SP Gupta v. Union of India*,[16] and drawing an analogy with the 'next friend' provisions in the existing rules of civil procedure, the court noted that:

> [a]fter all the law is not a closed shop and, even in adversary procedure, it is permissible for the next friend to move the Court on behalf of a minor or a person under a disability. . . . why not then a person, if he were to act bona fide, activise the Court for several reasons. This is what public interest litigation seeks to achieve as it goes further to relax the rule on *locus standi*. . . .

Although the wording of public interest litigation has been used here, it does not sit well with the background of the case inasmuch as Ms Bhutto was a wealthy person and one of the country's most powerful politicians. It could accordingly be argued that the first 'genuine' public interest litigation case in Pakistan was *Darshin Masih v. The State*.[17] In factual circumstances reminiscent of those in *Bandhua Mukti Morcha v. Union of India*,[18] the Supreme Court founded jurisdiction on a telegram sent by a group of brick kiln bonded labourers and their families. The court noted that the assumption of jurisdiction in the case was a permissible extension of the principle laid down in the *Benazir Bhutto* case but that: '[S]uch extension/s would depend on the facts and the circumstances of each case and nature of public importance involved and importance thereof'.

The record of the superior courts in Pakistan shows that public interest litigation has been applied successfully to a broad spectrum of social ills; from discriminatory laws and regulations affecting women and children to the humiliating treatment of prisoners. These cases arose from three major sources: letters written to the Chief Justice of the superior courts of Pakistan; newspaper reports (which

---

16. 1982 AIR SC 149.
17. 1990 PLD SC 513.
18. 1984 AIR SC 802.

become the basis of *suo motu* actions by the courts); and cases filed by petitioners that raised questions concerning human rights.

As in India, a novel approach had to be taken by the Pakistani courts with respect to both the initiation of cases (for example, recognizing an epistolary jurisdiction) and their subsequent conduct since the traditional system of pleadings could not accommodate this new form of litigation. As the human rights cases typically involved a factual and sometimes technical enquiry, the appellate courts had to resort to the use of expert commissions, whose findings could become the basis for further action.

Once a general jurisdiction tailored to human rights abuses was established, it was only a matter of time before the courts of Pakistan would be required to exercise it with respect to all manner of public injury, including threats to the environment.

5.2   COURT STRUCTURE AND HIERARCHY OF COURTS

5.2.1   Supreme Court of Pakistan

The Constitution contains elaborate provisions on the composition, jurisdiction, powers and functions of the Supreme Court, entrusting it to 'preserve, protect and defend' the Constitution. Not only does the Supreme Court exercise original, appellate and advisory jurisdiction, but also acts as the court of ultimate appeal and therefore is the final arbiter of law and the Constitution. The Supreme Court also exercises original jurisdiction (concurrently with High Courts) for the enforcement of fundamental rights, where a question of 'public importance' (including environmental issues) is involved.

Article 184(3) of the Constitution, which sets out the jurisdiction of the Supreme Court in respect of public interest litigation, provides:

> Without prejudice to the provisions of Article 199, the Supreme Court shall, if it considers that a question of public importance with reference to the enforcement of any of the Fundamental Rights, conferred by Chapter 1 of Part-II, is involved, have the power to make an order of the nature mentioned in the said Article.

Article 189 of the Constitution prescribes that the decisions of the Supreme Court are binding on all other courts in Pakistan.

5.2.2   Provincial High Courts

There is a High Court in each province. Each High Court consists of a Chief Justice and puisne judges. The court exercises original jurisdiction in the enforcement of fundamental rights and appellate jurisdiction in judgments/orders of the subordinate courts.

Provincial High Courts have jurisdiction under Article 199 of the Constitution to entertain various petitions of judicial review in writ jurisdiction. Moreover, the

High Court also acts as an appellate court under section 22 of the 1997 Act to adjudicate against the orders of the Environmental Tribunals.[19] Under Article 201 of the Constitution, the decisions of the High Court are binding on all the subordinate courts.

5.2.3   Environmental Tribunals

The Environmental Tribunals constituted under section 20 of the 1997 Act have exclusive jurisdiction to try serious environmental offences and to hear appeals in this respect. Environmental Tribunals[20] are federal bodies (comprising of a chairperson, member legal and member technical) constituted under section 20 of the 1997 Act. They have exclusive jurisdiction to try serious offences provided by section 17(1),[21] and further to hear appeals against the orders of EPAs under section 22. The tribunals are established in all the provinces. The Environmental Tribunals were not constituted immediately after the promulgation of the PEPA, but rather in 1999, on the direction of the Supreme Court of Pakistan.

In *Shaheen Welfare Society v. Environmental Protection Agency Punjab, Lahore*,[22] the Punjab Environmental Tribunal, Lahore, held that the tribunal is competent to hear criminal matters punishable under section 17(1) of the 1997 Act. Moreover, such powers vest exclusively with this special tribunal as no other authority, court or special court has so far been afforded jurisdiction to entertain such matters.

The Environmental Tribunal can adjudicate on complaints lodged by the following:[23] the federal or provincial EPA; private individuals (a private complaint can be lodged after a period of thirty days has lapsed following the issue of a notice to the relevant EPA); Nazims (through the District Co-ordination Officer or Executive District Officer Works[24] of local government under the *Local Government Ordinance*, 2001; and private individuals who feel aggrieved by the actions of EPAs.

5.2.4   District and Session Courts

This subordinate judicial organ may broadly be divided into two parts, namely: civil courts established under the *West Pakistan Civil Court Ordinance* 1962; and

---

19. See the discussion below.
20. Government of Pakistan, Ministry of Law, Notification No. F. 22(1)/97-A-III (A) of 2 June 1999.
21. These cover: prohibited discharge and emissions, the prohibited import of hazardous wastes, violations of the requirements of an IEE and EIA, and non-compliance with an environmental protection order (EPO) issued by an EPA.
22. 2005 CLD Punjab Environmental Protection Tribunal, Lahore, 1267.
23. Government of Pakistan, Law, Justice, & Human Rights Division, *Year Book 2004-05* (Islamabad: LJ&HR, 2005).
24. *District Nazim Sheikhupura v. Shafi Spinning Mills Ltd* 2004 Punjab Environment Protection Tribunal, Lahore. Judgment passed on 11 October 2004.

criminal courts created under the Criminal Procedure Code 1898. In addition, there also exist other courts and tribunals of civil and criminal nature, created under special laws and enactments.[25] Their jurisdiction, powers and functions are specified in the statutes creating them. The decisions and judgments of such special courts are assailable before the superior judiciary (High Courts and/or Supreme Court) through revision or appeal.

The District and Session Courts act as the appellate *fora* against the judgments of the Environmental Magistrates under section 23 of the 1997 Act.

5.2.5   Environment Magistrates

Civil judges and magistrates have been empowered as environmental magistrates under section 24(1) of the 1997 Act by all four High Courts to deal with minor offences such as: handling/disposing of hazardous waste; pollution from motor vehicles; and enforcing compliance with orders of the EPAs. Under section 24 of the 1997 Act, a special Office of the Environmental Magistrate has been constituted to try offences punishable under section 17(2) of the 1997 Act. The 1997 Act provides that environmental magistrates shall be empowered in this respect by the High Court.[26]

The Lahore High Court in *Allah Ditta v. M. Ramzan*,[27] held that only senior civil judges of the districts, appointed by notification, can entertain these cases under the 1997 Act.

5.2.6   Quasi Judicial Forums

The Director-General and the directors of the PEPA and the provincial EPAs, can adjudicate all environmental matters and can summon any person to appear before them. Section 16 of the 1997 Act provides a quasi-judicial mechanism to curb the harmful effects of pollution caused by any activity, in the form of an environmental protection order (EPO), which can be issued by the federal or provincial EPA. The pollution causing activities against which an EPO can be issued include polluting discharges/emissions and any other act contravening the provisions of the 1997 Act and the rules and regulations made under it.

5.3   Analysis of Significant Environmental Judgments

The following sections analyse a selection of some of the most significant environmental judgments in Pakistan.

---

25. Special laws setting up special tribunals in other areas include: the Banking Courts under the Financial Institutions (Recovery of Finances) Ordinance 2001; the Labour Court under the Industrial Relations Ordinance 2002; the Services Tribunal under the Service Tribunal Act 1974; and the Income Tax Tribunal under the Income Tax Ordinance 2001.
26. Government of Pakistan, Ministry of Law, Notification No. 293 of 15 July 1998.
27. 2005 YLR Lahore 650.

5.3.1   Supreme Court of Pakistan

In 1994, the Supreme Court of Pakistan delivered its landmark judgment in *Shehla Zia and Others v. WAPDA*,[28] (*Shehla Zia* case), where a petition was made against the construction of a high voltage grid station by WAPDA in a residential area of Islamabad. The residents of this neighbourhood, led by Ms Shehla Zia, contended that the electro magnetic radiation of the grid station would likely be harmful to the health of the residents. The residents were also concerned about the violation of the city's much prized green belt regulations.[29] The absence of specific environmental provisions in the Constitution posed a serious problem for the applicants in this case. The present co-author, Dr Parvez Hassan, who acted as counsel for the petitioners, had to rely on the extensive comparative environmental case law of India which had held that the 'right to life' included and embraced a 'quality' of life. The fact that the Pakistan Constitution protected the 'right to dignity' (Article 14), was further used to argue for a broad interpretation of the right to life entrenched in Article 9 of the Constitution.[30] The Supreme Court, speaking through Justice Saleem Akhtar, accepted these arguments and held that the right to life guaranteed by Article 9 of the Constitution included the right to a healthy environment.

The first major legal consequence flowing from this judgment was that the right to a quality of life was held to be guaranteed by the Constitution:

> The word life has not been defined in the Constitution but it does not mean nor can it be restricted only to the vegetative or animal life or mere existence from conception to death. Life includes all such amenities or facilities which a person in a free country is entitled to enjoy with dignity, legally and constitutionally.[31]

The receptivity of the court to the precautionary principle covered in Principle 15 of the Rio Declaration on Environment and Development 1992, was another significant development.[32] The applicant's counsel took the Supreme Court through an extended personal report of Pakistan's leadership, as the chair of the Group of 77, of the developing countries at the Rio Earth Summit in 1992 and of its role as one of the principal architects of the Rio success. The historical exposition was reflected in the court's judgment:

> The concerns for protecting [the] environment were first internationally recognized when the declaration of [the] United Nations Conference on the

---

28. 1994 PLD SC 693.
29. *Id.*
30. P. Hassan & A. Azfar, 'Securing Environmental Rights through Public Interest Litigation in South Asia', *VELJ* 22, no. 3 (2004): 216-236.
31. *Supra* n. 28, 712.
32. The impact of the Shehla Zia case in the environmental jurisprudence of Pakistan has been discussed in P. Hassan, 'Shehla Zia v. Wapda: Ten Years Later', *PLD Journal* (2005): 48-57. See also, generally, P. Hassan, 'From Rio 1992 to Johannesburg 2002: A Case Study of Implementing Sustainable Development in Pakistan', *SJICL* 6 (2002): 683-722.

Human Environment was adopted at Stockholm on 16 June, 1972. Thereafter it has taken two decades to create awareness and consensus among the countries when in 1992 Rio Declaration was adopted. Pakistan is a signatory to this declaration and according to Dr Parvez Hassan although it has not been ratified or enacted, the principle so adopted has its own sanctity and it should be implemented, if not in letter, at least in spirit.[33]

The court readily accepted the thrust of these submissions. While recognizing the fact that the Rio Declaration was not a formal part of Pakistani law, the court nonetheless stated that it commanded respect as a major international treaty of far-reaching significance for human progress:

The Rio Declaration is the product of hectic discussion among the leaders of the nations of the world and it was after negotiations between the developed and the developing countries that an almost consensual declaration had been sorted out. [The] Environment is an international problem having no frontiers creating trans-boundary effects. In this field every nation has to cooperate and contribute and for this reason the Rio Declaration would serve as a great binding force and to create discipline among the nations when dealing with environmental problems.[34]

With respect to the precautionary principle adopted in the Rio Declaration, the Supreme Court approvingly declared:

[i]t would not be out of place to mention that Principle No. 15 envisages rule[s] of precaution and prudence. According to it if there are threats of serious damage, effective measures should be taken to control it and it should not be postponed merely on the ground that scientific research and studies are uncertain and not conclusive. It enshrines the principle that prevention is better than cure. It is a cautious approach to avert a catastrophe at the earliest stage. Pakistan is a developing country. It cannot afford the researches [sic] and studies made in developed countries on scientific problems particularly the subject at hand. However, the researches [sic] and their conclusions with reference to specific cases are available, the information and knowledge is at hand and we should take benefit out of it. In this background if we consider the problem faced by us in this case, it seems reasonable to take preventive and precautionary measures straightaway instead of maintaining [the] status quo because there is no conclusive finding on the effect of electromagnetic fields on human life. One should not wait for conclusive finding[s] as it may take ages to find it out and, therefore, measures should be taken to avert any possible danger and for that reason one should not go to scrap the entire scheme but could make such adjustments, alterations or additions which may ensure safety and security or at least minimize the possible hazards.[35]

---

33. *Supra* n. 28, 710.
34. *Ibid.*
35. *Ibid.*

Respect for sustainable development can also be gleaned from the following passage where the court stated that the energy needs of a developing country, though essential, cannot justify injurious projects:

> One cannot ignore that energy is essential for present-day life, industry, commerce, and day-to-day affairs. The more energy is produced and distributed, the more progress and economic development become possible. Therefore, a method should be devised to strike [a] balance between economic progress and prosperity and to minimize possible hazards. . . . our need is greater as it is bound to affect our economic development, but in the quest of economic development one has to adopt such measures which may not create hazards to life, destroy the environment and pollute the atmosphere.[36]

In its order, the Supreme Court afforded significant relief to the petitioners by staying the construction of the grid station until further studies had been conducted to establish the nature and extent of the threat posed by electro-magnetic radiation emitted by power plants.

A further important implication of the *Shehla Zia* case for the further development of environmental law in Pakistan, is that the word 'life' as contained in Article 9 of the Constitution, read together with the requirement for dignity of man (human dignity) contained in Article 14, denotes the fundamental right to an unpolluted environment. The case also established the application of the precautionary principle where there is a threat to these rights.

The *Shehla Zia* case has been cited with approval in many subsequent cases in the Supreme Court and in subordinate courts. In *General Secretary Salt Miners Labour Union (CBA) Khewra, Jhelum v. The Director, Industries and Mineral Development, Punjab, Lahore*,[37] (*Khewra Mines* case), the petitioners sought to enforce the right of the residents to clean and unpolluted water which was being undermined by upstream coal mining activities. The Supreme Court, citing the *Shehla Zia* case, stated that '[T]he right to have unpolluted water is the right of every person wherever he lives'.[38] In this case the court, speaking again through Justice Saleem Akhtar, also took the opportunity to reiterate its openness to removing procedural constraints in public interest litigation cases and the broad and flexible powers it enjoys in this regard:

> It is well settled that in human rights cases/public interest litigation under Article 184 (3), the procedural trappings and restrictions, precondition of being an aggrieved person and other similar technical objections, cannot bar the jurisdiction of the Court. The Court has vast power, under Article 184 (3), to investigate into questions of fact as well as independently by recording evidence, appointing a commission or any other reasonable and legal manner to ascertain the correct position.[39]

---

36. *Supra* n. 28, 711.
37. 1994 SCMR 2061.
38. *Id.*, 2070.
39. *Id.*, 2071.

This was another case in which the Supreme Court appointed a five member commission to: inspect the stream and reservoir supplying the Khewra region to ensure that water supplies were not being polluted by effluent of the mines operating in the area; and to recommend methods of preventing further damage. The commission undertook a detailed inspection of the area during which it also conducted hearings involving the parties to the case, the mine operators and members of the general public. In subsequent months, laboratory tests and maps of catchment areas were procured, and two lists were prepared, one to identify mines recommended for closure and the other for those which should be allowed to continue operating. The commission kept the Supreme Court informed through interim reports and also submitted its final report for the court's insight.

In 1994, in the *Human Rights Case (Environment Pollution in Balochistan)*,[40] the Supreme Court of Pakistan moved *suo motu* to prevent the dumping of imported industrial and nuclear waste in Pakistan. The Supreme Court noticed a report in a daily newspaper regarding the purchase of coastal areas of Balochistan for the purpose of dumping industrial and nuclear waste. It reasoned:

> The coast land of Balochistan is about 450 miles long. To dump waste materials including nuclear waste from the developed countries would not only be a hazard to the health of the people but also to the environment and the marine life in the region. . . . In my view, if nuclear waste is dumped on the coastal land of Balochistan, it is bound to create environmental hazard[s] and pollution. This act will violate Article 9 of the Constitution.[41]

The court found that Article 9 of the Constitution had been violated. It ordered the government of Balochistan to explain whether coastal lands of Balochistan or any area within the territorial waters of Pakistan had been allotted to any person for the purpose of dumping such waste. The Supreme Court ordered that the allottees must not engage in dumping industrial or nuclear waste of any nature on the land or in the sea, or by destroying it by any device. The Supreme Court further directed all concerned government agencies to include a condition in the allotment letters that the allotted land should not be used for dumping industrial or nuclear waste.

In dealing with noise pollution, the Supreme Court in *Islamuddin v. Ghulam Muhammad*,[42] restrained the defendants from creating a public nuisance in their workshop, stating that even noise made in carrying on a lawful trade, if injurious to the comfort of the community, is a public nuisance.

The Supreme Court took *suo motu* action in *Islamabad Chalets and Pir Sohawa Valley Villas*,[43] restraining the construction of chalets and villas situated two kilometres from the Margalla Hills. The housing scheme in question would have had a direct bearing on the eco-system of the Margalla Hills, and the overall environment of Islamabad, because of increased traffic congestion, noise pollution,

---

40. 1994 PLD SC 102.
41. 1994 PLD SC 103.
42. 2004 PLD SC 633.
43. Suo Motu Case No. 13 of 2005, Report 2005-2006, SC of Pakistan, Golden Jubilee Edition, 106.

diminishing greenery, the annihilation of wildlife, unhygienic conditions caused by sewerage, and frequent landslides due to the loosening of soil and removal of rocks.

The Supreme Court also took *suo motu* action in the *New Murree Project* case.[44] It stated that the New Murree Project posed grave environmental hazards. The project would have destroyed 4,111 acres of reserve forest in the area north of Islamabad. This would have in turn adversely affected the annual rainfall in Islamabad, resulted in the depletion of the supply of water to nearby dams and a 50% reduction in the availability of drinking water to the twin cities of Rawalpindi and Islamabad. The government undertook, before the Supreme Court, not to cut any trees or commence any construction until the requirements of the 1997 Act have been complied with. The court also ordered the government to demolish the project buildings and to keep the court up to date on their progress.

In *Sheri-CBE v. LDA*,[45] the Supreme Court held that in view of the provision of section 12 of the 1997 Act, the very commencement of construction without filing an IEE with the PEPA was grossly illegal and an offence under the 1997 Act. It was further held that the provincial High Courts must strictly enforce the provisions of the 1997 Act and stay projects that have not filed EIAs and obtained the necessary 'no objection certificates' (NOCs). The Supreme Court accordingly stayed the construction of a multiplex cinema on an area used by residents for recreation.

The Supreme Court, by taking *suo motu* action in *Moulvi Iqbal Haider v. Capital Development Authority*,[46] restrained and cancelled a lease agreement for developing a mini golf course in Islamabad on the site of Jubilee Park. The basis of the court's decision was that the project contravened the fundamental rights of the general public, enshrined under Article 26 of the Constitution.

5.3.2   The High Courts

Margala Hills have been declared a national park under section 21 of the *Islamabad Wildlife (Protection, Preservation, Conservation and Management) Ordinance*, 1979. In 1990, a petition was filed by the Margala Hills Society in the Lahore High Court in *Roedad Khan v. Federation of Pakistan and 41 others*.[47] The complaint was that the construction of a large complex, the quarrying activities carried out by a cement company and various other stone crushing activities undertaken in the Margala Hills National Park had resulted in the breaking up and clearing of land, the felling of trees and the discharge of effluents into the park. It was argued that these activities accordingly posed a serious health hazard to the residents of Islamabad. It was contended that this would result in a depletion of the natural habitat, dislocating the wildlife of the area and causing ecological imbalance and

---

44. Suo Motu Case No. 10 of 2005, Report 2005-2006, SC of Pakistan, Golden Jubilee Edition, 104.
45. 2006 SCMR 1202.
46. 2006 PLD SC 394.
47. Writ Petition No. 642 of 1990.

degradation. The national media had at that stage become an important ally of the environmentalists, and the publicity of the case alone deterred the impugned action. It was, as a result, not necessary to pursue the petition. Nasim Hasan J commented:

> In the well-known case relating to the Margala Hills, the complaint was that the stone crushing plants established there were not only destroying these lovely Hills but were also posing a serious health hazard to the people living all around. The approach of the Lahore High Court Bench seized of this matter has been very positive and the attendant publicity to the proceedings of the Court has resulted in the initiation of remedial action by the Government itself in this matter.[48]

The impetus provided by the Supreme Court in *Shehla Zia* and the judgments that followed, began to drive results in the country's high courts as well. The Lahore High Court in *Rana Ishaque v. DG, EPA and others*[49] restrained 121 industrial units of Punjab, excluding those that had already installed treatment plants, from discharging untreated effluent into drains and canals. Consequently, most of the industries have been forced to install treatment plants to avoid any future litigation.

With respect to water pollution, in *Mst. Ameer Bano v. S.E.Highways*,[50] the petitioner alleged that the sewerage system in Bahawalpur had become totally unserviceable. As a result, dirty polluted water had collected in ponds and the construction of roads in the area by the highway department was threatening to displace the water into residential houses. The court was of the opinion that human life in the area might be endangered and thus the right to life would be undermined if the court did not order the highway department to cease its construction activity.

The influence of the *Shehla Zia* case on Pakistani environmental jurisprudence continues to this day as reflected in *Anjum Irfan v. LDA*.[51] This case, heard in the Lahore High Court, concerned the setting of air and noise pollution standards under the 1997 Act. In February 2001, the Lahore High Court appointed the co-author, Dr Parvez Hassan as the *amicus curiae* to assist the court in the writ petition. Proposals were submitted for controlling vehicular and other pollution in Lahore. It was suggested that the new industries be compelled to install devices used for checking and controlling pollution. The court further suggested various measures for combating pollution, which included: promoting the efficient use of solar energy; increasing tree plantations; adopting measures to introduce electric rail cars, and increasing the role of the media in promoting public awareness.

The issue of air pollution was also considered in *Pakistan Chest Foundation v. Government of Pakistan*,[52] where the petitioners had filed a writ petition with the

---

48. N.H. Shah, 'Environment and the Role of the Judiciary', *PLD Journal* 21 (1992): 27.
49. Writ Petition No. 671 of 1995.
50. 1996 PLD Lahore 592.
51. 2002 PLD Lahore 555.
52. 2003 PLD Lahore 439.

aim of stopping tobacco advertisements on Pakistani television. The Lahore High Court, while accepting the writ petition, brought the case within the 'right to life' principle set out in the *Shehla Zia* case:

> Applying the principle of law enunciated in Shehla Zia's case . . . to the facts and circumstances of the present case, the citizens of this country and particularly the younger generation are entitled to protection of law from being exposed to the hazards of cigarette smoking, by virtue of the command contained in Article 4 (2) of the Constitution.[53]

The model of using expert commissions in complex issues has proved to be an effective device. In *City District v. Muhammad Yusaf*,[54] the petitioners sought to ensure that a solid waste disposal site in Mahmood Booti in Lahore operated in an environmentally appropriate manner. The Division Bench of the Lahore High Court appointed a Solid Waste Management Commission in February 2003, to investigate the grievances of the petitioners, to review the suitability of the solid waste disposal measures in Mahmood Booti, and to recommend remedial measures for ensuring environmentally appropriate solid waste management. Following the lead of the Supreme Court in the *Khewra Mines* case,[55] the court appointed a commission comprising government officials and city administrators, academics and scientists, parliamentarians, specialists, environmentalists, and members of civil society. The Solid Waste Management Commission set up a sub-committee for hospital waste disposal under the Provincial Secretary of Health, who is in charge of all public sector hospitals. The effective functioning of the commission persuaded the City Government Lahore to arrange and finance the EIA of Mahmood Booti by NESPAK, a consultancy firm selected by the commission itself. Based on the EIA, the commission filed its recommendations to the court.

The High Court further considered the issue of water pollution in a number of judgments. In *Nizam v. The State*,[56] the court held that the right to unpolluted water was a right of every citizen wherever he or she lived. In this judgment, the word 'life' had to be afforded an extended meaning and could not be restricted to vegetative life or mere animal existence. In hilly areas where access to water was scarce, difficult or limited, the court held that the right to have water free from pollution and contamination was a right to life itself. The court held further that a fundamental right to preserve and protect the dignity of man under Article 14 of the Constitution was unparalleled and could be found only in a few foreign national constitutions. Under provisions of Article 38(d) of the Constitution, the court concluded that the primary duty of the government was to provide people basic necessities of life, which included unpolluted water for their consumption.

---

53. *Supra* n. 49.
54. 2003 CLC Lahore 576.
55. *Supra* n. 37.
56. 2004 YLR Lahore 2077.

In *Sindh Institute of Urology and Transplantation and others v. Nestle Milkpak Limited and others*,[57] the Sindh High Court held that a landowner has a right to collect and dispose of all water within his or her own limits but that this right is not unfettered. The court held that the common law 'public trust' doctrine meant that all natural resources are held in the public trust, and being a gift of nature, should be made freely available to everyone irrespective of their status. Even under Islamic law, certain water resources are to be protected from misuse and over-exploitation. Nestle filed an appeal before the Division Bench of the Sindh High Court, (*Nestle Milk Pack v. SIUT*),[58] which was dismissed on the ground that the extraction of the water from the aquifer in huge quantities would disturb the environment of the area.

The issue of air pollution in the city of Lahore was dealt with in *Syed Mansoor Ali Shah v. Government of Punjab*.[59] In this matter, Mr Justice Muhammad Sair Ali of the Lahore High Court appointed, in July 2003, the Lahore Clean Air Commission to recommend measures for the improvement of Lahore's air quality. The commission set up sub-committees to look at clean fuel, rickshaws, public transport and coordination with local councils. The Rickshaws Sub-committee, for example, worked under the chairmanship of the Provincial Secretary, Environment. The Clean Fuel Sub-committee, however, worked under the chairmanship of the District Coordination Officer, Lahore. All the oil companies were invited by the Clean Fuel Sub-committee to support the work of the commission, and some of their representatives attended a national workshop in Lahore convened by the commission to formulate a joint strategy for air quality. The court disposed of the petition by giving directions to the Transport Department, City District Government Lahore and the EPA to: introduce CNG Euro II buses for public transport; phase out existing buses within two years; set up dedicated bus lanes; implement a cap age of ten years for buses; and ban four stroke rickshaws.

The Sindh High Court in *Islam Hussain v. City District Government Karachi*,[60] directed the DIG Traffic Police to ensure that no smoke-emitting vehicle or one causing noise pollution ply the city of Karachi roads within three months of the handing down of the judgment. The court furthermore directed the authority to take strict action against offenders.

The aspect of the application and implementation of the provisions of the 1997 Act were raised in a number of judgments. In *Amer Azam Bakhat v. Corporative Societies*,[61] the Lahore High Court stayed the proposed construction of a supermarket until such time as an EIA had been obtained from the EPA in terms of section 12 of the 1997 Act.

In *Shehri-CBE v. Government of Pakistan*,[62] the Division Bench of the Sindh High Court rejected an EIA prepared by the government and referred the case back

---

57. 2005 CLC Karachi 424.
58. 2007 PLD Karachi 11.
59. 2007 PLD Lahore 411.
60. 2007 CLC Karachi 530.
61. 2007 CLC Lahore 374.
62. 2007 PLD Karachi 293.

to the Sindh EPA for considering all the objections raised by aggrieved parties. This case concerned an objection raised by residents to the construction of a 94 MW natural gas-fire power plant and 3 million MGD desalination plant on the coastal avenue of DHA Karachi.

The Peshawar High Court, in *Tandlianwala Sugar Mill v. NWFP*,[63] held that after considering the feasibility of the number of sugar mills in the area, and considering hazards to the environment, the provincial government had the authority to allow any number of sugar mills to operate.

6   CRITICAL SURVEY

In 1994, the Supreme Court of Pakistan delivered its landmark judgment in *Shehla Zia*. Through this judgment, the Supreme Court accorded environmental rights constitutional legitimacy and status, which is the highest legal status in Pakistani law. Such legitimacy is of course coveted not for its legal consequences alone, but for what it represents, namely an almost sacred imperative that articulates the most fundamental values of a society. Further, as a result of recent *suo motu* judgments by the Chief Justice of the Supreme Court of Pakistan discussed above, environmental law has further been strengthened since the landmark judgment in *Shehla Zia*.

Notwithstanding all the national and international milestones, there remains in Pakistan a wide gap between legislative goals, declared national policies, and their implementation. Whether it is a constraint of resources (financial or technical), or lack of capacity, or even lack of will to commit to environmental protection and sustainable development, the harsh reality is that the laws and policies of Pakistan generally, are not effectively enforced. A major cause of the serious deterioration in Pakistan's urban environmental management is the failure of government planning and the prioritization afforded to commercial growth over ecological considerations. Moreover, the role and functions of the Environmental Tribunals are not well understood and aggrieved persons frequently seek justice from avenues other than the Environmental Tribunals.

To generalize, the result is therefore that Pakistan has framework environmental protection legislation that is not adequately enforced. The federal PEPA, supported by provincial EPAs, do not act effectively. The Environmental Tribunals are not adequately resourced. The above is typical of most developing countries that prioritize economic development and consider environmental regulation as an impediment to development and economic growth. There is accordingly a lack of capacity and political will within established EPAs. On the upside, such apathy has, as evidenced in the cases discussed above, led to a higher degree of scrutiny by the judiciary.

---

63. 2007 PLD Peshawar 68.

7 THE WAY FORWARD

7.1 KEY CHALLENGES

The lack of tangible results in environmental protection in Pakistan is often attributed to a dearth of professional and scientific capacity in developing countries. After all, a provision in EIA law is of no use if the country does not have the professional and technical ability or capacity to conduct and evaluate such assessments. Setting environmental quality standards for industrial emissions and effluents can similarly only make a difference if the EPAs have the laboratories, equipment and technical administrators to police such standards. The problem of weak agencies is compounded by a colonial legacy of unregulated industry governance.

It is now generally accepted that the prescription of legislative and administrative frameworks for environmental protection is not enough. Independent monitoring and enforcement agencies cannot function optimally without adequate resources, capacity and political support. There is, generally speaking, inadequate implementation of the domestic environmental regime. The above challenges are symptomatic of a deeper malaise that environmental protection is typically accorded a low priority within domestic policy and accordingly environmental portfolios and ministries seldom carry the influence or prestige necessary to advance their environmental agenda.

The administrative power centers in Pakistan are ministries concerned with economic growth. For instance, the National Housing Policy of Pakistan 2001, places central importance on the role of the construction sector in promoting economic growth. As a result, the government has declared housing to be a priority and introduced a range of subsidies and tax relief measures to support the sector.[64] Economic growth imperatives clearly outweigh ecological imperatives.

The primacy afforded to commercial considerations is also evident in other sectors of national planning. Textiles is the backbone of the country's industrial sector and it is interesting to note that environmental considerations are entirely absent from relevant policy documents governing this sector, notwithstanding its significant contribution to industrial pollution. In the banking sector, consumer finance is being given top priority by the State Bank of Pakistan and motor vehicle loans accordingly reached an all-time high. No policy has, however, been created to consider the horrendous effects on air quality associated with increased motor vehicle sales.[65]

---

64. Incentives include soft-term loans, reduction in levies on raw material, an increase in the budgetary allocations for Public Sector Development Programmes (PSDP) and reductions in the central excise duty on cement by 25% in the 2003-2004 budget.
65. The World Bank Urban Strategy acknowledges that '[m]otor vehicles, the number and use of which are growing much faster than urban population, contribute about a third of the air pollution from fossil fuel combustion; other energy use and waste incineration account for half of air pollution ... Policies to curb environmental deterioration resulting from motorization and other energy consumption will have limited effect if focused only on fuel choice or internal production efficiency. Effective solutions will require addressing broader issues, including transport demand, land use planning, industrial development and location, and household

Pakistan does appear to have appropriate environmental legislation notwithstanding the lack of political will, resources and capacity to implement it. The 1997 Act is a good example of framework legislation that provides for a high-level policy making body (PEPC) and an enforcement arm in the form of federal and provincial EPAs. Notwithstanding this legislative and institutional framework, it is interesting to note that it is the activism of the judiciary that has partly shown the way forward for improved environmental governance in Pakistan. In many *suo motu* public interest matters, the judiciary has appointed expert commissions to resolve environmental disputes. It is heartening to see how the public and private sector partnerships reflected in the membership of many of these commissions (such as the Solid Waste Management Commission established in the *City District vs. Muhammad Yusaf* case) have achieved success and provide a valuable alternative to protracted, contentious, divisive and adversarial proceedings before the courts of Pakistan. The model adopted by the judiciary in these proceedings was to resolve complex disputes through the use of science, technology and dispassionate technical advice with the willing co-operation and support of the city government. Each metropolis is unique, but it is hoped that the experience of the Solid Waste Management Commission in Lahore may provide some useful lessons for urban environmental management in Pakistan. Equally useful in this respect would be the consensus-building approach of the Lahore Clean Air Commission.[66]

The use of court-appointed commissions to resolve complex environmental issues in Pakistan has already shown promise. It moves away from adversarial court proceedings and rather encourages dialogue and discussion between stakeholders. Ensuring that relevant commissions have a broad and inclusive membership would appear to promote their credibility and success. It would also appear particularly important to include representatives from relevant government departments and ministries in the commission membership. Eminent scientists and experts drawn from universities can anchor the work of these commissions by providing 'neutral', contemporary technical and scientific advice. The careful selection of the commission chairperson also appears vital for ensuring its impartiality, transparency and ultimate success. Allowing public participation during commission hearings can significantly contribute to such transparency. Cumulatively, the above should go a long way toward ensuring that future commissions are able to fulfil their mandate entrusted to them by the judiciary.

However, the use of judicial commissions is by no means a *panacea* as the technique can only work effectively where expert opinion is not divided[67] and a

---

income growth and distribution – all central to the urban development agenda.' World Bank, *Cities in Transition: World Bank Urban and Local Government Strategy* (Washington: The World Bank, 2000), 39.

66. P. Hassan, 'The Role of the Judiciary and Judicial Commissions on Sustainable Development Issues in South Asia', *EPL* 3, no. 2 (2007): 185-193.

67. In the *Indian Dam* case titled *Tehri Bandh Virodhi Sangarsh Samiti v. State of UP* (1992) Supp. 1 SCC 44, the Supreme Court held that it did 'not possess the requisite expertise to render any

fair chance exists that consensus can emerge amongst a diverse range of stake-holders. Even though the advent of public interest litigation and innovative procedural mechanisms (such as judicial commissions) threaten to obliterate the law/policy divide, the success of the new approach in Pakistan has been welcomed by a public long used to an apathetic legislature and a weak executive.[68]

Good environmental governance also promotes policies aimed at alleviating poverty, itself a significant cause of environmental degradation. In the Asia-Pacific region, the poor bear the majority of adverse effects of environmental degradation as they frequently reside in rural areas and depend directly or indirectly on the natural systems and resources situated in these areas for their livelihoods. As has been illustrated in the discussion of significant Pakistani jurisprudence above, the superior courts have used their jurisdiction, including *suo motu*, to protect these poor and marginalized communities and the natural resources upon which they are dependant.

As long as environmental protection remains a low priority for the political establishment and the State machinery, courts in Pakistan will increasingly be called upon to give practical significance and effect to the fundamental rights guaranteed under the Constitution. It should, however, be borne in mind that the activism of the courts is not a substitute for proper policy making and imple-mentation as judicial intervention is by its very nature reactive and hemmed in by the procedural pathways that are peculiar to the legal process.

BIBLIOGRAPHY

Desai, A. & S. Muralidhar. 'Public Interest Litigation: Potential and Problems'. In *Supreme But Not Infallible: Essays in Honour of the Supreme Court of India*, edited by B.N. Kirpal et al. New Delhi: Oxford University Press, 2000.
Government of Pakistan, Law, Justice, & Human Rights Division. *Year Book 2004-05*. Islamabad: LJ&HR, 2005.
Hassan, J. 'Country National Report'. *Asia Pacific Journal for Environmental Law* 3/4 (2001): 319-332.

---

final opinion on the rival contentions of the experts. In our opinion the Court can only investigate and adjudicate the question as to whether the Government was conscious to the inherent danger as pointed out by the petitioners and applied its mind to the safety of the dam. We have already given facts in detail, which show that the Government has considered the question on several occasions in the light of the opinions expressed by the experts. The Government was satisfied with the report of the experts and only thereafter clearance has been given to the project.'

68. See A. Desai & S. Muralidhar, 'Public Interest Litigation: Potential and Problems', in *Supreme But Not Infallible: Essays in Honour of the Supreme Court of India*, ed. B.N. Kirpal et al. (New Delhi: OUP, 2000), 159, on the appeal of public interest litigation in India despite the lingering questions about its constitutional legitimacy. For the Pakistan over-view, see generally Hassan & Azfar, *supra* n. 30, 216-217. See also, P. Hassan, 'Judiciary Leads the Way', *TEF* 15, no. 1 (1998): 48. An earlier recognition of the evolving role of the Pakistan judiciary is noted in P. Hassan, 'From Lyon to Otsu: Laws on Conservation and Wise Use of Wetlands', in *Towards Wise Use of Wetlands*, ed. H. Isozaki, M. Andi & Y. Natori (Kusatsu: ILEC, 1993).

Hassan, J. *Environmental Laws of Pakistan*. Lahore, Bookbiz Publications, 2006.

Hassan, P. & A. Azfar. 'Securing Environmental Rights through Public Interest Litigation in South Asia'. *Virginia Environmental Law Journal* 22, no. 3 (2004): 216-236.

Hassan, P. 'Environmental Rights as Part of Fundamental Human Rights: The Leadership of the Judiciary in Pakistan'. *PLJ Magazine* (2003): 209-231.

Hassan, P. 'From Lyon to Otsu: Laws on Conservation and Wise Use of Wetlands'. In *Towards Wise Use of Wetlands*, edited by H. Isozaki, M. Andi & Y. Natori. Kusatsu: ILEC, 1993.

Hassan, P. 'From Rio 1992 to Johannesburg 2002: A Case Study of Implementing Sustainable Development in Pakistan'. *Singapore Journal of International and Comparative Law* 6 (2002): 683-722.

Hassan, P. 'Judiciary Leads the Way'. *The Environmental Forum* 15, no. 1 (1998): 48-49.

Hassan, P. 'Shehla Zia v. Wapda: Ten Years Later'. *PLD Journal* (2005): 48-57.

Hassan, P. 'The Role of the Judiciary and Judicial Commission on Substantial Development Issues in Pakistan'. *PLD Journal* (2006): 45-59.

Hassan, P. 'The Role of the Judiciary and Judicial Commissions on Sustainable Development Issues in South Asia'. *Environmental Policy and Law* 37, no. 2 (2007): 185-193.

Khan, M.A. *Government of Pakistan, Environment and Urban Affairs Division, Environmental Profile of Pakistan*. Islamabad: Government of Pakistan, Environment and Urban Affairs Division, 1986.

Kirpal, B.N. et al., (eds). *Supreme But Not Infallible: Essays in Honour of the Supreme Court of India* New Delhi: Oxford University Press, 2000.

Menski, W. Public Interest Litigation in Pakistan. Karachi: Pakistan Law House, 2000.

PEPA. 'Publications'. <www.environment.gov.pk/Publications.htm>, 21 September 2008.

Robinson, N. & Hassan, J. *Chapter on Pakistani Environmental Law, Comparative Environmental Law and Regulation*. New York: Oceana Publications, 1997.

Shah, N.H. 'Environment and the Role of the Judiciary'. *PLD Journal* 21 (1992): 21-29.

World Bank. *Cities in Transition: World Bank Urban and Local Government Strategy*. Washington D.C.: The World Bank, 2000.

TABLE OF LEGISLATION AND AUTHORITIES

Agricultural Pest Ordinance 1971
Canal and Drainage Act 1873
Code of Criminal Procedure 1868
Constitution of Pakistan 1973
Criminal Procedure Code 1898
Environmental Laboratories Certification Regulations 2001

TABLE OF CASES

Human Rights Case (Environment Pollution in Balochistan), Re 1994 PLD SC 102
Imtiaz Ahmed v. Ghulam Ali 1963 PLD SC 382
Islam Hussain v. City District Government Karachi 2007 CLC Karachi 530
Islamabad Chalets and Pir Sohawa Valley Villas Suo Motu Case No. 13 of 2005,
    Report 2005-2006, SC of Pakistan, Golden Jubilee Edition
Islamuddin v. Ghulam Muhammad 2004 PLD SC 633
Moulvi Iqbal Haider v. Capital Development Authority 2006 PLD SC 394
Mst. Ameer Bano v. S.E.Highways 1996 PLD Lahore 592
Nestle Milk Pack v. SIUT 2007 PLD Karachi 11
New Murree Project Suo Motu Case No. 10 of 2005, Report 2005-2006, SC,
    Golden Jubilee Edition
Nizam v. The State 2004 YLR Lahore 2077
Pakistan Chest Foundation v. Government of Pakistan 2003 PLD Lahore 439
Province of East Pakistan v. MD Mehdi Ali Khan 1959 PLD SC 387
Rana Ishaque v. DG, EPA and others Writ Petition No. 671 of 1995
Roedad Khan v. Federation of Pakistan and others Writ Petition No. 642 of 1990
SP Gupta v. Union of India 1982 AIR SC 149
Shaheen Welfare Society v. Environmental Protection Agency Punjab, Lahore
    2005 CLD Punjab Environmental Protection Tribunal 1267, Lahore
Shehla Zia and Others v. WAPDA 1994 PLD SC 693
Shehri-CBE v. Government of Pakistan 2007 PLD Karachi 293
Sheri-CBE v. LDA 2006 SCMR 1202
*Sindh Institute of Urology and Transplantation and others v. Nestle Milkpak Ltd
    and others* 2005 CLC Karachi 424
Syed Mansoor Ali Shah v. Government of Punjab 2007 PLD Lahore 411
Tandlianwala Sugar Mill v. NWFP 2007 PLD Peshawar 68
Tehri Bandh Virodhi Sangarsh Samiti v. State of UP (1992) Supp 1 SCC 44

TABLE OF INTERNATIONAL INSTRUMENTS

Agreement for the Establishment of a Commission for Controlling the Desert
    Locust in the Eastern Region of its Distribution Area in South-West Asia
    (1963)
Convention Concerning the Protection of World Culture and Natural Heritage
    (1972) 11 *ILM* 1358
Convention on Biological Diversity (1992) 31 *ILM* 818
Convention on International Trade in Endangered Species of Wild Fauna and Flora
    (1973) 46 *ILM* 1178
Convention on Wetlands of International Importance Especially as Waterfowl
    Habitat (1972) 11 *ILM* 969
International Plant Protection Convention (1951)
Plant Protection Agreement for South-East Asia and Pacific Region (1956)
Rio Declaration on Environment and Development (1992) 31 *ILM* 874
Stockholm Declaration on Human Environment (1972) 11 *ILM* 1416
United Nations Framework Convention on Climate Change (1992) 31 *ILM* 841

ABBREVIATIONS

EIA	Environmental Impact Assessment
EPA	Environmental Protection Agency
EPO	Environmental Protection Orders
IEE	Initial Environmental Examination
MINFAL	Ministry of Food, Agriculture and Livestock
MPCB	Marine Pollution Control Board
NECC	National Environmental Co-ordination Committee
NEQS	National Environmental Quality Standards
NGO	Non-governmental Organization
NOC	No Objection Certificate
PLD	Pakistan Legal Decisions
PEPC	Pakistan Environmental Protection Council
PEPA	Pakistan Environmental Protection Agency
PLGO	Provincial Local Government Ordinance
PSDP	Public Sector Development Programmes
SC	Supreme Court
SCMR	Supreme Court Monthly Review
UN	United Nations
VELJ	Virginia Environment Law Journal

Chapter 13

The People's Republic of China

Qun Du

1   INTRODUCTION

The environmental governance regime is a complex of multiple disciplines embedded within the contexts of both the public and the private sector. In the former, in the People's Republic of China (PRC), environmental governance takes place by means of legislation enacted by the people's congresses and their standing committees, the administration of the people's governments and their related authorities, the judgments and rulings of the people's procuratorates, and most importantly, the adjudication of the people's courts. In contrast, in the private sector, the work of scientists and technologists and the participation of civil society appear to play an important role.

This chapter discusses the performance of the Chinese judiciary in matters relating to environmental governance. The investigation is to be approached through examining the judgments of the people's courts over environmental pollution torts, judicial review cases, and criminal cases concerning environmental pollution control, natural resources, and the conservation of wild animals. As a general background, the chapter first sets out principal environmental challenges, the main environmental laws, and the Chinese governance structure with specific focus on the judicial institutions. The chapter concludes by critically reflecting on the challenges and opportunities facing the Chinese judiciary as an important element in environmental governance.

Louis J. Kotzé and Alexander R. Paterson (eds), *The Role of the Judiciary in Environmental Governance: Comparative Perspectives*, pp. 411–449.
© 2009 Kluwer Law International BV, The Netherlands.

2   ENVIRONMENTAL ISSUES

The PRC's economy has been developing very rapidly in recent times. In fact, it is one of the fastest growing economies in the world. Whilst the benefits of economic growth are self-evident so far as socio-economic development is concerned, such inordinate growth poses a severe threat to the environment, particularly because of the increased pressure it exerts on the PRC's natural resources. Some of the most significant current environmental concerns include: increased pollution, the loss of soil and desertification, the loss of biodiversity, and the adverse effects of increased trade. These concerns are discussed in turn below.

Pollution poses a serious threat to environmental quality in the PRC, especially as it manifests in water and air pollution. In the year 2000, the country's total emissions of carbon dioxide and nitrogen chlorine hydrocarbons were respectively ranked as the world's second and largest (40% of the mainland area was affected by acid rain).[1] This situation is reportedly deteriorating.[2] By 2005 sulphur dioxide emissions had increased by 27% and carbon dioxide emissions by 2%.[3]

Water pollution is another serious concern. The water in 42% of the watercourses in seven major river basins is below water quality Class III as described in the PRC's national standards (not fit for human consumption). 36% of fresh river water in urban areas does not reach water quality Class IV (its bio-function being lost). The water quality of large-scale freshwater basins such as the lakes and reservoirs in urban areas, is generally very poor and more than 75% of the lakes suffer from eutrophication caused by industrial and agricultural activities. Access to suitable water resources for human consumption also is a great concern, since 300 million rural people in the PRC have difficulty in accessing clean drinking water.

Pollution by garbage and persistent organic pollutants has become an ever-increasing concern. Industry annually generates 820 million tons of solid waste, and only 46% of this is re-used. Urban households discharge 140 million tons of garbage per year, and less than 10% of this is disposed in a manner that meets the requirements of innocuous treatment. The waste of plastic packaging and plastic sheeting for use in agricultural greenhouses and more general use (so-called 'white pollution'),[4] has significantly increased in recent years. Most of the substances listed by the Convention on Persistent Organic Pollutants, 2001 (Stockholm

---

1. EPAC, 'Analysis of Implementation of the Eleventh Five-Year National Environmental Protection Planning targets', <www.chinanews.com.cn/news/2006/2006-04-12/8/715966.shtml>, 12 April 2006.
2. China's Environmental Public Bulletin in 2005 reported that the targets of main pollutants and their indicators, which were set out as national environmental protection objectives in the 10th Five-Year Plan of the PRC, have not been achieved.
3. EPAC, *supra* n. 1.
4. This name reflects the fact that most plastic waste is in fact white. The production and sale of plastic bags for use by shoppers have been restricted by the State Council since 1 May 2008. See L.H. Yu, 'State issues "plastic limit order" to speed up China's plastic bag industry', <news.xinhuanet.com/newscenter/2008-01/12/content_7411275.htm>, 12 January 2008.

Convention), as prohibited, have been detected in the PRC's environment. Chemicals containing these organic pollutants are in fact increasingly used in industry, agriculture and urban construction, and this upward trend is set to continue.

The deterioration of the natural environment in the PRC is severe. The annual loss of soil through water and wind erosion and poor agricultural practices amounts to more than 5 billion tons, which is equivalent to the loss of 40 million tons of standard fertilizer.[5] Severe natural disasters are occurring more frequently than ever before. Strong sandstorms in Northern China occurred twenty-three times per annum in the 1990s; four times more frequently than in the 1950s. The amount of arable land affected by natural drought in the 1990s has trebled in comparison with the incidence in the 1950s. The situation has become so dire that desertification in some areas of Inner Mongolia has even forced residents to resettle elsewhere in search of better livelihoods.[6] Researchers predict that in the next fifteen years, Northern China will increasingly be threatened by severe droughts, while floods will occur more frequently in Southern China.[7]

The loss of biodiversity is another concern. The Convention on International Trade in Endangered Species of Wild Flora and Fauna, 1973 (CITES), lists 740 endangered species of which 189, around one quarter of the total, are located in the PRC. Between 4,000 to 5,000 of the country's plant species are endangered or approaching endangerment. This constitutes between 15% and 20% of the country's total number of plant species.[8]

Since the PRC's entry into the World Trade Organization (WTO), recent trade-associated environmental problems have been exacerbated. In particular, the foreign demand for the country's minerals, medicinal plants, and agricultural and pastoral products has resulted in the PRC becoming a major supplier and processor of raw materials. This places significant pressure on the country's natural environment and has occasioned severe destruction of its ecosystems and natural resources.

3   PRINCIPAL ENVIRONMENTAL LAWS

3.1   INTRODUCTION

Environmental protection was declared a basic national policy of the PRC in the early 1980s. This declaration was followed by the development of a comprehensive framework of environmental legislation, the framing of primary policies, and the

---

5. Environmental Protection Bureau of Xiamen City, 'China's Environmental Problems', <www.xmepb.gov.cn/environment/10.htm>, 28 December 2007.

6. *Ibid.*

7. See C.Q. Song, 'The researchers predict: the North China over the next 10 years will be relatively drought', <news.xinhuanet.com/newscenter/2004-10/19/content_2111006.htm>, 19 October 2004.

8. G.M. Jiang & G.X. Gao, 'The terrible cost of China's growth', <www.chinadialogue.net/article/show/single/ch/684>, 12 January 2007.

establishment of environmental institutions. The rapid growth of the economy in a less than environmentally friendly manner, and the transition from a centrally planned economy to a market economy, has created the need to resolve the conflict between unbridled economic development and environmental protection. The legislative framework with regard to environmental protection and natural resource conservation, as the principal mechanism to ensure sustainable development, has been under construction and revision for more than three decades. The PRC's legislative framework comprises of national and local laws and regulations and structures at four levels, namely: (a) constitutional law provisions and international conventions and agreements to which the PRC has become a party; (b) national laws promulgated by the National People's Congress (NPC) and its Standing Committee; (c) national regulations, orders, decisions and other normative documents with the binding force of law, promulgated by the State Council (SC); and (d) local regulations, decisions and orders promulgated by the people's congress of provinces, autonomous regions/cities/counties, SC-directed municipalities, authorized municipalities and other local organs with local legislative power. This environmental legislative framework can be variously categorized as environmental protection and pollution control law, environmental impact assessment (EIA) law, marine protection law, and natural resources conservation law relating to water, land, forests, and grasslands. The following discussion briefly reflects on some of the most important laws which have also been the subject of recent judicial scrutiny.

3.2   FRAMEWORK LEGISLATION

The *Environmental Protection Law* 1989 (EPL), is the basic law for environmental governance in the PRC and is the foundation of all other sectoral environmental laws. Its purpose is to protect the human and ecological environment and to prevent pollution. This law contains provisions dealing with the following: environmental protection procedures in national economic and social plans; national and local environmental protection standards; monitoring systems; the protection of ecological systems; legal procedures relating to liability for environmental violations; and various compensatory and administrative sanctions and remedies. The main legal rules for referring civil environmental issues to court are contained in Article 41 of the EPL, specifically the three following paragraphs:

> A unit that has caused an environmental hazard shall have the obligation to eliminate it and make compensation to the unit or individual that suffered direct losses. (Para. 1.)
>   A dispute over the liability to make compensation or the amount of compensation may, at the request of the parties, be settled by the competent department of the environmental protection administration or another department vested by law with the power to conduct environmental supervision and management. If a party refuses to accept the decision on the settlement, it may bring a suit before a people's court. The party may also bring a suit directly before the people's court. (Para. 2.)

If environmental pollution losses result solely from irresistible natural disasters which cannot be averted even after the prompt adoption of reasonable measures, the party concerned shall be exempted from liability. (Para. 3.)

Articles 41(1) and (3) of the EPL have been acknowledged as setting out strict norms pertaining to liability in civil matters concerning environmental pollution. In practice, however, these provisions have been differently interpreted in the people's courts, as discussed below. The first sentence of Article 41(2) refers to the competence of civil tribunals of the people's courts to rule in disputes that parties bring to them directly. Notably, Article 41(2) empowers administrative tribunals of the people's courts to conduct judicial review of the 'decision on the settlement' arrived at by the environmental protection authorities, based on the rules of Article 41(2).[9] In 1992, however, a special legislative interpretation from the Legal Working Committee of the NPC,[10] determined that issues resolved by the environmental protection administration authority should not be brought to the people's courts for their 'decision on the settlement'. The implication was that such a settlement is a civil mediation rather than an administrative decision.[11] Consequently, since 1992, the people's courts have ceased undertaking judicial review of such 'decisions on the settlement', and have let civil tribunals deal with the civil disputes in terms of Article 41(2).

Article 42 of the EPL contains another important provision concerning the courts' jurisdiction in environmental civil cases. It establishes a three year limitation period for petitioning for compensation for losses sustained through environmental pollution. This is longer than the period which applies in general civil cases, which is two years according to Article 135 of the *General Principles of Civil Law* 1991.[12]

3.3   POLLUTION LEGISLATION

Pollution control laws include: the *Water Pollution Prevention and Control Law* 2008 (WPPCL) (amended from WPPCL 1984 and 1996); the *Air Pollution Prevention and Control Law* 2000 (APPCL) (amended from APPCL 1987 and 1995);

---

9. This was reflected in a report delivered by Jianxin Ren, the President of the Supreme People's Court on 18 July 1988; see J.X. Ren, Report of the 14th National Conference of Courts' Work (Beijing: National Publishing House, 1988).
10. Legal Working Committee of the NPC, *Reply to State Environmental Protection Agency on the Application of Article 41(2) of Environmental Protection Law 1989* (Beijing: NPC, 1992).
11. Part of the intention of the legislative interpretation of Art. 41(2) of the EPL is to avoid environmental protection administration agencies or other departments from being brought to people's courts as defendants in such civil cases. It is thought that this legislative interpretation is not in line with the original intent of the EPL. It exempts environmental protection administration agencies and other departments from exercising diligence in resolving disputes concerning environmental pollution hazards, and is therefore of less assistance to the victims of pollution. See: Z.M. Lv, (ed.), *Environmental Law Case Studies* (Beijing: HEP, 2006), 282-287.
12. This is a basic law in civil matters in China.

the *Noise Pollution Prevention and Control Law* 1996 (NPPCL); and the *Law for Prevention and Control of Solid Wastes Polluting the Environment* 2004 (amended from 1995). These laws reflect the command and control approach and make provision for pollution registers and reports, EIA, liability provisions dealing with pollution damage, preventive measures, on-site monitoring and inspection, and various environmental protection standards. In each of these pollution control laws the provisions governing the jurisdiction of the people's courts in environmental civil disputes largely mimic Article 41 of the EPL,[13] with the exception of the WPPCL, which is discussed further below.

Legislation on the prevention of marine pollution and pollution control was developed as early as the 1970s. The *Marine Environment Protection Law* 1999 (MEPL)[14] comprehensively regulates the prevention and remediation of marine pollution. A broad range of regulations has been enacted which currently constitutes a comprehensive legal framework dealing with specific issues regarding protection of the marine environment.[15] The MEPL was amended in 2000 to provide, inter alia, for the supervision and management of the marine environment, the protection of the marine ecology, the prevention and treatment of marine damage caused by land-based pollution, coastal and marine construction projects, and measures to regulate the dumping of certain wastes.

3.4   ENVIRONMENTAL IMPACT ASSESSMENT

The *Environmental Impact Assessment Law* 2002 (EIAL) requires most programmes and activities of government,[16] and all activities of entities affecting the environment and natural resources, to be subjected to EIA and for remedial measures to be applied to reverse evident impacts. The law makes it incumbent on all concerned parties to prepare environmental impact reports for all major development activities relating to industry, agriculture, animal husbandry, forestry, energy, water conservancy, communications, municipal construction, tourism, and the development of natural resources. The law also regulates other procedural aspects such as the private sector's right to access to information. Together with the Regulation for Governments Opening Information, 2007 and the Interim Provisions of Public Participation in Environmental Impact Assessment of the National People's Congress 2006 (Decree No. 2006/26), this law endows the public with the

---

13. See WPPCL 2008, Art. 84; APPCL 2000, Arts 62-63; and NPPCL 1996, Art. 61.
14. Passed in 1982 and amended twice in 1982 and 1999.
15. These include: Regulations Pertaining to the Prevention and Control of Pollution of the Sea by Vessels 1983; Regulations Pertaining to Environmental Protection in Offshore Oil Exploration and Exploitation 1983; Regulations Pertaining to Controlling the Dumping of Waste in the Ocean 1985; Regulations Pertaining to Prevention of Pollution from Ship Breaking 1988; Regulations Pertaining to the Prevention and Treatment of Land-Source Pollution 1990; and Regulations Pertaining to the Prevention and Treatment of Pollution Damaging Marine Environment by Coastal Construction Projects 1990.
16. Strategic programmes are exempted from this.

right to access environmental information and to participate in decision-making. These laws and regulations do not, however, contain provisions allowing members or groups of the public who have no direct interest in the particular environmental issue to bring a suit to the people's courts in the interests of the public at large. Thus, there are legal constraints preventing representatives of the public, acting through autonomous civic bodies, from gaining access to justice in both administrative proceedings and civil proceedings.

3.5   LAND USE AND FORESTRY LAWS

Land use and property laws are mainly contained in the *Land Administration Law* 1998 and the *Country Land Contracting Law* 2002. These laws provide rules and regulations for land ownership, land-user provisions, and contracting entitlements. The former law specifically regulates State-owned land with regard to land-use rights, and makes provision for transfer and trading operations. The latter regulates collectively owned land (generally referred to as 'responsibilities land'), that has been contracted to farmers and herders since the agricultural land reforms of the 1980s.

Important provisions pertaining to the use of land are also found in the *Forest Law* 1998 (amended from that of 1984) and the *Grassland Law* 2002 (amended from that of 1985). The *Forest Law* takes the concept of 'conservation for development' and establishes a complex legal and institutional framework for forest utilization, conservation and administration. It provides, inter alia, for the categorization of forests based on their function or use, financial instruments, a compensation fund for public-interest forests, and forestation programmes and policies. The *Grassland Law* provides rules for: grassland ownership and use; administrative procedures; measures relating to supervision; protection measures; and requirements for rational utilization, scientific management and conservation. It also addresses the resolution of disputes concerning grassland rights, the prevention of over grazing, the restriction of reclamation from grassland to farmland, the rehabilitation of grasslands, and legal liability for grassland conservation.

3.6   NATURE CONSERVATION LAWS

Nature conservation laws include the *Soil and Water Conservation Law* 1991 and the *Desertification Prevention and Control Law* 2001. The former law and its accompanying Implementation Regulation of 1993, provide basic rules for countering water and soil loss, including: the rights and duties of entities or individuals; measures for preventing and restoring water and soil loss; financial arrangements; and legal liability. The latter is a national law aimed specifically at desertification control in accordance with the Convention to Combat Desertification 1994. It provides two strategic tools to achieve its aims, namely: the National Plan for Combating Desertification and Action Plans for Combating Desertification; and specific measures to combat desertification which include monitoring, the reporting of statistics describing desertification, early warning of droughts and dust storms, engineering measures, and policies prohibiting certain land uses.

3.7   PROCEDURAL LAWS AND ENVIRONMENTAL LITIGATION

The *Civil Procedure Law* 1991 (CPL), the *Administrative Procedure Law* 1989 (APL) and the *Criminal Procedure Law* 1996 (CPL) (amended from that of 1979) are relevant to environmental issues insofar as they relate to litigation on environmental issues in people's courts (including civil, administrative and criminal litigation). Notably, the APL in particular has revitalized procedures for litigation by providing formal legal rules for administrative lawsuits, and has incidentally given administrative tribunals a permanent seat in the people's courts. The law now enables citizens to participate in and supervise specific decision-making processes to safeguard their own interests, including environmental interests. Since 1989, there has been a rapid growth in the number of administrative lawsuits, particularly in the field of environmental protection. These are further discussed below.

4   INSTITUTIONS AND GOVERNANCE STRUCTURES

4.1   GENERAL GOVERNANCE INSTITUTIONS AND ENVIRONMENTAL
               AUTHORITIES

This section explains the power structure of the various public sectors in order to present a clear picture of the institutions playing a role in environmental governance in the PRC.

    The doctrine of the separation of powers has not found favour in the PRC. Instead, the PRC has developed a unique centralized power system with four levels: the central, provincial, prefecture and county levels.[17] Each level contains the same four interactive public sectors, namely: the people's congress and its Standing Committee, the people's government, the people's court and the people's procuratorate. At the central level, for example, there are the NPC and its Standing Committee, the State Council, the Supreme People's Court (SPC) and the Supreme People's Procuratorate (SPP). At each local level, the NPC and the people's congress are responsible not only for legislation and decision-making on significant issues in the county or region, but are in themselves also the source of the State's power to create other sectors. Considered vertically, the higher levels in the public sector take the lead and supervise the lower levels.

---

17. The province, prefecture and county are various local government levels.

The NPC and its Standing Committee is the legislator of national laws, including those dealing with environmental matters and issues relating to natural resources. Generally, substantive laws and procedural laws concerning administrative, civil and criminal issues are legislated by the NPC itself. Laws concerning professional issues, such as all laws concerning the environment and natural resources, are legislated by the Standing Committee of the NPC. The NPC comprises several professional committees which carry out its functions, including, the Environmental Protection and Resource Conservation Committee (EPRCC). The EPRCC was established on 29 March 1993 in response to the call by the NPC for enhanced environmental protection, and is an organization responsible for legislative affairs concerning the protection of the environment and natural resources and the supervision of related law enforcement.[18] It is widely acknowledged that the EPRCC has played a significant role in developing the legal framework of environmental and natural resource laws in the past two decades, and that it continues to do so.

One feature of Chinese environmental governance is the preponderance of the command and control approach. This reflects the strong empowerment of the people's governments to administer environmental policy. The department in charge of environmental pollution, urban environmental protection and overall ecosystem conservation within the people's government system and at the central level is the Ministry of Environmental Protection (MEP), which has in reality only recently emerged as a key role player and which bears an increasing weight of power in the State Council.[19]

Other departments in the State Council, for example, the Ministry of Water and Hydrological Resources, the State Forestry Agency, the Ministry of Agriculture, the State Marine Agency, and the Maritime Traffic Authority are administrators of their own respective areas of natural resource utilization and conservation. In accordance with the principles of socialist planning, the departments in charge of overall planning and development, specifically the State Development and Reform Commission and the Ministry of Finance in the State Council, play key roles in overall planning and policy making relating to expenditure.

---

18. See Greener Beijing Institute, 'EPRCC', <www.grchina.org/gbj/spot/orgpcepc.htm>, 8 August 2008, for more details.
19. The evolution of the MEP is a history of the institutional enhancement of Chinese environmental governance. The initial form of the MEP can be traced back to 1973 in the office of the Leading Group for Environmental Protection of the SC – a temporary organ with relatively comprehensive powers under the direct lead of the SC. Since then, in response to the increased attention paid to environmental protection by the SC, it has evolved as follows: in 1988 it became the Bureau of Environmental Protection of the Construction Ministry – a permanent department with competence but dependent on the Ministry; later in 1988 it became the State Environmental Protection Agency – a permanent and independent department; in 1998 it was elevated to the State Environmental Protection Administration; and in 2008 it became the MEP. See Y.D. Guo, 'State Environmental Protection Administration to be upgraded to the Ministry of Environmental Protection', <env.people.com.cn/GB/6971602.html>, 1 July 2008.

4.2   JUDICIAL INSTITUTIONS: GENERAL REMARKS

Among the public sector institutions referred to above, the people's courts (the judicial organs of the county) and the people's procuratorates (the legal supervision organs of the county) fulfil the main judicial function, including presiding over environmental matters. In general, the institution of the people's courts is composed of the SPC, the people's courts at various local levels, military courts, and other special people's courts. The SPC is the highest judicial organ. It supervises the administration of justice by the people's courts and special people's courts at various local levels. People's courts at higher levels supervise the administration of justice by those seated at lower levels. The SPC is responsible to the NPC and its Standing Committee. Local people's courts at various levels are responsible to people's congresses at the same level.

The procuratorates system, established in parallel to the people's courts system, encompasses the SPP, the people's procuratorates at various local levels, military procuratorates, and other special people's procuratorates. Its legal status is similar to that of the people's court system in the hierarchy of overall public power. The people's procuratorates exercise procuratorial power independently. The SPP is the highest procuratorial organ and directs the work of the people's procuratorates at various local levels and of the special people's procuratorates. People's procuratorates at higher levels direct the work of those at lower levels. The SPP is responsible to the NPC and its Standing Committee. The people's procuratorates at various local levels are responsible to the respective people's congresses at the same level.

The system of procuratorates is unusual in the sense that it was copied from the former Soviet Union. The procuratorates have the power to inspect the people's courts' adjudication activities in order to ensure that they are correctly upholding justice. The functions of the people's procuratorates in criminal cases are to initiate public prosecution in criminal cases, to support such prosecutions, to exercise supervision over the judicial activities of the people's courts, and to determine whether they conform to the law. If the SPP or a people's procuratorate at a higher level finds some definite error in a judgment or court order made by a people's court at a lower level, it has the power to protest against it through the procedure of trial supervision. In the trial supervision procedure, the people's procurator must appear in court and hear the case.[20] The procuratorial power in civil cases is expressed in Article 185 of the *Civil Procedure Law* 1991, which provides that if: the evidence on which a judgment or court order is based is not sufficient; there is a definite error in the judgment or order; the trial court did not follow the established legal procedure and this affected the fair judgment or order; or a judge behaved improperly and perverted the law in trying the case – the procuratorate at the same level as the court has the power to protest against the judgment or court order through the procedure of trial supervision. In this procedure, a

---

20.   Art. 135 of the *Organizational Law of the People's Procuratorates* 1983.

people's prosecutor must appear in court and hear the case. The practice of this procedure in civil tort cases is further discussed below.

5   AN OVERVIEW OF THE PEOPLE'S COURT SYSTEM

5.1   HISTORICAL DEVELOPMENT OF THE JUDICIARY

An outcome of the communist party's victory in the domestic Liberation War from 1946 to 1949, was the establishment of the PRC on 1 October 1949. The PRC abolished the old legal and judicial system and created a new, socialist legal and judicial system representing the people's interests.[21] With the establishment of the superior government of the PRC in 1949,[22] the formation of the SPC was initiated by appointing to it members from key interest groups, including the army, the trade unions and the Women's Federation. The SPC was structured into three sections charged with dealing with criminal, civil and administrative cases. In 1952, the people's courts were established within every major administrative region.[23]

The first five years of the PRC were the nascent period of the people's court system. Many institutions and procedures that the people's courts currently operate were initiated during the period including, for example: the hierarchy of courts, open trials, the appeal system, the separate review for death penalty cases, circuit tribunals in smaller cities and rural areas, and the adjudication committees.

The NPC, the State Council, the people's courts and the people's procuratorates (i.e. the entire judicial system of the PRC), were formally established with the enactment of the first Constitution in 1954. In particular, the *Organizational Law of People's Courts* 1954 (OLPC) stipulated the nature, tasks, institutions, organic structure, working principles and procedures for trial of the people's courts. This law contained many stipulations of significance to the current court structure. It transferred the leadership of the people's courts from the people's governments to the people's congresses at all levels. In other words, the people's courts no longer functioned as a branch of government, but rather as an independent judicial organ exercising exclusive judicial power to conduct trials free from any political interference. It also constituted the fundamental basis of the rule of law for the modern judiciary. This law sets up adjudication committees for people's courts at all levels, and empowers adjudication committees as leading trial organs for general trial work. Moreover, all the working principles for trials, such as the jury system, the open trial system, the collegial system, and the system of defence

---

21. Directive to Abolish the Code of Six Laws by Guo-min-tang and Establish Judicial Principle for the Liberated Areas, North China Regional Government, March 31, 1949. See B.W. Dong, *Collection of Papers on Politics and Law* (Beijing: Law Press, 1986), 45 *et seq.*
22. It was called the Central People's Committee at that time, and later became the State Council.
23. There were six large administrative regions in China, i.e., the Northeast, Northwest, East, Middle South, Southwest and North China.

and withdrawal, were formally established at that stage primarily to protect the rights of the people and to ensure that the courts made appropriate judgments.

The advent of the anti-rightist political campaigns, the Great Leap Forward Movement and the Cultural Revolution (from 1957 to the late 1970s), damaged the structure of the people's courts and the independence of the judiciary. In many instances the people's police, the procuratorates and the courts were merged into a single organization called the Department of Public Security, Politics and Law. The various special courts were abolished which signaled a catastrophic period for the rule of law and justice in the PRC. The new OLPC was introduced in 1979, when the Cultural Revolution ended, and was amended in 1983.[24] Since then, the system of people's courts has been firmly reconstructed with the intention of championing judicial freedom.

5.2   COURT STRUCTURE AND HIERARCHY

5.2.1   Structure

According to the OLPC of 1983, the people's courts are organized into local people's courts, special courts, and the SPC.[25] Local people's courts, which are also called general courts as against special people's courts, comprise of: (a) basic people's courts at the level of county and district; (b) intermediate people's courts at city level with districts and prefectures; and (c) high people's courts at provincial levels including autonomous regions and the Standing Committee-directed municipalities.

Local people's courts deal with most cases except for those that are exclusively subject to the jurisdiction of special courts. Each people's court possesses four sorts of trial tribunals, namely: civil, criminal, commercial, and administrative. The people's court may establish other tribunals if necessary,[26] such as a juvenile tribunal or an intellectual property tribunal, or possibly even an environmental tribunal. There is no permanent tribunal for environmental cases in terms of the OLPC. An environmental case is usually filed with the civil, criminal, commercial or administrative tribunal, subject to the nature of the matter in dispute.

There have, however, been continuous attempts to create environmental tribunals in some cities, and these attempts are ongoing. The number of environmental administrative cases to be heard annually increased since the 1990s after the creation of the administrative trial tribunal in terms of the APL in 1989 and the EPL in 1989. In order to strengthen the enforcement of the EPL through environmental litigation, some cities established environmental tribunals in people's courts to

---

24. The OLPC 1983 was amended in 2006 with the change of only one article, namely the approval procedure for the death penalty.
25. OLPC 1983, Art. 2.
26. OLPC 1983, Art. 24(2).

hear environmental administrative lawsuits (for example, the basic people's court of Qiaokou District of Wuhan City). From an institutional point of view, this environmental tribunal was a union of the people's courts and the environmental administrative department of the people's government. Its nature and purpose were, however, extensively questioned. It was soon declared to lack legitimacy and it was disbanded on the grounds that it violated the rules of the OLPC of 1983.

Special people's courts include military courts, maritime courts, railway transport courts, forestry courts and agricultural reclamation courts. They differ from local people's courts in that they are designed to meet the needs of sectoral or professional enterprise, whereas local people's courts were established in line with the geographical area of the administrative jurisdictions of the local people's governments. As the activities in sectoral or professional enterprises are unavoidably conducted in one or more administrative jurisdictions, there inevitably is an overlap between the jurisdictions of special people's courts and local people's courts, though the SPC has provided guidance on how to deal with such overlap.[27]

Special people's courts are closely concerned with resolving environmental matters. Maritime courts are responsible for commercial cases and civil cases dealing with marine business relating to coastal waters and watercourses that flow into the sea.[28] Matters concerning the pollution of such watercourses and coastal waters by ships or shipping, or through any other activities, are also subject to the jurisdiction of the maritime courts.[29] Forestry courts deal with civil, administrative and criminal matters relating to the harvesting, use and conservation of forests and forest products. Railway transport courts are also involved in environmental matters. Many of the cases these courts deal with have to do with noise nuisance emanating from railways. Military courts are empowered to resolve only criminal cases linked with the activities of members or entities of the People's Liberation Army. As for environmental matters, military courts have the power to deal with criminal cases related to activities directed to the compliance with and enforcement of the Regulations for Environmental Protection of the People's Liberation Army of the PRC 1990.[30]

---

27. It has raised debates on the overlapping jurisdictions of special people's courts and local people's courts. Many recommend the reform of the people's court system and the revision of the OLPC 1979 and its amendments 1983 and 2006, with one sound proposal that it retains military courts and maritime courts as special people's courts, and include other existing special courts into the scope of local people's courts. See Xinhua News Net, 'People's Representatives Zhou Shuo and Chen Yan-ping proposed to amend the Organic Law of the People's Court', <fl.pub.cqnews.net/system/2008/03/17/001113885.shtml>, 17 March 2008.
28. Maritime courts handle only commercial and civil cases in the first instance. The high people's court, in which the maritime court is located, deals with appeals.
29. See SPC, *Some Provisions on the Scope of Cases that are Subject to the Jurisdiction of Maritime Courts* (Beijing: National Publishing House, 2001).
30. Very few cases on environmental issues in the military sector have been reported. This may be the consequence of national security concerns, but is more likely to emanate from other reasons. E.g., there is a dearth of provisions directing the involvement of military courts in the justice function.

Each case can be heard only twice in all types of people's courts; the second instance being the final instance. Also, each court establishes its own adjudication committee for all types of people's courts. The adjudication committee is the court's highest decision-making organ for judicial work.[31] Its task is described as being to track judicial experience and to discuss significant or difficult cases and issues relating to judicial work.[32] As will be illustrated below, many judicial interpretations approved by the adjudication committees of the SPC provide significant and practical guidance to judges when trying environmental cases.

5.2.2   Operation of the Courts

There are some aspects of the operation of the people's courts that are rather unusual. When they consider environmental cases, especially those concerning injury and damage arising from pollution, people's courts face the challenge of developing novel techniques of justice in a fairly new field of law in the PRC.

As was stated earlier, the SPC has the power to issue judicial interpretations which will direct judicial work. So does the SPP, but only in relation to the work of the procuratorates. It is commonly acknowledged that the statutes of the NPC, the administrative regulations of the State Council, and the judicial interpretations of the SPC and the SPP, constitute the principal sources of law in the PRC. As legislative interpretations are retained in issues concerning compliance with statute law, judicial interpretations by the SPC are limited to issues dealing with the application and enforcement of statute law which do not satisfy actual practice in court (where, for instance, they are too abstract or vague for use in complicated cases). Judicial interpretations by the SPP deal with issues on the application of statute law that relate to procuratorate work. At this point, the legislature may have reason to be concerned and may ask how far the judicial interpretations can legitimately go in challenging the legislative power of the NPC and its Standing Committee.[33] This is so because, among others, there is still considerable opportunity to develop and enact new statute law to improve justice in environmental cases. Two questions accordingly arise in this respect. Would judicial interpretations be a rational or reliable means to effectively close the loopholes in statute law? Should the SPC and SPP more actively address environmental issues by means of judicial interpretations? The success of some key judicial interpretations in civil environmental cases, discussed below, appear to suggest that the answer should be in the affirmative. However, statute law may perhaps still be a better instrument for environmental governance than relying on judicial interpretation.

---

31. The members of the judicial committee are nominated by the people's court itself from senior judges and experienced senior executives in the people's court; and their appointment is made by the people's congress at the same level.
32. OLPC 1983, Art. 11.
33. C.Y. Xin, *Chinese Courts: History and Transition*, 2nd ed. (Beijing: Law Press, 2004), 103.

Most cases are heard in the people's court in the first instance and on appeal are tried by a collegial panel consisting of judges and a jury.[34] The president of the court or the chief judge usually appoints a judge to preside over the collegial panel unless he or she is sitting in the trial. Members of the collegial panel enjoy equal rights as far as participation in the trial, discussions and judgment are concerned. The jury in the collegial panel consists of elected citizens who have the right to vote and are above twenty-three years of age.[35] In environmental cases, citizens who are environmental professionals are encouraged to become members of the people's jury and to play an active role in court proceedings. The people's courts have realized the necessity to tap special expertise, but there is room to further develop this opportunity by refining the election procedures for the people's jury.

6   ANALYSIS OF SIGNIFICANT ENVIRONMENTAL JUDGMENTS

6.1   INTRODUCTION

As the Chinese judicial system upholds the tradition of statute law, the people's courts adjudicate cases strictly in accordance with specific rules determined by the statutory regime. As they do not have the status of statute law, the judgments delivered in environmental cases cannot be applied or even referred to in successive similar cases. However, they provide a trace of the evolution of judicial practice concerning environmental matters and accordingly may be somewhat persuasive in subsequent matters brought before the court. The following section analyses some significant environmental judgments that the people's courts in the PRC have adjudicated to date. The discussion is arranged to respectively focus on issues of a civil, administrative and criminal nature.

6.2   CIVIL ISSUES

6.2.1   Pollution Torts: General Remarks

Matters involving environmental pollution have been widely recognized in the environmental law regime as issues requiring the adoption of special legal rules and doctrines. The most significant doctrine applied in cases involving environmental pollution damage worldwide, is strict liability, whereby the violation of law or the subjective fault of the polluter is ignored as a fact of causality. However, its interpretation in Chinese environmental legislation has varied from the inception of the EPL Interim 1979 to date. The doctrine of fault has been entrenched in the

---

34. Except for fairly simple civil cases, for instance, minor criminal cases, and cases that a single judge could deal with alone.
35. See CPL 1996, Art. 13; and APL 1989, Art. 40.

PRC's environmental regime for a long time. This is typically reflected in the EPL Interim 1979. Looking back on it now, the EPL Interim 1979 seems more like a policy document than pure statute law, but in the chapter on 'Praise and Penalty' it provided the initial norms concerning general legal responsibilities in environmental protection. Although its reference to environmental pollution tort and court's jurisdictions is vague, its stipulations[36] nevertheless helped to situate the violation of the law as the precondition for the imposition of all sorts of penalties. By implication, it accordingly entrenched the doctrine of fault as a necessary prerequisite to found liability in environmental pollution torts. This was altered by the WPPCL 1984, the PRC's first environmental law, which introduced the doctrine of relative strict liability in environmental pollution torts. However, the basic civil law (the General Rules of Civil Law 1986) subsequently stipulated fault liability for all torts, and especially pollution torts.[37] The EPL resurrected the restriction of relative strict liability prescribed in the WPPCL 1984, in which 'natural disasters' and the 'prompt adoption of reasonable measures' were retained as instances leading to exemption from liability.[38] The question facing the judiciary during this period was how to apply such contradictory legal doctrines and deal with pollution tort cases when the law was incapable of application.

6.2.2   Liability and Burden of Proof

The judiciary heard various cases dealing with environmental liability between the late 1970s and 1992,[39] including: *Hexin Village Fishery Farm v. Tianjing 2nd Steel Strings Manufacture*[40] (damage to a fishery by water pollution); *Five Star Unit in Baqiao District of Xi'an City v. Xi'an Electricity Manufacture*[41] (compensation for the cost of resettlement away from noise pollution); *Ledu County People's Government of Gansu Province v. Liancheng Aluminium Manufacture of Qinghai Province*[42] (compensation for damage caused by air pollution to victims in Ledu County); and *Four Villages of Datong County of Qinghai Province v. The*

---

36. Art. 32(1) stipulated that after receiving the approval of the people's government at the same level, the environmental protection departments could release a compensation order to the entities who violated this law or other environmental regulations, thus polluting and damaging the environment, and harming people's health. Further in Art. 32(2), it provided that those persons who caused great harm because of pollution and serious damage as described by law, were to be charged for administrative, economic and criminal responsibility.
37. Art. 124 of the GRCL stated that 'any person who pollutes the environment and causes damage to others in violation of state provisions for environmental protection and the prevention of pollution shall bear civil liability in accordance with the law'.
38. See EPL, Art. 42(1) and (3).
39. In 1992, the SPC issued specific judicial interpretations concerning burden of proof of environmental pollution tort cases as discussed later in this section, which supported practices of relative strict liability.
40. [1988] Zhang 1993, 383-395. See K.M. Zhang (ed.), *Handbooks of China's Environmental Law Enforcement* (Beijing: Publishing House of China University of Law and Politics, 1993).
41. [1984] Zhang 1993, 399-400.
42. [1989] Zhang 1993, 409-411.

Cement Manufactory of Qinghai Province[43] (damage to property and health arising from dust pollution). What is noteworthy about most of these judgments is that the courts did not rely on fault liability, but instead on strict liability. A further example is that of *Wang Juan v. Qingdao City Chemical Plant.*[44] The plaintiff was an employer of the defendant. On the evening of 1 July 1978, a lightning strike caused a large chlorine leak on the defendant's premises. More than ten residents living in the vicinity were poisoned and sent to hospital for medical care. The plaintiff suffered from serious chlorine poisoning and was hospitalized for over a year. The defendant covered all her medical expenses and compensated her for her loss of income. Later the plaintiff was diagnosed as having allergic bronchial asthma and was subject to ongoing treatment. The plaintiff's claim for reimbursement of her medical expenses and compensation for loss of income was in this instance rejected by the defendant on the grounds that her allergic bronchial asthma had no causal link with the pollution accident. The Intermediate People's Court of Qingdao City established the following grounds for later adjudication: first, neither the plaintiff nor any members of her family had previously had allergic bronchial asthma; second, medical trials proved that chlorine poisoning could result in allergic bronchial asthma; and third, she contracted allergic bronchial asthma immediately after the chlorine spill. The court accordingly held that the plaintiff's allergic bronchial asthma was caused by the chlorine spill from the defendants premises and that the defendant had to compensate her. The matter was ultimately settled with the defendant agreeing to compensate the plaintiff. This case was the first lawsuit heard after the EPL Interim 1979 came into effect. Even by today's standards, the approach taken by the people's court took was innovative and commendable. First, the people's court applied absolute strict liability and even excluded *force majeure* as an instance leading to exemption (in this case, the cause of the chlorine pollution was a lightning strike); an approach which was strongly in favour of the victim. Second, in establishing the causal link between the conduct and the consequences, the burden of proof was imposed neither on the plaintiff nor on the defendant, but was voluntarily undertaken by the people's court itself. This approach certainly favoured the plaintiff. Third, the people's court took the deductive approach to prove that the chlorine spill caused the allergic bronchial asthma, using the theory of epidemiology.[45] What is especially admirable in the context of the then inadequacy of the rules of law to be applied in environmental pollution tort cases, is that the people's court broke the bounds of existing statutes by considering Japanese cases of the same sort, and rendered a judgment favourable to the plaintiff in accordance with the principle of fairness and justice.

---

43. [1990] Zhang 1993, 411-418.
44. [1978] Zhang 1993, 395-399.
45. This is the method relied on by medical experts to identify the probability of the occurrence of epidemic diseases in certain areas where pollutants exist. The probability of disease occurrence can be concluded when a case is comprehensively analyzed, through establishing elements such as the factors in an area which could result in a particular disease, or that pollutants had been present in the area before the occurrence of an epidemic.

6.2.3   Damages and Causality

In the case of *Four Villages of Datong County of Qinghai Province* (see above), the
plaintiff had endured dust pollution from the defendant for almost ten years and
claimed for damages to crops, animal husbandry, health and loss of income. The
difficulty in this case lay in finding a technical method to measure the actual
damages caused by the dust emanating from the defendant's premises. The
court used scientific reports and expert laboratory results as its reference in measuring the plaintiff's loss in crops and animal husbandry, and upheld the plaintiff's
crop loss claim. It did not, however, uphold the claims for loss of animals and
human health injuries as it was not technically feasible to prove these damages. In
relation to the claim for damage to human health, for example, the medical examination of individuals had not demonstrated that the disease symptoms actually
occurred after the act of pollution.

6.2.4   Resolution through Administrative Means

In the period from the late 1970s to the mid-1990s, the people's courts did not face
many environmental pollution tort cases. Of all the hundreds of thousands of annual
petition cases, less than 1% was brought to the people's courts in the year 2000
according to the statistics of the State Environmental Protection Administration.[46]
The environmental protection administrative bodies were handling most of the
environmental pollution tort cases through administrative processes in accordance
with Article 42(2) of the EPL discussed above. It is obviously not feasible to reflect
on the details of all of the cases in which the people's courts considered matters
relating to damages arising from pollution, but from a brief scrutiny of the cases
reported by the public media, one may conclude that the people's courts acquitted
themselves well in such cases, or at least that judgments were made in an open-
minded and innovative manner. In the mid 1990s, an increased number of matters
dealing with environmental torts were brought to the people's courts. According to a
survey,[47] from 1998 to 2001, 20,000 environmental pollution tort disputes were
lodged and settled by civil, administrative and criminal proceedings of the people's
courts.[48] Since then the number has annually increased by 25%. As environmental
pollution tort cases are often a complicated mix of scientific, social and economic
issues, and considering the sudden increased case load in environmental torts, the
people's courts are under immense pressure to deal with the increased case load.

---

46.   S.H. Qi & J.W. Lin (eds), *Environmental Dispute Resolution* (Xiamen: XUP, 2005), 222.
47.   C.F. Wang, 'Existing problems of defending environmental rights and the way-out',
      <www.greensos.cn/?action_viewnews_itemid_4302.html>, 28 December 2007.
48.   In comparison, the total number of petitions nationwide to the environmental protection author-
      ity for administrative mediation amounted to 180,000 in 1998, 250,000 in 1999, 300,000 in
      2000, and 400,000 in 2001. See, State Environmental Protection Administration, Public Reports
      of State Environmental Statistics 1998-2001 (Beijing: National Publishing House, 2001).

6.2.5   Strict Liability

Generally, the doctrine of relative strict liability would need to have supplementary rules added to it for use in the people's courts. The absence of such rules (including, for example, rules pertaining to causality, the burden of proof, and the quantification of pollution-affected damages), has always hindered the people's court in dealing with environmental pollution tort cases. The SPC responded to the need for a ruling on the issue of the burden of proof through its judicial interpretations. The first important judicial interpretation in this regard was in *The Opinions of the SPC on Several Issues of the Application of Civil Procedure Law*, which reversed the burden of proof in environmental pollution tort litigation. Article 74 reads:

> ... in lawsuits each party has liability to provide proof of what he/she claims for, except for in the following lawsuits where the defendant bears the burden of proof of the tort fact that the plaintiff lodges but he/she denies: ... (c) lawsuit for damages by environmental pollution.

This judicial interpretation clearly states that the court should apply the principle of strict liability in environmental pollution torts despite the conflict of legislation. There is, however, still a *lacuna* with regard to the extent to which the burden of proof reverts to the polluter and the extent to which it remains a duty of the victim. The determination of these evidentiary issues remains a matter for the judge's discretion. This dynamic was practically illustrated in *Pinghu Normal Farm of Zhejiang Province v. Five Corporations of Buyun Dye Chemical,*[49] which dealt with damage caused to a fishery by water pollution. The case is unique in that it twice went through the procedure of trial supervision for consideration of the issue of burden of proof with regard to water pollution torts. The Pinghu Normal Farm was established in 1991 and specialized in the aqua-culture of a species of tadpole for an American partner enterprise. In April 1994, the plaintiff found that the tadpoles were dying in unusually high numbers. In September and October that year, almost all of the tadpoles died. As the farm was located in a watercourse into which the defendants had for some time been discharging pollutants above the level permitted by national emission standards, the plaintiff believed that the death of the tadpoles was caused by the defendant's pollution. The basic people's court of the Pinghu County undertook the trial in the first instance, and held that the plaintiff's claim could not be upheld because it had failed to provide proof that the tadpoles' death was caused by the defendant's conduct. Upon the petition of the plaintiff, the intermediate procuratorate of Jiaxin City protested a wrongful decision of the court on the ground that the court did not apply the reverse onus of proof as reflected in the SPC's judicial interpretation of 1992 (quoted above). The intermediate people's court of Jiaxin City then tried the case through the procedure of trial supervision with a procuratorate officer present. The intermediate court held that the reverse onus of proof had to be applied in this case, but only

---

49. [2000], PKU, Lawyee, 'Case', <edu.lawyee.net/Case/Case_Display.asp?RID=127871>.

to establish the subjective fault of the polluter. The plaintiff still had to prove two facts: that the pollution was caused by the defendants; and that the damages (the death of the tadpoles) were caused by the pollution. With regard to these two facts, the intermediate court held that the plaintiff had satisfied the former but not the latter element and accordingly dismissed the plaintiff's claim. The High Procuratorate of Zhejiang Province was finally called upon to hear the matter. The plaintiff argued that both the basic court and the intermediate court had failed to take fault liability and the general doctrine of causality into account in trying the matter. It further argued that both courts had failed to apply strict liability and reverse the onus of proof that was to be applied in environmental pollution torts. In the appeal trial the defendant provided proof that other tadpole farms in the same area had not experienced tadpole deaths on the same scale as the plaintiff. The High People's Court of Zhejiang Province accordingly held that the plaintiff was not entitled to compensation. It is interesting to note that with regard to the issue of causality, the court adopted the same approach as the intermediate court.

It is fair to infer from the above jurisprudence that the people's courts are rather conservative in employing the new legal rule of reversed onus of proof in trying pollution tort cases. This jurisprudence further illustrates the inherent weakness of the legal rules, including the judicial interpretations, relating to strict liability, deductive causality and the onus of proof. Pollution tort cases heard by the people's courts are accordingly seldom decided in favour of the victim.

In light of the manner in which the courts had treated the rule reversing the onus of proof in pollution tort cases, the SPC released its second related set of judicial interpretations in *The Several Provisions of the SPC Concerning the Proof of Civil Lawsuit* dated 1 April 2002. These sought to again address the onus of proof conundrum and furthermore the deductive causality doctrine, described as 'no existence of causality of conduct and damage' in environmental pollution torts cases. Article 4 reads:

> . . . in the following tort lawsuits, the burden of proof applies the following rules: . . . (c) in the lawsuit for damages by environmental pollution, the inflictor bears the burden of proof over matters that are subject to exemption explicated by law, and proof over no existence of causality of conduct and damage.

These two judicial interpretations by the SPC appear to have created the impetus for the people's courts to reach agreement on how to decide environmental pollution tort cases. In most decisions following their release (for example, *Liu Jun and Liu Rong v. Liulu Enterprise Limited Corporation of Jinzhou Economic and Technology Development District*,[50] which dealt with damage caused to a coastal fishery by an oil leak; and the appeal case of *Di Minze v. Chen Hongshen*[51] relating to noise torts), the people's courts have invoked the relevant judicial interpretations released in 2002.

---

50. [2003] PKU, Lawyee, 'Case', <edu.lawyee.net/Case/Case_Display.asp?RID=79626>.
51. [2005] PKU, Lawyee, 'Case', <edu.lawyee.net/Case/Case_Data.asp?RID=158104>.

Benefiting from the years of practice that the people's courts and other authorities have had in dealing with environmental pollution torts cases, the legal rules on strict liability and related doctrines have been developed and better presented in the WPPCL 2008. Article 87 of the WPPCL 2008 prescribes various instances in which the polluter bears the onus of proof in lawsuits for compensation for damages caused by water pollution.[52] It is fair to say that the WPPCL 2008 has adopted part of the judicial interpretations of SPC as described above. One hopes that this law will better assist the judiciary to uphold justice in water pollution tort matters, and furthermore influence air and noise pollution torts cases through the operation of judicial discretion.

6.3   ADMINISTRATIVE ISSUES

6.3.1   Introduction

The people's courts in the PRC are generally not averse to reviewing the issue of administrative permits, orders or penalties to public and private entities. The APL 1989 created administrative procedures for the people's courts to comply with in dealing with judicial review cases. Administrative tribunals were consequently established in the people's courts. These were initiated at the local level and specialized in trying judicial review cases and other administrative issues.

6.3.2   Administrative Enforcement of Environmental Laws

In the 1980s the people's courts played an important role, through judicial review, in supporting the implementation of environmental law (the interim EPL 1979 and the EPL) the operation of the newly established environmental administration authorities. In terms of the *Civil Procedure Law* 1982, both the environmental administrative authorities and citizens or entities directly involved in an issue, could take the other to court over disputes relating to administrative conduct. The people's courts were eager to support environmental protection and administration. This is well illustrated by the case of *Shekou Environment Monitoring Station v. Hong Kong Kaida Company.*[53] The defendant, the Hong Kong Kaida Company, invested in a toy factory in the Shekou Industrial District in 1982. The factory went into operation in February 1982. It emitted high levels of noise and poisonous and malodorous gas without any apparent attempts at prevention or

---

52. These instances are defined in Art. 85 of this law as follows: in the instance of *force majeure,* or that victims on purpose conduct water pollution, the polluter is free from liability for damages to victims; and in the instance that third parties cause water pollution, the polluter first bears liability but can then revert to the third party for the liability; and in the instance that the victim causes water pollution due to significant negligence, the polluter can mitigate the liability for damages.
53. [1983] PBSPC, 1985, 3.

mitigation. Residents complained that they were being affected and had developed respiratory diseases and other health problems. The plaintiff, the Shenzhen City Shekou District Environment Monitoring Station, urged the defendant to take measures to eliminate all forms of nuisance under a pollution control plan, and offered to provide technical assistance to the defendant to detect and monitor pollutants. Having received no response from the defendant, the plaintiff issued an order compelling the defendant to take various pollution prevention measures by a prescribed date. The defendant failed to comply with the order and the plaintiff accordingly approached the Shenzhen Intermediate People's Court for a court order. The plaintiff pleaded that the defendant had to eliminate the noise and gas to the extent that it met national emission standards, and had to pay for the related costs in detecting and monitoring pollutants and nuisance. The defendants argued that they had never been informed of any national standards with respect to environmental pollution, and that the onus to prove nuisance, noise, and the existence of odors rested on the plaintiff. The defendants argued further that the deadline by which the factory was required to treat the pollution was unrealistic. The people's court held that according to the EPL Interim 1979, the defendant was obliged to report to the environmental authority any environmental impacts resulting from the activities of the factory, including pollution data. The defendant also had to prevent and treat pollution. The defendant had ignored the plaintiff's order and failed to comply with the deadline which clearly constituted a violation of the EPL. The plaintiff's order was upheld by the court. This judgment was highly influential with respect to judicial enforcement of the EPL Interim 1979. The primary aim of the environmental protection authority was the effective implementation of the EPL. This judgment was hailed by the Adjudication Committee of the SPC in 1985, when it praised the approach and efforts of the people's court to protect human health, safeguard environmental standards and uphold the EPL.

Another example was the appeal case of *Chen Weiqiang v. Environmental Protection Office of Zengcheng County of Guangdong Province*;[54] the first administrative case that the intermediate people's court of Guangdong Province tried. The plaintiff conducted trade in wastes that contained hazardous substances. He stored the goods inappropriately and caused accidental pollution. He received a penalty from the defendant that he did not accept. The people's court upheld the decision of the defendant to issue the penalty.

It can be observed from the above cursory survey, that the people's courts have tended to favour the victims in environmental cases and to support the environmental administrative authority by making genuine efforts to enforce the EPL. For this purpose, especially after 1989, the people's courts were empowered by the EPL and the APL to employ the judicial procedures to enforce the decisions of the environmental administrative authority, which had become effective but not been complied with by the parties concerned. In contrast, those administrative decisions that had been rendered to the parties concerned, but which were not yet effective,

---

54. [1985] Xie 1995, 124-125. See Z.H. Xie, *Concise Book of Classic Environmental Lawsuits and Law Enforcement in China* (Beijing: CEPSP, 1995).

were subject to judicial review through the administrative procedures in the APL. The focus of these cases is on strict implementation of and compliance with environmental law, and bears testimony to the fact that the judiciary will intervene, even in an age when non-compliance with environmental laws is the order of the day. Where an administrative organ of state is not able to enforce environmental laws, the people's courts will not hesitate to assume the role of an enforcement authority. This approach should also be welcomed.

It can further be observed that although the function of judicial review by the people's court is unchanged today, and still relates to the enforcement of and compliance with environmental law, Chinese society has now adjusted its focus to include challenging the manner in which environmental administrative authorities fulfil their statutory functions.

6.3.3   Environmental Impact Assessment

In 2005, the State Environmental Protection Administration suspended thirty large projects in thirteen provinces and cities, including the Xiluodu Hydraulic Power Station on the Upper Yangtze River, for violating national laws on EIA and the EIAL 2002.[55] Construction on these projects had commenced without EIA review and approval. The blame for the violations of the EIA laws cannot only be laid at the door of the project developers. It could partially be attributed to the fragmented and complex EIA and permitting regime enacted in the PRC which causes immense confusion and delay. This is illustrated by the case of *Shen Xixian, 182 Residents v. Planning Committee of Beijing Municipality*.[56] The defendant issued a construction permit to a third party to build an animal laboratory in the middle of two residential buildings without EIA permission. The animal laboratory was very close to the residential buildings and consequently in breach of national standards concerning safety. The plaintiffs pleaded that the basic people's court of Dongcheng District in Beijing ought to order the defendant to withdraw the construction permit. The defendant argued that the approval of the EIA was not a precondition for the issue of a construction permit, according to the established procedure in such matters. The basic court invoked Article 13 of the EPL and asserted that EIA approval had to be granted prior to the issuing of the construction permit for the project. The court hence ordered the defendant to withdraw the construction permit pending finalization of the EIA approval process. This case clearly illustrates the relative weight the court ascribes to the EIA approval process in contrast to other relevant permitting processes. The SPC public bulletin publicized this case to illustrate the willingness of the people's courts to uphold the EIA legislation and to encourage its implementation by relevant authorities.

---

55. X.J. Yang (ed.), *Selection of Significant Administrative Cases* (Beijing: PHCUPL, 2006), 373-374.
56. [2003] PBSPC, 2004, 3; Yang, *supra* n. 55, 270-273.

6.3.4   Administrative Duties to Protect the Environment

Since the late 1990s, rapid urbanization, large-scale development and the exploitation of natural resources have compounded the challenge of finding a balance between development and environmental protection. The frequent non-performance or wrongful conduct of people's governments, environmental watchdogs and environmental authorities has become a new social concern. Those who damage the environment or fail to perform their function of protecting the environment are more frequently being arraigned in the people's courts. Two trends have become evident in this context.

The first is for citizens who are directly affected by administrative non-performance, to initiate judicial review proceedings. The people's courts are taking a cautious approach in responding to this trend, both in their examination of the relevant facts and in their application of the relevant legislation. This was clearly illustrated in the appeal case of *Tong Huancheng, 78 villagers v. The People's Government of Xing Rong County of Chende City, Hebei Province*.[57] The plaintiffs lived in the village where the Xinye vitriol chemical factory was located. The factory heavily polluted the village and twice received orders from the environmental bureau of Chende City to replace its old facilities. The plaintiffs alleged that the defendant knew that the factory was the source of heavy pollution but colluded with the polluters by failing to enforce its relevant bylaw. The plaintiffs requested the basic people's court of Xinrong County to order the defendant to issue an administrative order to suspend or close the factory. The court cautiously examined the facts and held as follows: the factory was the major cause of pollution; the defendant had organized many meetings to discuss this issue and initiated a plan to assist the factory in technological reconstruction; the environmental protection bureau had frequently urged the factory to conduct such reconstruction or suspend operations; the electricity bureau had stopped the electricity power supply; and the factory was currently undergoing reconstruction. The court accordingly held that the defendant had been actively performing its bylaw duty to solve the pollution problem at the factory. The plaintiffs' suit was accordingly dismissed. In another similar case, *Sun Datao, 101 villagers v. Environmental Protection Bureau of Pingdingshan City*,[58] the people's court of the Weidong District of Pingdingshan City upheld the plaintiff's claim. In this matter, a coking plant polluted the plaintiffs' properties, even after a fine was levied on it by the defendant in response to prior complaints about pollution. The plaintiffs accused the defendant of being negligent in not performing its bylaw duty of monitoring pollution and directing a treatment order to the polluter. The basic people's court upheld the plaintiffs' plea and ordered the defendant to impose a treatment order on the coking plant and carry out regular inspections of it. It is worth noting that it was the people's court of Weidong District that adjudicated the first of these administrative cases, namely: *Li Xinfang, 295 Residents v. Environmental Protection Bureau of Pingdingshan*

---

57.   [2006] PKU, Lawyee, 'Case', <edu.lawyee.net/Case/Case_Display.asp?RID=101402>.
58.   [2001] PKU, Lawyee, 'Case', <edu.lawyee.net/Case/Case_Display.asp?RID=25587>.

City.[59] This matter dealt with the defendant's alleged failure to enforce relevant pollution legislation. The residents' claim was upheld by the people's court.

6.3.5   Public Interest Environmental Litigation

Another emerging trend is for citizens and civic entities to litigate in the public environmental interest. This is true in particular of environmental non-governmental organizations (NGOs) representing the public at large, which have no direct civil or administrative interest in the particular environmental matter, but initiate judicial proceedings in defence of the public interest. In recent years, the strength of NGOs' advocacy and the prominence of their victories (for example, in the Yuanmingyuan Park public hearings of 2005[60] and the Nujiang hydraulic power station planning between 2003-2005),[61] has drawn society's attention to the benefits to be derived from public participation in environmental decision-making processes. It has further drawn the judiciary's attention to the need to safeguard citizens' rights or opportunities to access justice in matters pertaining to public environmental interests.

The main hindrance facing citizens seeking to litigate in the public environmental interest relates to standing. Article 6 of the EPL is considered the principal legal basis for providing rights to citizens in prosecution and in bringing public interest cases to court. Owing to the nature of its allusion to individual litigation rights in environmental matters of public interest, the application of Article 6 of the EPL still has to rely on special litigation laws. Civil and administrative litigation laws require a person of standing to have a direct civil or administrative link with, or interest in, the suit. These legislative constraints have proven to be serious obstacles to public interest litigation in environmental matters.[62] In 2005, two citizens sued the Planning Bureau of Nanjin City for issuing a permit that allowed the Zijinshen Administrative Bureau to build a viewing tower in a protected area. The court rejected this suit because the applicants lacked standing to sue.[63] This illustrates the reticence of the people's courts to exercise their protective jurisdiction in this field.

---

59. [1994] Wang 2004, 33-34. See S.Y. Wang (ed.), *Case-interpreted Textbook of Environmental and Natural Resource Law* (Beijing: IRP, 2004).
60. The case of Yuan-min-yuan Park created the first environmental public hearing and procedures for public participation in EIA in China. In August 2003, this park conducted a large-scale environmental improvement project with no EIA review. In March 2006, Prof. Zhang of Lanzhou University led media and NGOs to campaign for a review. See Chinaxys, 'Review', <www.chinaxys.net/dajia/yuanmingyuan.html>, 19 December 2006.
61. The Nujiang hydraulic power station planning campaign 2003-2005 was a case in which the public used an EIA to correct the governmental planning proceedings. See China Energy Net, 'News', <www.china5e.com/focus/focus.php?type=nujiang>, 19 November 2006.
62. S.Q. Cai, 'Policy framework of resolution of environmental disputes and enforcement of environmental liabilities', *proceedings of the International Symposium on Legislation For Environmental Damage Compensation* (Beijing: EPNRC, 2004); and Z.M. Lv, 'Probing Environmental Litigation: Does Environmental Litigation Exist?', in Z.M. Lv (ed.), *Environmental and Natural Resource Law Study*, vol. 3 (Beijing: LSP, 2004), 12-18.
63. Xinhua Net, 'Viewing Tower Construction in Zijing Mount: State-invested Capital in Vain', <www.xinhua.net>, 25 January 2002.

6.4   CRIMINAL LAWSUITS

6.4.1   Introduction

In the 1980s, environmental resources were in short supply and there was a dearth of adequate resources to sustain people in the PRC. This situation brought pressure to bear in the area of natural resource conservation, as evidenced by the prevalence of the common crimes of illegal logging and the killing of protected rare and endangered wildlife for profit.[64] While the *Criminal Law* 1979 (CL) provided limited and vague provisions relating to these issues,[65] most violations of environmental protection and natural resource conservation were more frequently prescribed in sectoral environmental and natural resources laws, which at that time were insufficient for effective judicial prosecution and adjudication purposes. To close the legislative loophole, the Standing Committee of the NPC released supplementary provisions addressing specific issues, and the SPC and the SPP issued related judicial interpretations. The judicial institutions were able to use these legal rules to fairly effectively suppress the crimes. In *People's Procuratorate of Fuping County of Shaangxi Province v. Li Chuancai*[66] the severe punishment imposed by the court virtually put an end to the crime of killing pandas and other similar crimes. In this case, the defendant colluded with others and shot a panda. The people's court of Fuping County held that: the panda was a rare and endangered wild animal; the defendant illegally shot the panda in a protected area for the sake of the high profit to be derived from the sale of its fur; and that the conduct of the defendant violated Article 130 of the CL 1979[67] and the supplemental provision of the NPC (of 1988) on punishing the crime of killing State-protected key, rare, and endangered wild animals. The court, employing the particular SPC's judicial interpretation in 1987 on strictly punishing the crime of killing a panda and the smuggling and sale of panda fur, issued a death sentence to the defendant, with a two year reprieve.

6.4.2   The Evolution of Environmental Crimes

The adjudication of criminal cases in the field of environmental protection and pollution control in the 1980s seemed unable to respond to the new patterns of crime. This was largely owing to the fact that the CL 1979 contained no provisions relating to pollution and environmental harm. The relevant legal provisions were fragmented across many different laws, especially in newly promulgated sectoral

---

64. The classic criminal cases that were adjudicated in this period were Qian Pu (killing filefish in the Yangtze River in 1984), Gao Lianshan (killing swans in Shangdong Province in 1986), and Wang Yong (killing golden monkeys in Hubei Province in 1988). See Xie, *supra* n. 54, 23-43.
65. CL 1979, Arts 128, 129 and 130. In general these included crimes against the regulation and conservation of forest resources, aquatic resources and wild animals.
66. [1984] Xie 1995, 21-23.
67. This concerned the crime against the conservation of wild animals in general. The longest limit of imprisonment related to this crime was two years.

laws governing environmental protection and pollution control, with which the people's procuratorates and courts were not conversant. As a result, criminal cases relating to environmental pollution and degradation were not readily lodged in the people's courts. Where they were lodged, the people's courts faced difficulties in determining whether the action constituted an environmental crime, and what the appropriate penalty should be. In the mid-1980s several cases were incorrectly decided, where judges mistook environmental crimes to be crimes against production and public security.[68] The case of *People's Procuratorate of Xiangxiang County of Hunan Province v. Tan Liangui,*[69] (reported in Xiang Xiang County) is a typical example. Several aluminum and phosphor fertilizer factories discharged waste water into a stream which farmers in Xiang Town relied on for drinking water and irrigation. Ten years of this pollution caused great harm to the farmers' living environment, their health and their crops. Farmers in three villages frequently urged the two factories to treat their waste water and to compensate them for their loss, but never received a reply. In 1980, the farmers took the matter into their own hands and cut the discharge pipes as part of a campaign to sabotage the aluminum factory's production. Tan Liangui (the leader of the farmers) and others were arraigned by the people's procuratorate of Xiang Xiang County. The basic people's court of Xiang Xiang County held that the accused farmers had committed a 'crime against production', according to Article 125 of the CL 1979, and imposed a sentence of imprisonment. On appeal, the intermediate people's court of the Xiangtan Prefecture agreed with the verdict of the basic court. The court's decision took immediate effect but protests against the verdict continued until 1988. In 1990, the intermediate people's court of Xiangtan City (Prefecture) had to conduct the procedure of trial supervision to hear this case again. Eventually the court found the accused farmers not guilty. Mistakes of this nature seldom occur nowadays, especially given the further development of the knowledge and techniques of the people's courts in trying environmental crimes.

The introduction of the *Criminal Law* 1997 (CL) created a new category of crimes namely, 'crimes against environmental protection and natural resources conservation'.[70] The CL 1997 and its five amendments from 1999 to 2005, effectively codify crimes in the environmental and natural resources contexts into a single source. Cumulatively, they provide the first general criminal statute and prescribe the principal mechanisms for raising the awareness and capacity of prosecutors and judges dealing with criminal lawsuits in this field. In addition, the SPC has released several judicial interpretations relating to frequently

---

68. Similar incorrect judgments can also be found in: *Mr Wus for destruction of production 1983* by the People's Court in Shupu County, Huaihua Prefecture, Hunan Province; *Zhang Daichao for destruction of public property* by the basic People's Court of Huaining County, Anhui Province 1984; and *Guo Hesheng for a breach of social order* 1983 by the basic People's Court of Jiyuan County, Henan Province. All of these were corrected sooner or later. See: Zhang, *supra* n. 40, 461-481.
69. [1980] Zhang 1993, 470-472.
70. Ch. VI, s. VI of CL 1997.

committed 'modern' crimes concerning natural resource conservation, namely: the destruction of land resources[71] and forest resources;[72] the spoliation of wild animal resources;[73] and the destruction of forest resources.[74] The above have significantly expanded the role of the people's courts in adjudicating criminal cases in the contexts of environmental protection and the conservation of natural resources.

6.4.3   Specific Environmental Crimes

Of all the crimes relating to the environment, those involving significant environmental pollution accidents are probably adjudicated most frequently by the people's courts. The case of *People's Procuratorate of Yunchen City of Shanxi Province v. Yang Junwu*,[75] was the first criminal lawsuit to be publicized by the SPC following the commencement of the CL 1997. In this case, the defendant's paper manufacturing factory was located near a channel that conveyed drinking water to a reservoir. The defendant did not construct facilities to treat wastewater. Instead, he stored it in a sewage pit near the factory. In October 1997, the pit burst and sewage containing poisonous substances spilled into the channel and contaminated the reservoir containing water the local people relied on for drinking and irrigation. During the accident, the defendant took some rehabilitation measures. These measures were insufficient to eliminate the sewage contamination to the reservoir. The defendant was prosecuted by the basic people's procuratorate for having negligently caused a contamination accident that gave rise to significant loss of private and public property. The basic people's court examined the above facts and found that the defendant was guilty of committing the crime of causing significant environmental pollution by accident. The court invoked Article 338 of the CL 1997 and sentenced the defendant to two years imprisonment and a 50,000 Yuan fine. The court also adjudicated the civil tort aspect in this lawsuit, and concluded that the defendant had to compensate the victim (the reservoir committee) for damage to the drinking water based on its market value. In the appeal, the intermediate people's court of Yunchen Prefecture upheld the decision of the first court.

    Given the improved regulation of crimes against rare and endangered animals, arising from the stringent punishments handed down by the courts, the general pattern seems to reflect a shift towards crimes relating to the illegal use and exploitation of other natural resources, such as timber. In the case of *The Basic People's Procuratorate of Xixian County of Shaanxi Province v. Peng Fangrong*,[76] the defendant was prosecuted for the illegal and larcenous logging of trees. Without a logging permit from the forestry authority of the people's government,

71. Effective from 22 June 2000.
72. Effective from 30 December 2005.
73. Effective from 11 December 2000.
74. Effective from 11 December 2000.
75. [1997] PBSPC, 1999, 3; Lawyee, 'Case', <edu.lawyee.net/Case/Case_Display.asp?RID =26273>.
76. [2005] PKU, Lawyee, 'Case', <edu.lawyee.net/Case/Case_Display.asp?RID=101761>.

the defendant logged fifty trees that had been planted in collectively owned land under the stewardship and permission of his neighbour.[77] He logged a further nine trees on the same land but without the permission of the neighbour. Invoking the CL 1997 and the SPC's judicial interpretation on the destruction of forest resources (of 2000),[78] the basic people's court concluded that the defendant had committed two crimes: first, illegal logging; and second, larcenous logging with regard to nine trees without permission.[79] The defendant was sentenced to two years imprisonment.

In the area of wildlife conservation, current criminal justice has expanded the scope of activities attracting criminal punishment from the hunting and killing of protected wild animals, to the transport and sale of protected wild animals and products made from them. In the criminal case of *The Basic People's Procuratorate of Heshan City of Guangdong Province v. Li Yayang*,[80] the defendant was prosecuted for illegally transporting eighteen live pangolins, a protected, rare and endangered wild animal. After invoking Article 341(1) of the CL 1997 and employing the relevant Articles[81] of the SPC's judicial interpretations on crimes concerning rare and endangered wild animals, the basic people's court found that the defendant was guilty and sentenced him to ten years imprisonment and a 5,000 Yuan fine. The court also confiscated the vehicle which had been used to transport the animals.

7   CRITICAL SURVEY

The judiciary serves as a vital agent in the process of guiding the administration of environmental legislation, enforcing it and facilitating and promoting societal

---

77. It is worth noting that all logging, including the logging of trees that the logger himself/herself owns, requires an official permit issued in advance. Whether an action that violates this regulation is a crime or not, is determined by reference to various elements of criminal jurisprudence, inclusive of the number of trees logged.
78. The illegal logging crime was determined mainly through the application of statutes such as Art. 355(1) of the CL 1997, Art. 3(1) and Art. 6 of the SPC's judicial interpretations on forest resource crimes 2000. The crime of larcenous logging was determined in accordance with Art. 355(2) of the CL 1997, and Arts 5(1) and 4 of the same SPC's judicial interpretations.
79. Nine trees would yield more than two cubic meters of timber, meeting the range of quantity (two to five cubic meters) for basic punishment (under three years imprisonment) for the crime of larcenous logging as prescribed by Art. 4 of the SPC's interpretation.
80. [2006] PKU, Lawyee, 'Case', <edu.lawyee.net/Case/Case_Display.asp?RID=100383>.
81. According to Art. 341(1) of the CL 1997, this crime has three instances: the crime with general instance, severe instance and extra-severe instance. The SPC's judicial interpretations provided standards by which to distinguish the three instances. In this case, the number of pangolins in illegal transport was the key element that defined the instance of crime and the related sentence, as follows: fewer than eight pangolins – general instance: under five years imprisonment; eight to sixteen – severe instance: five to eight years; and more than sixteen – extra-severe instance: more than ten years. This example demonstrates how the SPC's judicial interpretations are particularly useful in adjudicating criminal cases.

involvement. The judiciary is also a crucial partner in upholding the rule of law to ensure justice in environmental, social and economic matters.

Chinese environmental legislation is oriented towards protecting governmental or collective interests rather than civil and individual concerns. Consequently, it lacks legal rules concerning pollution torts and civil matters. It also lacks provisions relating to standing in public interest litigation. The judiciary has accordingly generally adopted a conservative approach in civil lawsuits, making little use of its wide discretionary powers to create law (except in a few cases such as *Wang Juan*). The reluctance of the people's courts to exercise their protective jurisdiction, for example, in public environmental interest litigation, is one of the many reasons why the bulk of environmental disputes are resolved through governmental mediation rather than through litigation.[82] The role of the people's courts in environmental civil tort justice has lagged behind the public's expectation of what it should or could be.[83] In civil tort cases, the judiciary's contribution has improved significantly through the SPC's judicial interpretations championing strict liability and the doctrine of deductive causality in environmental pollution tort cases. This is despite the conflict between national tort law and environmental law. In light of the judiciary's continued failure in various cases (such as the *Pinghu Normal Farm* case) to find in favour of those suffering environmental damage, it seems fair to conclude that the judiciary requires more time and experience to be able to optimally apply the SPC's judicial interpretations in pollution tort cases.

Through the process of judicial review, the courts have traditionally played an important role in the administrative aspects of environmental governance. As civil society has become more active, the functioning of the people's governments and the environmental administrative authorities has gradually been brought within the purview of judicial review. The people's courts do, however, tend to take a fairly cautious approach in trying various cases, particularly those cases in which citizens sue governmental authorities for non-performance and wrongful administration (such as in the *Tong Huancheng* case). This may partly be owing to the strong relationship between the people's courts and the people's government.

EIA is potentially one of the most effective administrative measures for promoting environmental protection and one would accordingly expect the judiciary to seek to uphold its value. However, if one considers the many cases which have been brought before the judiciary dealing with the application of the EIAL, there appears to be a problem regarding the review and enforcement of this law by the judiciary. The judiciary has specifically failed to actively respond to the EIAL and uphold its provisions promoting the public's rights to access environmental information, participate in decision-making and access justice.

---

82. J. Luo & Q. Du, 'Environmental Disputes' Resolution in China', *paper given at the 4th Annual Conference of IUCN Academy of Environmental Law* (Pace: Pace University, 2006).
83. EPNRC Committee, Proceedings of the International Symposium on Legislation for Environmental Damage Compensation, National People's Congress, 20-21 August 2004 (Beijing: EPNRC, 2004).

In the field of criminal law, despite various problematic trends which emerged in pollution cases heard in the 1980s, the judiciary has mostly played an adequate role in prosecuting crimes relating to endangered wildlife species, pollution and waste management. The move by the judiciary to impose significant penalties for environmental offences should increasingly deter would-be offenders in all environmental contexts.

8 THE WAY FORWARD

8.1 KEY CHALLENGES

In order to improve the rule of law in the PRC, the legal rules for civil and administrative lawsuits relating to environmental harm and pollution need to be clarified. This is notwithstanding the prescription of the SPC's judicial interpretations, which have addressed some of the loopholes with respect to the burden of proof in such matters. However, the rules remain too abstract, vague and ambiguous and the following specific issues require attention in future legislative reform:

(a) The scope of the reverse burden of proof. The relevant judicial interpretation needs to be more specific and more practical. It is proposed that plaintiffs ought to bear the burden of proof to establish that they are affected by the harm, the extent of such harm and resultant damage, and that they did not themselves contribute to it.

(b) Deductive causality. This is closely related to, but distinct from, the above. This doctrine states that if the person accused of inflicting harm and damage fails to provide proof that their conduct did not cause it, it is inferred that their conduct was in fact the cause of such harm and damage. This doctrine has been approved by the WPPCL 2008 in principle, but it needs to be expanded into other areas of pollution control such as air pollution. The doctrine of deductive causality also needs to be clarified through a set of procedural rules in order to facilitate its application.

(c) The public duty of providing and collecting proof. The issue requiring attention is which public authorities or sectors are responsible for providing relevant information to pollution victims, especially those victims who have difficulty in accessing the relevant environmental information. It is proposed that the public watchdogs, the environmental protection authorities should bear such a duty upon the request of a court or application by the private sector; and that the people's courts should also accept the duty of requesting or ordering the responsible public or private entity to provide the information.

(d) Standing of citizens in public interest environmental litigation. By nature, this type of litigation does not ordinarily require that the litigator have a direct link or interest in the matter. The PRC's existing legal regime limits standing to those having a direct link or interest in the matter. It is therefore proposed that in order to promote public interest environmental litigation, the rules on standing need to be revised and expanded by, for example, affording people's procuratorates or NGOs special standing.[84]

More generally, when comparing the decisions of the people's courts with those of the environmental protection authority in the mediation of tort disputes, the former appear to be relatively weak. This could possibly be attributed to the people's courts lack of capacity. They generally lack both the technical capacity and resources to source relevant information, investigate matters, gather testimony and undertake site inspections. From an institutional point of view, the existing structure of people's courts does not yet include a special trial tribunal for environmental matters; a fact which suggests that the courts may be indifferent to environmental pollution torts.[85] Considering the often technical nature of environmental matters, it may be advisable and necessary to establish a trial tribunal in the judicial structure exclusively dedicated to the adjudication of environmental cases.

The judiciary is the key guardian of environmental justice and should accordingly function independently. However, in the pursuit of economic growth, the people's governments often put pressure on the judiciary, directly and indirectly, to adjudicate cases in favour of generators and not victims of pollution. This is illustrated by the fact that the judiciary has failed to uphold the claims of pollution victims in between 60% to 70% of pollution cases in some areas.[86] Part of the problem stems from the fact that the people's courts are funded by the people's governments. This may also be the reason why the judiciary has taken such a cautious approach in the adjudication of judicial review cases. Recent proposed judicial reform advocated by the SPC and the Ministry of Justice is, however, expected to overcome this challenge.

8.2   KEY OPPORTUNITIES

There is still cause for optimism that the Chinese judiciary will in future be able to overcome the present challenges and perform in a sound and just manner in protecting the environment in the PRC. Inadequate legal rules could gradually be replaced by new laws, or existing laws could be reformulated or revised. A special law for dealing with disputes concerning environmental harms and compensation for damages arising from pollution has for some time been widely discussed amongst the legislature, academics and practitioners.[87] The absent substantive

---

84. C.X. Li, 'Prosecutorate Office Intervening Public Litigation', *China Lawyer* 3 (2006): 23; Y.T. Liu, 'Standings of Environmental Public Litigation', *Frontier* 10 (2006): 93-95.
85. L. Wang, 'Problems in the Trial of Cases Concerning the Environment and Natural Resources and Countermeasures', *Law Application* 3 (2003): 60-62.
86. Y.X. Zhao, 'Victims Always Lose Lawsuits: How to Interpret Dilemmas in Environmental Litigation', <past.people.com.cn>, 10 December 2007.
87. In 2005, the EPRCC of the NPC hosted an international workshop to discuss the feasibility of a national law for environmental pollution compensation and dispute resolution.

civil rules for environmental consideration, the duty of collecting proof, the reverse burden of proof, the deduction of causality, and the matter of standing in environmental public interest litigation are expected to be accommodated in this law. The revision of two major procedural laws relating to administrative and civil lawsuits provides a timely opportunity to improve the existing procedural rules pertaining to environmental lawsuits. For example, the development of the public litigation rule of law has been taken into account by the legislature in revising the Civil Procedural Law.

Improving the courts' capacity to apply environmental law will depend on the continuous training and education of the judiciary. Annual training programmes for judges and juries, run by the people's courts themselves, should include environmental judicial perspectives from independent experts in environmental law. As the United Nations Environmental Programme has expanded its project to improve the environmental legal training of judges worldwide, relevant judicial training materials have been introduced into the PRC.[88] Moreover, the consideration and application of foreign jurisprudence and experience in domestic courts and tribunals may provide an excellent source of reference for Chinese judges and juries, and the people's courts.

Various initiatives have been undertaken to address some of the above challenges. The 1980s and 1990s saw, for example, the establishment of 'environmental tribunals' or 'environmental enforcement tribunals'. The call for the establishment of a special trial branch (and for the establishment of environmental tribunals within the system) is being driven by the need to: strengthen the capacity of the courts to effectively settle environmental disputes; to provide judicial customary rules; and to uphold the rule of law. It is encouraging to note that such judicial institutional reform is taking place at local level. On 11 November 2007, the intermediate people's court of Guiyang City established a trial division for environmental protection with the approval of the people's congress of Guiyang City, while the basic people's court of Qingzhen City established an environmental protection tribunal. Both of these are responsible for hearing environmental matters concerning civil, administrative and criminal lawsuits.[89] As these were launched wholly within the judicial structures, their establishment is in accordance with the OLPC 1983 and their legitimacy has accordingly not been challenged.[90]

This ongoing judicial reform could serve as an impetus to build greater judicial capacity in environmental law and to create a sounder judicial environment in the PRC.[91] Finally, the rise of environmental NGOs and the increase in public

---

88. See Q. Du, J. Luo & K.L. Cao, *Judicial Training Modules on Environmental Law-Application of Environmental Law by National Courts and Tribunals* (translation) (Beijing: UNEP, 2007).
89. Z.Q. Wang, 'Environmental Protection Tribunals in Guiyang City', <www.zhb.gov.cn/ hjyw/ 200711/t20071122_113254.htm>, 28 December 2007.
90. OLPC 1983, Arts 19, 24, 27 and 31. The people's court can set up special trial divisions or tribunals if necessary.
91. By 2002, led by the Supreme People's Court, judicial reform had completed its first five-year phase. The second phase of five-year reform (2004-2008) has also been completed. In the second phase the targets have been, inter alia, to improve procedures in order to intensify

participation in environmental governance should go some way toward safeguarding the independence and impartiality of the judiciary when presiding over environmental issues.[92]

BIBLIOGRAPHY

Cai, S.Q. 'Policy framework of resolution of environmental disputes and enforcement of environmental liabilities'. *Proceedings of the International Symposium on Legislation for Environmental Damage Compensation*. Beijing: Environmental Protection and Natural Resource Conservation, 2004.

China Energy Net. 'News'. <www.china5e.com/focus/focus.php?type=nujiang>, 19 November 2006.

Chinaxys. 'Review'. <www.chinaxys.net/dajia/yuanmingyuan.html>, 19 December 2006.

Dong, B.W. *Collection of Papers on Politics and Law*. Beijing: Law Press, 1986.

Du, Q. 'Environmental Justice and Public participation in the PRC'. *Paper given at the International Conference on Environmental Justice of Stockholm University*. Stockholm, ICEJ, 2006.

Du, Q., J. Luo & K.L. Cao. *Judicial Training Modules on Environmental Law-Application of Environmental Law by National Courts and Tribunals*, Chinese edition. Beijing: United Nations Environmental Program, 2007.

Environmental Protection Bureau of Xiamen City. 'China's Environmental Problems'. <www.xmepb.gov.cn/environment/10.htm>, 28 December 2007.

EPAC. 'Analysis of Implementation of the Eleventh Five-Year National Environmental Protection Planning targets', <www.chinanews.com.cn/news/2006/2006-04-12/8/715966.shtml>, 12 April 2006.

EPNRC Committee. Proceedings of the International Symposium on Legislation for Environmental Damage Compensation. National People's Congress, 20-21August 2004. Beijing: EPNRC, 2004.

Greener Beijing Institute. 'EPRCC'. <www.grchina.org/gbj/spot/orgpcepc.htm>, 8 August 2008.

Guo, Y.D. 'State Environmental Protection Administration to be upgraded to the Ministry of Environmental Protection'. <env.people.com.cn/GB/6971602.html>, 1 July 2008.

Jiang, G.M & G.X. Gao. 'The terrible cost of China's growth'. <www.chinadialogue.net/ article/show/single/ch/684>, 12 January 2007.

---

judicial justice and efficiency, to enhance adjudication enforcement, to reform trial organs and trial institutions, to improve personnel administration, and to increase judges' professional capacity. See: SPC, The 2nd Five-Year People's Courts' Reform Outlines 2004-2008 (Beijing: National Publishing House, 2004).

92. Q. Du, 'Environmental Justice and Public participation in the PRC', *paper presented at the International Conference on Environmental Justice of Stockholm University* (Stockholm, ICEJ, 2006).

Judicial Training Module on Environmental Law: Application of Environmental Law by National Courts and Tribunals. English edition. Beijing: United Nations Environmental Program, 2007.

Legal Working Committee of the NPC. *Reply to State Environmental Protection Agency on the Application of Article 41(2) of Environmental Protection Law 1989*. Beijing: NPC, 1992.

Li, C.X. 'Prosecutorate Office Intervening Public Litigation'. *China Lawyer* 3 (2006): 23-27.

Liu, Y.T. 'Standings of Environmental Public Litigation'. *Frontier* 10 (2006): 93-95.

Luo, J. & Q. Du. 'Environmental Disputes' Resolution in China'. *Paper given at the 4th Annual Conference of IUCN Academy of Environmental Law*. Pace: Pace University, 2006.

Lv, Z.M. (ed.). *Environmental Law Case Studies*. Beijing: Higher Education Press, 2006.

Lv, Z.M. 'Probing Environmental Litigation: Does Environmental Litigation Exist?'. In *Environmental and Natural Resource Law Study*, edited by Z.M. Lv. Vol. 3. Beijing: Law Science Press, 2004.

Peking Uiversity. 'Lawyee database'. <edu.lawyee.net/Case/Case>, 21 September 2008.

Qi, S.H. & J.W. Lin. (eds). *Environmental Dispute Resolution*. Xiamen: Xiamen University Press, 2005.

Ren, C. & G. Piao. (eds.). *The basic theory of Environmental Law Enforcement*. Beijing, Law Press, 1997.

Ren, J.X. Report of the 14th National Conference of Courts' Work. Beijing: National Publishing House, 1988.

Song, C.Q. 'The researchers predict: The North China over the next 10 years will be relatively drought'. <news.xinhuanet.com/newscenter/2004-10/19/content_2111 006.htm>, 19 October 2004.

SPC. Some Provisions on the Scope of Cases that are Subject to the Jurisdiction of Maritime Courts. Beijing: National Publishing House, 2001.

SPC. The 2nd Five-Year People's Courts' Reform Outlines 2004-2008. Beijing: National Publishing House, 2004.

State Council. The National Plan for Building Ecological Environment. Beijing: National Publishing House, 1999.

State Environmental Protection Administration. Public Reports of State Environmental Statistics 1998-2001. Beijing: National Publishing House, 2001.

Wang, C. & K. Xu. 'Settlement of Environmental Disputes in China and Environmental Enforcement Supervised by the Public'. *Environmental Protection* 5 (2003): 5-8.

Wang, C.F. 'Existing problems of defending environmental rights and the way-out'. <www.greensos.cn/?action_viewnews_itemid_4302.html>, 28 December 2007.

Wang, L. 'Problems in the Trial of Cases Concerning the Environment and Natural Resources and Countermeasures'. *Law Application* 3 (2003): 60-62.

Wang, S.Y. (ed.). *Case-interpreted Textbook of Environmental and Natural Resource Law*. Beijing: Intellectual Right Press, 2004.

Wang, Z.Q. 'Environmental Protection Tribunals in Guiyang City'. <www.zhb.gov.cn/ hjyw/200711/t20071122_113254.htm>, 28 December 2007.

Xie, Z.H. (ed.). *Concise Book of Classic Environmental Lawsuits and Law Enforcement in China*. Beijing: China Environmental Protection Science Press, 1995.

Xin, C.Y. *Chinese Courts: History and Transition*. 2nd ed. Beijing: Law Press, 2004.

Xinhua Net. 'Viewing Tower Construction in Zijing Mount: State-invested Capital in Vain'. <www.xinhua.net>, 25 January 2002.

Xinhua News Net. 'People's Representatives Zhou Shuo and Chen Yan-ping proposed to amend the Organic Law of the People's Court'. <fl.pub.cqnews.net/system/2008/ 03/17/001113885.shtml>, 17 March 2008.

Yang, X.J. (ed.). *Selection of Significant Administrative Cases*. Beijing: Publishing House of China University of Politics and Law, 2006.

Zhang, K.M. (ed.). *Handbooks of China's Environmental Law Enforcement*. Beijing: Publishing House of China University of Law and Politics, 1993.

Zhao, Y.X. 'Victims Always Lose Lawsuits: How to Interpret Dilemmas in Environmental Litigation'. <past.people.com.cn>, 10 December 2007.

TABLE OF LEGISLATION

Administrative Procedure Law 1989
Air Pollution Prevention and Control Law 2000
Civil Procedure Law 1982
Country Land Contracting Law 2002
Criminal Procedure Law 1996
Desertification Prevention and Control Law 2001
Environmental Impact Assessment Law 2002
Environmental Protection Law 1989
Forest Law 1998
General Principles of Civil Law 1991
Grassland Law 2002
Interim Provisions of Public Participation in Environmental Impact Assessment of the National People's Congress 2006 (Decree No. 2006/26)
Land Administration Law 1998
Law for Prevention and Control of Solid Wastes Polluting the Environment 2004
Marine Environment Protection Law 1999
Noise Pollution Prevention and Control Law 1996
Organizational Law of People's Courts 1954
Organizational Law of the People's Procuratorates 1983
Regulation for Governments Opening Information 2007
Regulations Pertaining to Controlling the Dumping of Waste in the Ocean 1985

TABLE OF STATUTORY INSTRUMENTS

TABLE OF CASES

People's Government of Ledu County of Gansu Province v. Liancheng Aluminium Manufacture of Qinghai Province [1989] Zhang 1993, 409-411

People's procuratorate of Fuping County of Shaangxi Province v. Li Chuancai [1984] Xie 1995, 21-23

People's procuratorate of Heshan City of Guangdong Province v. Li Yayang [2006] PKU

People's Procuratorate of Xiangxiang County v. Tan Liangui and Others [1980] Zhang 1993, 470-472

People's procuratorate of Xixian County of Shaanxi Province v. Peng Fangrong [2005] PKU

People's procuratorate of Yunchen City of Shanxi Province v. Yang Junwu [1997] PBSPC, (1999) 3

Pinghu Normal Farm of Zhejiang Province v. Five Corporations of Buyun Dye Chemical and Others [2000] PKU

Shekou Environment Monitoring Station v. Hong Kong Kaida Company [1983] PBSPC, (1985) 3

Shen Xixian and Others, 182 Residents v. Planning Committee of Beijing Municipality [2003] PBSPC, (2004) 3

Sun Datao and Others, 101 villagers v. Environmental Protection Bureau of Pingdingshan City [2001] PKU

Tong Huancheng and Others, 78 villagers v. The People's Government of Xing Rong County of Chende City, Hebei Province [2006] PKU

Wang Juan v. the Qingdao City Chemical Plant [1978] Zhang 1993, 395-399

ABBREVIATIONS

APL	Administrative Procedure Law
APPCL	Air Pollution Prevention and Control Law
CEPSP	China Environmental Protection Science Press
CITES	Convention on International Trade in Endangered Species of Wild Flora and Fauna
CL	Criminal Law
CPL	Civil Procedure Law
EIA	Environment Impact Assessment
EIAL	Environmental Impact Assessment Law
EPAC	Environment Planning Academy of China
EPL	Environmental Protection Law
EPNRC	Environmental Protection and Natural Resource Conservation
EPRCC	Environmental Protection and Resource Conservation Committee
GRCL	General Rules of Civil Law
LAL	Land Administration Law
MEP	Ministry of Environmental Protection
MEPL	Marine Environment Protection Law
NGO	Non-governmental Organization

NPC	National People's Congress
NPPCL	Noise Pollution Prevention and Control Law
OLPC	Organizational Law of People's Courts
PBSPC	Public Bulletin of Supreme People's Court
PHCULP	Publishing House of China University of Law and Politics
PKU	Peking University
PRC	People's Republic of China
SC	State Council
SPC	Supreme People's Court
SPP	Supreme People's Procuratorate
WPPCL	Water Pollution Prevention and Control Law
WTO	World Trade Organization

Chapter 14
Kenya

Patricia Kameri-Mbote

1   INTRODUCTION

1.1   Background

Kenya is situated on the East African highlands with a total area of 225,000 square miles. It has wide differences in the amount, reliability and seasonal distribution of rain. There is also great elevation variation which has produced regions with sharply contrasting environments.[1] The terrain consists of low plains rising to the central highlands which are bisected by the Rift Valley, leading on to the fertile western plateau. Forest vegetation is confined to areas that are 5,000 feet above sea level while savannah, comprising tall grass with scattered trees and shrubs or acacia trees, are a characteristic of the plateau area to the south and south west of Kenya. The most common vegetation is the dry bush land and thorn scrub.[2]

Kenya lacks major exploitable mineral resources and arable land is scarce. The main economic activities are based on the primary sector, predominantly

---

1. See D.C. Edwards, 'The Ecological Regions of Kenya: Their Classification in Relation to Agricultural Development', *Empire J. Experimental Agriculture* 24 (1956): 96.
2. See C.G. Trapnell & I. Langdale-Brown, 'The Natural Vegetation of East Africa', in *The Natural Resources of East Africa*, ed. E.W. Russell (Nairobi: DA Hawkins, 1962), 92. See also J.F. Griffiths, 'The Climate of East Africa', in *id.*, 79, noting that most of it however, has extremely arid climate with too little rain to sustain any form of agriculture.

Louis J. Kotzé and Alexander R. Paterson (eds), *The Role of the Judiciary in Environmental Governance: Comparative Perspectives*, pp. 451–478.
© 2009 Kluwer Law International BV, The Netherlands.

agriculture,[3] which is both a source of food as well as a foreign revenue earner. The agricultural sector employs over 70% of the country's population and in the 1990s, agricultural products accounted for as much as 25% of the gross domestic product (GDP) compared to manufacturing which contributed 14%.[4] The country can be divided broadly into three land categories based on agricultural production and the amount of rainfall received. These are the high, medium and low potential areas. Over 75% of the human population lives in the high potential area to the south and west. Much of north and east Kenya is too dry to support any agriculture.[5] Kenya has great faunal and floral diversity including forests, woodlands, swamps, grasslands of many different varieties and plant and animal species. It is endowed with unique and economically valuable wildlife resources.

Kenya's population is currently estimated to be thirty-seven million people.[6] Only 25% of this population live in urban areas, the remainder live in the rural areas and consequently depend directly on land for a living.[7] The rural population depends mainly on biological resources, which has resulted in biodiversity erosion owing to over-cultivation, over-grazing and the clearing of forestlands and crop plantation areas to make way for urban expansion. Further, population growth has outstripped the agricultural capacity of the land in adequately watered areas and resulted in migration to drier low agricultural potential areas designated in official policy as arid and semi-arid areas (ASALs). ASALs comprise 88% of Kenya's total land area and carry over 20% of the country's total human population and more than 50% of its livestock.[8] Traditional pastoral systems of land use still prevail in these areas and temporary out-migration is common due to climate and insecurity. Pastoralists are, however, increasingly settling permanently in these areas due to interventionist activities of the government, donors and non-governmental organizations (NGOs) which develop means of communications and permanent water sources.[9]

1.2   MAJOR ENVIRONMENTAL CHALLENGES

Kenya's main environmental challenges include: degradation of habitat; loss of biological diversity;[10] pollution; management of water, wildlife and forest

---

3. The term 'agriculture' denotes cultivation and livestock keeping. We use the term 'settled agriculture' when we discuss areas where livestock keeping is practiced alongside cultivation.
4. See Republic of Kenya, *Economic Recovery Strategy* (Nairobi: Government Printer, 2003), 12.
5. See, e.g., Griffiths *supra* n. 2.
6. Republic of Kenya, *Economic Survey 2007* (Nairobi: Ministry of Planning and National Development KNBS, 2007).
7. See Republic of Kenya, *supra* n. 4.
8. Republic of Kenya, *Environmental Action Plan for Arid and Semi-Arid Lands in Kenya* (Nairobi: Government Printer, 1992).
9. *Ibid.*
10. See generally P. Kameri-Mbote, *Property Rights and Biodiversity Management in Kenya* (Nairobi: ACTS Press, 2002).

resources; and competition between environmental conservation and land uses inimical to such conservation. By 1994, deforestation had reduced Kenya's forest cover to a meager 1.7% (1,4 million hectares).[11] Continued deforestation[12] has also impacted negatively on indigenous forests which are now only found in the Aberdare range (250,000 hectares), Mount Kenya (220,000 hectares), the Mau complex (400,000 hectares), Mount Elgon (74,000 hectares) and the Cherangani Hills (120,000 hectares).[13] The loss of forest cover (a critical habitat for many species), has also entailed loss of genetic resources. Other related issues comprise: biopiracy; absence of a national legal framework for protecting indigenous knowledge that can be used for sustainable environmental management; lack of an implementation framework for bioprospecting activities and equitable benefit sharing; and the absence of a national legal framework for genetic modification of organisms and related threats, principally to the environment and human health (allergenicity and toxicity).[14]

As a developing country with a growing population, the imperatives of economic development and environmental protection are in constant tension. Indeed, land use is a major challenge to sustainable environmental management impacting both on habitat as well as being a source of pollution. Not surprisingly, there are conflicts between humans and conservation agencies especially around protected wildlife reserves and gazetted forests. Kenya's population largely depends on land for subsistence as well as economic activities. Environmental degradation consequently has implications for the well-being of individuals and the country as a whole. Moreover, wildlife based tourism significantly contributes to Kenya's GDP.

Agriculture, water and sanitation, the physical planning and biodiversity management interface with environmental management, together with the governance frameworks put in place for these activities, have implications for general sustainability. For instance, the *Agriculture Act*[15] provides for soil quality and use while the *Physical Planning Act*[16] provides for rational use of space. Kenya is also concerned about the management of national and international waters. Being endowed with a coastal zone, a share of Lake Victoria, and river basins such as the Nile with other countries, the concerns about water quantity, quality and sustainable use, are major issues in Kenya. Being a country prone to cyclic droughts

11. P. Wass, *Kenya's Indigenous Forests: Status, Management and Conservation* (Paris: IUCN, 1994).
12. V. Matiru, Forest cover and forest reserves in Kenya: Policy and Practice: EPA working paper no. 5 (Nairobi: IUCN, 2002).
13. KFWG, *Changes in Forest Cover in Kenya's Five 'Water Towers' 2000-2003* (Nairobi: KFWG, 2004).
14. This is notwithstanding the fact that genetic modification activities are continuing in the country whilst Kenya has both signed and ratified the Cartagena Protocol on Biosafety (2000) 6 *ILM* 1027. For more discussions on this, see generally, P. Kameri-Mbote, G. Tumushabe & I. Sithole-Niang, *Biotechnology and Law: Africa's Dilemma* (Forthcoming, 2008).
15. Cap. 318 of the Laws of Kenya.
16. Cap. 286 of the Laws of Kenya.

and having a substantial part of its territory as ASALs, Kenya's management of its water resources is an issue of major concern. Related to this is the concern to reduce the country's dependence on hydrocarbons for energy and to facilitate research and development on renewable energy resources.

Other environmental challenges include sustainable management of fisheries to ensure that fishing activities are within the maximum sustainable yield in both inland waters and the territorial sea (*ca.* 9,700 km^2); legal facilitation of carbon trading and sequestration; control of indoor and outdoor pollution; and marine pollution.

2 PRINCIPAL ENVIRONMENTAL LAWS

2.1 INTRODUCTION

Kenya's environmental legislation is contained in the Constitution,[17] the *Environment Management and Coordination Act* 1999 (EMCA),[18] and resource or sector specific laws.[19] It is expected that all sectoral laws will be reviewed or amended to ensure their consistency with EMCA. Section 148 of EMCA states that:

> Any written law, in force immediately before the coming into force of this Act, relating to the management of the environment shall have effect subject to modification as may be necessary to give effect to this Act, and where the provisions of any such law conflict with any provisions of this Act the provisions of this Act shall prevail.

A number of sectoral environmental laws have been revised after the promulgation of EMCA. These include the *Water Act*,[20] *Forests Act*,[21] and *Energy Act*.[22] The *Wildlife Management and Conservation Act*,[23] is in the process of being reviewed and one of the reasons for the review is to align it to EMCA. There is also a draft Mining Bill 2007.

Additionally, common law and criminal law are integral components of Kenya's environmental law. Even though statute law is now dominant in the environmental field, common law still has residual functions in sustainable development. Common law arises from the English tradition laying supremacy on case law or decided cases, especially from superior courts, which provide precedence over succeeding cases by virtue of the doctrine of *stare decisis*. A common law action may be brought in the form of judicial review – an action in public law challenging

---

17. Act 5 of 1969 (amended in 2008).
18. Act 8 of 1999.
19. J.B. Ojwang, *Environmental Law and the Constitutional Order* (Nairobi: ACTS Press, 1993), 35.
20. Act 8 of 2002.
21. Act 7 of 2005.
22. Act 12 of 2006.
23. Cap. 376 of the Laws of Kenya (amended in 1989).

the legal validity of the decisions or actions of public bodies when they result in injuries. Judicial review may be used to: (a) quash a decision (*certiorari*); (b) stop an unlawful action (prohibition); (c) require performance of a statutory duty (*mandamus*); (d) declare the legal position of a litigant (declarations); (e) monetary compensation; or (f) declare the *status quo*. Common law also provides for causes of action in private law, which include trespass, nuisance, negligence and the rule in *Rylands v. Fletcher*, or strict liability.[24]

Criminal enforcement of environmental law is necessary to protect the integrity of the regulatory system, to prevent harm to the environment, to protect public health and welfare and to punish culpable violations. Other reasons for using criminal law to enforce environmental law are: the inadequacy or failure of civil/administrative law to adequately deter violations; the use of criminal sanctions as a back-up where civil remedies are not suitable or cannot remedy the situation; societal preference to criminalize actions as an expression of moral outrage; and to prohibit the activity. In the case of moral outrage, the commonality of interest in an issue forms the basis for prosecuting the wrong. Criminal sanctions punish the responsible party and make it clear that non-compliance is a crime. Kenya's Penal Code[25] has been used to deal with environmentally harmful activities that also constitute criminal activities. Moreover, EMCA makes provision for both substantive as well as administrative offences.[26]

The following sections investigate the Constitution's provisions pertinent to environmental governance, as well as EMCA and a selection of sectoral environmental statutes. Apart from these laws, customary law is recognized as one of the legal orders governing people's life in Kenya. To the extent that such customary law impacts on the environment, it is critical for effective environmental governance. The adjudication of customary law matters is carried out largely by traditional governance institutions and also by Magistrates' Courts. The customary law provisions are reflected on where appropriate.

2.2 CONSTITUTION

2.2.1 The Constitution of Kenya, 1969

Kenya's Constitution of 1969 does not contain explicit environmental provisions.[27] It does, however, place importance on the right to life, which experts

---

24. C.O. Okidi, 'Concept, Structure and Function of Environmental Law', in *Environmental Governance in Kenya: Implementing the Framework Law*, ed. C.O. Okidi, P. Kameri-Mbote & M. Akech (Nairobi: EAEP 2008), 3.
25. Cap. 63 of the Laws of Kenya.
26. P. Kameri-Mbote, 'The Use of Criminal Law in Enforcing Environmental Law', in *Environmental Governance in Kenya: Implementing the Framework Law*, ed. C.O. Okidi, P. Kameri-Mbote & M. Akech (Nairobi: EAEP, 2008), 110.
27. Act 5 of 1969 (amended in 1992, rev. in 1998 and 2008).

argue encompasses the right to a clean and healthy environment.[28] It protects individual fundamental rights and freedoms which are relevant in accessing justice in environmental matters. These include: freedom of speech, assembly and association; the right to life; and the right to the protection of the law, which appear in Chapter V of the Constitution. Of particular significance is section 80, which guarantees every person the right to assemble freely and to associate with other persons, and further includes the right to form or belong to associations. The Constitution also includes the right to access to the High Court for redress regarding enforcement of fundamental individual rights and freedoms.

The legal provision of rights does not guarantee enjoyment of those rights if one has no access to justice. It is therefore instructive to note that the Constitution also provides for the right to sue.[29] The issue as to whom this right belongs to is one that is widely debated especially in environmental cases. It has been ruled that the Constitution's provisions for the protection of fundamental rights and freedoms of the individual cover both natural and legal persons. The word 'person' is defined in the Constitution to include 'any body of persons corporate or unincorporate'.[30] There has been detailed judicial pronouncement on what may be regarded as a 'person' within the meaning of the fundamental rights provisions or the Constitution. This was the case in *Shah Vershi Devshi & Co. Ltd v. The Transport Licensing Board*,[31] where the High Court of Kenya held the constitutional references to 'person' covered both natural and legal persons. The applicant company had been refused renewal of a license under the Policy of Africanization. It appealed to the High Court claiming breach of its fundamental rights. The court observed:

> a company is a 'person' within the meaning of Chapter V. [of the Constitution of Kenya] and would be entitled to all the rights and freedoms given to a 'person' which it is capable of enjoying. . . . If a right or freedom is given to a 'person' and is, from its nature, capable of being enjoyed by a 'corporation' then a 'corporation' can claim it, although it is included in the list of 'rights and freedoms of the individual'. The word 'individual' like the word 'person', does, where the context so requires, include a corporation.[32]

These rights and freedoms are subject to respect for the rights and freedoms of others and for the public interest. In democratic societies, justifiable and reasonable limitations to freedoms must be provided under the law. The Constitution specifies that freedom of assembly and association may be curtailed to protect public defence, safety, health, order, morality, and the rights and freedoms of other

---

28. G.M. Wamukoya & F.D.P. Situma (eds), *Environmental Management in Kenya: A Guide to the Environmental Management and Coordination Act* (Nairobi: Centre for Research and Education Environmental Law, 2000), 2.
29. S. 84(1) of the Constitution.
30. S. 123.
31. (1971) EALR 289.
32. *Ibid.*, 298.

persons; or to impose reasonable conditions relating to, for example, registration of trade unions and martial law.[33] The rights to freedom of expression, assembly, and association, are inextricably linked to the right to information. However, numerous obstacles impede access to environmental information in Kenya, as the Constitution contains no express provision covering the right to information. This right is only implied in provisions that address the protection of the fundamental rights and freedoms of the individual. Indeed, until recently, the government did not play an active role in informing the public about pertinent issues relating to public participation and decision making in the environmental context.

Various groups feel that the constitutional weaknesses are the primary reason behind the government's failure to make environmental information readily available to the public.[34] This perception is partially based on the lack of a constitutional mandate for the government to collect and disseminate relevant information. Furthermore, while some of the Constitution's provisions lay the basis for access to information, they also contain exceptions that negate this right. As a result, there is a seemingly adversarial relationship between citizens who seek information and government officials who use legal arguments to restrict the flow of information. This impedes access to justice where information is critical to prosecuting offences and bringing civil claims.

2.2.2   The Draft Constitution of Kenya, 2004

The stalled constitutional review process was expected to define a more explicit basis for environmental rights. The draft Constitution includes explicit provisions on the environment, including the right to a healthy environment, public participation in environmental decision making, and access to information. For instance, the chapter on national values, principles and goals includes principles on the promotion of public participation in public affairs, sharing and the devolution of power; and access of the people to independent, impartial, competent, timely and affordable institutions of justice.[35] The Bill of Rights further reinforces these rights and provides that 'every citizen has the right of access to information held by the state',[36] and requires parliament to enact legislation providing for access to information.[37] It also explicitly provides for the right to a healthy environment and free information about the environment,[38] and access to courts.[39] The provision on

---

33. S. 80(2) of the Constitution.
34. See N. Rukuba-Ngaiza et al., *Public Involvement in Environmental Decision-making in Asia and East Africa: Law and Practice* (Washington DC: Legal Vice Presidency IBRD/WB, 2003), 60.
35. The Draft Constitution of Kenya adopted by the National Constitutional Conference on 15 March 2004.
36. *Ibid.*, Art. 51(1).
37. *Ibid.*, Art. 51(4).
38. *Ibid.*, Art. 67(a) & (c).
39. *Ibid.*, Art. 72.

access to courts makes room for access to justice through other non-State justice systems such as councils of elders and other local community institutions.[40]

2.3   THE ENVIRONMENT MANAGEMENT AND COORDINATION ACT, 1999

2.3.1   Normative Provisions

EMCA[41] creates an overall and all-embracing agency for environmental management as opposed to previous legislation that set up sectoral agencies often leading to regulatory competition.[42] It also provides for public participation and access to justice. The Act establishes the National Environment Council (NEC); the National Environment Management Authority (NEMA); the Provincial and District Environment Committees; the National Environment Tribunal; and the Public Complaints Committee. In all these administrative structures, access to justice remains a concern.

2.3.1.1   Right to a Healthy Environment

Significantly, EMCA provides for the right of every person to a clean and healthy environment.[43] It also imposes an obligation on every person to protect and manage the environment.[44] Any person may bring an action in the High Court to enforce the right to a clean and healthy environment. Redress may be sought if the right has been violated, is being violated, or is likely to be violated. In determining the dispute, the court will be guided by the principles of sustainable development including public participation in the development of policies, plans and processes for environmental management.

2.3.1.2   Locus Standi

One great innovation of EMCA is that it overcomes most of the limitations on standing to sue. It explicitly provides that an aggrieved person need not show special damage or peculiar injury beyond that which is suffered by other affected people.[45] Effectively, this provision grants every person the right to protect the environment. Further, the provision in EMCA for the publication of annual state of

---

40. It provides that 'every person has the right to have any dispute that can be resolved by the application of law decided in a fair public hearing before a court or, where appropriate, another independent tribunal or forum', *Ibid.*
41. EMCA 1999.
42. See C.O. Okidi & P. Kameri-Mbote, *The Making of a Framework Environmental Law* (Nairobi: ACTS Press, 2001).
43. S. 3(1) of EMCA.
44. S. 3 of EMCA.
45. S. 3(3) of EMCA.

the environment reports,[46] which are expected to inform the budget, facilitates proper environmental governance by providing access to information. This will empower the citizenry to carry out the duty placed on them by section 3 of EMCA. The timeous publication and wide availability of the state of the environment report should go a long way towards enhancing sustainable environmental management.

2.3.1.3 Environment Impact Assessment

Another mechanism that fosters sustainable environmental management is environment impact assessment (EIA). EMCA states:

> Notwithstanding any approval, permit or licence granted under this Act or any other law in force in Kenya, any person, being a proponent of a project, shall, before financing, commencing, proceeding with, carrying out, executing or conducting or causing to be financed, commenced, proceeded with, carried out, executed or conducted by another person any undertaking specified in the Second Schedule to this Act, submit a project report to the Authority, in the prescribed form, giving the prescribed information and which shall be accompanied by the prescribed fee.[47]

The essence of EIA is to gather information and the use of that information in the decision-making process. If, after studying the report, it becomes clear to NEMA that the proposal will result in, or is likely to have, significant impacts on the environment, then an EIA must be undertaken.[48] No other licensing authority can lawfully issue any license in respect of a project for which an EIA is required under EMCA. Only a license issued by the Director General of NEMA is valid.[49] The EIA is undertaken by the project proponent at her/his own expense.

EMCA identifies the categories of projects that must undergo an EIA and these are broad enough to accommodate any projects which may result in significant impacts.[50] The minister responsible for matters relating to the environment has powers to amend the list of projects after consultations with the key actors in the environmental field. The Act also makes extensive provision for public participation,[51] which ensures inclusive and accountable environmental governance.

2.3.2 Institutions under EMCA

A number of institutions are established under EMCA to facilitate sustainable environmental governance. The first of these is the NEC which is responsible

---

46. S. 58(1) of EMCA.
47. S. 9 of EMCA.
48. S. 58(2) of EMCA.
49. S. 158 of EMCA.
50. These are specified in the Second Schedule to EMCA.
51. Ss 52 and 59 of EMCA.

for formulating policy on matters relating to environment management in Kenya. Its membership comprises of two representatives of public universities in Kenya, two representatives of specialized research institutions in Kenya, three representatives of the business community, and two representatives of NGOs active in the environmental field.

The second institution is NEMA, the principal government institution responsible for the implementation of all policies relating to the environment. NEMA is responsible for dealing with EIA (see also the discussion above). The third group of institutions is the Provincial and District Environment Committees. The Provincial Environment Committees draw their membership from: each local authority within the province; representatives of farmers or pastoralists; representatives of NGOs involved in environmental management programmes in the province; and a representative of every regional development authority in the province. The District Environment Committees also include: a representative of each local authority within the district; representatives of farmers, women, youth and pastoralists; representatives of NGOs involved in environmental management programmes in the district; representatives of community-based organizations involved in environmental management programmes in the district; and representatives of the business community in the district. The function of the Provincial and District Environment Committees is the proper management of the environment at the provincial and district levels.

The Kenyan judiciary has at times not given due recognition to decisions of District Environmental Committees, thereby reducing their efficacy. In the case of *Gathoni v. Republic*,[52] for instance, it was held that a failure to obey an order of the District Environmental Committee was not an offence under the Penal Code's section 131, which deals with failure to obey a lawful order. In the court's opinion, this section of the Penal Code applied in situations where public peace and harmony were at risk. The court did not regard the transportation of timber by a motor vehicle on a public road as falling within this ambit. A more positive reading of the decision may be to infer that in the court's opinion, EMCA had provisions dealing with infractions under it, and that bringing the action under the Penal Code was erroneous. It is, however, necessary to have synergy between different laws that impact on environmental management if proper governance is to be achieved.

EMCA also establishes the Public Complaints Committee (PCC) under section 31. Its members include representatives of the Law Society of Kenya (LSK), the NGO sector and the business community. The function of the PCC is to investigate complaints relating to environmental damage and degradation generally, but it can also investigate issues under NEMA. These investigations can be initiated *mero motu* or following receipt of a complaint, and its findings are reported to the NEC. Some of the problems currently encountered by the PCC are the non-appearance by witnesses in response to summons, hostility between parties during hearings, hostility towards PCC investigators, lack of understanding of EMCA, and the abdication of duty by sectoral lead agencies. Given that the

---

52. Criminal Appeal No. 297 of 2004 reported in (2006) KLR (Environment and Land) 697.

duty of the PCC is only to file its report with the NEC, it also lacks the necessary authority to see that the recommendations are formally implemented.

The final institution established under EMCA, is the National Environment Tribunal (NET), which is a specialized dispute settlement institution.[53] NET is set up to hear appeals from administrative decisions taken by organs responsible for enforcing environmental standards. The appeals may be launched by the proponent of a project against the rejection of an EIA and against a denial of a license. An appeal may also be launched by a local community against the grant of a license by an administrative body such as NEMA. The limited mandate of NET has hampered its effectiveness as its work is predicated on work undertaken by NEMA.[54] Access to justice in Kenya could be enhanced by giving NET original jurisdiction in environmental matters. This would position it as the best forum for hearing environmental disputes before these are taken to the High Court. The tribunal sits in Nairobi, but it has powers to sit anywhere else in the country as long as it gives notice to the public to that effect. EMCA is silent on the enforcement status of NET's orders. It would appear advisable for NET to be afforded power to enforce its orders rather than being required to file these through the formal courts.

2.4　　　SECTORAL STATUTES

Alongside the Constitution and EMCA, Kenya has an elaborate mosaic of sectoral environmental laws. These include laws on wildlife, biodiversity, forests, mining, fisheries, water, energy, marine resources and public health. Laws on agriculture, the working environment, land tenure and land use planning also have implications for environmental governance in Kenya. Many of these laws were part of the colonial legacy and predate EMCA. Indeed, the colonization of Kenya by Britain in 1895 was followed by the importation of institutions for the management of resources. The laws on wildlife and forests were, at inception, mainly concerned with the extraction of resources and conservation was only carried out in selected landscapes. These laws have now incorporated concerns for sustainable management of resources in light of increased resource degradation.

The sectoral ministries, departments and agencies continue to operate under the sectoral laws and policies inherited from the colonial era. They have, however, recognized the need to cooperate with other agencies as well as to involve stakeholders.[55] Revised sectoral forest and water laws have redefined the role of lead

---

53. S. 125 of EMCA.
54. If NEMA and other administrative organs are inactive, as has been the case until recently, NET has no work to do.
55. The Fisheries Department and the Kenya Wildlife Service (KWS) have, using limited provisions in the sectoral laws and their discretion, introduced elaborate schemes for involving local communities in natural resource management. Examples of these can be seen in the cooperative arrangements between KWS and local communities in developing wildlife sanctuaries and preserving wildlife corridors. Similar arrangements are being institutionalized in the fisheries sector through introducing beach management units.

agencies. The *Forest Act*[56] establishes a comprehensive institutional framework for managing forests in Kenya. It creates the Kenya Forest Service (KFS) responsible for overseeing the sustainable development of the nation's forests; makes elaborate provision for involving local communities in forest management through forest community associations; and creates a system of incentives for co-opting compliance. Similarly, the *Water Act* (2002) establishes the National Water Board, a central body responsible for: allocating water rights; coordinating the River Basin Boards and the District Water Boards; managing data banks; monitoring water resources; and undertaking all other key functions ascribed to it by the responsible ministry. In addition, the policy framework envisages delegation of many of the functions of the National Water Board to the River Basin Boards. River Basin Boards are accordingly responsible for approving applications for water permitting, formulating recommendations on water use and conservation, and monitoring and enforcing water use in their respective catchment areas.

3	JUDICIAL AND NON-JUDICIAL FORMS OF ENVIRONMENTAL DISPUTE RESOLUTION

3.1	An Overview of the Court System

Kenya attained independence in 1963 and adopted the Constitution of Kenya in 1964 which provides for the separation of the powers between the executive, legislative and judicial arms of government. Having been a British colony, Kenya's laws have been inherited from Britain with some modifications to reflect local conditions. The Kenyan legal system is thus based on English common law but has elements of customary law and religious law (mainly Islamic law). Chapter IV of the Constitution sets out the court structure which is further elaborated on by both the *Judicature Act*,[57] and the *Magistrates' Courts Act*.[58]

The Constitution establishes the High Court as a superior court of record with: unlimited original jurisdiction in civil and criminal matters and to hear appeals from subordinate courts; powers of constitutional interpretation; and such other jurisdiction and powers as may be conferred on it by the Constitution or any other law.[59] It also establishes the Court of Appeal as the highest appeal court immediately above the High Court.[60] Under section 65, the Constitution bestows on parliament the power to establish other courts subordinate to the High Court and court-martial with such jurisdiction and powers as conferred on them under the Constitution or any other law.[61] Magistrates' Courts have been created as the

---

56. Act 7 of 2006.
57. Cap. 8 of the Laws of Kenya.
58. Cap. 10 of the Laws of Kenya.
59. S. 60 of the Constitution.
60. S. 64 of the Constitution.
61. S. 65(1) of the Constitution.

primary subordinate courts and decide on the majority of legal disputes in the country.[62] Section 65(2) of the Constitution vests the High Court with jurisdiction to supervise any civil or criminal proceedings before a subordinate court or court-martial. In such cases, the High Court may make such orders, issue such writs and give such directions as it may consider appropriate for the purpose of ensuring that justice is duly administered by those courts. The Constitution formally recognizes Kadhi's Courts at section 66. The jurisdiction of these courts is elaborated in section 66(5) as: '...the determination of questions of Muslim law relating to personal status, marriage, divorce or inheritance in proceedings in which all the parties profess the Muslim religion'.

Specialized judicial divisions have been created to deal with constitutional matters, commercial matters, criminal matters, family matters and more recently, land and environmental matters. The land and environment division was established at the High Court and Magistrates' Court levels in February 2007 to deal with land and environment matters.[63] The presiding officers of the different courts are designated as justices, judges, magistrates and Kadhis.[64]

The *Judicature Act* prescribes the laws to be applied by the courts in Kenya. It states that:

> The jurisdiction of the High Court, the Court of Appeal and of all subordinate courts shall be exercised in conformity with –
>
> (a) the Constitution;
> (b) subject thereto, all other written laws, including the Acts of Parliament of the United Kingdom cited in Part I of the Schedule to this Act, modified in accordance with Part II of that Schedule;
> (c) subject thereto and so far as those written laws do not extend or apply, the substance of the common law, the doctrines of equity and the statutes of general application in force in England on the 12th August, 1897, and the procedure and practice observed in courts of justice in England at that date; but the common law, doctrines of equity and statutes of general application shall apply so far only as the circumstances of Kenya and its inhabitants permit and subject to such qualifications as those circumstances may render necessary.[65]

---

62. ICJ, *Kenya: Judicial Independence, Corruption and Reform* (Nairobi: ICJ Kenya Chapter, 2005), 6.
63. In his announcement on the establishment of these courts, the Chief Justice also pointed out that 'the court would waive filing fees for the environmental suits due to public interest' and that 'a litigant would also be allowed to sue as a pauper without paying the cost of the suit under the provisions of the Civil Procedure Rules'. See Judiciary of Kenya, 'New Courts Set Up to Handle Land Cases', <www.judiciary.go.ke/ news_info/view_article.php?id=408673>, 23 September 2008.
64. ICJ, *supra* n. 62.
65. S. 3(1) of the Judicature Act.

The Act further provides that:

> ...the High Court, the Court of Appeal and all subordinate courts shall be guided by African customary law in civil cases in which one or more of the parties is subject to it or affected by it, so far as it is applicable and is not repugnant to justice and morality or inconsistent with any written law, and shall decide all such cases according to substantial justice without undue regard to technicalities of procedure and without undue delay.[66]

Magistrates' Courts are established under the *Magistrates' Courts Act*. Section 3 of the Act establishes Resident Magistrates' Courts with jurisdiction throughout Kenya; subordinate to the High Court; and duly constituted when held by chief, senior principal, principal, senior resident and resident magistrates. These courts have jurisdiction over criminal[67] and civil matters. With respect to civil matters, the jurisdiction of Resident Magistrates' Courts is limited to matters where the value of the subject matter in question does not exceed Kshs 500,000.[68]

District Magistrates' Courts, established under section 8 of the *Magistrates' Court Act*, also have jurisdiction in criminal and civil proceedings. In civil proceedings, section 9 provides that a District Magistrates' Court shall have and exercise jurisdiction and powers in proceedings of a civil nature where either the proceedings concern a claim under customary law; or the value of the subject matter in dispute does not exceed Kshs 5,000, or Kshs 10,000 where the court is constituted by a district magistrate having power to hold a Magistrates' Court of the first class.

With respect to customary law, the *Magistrates' Court Act* provides that a Magistrates' Court 'may call for and hear evidence of the African customary law applicable to any case before it'.[69] Many environmental matters are heard at the Magistrates' Courts level as criminal or civil matters. This underscores the crucial role of these courts in environmental governance. Unfortunately, the low levels of understanding of environmental matters and the heavy workload at this level can negatively impact on environmental governance. Indeed the judicial officers at this level have limited understanding of environmental issues which raises the need for training.

3.2   QUASI-JUDICIAL TRIBUNALS

As pointed out above, EMCA has established NET to offer specialized, expeditious and cheaper justice than the ordinary courts of law. By their nature, tribunals are

---

66. S. 3(2) of the Judicature Act.
67. S. 4 of the Magistrates' Courts Act.
68. *Ibid.*, s. 5.
69. *Ibid.*, s. 17.

designed to be more accessible, informal and free from legal technicalities. There is increased use of the Tribunal to challenge decisions of NEMA.

Several sectoral statutes, such as the *Water Act* 2002, the *Energy Act* 2006 and the *Forests Act* 2005, similarly provide for the establishment of tribunals to resolve matters relating to water, energy and forestry matters. Appeals from the decisions of these tribunals lie to the High Court of Kenya. To date, not one matter has been considered by any of these tribunals. The tendency is likely to be for lawyers to file environmental matters in the High Court unless there is a concerted effort to mandate parties to go through the tribunals prior to approaching the High Court.

3.3   Non-Judicial Environmental Dispute Resolution

Over and above judicial and quasi-judicial dispute resolution forums, there exist community level organizations that are used to resolve disputes at local levels. These differ from place to place and context to context. The nature of community groups in a pastoral setting is different from those in an agricultural setting, and these differences are linked to the nature of land tenure systems and the cohesion of community members. There is not yet a detailed study of traditional governance institutions that are used in environmental management activities in Kenya but they do exit; they are dynamic and acquire new roles as the need arises, making a generalization both undesirable as well as too simplistic.

It is, however, possible to identify institutions that one finds among most communities in Kenya, whose mandate increasingly includes environmental matters. Being accessible and accepted at the lowest level of society where most environmental resources are found, these institutions compete with national, provincial and district mechanisms and can impact on the efficacy of the latter where their objectives are not the same. This raises the need to incorporate them in national environmental policy planning and implementation to ensure proper governance of the environment in those areas where access to formal courts is limited by physical distance, linguistic and cost barriers.

3.3.1   Elders

In almost all communities in Kenya, the institution of *Wazee* (elders) exists. This is ordinarily the first point of call when any dispute arises in a community. Since most Kenyans' lives are closely linked to environmental resources, it is not surprising that most of the issues that elders deal with touch on the environment. In north eastern Kenya, the elders' role in managing water resources as custodians is noteworthy. They manage water extraction from boreholes and determine community members' entitlements to water. District umbrella water users' associations include these elders in their membership as they know the status of the water resources and are revered among their communities. Among most of the communities in north eastern Kenya, referral of a matter to the formal dispute resolution mechanisms such as courts, is analogous to taking your dispute to the 'enemy'.

Only persons that refuse to accept the elders' verdict will be turned over to the chief and to the courts.[70]

The procedures adopted by the elders' courts are *ad hoc* and typically involve only older men. Although the exclusion of women and youth from the court process may undermine their human rights, these members of the community appear to accept the process. Among the Rendille tribe for instance, the two most important organs of the community are *geeyi makhabaale* and *nabo*, both of which are an exclusive male preserve and whose mandate includes formulating community strategy and dispute resolution.[71]

3.3.2   The Chief

The institution of the chief plays an integral role in regulating people's affairs at community level. Having started as a formalization of the traditional chief, the chief remains the most powerful person in a local setting in modern day Kenya. His duties are multi-faceted including the resolution of environmental disputes.[72]

3.3.3   Peace Committees

Peace committees are typically found in pastoral communities that have histori-cally had sour relations with their neighbours. While most of the members will be the elders, there is representation from other members of the community. Most disputes revolve around livestock and pasturelands and consequently, the mandate of these committees includes handling environmental matters.

3.3.4   Provincial, District and Local Environment Committees

These environmental committees are critical to access to justice as they act as the link between the formal and informal structures. The membership of these commit-tees is drawn from governmental agencies, district and local governance institutions, civil society organizations and community-based organizations engaged in environ-mental programmes, representatives of women, youth, farmers, pastoralists and the business community, and representatives of regional development authorities.[73]

The Provincial and District Environment Committees are responsible for the proper management of the environment within the province or district in respect of which they are appointed. They are also expected to perform such additional functions as may be prescribed by EMCA or assigned by the minister by notice

---

70. P. Kameri-Mbote, 'Towards Greater Access to Justice in Environmental Disputes in Kenya: Opportunities for Intervention', *Law Society Digest* July 2005, <www.ielrc.org/content/w0501.pdf>, 23 September 2008.
71. *Ibid.*, 42.
72. *Ibid.*
73. S. 29 of EMCA.

in the Gazette.[74] Since these committees operate at lower levels, they are closer to the communities and can easily interface with both the formal and informal structures as the membership is drawn from both. They have the potential to promote access to justice by taking the best from both sides.[75]

4	ANALYSIS OF SIGNIFICANT ENVIRONMENTAL JUDGMENTS

4.1	*Locus Standi*

Judicial pronouncements on environmental decision making have not helped remedy the absence of explicit environmental provisions in the Constitution. For instance, Kenyan courts were unable to establish a clear jurisprudence on matters of *locus standi* (right to sue) before the promulgation of EMCA in 1999. In the public interest case of *Maina Kamanda v. Nairobi City Council*, the High Court adopted a fairly liberal position on *locus standi* and granted the plaintiff the right to be heard.[76] This was in stark contrast to *Wangari Maathai v. Kenya Times Media Trust*,[77] an environmental case brought before the court as a public interest matter, in which *locus standi* was denied. The plaintiff was a resident of Nairobi and the coordinator of the Greenbelt Movement, a NGO working in environmental conservation. She filed suit on her own behalf seeking a temporary injunction to restrain the defendant from constructing a proposed complex in a recreational park in Nairobi. The court upheld the defendant's objection that the plaintiff lacked standing to bring the suit, because the plaintiff would not be affected more than any other resident of Nairobi. The court pointed out:

> it is not alleged that the Defendant Company is in breach of any rights, public or private in relation to the plaintiff nor has the company caused damage to her nor does she anticipate any damage or injury.[78]

Furthermore, in *Law Society of Kenya v. Commissioner of Lands and Others*,[79] the court adopted a highly restrictive approach to *locus standi*. The matter involved public land that had allegedly been improperly allocated to the Law Society. The judge opined that matters of public interest are the domain of the Attorney General and held that:

> If the interest issue is a public one, then the litigant must show that the matter complained of has injured him over and above injury, loss or prejudice suffered by the rest of the public in order to have a right to appear in court and to

---

74. *Ibid.*
75. Kameri-Mbote, *supra* n. 70, 43.
76. HCK Civ. Case No. 6153 (1992).
77. HCK Civ. Case No. 5403 (1989).
78. *Ibid.*, 24.
79. HCK Civ. Case No. 464 (2000).

be heard on the matter. Otherwise, public interest [issues] are litigated upon by the Attorney-General or such other body as the law sets out.[80]

In *Albert Ruturi & Another v. The Minister for Finance and Others*,[81] the Kenya Bankers Association challenged the constitutionality of the *Central Bank of Kenya (Amendment) Act* 2000. The Attorney General challenged the *locus standi* of the association to bring the application since it had no right to litigate on behalf of its member banks. The court held that representative suits brought by an organization on behalf of its members were permissible provided that: (i) the organization's members have standing to sue in their own right; (ii) the interest which the organization seeks to protect is germane to the organization's purpose; and (iii) neither the claim nor the relief sought requires the individual participation of the members. The court added that where an organization was formed for the very purpose of promoting a particular interest, it would be ridiculous to hold that it does not have the right to litigate to protect such interest of its own. Although not dealing with an environmental issue, this case provided an important precedent for environmental associations and organizations seeking to bring applications on behalf of their members.

4.2   SUITS AGAINST GOVERNMENT AGENCIES

In *Lereya and 800 Others v. Attorney General and 2 Others*,[82] the plaintiffs, describing themselves as the affected residents of Marigat Division, sought an order against the Attorney General, the Minister of Environment and Natural Resources and NEMA, compelling them to eradicate the weed *Prosopis Juliflora* from their land. The weed had been introduced by the United Nations Food and Agriculture Organization (FAO) ostensibly to curb desertification. It had, however, invaded large tracts of land causing harm to local vegetation, livestock, people and the environment. The defendants objected to the suit on three main grounds. First, that the plaintiffs had not served the statutory notice of intention to sue on the Attorney General as required under the requisite legislation. Secondly, that the application was barred by statutory limitation having been filed in 2006 when the weed was introduced in 1983. Thirdly, the defendants argued that the plaintiffs lacked *locus standi*. The High Court ruled that the suit be struck off the court role owing to the failure of the plaintiffs to serve the mandatory notice on the defendant. However, the court noted that *Prosopis Juliflora* is an invasive weed with a long-term and continuing impact on the environment. It according held that the application was not barred by statutory limitation. Finally, with regard to *locus standi*, the court noted that EMCA filled a gap existing in Kenyan law by being the first statute with provisions specifically tailored to address *locus standi* in

---

80. *Ibid.*, 12.
81. Nairobi High Court Misc. Civ. Appl. No. 908/2001 1 KLR 54 (2002).
82. High Court at Nairobi, July 11, 2006, KLR (Environment & Land) 1 (2006) 761.

environmental matters. The court accordingly held that the plaintiffs had *locus standi* to bring the application as spelt out in sections 3(3) and 3(4) of EMCA.

A second case relating to the same weed was brought before the High Court in *Charles Lekuyen Nabori and Others v. The Attorney General and Others.*[83] The applicants sought a declaration from the court that the right to life embodied in the Constitution entitled the applicants to a clean and healthy environment, free from the damage occasioned by the weed *Prosopis Juliflora.* The applicants also sought to have the weed declared a noxious weed; and an order that the respondents be held liable for breach of the right to property on account of their failure to eradicate the weed. The court held that the right to life includes a clean and healthy environment which guarantees the full enjoyment of natural resources.[84] The judges also noted that 'the failure by the Ministry of Environment and Natural Resources to take affirmative steps towards eradication of the weed/plant *Prosopis Juliflora* amounts to a breach of property'.[85] Most interestingly, the court affirmed recommendations of the PCC calling for the creation of a commission of technical and local experts by the government to assess and quantify the loss caused to the environment by the weed and the injury suffered by the petitioners; and recommended commensurate monetary compensation.[86]

In the case of *John Peter Mureithi and Others v. The Attorney General and 4 Others,*[87] the applicants, acting on behalf of the Mbari-ya-Murathimi clan, sought to challenge the acquisition of the clan's ancestral land by the Catholic Consolata Mission when the community was moved from the land to emergency villages by colonial authorities in 1955. The applicants argued that the land belonged to the clan under Kikuyu customary law. The respondents argued that: the applicants had no *locus standi*; the applicants' remedy lay in private law rather than public law; and the applicants had unduly delayed the assertion of their claim for up to forty years and were accordingly barred from bringing the suit. The court held that:

> . . . the clan members and their successors are sufficiently aggrieved since they claim an interest in the parcels of land which they allege was clan and trust land and which is now part of a vibrant Municipality. I find it in order that the applicants represent themselves as individuals and the wider clan and I unequivocally hold that they have the required standing to bring the matter to this court. Moreover in this case I find – the claim that the land belonged to the clan and finally there cannot be a better challenger than members of the affected clan.[88]

---

83. HCK Nairobi (Nairobi Law Courts) Petition No. 466 of 2006 (Eklr) 2007.
84. *Ibid.* See Rawal's J judgment, 54.
85. *Ibid.*
86. *Ibid.*, 66.
87. High Court at Nairobi, Misc. Civil Appl. No. 158 of 2005, 2 June 2006 KLR (Environment & Land) 1 (2006) 707.
88. *Ibid.*, 708.

4.3   RIGHT TO A HEALTHY ENVIRONMENT

In *Waweru v. Republic*,[89] the applicants, property owners in the Kiserian Township, had been charged with discharging raw sewerage into a public water source and the environment contrary to the *Public Health Act*;[90] and failing to comply with a statutory notice issued by the public health authority. The applicants challenged the charge and contended that: the selection of accused persons was discriminatory; they could not comply with the health requirements concerning wastewater as the cost would be prohibitive; and that it was the responsibility of the local authority to construct and maintain the drainage system and sewerage plant. In dismissing the criminal charges against the applicants, the High Court confirmed that it was the duty of the local authority to build and maintain a sewerage and drainage system. The court, however, rejected the applicants' argument that the cost of complying with health requirements was prohibitive: 'Firstly because sustainable development has a cost element which must be met by developers and secondly, because they had not stated other alternatives which could have been more environmentally friendly to deal with the problem'.[91] Interestingly, the court noted at the end of its judgment:

> Our inspiration to take up the challenge should spring from the fact that our generation has perhaps witnessed the greatest degradation of the environment more than any other past generation . . . we have witnessed the steepest drift from Grace (call it the Garden of Eden if you may) to the bottled water type of environment! We were created for greater things and no effort should be spared in restoring the lost grace.[92]

Furthermore, the court having stated that 'development that threatens life is not sustainable development and it ought to be halted,' went beyond the applicants' prayers and ordered the Ministry of Water, Nairobi Water Services Board and Olkejuado County Council to construct sewerage treatment works.[93] It also directed that its judgment be served on the Ministry of Water, Ministry of Local Government, Olkejuado County Council, NEMA, Attorney General's Office and the ministry responsible for physical planning; and further that NEMA be urged to consider making appropriate restoration orders.[94]

This case has been held as a landmark decision in environmental jurisprudence in Kenya. It confronted issues that affect the environment drawing from examples in Pakistan and also the documents emanating from the UN National Conference on Environment and Development held in 1992. Quoting Klaus Topfer, the former

---

89. HCK Nairobi, Misc. Civil Appl. No. 118 of 2004, 2 March 2006, KLR (Environment & Land) 1 (2006) 677.
90. Cap. 242 of the Laws of Kenya.
91. *Supra* n. 90, 678.
92. *Ibid.*, 696.
93. *Ibid.*, 693 and 688.
94. *Ibid.*, 687.

UN Environment Programme's Executive Director's address to the Global Judges Programme in 2005, the Court noted that:

> The judiciary is also a crucial partner in promoting environmental governance, upholding the rule of law and in ensuring a fair balance between environmental, social and developmental consideration through its judgments and declarations.[95]

4.4   ENVIRONMENT IMPACT ASSESSMENT

The judiciary has also had to make pronouncements on EIAs as instruments for ensuring access to justice in cases involving mining; forestry excisions; and environmental resources held in trust by the government.

In the mining context, the case of *Rodgers Muema Nzioka and Others v. Tiomin Kenya Ltd*,[96] is noteworthy. A Canadian mining company, Tiomin, sought to mine titanium in the Kwale district. Environmental lobby groups disputed the legitimacy of the authorization process on the basis that no EIA report had been provided as required by section 3 of EMCA. The High Court granted: first, an injunction in favor of the applicants restraining the company from undertaking mining activities in the Kwale District; second, a declaratory order that the company's existing mining activities in the Kwale District were illegal; and third, general damages. In granting the injunction, the court noted that although the defendant had obtained the required licenses under the mining legislation, it had not complied with the provisions of EMCA, specifically section 58 which provides that a person intending to carry out any activity under the second schedule to the Act (including mining and quarrying), must submit a project report to NEMA. Following the above court wrangling, the Minister of Environment stepped in to personally resolve the issue extra-judicially, with allegations of bribery and corruption following. While NEMA had a basis for pursuing the issue, it is important to note that the Minister's intervention effectively undermined the role of the regulatory authorities and the judiciary as well as citizens' access to justice.

4.5   PUBLIC TRUST

In the context of forestry, the Kenyan judiciary has also been called upon to consider the validity of the government's decision to de-gazette state forests, thereby effectively removing them from protection. In the case of *Republic v. Minister for Environment and Natural Resources and Others ex parte Kenya Alliance of Residents Associations and Others*,[97] the applicants sought to review such a decision and sought *writs of certiorari* to quash the relevant government notice and prohibit the

---

95. *Ibid.*, 688-689.
96. HCK Mombasa, Civ. Case No. 97, 2001.
97. HCK Misc. Civ. Appl. No. 421 of 2002.

government from dealing with the forest areas in a manner detrimental to Kenya's environmental health. The court granted the orders, thereby stopping the government from proceeding with the exercise until such time as the issue was fully heard and determined. The procedure for bringing this matter to court was very cumbersome owing to the fact that the respondent was the Kenyan government. To be able to bring a civil action against the government, one has to give notice.[98] This is a matter of grave concern given that many of Kenya's environmental resources are held in (public) trust by the State and its organs; and the cumbersome procedures could therefore effectively act as a bar to accessing justice in environmental matters. Interestingly, in the *Waweru* case, the court held that 'in the case of land resources, forests, wetlands and waterways . . . the Government and its agencies are under a public trust to manage them in a way that maintains a proper balance between the economic benefits of development with the needs of a clean environment'.[99]

4.6 REGULATION OF PROPERTY RIGHTS

The judiciary has also been called upon to consider the boundaries between private property rights and broader public environmental imperatives. In *Park View Shopping Arcade Limited v. Charles M. Kang'ethe and 2 Others*,[100] the High Court had to determine how to balance constitutionally guaranteed private property rights in the face of public environmental concerns. The case concerned a wetland, which the applicant argued it was the *bona fide* registered owner of. The applicant further argued that as owner, it had the right to enjoy, occupy and use the land. The problem was that the land was occupied by the respondents. The applicant wished to develop the land and sought an order evicting the respondents. The respondents opposed the application and argued that: the land constituted a sensitive marshland and wetland along one of the tributaries of the Nairobi River; they were not trespassers, and had a permit to conduct their business on the land which enhanced the environmental quality of the area; and the applicant's proposed construction was a threat to a clean and healthy environment. The court resolved the matter by compelling the Minister of the Environment to 'ensure the conduct of a professional and policy assessment' of the land in question in accordance with section 42 of EMCA. The resolution of the other matters in the case was predicated on the carrying out of an EIA.

5 CRITICAL SURVEY

As has been highlighted above, the judiciary is increasingly contributing to environmental governance in Kenya. This trend seems to have followed the

---

98. S. 13A of the Government Proceedings Act, Cap. 40 of the Laws of Kenya.
99. *Supra* n. 89, 692.
100. Civil Suit No. 438 of 2004.

promulgation of EMCA which provides an explicit foundation for environmental governance. The *Maathai* case highlighted the *lacuna* in Kenyan laws for public spirited attempts to protect environmental resources that were held in trust by the government for the entire country. The *Waweru* case illustrates how far the judiciary has come in understanding its key role in environmental governance. One of the reasons for this recent judicial activism is the environmental legal training provided to all High Court judges by the United Nations Environmental Programme; the Centre for Advanced Studies in Environmental Law and Policy of the University of Nairobi; and the Institute for Law and Environmental Governance. The training was conducted between 2005 and 2007 and it is noteworthy that many of the landmark environmental decisions discussed above coincide with this period and were handed down by judges who had attended the training programme. By 2007, all High Court and Court of Appeal members had received training on environmental law. In the interests of consistency and continuity, it would appear advisable to ensure that all judicial officers appointed since 2007 receive similar training.

It is also interesting to note that shortly after EMCA's promulgation; many environmental cases were dismissed on technical grounds. This no longer appears to be the case. For example, in the *Lereya* case, where the court – while pointing out the need to properly serve the Attorney General – was also clear on the issue of *locus standi* and the gravity of the matter before it. Similarly, if one reads the full judgment of the *Waweru* case, one senses the court's frustration that both parties' lawyers failed to furnish the court with all relevant information or join key parties to the proceedings.[101] There appears to be a lack of symmetry in the knowledge of environmental law between the judges and the members of the bar, which needs to be addressed. The reason for the above is no doubt the fact that until recently, environmental law was not part of the formal legal curriculum at universities and even now, it remains a final year elective, not a compulsory course. It is also not among the mandatory courses that the Council for Legal Education sets for admission to the Kenyan Bar. It is therefore not surprising that many lawyers have no environmental law knowledge. Another factor limiting the Kenyan Bar's engagement in environmental law matters is that the matters are predominantly public in nature and the country does not have a culture of public interest litigation. If there is no client able to pay for instituting the legal proceedings, an environmental issue may remain unaddressed in perpetuity. Similarly, Kenya does not have the epistolary institution of cases in court, as is the case in other jurisdictions such as India.

It is disturbing that *locus standi* continues to be used by parties to thwart environmental actions, even though EMCA, which resolves the issue of legal standing in the environmental context, was promulgated almost ten years ago. This is significant considering that, in sharp contrast to the High Court and Appeal Court judges, only a small number of magistrates have received environmental law

---

101. *Ibid.*, 12.

training. The magistrates may, therefore, be ignorantly dismissing environmental cases on the grounds of standing. Given that the majority of cases begin their life in the Magistrates' Courts, implementing environmental law training for magistrates requires urgent attention. Besides, environmental issues may come to the court not as environmental case, but as general civil and criminal case. This is epitomized by, for example, the *Waweru* case; a criminal case that turned out to have great implications for environmental jurisprudence in Kenya.

In light of the above, it is essential that all members of the judiciary are trained in environmental law to ensure that there is an overall context for promoting environmental governance. These training interventions should not, however, be limited to formal judicial institutions, but should extend to quasi-judicial and informal dispute resolution *fora*, as these latter two *fora* are where many environmental-related disputes are resolved. The training needs to be continuous to appraise the personnel on new issues and to cater for those joining after the completion of the initial training. The training should also illustrate the linkages between the different dispute resolution *fora*. For instance, it is important for judicial officers to understand the mandate of NET with the objective to promote synergy; not unnecessary duplication and conflict.

As has been mentioned above, legal practitioners also require training in environmental law. In this regard, it is heartening to note that the LSK has introduced continuing legal education to build the capacity of Kenya's lawyers and as a requirement for obtaining an annual practicing certificate. Environmental law is one of the courses offered. However, the current structure of these courses and their non-compulsory status may undermine their role in transferring the requisite environmental law skills to legal practitioners.

6   CONCLUSION AND WAY FORWARD

As should be evident from the preceding analysis, the role of Kenya's judiciary in environmental governance is growing. With the proliferation of international environmental treaties and the domestication of these into Kenya's national law, the role of the judiciary will no doubt continue to grow. Indeed, the role of the judiciary is well captured in the following statement:

> The judiciary plays a critical role in the enhancement and interpretation of environmental law and the vindication of the public interest in a healthy and secure environment. Judiciaries have and will most certainly continue to play a pivotal role both in the development and implementation of legislative and institutional regimes for sustainable development.[102]

---

102. D. Kaniaru, L. Kurukulasuriya & C.O. Okidi, 'UNEP Judicial Symposium on the Role of the Judiciary in Promoting Sustainable Development', paper presented at the 5th International Conference on Environmental Compliance and Enforcement, (California: ICECE, 1998), 22.

The development of Kenya's environmental jurisprudence has clearly begun. The increased participation of all its judicial officers in *fora* where they can exchange views between themselves, with judicial officers from other jurisdictions, and environmental law academics and specialists, will play an invaluable role in building their capacity to develop this jurisprudence. As Kaniaru, Kurukulasuriya and Okidi note:

> A judiciary, well informed on the contemporary developments in the field of international and national imperatives of environmentally friendly development will be a major force in strengthening national efforts to realise the goals of environmentally friendly development and, in particular, in vindicating the rights of individuals substantively and in accessing the judicial process.[103]

Building this environmental capacity and jurisprudence may not always be easy. Key challenges include: the imbalance between demand for judicial services compared to the available judicial officers; the limited public awareness of the quasi judicial and informal dispute resolution mechanisms; the minimal awareness of the citizenry and legal practitioners of environmental law; the absence of a culture of public interest litigation; and developing synergies between the myriad of different bodies charged with environment governance and the judiciary. Key opportunities do currently exist for overcoming these obstacles and these include: the willingness of the judiciary to learn; the increasing implementation of EMCA and NEMA's activities; renewed interest in traditional justice delivery institutions; the governance, justice, law and order sector reforms aimed at enhancing environmental governance through improved access to justice; and increased interest by civil society in environmental matters. If properly overseen, these opportunities and challenges will take environmental governance to a higher level in Kenya. The seeds have been sown and improvements can be made if the existing efforts are sustained.

BIBLIOGRAPHY

Edwards, D.C. 'The Ecological Regions of Kenya: Their Classification in Relation to Agricultural Development'. *Empire Journal of Experimental Agriculture* 24 (1956): 89-108.

Griffiths, J.F. 'The Climate of East Africa'. In *The Natural Resources of East Africa*, edited by E.W. Russell. Nairobi: DA Hawkins, 1962.

ICJ. *Kenya: Judicial Independence, Corruption and Reform*. Nairobi: ICJ Kenya Chapter, 2005.

Judiciary of Kenya. 'New Courts Set Up to Handle Land Cases'. <www.judiciary.go.ke/news_info/view_article.php?id=408673>, 23 September 2008.

---

103. *Ibid.*

Kameri-Mbote, P. *Property Rights and Biodiversity Management in Kenya.* Nairobi: ACTS Press, 2002.

Kameri-Mbote, P. 'The Use of Criminal Law in Enforcing Environmental Law'. In *Environmental Governance in Kenya: Implementing the Framework Law*, edited by C.O. Okidi, P. Kameri-Mbote & M. Akech. Nairobi: East African Education Publishers, 2008.

Kameri-Mbote, P. 'Towards Greater Access to Justice in Environmental Disputes in Kenya: Opportunities for Intervention'. *Law Society Digest* July 2005. <www.ielrc.org/content/w0501.pdf>, 23 September 2008.

Kameri-Mbote, P., G. Tumushabe & I. Sithole-Niang. *Biotechnology and Law: Africa's Dilemma.* Forthcoming, 2008.

Kaniaru, D., L. Kurukulasuriya & C.O. Okidi. 'UNEP Judicial Symposium on the Role of the Judiciary in Promoting Sustainable Development'. Paper presented at the 5th International Conference on Environmental Compliance and Enforcement. California: ICECE, 1998.

KFWG. *Changes in Forest Cover in Kenya's Five 'Water Towers' 2000-2003.* Nairobi: KFWG, 2004.

Matiru, V. Forest cover and forest reserves in Kenya: Policy and Practice. EPA working paper no. 5. Nairobi: IUCN, 2002.

Ojwang, J.B. *Environmental Law and the Constitutional Order.* Nairobi: ACTS Press, 1993.

Okidi, C.O. & P. Kameri-Mbote. *The Making of a Framework Environmental Law.* Nairobi: ACTS Press, 2001.

Okidi, C.O. 'Concept, Structure and Function of Environmental Law'. In *Environmental Governance in Kenya: Implementing the Framework Law*, edited by C.O. Okidi, P. Kameri-Mbote & M. Akech. Nairobi: East African Education Publishers, 2008. EAEP, Forthcoming 2008: 3-60.

Republic of Kenya. *Economic Recovery Strategy.* Nairobi: Government Printer, 2003.

Republic of Kenya. *Economic Survey 2007.* Nairobi: Ministry of Planning and National Development KNBS, 2007.

Republic of Kenya. *Environmental Action Plan for Arid and Semi-Arid Lands in Kenya.* Nairobi: Government Printer, 1992.

Rukuba-Ngaiza, N., et al. *Public Involvement in Environmental Decision-making in Asia and East Africa: Law and Practice.* Washington DC: Legal Vice Presidency IBRD/WB, 2003.

Trapnell, C.G. & I. Langdale-Brown. 'The Natural Vegetation of East Africa'. In *The Natural Resources of East Africa*, edited by E.W. Russell. Nairobi: DA Hawkins, 1962.

Wamukoya, G.M. & F.D.P. Situma (eds). *Environmental Management in Kenya: A Guide to the Environmental Management and Coordination Act.* Nairobi: Centre for Research and Education Environmental Law, 2000.

Wass, P. *Kenya's Indigenous Forests: Status, Management and Conservation.* Paris: IUCN, 1994.

TABLE OF LEGISLATION

TABLE OF CASES

TABLE OF LEGISLATIVE INSTRUMENTS

Cartagena Protocol on Biosafety (2000) 6 *ILM* 1027

ABBREVIATIONS

ASAL(s)	Arid and Semi-arid Area(s)
BMU	Beach Management Unit
CREEL	Centre for Research and Education Environmental Law
EAEP	East African Education Publishers
EAP	Eastern Africa Program
EIA	Environmental Impact Assessment
EMCA	Environment Management and Coordination Act
FAO	Food and Agricultural Organization
FD	Forest Department
GDP	Gross Domestic Product
HCK	High Court of Kenya
IBRD/WB	International Bank for Reconstruction and Development/ World Bank
ICJ	International Commission of Jurists
KFS	Kenya Forest Service
KFWG	Kenya Forest Working Group
KLR	Kenya Law Reports
KNBS	Kenya National Bureau of Statistics
KWS	Kenya Wildlife Service
LSK	Law Society of Kenya
NEC	National Environment Council
NEMA	National Environment Management Authority
NET	National Environment Tribunal
NGO(s)	Non-governmental Organization(s)
PCC	Public Complaints Committee
UN	United Nations

Chapter 15

Uganda

Emmanuel Kasimbazi

1   INTRODUCTION

Uganda is a land-locked country located in Eastern Africa. It occupies an area of about 241,500 km², of which approximately 15% is open water, 3% permanent wetlands, 9% seasonal wetlands, 6% game reserves and national parks, and a further 6% forest reserves.[1] It is bordered by the Republic of Kenya in the east, Tanzania and Rwanda in the south, Democratic Republic of Congo (former Zaire) in the west, and Sudan in the north. Nearly one-fifth of the country's total area comprises of open water or wetlands and four of East Africa's Great Lakes (Lake Victoria, Lake Kyoga, Lake Albert and Lake Edward) lie within or adjacent to its borders.

Uganda generally has an equatorial climate that provides plentiful sunshine, moderated by the relatively high altitude of most regions in the country. With the exception of the northeastern corner of the country, rainfall is well distributed. The southern region has two rainy seasons, usually beginning in early April and again in October. Little rain falls in June and December. In the north, occasional rains occur between April and October, while the period from November to March is often very dry.[2]

---

1. Visiting Uganda, 'The Essential Guide to Uganda', <www.visiting-uganda.com>, 21 September 2008.
2. USLC, 'The Library of Congress Country Studies: The Geography of Uganda', <lcweb2.loc.gov/frd/cs/>, 21 September 2008.

Louis J. Kotzé and Alexander R. Paterson (eds), *The Role of the Judiciary in Environmental Governance: Comparative Perspectives*, pp. 479–504.
© 2009 Kluwer Law International BV, The Netherlands.

2   MAIN ENVIRONMENTAL ISSUES

Uganda is endowed with a wealth and diversity of natural resource. These natural resources are, however, under significant threat largely as a result of human activities. Deforestation is caused by: high demands placed on wood as a source of fuel for cooking, brick making and mining; clearing forests for agriculture; uncontrolled pit-sawing; poor logging methods; and the inefficient use of wood. Soil erosion and leaching, especially in highland areas, is caused by overstocking and overgrazing; uncontrolled bush burning; and the improper use of agro-chemicals. Loss of wildlife is predominantly caused by: the poaching of animals for their hides, ivory and meat; and the encroachment and degradation of natural habitats for ranching, crop production and human settlement. Additional environmental challenges include: loss of biodiversity; wetland degradation; and the pollution of the country's terrestrial, atmospheric and freshwater resources as a result of industrialization and urbanization.

The degradation of Uganda's environment has directly impacted on the health and wellbeing of its citizens. Reduced agricultural production has led to food shortages, poverty, urbanization and in extreme cases, famine. Building materials, particularly wooden poles, are in short supply; so too is one of the population's major sources of fuel, firewood. A lack of access to adequate and safe drinking water and sanitation services has led to the spread of disease. This has been aggravated by many communities living in, or adjacent to, unhygienic and polluted environments. Land degradation, the unsustainable consumption of natural resources and the pollution of its natural environs, have not only destroyed various rural economies but have also undermined one of Uganda's potential sources of significant foreign exchange, namely its eco-tourism industry. The impacts of climate change are also visible in Uganda with un-seasonal flooding in some parts of the country leading to loss of life and property, and the displacement of people.

3   DEVELOPMENT OF ENVIRONMENTAL LAW: AN
           OVERVIEW

The development of environmental law in Uganda can be divided into five periods. The first period was that which preceded the establishment of colonial rule in Uganda. During this period, indigenous communities had various customary rules which governed their use of natural resources, such as forests and wetlands. These rules were founded on notions such as common resources, communal use, nomadic pastoralism, and shifting cultivation. Certain species of flora and fauna were afforded special protection due to their medicinal qualities or religious significance. It is presumed that during this period, Uganda's population achieved a delicate equilibrium between using and conserving their environment.[3]

---

3. J.R. Kamugisha, *Management of Natural Resources in Uganda: Policy and Legislation Land Marks, 1890-1990* (Nairobi: Swedish Industrial Development Agency Regional Soil Conservation Unit, 1993), 15.

The second period was that under colonial rule during which state ownership of the country's natural resources (including its forests, wildlife and minerals) was introduced.[4] During this period, several laws were enacted in an attempt to regulate the use of specific natural resources and derive revenue from such use.[5] These laws did not entrench notions of sustainability and were founded on command and control forms of regulation.

The third period was that following Uganda gaining independence in 1962. Most of the policies and laws applicable under colonial rule remained intact and all that appears to have been amended was the substitution of various words and names such as 'public' for 'crown', and 'Uganda' for 'Britain.'[6]

The fourth period was that endured under Idi Amin's dictatorial reign. During this period, Uganda's economy and infrastructure started to crumble and its environment was rapidly degraded as a result of: the political instability surrounding Amin's rule; the absence of a coherent development agenda; the lack of relevant environmental policies; and minimal state investment in the regulation and conservation of the country's natural resources.

The fifth period is that following the National Resistance Movement securing power in 1986. Following its assumption of power, a number of measures to address Uganda's environmental problems were implemented. These notably included the establishment of the Ministry of Environmental Protection whose responsibility it is to: coordinate and enhance natural resources management; harmonize the interests of natural resource users; monitor pollution levels; and advise the government on policy and legislative reforms for ensuring sound environmental governance in Uganda.

In 1991, the government initiated a consultative process to develop Uganda's first National Environment Action Plan[7] (NEAP). The NEAP was a major milestone in Uganda's development of environmental law because it incorporated strategies for addressing concerns in the areas of policy, legislation, institutional reform and new investments for promoting sustainable development. The NEAP process was followed by the adoption of the National Environment Management Policy[8] (NEMP) in 1994. It set out the country's overall policy goals, objectives and principles for environmental management; and recommended some initial actions including: the creation of an appropriate institutional and legal framework; and the revision and modernization of sectoral policies, laws and regulations.

---

4. Crown ownership of natural resources was introduced by the Buganda Agreement 1900, the Toro Agreement 1900, the Ankole Agreement 1901 and the Bunyoro Agreement 1933.
5. These laws included: *Forests Act* 1947; *Timber Export Act* 1950; *Plant Protection Act* 1937; and *Game (Preservation and Control) Act* 1959.
6. The 'colonial acts' (*supra* n. 5) were re-enacted by the Independence Parliament and became known as the *Laws of Uganda* 1964.
7. The Republic of Uganda Ministry of Water Lands and Environment, *The National Environment Action Plan for Uganda* (Kampala: MWLE, 1994).
8. The Republic of Uganda, *The National Environment Management Policy* (Kampala: Ministry of Natural Resources, 1994).

It was as a result of these two processes that Uganda's current environmental regime emerged.

4   PRINCIPAL ENVIRONMENTAL LAWS

4.1   THE CONSTITUTION OF THE REPUBLIC OF UGANDA, 1995

The Constitution of the Republic of Uganda (1995 Constitution),[9] in its National Objectives and Directive Principles of State Policy, enjoins the government to protect natural resources (including land, water, wetlands, minerals, oils, fauna and flora) on behalf of the people of Uganda.[10] The government is under a duty to promote sustainable development and public awareness of the need to manage land, air and water resources in a balanced and sustainable manner for present and future generations.[11] It is further required to promote and implement energy policies that will ensure that people's basic needs and those of environmental preservation are met.[12] Finally, the government is obliged to: create and develop parks, reserves and recreation areas; ensure the conservation of natural resources; and promote the rational use of natural resources so as to safeguard and protect the biodiversity of Uganda.[13]

In its substantive provisions, the 1995 Constitution provides that every Ugandan has a right to a clean and healthy environment[14] and compels parliament by law to: provide measures to protect and preserve the environment from abuse, pollution and degradation; manage the environment for sustainable development; and to promote environmental awareness.[15] In fulfilment of this obligation, the government has passed a number of environmental laws. These are summarized below.

4.2   FRAMEWORK ENVIRONMENTAL LEGISLATION

The *National Environment Act*[16] (NEA) is Uganda's framework environmental law. The central tenet of the NEA is sustainable environmental management and it prescribes a set of environmental management principles which include assuring all people living in the country the fundamental right to an environment adequate for their health and well-being.[17] The NEA establishes the National Environment

---

9. *Constitution of the Republic of Uganda* 1995.
10. *Ibid.*, Principle XIII.
11. *Ibid.*, Principle XXVII.
12. *Ibid.*, Principle XXVII (iii).
13. *Ibid.*, Principle XXVII (iv).
14. *Ibid.*, Art. 39.
15. *Ibid.*, Art. 245.
16. Cap. 153 *Laws of Uganda* 2000.
17. *Ibid.*, s. 2(2)(a). The right to a clean and healthy environment is further guaranteed by s. 3 of the NEA which imposes a duty on all citizens to maintain and enhance the environment, including a

Management Authority (NEMA),[18] Uganda's lead environmental agency. The NEA also provides for various environmental regulatory tools in Part IV including: environmental impact assessment (EIA) which must be conducted prior to under-taking all projects that are likely to have adverse effects on the environment;[19] environmental auditing;[20] and environmental monitoring.[21] The NEA requires the NEMA to establish standards for air quality,[22] water quality,[23] the discharge of effluent into water,[24] the control of noxious smells,[25] the control of noise, vibration and pollution,[26] soil quality[27] and standards for minimization of radiation.[28] Part VIII of the NEA deals with pollution control.

4.3   Sectoral Environmental Laws

The NEA is complemented by an array of sectoral environmental laws regulating forestry, water resources and wildlife. The *National Forestry and Tree Planting Act*[29] provides for the: conservation, sustainable management and development of forests for the benefit of the people of Uganda; declaration of forest reserves for purposes of protection and production of forests and forest produce; sustainable use of forest resources and the enhancement of the productive capacity of forests; promotion of tree planting; and the establishment of the National Forestry Authority.[30]

 Water resources are regulated under the *Water Act*,[31] which governs: the use, protection and management of water resources and water supply; the establishment of water and sewerage authorities; and the devolution of water supply and sewer-age functions to these authorities. The *Water Act* vests all rights to investigate, control, protect and manage the nation's water in the government.[32] The Act also makes it an offence for a person to cause or allow waste to come into contact with any water; waste to be discharged directly or indirectly into water; or water to be polluted.[33] Subsidiary legislation relating to water resources management include

---

  duty to inform the relevant authority or Local Environment Management Committees of all activities and phenomena that may significantly affect the environment.
18. *Ibid.*, s. 4.
19. *Ibid.*, s. 19.
20. *Ibid.*, s. 22.
21. *Ibid.*, s. 23.
22. *Ibid.*, s. 24.
23. *Ibid.*, s. 25.
24. *Ibid.*, s. 26.
25. *Ibid.*, s. 27.
26. *Ibid.*, s. 28.
27. *Ibid.*, s. 30.
28. *Ibid.*, s. 31.
29. *National Forestry and Tree Planting Act* 8 of 2003.
30. The National Forestry Authority is established under s. 52.
31. Cap. 152 *Laws of Uganda* 2000.
32. *Ibid.*, s. 5.
33. *Ibid.*, s. 31.

the Water Resources Regulations,[34] Water (Waste Discharge) Regulations,[35] and
the National Environment (Standards for Discharge of Effluent into Water or on
Land) Regulations.[36]

Other relevant sectoral environmental laws are: the *Uganda Wildlife Act*
(UWA),[37] which provides for the sustainable management of wildlife and estab-
lishes a coordinating, monitoring and supervisory body to fulfil this purpose; the
Fish Act,[38] which seeks to conserve Uganda's fish stocks and regulate the catching,
purchasing, sale, marketing and processing of fish; and the *Prohibition of the
Burning of Grass Act*,[39] which prohibits the burning of grasslands.

These laws provide for the creation of a strong institutional framework
to facilitate their implementation. The NEMA is the principal agency responsible
for environmental management and protection in Uganda.[40] Additional key
environmental agencies established under the above sectoral laws are the
Uganda Wildlife Authority,[41] the National Forestry Authority,[42] the Directorate
of Water Development and the Wetlands Inspection Division.[43] Cumulatively,
these institutions seek to ensure that Uganda's environment is managed in a
sustainable manner. The realization of this objective is, however, somewhat
dependant on an activist and well informed judiciary willing to assist them in
their environmental governance effort. The chapter now turns to a discussion of
the Ugandan judiciary and further reflects on the role of the judiciary in domestic
environmental governance efforts.

5   OVERVIEW OF COURT SYSTEM

5.1   INTRODUCTION

In Uganda's pre-colonial era, each community had its own customary law system.
These customs were uncodified and passed from generation to generation by the
use of folk tales, proverbs and cultural counselling sessions. The customs were
enforced by elders, clan leaders and kings.[44] These traditional legal systems were

---

34. Water Resources Regs SI No. 33 of 1998.
35. Water (Waste Discharge) Regs SI No. 32 of 1998.
36. National Environment (Standards for Discharge of Effluent into Water or on Land) Regs SI
    No. 5 of 1999.
37. Cap. 200 *Laws of Uganda* 2000.
38. Cap. 197 *Laws of Uganda* 2000.
39. Cap. 33 *Laws of Uganda* 2000.
40. The NEMA is established under s. 4 of NEA.
41. The Uganda Wildlife Authority is established under s. 4 of UWA, *supra* n. 37.
42. The National Forestry Authority is established under s. 52 of the *National Forestry and Tree
    Planting Act*.
43. The Republic of Uganda Ministry of Water, Lands and Environment, Wetland Inspection
    Division.
44. J. Oloka Onyango, Judicial Power and Constitutionalism in Uganda: Working Paper No. 3
    (Kampala: CBR, 1993), 4.

significantly undermined during the colonial era in which the English common law, together with the English court system, was introduced into Eastern Africa by the inception of the African Order in Council of 1889.[45] The African Order was imported into Uganda by the Order in Council of 1902, with its repugnancy clause (Article 20) being directly responsible for watering down the traditional legal systems.

In the post-colonial era, a series of constitutions were promulgated which included: the independence Constitution of 1962;[46] 1966 Constitution;[47] the Republican Constitution of 1967,[48] and the 1995 Constitution. Each of these constitutions provided for distinct organs of the State, including the judiciary. The current judiciary is regulated by the 1995 Constitution and other related laws such as the *Judicature Act*[49] and the *Magistrates' Courts Act*.[50]

The vision of Uganda's judiciary is to: improve access to justice for all the people in Uganda by reforming the composition, structure and procedures of the judicial system; improve the efficiency, effectiveness and transparency of case administration; enhance the effectiveness of judicial officers/staff; maintain, improve and increase the infrastructure and equipment of the courts; and support the reform of legislation and the administration of justice.[51] The mission of the judiciary is 'to develop and administer an efficient and effective judicial system, accessible to all the people in Uganda, respectful of their traditions, mindful of their aspirations, serving them without bias or discrimination, fear of favour.'[52] The practical application of this vision and mission in the environmental context should ensure the active participation of the judiciary in Uganda's environmental governance effort.

5.2   STRUCTURE OF THE COURT SYSTEM

The Supreme Court sits at the top of Uganda's judicial hierarchy. The Supreme Court is established by Article 130 of the 1995 Constitution and is the court of last instance. The Supreme Court is constituted by the Chief Justice and not less than six additional justices.[53] The Chief Justice is the head of the Supreme Court, and in his or her absence, the most senior member of the court presides.[54] The Supreme Court, as the last appellate court, has no original jurisdiction in any matter except

---

45. *Ibid.*, 6.
46. The *Constitution of Uganda* 1962.
47. The *Constitution of Uganda* 1966.
48. The *Constitution of the Republic of Uganda* 1967.
49. Cap. 13 *Laws of Uganda* 2000.
50. Cap. 16 *Laws of Uganda* 2000.
51. Republic of Uganda Courts of Judicature, 'Mission, Objectives and Values', <www.judicature. go.ug/mission.php>, 14 September 2007.
52. *Ibid.*
53. The 1995 Constitution, Art. 130.
54. *Ibid.*, Art. 131(3).

as may be conferred on it by law. The jurisdiction of the Supreme Court is limited to hearing criminal and civil appeals from the Court of Appeal.[55] When hearing appeals of a constitutional nature, the Supreme Court sits as a Constitutional Court, and must be constituted by a full bench of members of the court.[56] If any justice is unable to attend, the president must appoint an interim acting justice for the purpose of hearing the matter.[57] The Supreme Court has powers to confirm or vary the decision of the Court of Appeal and issue such directions as may be appropriate. It may alternatively order a retrial or rehearing of the matter by the court *a quo*. No appeal is allowed regarding a decision of the Supreme Court.[58]

The Court of Appeal of Uganda is positioned between the Supreme Court and the High Court in the court hierarchy.[59] It came into being following the promulgation of the 1995 Constitution and the enactment of the *Judicature Act* in 1996. The structure of the Court of Appeal is prescribed by the 1995 Constitution and comprises of the Deputy Chief Justice, and such number of Justices of Appeal, not being less than seven, as parliament may prescribe by law.[60] The Court of Appeal, as the title suggests, has appellate jurisdiction over the High Court and is generally not a court of first instance.[61] It can, however, sit as court of first instance when hearing constitutional matters in which case it similarly sits as a Constitutional Court.[62]

The High Court is on the third tier of the court hierarchy and has unlimited jurisdiction to hear both criminal and civil cases.[63] In addition, it hears appeals from Magistrates' Courts and exercises general supervisory powers over them.[64] The Principal Judge is the head of the High Court and subordinate courts and in that capacity, assists the Chief Justice in the administration of the High Court and subordinate courts.[65]

The High Court is divided into civil, criminal, commercial, family and circuit divisions. The divisions of the High Court are not regarded as different courts, even though they exercise separate jurisdiction. A judge from any division may exercise jurisdiction over another division. Each judge of the High Court is assigned a particular division and is eligible to transfer to another division. Although each

---

55. *Ibid.*, Art. 132(2).
56. *Ibid.*, Art. 131(2).
57. *Ibid.*
58. *Ibid.*, Art. 132(1).
59. *Ibid.*, Art. 134.
60. *Ibid.*, Art. 134(4).
61. Art. 134(2) of the Constitution affords the Court of Appeal jurisdiction to hear appeals from decisions of the High Court. The provisions of Art. 134 were incorporated in the *Judicature Act*. See further ss 10-12 of the *Judicature Act* which set out the details regarding the Court of Appeal's jurisdiction.
62. *Ibid.*, Art. 137(1) of the 1995 Constitution.
63. *Ibid.*, Art. 139.
64. *Ibid.*, Art. 139(2).
65. *Ibid.*

division has its administrative head, they are under the supervision and control of the Principal Judge.[66]

In addition to these divisions, the High Court has created circuit divisions in regional centres in an effort to improve its service delivery. There are now seven High Court circuit divisions at Mbarara, Fort Portal, Masaka, Jinja, Mbale, Gulu and Nakawa. Each circuit division has jurisdiction to handle all matters within its territorial jurisdiction. There are plans to open up more circuit divisions in the near future to further decentralize the jurisdiction of the High Court.

Magistrates' Courts are situated on the fourth tier of the judicial hierarchy and are responsible for hearing the bulk of Uganda's cases. The country is divided into many magisterial areas in respect of each of which a Magistrates' Court presides. A magistrate is assigned to a magisterial area and cannot sit to hear a matter in another magisterial area without the authority of the Chief Justice. The jurisdiction of Magistrates' Courts is not only geographically limited, but also circumscribed in respect of the nature of the case or claim it can hear. The *Magistrates Courts Act* limits the jurisdiction of the Chief Magistrates' Courts[67] to criminal offences other than those of a capital nature which are entertained by the High Court.[68] The jurisdiction of other Magistrates' Courts in criminal matters is limited to offences which are not of aggravated or serious nature.[69]

The judicial system also comprises of Local Council Courts established to hear simple civil cases falling within their local jurisdiction. Uganda also makes extensive use of the military court system, established under the *Uganda Peoples' Defence Forces Act*,[70] but these courts hear military matters and accordingly play almost no role in environmental governance.

6   ANALYSIS OF SIGNIFICANT ENVIRONMENTAL JUDGMENTS

The Ugandan judiciary has played, and will no doubt continue to play, a critical role in developing, enhancing and interpreting environmental law; protecting public environmental interests; and supporting the governance efforts of Uganda's environmental authorities.[71] The main court judgments which are indicative of the above, are reviewed below under various themes.

---

66. *Ibid.*
67. Magistrates' Courts are divided into three layers: Chief Magistrates' Courts; Magistrates' Grade I Courts; and Magistrates' Grade II Courts.
68. *Magistrates' Courts Act*, s. 161(1)(a).
69. *Ibid.*, s. 161(1)(b)-(d).
70. The *Uganda Peoples' Defence Forces Act* Cap. 307 *Laws of Uganda* 2000.
71. D. Kaniaru, L. Kurukulasuriya & C. Okidi, 'The Role of the Judiciary in Promoting Sustainable Development', paper presented to the Fifth International Conference on Environmental Compliance and Enforcement (Monterey California: ICECE, 1998), 22.

6.1   USE OF COMMON LAW PRINCIPLES

Common law torts, particularly nuisance, have been successfully used by parties to achieve environmental objectives in Uganda. The Ugandan judiciary has had to grapple with the application of these torts, particularly in the context of odour and pollution.

In *Dr Bwogi Richard Kanyerezi v. The Management Committee of Rubaga Girls School,*[72] the applicant sought an injunction to restrain the respondents from using twelve latrines situated on the school's premises. The applicant contended that the foul smell emanating from the latrines constituted a nuisance as it unreasonably interfered with, and diminished, the applicant's ordinary use and enjoyment of his adjacent home. It was established that the toilets were being used by over 600 students and constantly emitted odours which drifted directly into the applicant's house, making life uncomfortable for the inhabitants. The court held that these odors constituted a nuisance and an injunction was accordingly granted.

A further case to consider the application of common law torts in the environmental context was *Seezi Huiya Munghereza and 11 Others v. Kampala City Council.*[73] In this case, a representative action was bought against the respondent in nuisance and trespass, relating to its disposal of garbage in a residential area of Kampala. The respondent did not enter appearance to defend the matter and the court accordingly handed down a default judgment compelling it to stop its improper garbage disposal. Although the respondent successfully appealed the matter on procedural grounds, this case is indicative of the judiciary's appreciation of the tort of nuisance as a tool for achieving effective environmental governance.

6.2   EXTENDING *LOCUS STANDI*

The right to a clean and healthy environment enshrined in the 1995 Constitution has a corresponding duty to protect the environment. As enunciated in the NEA, the duty imposes an obligation on citizens to take action where they perceive a threat to the environment.[74] However, in order for citizens to seek to challenge environmentally deleterious actions in the courts, they need to have *locus standi* to bring the action. The common law position was stated by Lugakingira J in *Mtikila v. Attorney General*[75] as follows:

> In English common law the litigants' *locus standi* was the hand maiden of judicial review of administration actions. Whenever a private individual challenged the decision of an administrative body the question always arose whether that individual had sufficient interest in the decision to justify the courts intervention, traditionally, common law confines standing to litigation

---

72. Civ. Appl No. 3 of 1996.
73. HCCS No. 609 of 1997.
74. S. 3 of the NEA.
75. Civ. Suit No. 5 of 1993 (High Court of Tanzania) (unreported).

protection of public rights to the Attorney General and the Attorney General's discretion in such cases may be exercised at the instance of an individual.

However, public interests and the interests of the government are not necessarily the same. The Attorney General may not be interested in taking up a matter which is of concern to the public. The Ugandan judiciary has acknowledged this and adopted a liberal approach to *locus standi* on the basis of provisions contained in the 1995 Constitution and the NEA. Article 50(2) of the 1995 Constitution provides that any person or organization may bring an action against the violation of another person's or group's human rights. Section 71 of the NEA provides that the court may in proceedings brought by any person, issue an environmental restoration order against a person who has harmed the environment and that '*it shall not be necessary for the plaintiff to show that he or she has a right of or interest in, the property, in the environment or land alleged to have been harmed* or in the environment or land contiguous to such environment or land'.[76] A number of cases have considered the above provisions relating to *locus standi*. These are analysed below.

The case of *Environmental Action Network (Ltd) v. Attorney General and National Environment Management Authority (NEMA)*[77] concerned an application for a court declaration to the effect that smoking in public places constituted a violation of the right of the non-smoking members of the public to a clean and healthy environment. In its founding affidavit, the applicant was described as a public interest litigation group bringing the application *bona fide* on its own behalf and on behalf of the non-smoking members of the public under Article 50(2) of the 1995 Constitution, to protect their rights to a clean and healthy environment, their right to life and for the general good of public health in Uganda. The respondents objected and argued that the applicant did not have *locus standi* and could not claim to represent the non-smoking members of the public. Ntabgoba J held that Article 50(2) nullified the respondent's objection and stated that 'the applicants say they are especially interested in the infringement of the rights and freedoms of those who cannot appreciate their rights and freedoms and those who do not know where to go and how to go there for redress'.[78] The court accordingly held that the applicants were entitled to a hearing. By giving a courageous and liberal interpretation to the 1995 Constitution's *locus standi* provisions, this decision appears to have potentially opened the floodgates for public interest litigation, including that of environmental interest, in Uganda.

In a related matter, *Environmental Action Network v. British American Tobacco*,[79] the same applicant brought an application under Article 50(2) of the 1995 Constitution and rule 3 of the Fundamental Rights and Freedoms (Enforcement Procedure) Rules,[80] for a court order compelling the respondent, a manufacturer of

---

76. Own emphasis.
77. HC Misc. Appl. No. 39 of 2001.
78. *Ibid.*, 5.
79. HC Civ. Suit No. 27 of 2003 (Arising from Misc. Appl. No. 70 of 2002).
80. Fundamental Rights and Freedoms (Enforcement Procedure) Rules SI No. 26 of 1992.

'dangerous products' (cigarettes), to fully and adequately warn consumers of the health risks associated with its products. Although the order was ultimately denied, the court did confirm the *locus standi* of the applicant, as Article 50(2) enabled individuals to bring public interest matters to court on behalf of those who were not in a position to do so.

6.3   ENVIRONMENTAL IMPACT ASSESSMENT

EIA is defined in NEA as a 'systematic examination conducted to determine whether or not the proposed project will have an adverse impact on the environment'.[81] Owing to its entrenchment in the NEA, EIA has become an essential management tool for ensuring environmentally sound development planning in Uganda. It has also become the fertile ground for court action by litigants seeking to challenge development proponents who fail to comply with the statutory EIA requirements, as illustrated in *National Association of Professional Environmentalists v. AES Nile Power (Ltd).*[82] The applicant in this matter sought a temporary injunction to stop the respondent from concluding a power purchase agreement with the government of Uganda, until such time as the NEMA had approved the project's EIA. It further sought a declaration to the effect that: the EIA approval was a legal prerequisite for the development; and that the endorsement of the project by parliament without the NEMA's prior approval of the EIA, was illegal, null and void and of no effect. Okumu Wengi J held:

> I am able to declare though not in terms of the declaration sought that the EIAs presented by the respondents' consultant in this project must be approved by the lead agency and the National Environment Management Authority. The declaration sought by the applicant relating to parliamentary approval is unnecessary to consider since parliament would equally be advised and is capable of knowing their power. Since no approval has been given by Parliament, this court can't inquire as to whether it will or will not grant the approval in contravention of the law. In the circumstances, the declarations sought in the motion are not granted; save that this court declares that approval of the EIA by NEMA is required under section 20 of the NEMA Statute (now section 19 of NEA).[83]

6.4   APPLICATION OF THE PUBLIC TRUST DOCTRINE

The public trust doctrine refers to the government's responsibility to hold the nation's natural resources in trust for the benefit of its citizens. It is clearly reflected

---

81. S. 1 of NEA.
82. Misc. C. No. 60 of 1999.
83. *Ibid.*, 1.

in the 1995 Constitution[84] and as a result has filtered down into a number of the country's sectoral laws such as the *Land Act*,[85] National Environment (Wetlands, River Banks and Lake Shores Management) Regulations,[86] and the *National Forestry and Tree Planting Act*.[87] The public trust doctrine, as enunciated in these laws, has been the subject of judicial scrutiny.

In *Siraji Waiswa v. Kakira Sugar Works Ltd*,[88] the applicant sought a temporary injunction prohibiting the respondent from acquiring and uprooting the Butamira Forest Reserve for the purpose of establishing a sugarcane plantation; and restraining the respondent from evicting, intimidating, threatening or in anyway interrupting the applicant's and other residents' use and occupation of Butamira forest reserve. Y. Bamwine J held:

> I would grant the remedy sought herein and order restraint on the part of the defendant from uprooting the forest to establish a sugarcane plantation during the pendency of the main suit. The defendant would be restrained from evicting, intimidating, threatening or in any way interrupting the status quo during

---

84. The 1995 Constitution's National Objectives and Directive Principles of State Policy (Principle 13) require the State to 'protect important natural resources, including land, water, wetlands, minerals, oil fauna and flora on behalf of the people of Uganda'. Art. 237(2)(b) further provides that 'the Government or a Local Government as determined by Parliament by law, shall hold in trust for the people and protect, natural lakes, rivers, wetlands, forest reserves, game reserves, national parks and any land to be reserved for ecological and touristic purposes for the common good of all citizens'.

85. Cap. 227 *Laws of Uganda* 2000. S. 44(1), e.g., states that: 'The Government or a local government shall hold in trust for the people and protect natural lakes, rivers, ground water, natural ponds, natural streams, wetlands, forest reserves, national parks and any other land reserved for ecological and tourist purposes for the common good of all citizens.' The Act appears to go further then the 1995 Constitution by providing that any resource that is not covered under the above provision may, upon request to the government and with the approval of parliament, be held in trust for the people and for the common good of the citizens of Uganda by a local government (s. 44(3)). The government or a local government is prohibited from leasing or otherwise alienating any of these natural resources unless authorized by law to do so (s. 44(5)). Furthermore, parliament or any other authority empowered by parliament may from time to time review any land held in trust by the government or a local government, whenever the community in the area or district where the reserved land is situated so demands (s. 44(6)).

86. The National Environment (Wetlands, River Banks and Lake Shores Management) Regs No. 3 of 2000 also recognizes the public trust doctrine under Reg. 18 by stating that the government or a local government shall hold in trust for the people and protect river banks and lake shores for the common good of the citizens of Uganda, and that the government or a local government shall not lease or otherwise alienate any river bank and lake shore.

87. The *National Forestry and Tree Planting Act* 8 of 2003. The Act provides that the government, or a local government, shall hold in trust for the people and protect forest reserves for ecological, forestry and tourism purposes for the common good of the citizens of Uganda. In furtherance of this goal, the Act enables any person or responsible body to bring an action against a person whose actions or omissions have had, or are likely to have, a significant impact on a forest; or to protect a forest (s. 5(2)).

88. Misc. Appl. No. 230 of 2001 (arising from Civ. Suit No. 69 of 2001).

the pendency of the main suit or until a lasting solution shall be provided by Government, whichever comes first.[89]

The application of the public trust doctrine was also considered in *Advocates Coalition for Development and Environment v. Attorney General and NEMA.*[90] The facts of this matter were as follows. The government had issued Kakira Sugar Works with a fifty year sugar cane growing permit in the Butamira Forest Reserve in contravention of the 1995 Constitution and a number of environmental laws. The government had also *de facto* de-gazetted the Butamira Forest Reserve notwithstanding protest by the local communities who depended on the reserve for their livelihood. No project brief, EIA or environmental impact statement had been undertaken by, or submitted to, the respondents as required by law. The respondents had not even ordered Kakira Sugar Works to prepare and submit such documents and had entirely disregarded the local community's views and concerns throughout the approval process. The applicant, a coalition representing local communities in the area, sought a court order setting aside the grant of the permit to Kakira Sugar Works on the basis that it contravened provisions contained in the 1995 Constitution, *Land Act* and the NEA (specifically those relating to EIA). The applicant furthermore sought an order compelling the second respondent to restore or take such measures as statutorily required to restore the environment and preserve the ecological integrity of the Butamira Forest Reserve. Aweri Opio J held that:

> [The] Butamira Forest Reserve is land which [the] Government of Uganda holds in trust for the people of Uganda to be protected for the common good of the citizens. Government has no authority to lease out or otherwise alienate it. However, Government or a local government may grant concessions or licenses or permits in respect of land held under trust with authority from parliament and with consent from the local community in the area or district where the reserved land is situated. In the instant case there was evidence that the permit was granted to Kakira Sugar Works amidst protests from local communities which raised a pressure group of over 1500 members who depended on the reserve for their livelihood through agro-forestry, and source of water, fuel and other forms of sustenance. There was therefore breach of [the] public Trust doctrine. . . . [The] Butamira permit if it was ever granted at all was null and void by the fact that no project brief and Environmental Impact Assessment were ever carried out as required by the law. The aliena-tion of the Reserve could only be done with due consultation of the local community and the relevant district as provided by the law. If the project is very vital for the development of the nation, proper procedure outlined above should have been followed to put it in place. For the above reasons I find that the applicants are entitled to all the orders sought above except the restoration

---

89. *Ibid.*, 5.
90. Misc. C. No. 0100 of 2004.

orders against the respondents. Such orders are only relevant to the party who is guilty of the environmental damage.[91]

6.5 THE PRECAUTIONARY PRINCIPLE

The precautionary principle is one of the most important general environmental law principles for avoiding environmental damage and achieving sustainable development. As enunciated in the Rio Declaration,[92] the precautionary principle states that where there are threats of serious or irreversible damage, lack of full scientific certainty shall not be used as a reason for postponing cost-effective measures to prevent environmental degradation.

The precautionary principle was expressly considered in *Uganda Electricity Transmission Co. Ltd v. De Samaline Incorporation Ltd.*[93] This case arose as a result of dust emanating from the respondent's premises which caused damage to the applicant. The NEMA was called upon to prepare a report on the situation. It found that the discharge of dust significantly exceeded the statutorily prescribed levels. The judge stated that when a person complains that his or her right to a clean and healthy environment has been violated, he or she does not necessarily need medical evidence to prove his or her case. All that is required is proof of degradation or threats of degradation. The NEMA's report satisfied such proof and therefore the respondent was found liable. Applying the precautionary principle, the judge stated:

> The precautionary principle is premised on the notion that it is not always possible to predict with scientific precision the probable impact of activities, processes, technologies or chemicals on the environment. Therefore if preventive and corrective measures were to be based only on the availability of hard and fast scientific evidence, substantial and or irreversible damage would be occasioned before such evidence would be available. Therefore the precautionary principle stipulates that preventive action should be taken notwithstanding the lack of full scientific certainty about the environmental consequences.[94]

6.6 ACCESS TO INFORMATION

Complete, accurate and current information is considered to be at the heart of sound environmental protection and sustainable development, especially as regards the decision-making process.[95] Access to information enables citizens

---

91. *Ibid.*, 8.
92. 31 *ILM* 874, Principle 15.
93. Misc. C. No. 181 of 2004.
94. *Ibid.*, 6.
95. R. Mwebaza, 'Access to Information, Public Participation and Justice in Environmental Decision Making in Uganda', *E. Afr. JPHR* 9 (2003): 37-86; G. Tumushabe, 'Towards

to participate meaningfully in decisions that directly affect their livelihoods, and enables them to monitor public and private sector activities. The nature of environmental degradation is such that its causes and impacts may often only be understood or become visible long after the damage-causing project or activity is complete. Consequently, there is a need for early and comprehensive access to relevant data to enable those concerned to make informed decisions. Access to information is also critical for holding governments accountable for their omissions or actions that prove deleterious to the environment.

Pursuant to Article 41(2) of the 1995 Constitution, parliament passed the *Access to Information Act*,[96] which provides for the right to access to information and sets out the procedure for obtaining such information.[97] In addition, the NEA guarantees 'freedom of access to any information relating to the implementation of this Act submitted to NEMA or to a lead agency'.[98] However, a person who desires to access this information must pay a prescribed fee,[99] and the NEA exempts 'proprietary information which shall be treated as confidential'.[100]

In *Greenwatch (U) Ltd v. Attorney General & Uganda Electricity Transmission Co. Ltd*,[101] the applicant sought to obtain a copy of a Power Purchase Agreement (PPA) from the government. The government had entered into an Implementation Agreement (IA) with AES Nile Power Ltd, covering the building, operation and transfer of a hydroelectric power complex. As a result of the conclusion of the IA, AES Nile Power Ltd and the Uganda Electricity Board (a statutory corporation) executed a PPA. The applicant requested a copy of the PPA but its request was declined. The applicant accordingly approached the court for an order directing the disclosure of the PPA. The respondents raised three defences in court. First, they argued that the PPA was a confidential document which included the sponsor's technical and commercial confidential information. Second, the first respondent argued that the PPA was not a public document within the meaning of the *Evidence Act*,[102] and since the second respondent was not an organ of State, it was not obliged to release the information. Third, they argued that according to Article 41 of the 1995 Constitution, only citizens were entitled to have access to information held by the government or its agents or organs; the applicant was not a natural person and could therefore not invoke Article 41.

    Environmental Accountability: Freedom of Access to Information Legislation for Uganda', in *Handbook on Environmental Law in Uganda*, ed. Greenwatch Environmental Law Institute (Kampala: GELI, 2004), 163, R.A. Wabunoha (ed.), *Handbook on Environmental Law in Uganda*. 2nd ed. (Kampala: GELI, 2005), <www.greenwatch.or.ug/pdf/news/HandBook_on_Environmental_Law_VolI_Sept05.pdf>, 2 September 2008.

  96. Act 6 of 2005.
  97. *Ibid.*, s. 5.
  98. NEA, s. 85(1).
  99. *Ibid.*, s. 85(2).
100. *Ibid.*, s. 85(3).
101. HCCT-00-CV-MC-0139 of 2001.
102. Cap. 6 *Laws of Uganda* 2000.

The court held that since the Minister of Energy, acting on behalf of the government, had signed the IA, it was a public document. The judge noted that the PPA relating to the IA, was in possession of the government, and accordingly amounted to information in possession of the government. As to the question whether a corporate body is a citizen for purposes of access to information, the court held that corporate bodies could enforce rights under the 1995 Constitution as they are persons in law, though not natural persons. However, the judge refused to grant the order as the applicant had not supplied sufficient evidence as to its membership to enable the court to determine whether it was a citizen for purposes of invoking Article 41.

6.7   GRANT OF APPROPRIATE REMEDIES

The grant of an appropriate remedy is an essential element of litigation. The remedies that are usually granted in environmental matters include: injunctions (interlocutory or permanent); declarations; damage orders; and judicial review. Courts have in a number of cases granted such remedies in environmental matters.[103] This is not, however, always the case, and the Ugandan courts have shown a reluctance to grant substantive and effective orders in various environmental matters.

In *Greenwatch and Advocates Coalition for Development and Environment v. Golf Course Holdings Ltd*,[104] the applicant sought an interlocutory injunction against the respondent, prohibiting it from building a hotel on certain plots owned by the respondent in Kampala. The applicant claimed that the construction of the hotel would cause environmental degradation as the proposed site was situated on a wetland and green belt. Akiiki Kiiza J declined to issue the interlocutory injunction on the basis that it could not be issued against a landowner who held a certificate of title; as this would amount to violating the provisions of the *Registration of Titles Act* relating to indefeasibility of title. The court stated that:

> It was held in the case of *David Bakirirahakye v. A.G. and 7 Others*. H.C.C.S. NO. MMB 14/90 (MBARARA REGISTRY) per Karokora J, as he then was, that granting an interim (temporary injunction) to restrain a respondent from using the land to which he has a certificate of title, which in law is conclusive evidence of ownership, when no fraud has been proved, would be tantamount to contravening the provisions of S. 184 of R.T.A. I entirely agree with the learned judge. This is more so in this case, where the applicants/plaintiffs are not claiming any proprietary interest at all, in the plot on which the construction is taking place. Their interest is stated to be in public of nature. I am aware that the NEMA Statute gives them the right to sue but in my view this does not

---

103. B.K. Twinomugisha, 'Some Reflections on Judicial Protection of the Right to a Clean and Healthy Environment in Uganda', *LEAD* (2007): 244, <www.lead-journal.org/content/07244.pdf>, 26 June 2008.
104. HC Misc. Appl. No. 390 of 2001.

diminish the fact that the suit property belongs to the respondents and in absence of fraud, their title can not be impeached![105]

The judge's reasoning is to be questioned as he appears to have failed to apply his mind to particularly section 43 of the *Land Act*, which provides that the use of land must comply with all relevant laws, including the environmental laws of Uganda, irrespective of whether one is dealing with private or public land. Moreover, the principle of indefeasibility admits, as an exception, overriding statutory provisions. The judge was hesitant to grant an appropriate remedy to protect the environmental interest, and went on to state that:

> As to whether the applicants will suffer irreparable damage, which would not be adequately compensated by way of damages, I do not see how the applicants are likely to suffer any irreparable damage. As I have already said, they don't have any proprietary interest in the suit property. What they appear to be claiming is that, the respondents are using their property wrongly. That they should not use it for something else. They claim further that the construction of the hotel now going on is contrary to public interest, as the area is a wetland and a green area. On the other hand, the respondents are maintaining that both the controlling authority (KCC) and the regulatory authority (NEMA) gave a go ahead after carrying out [an] impact assessment. In my view, these public bodies are in place to ensure that the provisions of the NEMA statute are complied with and hence they take care of the public interest the applicants are claiming to protect. It is in my view that there is no irreparable damage to be suffered by the applicants or for that matter the public whose interest they claim to represent. Even if the damage is caused, this could be put right under the provisions of s. 68 of the NEMA statute. This section provides for restoration. This restoration would be definitely at the respondents' expense. All in all I find that the applicants have failed to prove irreparable damage which can not be adequately compensated in damages.[106]

Three further issues emerge from this statement. First, as regards 'irreparable damage', the judge took the position that the applicant could not suffer irreparable damage because the land belonged to the respondent. The judge appears to have failed to understand the nature of environmental damage and the fact that the applicant was seeking to protect the broader environmental interest, not its own personal interest. To restrict the notion of irreparable damage to proprietary interests in land would effectively undermine all interlocutory injunctions sought by public interest organizations in the environmental interest. The judge also appears to have failed to understand and apply the common principle that although a person has a right to use his property, he or she should not use it in such a way as to injure his or her neighbors.

---

105. *Ibid.*, 4.
106. *Ibid.*, 5.

Second, the judge declined to grant the remedy prayed for on the ground that the NEMA had given a go-ahead to the project after considering an EIA. Although the NEA effectively precludes judicial review of the NEMA's decisions following an EIA process, this is not absolute.[107] The NEA itself acknowledges the residual jurisdiction of the High Court.[108] Furthermore, the EIA Regulations[109] provide that the grant of an EIA approval provides no defence to any civil or criminal action related to the approved development. The judge therefore appeared to err in his ruling that the NEMA's approval of the development precluded any subsequent civil or criminal action.

Third, the judge viewed the possibility of a subsequent environmental restoration order under the NEA[110] as a suitable alternative remedy. However, surely it would have been far more preferable and logical for the court to have halted the development at the outset, rather than letting it proceed and then having the environmental authorities seek to order the respondent to rehabilitate the site sometime in the future. Even if one were to accept the judge's reasoning that a future environmental restoration order would have been more appropriate in the circumstances than an interlocutory injunction, the judge appears to have failed to understand the nature of the remedy. Under section 67 of the NEA, environmental restoration orders can be issued both prospectively (preventing persons taking any action that may cause damage) and retrospectively (ordering persons to rehabilitate damage). In the former sense, they effectively operate as an injunction.

7   CHALLENGES FACING THE JUDICIARY IN ENVIRONMENTAL GOVERNANCE

7.1   POLITICAL INTERFERENCE

Although the judiciary has to some degree contributed to environmental governance in Uganda, its current and future role may be undermined by the country's current political climate. A clear example of this is the case of *Advocates Coalition for Development and Environment v. Attorney General and NEMA*[111] where, although the court effectively halted the clearing of portions of the Butamira Forest Reserve for agriculture, parliament, subsequent to the judgment, approved the clearing activity by granting a permit to Kakira Sugar Works Co. While it is

---

107. S. 104(a) of the NEA provides that where this Act empowers the NEMA or any of its organs to make a decision, the decision may be subject to appeal within the structure of the authority in accordance with such administrative procedures as may be established for the purpose, and the decision shall not be called into question by any court. From this section it can be deduced that the decision of the NEMA cannot be subject to judicial review.

108. S. 104(b) of the NEA provides that nothing in s. 104(a) impairs the High Court in the exercise of its supervisory jurisdiction, thereby affirming the supervisory jurisdiction on the High Court.

109. The Environmental Impact Assessment Regs SI No. 13 of 1998, Reg. 35(2).

110. S. 67(2)(a) of the NEA.

111. Misc. C. No. 0100 of 2004.

acknowledged that parliament has authority to review any land held in trust by the government under section 44 (5) of the *Land Act*,[112] these powers should be executed in a judicious manner. Where the judiciary has already ruled on a matter, it does not appear prudent or judicious for parliament to simply trump their ruling, thereby undermining the judiciary's authority. This does not bode well for the future role of the judiciary in environmental governance, especially where its rulings do not coincide with the government's development agenda.

7.2   CAPACITY CONSTRAINTS

The Ugandan judiciary is seeking to promote access to justice by increasing the number and geographical spread of High Courts. Their efforts are, however, currently being undermined by resource constraints. Although seven High Court circuit divisions have been created, with the exception of Mbale, all are manned by only a single judge. Given their jurisdictional areas, these circuit divisions should ideally be served by a minimum of two judges in order to be efficient; something which current resources do not allow.[113] This has caused significant delays in the hearing of matters in these circuit divisions.

7.3   INADEQUATE FINANCIAL RESOURCES

In additional to human resources, the majority of Uganda's courts lack financial resources to ensure that justice is efficiently administered. Key problems in this regard include resources to summon witnesses and recall circuit judges to rural stations to hear partially completed criminal and civil matters. The future does not appear favourable in this regard as the judiciary's budget has been drastically cut since 2005/2006.[114] As a result, funds are wholly inadequate to support both civil and criminal sessions, and this has reduced the court's case output and increased the frustration on the part of litigants and other stakeholders.

The resource crisis has been exacerbated by increasing the nominal allowance rates for public servants, without simultaneously increasing the monthly release of funds to the judiciary. The monthly cost to maintain a judge, driver and body guard at a non-resident court station, for example, has risen from Uganda Shs 3,510,000 (approximately US$ 2,193) to Uganda Shs 5,700,000 (approximately US$ 3,562). This figure does not include fuel, stationery and other facilities.[115] As a result, a number of planned sessions have had to be postponed or even terminated. This, in

---

112. Cap. 227 *Laws of Uganda* 2000.
113. Justice J. Ogoola, 'The Current State of Affairs in the High Court and the Role of Division Heads and Registrars', unpublished paper presented at the Judge's Conference (Kampala, 6 February 2006).
114. *Ibid.*
115. *Ibid.*

turn, has resulted in disillusionment among litigants. The problem is further compounded by the fact that backlog funding is only released on a quarterly basis upon satisfactory accountability and submission of accurate case returns. Many returns are often submitted late, not at all, and are frequently inaccurate, thereby precluding the timeous release of necessary funds.[116]

7.4	POOR CASE FLOW MANAGEMENT

Poor case flow management remains the leading cause of the courts' case backlog.[117] In the High Courts, for example, effective case flow management has been undermined by judges: not taking an active part in case management prior to hearings; granting unnecessary adjournments; failing to apply procedural rules; not keeping up to date on legislative procedural amendments; and not balancing work schedules between civil and criminal work. More time is spent on criminal cases as opposed to civil cases, causing significant delays in finalization of the latter matters. The Civil Procedure Rules[118] should ensure that civil matters are dealt with expediently. However, the courts have been reluctant to consistently apply these rules resulting in chronic backlogs.[119]

7.5	EXTRA-CURRICULA ACTIVITIES OF THE JUDICIARY

Perpetuating the human resource crises in the judiciary is the fact that many of Uganda's judges have taken on international assignments or are on sabbatical leave. Many others have taken leave to chair controversial and politically sensitive commissions of enquiry. Although these judges are no doubt the most suitable persons to lead these inquiries (given their integrity, impartiality, judicial skills of inquiry and public credibility) their continued absence from the formal judiciary undermines its functioning.

7.6	LACK OF MOTIVATION

The motivation of judicial staff is extremely low due to: poor remuneration; inadequate court facilities; the absence of adequate administrative, public and political support; and public and executive criticism of the judiciary, not forgetting the infamous siege of the High Court by the 'Black Mambas' in 2006.[120] This has led

---

116. *Ibid.*
117. *Ibid.*
118. The Republic of Uganda Civil Procedure Rules Statutory Instrument 71-1. See, e.g., Order 9 r.r 14 and 19; Order 15 r.r 1(i) (b) and 16; Order 10; and Order 10B.
119. Ogoola, *supra* n. 113.
120. In November 2005 there was a siege on the High Court of Uganda in Kampala by the army's 'Black Mamba' anti-terrorism unit that prevented the release on bail of twenty-two suspected

to a substantial decrease in productivity and job satisfaction amongst members of the judiciary; and an associated increase in tardiness, grievances, absenteeism, and case backlogs.

7.7   Reliance on Technicalities and Limited Judicial Activism

Effective environmental governance requires a well-informed judiciary that responds actively and positively to public concerns about environmental issues. As was illustrated in the discussion of *Greenwatch and Advocates Coalition for Development and Environment v. Golf Course Holdings Ltd*[121] above, various members of the judiciary do not have a clear understanding of Uganda's environmental law framework which significantly undermines their potential role in environmental governance.

   Furthermore, the Ugandan judiciary does not appear to have yet fully understood its broader role in the environmental governance effort. All too frequently, it relies on procedural technicalities to dismiss environmental matters rather than delving deeper into the substantive issue underlying them. A good example of this is the case of *Byabazaire v. Mukwano Industries*[122] in which the court strictly applied section 3 of the NEA to deny the applicant *locus standi* on the basis that this section reserved the right to prosecute an environmental offender for the NEMA or Local Environment Committees. Whilst this does appear to be a correct interpretation of the law, the court failed to proactively consider other sections of the law, specifically section 71, which would have granted the applicant *locus standi* in the proceedings.

7.8   High Cost of Litigation

One of the major barriers to environmental justice is the cost of legal action. Individuals or organizations may be reluctant to bring environmental matters to court for fear of being lumped with a large cost order if they do not succeed in their action. A further financial impediment relates to the potential of having to file security for costs prior to bringing the action. In *Greenwatch and Advocates Coalition for Development and Environment v. Golf Course Holdings Ltd*,[123] for example, the court ordered the applicant to pay Uganda Shs 50,000,000 as security

---

rebels including Besigye, who was the leading opposition candidate running against President Yoweri Museveni in the February 2006 election. The security forces surrounded the High Court to intimidate the judges and thwart their decision to release the men on bail. See Human Rights Watch, 'Uganda: Government Gunmen Storm High Court Again – Security Forces Used to Intimidate Judiciary in Case of "PRA Suspects" ', <hrw.org/english/docs/2007/03/05/uganda15449.htm>, 21 September 2008.
121. *Supra* n. 104.
122. Misc. Appl. No. 909 of 2000.
123. *Supra* n. 104.

for costs prior to the matter being heard. These financial realities significantly impact on access to environmental justice in Uganda, especially by the poor, indigent and disadvantaged members of society.

8   CONCLUSION AND THE WAY FORWARD

It is evident from the analysis of the judgments above that the Ugandan judiciary has played a significant role in environmental governance through interpreting the country's environmental laws and giving effect to the principles, standards and rights contained therein. The relaxation of *locus standi* following the implementation of the 1995 Constitution and the NEA has significantly facilitated and encouraged the role of the judiciary in this regard. As has been further observed above, however, the Ugandan judiciary faces a number of challenges in administering justice in Uganda, including environmental justice. The remainder of this section sets out proposals for addressing some of the challenges discussed above.

First, the jurisdiction of the courts in respect of applications under Article 50 of the 1995 Constitution could be extended to Magistrates' Courts.[124] Given that the High Court has unlimited jurisdiction, it is always flooded with cases which leads to a delay in the administration of justice. Environmental matters could, for instance, be settled by a Chief Magistrate who, in any event, can award similar relief to a High Court judge. Extending the jurisdiction of the Magistrates' Courts may speed up the administration of justice.

Second, the judiciary should be more flexible in their interpretation of the law in matters of public importance. Take for instance the approach adopted by the court in the *Byabazaire's* case[125] which potentially undermines future environmental litigation. A more flexible interpretation of the relevant enabling provisions could have enabled the court to hear the application.

Third, the government should increase its funding to the judiciary. These funds are essential for recruiting additional judicial officers, holding sessions, improving facilities, enhancing administration and increasing the salaries of judicial officers. The latter will, in turn, potentially improve the motivation of judicial officers, improve service delivery and increase access to environmental justice.

Fourth, in cases where it is clear to the court that the applicant is acting *bona fide* out of an interest for the environment, the judiciary should exercise its discretion and not compel such litigants to file bonds of security and pay the statutory court fees. These economic hurdles undermine litigation in the environmental interest, and should accordingly be removed.

---

124. Art. 50 (1) provides that a person who claims that a constitutional right has been violated can apply to *a competent court* for redress (emphasis added). Under the Fundamental Human Rights (Enforcement Procedure) Rules SI No. 26 of 1992, applications for human right's violations (including the right to clean and healthy environment) must be made to the High Court. The High Court therefore is the competent court in respect of human rights applications.
125. *Supra* n. 122.

However, even were these changes to be made, a failure by the executive to consistently support and respect the decisions of the judiciary, will not only undermine democracy in Uganda, but also the key role of the courts in environmental governance.

BIBLIOGRAPHY

Human Rights Watch. 'Uganda: Government Gunmen Storm High Court Again – Security Forces Used to Intimidate Judiciary in Case of "PRA Suspects" '. <hrw.org/english/docs/2007/03/05/uganda15449.htm>, 21 September 2008.

Kamugisha, J.R. *Management of Natural Resources in Uganda: Policy and Legislation Land Marks, 1890-1990*. Nairobi: Swedish Industrial Development Agency Regional Soil Conservation Unit, 1993.

Kaniaru, D., L. Kurukulasuriya & C. Okidi. 'The Role of the Judiciary in Promoting Sustainable Development'. Paper presented to the Fifth International Conference on Environmental Compliance and Enforcement. Monterey California: ICECE, 1998.

Mwebaza, R. 'Access to Information, Public Participation and Justice in Environmental Decision Making in Uganda'. *East African Journal of Peace and Human Rights* 9 (2003): 37-86.

Ogoola, J. 'The Current State of Affairs in the High Court and the Role of Division Heads and Registrars'. Unpublished paper presented at the Judge's Conference. Kampala, 6 February 2006.

Oloka Onyango, J. Judicial Power and Constitutionalism in Uganda: Working Paper No. 3. Kampala: Centre for Basic Research, 1993.

Preston, B.J. Hon, J. 'The Role of the Judiciary in Promoting Sustainable Development: The Experience of Asia and the Pacific'. Paper Presented to the Second Kenya National Judicial Colloquium on Environmental Law. Mombasa, 17-22 April 2006.

Republic of Uganda. *The National Environment Management Policy*. Kampala: Ministry of Natural Resources, 1994.

Republic of Uganda Courts of Judicature. 'Mission, Objectives and Values'. <www.judicature.go.ug/mission.php>, 14 September 2007.

Republic of Uganda Ministry of Water Lands and Environment. *The National Environment Action Plan for Uganda*. Kampala: MWLE, 1994.

Tumushabe, G. 'Towards Environmental Accountability: Freedom of Access to Information Legislation for Uganda'. In *Handbook on Environmental Law in Uganda*, edited by Greenwatch Environmental Law Institute. Kampala: GELI, 2004.

Twinomugisha, B.K. 'Some Reflections on Judicial Protection of the Right to a Clean and Healthy Environment in Uganda'. *Law Environment and Development Journal* (2007). <www.lead-journal.org/content/07244.pdf>, 26 June 2008.

USLC. 'The Library of Congress Country Studies: The Geography of Uganda'. <lcweb2.loc.gov/frd/cs/>, 21 September 2008.

Visiting Uganda. 'The Essential Guide to Uganda'. <www.visiting-uganda.com>, 21 September 2008.

Wabunoha, R.A., (ed.). *Handbook on Environmental Law in Uganda*. 2nd ed. Kampala: GELI, 2005. <www.greenwatch.or.ug/pdf/news/HandBook_on_Environmental_Law_VolI_Sept05.pdf>, 2 September 2008.

TABLE OF LEGISLATION

Constitution of the Republic of Uganda 1995
Environmental Impact Assessment Regulations SI No. 13 of 1998
Evidence Act Cap. 6 *Laws of Uganda* 2000
Fish Act Cap. 197 *Laws of Uganda* 2000
Fundamental Rights and Freedoms (Enforcement Procedure) Rules SI No. 26 of 1992
Judicature Act Cap. 13 *Laws of Uganda* 2000
Land Act Cap. 227 *Laws of Uganda* 2000
Laws of Uganda 1964
Magistrates Courts Act Cap. 16 *Laws of Uganda* 2000
National Environment (Standards for Discharge of Effluent into Water or on Land) Regulations SI No. 5 of 1999
National Environment Act Cap. 153 *Laws of Uganda* 2000
National Forestry and Tree Planting Act 8 of 2003
Prohibition of the Burning of Grass Act Cap. 33 *Laws of Uganda* 2000
Uganda Peoples' Defence Forces Act Cap. 307 *Laws of Uganda* 2000
Uganda Wildlife Act Cap. 200 *Laws of Uganda* 2000
Water (Waste Discharge) Regulations SI No. 32 of 1998
Water Act Cap. 152 *Laws of Uganda* 2000
Water Resources Regulations SI No. 33 of 1998

TABLE OF CASES

Advocates Coalition for Development and Environment v. Attorney General and National Environmental Management Authority Misc. C. No. 0100 of 2004 (High Court of Uganda)
Byabazaire v. Mukwano Industries Misc. Appl. No. 909 of 2000
David Bakirirahakye v. AG and 7 Others High Court Civ. Suit 14 of 1990
Dr Bwogi Richard Kanyerezi v. The Management Committee of Rubaga Girls School Civ. Appeal No. 3 of 1996
Environmental Action Network v. British American Tobacco High Court Civ. Suit No. 27 of 2003

Greenwatch (U) Ltd v. Attorney General & Uganda Electricity Transmission Co. Ltd HCCT-00-CV-MC-0139 of 2001
Greenwatch and Advocates Coalition for Development and Environment v. Golf Course Holdings Ltd High Court Misc. Appl. No. 390 of 2001
Mtikila v. Attorney General Civ. Suit No. 5 of 1993 (High Court of Tanzania)
National Association of Professional Environmentalists v. AES Nile Power (Ltd) Misc. C. No. 60 of 1999
Seezi Huiya Munghereza and 11 Others v. Kampala City Council High Court Civ. Suit No. 609 of 1997
Siraji Waiswa v. Kakira Sugar Works Ltd Misc. Appl. No. 230 of 2001
The Environmental Action Network (Ltd) v. Attorney General and National Environment Management Authority High Court Misc. Appl. No. 39 of 2001
Uganda Electricity Transmission Co. Ltd v. De Samaline Incorporation Ltd Misc. C. No. 181 of 2004

TABLE OF INTERNATIONAL INSTRUMENTS

Rio Declaration on Environment and Development 31 *ILM* 874
Buganda Agreement 1900
Toro Agreement 1900
Ankole Agreement 1901
Bunyoro Agreement 1933

ABBREVIATIONS

CBR	Centre for Basic Research
EIA	Environmental Impact Assessment
GELI	Greenwatch Environmental Law Institute
IA	Implementation Agreement
MWLE	Ministry of Water Lands and Environment
NEA	National Environment Act
NEAP	National Environment Action Plan
NEMA	National Environment Management Authority
NEMP	National Environment Management Policy
PPA	Power Purchase Agreement
UEB	Uganda Electricity Board
USLC	United States Library of Congress
UWA	Uganda Wildlife Act

Chapter 16

Tanzania

Palamagamba John Kabudi

1   INTRODUCTION

The courts and society at large are increasingly appreciating the role of the judiciary
in enhancing and guaranteeing environmental protection. Globally, the contribution
of the judiciary appears to be shifting from being purely reactive adjudicative bodies
trying environmental offences and hearing civil environmental disputes, to more
proactive institutions playing an active role in environmental governance through:
defining the bounds of just administrative environmental action; incorporating
international environmental principles within their jurisprudence; interpreting and
remedying anomalies in contemporary environmental laws; moulding common law
torts to suit environmental contexts; and shaping the common law rules of *locus
standi* to facilitate increased access to environmental justice. A further key role
played by the judiciary in many commonwealth jurisdictions, including India and
Tanzania for example,[1] is in articulating, developing and promoting citizens' rights
to a clean and healthy environment. This has either transpired through interpreting
the express environmental provision contained in their constitutions or through

---

1. See E.O. Awuku, 'The Right to Clean Environment: Lessons from India and Tanzania',
   Verfassung und Recht in Uebersee 27 (1994): 16.

Louis J. Kotzé and Alexander R. Paterson (eds), *The Role of the Judiciary in
Environmental Governance: Comparative Perspectives*, pp. 505–526.
© 2009 Kluwer Law International BV, The Netherlands.

adopting creative interpretations of analogous rights, such as the right to life, and directive principles of state environmental policy.[2]

It has been argued by some scholars that for the judiciary to contribute positively to environmental rights jurisprudence, clear strategies must be formulated to guide them in fulfilling this role.[3] There are those who opine that non-litigious forms of dispute resolution, such as mediation, reconciliation and arbitration, should also be used to resolve environmental rights issues and that litigation should be a measure of last resort.[4] It must be remembered, however, that the courts do not only play an adjudicative role, but also an educative role[5] in their articulation and development of jurisprudence in different fields, including environmental rights. Their educative role is vast when account is taken of the so-called 'radiating effects of courts' as explained by Galanter[6] in his treatise on the theory of courts and the process of litigation. The impact of a court decision can extend well beyond the doctrine of precedent and impact not only on the specific litigants, but also on broader society.[7] However, as cautioned by Gutto,[8] the usefulness of this 'radiating role' depends on the legitimacy of the interests involved in the matter before the court, the level of publicity surrounding the matter and its relevance to the community.

2   BACKGROUND

The United Republic of Tanzania is the largest country in Eastern Africa, with a total area of 945,087 km^2 comprising of: 883,749 km^2 of land (881,289 km^2 mainland and 2,460 km^2 Zanzibar Island) and 59,050 km^2 of inland water bodies.[9] It shares borders with eight countries, namely: Kenya and Uganda in the north; Rwanda, Burundi and Democratic Republic of Congo in the east; Zambia and Malawi in the south west; and Mozambique in the south. Mainland Tanzania borders the main water bodies of Africa: to the east is the Indian Ocean; to the north, Lake Victoria; to the west, Lake Tanganyika; and to the south-west, Lake Nyasa. Mainland Tanzania also has the highest point in Africa, the snow capped Mount Kilimanjaro standing 5,895 m high.[10]

---

2. See A. Rosencranz, S. Divan & M.L. Noble (eds), *Law and Policy in India: Cases, Materials and Statutes* (Delhi: Tripathi, 1995).

3. S.B.O. Gutto, 'Environmental Rights Litigation, Human Rights and the Role of Non-Governmental and Peoples' Organisations in Africa', *SAJELP* 1 (1995): 7.

4. *Ibid.*

5. See R.H. Kisanga, *A Critical Assessment of the Adjudicatory and Educative Role of the Court of Appeal as the Highest Judicial Organ in Tanzania* (mimeo) (Dar es Salaam: UDS Faculty of Law, 1985).

6. See M. Galanter, 'The Radiating Effects of the Courts', in *Empirical Theories about Courts*, ed. K.O. Boyum & Mather, L. (New York: Longmans, 1983), 117-142.

7. Gutto, *supra* n. 3, 7-8.

8. *Ibid.*

9. A.M. Kabudi, *The Development and Provision of Scientific and Technical Information Services in Tanzania* (Berlin: Koester, 1997), 8.

10. P. Johnson-Hicks, *Tanzania: A Portrait of a Nation* (London: Quiller Press, 1998), 26.

Tanzania shares large important ecosystems with its neighbours which straddle national boundaries such as: Lake Victoria with Kenya and Uganda; Lake Tanganyika with Burundi, the Democratic Republic of Congo and Zambia; Lake Nyasa with Malawi and Mozambique; and the Nile Basin with nine other countries. These transboundary ecosystems pose significant governance challenges and require Tanzania and its neighbours to establish a range of protocols, agreements and mechanisms to ensure their conservation, sustainable use and the equitable sharing of benefits derived from such use. Several of these transboundary resources are currently subject to such regional instruments and mechanisms.[11]

The people of Tanzania, who constitute a peaceful, politically stable and vibrant democracy in Africa, are drawn from more than 120 major ethnic groups with varying cultures, languages and dialects. If the sub-ethnic groups are included in the equation, the figure grows to over 150 different groups. The majority of these groups are composed of Bantu speaking people but there are also Cushites and Nilotic speaking ethnic groups and a few thousand Khoisan people. Furthermore, there are many Tanzanians of Asian, Arabian and European origins. As a result, Tanzania is one of the least culturally homogeneous nations with an estimated 7% homogeneity.[12]

Tanzania has in the past forty-five years of independence, notwithstanding this heterogeneity, been able to forge a sense of nationhood and discard negative tendencies of tribalism that have plagued other African countries leading to internecine wars and genocide. The cultural and linguistic diversity of the Tanzanian people has blended a unique sense of togetherness and solidarity consolidated by the use of Kiswahili by almost all its people as the national language.[13] People of different races and religions live side by side without acrimony, respecting each other and cooperating in social events and activities. It is a taboo in Tanzania to use or exploit ethnicity or religion for political or public gain.[14] The above attributes have led to Tanzania becoming a haven of peace for many African asylum seekers. The influx of refugees has, however, resulted in significant stress on the country's environment, leading to catastrophic environmental degradation in certain areas.

Tanzania is a union of two former independent sovereign States; the Republic of Tanganyika and the People's Republic of Zanzibar. They united on 26 April 1964 to form one sovereign United Republic of Tanzania. The Articles of Union did not, however, expressly state what the nature of the new State was: a federation or unitary State.[15] The Court of Appeal of Tanzania in the case of *Machano Khamis*

---

11. See, e.g., the East African Community Protocol for Sustainable Development of Lake Victoria Basin 2003, see EAC, 'Lake Victoria Basin Commission', <www.eac.int/index.php/lvdc.html>, 21 September 2008.

12. Kabudi, *supra* n. 9, 12.

13. E. Broszinsky-Schwabe, *Kulture in Scwarzafrika* (Leipzig: Urania Verlag, 1982), 35.

14. C.K. Omari, 'The Management of Tribal and Religious Diversity', in *Mwalimu: The Influence of Nyerere*, ed. C. Legum & G.V. Mmari (London: James Currey, 1995), 23.

15. P.J. Kabudi, 'The Union of Tanganyika and Zanzibar: Examination of the Treaty of a Political Legal Union, MAWAZO', *JFASS* 6, no. 3 (1985): 11; *Id.*, 'The United Republic of Tanzania after a Quarter of a Century: A Legal Appraisal of the State of the Union of Tanganyika and Zanzibar', *AJICL* 5, no. 2 (1993): 310.

Ali and 18 Others v. Serikali ya Mapinduzi Zanzibar[16] ruled that Zanzibar is not a State, and sovereignty resides with the United Republic of Tanzania. However, taking into account the small population and size of Zanzibar compared to Mainland Tanzania, and to avoid Zanzibar being swallowed up or loosing its identity, Tanzania's relevant constitutions, discussed below, allow Zanzibar to retain semi-autonomy in respect of various matters.

The United Republic of Tanzania currently has two constitutions, creating two governments and effectively covering three jurisdictions within the country. The *Constitution of the United Republic of Tanzania* 1977 (Constitution), governs all Union matters and non-Union matters in relation to Mainland Tanzania (previously the Republic of Tanganyika). Article 4(2) of the Constitution provides for twenty-two union matters listed in the first schedule to the Constitution. In the list relating to the union, matters relevant to the environment include minerals and oil resources (incorporating crude oil and gas). Relevant items such as fisheries, wildlife, forestry and land use management are not union matters. The Constitution of Zanzibar 1984 governs all non-union matters as far as Zanzibar is concerned and creates the Revolutionary Government of Zanzibar.

The legal system is a non-union matter and therefore Mainland Tanzania and Zanzibar each has its own judiciary. In addition, Zanzibar has its own executive and legislature. External relations are union matters and therefore the competence to negotiate, sign and ratify treaties lies with the union government. However, when it comes to incorporating international instruments into domestic law, Zanzibar is competent to make laws governing all aspects that are designated in the Constitution as non-union matters such as forestry, fisheries and wildlife.

This chapter exclusively focuses on the environmental laws, policies and court decisions of Mainland Tanzania and not on Zanzibar, as to the knowledge of the author, there has not been a single environmental case brought before the latter's judiciary.[17]

3   ENVIRONMENTAL POLICIES AND CHALLENGES

Tanzania faces an array of environmental challenges, some of which are clearly outlined in policies and reports recently published by the government. Among these, one of the greatest is deforestation. It is estimated that about 70% of the original forest cover of Tanzania has been converted to settlements and agricultural land.[18] Tanzania is endowed with rich deposits of minerals which were for many years allowed to lie fallow. Since 1995, however, mining activities have gained momentum with the participation of big mining companies and small scale or

---

16. Court of Appeal of Tanzania, Crim. Appl. No. 8 of 2000 (unreported).
17. The *Environmental Management Act*, Cap. 191 of 2002, only applies to Mainland Tanzania. Zanzibar has enacted a comprehensive framework environmental law, the *Environmental Management for Sustainable Development Act* 2 of 1996 and the *Forest Resources Management and Conservation* Act 10 of 1998.
18. United Republic of Tanzania, State of the Environment Report 2007 (Dar es Salaam: VPO, 2007), 28.

artisanal miners. Mining activities by small-scale miners pose significant environmental challenges as this sector frequently does not have the resources to put in place comprehensive mitigation measures when compared with large mining companies. The discharge of mining effluent and raw sewage during the mining process frequently pollutes groundwater and surface water resources.[19]

In the post-independence political era of Tanzania (following the introduction of a one party State in 1965 until it was abolished in 1992, and the introduction of socialism in 1967 until it was quietly abandoned in 1989), the ruling party policies enjoyed prominence and legitimacy above executive decisions and were sometimes more respected than legislative enactments. For example, although Tanzania had no law providing for environmental impact assessment (EIA), these were conducted and reviewed because that was the directive of the government. The reintroduction of a multi-party government necessitated the need to replace previous party policies with national sectoral policies approved by cabinet and parliament.

The union government promulgated a number of framework and sectoral environmental policies in the 1990s. These policies guide State action at all governance levels in Tanzania. Tanzania's governance structure is very complex and fragmented along both the horizontal (different sectors of governance) and vertical (different levels of governance) plain. Effective environmental governance is therefore dependant on integrating and coordinating many different environmental actors, institutions and laws.

Tanzania introduced a National Environmental Policy[20] in 1997. This framework policy, aimed at facilitating the coordination and implementation of Tanzania's environmental regime, is complemented by an array of sectoral policies relating to forestry, wildlife and water.[21] The *Environmental Management Act* (EMA)[22] provides in section 9 that all persons exercising powers under the Act or any other written law that have a bearing on environmental management, must strive to promote and have regard to the National Environmental Policy. The express objectives of the policy include the following:

a) Developing consensual agreement at all levels of government for the challenge of making trade-offs and the right choices between immediate economic benefits to meet short term and urgent development needs, and long term sustainability benefits;

b) Developing a unifying set of principles and objectives for integrated multi-sectoral approaches necessary for addressing the totality of the environment;

c) Fostering government-wide commitment to the integration of environmental concerns in sectoral policies, strategies and investment decisions, and to

---

19. *Ibid.*, 83.
20. United Republic of Tanzania, National Environmental Policy (Dar es Salaam: VPO, 1997).
21. E.g., United Republic of Tanzania, National Forest Policy (Dar es Salaam: MNRT, 1998); *Id.*, Wildlife Policy of Tanzania (Dar es Salaam: MNRT, 1998); and *Id.*, National Water Policy (Dar es Salaam: MWI, 2002).
22. Cap. 191 of *Laws of Tanzania* rev. ed. 2002.

develop and use relevant policy instruments best suited for achieving this objective; and

d) Creating the context for planning and coordinating at a multi-sectoral level, to ensure a more systematic approach, focus and consistency; for the ever-increasing variety of players and intensity of environmental activities.[23]

As is evident from the above, a central tenet of the National Environmental Policy is the development and implementation of a holistic multi-sectoral approach to environmental governance, and ensuring that this approach filters down through sectoral policies, strategies and decisions. In this way, the policy seeks to create a context for cross-sectoral planning and coordination.[24] It articulates the concept of shared responsibility and distinct accountability for environmental management, so as to inculcate collective responsibility in environmental management without blurring specific mandates and responsibilities that have been assigned to each institution.[25] The National Environmental Policy is exceptionally broad in scope, and in the interest of integration, cross refers to many associated sectoral environmental policies covering agriculture, livestock, water and sanitation, health, transport, energy, mining, human settlement, industry, tourism, wildlife, forestry and fisheries.[26] Several of the sectoral policies in turn cross-refer back to the National Environmental Policy.[27] Cumulatively, the above provides Tanzania with a solid policy framework for ensuring that environmental management and sustainability issues are mainstreamed in all sectors of governance.

The above is essential given the many environmental challenges facing Tanzania. The National Environmental Policy contains a diagnosis of the state of Tanzania's environment and identifies the following six major environmental problems requiring urgent attention: land degradation; lack of accessible, good quality water for both urban and rural inhabitants; environmental pollution; loss of wildlife habitats and biodiversity; deteriorating aquatic systems; and deforestation.

---

23. National Environmental Policy, *supra* n. 20, 4.
24. *Ibid.*
25. *Ibid.*
26. *Ibid.*, para. 45-60.
27. National Forest Policy, *supra* n. 21, and United Republic of Tanzania, National Beekeeping Policy (Dar es Salaam: MNRT, 1998), cross refers to National Environmental Policy, *supra* n. 20, 4 and 5, respectively. The rest do not make cross-reference, and include: *Id.*, Agriculture and Livestock Policy (Dar es Salaam: Ministry of Agriculture and Food Security, 1997), *Id.*, National Health Policy (Dar es Salaam: Ministry of Health and Social Welfare, 1990), *Id.*, National Transport Policy (Dar es Salaam: Ministry of Communication and Transport, 2003), *Id.*, Energy Policy of Tanzania (Dar es Salaam: Ministry of Energy and Minerals, 2002), *Id.*, Mineral Policy of Tanzania (Dar es Salaam: Ministry of Energy and Minerals, 1998), *Id.*, National Human Settlements Development Policy (Dar es Salaam: Ministry of Lands, Human Settlements and Housing, 2000), *Id.*, Sustainable Industrial Policy (Dar es Salaam: Ministry of Industry and Trade, 1996), *Id.*, National Tourism Policy (Dar es Salaam: MNRT, 1999), and *Id.*, National Fisheries Sectoral Policy and Strategy Statement (Dar es Salaam: MNRT, 1997).

These challenges require urgent attention and it is noteworthy that the National Environmental Policy outlines an array of broad objectives specifically aimed at overcoming these challenges. These include:

a) To ensure sustainability, security and equitable use of resources for meeting the basic needs of the present and future generations without degrading the environment or risking health or safety;
b) To prevent and control the degradation of land, water, vegetation, and air which constitute life support systems;
c) To conserve and enhance our natural and man made heritage, including the biological diversity of the unique ecosystems of Tanzania;
d) To improve the condition and productivity of degraded areas including rural and urban settlements in order that all Tanzanians may enjoy aesthetically pleasing surroundings;
e) To raise public awareness and understanding of the essential linkages between environment and development, and to promote individual and community participation in environmental action; and
f) To promote international cooperation on the environment agenda, and expand participation and contribution to relevant bilateral, sub-regional, regional, and global organizations and programs, including implementation of Treaties.

In order to achieve these environmental objectives, the National Environmental Policy identified the need for a new environmental law but stressed that in order for such a law to be effective it:

> must be understood and appreciated by the people to whom it is aimed. It is therefore stressed that other instruments like public education and public awareness are essential and complimentary policy instruments. Furthermore environmental standards and procedures have to be in place before or as a result of legislation for this instrument to be effective.[28]

These statements informed the content of Tanzania's framework environmental law, the EMA,[29] which was enacted in November 2004.

4   PRINCIPAL ENVIRONMENTAL LAWS

4.1   INTRODUCTION

The sources of environmental law in Tanzania include the Constitution, statute law, common law and customary law. Prior to discussing the above sources, it must be noted that the environment and its protection is not a union matter and therefore

---

28. National Environmental Policy, *supra* n. 20, para. 70.
29. Cap. 191 of *Laws of Tanzania* rev. ed. 2002.

both Mainland Tanzania and Zanzibar are competent to promulgate environmental laws governing their regions.

Neither the Constitution nor the Constitution of Zanzibar includes a right to a clean and safe environment. However, as will be illustrated below in the discussion of Tanzania's emerging environmental jurisprudence, the lack of such an express environmental right has not hampered the Tanzanian judiciary from inferring such a right through other entrenched constitutional rights. The Tanzanian judiciary has adopted a generous approach to the right to life,[30] interpreting it to include the right to live in a healthy environment.[31]

Although the Constitution and the Constitution of Zanzibar make no express provision for an environmental right, they both contain clauses dealing with the protection of natural resources. Article 27(1) of the Constitution stipulates that: 'Every person is obliged to safeguard and protect the natural resources of the United Republic, State property and all property jointly owned by the people, as well as to respect another person's property'.[32] The natural resources referred to in Article 27(1) include: forests; other biological resources; landscapes; lakes, rivers and other water bodies; land, soil and minerals; terrestrial wildlife; and fish. The protection of natural resources is further fortified by Article 27(2) of the Constitution which provides that:

> All persons shall be by law required to safeguard state and communal property, to combat all forms of misappropriation and wastage and to run the economy of the nation assiduously, with the attitude of people who are masters of their fate of their own nation.

These constitutional provisions are of key relevance to protecting the environment and are complemented by the Directive Principles of State Policy enshrined in the Constitution. These mandate the union government to ensure that the natural resources and heritage are harnessed, preserved and applied for the common good of all Tanzanians.[33] Furthermore, they require the union government and all its agencies to direct their policy and business towards securing the 'conduct of public affairs in a manner designed to ensure that the national resources and heritage are harnessed, preserved and applied toward the common good and the prevention of the exploitation of one man by another'.[34]

---

30. Art. 14 of the *Constitution of the United Republic of Tanzania* 1977 (Constitution) states that: 'Every person has the right to life and to the protection of his life by the society in accordance with law.'
31. See the cases of *Joseph D. Kessy and Others v. The City Council of Dar es Salaam*, HC of Tanzania, Civ. Case No. 299 of 1998 (unreported); and *Festo Balegele and 794 Others v. Dar es Salaam City Council*, HC of Tanzania, Misc. Civ. C. No. 90 of 1991 (unreported). The two decisions of the High Court of Tanzania are discussed in C.M. Peter, *Human Rights in Tanzania: Selected Cases and Materials* (Koeln: Ruediger Koeppe Verlag, 1997), 157-163. They are also commented on in Awuku, *supra* n. 1, 27.
32. The same is provided for under Art. 23(2) of the Constitution of Zanzibar.
33. Constitution, Art. 27 (2).
34. *Ibid.*, Art. 9(1)(c).

The Directive Principles of State Policy are not legally enforceable.[35] However, Article 7(1) of the Constitution compels all organs of State (the executive, legislature and judiciary) to take cognisance of, observe and apply these in their activities and decision-making. As a result, the Directive Principles of State Policy have played a significant role developing Tanzania's human rights and environmental jurisprudence.[36] This is comprehensively discussed later in this chapter, but what is relevant to note at this stage, is the proactive approach of the High Court and the Court of Appeal toward the application of these fundamental duties and directive principles in the promotion of environmental rights.[37] Notwithstanding this approach, the prescription of an express environmental right in the Constitution remains a future imperative.

In the interim, the provisions contained in Tanzania's EMA will have to suffice. It contains three very important provisions of general relevance to environmental governance. First, in the absence of a constitutional environmental right, the EMA prescribes that: 'Every person living in Tanzania shall have a right to [a] clean, safe and healthy environment'.[38] Second, the Act has expanded the application of *locus standi* in Tanzania and states that:

> An individual or legal persons may bring action and seek appropriate relief in respect of any breach, violation or threatened breach or violation of any provision of this Act or any use of article, substance or natural resources –
>
> a) in that individual's or legal persons own interest;
> b) in the interest or on behalf of a person who is, for practical reasons, unable to bring such action;
> c) in the interest of or on behalf of a group or class of person whose interest are affected;
> d) in the public interest; and
> e) in the interest of the environment or other habitats.[39]

Third, the EMA recognizes the role of the courts in enhancing sustainable environmental management and compels courts exercising jurisdiction under the Act to be guided by the following international environmental principles: precautionary principle; polluter pays principle; principle of ecosystem integrity; public participation in the development of policies, plans and processes for the management of the environment; access to justice; inter-generational equity and intra-generational equity; international co-operation in management of environmental

---

35. *Ibid.*, Art. 7(2).
36. P.J. Kabudi, 'The Directive Principles of State Policy in Tanzania', in *Human Rights, Constitutionalism and the Judiciary: Tanzanian and Irish Perspectives*, ed. W. Binchy & C. Finnegan (Dublin: Clarus Press, 2006), 37-38.
37. P.J. Kabudi, *Human Rights Jurisprudence in East Africa: A Comparative Study of Fundamental Rights and Freedoms of the Individual in Tanzania, Kenya and Uganda* (Baden-Baden: Nomos Verlag, 1995), 94-95.
38. EMA, s. 4(1).
39. *Ibid.*, s. 202.

resources shared by two or more States; and the principle of common but differentiated responsibilities.[40]

In undertaking the study of institutional arrangements for environmental management in Tanzania, a report prepared by the vice president's office, which is responsible for environmental management and coordination, identified two basic types of environmental management functions, namely: sectoral functions; and coordinating and supporting functions.[41]

4.2   SECTORAL ENVIRONMENTAL MANAGEMENT FUNCTIONS

These functions concern the management of specific natural resources or environmental services (such as agriculture, fisheries, mining and waste management) and are to a large extent directly operational and regulated by laws such as the *Forest Act*;[42] *Fisheries Act*;[43] *Wildlife Conservation Act*;[44] and *Mining Act*.[45]

Most of the sectoral laws aimed at regulating the use and management of natural resources, are based on the command and control or 'fences and fines' approach. However, more contemporary environmental laws have shifted from solely depending on the above approach and have included other environmental management instruments such as EIA, general management plans (GMPs) and pollution control plans. Laws that include environmental management instruments of this nature include the *Marine Parks and Reserves Act*;[46] *Beekeeping Act*,[47] *Industrial and Consumer Chemicals (Management and Control) Act*,[48] *Mining Act, Forest Act* and *Fisheries Act*.

4.3   COORDINATING AND SUPPORTING ENVIRONMENTAL
             MANAGEMENT FUNCTIONS

Coordinating and supporting functions involve: facilitating coordination between the different, and sometimes conflicting, sectoral functions; integrating them into an overall sustainable system; and providing central support for them. They concern the overall organization and establishment of a coherent general context for environmental management which the National Environmental Policy and the EMA aim to facilitate.

---

40. *Ibid.*, s. 5(3).
41. United Republic of Tanzania, Institutional and Legal Framework for Environmental Management Project Institutional Report (Dar es Salaam: VPO, 2000), 14.
42. Cap. 323 of 2002.
43. Cap. 279 of 2003.
44. Cap. 283 of 1974.
45. Cap. 123 of 1998.
46. Cap. 146 of 1994.
47. Cap. 224 of 2002.
48. Cap. 182 of 2003.

The EMA further aims to create a legal and institutional framework for ensuring the sustainable and coordinated management of the nation's environment and natural resources. The Act sets out the institutional roles, functions and responsibilities of various institutions ranging from the minister down to the village or street environmental management coordinator. The Act also includes a range of regulatory tools providing for EIA, strategic environmental assessment, pollution prevention and control, waste management, environmental quality standards, state of the environment reporting, enforcement, and the establishment of a national Environment Trust Fund.

5   THE COURT SYSTEM

Mainland Tanzania, although not previously a British colony, but rather a United Nation's Trusteeship Territory under British administration, adopted the English common law legal system. Prior to British administration, it constituted the Germany colony known as German East Africa (*Deutsch Ost-Afrika*). In the case of Zanzibar, it was a British protectorate under the Abusaidy Arab dynasty from Oman, and therefore also applied the English common law system. As has been mentioned above, following the union and independence of the Republic of Tanganyika and the People's Republic of Zanzibar in 1964, each part of the union retained a significant degree of autonomy, including its legal jurisdiction. Accordingly, both Mainland Tanzania and Zanzibar have their own High Court established under their respective constitutions,[49] and hierarchy of subordinate courts. Both high courts have unlimited civil and criminal jurisdiction, including environmental matters throughout the respective territories.[50] In order to fast track the hearing and disposition of commercial and land disputes, the High Court of Tanzania has established two specialized divisions. These are the Commercial Division and the Land Division of the High Court.

Although administration of justice is not a union matter, the Court of Appeal of the United Republic of Tanzania is a union matter; and accordingly, this court is the final appellate court for the whole of Tanzania with jurisdiction to hear appeals on all matters heard in the High Court of Mainland Tanzania and Zanzibar.[51]

---

49. Art. 108 of the Constitution establishes the High Court of Tanzania as the highest court of record on Mainland Tanzania with appeals lying to the Court of Appeal of Tanzania. Art. 114 of the Constitution expressly recognizes the High Court of Zanzibar. Art. 93(1) of the Constitution of Zanzibar establishes the High Court of Zanzibar as the highest court of record on Zanzibar with appeals lying to the Court of Appeal of Tanzania. Judicial powers of the High Court of Zanzibar are further elaborated in the *High Court Act* 2 of 1985.
50. *Jina Khatibu Haji v. Juma Selemani Nungu*, Court of Appeal of Tanzania, Civ. Appl No. 23 of 1986 (unreported).
51. The Court of Appeal is established under Art. 117(1) of the Constitution. Art. 117(3) confers on the Court of Appeal jurisdiction to hear and determine every appeal brought before it arising from the High Court or of a subordinate court with extended jurisdiction. However, the Constitution explicitly stipulates that the Court of Appeal of Tanzania has no jurisdiction in

The High Court of Tanzania enjoys original unlimited jurisdiction in all matters, including the environment. It also hears appeals from a three-tiered court system which exists under the High Court on Mainland Tanzania, comprising of Resident Magistrates' Courts, District Courts and Primary Courts in descending order. All three of these courts are established under the *Magistrates' Court Act*.[52] Resident Magistrates' Courts are on par with District Courts, the difference being that the former are headed by holders of a LLB degree. The District and Resident Magistrates' Courts have jurisdiction to hear cases dealing with environmental matters. Primary Courts are run by lay magistrates who are not in a position to handle complex and intricate cases. It is accordingly difficult to file an environmental case in these courts. However, where the matter involves a breach of a village by-law dealing with the environment,[53] it is the Primary Court which will be the appropriate court to deal with the matter.[54]

In the case of Zanzibar, the subordinate court structure to the High Court is very similar to that on Mainland Tanzania and includes: Magistrates' Courts; Primary Courts; and the Kadhi's Court. The latter court, established under the *Kadhi's Court Act*,[55] has jurisdiction to hear private civil suits dealing with issues such as marriage and divorce under Islamic law, where both parties are Muslim. It is accordingly unlikely that Zanzibar's Kadhi's Court will ever handle environmental matters.

6   ANALYSIS OF SIGNIFICANT ENVIRONMENTAL
              JUDGMENTS

6.1   INTRODUCTION

The commencement of the EMA in 2005 held significant potential for increasing the role of the judiciary in environmental governance by including an environmental right, extending *locus standi* to bring environmental matters before the court, and laying out a set of environmental principles which must guide judicial interpretation. However, despite being on the statute books for three years, the judiciary has not been afforded an opportunity to consider these innovative provisions. This is as a result of the fact that most recent incidents of environmental pollution have been handled by the National Environment Management Council,

---

      any dispute between the government of the United Republic and the Revolutionary Government
      of Zanzibar. Such disputes under the Constitution are referred to the Special Court established
      under Art. 125 of the Constitution when the need arises. For a discussion of the jurisdiction of
      the Court of Appeal see further G.M. Fimbo, 'The Court of Appeal of the United Republic of
      Tanzania: A Descriptive Essay', *EALR* 16, no. 2 (1989): 229.
52.   Ss 3, 4 and 5 of the *Magistrates' Court Act*, Cap. 11 enacted as Act 2 of 1984.
53.   Village by-laws are made by the Village Council by powers given under s. 163 the Local
      Government (District Authorities) Act, Cap. 287 of 1982.
54.   Constitution, Art. 108.
55.   Act 3 of 1985.

the institution responsible for enforcing the Act, using administrative measures such as compliance cessation orders, rather than referring these matters to court.

Prior to the introduction of the EMA, the judiciary had to be far more ingenious when environmental matters were brought before it, especially owing to the absence of a constitutionally guaranteed environmental right and the common law limitations on *locus standi*. This jurisprudence is considered below.

6.2   THE RIGHT TO LIFE AND THE ENVIRONMENT

The Tanzanian judiciary has adopted a very liberal and generous approach to interpreting the provisions of the Constitution. In the case of *Julius Ishengoma Ndyanabo v. The Attorney General*,[56] the Court of Appeal listed principles that should be applied in interpreting the Constitution. It pointed out that the Constitution is:

> a living instrument, having a soul and consciousness of its own as reflected in the Preamble and Fundamental Objectives and Directive Principles of State Policy. Courts must, therefore, endeavour to avoid crippling it by construing it technically or in a narrow spirit. It must be construed in tune with lofty purposes for which its makers framed it. So construed, the instrument becomes a solid foundation of democracy and the rule of law.[57]

In view of that position, the Court of Appeal held that:

> the provisions touching fundamental rights have to be interpreted in a broad and liberal manner thereby jealously protecting and developing the dimensions of those rights and ensuring that our people enjoy their rights, our democracy not only functions but also grows, and the will and dominant aspirations of the people prevail. Restrictions on fundamental rights must be strictly construed.[58]

The adoption of this liberal approach to interpreting the Constitution is very evident if one considers the manner in which the judiciary, in the absence of an express environmental right, has used the right to life to protect the environment in Tanzania. The link between the right to life and the right to live in a clean, safe and healthy environment was enunciated in two famous High Court decisions, namely: *Joseph A. Kessy and Others v. Dar es Salaam City Council*;[59] and *Festo Badegele and 794 Others v. Dar es Salaam City Council*.[60] Both cases generally dealt with

---

56. Court of Appeal of Tanzania, Civ. Appl No. 4 of 2001 (unreported).
57. *Ibid.*, 17.
58. *Ibid.*, 17-18.
59. Civ. C. No. 299 of 1988 HC of Tanzania, Dar es Salaam (unreported).
60. Misc. Civ. C. No. 91 of 1991 (unreported). The case is, however, reported in UNEP *Compendium of Judicial Decisions on Matters Related to Environment: National Decisions* (1998) Vol. 1.

the dumping of waste by the Dar es Salaam City Council. The residents living in areas where the waste had been dumped challenged City Council's actions.

In the *Kessy* case, several residents of the Tabata area of Dar es Salaam sought a High Court order prohibiting the City Council from continuing to dump and burn solid waste in Tabata, a designated residential area. The City Council simultaneously sought the court's permission to continue the waste dumping and burning activities. In dismissing the City Council's application, the High Court gave an expansive interpretation of the constitutional right to life as including the right to an environment free from pollution that would endanger life. Lugakingira J emphatically stated that:

> I have never heard it anywhere before a public authority, or even an individual, to go to court and confidently seek for permission to pollute the environment and endanger people's lives, regardless of their number. Such wonders appear to be peculiarly Tanzanian, but I regret to say that it is not given to any court to grant such a prayer. Article 14 of our constitution provides that every person has a right to life and to protection of his life by the society. It is, therefore, a contradiction in terms and a denial of this basis [sic] right deliberately to expose anybody's life to danger or, what is eminently monstrous, to enlist the assistance of the court in this infringement.[61]

The judge also pointed out that what had been done by the Dar es Salaam City Council at Tabata, did not only constitute a tort, but also a crime:

> Section 185 of the Penal Code makes it an offence punishable by imprisonment for any person voluntarily to vitiate the atmosphere in any place so as to make it noxious to the health of a person in general dwelling or carrying on business in the neighbourhood or passing along public way. This offence is known as fouling air; the offence of obstructing way under section 239 of the Code could similarly be cited in this context. In coming to court seeking to be permitted to continue using [the] Tabata site the way it has been doing, the Council is virtually asking for a license to contravene the law. I am not aware of any authority, and none was cited to me, which authorises a court of law to sanction criminal activity. I hold to the contrary, that a court cannot authorise an offence. In bringing this application it was claimed that the Council was seeking justice. Justice in this case is wholly on the side of [the] Tabata residents, and the Council in effect came to Court to enlist the Court's assistance in perpetuating an injustice. Ironically, the duty of the Court is to protect the individual from the excesses of executive power and in this duty it should not be seen to fail or to falter.[62]

Having been prohibited by the High Court from continuing to pollute the Tabata area, the Dar es Salaam City Council shifted the dump to Kunduchi Mtongani, another residential area on the outskirts of the city. The Kunduchi Mtongani

---

61. *Ibid.*, 15.
62. *Ibid.*, 16.

residents raised a similar challenge to the City Council's activities in the *Balagele* case. In this matter the City Council rather cynically argued that in dumping solid waste at Kunduchi Mtongani, it was 'reconditioning' the area and not polluting it. The applicant's argued that the City Council's activity did not constitute sanitary land filing or 'reconditioning'; but rather refuse dumping which attracted swarms of flies, bad odors and when set alight, emitted heavy smoke which posed a serious health hazard to residents living in the area. The High Court once again came to the rescue of the residents and the broader environment. Rubama J stated in no uncertain terms that: 'it is a statutory duty of the City Council . . . to stop nuisance and not to create it'.[63] The judge further opined that refuse collection and disposal, as one of the statutory duties of the City Council, should have been given the priority treatment it deserved, and that people's health and enjoyment of life were dependent on living in healthy surroundings. The court accordingly granted the orders of *certiorari*, prohibition and *mandamus*, and in doing so, stated that:

> In view of the findings, this Court brings into court the decision of the respondent of dumping refuse at Kunduchi Mtongani and quashes it. This court further prohibits the Dar es Salaam City Council from continuing to carry out its decision of using Kunduchi Mtongani as a refuse dumping site. This court lastly issues an order of mandamus and directs the Dar es Salaam City Council to discharge its functions properly and in accordance with the law by establishing an appropriate refuse dumping site and using it.[64]

The above decisions illustrate that the Tanzanian judiciary is certainly not ill-equipped or ill-adapted to hear and determine environmental disputes. If anything, the judiciary has shown that it can be relied upon to ply its role with remarkable intellectual vigour and with a deep conscientiousness and commitment to wider issues of social and environmental justice. Broadening the constitutional right to life to include the right to live in an unpolluted environment would not have been possible but for its willingness to be creative in its statutory interpretation, and flexible in its adherence to the common law *locus standi* rules and statutory procedural requirements. These latter aspects are discussed below.

6.3   *Locus Standi* and Public Interest Litigation

The High Court of Tanzania has been liberal in applying the common law rules relating to standing, especially in public interest cases concerning the application of constitutional rights. In the case of *Rev. Christopher Mtikila v. The Attorney General*,[65] the High Court, having undertaken a comprehensive survey of relevant jurisprudence in the United Kingdom, Canada, Gambia, Nigeria, India, Pakistan and Zimbabwe, held that the orthodox common law position regarding *locus standi*

---

63. UNEP, *supra* n. 60, 89-90.
64. *Ibid.*, 90.
65. [1995] TLR 31.

did not suit the context of 'constitutional litigation'. In the words of Lugakingira J: 'In the circumstances of Tanzania, if a public spirited individual springs up in search of the Court's intervention against legislation or actions that pervert the Constitution, the Court, as a guardian and trustee of the Constitution, must grant him standing'.[66]

Samatta J, who later rose to become the Chief Justice of Tanzania, further elucidated the position of Tanzanian courts on *locus standi* in the case of *Ballonzi v. Registered Trustees of Chama cha Mapinduzi*.[67] The judge, having pointed out areas where the common law rule of *locus standi* in Tanzania could be modified so as to make it suit local conditions and to cover new aspects which may include natural resources and environmental management, held that the rule of *locus standi*, insofar as it relates to human rights litigation, must be wide.[68]

A related issue in respect of which the judiciary has been very proactive, is its express support for public interest litigation. In the *Mtikila* case, Lugakingira J recognized the value of public interest litigation in Tanzania and stated that:

> The relevance of public interest litigation in Tanzania cannot be over-empha-sized. Having regard to our socio-economic conditions, this development promises more hope to our people than any other strategy currently in place. First of all, illiteracy is rampant. . . . By reason of this a great part of the population is unaware of their rights, let alone how same can be realised. Secondly, Tanzanians are massively poor . . . Public interest litigation is a sophisticated mechanism which requires professional handing. By reasons of limited resources the vast majority of our people cannot afford lawyers even where they were aware of the infringement of their rights and the per-vasion of the constitution . . . Given all these and other circumstances, if there should spring up a public spirited individual and seek the court's intervention against legislation or actions that pervert the constitution, the court, as guard-ian and trustee of the constitution and what it stands for, is under [an] obligation to rise up to the occasion and grant him standing.[69]

This liberal approach to *locus standi* in public interest litigation is evident in a number of High Court judgments dealing with environmental issues. *Felix Joseph Mavika and 4 Others v. Dar es Salaam City Commissioner and Ilala Municipal Commission*,[70] once again involved the dumping of waste (liquid and solid waste) by the Dar es Salaam City Council and Ilala Municipal Commission, this time in the Vingunguti area. The applicants (residents of the area), sought a temporary injunction against the respondents prohibiting them from dumping solid and liquid wastes in the Vingunguti area and using the abattoir located in the area. The respondents argued that the applicants had no *locus standi* to bring the matter to

---

66. *Ibid.*, 43.
67. [1996] TLR 203.
68. *Ibid.*, 211.
69. *Supra* n. 65, 42-43.
70. HC of Tanzania, Civ. C. No. 316 of 2000 (unreported).

court as they had not complied with section 66 of the Civil Procedure Code,[71] which required the prior consent of the Attorney General before bringing the matter to court. Ihema J, referring to the decisions in the *Kessy* and *Badegele* cases, supported the doctrine of public interest litigation enshrined in Article 26(2) of the Constitution and held that:

> On careful consideration of the respective submissions of both counsel on whether or not the applicants have *locus standi* to bring the matter before this Court, I am satisfied that the applicants do have a leg to stand on. There is authority in section 66(2) of the Civil Procedure Code as well as the doctrine of public interest litigation enshrined in Article 26(2) of the Constitution applied with approval of this Court in cases cited above. In the event that this ground of objection fails and is dismissed, this then disposes of the grounds of objection relating to *locus standi* and incompetence of the application.[72]

What is also noteworthy, is that the High Court's flexible approach to *locus standi* in public interest litigation has also influenced the jurisprudence of neighbouring jurisdictions with the High Court of Uganda, in the case of the *Environmental Action Network Ltd v. the Attorney General and the National Environment Management Authority*,[73] referring to the *ratio* in the *Mtikila* case as a persuasive authority.

6.4   APPLICATION OF THE POLLUTER PAYS PRINCIPLE

Following its entrenchment in the EMA, the polluter pays principle has been subject to judicial scrutiny in *Erick David Massawe v. The Tanzania National Roads Agency, Loi Langisho Mollel and the Attorney General*.[74] In this matter, the first respondent had deposited soil in the road reserve and built culverts which did not comply with legal specifications. As a result, there was an alleged divergence of national flow waterlines for which no alternative was provided. The applicant argued that the first respondent's action could have caused flooding in the area during the rainy season; and furthermore, that their deposition of soil and construction of a wall around the applicant's premises had interfered with natural flow water lines, resulting in the formation of ponds which had made access to her home impossible at times. In her ruling, Kileo J stated that:

> While I may agree that on the main the case centres on that part of the road reserve that was encroached upon by the plaintiff, nevertheless I consider it an obligation on the part of the court to be alert and sensitive to environmental degradation particularly where that ruin poses a danger to the lives of citizens.

---

71. Civil Procedure Code, Cap. 33 of *Laws of Tanzania* 1966.
72. *Supra*, n. 60, 9.
73. HC of Uganda, Kampala, Misc. Appl. No. 39 of 2001 (unreported).
74. HC of Tanzania (Land Division) at Arusha, Land Case No. 16 of 2004 (unreported).

I feel that I am obliged to comment and recommend or direct appropriate measures to be taken to remove the danger posed. For sure, I for one cannot be indifferent in situations where there is a likelihood danger may be caused to people in an area, which I have dealt with in the course of my adjudication of a matter before me.[75]

The court accordingly held that the applicant was at liberty to remove the soil deposited on the road reserve which interfered with the storm drainage or natural flow waterline. It further held that the respondents were liable for the applicant's costs occasioned by the removal of the obstruction.

7   CONCLUSION AND WAY FORWARD

One of the major challenges that have undermined the role of the Tanzanian judiciary in contributing to the nation's general governance and facilitating access to justice is that, for many years, there has been a shortage of judges to hear matters brought before the courts. This has resulted in case overload, delays in the conclusion of matters, and public disillusionment with the judiciary. In order to ameliorate these problems, the president of Tanzania, on recommendation of the Judicial Service Commission, appointed twenty new High Court judges in 2007. Overall, the number of High Court judges has increased from approximately forty to sixty-seven in the past two years. These judges have been more equitably distributed to all regions of Tanzania, thereby increasing the functioning of the High Courts and bringing access to justice to a greater geographical spread of citizens.

In the environmental context, a further challenge is that owing to the contemporary nature of environmental law in Tanzania, many members of the current judiciary did not study, and accordingly are not fully conversant with, environmental law. However, the Tanzanian judiciary has a continuous training programme for both High Court and Court of Appeal judges and one of the areas which have recently been integrated within these programmes is environmental law. The Tanzanian judiciary, in collaboration with the United Nations Environment Programme (UNEP) and the Faculty of Law (University of Dar es Salaam), offered an environmental law training and sensitization programme for thirty-five High Court judges in June 2003. Court of Appeal judges have received similar training whilst participating in another UNEP programme, namely the East Africa Regional Judicial Colloquium on Environmental Law held in Mombasa, Kenya, in April 2007. Specific aspects integrated within this training included: raising awareness of environmental issues and environmental legal frameworks; debating ways to relax the procedural requirements and impediments in environmental cases; and considering ways to improve the efficacy of the judicial system.

Notwithstanding these developments within the judiciary, a vital prerequisite for developing a vibrant environmental jurisprudence in Tanzania is the need to raise public awareness of environmental issues, relevant legal procedures and

---

75. *Ibid.*, 4.

remedies available to them to vindicate their right to live in a clean, safe and healthy environment. Tanzania's adversarial system of litigation precludes courts from entertaining a case *suo motu*, and therefore the role of the judiciary will continue to be somewhat frustrated if members of the public do not bring key environmental matters before it. In order to facilitate this process, UNEP, in collaboration with the Lawyers Environment Action Team, organized training workshops for eighty legal practitioners from different regions of Tanzania in 2004 and 2005. These efforts will hopefully culminate in increased environmental litigation in Tanzania.

Notwithstanding these potential impediments, several of which have been partially addressed in recent times, the analysis of cases undertaken in this chapter illustrates the significant role the Tanzanian judiciary has already played in environmental governance. The judiciary has shown ingenuity in developing Tanzania's environmental jurisprudence, and a willingness to draw on relevant jurisprudence from other common law jurisdictions where its realm was constrained by outdated or absent key legal provisions, most notably those relating to *locus standi* and environmental rights. With the enactment of the EMA, the judiciary's relaxation of the common law rules of *locus standi* and its apparent affinity for public interest litigation, the judiciary appears well placed to substantially contribute to environmental governance in Tanzania in the future.

BIBLIOGRAPHY

Awuku, E.O. 'The Right to Clean Environment: Lessons from India and Tanzania'. *Verfassung und Recht in Uebersee* 27 (1994): 16-27.
Broszinsky-Schwabe, E. *Kulture in Scwarzafrika*. Leipzig: Urania Verlag, 1982.
EAC. 'Lake Victoria Basin Commission'. <www.eac.int/index.php/lvdc.html>, 21 September 2008.
Fimbo, G.M. 'The Court of Appeal of the United Republic of Tanzania: A Descriptive Essay'. *Eastern Africa Law Review* 16, no. 2 (1989): 229-267.
Galanter, M. 'The Radiating Effects of the Courts'. In *Empirical Theories about Courts*, edited by K.O. Boyum & Mather, L. New York: Longmans, 1983.
Gutto, S.B.O. 'Environmental Rights Litigation, Human Rights and the Role of Non-Governmental and Peoples' Organisations in Africa'. *South African Journal of Environmental Law and Policy* 1 (1995): 1-14.
Johnson-Hicks, P. *Tanzania: A Portrait of a Nation*. London: Quiller Press, 1998.
Kabudi, A.M. *The Development and Provision of Scientific and Technical Information Services in Tanzania*. Berlin: Koester, 1997.
Kabudi, P.J. *Human Rights Jurisprudence in East Africa: A Comparative Study of Fundamental Rights and Freedoms of the Individual in Tanzania, Kenya and Uganda*. Baden-Baden: Nomos Verlag, 1995.
Kabudi, P.J. 'The Directive Principles of State Policy in Tanzania'. In *Human Rights, Constitutionalism and the Judiciary: Tanzanian and Irish Perspectives*, edited by W. Binchy & C. Finnegan. Dublin: Clarus Press, 2006.

Kabudi, P.J. 'The Union of Tanganyika and Zanzibar: Examination of the Treaty of a Political Legal Union, MAWAZO'. *Journal of Faculty of Arts and Social Sciences* 6, no. 3 (1985): 11-19.

Kabudi, P.J. 'The United Republic of Tanzania after a Quarter of a Century: A Legal Appraisal of the State of the Union of Tanganyika and Zanzibar'. *Africa Journal of International and Comparative Law* 5, no. 2 (1993): 310-339.

Kisanga, R.H. *A Critical Assessment of the Adjudicatory and Educative Role of the Court of Appeal as the Highest Judicial Organ in Tanzania* (mimeo). Dar es Salaam: UDS Faculty of Law, 1985.

Omari, C.K. 'The Management of Tribal and Religious Diversity'. In *Mwalimu: The Influence of Nyerere*, edited by C. Legum & G.V. Mmari. London: James Currey, 1995.

Peter, C.M. *Human Rights in Tanzania: Selected Cases and Materials*. Koeln: Ruediger Koeppe Verlag, 1997.

Rosencranz, A., S. Divan & M.L. Noble (eds). *Law and Policy in India: Cases, Materials and Statutes*. Delhi: Tripathi, 1995.

United Republic of Tanzania. Agriculture and Livestock Policy. Dar es Salaam: Ministry of Agriculture and Food Security, 1997.

United Republic of Tanzania. Energy Policy of Tanzania. Dar es Salaam: Ministry of Energy and Minerals, 2002.

United Republic of Tanzania. Institutional and Legal Framework for Environmental Management Project Institutional Report. Dar es Salaam: Vice President's Office, 2000.

United Republic of Tanzania. Mineral Policy of Tanzania. Dar es Salaam: Ministry of Energy and Minerals, 1998.

United Republic of Tanzania. National Beekeeping Policy. Dar es Salaam: Ministry of Natural Resources and Tourism, 1998.

United Republic of Tanzania. National Environmental Policy. Dar es Salaam: Vice President's Office, 1997.

United Republic of Tanzania. National Fisheries Sectoral Policy and Strategy Statement. Dar es Salaam: Ministry of Natural Resources and Tourism, 1997.

United Republic of Tanzania. National Forest Policy. Dar es Salaam: Ministry of Natural Resources and Tourism, 1998.

United Republic of Tanzania. National Health Policy. Dar es Salaam: Ministry of Health and Social Welfare, 1990.

United Republic of Tanzania. National Human Settlements Development Policy. Dar es Salaam: Ministry of Lands, Human Settlements and Housing, 2000.

United Republic of Tanzania. National Tourism Policy. Dar es Salaam: Ministry of Natural Resources and Tourism, 1999.

United Republic of Tanzania. National Transport Policy. Dar es Salaam: Ministry of Communication and Transport, 2003.

United Republic of Tanzania. National Water Policy. Dar es Salaam: Ministry of Water and Irrigation, 2002.

United Republic of Tanzania. State of the Environment Report 2007. Dar es Salaam: Vice President's Office, 2007.

United Republic of Tanzania. Sustainable Industrial Policy. Dar es Salaam: Ministry of Industry and Trade, 1996.

United Republic of Tanzania. Wildlife Policy of Tanzania. Dar es Salaam: Ministry of Natural Resources and Tourism, 1998.

TABLE OF LEGISLATION

TABLE OF CASES

Jina Khatibu Haji v. Juma Selemani Nungu Court of Appeal of Tanzania, Civ. Appl No. 23 of 1986

Joseph D. Kessy and Others v. The City Council of Dar es Salaam HC of Tanzania, Dar es Salaam, Civ. C. No. 299 of 1998

Julius Ishengoma Ndyanabo v. The Attorney General Court of Appeal of Tanzania, Civ. Appl No. 4 of 2001

Machano Khamis Ali and 18 Others v. Serikali ya Mapinduzi Zanzibar Court of Appeal of Tanzania, Zanzibar, Crim. Appl. No. 8 of 2000

Rev. Christopher Mtikila v. The Attorney General [1995] TLR 31

TABLE OF INTERNATIONAL/REGIONAL INSTRUMENTS

Protocol on the Sustainable Development of Lake Victoria Basin 2003

ABBREVIATIONS

EIA	Environmental Impact Assessment
EMA	Environmental Management Act
GMP(s)	General Management Plans
HC	High Court
MNRT	Ministry of Natural Resources and Tourism
MWI	Ministry of Water and Irrigation
UNEP	United Nations Environmental Programme
UDS	University of Dar es Salaam

Chapter 17

Nigeria

Muhammed Ladan

| 1 | INTRODUCTION |

Who should decide whether to build a road or a dam, or how much timber or fish to harvest? Would environmental governance decisions have different outcomes if the public was consulted in the decision-making process? Should local citizens or advocacy groups have the right to appeal a decision they believe harms an eco-system and negatively impacts on their environmental interests? What is the best way to fight corruption among government bureaucrats who manage forests, water, grasslands and parks? These are all questions concerning how we make environmental decisions and who makes them; the process we call environmental governance. How we decide and who gets to decide, often determine what we decide. Questions of environmental governance are therefore crucial and involve an intricate process of multiple public and private stakeholders. The significance of environmental governance is especially relevant today, when Nigeria's past environmental decisions (governance efforts)[1] stand in stark relief against the backdrop of vivid environmental crisis such as: dying reefs; degraded forests; species extinction, water scarcity, and climate change. Against this background, this chapter reflects on the role of the Nigerian judiciary in present day environmental governance efforts.

---

1. M.T. Ladan, *Materials and Cases on Environmental Law and Policy* (Zaria: ECONET Publishers, 2004), 117–244.

Louis J. Kotzé and Alexander R. Paterson (eds), *The Role of the Judiciary in Environmental Governance: Comparative Perspectives*, pp. 527–556.
© 2009 Kluwer Law International BV, The Netherlands.

1.1   MAIN ENVIRONMENTAL CHALLENGES

Nigeria, the most populous nation in Africa, rich in oil but underdeveloped,[2] has its own share of environmental problems which justify local and international attention. In terms of Nigeria's environmental challenges,[3] the four broad issues being accorded highest priority at present are briefly discussed below.

Industrial pollution: most industries, with the exception of the petroleum industry, do not have waste treatment facilities to deal with solid waste, effluent and air emissions they generate. The few treatment plants that do exist are outdated; not functioning effectively as a result of over use and a lack of proper servicing; or unable to cope with the vast amounts and types of industrial waste, effluents and emissions passing through them. The environmental problems associated with Nigeria's industrial sector include: air pollution (gas or particle emissions), especially from cement, steel and asbestos industries; and land and water pollution (effluent discharged onto land and into water has become a great concern particularly in view of the epidemic tendencies of such pollution) especially from the pharmaceutical, chemical, textile, food processing and oil industries; and noise pollution.

Desertification: Nigeria has lost about $351,000 \text{ km}^2$ of its land to the desert, which is estimated to be advancing at a rate of 0.6 km per year. Desertification is most prevalent in northern Nigeria, where entire settlements, and in some instances major access roads, have recently been buried by encroaching sand dunes.

Deforestation and loss of wildlife: deforestation and loss of wildlife resources are occurring throughout Nigeria. Deforestation affects timber production and the production of associated products such as medicines, food and paper. A ban was imposed on the export of wood obtained from natural forest in 1976. However, much of the current deforestation is the result of wood consumed for domestic purposes. The depletion of Nigeria's wildlife is an additional concern. Hunting is a major contributor to its demise and there is a dire need to protect wildlife and biodiversity by specifically providing for the protection of certain species and areas that are of scientific, recreational or aesthetic value.

Soil erosion: Nigeria's coastal and inland soil reserves have been greatly depleted by flooding and resultant erosion, which has had severe financial consequences for many local communities. Research into methods of controlling floods and erosion is accordingly being promoted by the government.[4]

In light of the above pressing environmental concerns, the need to use law as a vehicle in the regulation, management and protection of Nigeria's environment has become paramount.[5]

---

2. Underdevelopment is universally measured in terms of standard of living, gross domestic product (GDP), foreign exchange denominator, foreign reserves, political stability and the level of fundamental human rights of citizens.
3. See generally, the National Policy on the Environment, Rev. ed. (Lagos: FEPA, 1999), 30-37.
4. *Ibid.*
5. On the role of law in international environmental protection, see P.W. Birnie & A.E. Boyle, *International Law and the Environment*, 2nd ed. (Oxford: OUP, 2002), 7-9.

2   PRINCIPAL ENVIRONMENTAL LAWS AND
      INSTITUTIONS[6]

Environmental law in Nigeria, as in other countries, is that branch of public law that contains rules and regulations which have as their object (or effect) the protection of the environment.[7] During the colonial era, environmental protection was not deemed a priority in Nigeria and there was accordingly no policy and legal framework aimed at preserving and protecting it. Matters relating to the environment were dealt with as a tort of nuisance because disputes in environmental law were not viewed as public matters warranting State intervention. The few environmentally related laws that were applicable criminalized activities that could degrade the environment. These laws included the *Criminal Code Act*[8] of 1916, which prohibited water pollution and air pollution, and created the offence of nuisance. In 1917, the *Public Health Act*[9] was enacted. Although somewhat broad in scope, this act did contain provisions of relevance to the regulation of land, air and water pollution. It is, however, evident that at this time, matters relating to the environment were dealt with in a rudimentary manner, with the emphasis on environmental sanitation and only a limited array of available remedies in the form of criminal measures.

Following Nigeria's independence in 1960 and the discovery of oil in commercial quantities, it became apparent that existing laws dealing with the environment were grossly inadequate. This was because most of the provisions on environmental protection were scattered throughout different laws, resulting in an *ad hoc* response to different needs in different situations.[10] During the decade following independence, government criminalized polluting activities, particularly those relating to the discharge of oil in navigable waters and environmental degradation as a result of petroleum activities. The 1970s saw the further development of Nigeria's environmental law regime in response to the industrial growth associated with the oil boom.[11] River basin authorities[12] were created and environmental units were established in some government ministries.[13] The laws were, however, typically 'knee-jerk' responses to emergency situations.

The 1980s and 1990s witnessed the most drastic and systematic development of environmental law in Nigeria, partly owing to Nigeria's subscription to a

---

6. See generally, P.B. Ajibola, 'Protection of the environment through the Law', in *The Law and the Environment in Nigeria*, ed. F. Shyllon (Ibadan: UIP, 1999).
7. See generally, Y. Osinbajo, *Some Public Law Considerations in Environmental Law* (Lagos: UL Faculty of Law, 1990).
8. Cap. C. 38 *LFN* 2004.
9. Cap. P. 40 *LFN* 2004.
10. See F. Shyllon, 'Present and Future Institutional Framework for Environmental Management in Nigeria', in *The Law and the Environment in Nigeria*, ed. *id.* (Ibadan: UIP, 1999).
11. See, e.g., the laws listed *infra* n. 26, 28, 37 and 38.
12. See *infra* n. 29 for more detail on these authorities.
13. These ministries include the Ministry of Agriculture, Ministry of Water Resources and Ministry of the Environment.

number of international instruments during this period.[14] The main national laws and decrees developed during this period, and which are still in force today, include by way of summary the:[15] *Animal Diseases (Control) Act;*[16] *Bee (Import, Control and Management) Act;*[17] *Endangered Species Act;*[18] *Hides and Skins Act;*[19] *Live Fish (Control of importation) Act;*[20] *National Crop Varieties and Livestock Breeds Act;*[21] *Agricultural (Control of Implementation) Act;*[22] *Agricultural and Rural Management Training Institute Act;*[23] *Pests (Control of Produce) Act;*[24] *Quarantine Act;*[25] *Associated Gas Re-injection Act;*[26] *Civil Aviation Act;*[27] *Oil and Navigable*

---

14. These include: Convention on Biological Diversity (1992) 31 *ILM* 818; UN Convention to Combat Desertification in Countries Experiencing Serious Drought and/or Desertification (1994) 33 *ILM* 1328; Convention on International Trade in Endangered Species of Wild Fauna and Flora (1973) 46 *ILM* 1178; Convention on the Conservation of Migratory Species of Wild Animals (1980) 19 *ILM* 11; Vienna Convention on the Protection of the Ozone Layer (1987) 26 *ILM* 1516; Montreal Protocol on Substances that Deplete the Ozone Layer; Stockholm Convention on Persistent Organic Pollutants (2001) 40 *ILM* 532; and Basel Convention on the Control of Transboundary Movements of Hazardous Wastes and their Disposal (1989) 28 *ILM* 567. For a comprehensive discussion of the international and regional environmental instruments which Nigeria is party to, see: S. Simpson & O. Fagbohun (eds), *Environmental Law and Policy* (Lagos: LSU Faculty of Law, 1998), 10-49; I.A. Ayua & O. Ajai, *Implementing the Biodiversity Convention: Nigerian and African Perspectives* (Lagos: UL Nigerian Institute of Advanced Legal Studies, 1997); and I.L. Worika, *Environmental Law and Policy of Petroleum Development: Strategies and Mechanisms for Sustainable Management in Africa* (Portharcourt, Rivers State: Anpez CED, 2002), 62-80 and 311-328.
15. For a comprehensive discussion of Nigeria's environmental regime see M.T. Ladan, 'Human Rights and Environmental Protection', in *Text for Human Rights Teaching in Schools*, ed. A.O. Obilade & C. Nwankwo (Lagos: CRP, 1999), 100-102.
16. Cap. 18 *LFN* 1990. The main objective of the act is to prevent the spread and introduction of infections and contagious diseases among animals, hatcheries and poultry enterprises.
17. Cap. 33 *LFN* 1990. The act provides that bees and agricultural materials shall be imported by licensed persons only.
18. Cap. 108 *LFN* 1990. The act provides for the conservation and management of wildlife and the protection of species in danger of extinction as a result of over-exploitation.
19. Cap. 167 *LFN* 1990. The act provides for the regulation and control of the trade in and export of hides and skins.
20. Cap. 209 *LFN* 1990. The act prohibits the importation of live fish without a permit.
21. Cap. 249 *LFN* 1990. The act provides for the certification, registration and release of national crop varieties and livestock breeds.
22. Cap. 12 *LFN* 1990. The act seeks to control the spread of plant diseases and pests; and regulates the importation of specific articles.
23. Cap. 11 *LFN* 1990. The act establishes a training institute to identify management training needs in agricultural and rural development organizations throughout the country; and provides for the development and implementation of training programs to meet the needs of managers in agriculture and rural development.
24. Cap. 349 *LFN* 1990. The act provides for the inspection of produce for pests before export from all air and sea ports.
25. Cap. 384 *LFN* 1990. The act regulates quarantine procedures to prevent the introduction of infectious diseases.
26. Cap. 26 *LFN* 1990. The act prohibits gas flaring that will result in air and thermal pollution.
27. Cap. 51 *LFN* 1990. The act regulates atmospheric pollution resulting from aviation activities.

Waters Act;[28] *River Basin Development Authority Act;*[29] *Sea Fisheries Act;*[30] *Territorial Waters Act;*[31] *Exclusive Economic Zone Act;*[32] *National Water Resources Institute Act;*[33] *Kainji Lake National Park Act;*[34] *Harmful Waste Act;*[35] *Land Use Act;*[36] *Minerals Act;*[37] *Petroleum Act;*[38] *Criminal Code Act;*[39] *Energy Commission of Nigeria Act;*[40] *Federal Environmental Protection Agency Act;*[41] *Natural Resources Conservation Council Act;*[42] *Environmental Impact Assessment Decree;*[43] *Federal Environmental Protection Agency Decree;*[44] and the *Nuclear Safety and Radiation Protection Decree.*[45]

These laws and decrees are supported by an array of additional national regulations[46] and policies[47] of environmental significance. The most recent and

---

28. Cap. 337 *LFN* 1990. The act prohibits the discharge of oil into navigable waters.
29. Cap. 390 *LFN* 1990. The act establishes eleven river basin development authorities to undertake development of surface and underground water resources for multiple uses; especially for the control of floods and erosion and for watershed management.
30. Cap. 404 *LFN* 1990. The act provides for the regulation and protection of sea fisheries in territorial waters.
31. Cap. 428 *LFN* 1990. The act determines the limit of Nigeria's territorial waters.
32. Cap. 116 *LFN* 1990. The act defines the exclusive economic zone of Nigeria as extending 200 nautical miles seawards from the coast and enables Nigeria to exercise its sovereign rights, especially in relation to the conservation or exploitation of the resources of the seabed, subsoil and superjacent waters.
33. Cap. 284 *LFN* 1990. The act establishes the National Water Resources Institute to promote and develop training programs in water resource management and to advise government on training needs and priorities.
34. Cap. 197 *LFN* 1990. The act establishes Kainji Lake National Park for the conservation and preservation of wildlife and natural life.
35. Cap. 165 *LFN* 1990. The act prohibits the carrying, depositing and dumping of harmful waste on land or water.
36. Cap. 202 *LFN* 1990. The act vests all land in a State in the governor of that State, and further defines interests that can be held in land.
37. Cap. 226 *LFN* 1990. The act provides for environmental protection during mining activities.
38. Cap. 350 *LFN* 1990. The act provides for the protection of the environment during petroleum activities.
39. Cap. 77 *LFN* 1990. The act creates the offence of public nuisance which includes fouling of water and air.
40. Cap. 109 *LFN* 1990. The act establishes the Energy Commission of Nigeria to coordinate the development of Nigeria's energy resources.
41. Cap. 131 *LFN* 1990. The act establishes the Federal Environmental Protection Agency, which is charged with the responsibility for protecting and preserving the environment.
42. Cap. 268 *LFN* 1990. The act establishes the Natural Resources Conservation Council responsible for the conservation of natural resources and the formulation of a national policy for resource conservation.
43. No. 86 of 1992. The decree aims at infusing environmental considerations into development project planning and execution.
44. No. 58 of 1988 (amended by Decree No. 59 of 1992). The decree prescribes the powers and functions of the Federal Environmental Protection Agency.
45. No. 19 of 1995. The decree regulates nuclear safety and radiation protection.
46. Relevant regulations include: National Environmental Protection (Effluent Limitations) Regulation, 1991; National Environmental Protection (Pollution Abatement in Industries and Facilities Generating Wastes) Regulations, 1991; and Management of Solid and Hazardous Waste Regulations, 1991.
47. Relevant policies include: National Policy on the Environment, *supra* n. 3; and the Draft National Policy on Environmental Sanitation and its Guidelines (Lagos: FEPA, 2004).

important addition to Nigeria's environmental law regime is the *National Environmental Standards and Regulations Enforcement Agency (Establishment) Act*,[48] which came into force in 2007. The Act establishes the National Environmental Standards and Regulations Enforcement Agency, Nigeria's lead environmental protection agency.

Nigeria's formal environmental regime clearly has developed significantly from humble beginnings. Having been initiated in the colonial period, during which time environmental issues where generally couched within public health regulation;[49] and having developed in a rather *ad hoc* manner in the early days of independence (during which time heavy reliance was placed on the law of nuisance); Nigeria now has a relatively comprehensive environmental law regime. This regime is administered by an array of institutions. The Federal Ministry of Environment, Housing and Urban Development and the National Environmental Standards and Regulations Enforcement Agency are the main institutions responsible for the formulation of environmental policy and enforcement respectively. Their functions are supported by the following additional government institutions: Federal Ministry of Solid Minerals Development; Federal Ministry of Agriculture and Natural Resources; Federal Ministry of Water Resources; Federal Ministry of Science and Technology; and Ministry of Energy, Oil and Gas Resources.

3   AN OVERVIEW OF NIGERIA'S COURT SYSTEM

The Nigerian Constitution[50] of 1999 (1999 Constitution) provides for the establishment, composition, jurisdiction and powers of both federal and State courts. In terms of the Constitution's provisions,[51] the Nigerian courts generally have the mandate to: protect and enforce fundamental human rights; hear and determine civil and criminal cases; entertain and decide on appeal cases subject to their jurisdiction and powers; resolve inter-personal, institutional, and inter-governmental disputes; interpret and enforce constitutional provisions in the administration of justice; and review legislative and executive actions/decisions.

Nigeria's current court system is shaped like a pyramid, with the five main types of courts in descending order of status being: the Supreme Court; the Federal Court of Appeal; the Federal and State High Courts, the State Sharia and Customary Courts of Appeal; the Chief Magistrates' Courts, the Upper Area and Upper Sharia Courts; and the Lower Level Magistrates' Courts, Sharia, Customary and Area Courts. This hierarchy is illustrated by *Figure 1: Court Structure* (following page).

---

48. Act 57 of 2007.
49. O. Okediran, 'An appraisal of Environmental Sanitation Edicts in Nigeria', in *The Law and the Environment in Nigeria*, ed. F. Shyllon (Ibadan: UIP, 1999), 25.
50. The *Constitution of the Federal Republic of Nigeria* 1999, Cap. C. 23 *LFN* 2004.
51. The courts' jurisdiction is set out in s. 6 and ss 230-284.

At the top of the hierarchy, (see Figure 1), is the Supreme Court of Nigeria, the country's final court of appeal situated in Abuja, and presided over by the Chief Justice of Nigeria. The Federal Court of Appeal, established in 1976, is the second highest court in Nigeria and is governed by the *Federal Court of Appeal Act*.[52] This court, presided over by the President of the court, is primarily an appeal court which hears civil and criminal appeals from: the Federal High Court; the State High Court; the High Court of the Federal Capital Territory (Abuja); the State Sharia Courts of Appeal; the State Customary Courts of Appeals; and the Code of Conduct Tribunals and Election Tribunals (particularly the National Assembly Election Tribunals and Governorship and Legislative Houses Election Tribunals).

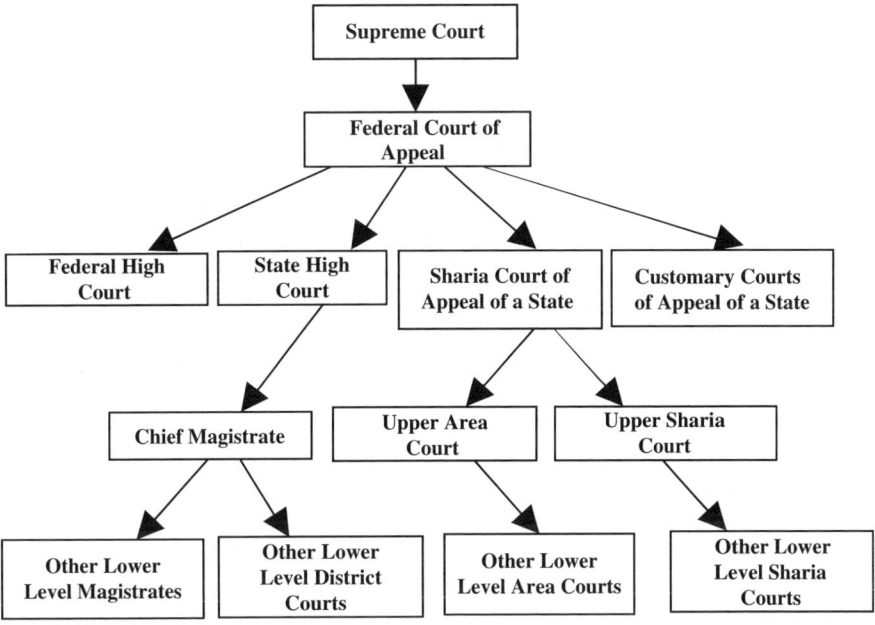

Figure 1. Court Structure

The Federal Court of Appeal started with three Divisions at Lagos, Kaduna and Enugu. An additional seven divisions have subsequently been established at Ibadan, Benin City, Jos, Port-Harcourt, Abuja, Illorin and Calabar. Seventy justices currently serve in these divisions. The original jurisdiction of the Court of Appeal is prescribed in section 239 of the 1999 Constitution and includes the determination of whether: any person has been validly elected to the office of president or vice president under the Constitution; the term of office of the president or vice

---

52. *Court of Appeal Act* Cap. C. 36 *LFN* 2004.

president has ceased; or the office of president or vice president has become vacant. Its appellate jurisdiction is set out in sections 240 and 241 of the 1999 Constitution and includes determining civil and criminal appeals from: the Federal High Court; the High Court of the Federal Capital Territory; the Abuja High Court of a State; the Sharia Court of Appeal of the Federal Capital Territory; the Abuja Sharia Court of Appeal of a State; the Customary Court of Appeal of the Federal Capital Territory; the Abuja Customary Court of Appeal of a State; and from decisions of a court martial or other tribunals as may be prescribed by an Act of the National Assembly.

The jurisdiction of the Federal High Court is provided under section 251 of the 1999 Constitution. Its exclusive jurisdiction covers matters relating to the following: revenue of the government of the federation; taxation of companies and other bodies; customs and excise duties and export duties; banks and other financial institutions; operation of the *Companies and Allied Matters Act*; copyright, patent, and design; admiralty jurisdiction, including shipping and navigation on the River Niger or River Benue; diplomatic, consular and trade representation; citizenship issues; bankruptcy and insolvency; aviation and safety of aircraft; arms, ammunition and explosives; drugs and poisons; mines and minerals (including oil fields, oil mining, geological surveys and natural gas); weights and measures; administration or the management and control of the federal government or any of its agencies; operation and interpretation of the 1999 Constitution insofar as it affects the federal government or any of its agencies; declaration or injunctions affecting the validity of any executive or administrative action or decision by the federal government or any of its agencies; and any other civil or criminal jurisdiction as may be conferred upon it by an Act of the National Assembly. The Federal High Court also exercises criminal jurisdiction over treason, treasonable felony and allied offences.

The jurisdiction of the High Court of the Federal Capital Territory, Abuja, is provided under section 257 of the 1999 Constitution and includes: civil proceedings in which the existence or extent of a legal right, power, duty, liability, privilege, interest, obligation or claim are in issue; and criminal proceedings involving or relating to any penalty, forfeiture, punishment or other liability in respect of an offence committed by any person.

The Sharia Court of Appeal of a State, as prescribed in section 277 of the 1999 Constitution, exercises both appeal and original jurisdiction in civil proceedings involving questions of Islamic personal law such as marriage, maintenance, guardianship, and succession.

In the customary context, the Customary Court of Appeal, as provided for under section 282 of the 1999 Constitution, has appellate and supervisory jurisdiction over the Customary Courts in Nigeria. The latter courts generally have jurisdiction to hear civil matters such as: land matters relating to ownership, occupation and possession; customary marriages; debt, demand or damages claimed between persons married under customary law or arising from a customary union; custody of children and other causes and matters relating to children under customary law; causes and matters relating to inheritance upon intestacy under customary law; grant of power or authority to any person to administer the estate of any intestate party under customary law; and disputes arising from contracts and torts at common or customary law.

The territorial jurisdiction of a Customary Court is usually delineated by the warrant establishing it. At present, there appears to be no set formula for determining the distribution and location of the Customary Courts within each State, but generally, consideration is given to a number of factors such as: ethnic, linguistic and historical links between communities; the similarity of the people's customs and traditions; the size, nature and proximity of the communities to be served by each court; and the expected volume of cases to be handled by a court if established within a given area. The law enforceable by a Customary Court is usually defined in the statute which provides for its establishment, and generally includes all rules and by-laws made by a local government body or a statutory corporation having authority in the locality. Furthermore, a Customary Court is usually authorized to apply a customary law which is neither repugnant to natural justice, equity and good conscience, nor incompatible with any written law in force in the area of the court's jurisdiction. Persons subject to the jurisdiction of a Customary Court are defined differently by different laws, but there are some similarities. The courts in Lagos, Oyo, Ogun, Ondo and the Cross River States have jurisdiction over all Nigerians regardless of their State of origin, residence or ethnicity.[53] In the Cross River States, the courts have further jurisdiction to try non-Nigerians who individually, or as members of a class, have been declared to be subject to the court's jurisdiction, or have at any time instituted proceedings in a Customary Court, or who voluntarily submitted to the court's jurisdiction. In Anambra State, every Customary Court is granted jurisdiction over all persons and classes of persons within the territorial limits of its jurisdiction.[54] This innovative approach is very different to the one adopted in the laws regulating the Customary Courts of the former Eastern Region, which empowered a Customary Court to exercise jurisdiction over a non-indigene of the area only if he or she was of African descent accustomed in his or her country of origin to living under a customary law or where a person, as an individual or a member of any class of persons, had been made subject to the court's jurisdiction by the regional executive council.[55]

Area courts in Nigeria exercise civil and criminal jurisdiction over matters expressly provided for in their enabling laws. In civil matters, these courts generally apply: the native law and custom prevailing in its area of jurisdiction or binding between the parties, provided it is neither repugnant to natural justice, equity or good conscience, nor incompatible with any written law in force in the area; any written law which it is empowered to enforce; the rules, orders and by-laws of local government bodies, as well as rules and orders made under the Native Authority Law of the former Northern Region or under any law repealed or

---

53. See, e.g., the *Customary Courts Law* Cap. 31 Western Region, s. 17.
54. *Customary Courts Edict* 1977, s. 12(1).
55. *Customary Court Law* Cap. 32 Eastern Region, s. 19.

replaced by it; and any principle of English law expressly or impliedly chosen or intended by the parties to regulate their transaction. In criminal cases, the courts generally apply: the Penal Code Law, the Criminal Procedure Code Law and any subsidiary law made thereunder; any written law which they are authorized by a Military Governor's order to apply; all rules, orders and by-laws of local government bodies; and rules and orders made under the Native Authority Law or under any enactment it replaced or repealed.[56]

Upper and Lower Area Courts can hear both civil and criminal cases relating to: matrimonial causes and matters between persons married under native law and custom or arising from or connected with a union contracted under such law and custom; custody of children under native law and custom; civil actions for debts, demands or damages; succession to property and the administration of estates under native law and custom; and ownership, possession or occupation of land. The scale and form of sanctions and awards which Upper and Lower Area Courts can impose vary according to their grade.

A further form of courts which exist in Nigeria are the Magistrates' Courts, whose physical and substantive jurisdiction is strictly delimited. Magistrates are assigned to a specific magisterial district. While stationed there, the magistrate is not expected to exercise jurisdiction beyond the limits of that district, except when temporarily moved to another district to assist with the disposal of case backlogs.[57] A magistrate has jurisdiction to hear and determine civil cases if the defendant or one of the defendants resides or carries on business within his or her district, the cause of action arose wholly or in part within the district, or if the subject matter of the action is within the district. The magistrate can also deal with any contractual dispute if the contract was concluded, breach occurred, or performance was expected to take place within its jurisdiction.[58] A magistrate can further hear criminal matters provided that the offence was committed within the district or within a ship, boat or canoe which at the time of the offence was committed was in the district, or which called at the district after the commission of the offence. If a defendant, before entering a plea objects to the jurisdiction of the Magistrates' Court, the matter must be referred to the High Court.[59] Every magistrate has authority to apply relevant statutes and principles of equity, and to grant such legal and equitable remedies that are appropriate in the circumstances. In the event of a conflict arising between principles of equity and relevant statutory provisions, the former prevail. Magistrates are enjoined to observe and enforce the observance of every local custom, except those which are repugnant to natural justice, equity and good conscience or to any written law.[60] Magistrates in the

---

56. See, e.g., *Area Court Edict* 1967 of Kwara State, ss 22, 24 and 25.
57. The *Magistrates' Courts Law* Cap. 82 Eastern Nigeria, ss 7 and 8; *Magistrates' Court Law* Cap. 74 Western Nigeria, s. 8; and *Criminal Procedure Code Law* Cap. 30 Northern Nigeria, ss 9 and 10.
58. Cap. 82 Eastern Nigeria, s. 24.
59. *Ibid.*, s. 30. See also Cap. 74 Western Nigeria, s. 27.
60. Cap. 82 Eastern Nigeria, ss 40-42; Cap. 74 Western Nigeria, ss 31-32; and Cap. 82 Lagos State, s. 24.

southern States of Nigeria exercise both civil and criminal jurisdiction, whilst those in the northern States only exercise the latter. Matters which, in the southern States fall within the civil jurisdiction of Magistrates' Courts, include: personal actions arising from contract and/or tort; suits between landlord and tenant; actions for the recovery of any penalty, rates, expenses or contribution recoverable by virtue of any written law; guardianship; and disputes relating to immovable property. Magistrates' Courts throughout Nigeria exercise two forms of criminal jurisdiction. First, a magistrate can conduct preliminary investigations into indictable offences and, where appropriate, refer an accused for trial by a High Court. Second, a magistrate can summarily try certain matters that need not be referred to the High Court. The Magistrates' Courts therefore operate effectively as a sieve, disposing of less serious matters and referring more serious issues to the High Court for disposal.

The final form of courts in Nigeria's judicial structure is the District Court. Its jurisdiction is very similar to the civil jurisdiction of Magistrates' Courts and includes: personal actions arising from contract and/or tort; suits between landlord and tenant; actions for the recovery of any penalty, rates, expenses or contribution recoverable by virtue of any written law; disputes relating to immovable property; guardianship; civil proceedings in respect of which jurisdiction has been conferred upon the court by the Land Tenure Law; and civil proceedings in respect of which jurisdiction has been conferred upon the court by any other written law.

4   ANALYSIS OF SIGNIFICANT ENVIRONMENTAL JUDGMENTS

4.1   INTRODUCTION

At the heart of good environmental governance is decision-making that is transparent and accountable. Principle 10 of the Rio Declaration on Environment and Development[61] (Rio Declaration) states that environmental issues are best handled with participation of all concerned citizens, and that effective participation requires access to information; access to decision-making and the opportunity to participate. It also includes access to redress and legal remedy. The last point, namely access to redress and legal remedy, is a key aspect in respect of which the judiciary can play a significant role in bettering environment governance. Citizens may wish to approach the court seeking access to relevant environmental information. Citizens may wish to challenge procedurally or substantively unfair environmental decisions. Citizens may also wish to approach the court to prevent environmentally deleterious action or seek compensation for any damage caused thereby.[62]

---

61. Rio Declaration on Environment and Development (1992) 31 *ILM* 874.
62. See M.T. Ladan, *Biodiversity, Environmental Litigation, Human Rights and Access to Environmental Justice: A Case Study of Nigeria* (Zaria: FPP, 2007), 43-46.

Underpinning each of these, and thereby fulfilling Principle 10, is the need to ensure access to justice and associated components such as: entrenching relevant constitutional and other legal environmental guarantees; adopting broad and inclusive interpretations of *locus standi*; creating impartial administrative, judicial and alternative venues for resolving conflicts; providing affordable and timely legal services; promoting active education of government and citizens regarding environmental rights and duties; promoting the role of the judiciary in applying the rule of law; and entrenching relevant statutory provisions in national legal systems which promote active participation.[63]

What follows below, is an analysis of the manner in which the Nigerian judiciary has, during the course of the past twenty years, both promoted and undermined environmental governance and the dictates inherent in the Rio Declaration's Principle 10. This analysis is arranged according to various themes, namely: procedural and jurisdictional issues; *locus standi* and representative actions; human rights and the environment, pre-action notices and statutory limitations; prescription in civil claims; application of torts; and burden of proof and special damage claims.

4.2   PROCEDURAL AND JURISDICTIONAL ISSUES

Complying with statutory procedural prerequisites is essential because where an action is not initiated by due legal process, the court proceedings can be declared a nullity.[64] The Supreme Court held in *Yahaya v. The State*,[65] that once a mandatory provision of the law is not followed, the trial is rendered null and void *ab initio*. The pre-conditions for the exercise of jurisdiction in any case are whether the plaintiff has a valid and legally enforceable cause of action. The plaintiff must accordingly have *locus standi* to bring the matter to court.[66] Where the plaintiff brings the suit in a representative capacity, the plaintiff must have the requisite authorization to act on behalf of another,[67] and the person/s that is/are so represented, must have the requisite *locus standi*.[68] Where provision is made for serving a pre-action notice,[69]

---

63. *Ibid.*, 46-59.
64. See *Jika v. Akuson* (2006) All FWLR (pt 293) 276.
65. (2002) 3 MJSC 103.
66. In *ELF Nigeria Ltd v. Sillo & Anor* (1994) 6 NWLR (pt 350) 258, a case involving damage caused by an oil spill, the Supreme Court, relying on *Adeshina v. Lemour* (1965) 1 All NLR 233, held that the plaintiffs had proven the existence of their common fishing right in tidal waters and accordingly had *locus standi* to approach the court for damages. See generally T. Okonkwo, *The Law of Environmental Liability* (Lagos: AEDE, 2003), 115. Also see the following cases: *Senator Adesanya v. President of Nigeria* (1981) 2 NCLR 388; *Edjerode v. Ikine* [2002] 2 MJSC 163; *A-G Federation v. A-G of the 36 States* [2001] 6 MJSC 69; *Arabambi v. ABI Ltd* [2006] 3 MJSC 61; and *Yesufu v. Governor Edo State* [2001] 5 MJSC 128.
67. *Ndule v. Ibezim* [2002] 12 MJSC 150.
68. See generally: *SPDC Nigeria Ltd v. Chief Otoko & Others* (1990) 6 NWLR (pt 159) 693; *Amos v. Shell BP Nigeria Ltd* (1974) 4 ECSLR 486; and *Ejem v. Offiah* (2000) 7 NWLR (pt 666) 662.
69. See Federal Environmental Protection Agency Act, s. 29(2).

this notice must have been served prior to bringing the matter to court. The court held in *Asogwa v. Chukwu*[70] that where a statutory pre-action notice has not been issued, the courts cannot assume jurisdiction. In *Teno Engineering Ltd v. Adisa*,[71] the court held that service of court process is another precondition to vesting jurisdiction in the court. Furthermore, the court held in *Okolo v. U.B.N.*[72] that the payment of filing fees is another precondition for the courts assuming jurisdiction over the matter.

Where there are prescribed time limits for commencing an action, the plaintiff must comply therewith, and as illustrated in *Akibu v. Azeez*,[73] time runs from the date the cause of action arises. The determination of the commencement of a prescription period is frequently problematic in the environmental context where the evidence of degradation, pollution or damage may be delayed. This often happens in cases of oil spillages, where the long term impacts of the pollution may not be immediately evident. In dealing with this issue, the Supreme Court, in *Aremo 11 v. Adekanye*,[74] held that a fresh cause of action arises from time to time as often as the damage is caused. In summary, the above cases, all decided by the Supreme Court, illustrate the judiciary's strict attitude toward adherence to court rules and procedures. Only once the plaintiff has complied with all requisite procedures, will the court begin its assignment and ascertain whether it has jurisdiction to hear the matter.

In *7up v. Abiola*,[75] the Supreme Court held that 'it is trite that in all matters before the court the fundamental one is the issue of jurisdiction which must first be determined before anything else, otherwise all proceedings relating thereto will be a nullity and an exercise in futility'. The Supreme Court held in *Abu v. Odugbo*,[76] that what determines the court's jurisdiction to entertain a suit is the claim of the plaintiff. In *Menakaya v. Menakaya*,[77] the Supreme Court held that the competence of a court to hear a matter is a fundamental issue which cannot be waived. The court's competence to hear a matter can be challenged at any stage of the proceedings[78] and the approach of the court has accordingly been to carefully

---

70. (2003) 4 NWLR (pt 811) 540, 552. Also see the following cases: *Mobil Producing (Nig.) Unlimited v. LASEPA* (2002) 2 MJSC 69; *Eze v. Okechukwu* (2003) 2 MJSC 188; *Abakaliki Local Government Council v. Abakaliki Rice Mills Owners Enterprises Nigeria* (1990) 6 NWLR (pt 155) 182; *University of Ife v. Fawehinmi Construction Co. Ltd* (1991) 7 NWLR (pt 201) 26; *Nigeria Cement Co. Ltd v. Nigeria Railway Corporation & Anor* (1992) 1 NWLR (pt 22) 747; *Amadi v. NNPC* (2000) 10 NWLR (pt 674) 6; and *Nigerian Ports Plc. v. Oseni* (2000) 8 NWLR (pt 669) 410.
71. [2005] 7 MJSC 89. See further the following cases: *A-G Adamawa State v. A-G Federation* [2006] I MJSC 1, *Sken Consult v. Ukey* (1981) 1 SC 6; and *AIE v. Adebayo* [2003] 12 MJSC 44.
72. [2004] 2 MJSC 69.
73. (2003) 5 NWLR (pt 814) 643.
74. *Ibid.*
75. [2001] 5 MJSC 93 at 97.
76. [2001] 7 MJSC 87 at 91.
77. [2001] 8 MJSC 50.
78. *Eze v. A-G Rivers State* [2002] 1 MJSC 87.

scrutinize its jurisdiction at the outset of the matter so as to ensure certainty, preclude unfounded and protracted litigation, and protect litigant's interests.

An example of the jurisdictional conundrums faced by the Supreme Court is clearly illustrated in the case of *Shell Petroleum Development Company (Nigeria) Ltd v. Abel Isaiah.*[79] The facts of the case were as follows. In July 1988, an old tree fell on the appellant's oil pipeline and dented it. The indention apparently hindered the free flow of crude oil through the oil pipeline which ran across the respondent's swamp land and surrounding farmlands, and therefore needed to be replaced. The appellant engaged the services of a contractor to repair the dented pipeline. While attending to the repairs, the appellant's contractor did not construct an oil trap; a device made of soil used to trap oil leaking during a repair process. As a result, crude oil spilled freely onto the respondent's swampland and polluted the surrounding farmlands, streams and fishponds. In the court *a quo* (High Court), the respondent had instituted a claim against the appellant for the sum of N22 million in damages based on the appellant's negligent conduct. The High Court awarded N22 million to the respondent, a decision which was confirmed by the Court of Appeal. The appellant accordingly sought to appeal the decision to the highest court in the land, the Supreme Court, which was called upon to decide on a number of issues including: the jurisdiction of the High Court to hear the issue; the appellant's negligence; causation; the damages calculation; the respondent's *locus standi*; and the applicability of the rule in *Rylands v. Fletcher* [1866] LR 1 Ex. 265. The Supreme Court stated that the key issue to be resolved at the outset was whether the Court of Appeal was correct in holding that the trial court had jurisdiction to hear the matter, in other words: did the issue fall within the High Court's jurisdiction to hear claims pertaining to mines and minerals including oil fields, oil mining, geological surveys and natural gas and oilfields, as prescribed in various statutory provisions?[80] In dispute was the fact that the subject matter of the dispute was premised on federal law[81] and therefore, according to section 251(1) of the 1999 Constitution, the matter should have been filed in a federal High Court. The Supreme Court, having considered the enabling statutory framework, upheld the appellant's appeal, ruling that the issue was regulated by federal legislation and accordingly, the High Court had lacked jurisdiction to hear the matter. The court accordingly did not need to rule on the remaining issues. Although the outcome of the case had harsh consequences for the respondents, litigants now know that all oil pollution cases should be brought before a Federal High Court, and not the State High Court. The ability of the Federal High Court to cope with the volume of litigation arising from petroleum operations, however, remains a matter of concern.[82]

---

79. (2001) 5 SC (pt 11) 1.
80. These were: *Federal High Court (Amendment) Act* Decree No. 60 of 1991 and *Constitution (Suspension and Modification) Act* Decree No. 107 of 1993, specifically s. 230(1).
81. *Petroleum Act and Oil Pipe Lines Act* (1956) *LFN* 2004, Ch. 7.
82. See J.F. Fedumo, *Oil Pollution and the Problems of Compensation in Nigeria* (Port-Harcourt: F & F Publishers, 2001), 21.

The problem of jurisdiction in an oil pollution case also arose in *Shell Petroleum Development Company (Nigeria) Ltd v. Chief GBA Tiebo VII & Others.*[83] In this case the Supreme Court was similarly called upon to decide whether the decision of the Court of Appeal confirming the jurisdiction of the State High Court, was valid or not. The Supreme Court referred to the *Abel Isaiah* case and held that the court's *ratio* in this matter did not apply because at the time the cause of action arose, the statutory provisions which had precluded the court's jurisdiction in the *Abel Isaiah* case were not in force, and accordingly did not preclude the jurisdiction of the High Court to hear the matter.

4.3   LOCUS STANDI AND REPRESENTATIVE CAPACITY

Locus standi is an essential gate keeper to the courts. However, if it is formulated and construed in a very restricted manner, it can significantly undermine access to justice especially in environmental matters. The issue of *locus standi* will not generally present a problem to an individual litigant where their personal or proprietary interests have been affected by environmental pollution or natural resources depletion.[84] As is illustrated in the following analysis of the country's relevant jurisprudence, in order to have standing to sue in Nigeria, a plaintiff must exhibit 'sufficient interest'; i.e., 'an interest which is peculiar to the plaintiff and not an interest which he [or she] shares in common with general members of the public'. A plaintiff who sues for damages arising from an environmental polluting or damaging action must in addition show that he/she has suffered damage. These issues, although not troubling for individual litigants, may prove problematic for citizen organizations or environmental non-governmental organizations (NGOs). These organizations play a crucial role as environmental watchdogs, educators, motivators and defenders and are often the institutions which bring matters to court.[85] They may, however, because of an inability to show a direct interest other than that of their special environmental consciousness and common interest in the environment, lack the requisite standing to approach the court.[86]

In *Shell Petroleum Development Company (Nigeria) Ltd v. Chief Otoko and Others,*[87] the first respondent, acting on behalf of residents in the area, brought an application for damages against the appellant following a crude oil spill by the latter which allegedly significantly polluted and deprived the residents use of the rivers and creeks in the area. The respondents succeeded in the court *a quo*, but the appellant challenged the *locus standi* of the respondents on appeal. The Court of Appeal held that it was essential that the representative have the same interest of

---

83. [2005] 9 MJSC 158.
84. See generally, Ladan, *supra* n. 1, 117, 204.
85. L. Malone & P. Scott, *Defending the Environment: Civil Society Strategies to Enforce International Environmental Law* (New York: TPI, 2004).
86. *Ibid.*, 205-222.
87. (1990) 6 NWLR (pt 159) 693, 695.

those who he/she is representing; there be a common interest and common grievance; and the relief sought should be of a nature which would benefit all those who
the representative represents. The court ruled that the respondent had failed to
satisfy these requirements and accordingly the appeal was upheld.

A significant problem with the above formulation is the need for plaintiffs in a
group action to prove their common interest and grievance that they have suffered
equally. In *Amos v. Shell BP PDC Ltd*,[88] the plaintiff, acting in a representative
capacity, sued the defendant claiming special and general damages. It was alleged
that the defendant had, during the course of its oil mining operations, built a large
earth dam across the plaintiff's creek. As a result, farms in the area were flooded
and damaged; the movement of local canoes was hampered, and agriculture and
commercial life was effectively paralysed. One of the issues which the court had to
address was whether special damages could be claimed in a representative action,
where the plaintiffs had suffered different and unequal loss. In other words, could
members of the public claim for losses suffered by them individually in a collective
action? The court dismissed the claim and held that since the creek was a public
waterway, the blocking thereof constituted a public nuisance. The court stated that
no individual could recover damages unless he or she could prove that the defendant's conduct had caused special damage to his or her person or property. As the
interests and losses suffered by the plaintiffs were separate in character and not
communal, their collective action was not permitted.

In *NNPC v. Sele*,[89] the plaintiff sued for damages arising from a massive crude
oil spill from the defendant's pipeline. The oil spill had polluted and damaged
many trees, crops, fishing ponds, fishing contrivances, local gin distilleries and
fresh water wells in the area. The plaintiff, acting on behalf of the community,
claimed N20 million as fair and adequate compensation for the community's loss.
The court *a quo* awarded the plaintiffs approximately N15 million as special
damages and N3 million as general damages. The defendant took the matter on
appeal. The Court of Appeal referred to *Adreniran v. Interland Transport Ltd*[90] in
which the court stated: 'While in this case it has been shown that they have
common interest, the grievance of individuals is separated and distinct; consequently a representative action taken as in this case must fail.' The court nonetheless held that the plaintiff had disclosed common grounds and interests in the suit
and there were no individual claims. The implications of this judgment are significant because by allowing an individual to bring an action for damages in a
community's interest, the court effectively obviated the need for future similar
litigants to bring many individual actions as opposed to one collective action.

It has been argued that the court's approach in the *Sele* case was correct in that:

> unlike the non-communal English society in which the rule as to public nui-
> sance was developed, in Nigeria people live in communities, especially in the

---

88. (1974) 4 ECSLR 48, 51
89. (2004) ALL FWLR (pt 223) 1859 CA.
90. (1991) 9 NWLR (pt 214) 155, 161.

Niger-Delta region where the worst incidents of environmental pollution occur. So how they share the proceeds of special damages awarded, which is the true worry informing the dichotomy of who sues in respect of public nuisance, is not the business of anybody.[91]

4.4   HUMAN RIGHTS AND THE ENVIRONMENT

In *Jonah Gbemre v. SPDC Ltd and Others* (2005),[92] the court granted leave to the applicant to: institute proceedings in a representative capacity for himself and for each and every member of the Iweherekan Community in the Delta State of Nigeria; and apply for an order enforcing or securing the enforcement of their fundamental human rights to life and human dignity as provided by sections 33 (1) and 34(1) of the 1999 Constitution. The court held that these constitutionally guaranteed rights inevitably include the right to a clean, poison and pollution-free and healthy environment.[93] The judge further declared that the impact of the respondent's gas flaring activities on the applicant's community was a violation of the applicants' fundamental rights.[94] Furthermore, the court ruled that the failure of the respondent to carry out an environmental impact assessment (EIA) relating to its gas flaring activities, was a clear violation of the *Environmental Impact Assessment Decree*, and further had contributed to violating the applicant's and community's environmental rights. The court consequently ordered the respondents to cease their gas flaring activities. The court did not, however, award the applicant's damages, costs or compensation. Despite this, the case is considered a landmark judgment, as it was the first occasion that the Nigerian judiciary, in line with the approach of many other jurisdictions, referred to fundamental human rights in an environmental context.[95]

4.5   PRE-ACTION NOTICES AND STATUTORY LIMITATIONS

As has been noted above, a key procedural pre-requisite in bringing a matter to court is compliance with relevant pre-action notice procedures. The *Federal Protection Agency Act* generally provides that no action can be lodged against the Agency unless a period of one month, after written notice of intention to commence the suit has been served upon the Agency, has expired.[96] The relevant notice must expressly state the cause of action, particulars of the claim, name and place of abode of the plaintiff, and the form of relief claimed. The main aim of this

---

91. W.A. Chechey J, 'Judgment and Remedies in Environmental Cases', paper presented at the Judicial Training Workshop of 28-30 March 2006 (Abuja: UNEP & NJI, 2006), 41.
92. (2005) Suit No. FHC/B/CS/53/05.
93. *Ibid.*, 15.
94. *Ibid.*, 17-18.
95. See M. Dean, 'The Revolution in Indian Environmental Jurisprudence: Review Essay', *APJEL* 5, no. 3 (2000): 291-303.
96. S. 29(2) read with s. 30(2).

pre-notice procedure in the *Federal Protection Agency Act* is not necessarily to enable the Agency to prepare its case, but rather to determine whether the matter can be settled out of court.

These pre-notice provisions were an issue in *Mobil Producing (Nig.) Unlimited v. LASEPA, FEPA & Ors*,[97] where the Court of Appeal dismissed the applicant's claim on the basis that it had failed to comply with the statutory pre-action notice procedure. On appeal, however, the Supreme Court held that the service of a pre-action notice is at best a procedural requirement and not an issue of substantive law on which the right of an applicant depends.[98] It further held that the pre-action notice procedure was not an integral part of the process of initiating proceedings and that a party who has served a pre-action notice is not obliged to commence proceeding at all. Non-compliance with this procedure does not therefore appear to undermine the original jurisdiction of the courts to hear the matter or entitle the respondent to apply to have the proceedings dismissed. It merely places the matter on hold until such time as the pre-notice procedure has been complied with or the respondent elects to waive the irregularity.

It is worth noting that the *Federal Environmental Agency Act* also contains important statutory limitations which may undermine environmental action. Section 29(1) of the Act provides that no suit can be brought against the Agency (including its members and employees) for any act done in pursuance or execution of any law or any public duties; or in respect of any alleged neglect or default in the execution of such law, duties or authority. Furthermore, claims against the Agency (including its members and employees) prescribe twelve months after the alleged act, negligence or default; or in the case of a continuing damage or injury, twelve months after it ceases. The nature of suits which could be brought against the Agency, and therefore falling within the ambit of the above provision, would include applications for the recovery of damages and for injunctions.

4.6   Prescription of Civil Claims

The issue of prescription often arises in civil environmental matters because the impacts of the original damage-causing event (the pollution) may be delayed, continuous or periodic. The defence of prescription tends to urge the court to hold that time runs from when the pollution incident originally occurred. The rule in Nigeria is as follows:[99] for continuous pollution, accompanied by renewed damage, the cause of action is maintainable backwards for the statutory period of limitation, bar one day. For periodic pollution, the cause of action is maintainable for all previous occurrences falling within the statutory period of limitation. For an isolated occurrence, the cause of action is reckoned from when the actual damage occurs, but not the original act itself.

---

97. (2002) 18 NWLR (pt 798) 1.
98. *Mobil Producing (Nig.) Unlimited v. LASEPA* (2002) 2 MJSC 69.
99. See generally Chechey, *supra* n. 91, 44.

The issue of a continuing wrong arose in *Gulf Oil Company (Nigeria) Ltd v. Oluba.*[100] The appellant commenced oil exploration on the respondent's land in 1973 which continued until 1989. The exploration activity damaged swamps, channels and lakes resulting in a loss of income derived by the respondent's fishing and farming activities. The respondent only commenced its action some thirteen years after the oil exploration had ceased. The appellant sought to have the matter dismissed in the court *a quo* on the basis that the respondent's claim had prescribed. In terms of the applicable law governing torts (the *Limitation Law*[101] of Delta State), claims have to be brought to court within six years of the date on which the cause of action arises. The court nonetheless ruled that the cause of action was a continuing one and accordingly had not prescribed. The appellant took the matter on appeal to the Court of Appeal which held that the decision of the court *a quo* was 'outlandish' and could not have been based on a proper interpretation of the relevant statutory provisions. It accordingly held that the cause of action arose when the appellant ceased its damaging oil exploration activities in 1989, and accordingly, the respondent's claim had prescribed. This decision is somewhat problematic as there appears to have been sufficient evidence of ongoing damage to enable the Court of Appeal to take the opposite view; and thereby not effectively condemn a vast area of land to permanent ecological ruin, especially where the appellant had the necessary resources to rehabilitate it.

4.7   APPLICATION OF TORTS IN THE THE ENVIRONMENTAL CONTEXT

Torts of negligence have in the Nigerian context been used by litigants to recover damages occasioned by environmentally deleterious activities. In *Shell Petroleum Development Company (Nigeria) Ltd v. Chief Otoko and Others,*[102] the respondents sued the appellant for damages arising from an alleged negligent crude oil spill. The oil spill had severely polluted the Andoni River and Creeks, and impacted on the respondents' beneficial use of these water resources. The court *a quo* upheld their initial application and expressly applied the rule in the English case of *Rylands v. Fletcher.*[103] It stated that:

> It is noteworthy that the Rule in *Rylands v. Fletcher* which is alternatively pleaded by the plaintiffs in the case applies to the circumstances of this case.

---

100. (2003) FWLR (pt 145) 712.
101. *Limitation Laws* No. 1, 1999 Delta State of Nigeria.
102. *Supra* n. 87.
103. [1866] LR 1 Ex. 265. The rule in *Rylands v. Fletcher* reads: 'The person whose habitation is made unhealthy by the fumes and noisome vapours of his neighbour's alkali works is damnified without any fault of his own and seems but reasonable and just that the neighbour, who has brought something on his own property which was not naturally there, harmless to other so long as it is confined to his own property, but which he knows to be mischievous if it gets on his neighbour's should be obliged to make good the damage which ensures if he does not succeed confining it to his own property.'

The crude oil which passed through the pipe lines could not naturally have been there, the defendant gathered the crude oil into the pipes and it was a substance which was dangerous and likely to escape. It was not a natural user of land but was brought in there by the act of the defendant. Since therefore it had escaped and caused damages the defendant is liable. In the consequences of this case, the Rule in *Rylands v. Fletcher* applies and as there was no third party act which caused the escape of the oil.[104]

The matter was, however, overturned on appeal, where the Court of Appeal agreed with the court *a quo*'s application of the common law, but dismissed the matter on a procedural ground.[105]

In *Shell Petroleum Development (Nigeria) Ltd v. HRH Chief GBA Tiebo VII and Others*,[106] the respondents sued for damages occasioned by the appellant's oil spill. The court *a quo* similarly applied the rule in *Rylands v. Fletcher* and found in favor of the respondents. The appellants unsuccessfully sought to appeal the matter.

Another common law remedy that has been recognized by the Nigerian judiciary in environmental context is the tort of nuisance. In *Seismograph Service (Nigeria) Ltd v. Ogbeni*,[107] the applicant sought to use the tort of nuisance to obtain a court order compelling the respondent to cease exploding oil testing chemicals around its premises on the basis that it was causing excessive noise and damage to his buildings. In *Shell Petroleum Development Company (Nigeria) Ltd v. Chief Otoko and Others*[108] discussed above, the applicant successfully sought to plea the tort of nuisance in the alternative to its primary claim based on the tort of negligence. Finally, in *Adediran and Another v. Interland and Transport Limited*,[109] the applicant sued the respondent under the tort of nuisance for an injunction compelling it to cease its activities which were causing excessive noise, vibration, dust and obstructing roads in the area. Although the applicants in the first two matters failed, the applicant did succeed in the latter case where the court held that: 'It is well settled that a nuisance, whether public or private, is an injury which confers on the person affected a right of action ... The individual who suffers injury has a right of action because of the cause of action.'[110]

---

104. *Supra* n. 87, 699.
105. *Ibid.*, 701.
106. (1976) 4 NWLR (pt 445) 657.
107. (1976) 4 SC 85.
108. *Supra* n. 87.
109. (1991) 9 NWLR (pt 241) 155.
110. *Ibid.*, 180.

4.8   Burden of Proof and Special Damage Claims

The burden of proof in civil matters in Nigeria generally rests on the plaintiff[111] and is based on a balance of probabilities.[112] The nature of the evidence depends on the substantive elements which underlie the cause of action. In a claim for compensation as a result of deleterious environmental action, one of the aspects which a plaintiff must generally prove is ownership of the damaged property.[113] In a claim for loss or destruction of farm crops, farm land and fruit producing trees, the court held in *Uhunmwangbo v. Uhunmwangbo*,[114] that the plaintiff must adduce sufficient evidence to show inter alia: the name; nature; and number of productive trees allegedly destroyed. For an action in negligence or nuisance, the ingredients of the cause of action must be established.[115] For a claim in special damages,[116] the plaintiff must itemize and prove the *quantum* of every aspect of the claim. In *RCC (Nig.) Ltd v. Edonwonyi*,[117] the court held that a claim for loss of earnings is a claim for special damages and accordingly the plaintiff must provide full particulars of the loss suffered including the rate of remuneration. Where the claim is highly technical in nature, the courts generally require the plaintiff to go the extra mile and lead expert evidence to support the claim.[118] In *ARC v. JDP*,[119] the court stated that a counsel presenting a case is expected to argue his or her client's case convincingly and assist the court to arrive at the correct decision.

    Fulfilling the above judicial expectations regarding the submission of evidence is often difficult in cases dealing with environmental pollution. This problem was vividly reflected in *Shell Petroleum Development Company (Nigeria) Ltd v. Chief GBA Tiebo VII & Others*,[120] where the respondents had approached the High Court and claimed the sum of N64 million from the appellant. The

---

111. See ss 135, 136 and 137 of the *Evidence Act* Cap. E. 14 *LFN* 2004. See in addition the following cases: *NNPC v. Lutin Inv. Ltd* [2006] 2 MJSC 1; *Onyenge & Ors v. Ebere & Ors* [2004] 11 MJSC 184; *Ojo v. Philips* (1993) 5 NWLR (pt 296) 751; *Jalico Ltd v. Owoniboys* [1995] 4 SCNJ 256; *Nsirim v. Nsirim* [2002] 3 MJSC 26; *Ewo v. Ani* [2004] 4 MJSC 119; *Adams v. LSDPC* [2002] 5 NWLR (pt 656) 291; and *Bon Ltd v. Babatunde* (2002) 3 NWLR (pt 706).
112. See *Olujinle v. Adeagbo* (1988)2 NWLR (pt 75) 386.
113. *Sommer & Ors v. Federal Housing Authority* (1992) 1 NWLR (pt 219) 548.
114. (1992) 2 NWLR (pt 226) 709.
115. See: *Anya v. Concorde Hotel* [2003] 2 MJSC 160; *Royal Ade v. National Oil* [2004] 9 MJSC 40; and *Adediran & Another v. Interland & Transport Ltd* (1986) 2 NWLR (pt 20) 78.
116. Special damages require the claimant to establish his or her entitlement by credible evidence of such character, as would suggest that he or she is entitled to an award under that head. In some cases it may be unnecessary.
117. (2003) 4 NWLR (pt 811) 513. See further: *Arabambi v. ABI Ltd* [2006] 3 MJSC 61; *Gonzee v. NERDC* [2005] 12 MJSC 179; *Daniel Holdings v. UBA Plc* [2005] 11 MJSC 69; *Reynolds v. RockOnoh* [2005] 10 MJSC 159; *SPDC (Nig.) Ltd v. Chief GBA Tiebo VII & Ors.* [2005] 9 MJSC 158; and *Nwanji v. Coastal Services* [2004] 10 MJSC 154.
118. *Seismograph Services (Nig.) Ltd v. Kwarbe Ogbeni* (1976) 4 SC 85.
119. [2003] 5 MJSC 57.
120. [2005] 9 MJSC 158.

respondents argued that the appellant, whilst undertaking its oil mining activities, had negligently spilt oil on the respondents' land, creeks, lakes and shrines. The respondents claimed special damages for losses arising from the pollution of fishponds and damages to communal fishing nets and raffia palms. They also claimed specific amounts of money as general damages. The court *a quo* awarded the following damages to be paid by the appellant: N400,000 and N600,000 as general damage for loss of raffia palms and loss of drinking water respectively; N5 million as general damages; and N1 million to cover the respondents' legal costs. The appellant's initial appeal to the Court of Appeal was dismissed. The appellant accordingly lodged a second appeal to the Supreme Court which was required to consider whether it was proper for the court *a quo* to have awarded special damages in the absence of sufficient proof; and also whether the amount awarded as general damages was excessive. The Supreme Court stated that 'anyone making a claim in special damages must prove strictly that he did suffer such special damages claimed'.[121] It held that proof of special damages is strict and where a plaintiff is unable to prove special damages, 'his case crumbles and a trial court cannot compensate him by way of general damages'.[122] The Supreme Court further held that:

> ... special damages require the claimant to establish his entitlement by credible evidence of such character, as would suggest that he is entitled to an award under that head. In some cases it may be unnecessary. The important thing is that the evidence proffered must be qualitative and credible and as such lend itself to quantification. However, general damages need not be proved strictly as they are regarded as damages resulting from defendant's tortuous conduct.[123]

These *dicta* appear to be correct in law because in the absence of strict proof of special damages, the courts may be compelled to rely on unsubstantiated estimations. These undesirable estimations are evident in the decision of the court *a quo* above in which significant sums were awarded against the appellant for the damage to the raffia palms and the cost of purchasing alternative drinking water, notwithstanding the absence of proof quantifying the actual damage occasioned by the appellant's conduct. The Supreme Court went on to comment that the requirement of strict proof definitely excludes a situation where the court will be left to guess what the losses due to the plaintiff's actions should be. The Supreme Court distinguished between special and general damages,[124] and held that since the respondents had failed to prove their entitlement to special damages, the court *a quo* appeared to have simply awarded general damages *in lieu* of special damages.[125] It further criticized the statements of the court *a quo* to

---

121. *Ibid.*, 161.
122. *Ibid.*, 162.
123. *Ibid.*
124. See generally: *Storms Bruks Aktie Bolag v. Hitchinson* (1905) AC 515; *In the Sesquehuanna* (1926) AC 655 at 661; and *Prehin v. Royal Bank of Liverpool* (1870) LR 5 Ex. 92.
125. *Tiebo* case, *supra* n. 120, 163.

the effect that the award of general damages was a way of compensating the respondents for the loss of expected profits and freight of goods; claims which did not even appear in the respondents' initial pleadings.[126] With respect to general damages, the Supreme Court confirmed that these were granted at the court's discretion and that the Supreme Court would only interfere with the discretion of the court *a quo* where the award was patently too high or too low.[127] Based on the extensive damage and pollution to the crops, farms, farmlands, ponds and creeks, the Supreme Court elected not to interfere with the court *a quo's* award of general damages.[128] The decision of the Supreme Court not to interfere with the grant of general damages appears prudent as in many instances these damages are vital for financing the rehabilitation of the damaged or polluted environment. The Supreme Court was, however, very clear in its statement that although it understood the difficulty in proving special damages, 'general damages cannot be a compensation for special damages'.[129]

In the pursuit of justice, the Supreme Court has in some instances inferred negligence from the facts before it and dispensed with the requirement of proof. In *Machine Umudje v. Shell*,[130] for example, the Supreme Court stated that it could draw necessary inference of negligence even in the absence of proof and effectively applied the rule in *Rylands v. Fletcher* to hold the defendant strictly liable. In this case, the plaintiff complained that the defendant had blocked and diverted a natural stream, thus interfering with his fishing rights. Furthermore, he claimed that accumulated oil waste on land under the defendant's control had escaped on to his land and caused damage. The defendant was held not liable for the latter compliant, but liable for the former. This case is indicative of the manner in which the court's recognition of the rule in *Rylands v. Fletcher* has lightened the *onus* resting on the plaintiff to prove essential elements of the relevant cause of action.

The Supreme Court has also applied the presumption of *res ipsa loquitur* to assist victims of environmental damage. In *Royal Ade v. National Oil*,[131] for example, the court held that the presumption of *res ipsa loquitur* effectively 'fastens liability on the defendant' unless he or she can rebut it. The application of this presumption should feasibly aid victims of environmental pollution who, because of their limited knowledge, are unable to prove negligence on the part of the defendant.

5   CRITICAL SURVEY AND WAY FORWARD

The generic obstacles impeding effective access to environmental justice take many forms. Governments often devote meager public funds to the judiciary

---

126.   *Ibid.*, 165.
127.   *Ibid.*
128.   *Ibid.*, 169.
129.   *Ibid.*, 171.
130.   (1975) 9-11 SC 155.
131.   *Supra* n. 115, 43.

thereby undermining its accessibility, efficiency and credibility. Public access to relevant information to enable citizens to effectively exercise their rights is often limited. Litigation is expensive which is further compounded by the tendency of the legal profession to pursue profit motives and neglect their ethical duty to take on *pro bono* public interest litigation. Courts interpret procedural rules relating to security for costs, prescription, legal standing and proof in a very strict manner which frequently undermines the ability of the legally illiterate to bring matters to court, or to succeed when they do so. Generally speaking, the independence of the judiciary is also to be questioned in various jurisdictions. Lawmakers create laws which are unnecessarily complex and which delegate excessively wide powers to public officials imbued with a culture of secrecy. Law reform, including the simplification and modernization of the statute book is given a low priority. Ministers and public authorities frequently hold political sway which effectively immunizes them from public accountability and procedurally and substantively dubious decision-making therefore frequently evades judicial scrutiny.

Many of these obstacles are similarly prevalent in Nigeria, a developing nation fraught with balancing social, economic and environmental imperatives. There is accordingly a pressing need for the judiciary to take a more activist, critical and creative stance towards environmental governance to, among other things, ensure access to environmental justice.[132] As should be evident from the above analysis, the judiciary has heeded this call in a limited manner. Positive trends, however, include: the judiciary's recognition of the link between human rights and the environment; extended *locus standi*; the application of torts in environmental context; some judicial flexibility regarding representative actions and pre-action notice procedures; and the acceptance of the rules laid down in *Rylands v. Fletcher*.

In addition to the many generic problems discussed above, there are various challenges which further undermine the ability of the Nigerian judiciary to play an effective role in environmental governance. First, its role in prosecuting environmental offenders is minimal owing to the absence of effective statutory sanctions and compliance and enforcement by environmental authorities. This could be remedied through effective legal reform which should increase environmental offences and penalties. Building capacity and resources within environmental compliance and enforcement authorities would be a further necessary prerequisite.

Second, the ability of the judiciary to hold polluters to account significantly depends on litigants bringing matters to court. The high costs and procedural conundrums in bringing civil matters to court have undermined the ability and willingness of would-be litigants to do so; thereby effectively stifling the role of the judiciary in this respect. This is further undermined by general public apathy and a lack of awareness regarding environmental concerns. What is therefore required is an extensive public environmental awareness campaign, coupled with the introduction of novel procedures for reducing the pecuniary and procedural barriers to

---

132. M.T. Ladan, 'Enhancing Access to Justice on Environmental Matters: Public Participation in Decision-making and Access to information', paper presented at the Judicial Training Workshop of 6-10 Feb 2006 (Abuja: UNEP & NJI, 2006).

would-be litigants. Necessary safeguards will, however, need to be put in place to curb one problem inherent in environmental litigation in Nigeria, namely 'gold digging actions' brought for the sole purpose of financial gain. Actions of this nature waste the courts' time and resources; delay access to justice to *bona fide* litigants; and potentially taint the attitude of the judiciary towards environmental litigants.

Third, as was illustrated in *Allar Irou v. Shell BP Development Company (Nigeria) Ltd*,[133] some members of the Nigerian judiciary have in the past adopted a very paternalistic attitude to companies responsible for some of the worst environmental atrocities in Nigeria; namely those operating in the oil sector. In this matter, the court refused to grant an injunction in favour of the plaintiff whose land, fish pond and creek had been polluted by the defendant's operations. The court's contention was that nothing should be done to disturb the operations of an industry which is responsible for generating a significant portion of the nation's revenue. What the judge failed to acknowledge in this matter was the need to achieve a sustainable balance between social, economic and environmental factors; an imperative which is no doubt now engrained in many members of Nigeria's judiciary following recent workshops held with the country's leading environmental law academics.[134]

Whilst various challenges remain, it is evident that the Nigerian judiciary is increasingly willing to take a pro-environment stance. This is commendable and, on condition that remaining challenges facing judicial involvement in environmental governance are addressed sooner than later, Nigeria may well be on its way to a more sustainable environmental governance effort supported by prudent judgments of its courts.

BIBLIOGRAPHY

Ajibola, P.B. 'Protection of the environment through the Law'. In *The Law and the Environment in Nigeria*, edited by F. Shyllon. Ibadan: University of Ibadan Press, 1999.

Ajomo, M.A. 'An Examination of Federal Environmental Laws in Nigeria'. In *Environmental Law and Sustainable Development in Nigeria*, edited by M.A. Ajomo & O. Adewale. Lagos: NIALS & the British Council, 1994.

Ayua, I.A. & O. Ajai. *Implementing the Biodiversity Convention: Nigerian and African Perspectives*. Lagos: University of Lagos Nigerian Institute of Advanced Legal Studies, 1997.

---

133. Suit No. W/89/71 Warri High Court 26/11/73 (unreported). See M.A. Ajomo, 'An Examination of Federal Environmental Laws in Nigeria', in *Environmental Law and Sustainable Development in Nigeria*, ed. M.A. Ajomo & O. Adewale (Lagos: NIALS & the British Council, 1994), 22.

134. One example is the Judicial Training Workshop on Environmental Law in Nigeria, organized by the National Judicial Institute (Abuja) and UNEP.

Birnie, P.W. & A.E. Boyle. *International Law and the Environment.* 2nd ed.
    Oxford: Oxford University Press, 2002.
Chechey, W.A., J. 'Judgment and Remedies in Environmental Cases'. Paper pre-
    sented at the Judicial Training Workshop of 28-30 March 2006, unpublished.
    Abuja: UNEP & Nigerian Judges Institute, 2006.
Dean, M. 'The Revolution in Indian Environmental Jurisprudence: Review
    Essay'. *Asia Pacific Journal of Environmental Law* 5, no. 3 (2000):
    291-303.
Draft National Policy on Environmental Sanitation and its Guidelines. Lagos:
    FEPA, 2004.
Fedumo, J.F. *Oil Pollution and the Problems of Compensation in Nigeria.* Port-
    Harcourt: F & F Publishers, 2001.
Ladan, M.T. *Biodiversity, Environmental Litigation, Human Rights and Access to
    Environmental Justice: A Case Study of Nigeria.* Zaria: Faith Printers and
    Publishers, 2007.
Ladan, M.T. 'Enhancing Access to Justice on Environmental Matters: Public Par-
    ticipation in Decision-making and Access to information'. Paper presented
    at the Judicial Training Workshop of 6-10 Feb 2006, unpublished. Abuja:
    UNEP & Nigerian Judges Institute, 2006.
Ladan, M.T. 'Human Rights and Environmental Protection'. In *Text for Human
    Rights Teaching in Schools*, edited by A.O. Obilade & C. Nwankwo. Lagos:
    Constitutional Rights Project, 1999.
Ladan, M.T. *Materials and Cases on Environmental Law and Policy.* Zaria:
    ECONET Publishers, 2004.
Malone, L. & P. Scott. *Defending the Environment: Civil Society Strategies
    to Enforce International Environmental Law.* New York: Transnational
    Publisher Inc., 2004.
National Policy on the Environment. Rev. ed. Lagos: FEPA, 1999.
Okediran, O. 'An appraisal of Environmental Sanitation Edicts in Nigeria'. In *The
    Law and the Environment in Nigeria*, edited by F. Shyllon. Ibadan: University
    of Ibadan Press, 1999.
Okonkwo, T. *The Law of Environmental Liability.* Lagos: Afrique Environmental
    Development and Education, 2003.
Osinbajo, Y. *Some Public Law Considerations in Environmental Law.* Lagos:
    University of Lagos Faculty of Law, 1990.
Shyllon, F. 'Present and Future Institutional Framework for Environmental
    Management in Nigeria'. In *The Law and the Environment in Nigeria*, edited
    by F. Shyllon. Ibadan: University of Ibadan Press, 1999.
Simpson, S. & O. Fagbohun (eds). *Environmental Law and Policy.* Lagos: Lagos
    State University Faculty of Law, 1998.
Worika, I.L. *Environmental Law and Policy of Petroleum Development: Strategies
    and Mechanisms for Sustainable Management in Africa.* Portharcourt, Rivers
    State: Anpez Centre for Environment and Development, 2002.

TABLE OF LEGISLATION

TABLE OF CASES

Eze v. Okechukwu [2003] 02 MJSC 188
Gonzee v. NERDC [2005] 12 MJSC 179
Gulf Oil Company (Nigeria) Ltd v. Oluba (2003) FWLR
Jalico Ltd v. Owoniboys [1995] 4 SCNJ 256
Jika v. Akuson (2006) All FWLR 276
Jonah Gbemre v. Shell PDC Ltd and Others (2005) Suit No. FHC/B/CS/53/05
Machine Umudje v. Shell (1975) 9-11 SC 155
Menakaya v. Menakaya [2001] 8 MJSC 50
Mobil Producing (Nig.) Unlimited v. LASEPA (2002) 2 MJSC 69
Mobil Producing (Nig.) Unlimited v. LASEPA, FEPA & Ors (2002) 18 NWLR
Ndule v. Ibezim [2002] 12 MJSC 150
Nigeria Cement Co. Ltd v. Nigeria Railway Corporation & Anor (1992) 1 NWLR 747
Nigerian Ports Plc. v. Oseni (2000) 8 NWLR 410
NNPC v. Lutin Inv. Ltd [2006] 2 MJSC 1
NNPC v. Sele (2004) All FWLR 1859 CA
Nsirim v. Nsirim [2002] 3 MJSC 26
Nwanji v. Coastal Services [2004] 10 MJSC 154
Ojo v. Philips (1993) 5 NWLR (pt 296) 751
Okolo v. UBN [2004] 2 MJSC 69
Olujinle v. Adeagbo (1988)2 NWLR (pt 75) 386
Onyenge & Ors v. Ebere & Ors [2004] 11 MJSC 184
Prehin v. Royal Bank of Liverpool (1870) LR 5 Ex. 92
RCC (Nig.) Ltd v. Edonwonyi (2003) 4 NWLR
Reynolds v. RockOnoh [2005] 10 MJSC 159
Rylands v. Fletcher [1866] LR 1 Ex. 265
Seismograph Service (Nig.) Ltd v. Ogbeni (1976) 4 SC 85
Senator Adesanya v. President of Nigeria (1981) 2 NCLR 388
Shell Petroleum Development Company (Nigeria) Ltd v. Abel Isaiah (2001) 5 SC (Part 11) 1
Shell Petroleum Development Company (Nigeria) Ltd v. Chief GBA Tiebo VII & Others [2005] 9 MJSC 158
Shell Petroleum Development Company (Nigeria) Ltd v. Chief Otoko & Others (1990) 6 NWLR 693
Sken Consult v. Ukey (1981) 1 SC 6
Sommer & Ors v. Federal Housing Authority (1992) 1 NWLR (pt 219) 548
Storms Bruks Aktie Bolag v. Hitchinson (1905) AC 515; *In the Sesquehuanna* (1926) AC 655
Teno Engineering Ltd v. Adisa [2005] 7 MJSC 89
Uhunmwangbo v. Uhunmwangbo (1992) 2 NWLR
University of Ife v. Fawehinmi Construction Co. Ltd (1991) 7 NWLR 26
Yahaya v. The State (2002) 3 MJSC 103
Yesufu v. Governor Edo State [2001] 5 MJSC 128

TABLE OF INTERNATIONAL INSTRUMENTS

Basel Convention on the Control of Transboundary Movements of Hazardous
    Wastes and their Disposal (1989) 28 *ILM* 567
Convention on Biological Diversity (1992) 31 *ILM* 818
Convention on International Trade in Endangered Species of Wild Fauna and Flora
    (1973) 46 *ILM* 1178
Convention on the Conservation of Migratory Species of Wild Animals (1980) 19
    ILM 11
Montreal Protocol on Substances that Deplete the Ozone Layer (1987) 26 *ILM*
    1541
Stockholm Convention on Persistent Organic Pollutants (2001) 40 *ILM* 532
United Nations Convention to Combat Desertification in Countries Experiencing
    Serious Drought and/or Desertification (1994) 33 *ILM* 1328
Vienna Convention for the Protection of the Ozone Layer (1987) 26 *ILM* 1516

ABBREVIATIONS

CJN	Chief Justice of Nigeria
EIA	Environmental Impact Assessment
FEPA	Federal Environmental Protection Agency
GDP	Gross Domestic Product
ILM	International Legal Materials
JSC	Justice of the Supreme Court
LASEPA	Lagos State Environmental Protection Agency
LFN	Laws of the Federation of Nigeria
MJSC	Monthly Judgments of the Supreme Court of Nigeria
NESREA	National Environmental Standards, Regulations and Enforcement Agency
NGO	Non-governmental Organization
NNPC	Nigeria National Petroleum Cooperation
UBN	Union of Bank of Nigeria
UNEP	United Nations Environment Programme
SPDC	Shell Petroleum Development Company

Chapter 18

South Africa

Louis Kotzé and Alexander Paterson

1 INTRODUCTION

The release of Nelson Mandela and the abolition of apartheid in the early 1990s
marked a watershed in South Africa's history. The country was transformed from
an isolated, pariah state to one founded on the values of human dignity, equality,
non-racicism and non-sexism.[1] It holds dear the supremacy of the Constitution of
the Republic of South Africa, 1996 (Constitution) and places a high premium on
the rule of law.[2] South Africa's transition to a constitutional democracy did not
only alter the political landscape but simultaneously provided the impetus for the
transformation of South Africa's environmental law and governance regime.

South Africa currently has a comprehensive environmental governance framework underpinned by an extensive array of environmental laws.[3] As in most
countries, however, the interpretation, application and enforcement of these
laws remain a challenge.[4] This challenge is compounded in South Africa by the

---

1. S. 1 of the Constitution of the Republic of South Africa, 1996.
2. *Ibid.*
3. See generally, J. Glazewski, *Environmental Law in South Africa*, 2nd ed. (Durban: LexisNexis
   Butterworths, 2005), 67-81; and M.A. Kidd, *Environmental Law* (Cape Town: Juta, 2008).
4. See, generally, A.R. Paterson & L.J. Kotzé (eds), Environmental Compliance and Enforcement in
   South Africa: Legal Perspectives (Juta, 2009).

Louis J. Kotzé and Alexander R. Paterson (eds), *The Role of the Judiciary in
Environmental Governance: Comparative Perspectives*, pp. 557–602.
© 2009 Kluwer Law International BV, The Netherlands.

need to balance competing socio-economic needs[5] with pressing environmental imperatives.[6] It is mainly up to the three branches of South Africa's government, namely the executive, legislature and the judiciary, to address these challenges. The focus of this chapter is on the judiciary and the manner in which it has contributed to this process. South Africa does not have a specialized environmental court and it has accordingly been left to the general judicial structures to fashion their role in environmental governance. Judging from the environmental jurisprudence which has emerged during the course of the past twelve years following the country's transition to a constitutional democracy, the judiciary is increasingly asserting itself in the realm of environmental governance through: interpreting environmental legislation; pronouncing on the validity of relevant executive and legislative action; resolving civil environmental disputes between citizens, and/or citizens and the State; and sanctioning non-compliance with environmental legislation.

This chapter proceeds by highlighting various contextual issues such as the current environmental challenges facing the country, South Africa's principal environmental laws and key governance institutions. It then turns to critically analyse the prominent environmental jurisprudence which has arisen since 1996.[7] This was the year in which the Constitution and its environmental right, which have so shaped the nature and form of South Africa's contemporary environmental regime, were introduced. The chapter concludes with a brief reflection on several generic challenges which may shape the future role of the judiciary in environmental governance.

2   ENVIRONMENTAL ISSUES

South Africa is situated at the southernmost tip of Africa. It has a coastline of approximately 3,000 km and is bordered by the Indian and Atlantic oceans. The country has two major physiographic features separated by an escarpment, namely: the interior plateau and the stretch of land between the plateau and the coast. These features, together with the warm Mozambique-Agulhas current on the East and South Coast, and the cold Benguela current on the West Coast, significantly influence the climate and vegetation patterns in these areas. The West Coast and interior plateau are generally dry and arid, whilst the East and South Coast are generally wet and lush.

---

5. These include the need to reduce poverty through economic development and the provisions of basic services such as water; sanitation; housing; education and health care.
6. These include climate change, land degradation, pollution and the need to provide for the sustainable use of the nation's natural resources.
7. Some pre-1996 decisions are also included where these judgments remain relevant to the present legal position. The scope of this contribution does not allow for an exhaustive discussion of all environmental judgments that have been handed down to date. For a concise summary and discussion of these judgments, see generally, L.J. Kotzé et al., *South African Environmental Law through the Cases* (Durban: LexisNexis Butterworths, 2008).

South Africa has a temperate climate with sunshine almost all year round. These favorable climatic conditions coupled with the country's picturesque landscapes, pristine wilderness areas and world-renowned protected areas, make it a popular international tourist destination. South Africa is also blessed with biological resources and is ranked as the third most biologically diverse country in the world,[8] with 80% of its 18,000 plant species, for example, occurring nowhere else on earth.[9] The country is further renowned for its rich mineral wealth with the world's largest reserves of chrome, gold, manganese, platinum and vanadium.[10]

However, as is reflected in South Africa's most recent National State of the Environment Report,[11] these landscapes and resources are currently under significant threat as the country grapples with the realities of development. The country's marine resources continue to be exploited at an unsustainable rate.[12] Its rich diversity of fauna and flora is currently regarded as one of the most threatened on the planet owing to land transformation, alien invasive vegetation, and the burgeoning biofuels and genetic modification industry.[13] Many landscapes are scarred by soil erosion, mining activities and rapid urbanization.[14] This rapid urbanization and industrial development has in turn led to the proliferation of waste disposal sites and the ever-increasing pollution of South Africa's atmospheric, terrestrial and marine environments. However, perhaps South Africa's greatest future environmental challenges are posed by climate change and water scarcity. South Africa's energy economy is driven by coal and accordingly, the country ranks as the eighth highest global per capita emitter of CO_2.[15] This has compelled the government to seriously rethink its energy policy in order to reduce the country's contribution to climate change through diversifying energy sources, promoting the use of various sources of renewable energy, and improving energy efficiency.[16] In the water context, South Africa is a water stressed country with an average annual rainfall of only 464 mm. The country's freshwater resources are almost fully-utilized and

8. World Conservation Monitoring Centre, *Global Biodiversity Status of the Earths Living Resources* (London: Chapman & Hall, 1992).
9. *White Paper on the Conservation and Use of South Africa's Biodiversity*, GN 1095, 28 July 1997, 12.
10. DME, 'South Africa's Mineral Industry (2006/2007)', <www.dme.gov.za/minerals/sami_2005.stm>, 20 November 2008.
11. DEAT, 'National State of the Environment Report 2006', <www.ngo.grida.no/soesa/ nsoer/>, 20 November 2008.
12. *Ibid.*
13. R. Wynberg, 'A decade of biodiversity conservation and use in South Africa: Tracking progress from Rio Earth Summit to the Johannesburg World Summit on Sustainable Development', *SAJS* 98 (2002): 233.
14. As of 2001, 50% of South Africans lived in urban centres; a figure that is estimated to increase to 73% by 2010. Statistics South Africa. *Census 2001: Investigation into appropriate definitions of urban and rural areas for South Africa – Discussion document* (Pretoria: Statistics South Africa, 2003).
15. See DEAT, *National Air Quality Management Programme – Initial State of the Air Report* (Pretoria: DEAT, 2006).
16. See DEAT, *National Climate Change Response Strategy* (Pretoria: DEAT, 2004).

with an estimated increasing demand of 53% in the next thirty years, the government has similarly been compelled to rethink its approach to water resource management.[17]

As should be evident from the above, South Africa's environmental resources are currently under considerable stress. The public and private sectors accordingly urgently need to fashion sustainable environmental governance strategies and mechanisms to manage this stress. Environmental law is one of the key mechanisms for redirecting South Africa onto a more sustainable path.

3   PRINCIPAL ENVIRONMENTAL LAWS

The past decade has evidenced the wholesale reform of South Africa's environmental legal framework under the purview of the Constitution. This environmental legal framework prescribes the powers, functions and mechanisms available to South Africa's institutions tasked with environmental governance. The key constitutional, framework, sectoral and common law components of South Africa's environmental legal framework are briefly discussed below.[18]

3.1   CONSTITUTIONAL PROVISIONS

The Constitution is the supreme law of South Africa[19] and is particularly relevant to environmental governance for three main reasons. First, its Bill of Rights entrenches an environmental right together with an array of associated rights of relevance to protecting environmental interests. Second, it determines the status of various sources of law, including international environmental law. Third, it prescribes governance mandates and entrenches the dictate of co-operative governance.

3.1.1   Environmental Right

The Bill of Rights, contained in Chapter 2 of the Constitution, is the cornerstone of South Africa's democracy and the State is compelled to respect, protect, promote and fulfil the rights contained therein.[20] The rights are not absolute, however, and can be limited by a law of general application to the extent that the limitation is reasonable and justifiable in an open and democratic society based on human dignity, equality and freedom.[21]

---

17. DEAT, *supra* n. 11.
18. The authors are mindful of the possible injustice such a brief analysis may cause and therefore additional sources providing further insight on these laws are included as footnote references where appropriate.
19. S. 2.
20. S. 7.
21. Any such limitation must conform to the requirements laid down in s. 36 of the Constitution.

The key right, from an environmental perspective, is that enshrined in section 24.[22] It reads as follows:

Everyone has the right –

(a) to an environment that is not harmful to their health or well-being; and
(b) to have the environment protected, for the benefit of present and future generations, through reasonable legislative and other measures that –
   (i) prevent pollution and ecological degradation;
   (ii) promote conservation; and
   (iii) secure ecologically sustainable development and use of natural resources while promoting justifiable economic and social development.

This environmental right is unique in the sense that it comprises of both a classic first generation fundamental right and second generation socio-economic right.[23] People can accordingly directly invoke the right where, for instance, their 'health' or 'well-being' is threatened. In addition, the State has a duty to take 'reasonable legislative and other measures' to progressively realize the objectives contained in the right. Whilst the meaning of 'legislative measures' is self-evident, 'other measures' may be construed to include prescribing policy and taking measures of an administrative, technical, financial and educational nature.

The Bill of Rights applies to all law, and binds the legislature, executive, judiciary, and all organs of State.[24] It furthermore binds natural and juristic persons if, and the extent to that, it is applicable taking into account the nature of the right and any duty imposed by it. Commentators are generally of the view that the environmental right is of such a nature and accordingly applies on both the vertical (between citizens and the State) and horizontal plain (between citizens themselves).[25] The Constitution furthermore compels the judiciary, when applying a provision contained in the Bill of Rights to natural and juristic persons, to apply, and if necessary develop the common law, to give effect to the right.[26] When interpreting any legislation, and when developing the common law or customary law, the judiciary must promote the spirit, purport and objects of the Bill of Rights.[27]

The inclusion of the environmental right in the Bill of Rights therefore enables citizens to assert the right at the 'highest' possible constitutional level.

22. For a detailed discussion of this right, see Kidd, *supra* n. 3, 18-23; L.J. Kotzé, 'The Judiciary, the Environmental Right and the Quest for Sustainability in South Africa: A Critical Reflection', *RECIEL* 16, no. 16 (2007): 298-311; J. Glazewski, 'The environmental right', in *South African Constitutional Law: The Bill of Rights*, ed. M.H. Cheadle, D.M. Davis & N.R.L. Haysom (Durban: LexisNexis Butterworths, 2002); and T. Winstanley, 'Entrenching Environmental Protection in the new Constitution', *SAJELP* 2 (1995): 85.
23. See T.P. van Reenen, 'Constitutional Protection of the Environment: Fundamental (Human) Right or Principle of State Policy?', *SAJELP* 4 (1997): 270-273.
24. S. 8(1).
25. *Supra* n. 22.
26. S. 8(3).
27. S. 39(2).

Furthermore, it significantly enhances the nature and scope of potential legal remedies available to citizens seeking to enforce it.[28]

3.1.2   Other Rights

The Bill of Rights contains an array of other rights which are of potential relevance to the environmental context. These include: the rights to equality, human dignity and life;[29] the property clause;[30] the right to access to adequate housing;[31] the right to health care, food, water and social security;[32] the rights of children as a particularly vulnerable group in society;[33] the rights of access to information and administrative justice;[34] the access to courts clause;[35] the limitation of rights clause;[36] the enforcement of rights clause;[37] and the interpretation of the Bill of Rights clause.[38]

An extensive analysis of these rights, and the manner in which they intersect with the environmental right, unfortunately falls outside the ambit of this chapter.[39] However, what should be evident from the range of rights listed above, is that the environmental right is supplemented by an array of other key substantive and procedural rights which generally complement and facilitate its implementation.

3.1.3   International Environmental Law

South Africa is a party to numerous multilateral and bilateral environmental agreements and the government places a high priority on giving domestic effect to its commitments under these agreements.[40] The Constitution provides for the incorporation of these agreements and states that:

> Any international agreement becomes law in the Republic when it is enacted into law by national legislation; but a self-executing provision of an agreement

---

28. Citizens can for instance approach the judiciary on the basis of the environmental right to: have laws and regulations declared invalid; question the interpretation and application of legislation; challenge administrative action; obtain an interdict; seek a declaration of rights; and obtain a damages award. See further in this regard I. Currie & J. de Waal, *The Bill of Rights Handbook* (Lansdowne: Juta, 2005), 199-226.
29. Ss 9-11.
30. S. 25.
31. S. 26.
32. S. 27.
33. S. 28.
34. Ss 32 and 33 respectively. These rights are given practical effect by the *Promotion of Access to Information Act* 2 of 2000, and the *Promotion of Administrative Justice Act* 3 of 2000.
35. S. 34.
36. S. 36.
37. S. 38.
38. S. 39.
39. For a detailed discussion of these rights see: Glazewski, *supra* n. 3, 67-102; and Kidd, *supra* n. 3, 18-31.
40. For a comprehensive list and discussion of these agreements see Glazewski, *supra* n. 3, 29-63.

that has been approved by Parliament is law in the Republic unless it is inconsistent with the Constitution or an Act of Parliament.[41]

South Africa accordingly follows a dualist approach to incorporating international environmental agreements into domestic law.[42] These agreements will generally only have the force of law in South Africa if they are enacted by means of domestic legislation. This requirement does not, however, apply to self-executing provisions of an international agreement.

In relation to customary international law, the Constitution provides that it '... is law in the Republic unless it is inconsistent with the Constitution or an Act of Parliament'.[43] The principles of customary international environmental law accordingly apply in South Africa insofar as these principles have evolved and are considered to have the status of international customary law. Furthermore, when interpreting legislation, the judiciary is compelled to prefer any reasonable interpretation that is consistent with international law over that which it not.[44] The above potentially facilitates the development of domestic environmental governance practices that are in line with international norms and standards.[45]

3.1.4 Governance Mandates and Cooperative Governance

The South African government is divided into three separate but interdependent spheres, namely: national, provincial and local. The Constitution identifies which sphere of government is competent to make and administer laws on various functional areas of relevance to the environment. Certain of these functional areas fall within the concurrent competence of the national and provincial spheres of government;[46] other areas are exclusively national[47] or

---

41. S. 231(4). This provision needs to be read in conjunction with Ch. 16 of the *National Environmental Management Act* 107 of 1998 (NEMA), which elaborates on these procedures in relation to international environmental agreements.

42. See for a detailed discussion on the incorporation of international law into South African law, J. Dugard, *International Law: A South African Perspective*, 3rd ed. (Cape Town: Juta, 2005), 47-80.

43. S. 232.

44. S. 233.

45. These provisions must be read with s. 39 of the Constitution, which places an obligation on courts to consider international law when interpreting a right in the Bill of Rights. This would naturally include the environmental right and the other constitutional rights listed above.

46. These include: administration of indigenous forests; environment; nature conservation; pollution control; regional planning and development; soil conservation; air pollution; building regulations; municipal planning; stormwater management; and water and sanitation services limited to potable water supply systems and domestic waste-water and sewage disposal systems (Sch. 4).

47. These include: mining; freshwater resources; national parks, botanical gardens and marine resources. They are set out in Sch. 4 or fall within the residual competence of the national

provincial competences;[48] whilst certain areas are reserved for local government administration.[49]

There is considerable overlap between these functional areas[50] and the Constitution contains detailed provisions regulating the resolution of conflicts between legislation passed by these spheres of government.[51] In addition, the Constitution contains a set of principles of cooperative governance aimed at facilitating intergovernmental relations and co-ordination.[52] All spheres of government must observe and adhere to these principles and must conduct their activities accordingly.[53]

3.2   ENVIRONMENTAL FRAMEWORK LEGISLATION

As has been mentioned above, South Africa's transition to a constitutional democracy in the mid-1990s initiated the wholesale reform and expansion of South Africa's environmental regime. However, even prior to this transition, South Africa had enacted a framework environmental law, namely the *Environment Conservation Act* 73 of 1989 (ECA) which dealt, inter alia, with environmental impact assessment (EIA), pollution prevention and remediation, littering and waste management. The ECA has now been repealed virtually in its entirety by the *National Environmental Management Act* 107 of 1998 (NEMA), South Africa's principal framework environmental law enacted in partial fulfilment of the State's constitutional duty to take reasonable legislative measures to protect the environment. The array of issues regulated under NEMA is exceptionally broad and includes: national environmental management principles with which the actions

---

government owing to the fact that they have not been listed in any of the schedules to the Constitution (s. 44(1)(a)(ii)).

48. These include: provincial planning; beaches; cleansing; control of public nuisances; municipal parks; noise pollution; and refuse removal, refuse dumps and solid waste disposal (Sch. 5).

49. These include: air pollution; building regulations; municipal planning; stormwater management; water and sanitation services limited to potable water supply systems and domestic wastewater and sewage disposal systems (Sch. 4 (Part B) and Sch. 5 (Part B)).

50. For a further discussion on the overlap between these functional competences see: L.J. Kotzé, *A Legal Framework for Integrated Environmental Governance in South Africa* (Nijmegen: Wolf Legal Publishers, 2006); E. Bray, 'Legal Perspectives on Global Environmental Governance: South Africa's Partnership Role (Part 2)', *JCRDL* 3 (2005): 357-373; C. Bosman, L.J. Kotzé & W. du Plessis, 'The Failure of the Constitution to Ensure Integrated Environmental Management from a Co-operative Governance Perspective', *SAPL* 19 (2004): 411-421; and E. Couzens, 'NEMA: A Step Closer to Coherence?', *SAJELP* 6 (1999): 13-19.

51. See s. 146 (regarding the resolution of national and provincial conflicts) and s. 151(1) read with s. 156(3) (regarding the resolution of conflicts between national/provincial and local authorities).

52. Ch. 3. The provisions contained in Ch. 3 are given practical effect by the *Intergovernmental Relations Framework Act* 13 of 2005, which establishes structures and procedures to facilitate cooperative governance.

53. S. 40(2).

of all organs of State[54] must comply;[55] institutions, mechanisms and procedures for facilitating cooperative environmental governance;[56] fair decision-making and conflict management procedures;[57] EIA;[58] South Africa's international environmental obligations including the ratification of environmental treaties;[59] comprehensive provisions on compliance, enforcement, pollution prevention, and remediation;[60] and South Africa's primary environmental enforcement agency, the recently-established Environmental Management Inspectorate (EMI).[61] The Act also specifically provides for: a duty of care to avoid, minimize and remediate pollution;[62] the protection of workers refusing to do environmentally hazardous work;[63] the control of emergency incidents;[64] access to environmental information and the protection of whistle-blowers;[65] wide legal standing to enforce environmental laws;[66] private prosecution;[67] and criminal proceedings.[68]

The scope of this chapter regrettably does not allow for an extensive discussion of these important provisions.[69] However, those which have been the subject of judicial scrutiny are elaborated on below in the critical analysis of relevant jurisprudence. For present purposes it suffices to say that the promulgation of NEMA has been a very welcome addition to South Africa's environmental regime in that it establishes: an integrated framework for facilitating cooperative

---

54. 'Organ of state' is defined in s. 239 of the Constitution as: '(a) any department of state or administration in the national, provincial or local sphere of government; or (b) any other functionary or institution – (i) exercising a power or performing a function in terms of the Constitution or a provincial constitution; or (ii) exercising a public power or performing a public function in terms of any legislation, but does not include a court or a judicial officer.'
55. S. 2.
56. Chs 2, 3 and 8 read with Ch. 3 of the Constitution.
57. Ch. 4.
58. Ch. 5.
59. Ch. 6 must be read with the constitutional provisions on international law discussed above.
60. Ch. 7.
61. Ss 31A-31Q, and 34A-34G.
62. S. 28.
63. S. 29.
64. S. 30.
65. S. 31 read with the *Promotion of Access to Information Act* 2 of 2000 and s. 32 of the Constitution referred to above.
66. S. 32.
67. S. 33.
68. S. 34.
69. For further discussion and critical analysis of NEMA see: Paterson & Kotzé (eds), *supra* n. 4; Kidd, *supra* n. 3, 31-40; L. Feris, 'Compliance Notices – A New Tool in Environmental Enforcement', *PELJ* 3 (2006):1-18, <www.puk.ac.za/fakulteite/regte/per/ issue06v3.html>, 20 November 2008.; Glazewski, *supra* n. 3, Ch. 5; J.G. Nel & W. du Plessis, 'Unpacking Integrated Environmental Management – A step closer to effective co-operative governance', *SAPL* 19 (2004):181; T-L. Field, 'Realising the National Environmental Management Act's potential to bring polluters to book', *SALJ* 121 (2004):772; W. du Plessis & J.G. Nel, 'An Evaluation of NEMA based on a Generic Framework for Environmental Framework Legislation', *SAJELP* 8 (2001):1-2; and F. Soltau, 'The National Environmental Management Act and Liability for Environmental Damage', *SAJELP* 6 (1999): 33.

environmental governance; an extensive array of provisions for facilitating environmental management; novel compliance and enforcement mechanisms; and innovative institutions for administering and enforcing these provisions.

3.3   SECTORAL LEGISLATION

NEMA is complemented by many national laws which seek to regulate sector-specific environmental issues including: mining;[70] fresh water resources;[71] air quality;[72] protected areas;[73] biodiversity;[74] forestry;[75] nuclear energy;[76] land use and planning;[77] genetically modified organisms (GMOs);[78] and cultural heritage.[79] Additional national laws governing integrated coastal management[80] and waste management[81] will be promulgated in the near future. These national laws are in turn supplemented by several provincial laws such as those regulating land use planning and conservation.[82] At the local sphere, municipalities have promulgated bylaws governing issues such as noise pollution, waste management, recreation facilities, vehicular emissions, and local town and city planning.[83]

3.4   COMMON LAW

As a former Dutch and English colony, South Africa still recognizes common law principles originating from these legal systems.[84] The principle of *sic utere tuo ut alienum non laedas* forms the basis of neighbour law and the law of nuisance, and may, for example, be invoked by those aggrieved by environmental harmful

---

70. *Mineral and Petroleum Resources Development Act* 28 of 2002.
71. *National Water Act* 36 of 1998 and the *Water Services Act* 108 of 1997.
72. *National Environmental Management: Air Quality Act* 39 of 2004.
73. *National Environmental Management: Protected Areas Act* 57 of 2003.
74. *National Environmental Management: Biodiversity Act* 10 of 2004.
75. *National Forest Act* 84 of 1998.
76. *National Nuclear Regulator Act* 47 of 1999 and the *Nuclear Energy Act* 46 of 1999.
77. *Development Facilitation Act* 67 of 1995 and Ch. 5 of NEMA dealing with EIAs.
78. *Genetically Modified Organisms Act* 15 of 1997.
79. *National Heritage Resources Act* 25 of 1999. For a detailed discussion of these laws see generally: Glazewski, *supra* n. 3; and Kidd, *supra* n. 3.
80. National Environmental Management: Integrated Coastal Management Bill (2007).
81. National Environmental Management: Waste Management Bill (2007).
82. Examples of these provincial sectoral laws include the *Western Cape Land Use Planning Ordinance* 15 of 1985, *KwaZulu-Natal Nature Conservation Management Act* 9 of 1997 and *Mpumalanga Nature Conservation Act* 10 of 1998.
83. These by-laws are too numerous to list here. For a detailed list and description see: A.A. du Plessis, The Fulfillment of the Constitutional Environmental Right in the Local Sphere of Government (LLD thesis, NWU, Potchefstroom, South Africa, 2009).
84. S. 39(2) of the Constitution states: '[W]hen interpreting any legislation, and when developing the common law or customary law, every court, tribunal or forum must promote the spirit,

activities undertaken on neighbouring land. The law of delict, specifically the *actio legis Aquilia*, may be relied on to claim compensation for damages occasioned by environmentally deleterious activity. South African common law further provides the possibility to seek an interdict or *mandamus* to, respectively, stop a person from acting in a specific manner or to force a person to act in a specific manner. These common law remedies have been, and continue to be, regularly invoked to address environmental wrongs and the relevant jurisprudence is considered subsequently in this chapter.

4   GOVERNANCE STRUCTURES AND INSTITUTIONS

Government comprises of three branches, namely: the legislature, executive and judiciary. The doctrine of *trias politica* applies and accordingly the three branches of government are, at least theoretically, not allowed to encroach on the functional areas of one another. South Africa's institutional governance structure at the national, provincial and local level is primarily determined by the Constitution and is briefly described below.

4.1   LEGISLATURE

National legislative authority vests in parliament which consists of the National Assembly and National Council of Provinces.[85] Provincial and local legislative authority vests in the provincial legislatures and municipal councils respectively.[86] Public access to, and participation in, the law-making process is specifically recognized in the Constitution.[87]

4.2   EXECUTIVE

National executive authority vests in the president and cabinet and their functions include: implementing national legislation; developing and implementing national

---

purport and objects of the Bill of Rights.' A court will therefore only apply common law principles and remedies where they are consistent with the Constitution.

85. Ss 42 and 43 of the Constitution. The National Assembly is elected to represent the people at the national level. The National Council of Provinces represents the provinces to ensure that provincial interests are considered in the national sphere of government.
86. See s. 104 (provincial government) and s. 156 (local government).
87. See s. 59 (national government) and s. 118 (provincial government). The Constitutional Court has recently reaffirmed the importance of active public involvement in the law-making process in *Doctors for Life International v. Speaker of the National Assembly and Others* 2006 (12) BCLR 1399 (CC) at 1442. See further L.J. Kotzé, 'Promoting Public Participation in Environmental Decision-making through the South Africa Courts: Myth or Reality?', unpublished paper presented at the UNITAR-Yale Conference on Environmental Governance and Democracy, University of Yale (New Haven, May 2008), (on file with the authors).

policy; co-coordinating the functions of State departments and administrations; preparing and initiating legislation; and performing any other executive function provided for in the Constitution or in national legislation.[88] Provincial executive authority vests in the premiers of each of South Africa's nine provinces, and their functions and powers are very similar to those of the president and cabinet, but delimited to dealing with provincial matters.[89] The executive authority of local government (municipalities) vests in municipal councils.[90] The Constitution enables the national government to intervene where provincial government fails to or inadequately performs its duties;[91] and provincial governments may intervene where local government fails to or inadequately performs its functions.[92]

4.3   JUDICIARY

The Constitution similarly sets out South Africa's court structure and procedures for the administration of justice.[93] Section 165 specifically prescribes that:

(1) The judicial authority of the Republic is vested in the courts.
(2) The courts are independent and subject only to the Constitution and the law, which they must apply impartially and without fear, favour or prejudice.
(3) No person or organ of state may interfere with the functioning of the courts.
(4) Organs of state, through legislative and other measures, must assist and protect the courts to ensure the independence, impartiality, dignity, accessibility and effectiveness of the courts.
(5) An order or decision issued by a court binds all persons to whom and organs of state to which it applies.[94]

The above provision clearly emphasizes: the independence of the courts; the separation of powers doctrine; the supremacy of the Constitution which should guide judicial action; and the fact that both the State and citizens are subject to court rulings. Importantly, section 165(4) places an obligation on organs of state to assist and protect courts in their quest for justice, through 'reasonable legislative and other measures' to ensure the independence, impartiality, dignity, accessibility and effectiveness of the courts.

---

88. S. 85.
89. See generally Ch. 6 of the Constitution.
90. See generally Ch. 7 of the Constitution.
91. S. 100.
92. S. 139.
93. See generally Ch. 8 of the Constitution.
94. S. 165.

4.3.1   Structure of the Courts

South Africa's hierarchy of courts include: the Constitutional Court; the Supreme Court of Appeal; High Courts; Magistrates' Courts; and any other court established or recognized in terms of an act of parliament.[95]

The Constitutional Court is the highest court in all constitutional matters.[96] It has exclusive jurisdiction to decide: disputes between organs of State in the national and provincial sphere concerning the constitutional status, powers or functions of any organs of State; on the constitutionality of national and provincial legislation, any parliamentary or provincial bill; applications envisaged in sections 80[97] and 122;[98] on the constitutionality of any amendment to the Constitution; that parliament or the president has failed to fulfil a constitutional obligation; and certify a provincial constitution.[99] The Constitutional Court also 'makes the final decision whether an Act of parliament, a provincial Act or conduct of the president is constitutional, and must confirm any order of invalidity made by the Supreme Court of Appeal, a High Court, or a court of similar status, before that order has any force'.[100]

The Supreme Court of Appeal is the highest court in all appeal matters, with the exception of constitutional matters.[101] High Courts can generally decide any constitutional matter except a matter that only the Constitutional Court may decide; and any other matter not assigned to another court by an act of parliament.[102] There are currently thirteen divisions of the High Court established in South Africa. Magistrates' Courts may decide any matter determined by the *Magistrates' Court Act* 32 of 1944, but have no jurisdiction to hear constitutional matters. There are approximately 250 Magistrates' Courts established in South Africa.

In most instances, environmental matters are decided by the Constitutional Court, Supreme Court of Appeal and High Court. Regrettably, neither the Constitution, nor any other Act of parliament, provides for a specialized environmental court. In 2003 an Environmental Court was established in the Western Cape Province and despite a fairly successful track record,[103] it was shut down in 2006 'due to the unwillingness of the Department of Justice and Constitutional

---

95. S. 166. It is important to point out here that South African law recognizes the law of precedent or *stare decisis*, in that 'lower' courts are bound by the decisions of 'higher' courts unless the decision was subject to a material error.
96. S. 167(7) provides that '[A] constitutional matter includes any issue involving the interpretation, protection or enforcement of the Constitution'.
97. S. 80(1) enables members of the National Assembly to apply to the Constitutional Court for an order declaring that all, or part of, an act of parliament is unconstitutional.
98. S. 122(1) enables members of a provincial legislature to apply to the Constitutional Court for an order declaring that all, or part of, a provincial act is unconstitutional.
99. S. 167(4).
100. S. 167(5).
101. S. 168.
102. S. 169.
103. It has been estimated that during its three year tenure (2003-2006) more than 400 cases were disposed of and eight out of ten cases resulted in a conviction. Most were abalone related but other

Development to continue to provide extra personnel and facilities for a specialized court that was not mandated by specific legislation'.[104]Adjudication of environmental matters therefore still remains primarily with the courts listed above.

4.3.2   Judicial Powers and *Locus Standi*

Historically, the South African judiciary had no authority to test the constitutionality of legislation or administrative action.[105] However, since the advent of the Constitution in 1996, the courts have been afforded such power.[106] As will be illustrated in the discussion of relevant jurisprudence in part 5 of this chapter, the South African judiciary has relatively frequently invoked this power to pronounce on the validity of environmental laws and the manner in which environmental authorities have exercised their administrative authority.

The Constitution also provides for the requisite *locus standi* of those seeking to institute proceedings in a court of law.[107] In the pre-constitutional dispensation, where the common law still regulated legal standing, a person who approached the court for relief had to show that he or she was personally harmed by the action that was being challenged[108] or that his or her legal rights were affected.[109] Public interest litigation, which is characteristic of environmental disputes and litigation, was accordingly nearly impossible during this period. The current approach is far more liberal as the Constitution provides that:

> 38. Anyone listed in this section has the right to approach a competent court, alleging that a right in the Bill of Rights has been infringed or threatened, and the court may grant appropriate relief, including a declaration of rights. The persons who may approach a court are –
>
> (a) anyone acting in their own interest;
> (b) anyone acting on behalf of another person who cannot act in their own name;

---

environmental crimes were also prosecuted. F. Craigie, P. Snijman & M. Fourie, 'Chapter 4: Environmental Compliance and Enforcement Institutions', in Paterson & Kotzé (eds), *supra* n. 4.

104. *Ibid.*
105. For an insightful discussion on the historical development of the South African judiciary, the current court structure, possible future judicial reforms and the independence of the judiciary, see J. Orr, 'South Africa', in *The Judicial Institution in Southern Africa: A Comparative Study of Common Law Jurisdictions*, ed. L. van de Vijver (Cape Town: Siber Ink, 2006), 114-159.
106. S. 172 of the Constitution states that: '(1) When deciding a constitutional matter within its power, a court – (a) must declare that any law or conduct that is inconsistent with the Constitution is invalid to the extent of its inconsistency . . . '.
107. S. 38.
108. *Patz v. Greene & Co.* 1907 TS 427; *Director of Education Transvaal v. McCagie* 1918 AD 616; *Milani v. South African Medical and Dental Council* 1990 (1) SA 899 (T), and *Laskey and Another v. Showzone CC and Others* 2007 (2) SA 48 (C).
109. *Dalrympie v. Colonial Treasurer* 1910 TS 372 and *Bamford v. Minister of Community Development and State Auxiliary Services* 1981 (3) SA 1054 (C).

(c) anyone acting as a member of, or in the interest of, a group or class of persons;

(d) anyone acting in the public interest; and

(e) an association acting in the interest of its members.

As a result, an almost non-exhaustive list of persons now have the requisite standing to approach a court for relief opening up the opportunity for public interest litigation.[110] The above constitutional provision is reinforced in the environmental context by NEMA which grants almost the same array of persons and institutions (including those acting in the 'environmental interest') standing to approach courts for appropriate relief in respect of any breach or threatened breach of: NEMA; several other sectoral environmental management acts; and any other statutory provision concerned with the protection of the environment or the use of natural resources.[111] Accordingly, the judiciary generally has very little discretion to disallow people access to the courts.

4.4   ENVIRONMENTAL AUTHORITIES

Within the national sphere, there are a number of government departments which have a role to play in environmental governance. The Department of Environmental Affairs and Tourism (DEAT) acts, at least on paper, as South Africa's lead environmental agency. It oversees the administration of NEMA and most of the country's important sectoral environmental laws governing air quality, biodiversity, protected areas, living marine resources, and waste management. It is assisted by provincial environmental departments in South Africa's nine provinces.

However, due to the fragmented nature of South Africa's environmental governance regime and the existence of various sectoral environmental laws, numerous other government departments and statutory authorities are responsible for regulating certain key sectors including the following: water affairs is governed by the Department of Water Affairs and Forestry (DWAF); minerals and energy (including mining) by the Department of Minerals and Energy; cultural heritage matters by the South African Heritage Resources Agency; agriculture by the Department of Agriculture; nuclear energy by the National Nuclear Regulator; and transport by the Department of Transport. Furthermore, each municipality has its own internal environmental department which deals with those environmental issues over which local governments have competence.[112]

---

110. S. 38 should be read with s. 34 of the Constitution which provides that: 'Everyone has the right to have any dispute that can be resolved by the application of law decided in a fair public hearing before a court or, where appropriate, another independent and impartial tribunal or forum.'

111. S. 32.

112. See the discussion in part 3.1.4 above.

5   CRITICAL ANALYSIS OF SIGNIFICANT
              ENVIRONMENTAL JUDGMENTS

Seemingly spurred on by the country's transition to a constitutional democracy, the
past decade has seen a plethora of judgments emerge from South Africa's courts
which have directly or indirectly dealt with environmental matters. The judiciary is
clearly playing a key role in environmental governance.

Owing to their abundance, it is unfortunately impossible to canvas all these
judgments within a single chapter. Accordingly, the following analysis does not
purport to provide an exhaustive discussion of all relevant environmental judgments, but rather a consideration of several of the most significant which have
emerged during the course of the past decade. These judgments are arranged and
discussed under the following main themes: giving content to the environmental
right; promoting administrative justice; facilitating access to information; extending *locus standi*; linking land reform and environmental protection; statutory interpretation; criminal enforcement; common law remedies; and litigation costs.

5.1   GIVING CONTENT TO THE ENVIRONMENTAL RIGHT

The first occasion the judiciary had to consider the application of environmental
rights in South Africa was in *Minister of Health and Welfare v. Woodcarb (Pty) Ltd
and Another* (Woodcarb).[113] The respondent in this matter established a sawmill
and proceeded to incinerate sawdust generated in the milling process in a burner.
The respondent had the requisite permit to operate the burner which generated a
significant amount of smoke. Following a number of complaints from neighbours
regarding the air pollution emanating from the respondent's premises, the authorities conducted several investigations which indicated that the respondent was in
breach of some of the permit conditions. Negotiations with the respondent failed
and the authorities accordingly approached the court for an interdict compelling
the respondent to shut down its operations pending compliance with the permit.
In granting the interdict, the court held that: 'the generation of smoke in these
circumstances . . . is an infringement of the rights of the respondent's neighbours to
an environment which is not detrimental to their health or well-being'.[114]

While the environmental right has been mentioned in a number of subsequent
cases brought before the courts,[115] two particular judgments deserve further

---

113. 1996 (3) SA 155 (NPD). The court in this matter was applying the environmental right
       enshrined in s. 29 of the interim *Constitution of the Republic of South Africa* 200 of 1993,
       and not s. 24. The wording of the two provisions is, however, almost identical.
114. 1996 (3) SA 155 (NPD), 164F.
115. These include: *Bareki NO and Another v. Gencor Ltd & Others* 2006 (1) SA 432 (T); *Bato Star
       Fishing (Pty) Ltd v. Minister Environmental Affairs & Others* 2004 (4) SA 490 (CC); *Capital
       Park Motors CC and Another v. Shell South Africa Marketing (Pty) Ltd and Others* Case
       No. 3106/05 of 18 March 2005 (unreported judgment of the High Court of South Africa
       Transvaal Provincial Division); *Hichange Investments (Pty) Ltd v. Cape Produce Co. (Pty)*

consideration in that they contain the most comprehensive analyses of the nature and content of the environmental right undertaken by the South African judiciary to date.

The first is the case of *BP Southern Africa (Pty) Ltd v. MEC for Agriculture, Conservation and Land Affairs* (BP).[116] The applicant in this matter undertook a statutorily prescribed EIA and applied for a permit to establish a new petrol filling station. The environmental authority considered the EIA and applying various decision-making guidelines it had developed, turned down the application. One of the principal reasons for refusing to grant the permit was the close proximity of the proposed new filling station to similar existing facilities. The applicant unsuccessfully appealed the matter and accordingly approached the High Court to review and set aside the authority's decision not to grant the permit. In the review proceedings, the applicant contended that the authority's mandate was limited to considering environmental issues and did not extend to socio-economic issues, such as the economic impact of the proposed new petrol station on existing establishments. The authority, on the other hand, argued that as per the Constitution (section 24) and NEMA, its mandate extended to cover environmental and socio-economic issues, both of which had been taken into account when refusing the respondent's application. The court was accordingly compelled to embark on a lengthy analysis of the relevant constitutional provisions to determine the bounds of the authority's mandate. It stated that the Constitution reigns supreme and that the advancement of human rights is one of the foundations of South Africa's democracy.[117] It went further to state that the Bill of Rights plays a central role because it embodies a set of foundational values which should be promoted at all times. It also stressed that the Bill of Rights binds government, natural, and juristic persons; in other words, it applies vertically and horizontally.[118] The court reiterated that the authorities had a constitutional duty to give effect to section 24 of the Constitution, a duty which included taking reasonable legislative and other

---

Ltd t/a Pelts Products 2004 (2) SA 393 (E); *HTF Developers (Pty) Ltd v. Minister of Environmental Affairs and Tourism and Others* 2007 (5) SA 438 (SCA); *Khabisi NO and Another v. Aquarella and Others* 2008 (4) SA 195 (T); *MEC for Agriculture, Conservation, Environment and Land Affairs v. Sasol Oil (Pty) Ltd & Another* 2006 (5) SA 483 (SCA); *MEC: Department of Agriculture, Conservation and Environment and Another v. HTF Developers (Pty) Ltd* 2008 (2) SA 319 (CC); *Minister of Public Works and Others v. Kyalami Ridge Environmental Association and Others* 2001 (7) BCLR 652 (CC); *Oudekraal Estates (Pty) Ltd v. City of Cape Town and Others* 2004 (6) SA 222 (SCA); *City of Cape Town & Others v. Oudekraal Estates (Pty) Ltd and Others* Case No. 8112/2004 of 9 October 2007 (unreported judgment of Van Reenen J in the High Court of South Africa Cape Provincial Division); *Petro Props (Pty) Ltd v. Barlow and Others* 2006 (5) SA 160 (W); *Trustees, Biowatch Trust v. Registrar: Genetic Resources and Others* 2005 (4) SA 111 (TPD); and *The Trustees for the Time Being of the Biowatch Trust v. The Registrar: Genetic Resources and Others* Case No. A831/2005 undated (unreported judgment of Mynhardt J in the High Court of South Africa Transvaal Provincial Division).

116. 2004 (5) SA 124 (WLD).
117. Para. G-J at 140.
118. Para. A-E at 141.

measures, such as prescribing decision-making guidelines, to protect the environment. The court quoted from *Government of the Republic of South Africa and Others v. Grootboom and Others*,[119] where it was held that:

> The State is required to take reasonable legislative and other measures. Legislative measures by themselves are not likely to constitute constitutional compliance. *Mere legislation is not enough.* The State is obliged to act to achieve the intended results, and the legislative measures will invariably have to be *supported by appropriate, well-directed policies and programmes implemented by the Executive* [Authority]. These policies and programs must be reasonable both in their conception and their implementation.[120]

Apart from being reasonable, these measures must also be capable of progressively realizing the protected right in question.[121] As far as the environmental right was concerned, the court confirmed that:

> ... the constitutional right to environment is on par with the rights to freedom of trade, occupation, profession and property entrenched in ss 22 and 25 of the Constitution ... the environmental rights requirements should be part and parcel of the factors to be considered without any *a priori* grading of the rights. It will require a balancing of rights where competing interests and norms are concerned. This is in line with the injunction in s 24(b)(iii) that ecologically sustainable development and the use of natural resources are to be promoted jointly with justifiable economic and social development. The balancing of environmental interests with justifiable economic and social development is to be conceptualised well beyond the interests of the present living generation. This must be correct since s 24(b) requires the environment to be protected for the benefit of 'present and future generations'. The above principles of 'intergenerational equity', which qualifies the rights to ownership of land, has been recognised as far back as 1971 ...[122]

The court proceeded to analyze the importance of sustainable development in the South African legal order and confirmed that it will '...play a major role in determining important environmental disputes in future'.[123] It was regarded by the court as the 'fundamental building block' around which South African environmental legal norms have been designed. In its frequently quoted *dictum*, the court found that:

> Pure economic principles will no longer determine, in an unbridled fashion, whether a development is acceptable. Development, which may be regarded as economically and financially sound, will, in future, be balanced by its

---

119. 2001 (1) SA 46 (CC).
120. As quoted from the *Grootboom* judgment as per Yacoob J at para. 69B-D. Emphasis of the court.
121. 2004 (5) SA 124 (WLD), para. H-J at 142.
122. Para. B-E at 143.
123. Para. A at 144.

environmental impact, taking coherent cognisance of the principle of inter-generational equity and sustainable use of resources in order to arrive at an integrated management of the environment, sustainable development and socio-economic concerns. By elevating the environment to a fundamental justiciable human right, South Africa has irreversibly embarked on a road, which will lead to the goal of attaining a protected environment by an integrated approach, which takes into consideration, *inter alia*, socio-economic concerns and principles.[124]

The court accordingly held that the environmental authority was under a duty to give effect to the environmental right and further, that the authority's mandate extended to cover both socio-economic and environmental considerations.[125] Its decision to refuse the respondent's permit application was accordingly upheld.

The most recent and arguably influential case to have dealt with the environmental right is *Fuel Retailers Association of SA (Pty) Ltd v. Director-General Environmental Management Mpumalanga and Others* (Fuel Retailers).[126] The case similarly concerned the nature and scope of an environmental authority's governance mandate. In this matter, the environmental authority had granted a developer a permit to establish a new petrol filling station. The applicant, an institution representing existing fuel retailers in South Africa, challenged the authority's decision to grant the permit. Its applications in the High Court and Supreme Court of Appeal were unsuccessful, so it sought leave to appeal to the Constitutional Court. The applicant's challenge was primarily based on the ground that the environmental authority, when making its decision, had neglected to consider relevant socio-economic issues, such as the potential negative economic impact a new filling station would have on existing filling stations in the area. The court was accordingly once again compelled to consider the environmental right, together with relevant environmental legislation, in order to determine the ambit of the authority's mandate. In its judgment, the court reiterated the sentiments in the *BP* case to the effect that an environmental authority must consider environmental *and* socio-economic issues when making its decisions.[127] The court emphasized that:

> The need to protect the environment cannot be gainsaid. So, too, is the need for social and economic development. How these two compelling needs interact, their impact on decisions affecting the environment and the obligations of environmental authorities in this regard, are important constitutional questions.[128]

---

124. Para. B-D at 144.
125. Para. G-H at 151.
126. 2007 (10) BCLR 1059 (CC).
127. Para. 41 at 24.
128. *Ibid.*

The court, in an attempt to balance social, environmental and economic concerns, stated that:

> What is immediately apparent from section 24 is the explicit recognition of the obligation to promote justifiable 'economic and social development'. Economic and social development is essential to the well-being of human beings... But development cannot subsist upon a deteriorating environmental base. Unlimited development is detrimental to the environment and the destruction of the environment is detrimental to development. Promotion of development requires the protection of the environment. Yet the environment cannot be protected if development does not pay attention to the costs of environmental destruction. The environment and development are thus inexorably linked.[129]

The court went further to confirm that the Constitution recognizes the interrelationship between social, economic and environmental considerations and 'envisages that environmental considerations will be balanced with socio-economic considerations through the ideal of sustainable development'.[130] In seeking to give content to the notion of sustainable development, the court embarked on a lengthy analysis of relevant scholarly writing and international jurisprudence and ultimately confirmed that:

> ...decision-makers guided by the concept of sustainable development will ensure that socio-economic developments remain firmly attached to their ecological roots and that these roots are protected and nurtured so that they may support socio-economic developments.[131]

The court recognized that when seeking to balance socio-economic and environmental issues, conflicts will arise but that:

> Our Constitution does not sanction a state of normative anarchy which may arise where potentially conflicting principles are juxtaposed. It requires those who enforce and implement the Constitution to find a balance between potentially conflicting principles. It is founded on the notion of proportionality which enables this balance to be achieved. Yet in other situations, it offers a principle that will facilitate the achievement of the balance. The principle that enables the environmental authorities to balance developmental needs and environmental concerns is the principle of sustainable development.[132]

The court concluded that the obligation to ensure that the essence of sustainability is reflected in the governance processes of environmental authorities is primarily that of the judiciary.[133] This, the court stated, is mandated by the Johannesburg

---

129. Para. 44 at 25.
130. Para. 45 at 26.
131. Para. 58 at 33 and para. 79 at 45-46.
132. Para. 93 at 52.
133. Para. 102 at 56-57.

Principles adopted at the Global Judges Symposium during the World Summit on Sustainable Development (WSSD)[134] and the courts accordingly: '... have a crucial role to play in the protection of the environment. When the need arises to intervene in order to protect the environment, they should not hesitate to do so'.[135]

The judiciary has not, however, only been compelled to seek the illusive balance between the socio-economic and environmental components inherent in the environmental right. It had also been called upon to balance the intersection between the environmental right and other competing rights entrenched in the Constitution.

This was lucidly illustrated in *Petro Props (Pty) Ltd v. Barlow and Another* (Petro Props).[136] The applicant sought to establish a petrol filling station on land which it owned. It had allegedly obtained all the requisite environmental authorizations to do so. The first respondent, the chairperson of a local environmental non-governmental organization (NGO), was opposed to the development owing to its location adjacent to an ecologically sensitive wetland. She conducted a media campaign and held various public meetings to try and stop the development. The applicant alleged that the campaign had damaged the company's reputation and that it had as a result suffered severe financial loss. The applicant accordingly applied for an interdict restraining the first respondent from harassing and interfering with its right to use and enjoy its property. The first respondent invoked her right to freedom of expression enshrined in section 16(1) of the Constitution. The court held that: '[A]s in all cases involving competing rights, the task in this matter is to determine the point of balance appropriate to the pertinent facts'.[137] In determining this point of balance, the court stated as follows:

> Ms Barlow and the Association bear a standard that any vibrant democratic society would be glad to have raised in its midst. Their interest and motivation is selfless, being to contribute to environmental protection in the common good. None of them stands to gain material personal profit. Their *modus operandi* is entirely peaceful. It is mobilized within a self-funding voluntary association. It is geared towards public participation, information gathering and exchange, discussion and the production of community-based mandates. Its accompanying public discourse and media coverage have been fair, with participants and readers alike being presented in a balanced way with viewpoints of all sides. In my view, conduct of that sort earns the support of our Constitution. In this context, it should be borne in mind that the Constitution does not only afford a shield to be resorted to passively and defensively. It also provides a sword, which groups like the Association can and should draw to empower their initiatives and interests.[138]

---

134. *Ibid.*
135. Para. 104 at 58.
136. 2006 (5) SA 150 (WLD).
137. Para. D at 180.
138. Para. H at 183H to para. B at 184.

The court accordingly found that the campaign was not an unlawful infringement of the applicant's rights and as a consequence rejected the application.[139] In doing so it held that:

> it is difficult to conclude that a successful campaign in the field of public opinion could be held to be vexatious, *contra bonos mores* or actionable. It is, likewise, difficult to conclude that Petro Props [the applicant] has shown that its rights outweigh the rights of expression viewed in the light of the manner in which those rights have been exercised by Ms Barlow and the Association in this case.[140]

In *Minister of Public Works and Others v. Kyalami Ridge Environmental Association and Others* (Kyalami),[141] the Constitutional Court had to balance two different competing constitutional rights; the right of access to housing (section 26) and the environmental right (section 24). Heavy rains had destroyed an informal settlement and the government decided to relocate flood victims to a temporary transit camp located on government-owned land. Residents in the vicinity opposed its establishment on the basis that: they had not been afforded a statutorily prescribed hearing prior to the decision; and that the camp could pose significant environmental risks to the area. The applicant argued that it had a constitutional duty to assist flood victims and, as the owner of the land in question, was entitled and obliged to make the land available for such a purpose. The court *a quo* set the applicant's decision aside and ordered it to properly consult with all concerned citizens. The applicant sought leave to appeal the decision directly to the Constitutional Court on the basis that it raised important constitutional issues, such as the need to balance the right of access to adequate housing with the environmental right.

All parties agreed that the flood victims had a constitutional right to be provided with access to adequate housing and that there was a duty on government to fulfil this right.[142] This right and duty had, however, to be balanced with the opposing right and duty enshrined in the environmental right. In a somewhat disappointing judgment, the court did not endeavor to explore the nature of the environmental right or its interface with the right of access to adequate housing. The court rather chose to rely on a somewhat flawed interpretation and application of the relevant statutory framework, specifically the national environmental management principles enshrined in NEMA, to overturn the decision of the court *a quo* and uphold the government's decision to establish the temporary transit camp.[143] This judgment led commentators to speculate whether the court had purposively misconstrued the enabling environmental regime to achieve a socially and politically satisfactory outcome, or whether the decision was just the result of judicial error.[144]

---

139. Para. D-G at 190.
140. Para. C at 187.
141. 2001 (3) SA 1151 (CC).
142. Para. 28.
143. For a full critique of this judgment see M.A. Kidd, 'The Constitutional Court's Dilution of NEMA: Minister of Public Works and Others v. Kyalami Ridge Environmental Association and Another', *SAJELP* 8 (2001): 119-127.
144. M.A. Kidd, 'Greening the Judiciary', *PELJ* 3 (2006): 3, <www.puk.ac.za/fakulteite/ regte/per/ issue06v3.html>, 20 November 2008.

What should be evident from the above brief analysis of the emerging jurisprudence relating to the environmental right is that the judiciary has clearly acknowledged this right's centrality to shaping South Africa's broad environmental governance regime and the mandate of environmental authorities. Furthermore, the judiciary has acknowledged its own important role in promoting the fulfilment of the right and the principle of sustainable development, and has begun to give content to both. Its role has not, however, been free from criticism. According to Feris:

> The Constitution of South Africa provides for one of the most comprehensive environmental rights. Yet, we have little understanding on the nature of the right and how it operates vis-à-vis other rights. Whilst some South African cases have referred to the environmental right and some cases have even attempted some analysis of the right, very few have endeavoured to conceptualise the right in an in-depth manner. In fact, in a number of instances where the occasion for detailed scrutiny did arise, courts have chosen to simply avoid the matter. This paucity in jurisprudence not only feeds criticism related to indeterminacy and obscurity, it also potentially impedes lawyers from claiming violation of environmental rights and judges from going out on a limb to enforce them.[145]

This criticism appears to be largely founded on the tendency of the judiciary to on occasion resolve matters in which constitutional rights are at play on procedural and not substantive grounds, thereby effectively circumventing the opportunity to provide guidance on: how to give practical effect to the environmental right; how to practically implement the notion of sustainable development; and how to resolve matters in which competing rights are at play.[146] This criticism would appear to be somewhat severe owing to the relative novelty of the South Africa's constitutional dispensation. Furthermore, the judiciary is compelled to pronounce on the legal arguments presented before it and these frequently revolve around technical procedural issues. There is clearly significant room for improving the depth of jurisprudence regarding the matters listed above, but this will no doubt develop overtime.

5.2   Promoting Administrative Justice

It has been stated above, that environmental governance issues frequently turn on administrative decision-making and these procedural aspects more often than not give rise to conflicts between environmental authorities and citizens.

---

145. L. Feris, 'Constitutional Environmental Rights: An Underutilised Resource', unpublished paper presented at the 5th Annual IUCN Academy of Environmental Law Colloquium (Parati, Brazil, June 2007), 2 (on file with the authors).
146. Examples of such cases include the *Kyalami* case and the *Fuel Retailers* case.

These disputes were historically resolved through the application of the common law, a typical example being the case of: *Director Mineral Development, Gauteng Region and Another v. Save the Vaal Environment and Others* (Save the Vaal).[147] In this matter, the mining authority had granted a permit to a company to mine coal on the southern bank of the Vaal River. The respondent, a group of concerned residents in the area, sought to challenge the grant of the permit on the basis that the authority had not afforded them a hearing (as envisaged by the common law rule of *audi alteram partem*) prior to granting the permit. The respondents were successful, but the mining authority appealed the decision. The Supreme Court of Appeal upheld the decision of the court *a quo* and stated that:

> the application of the [*audi alteram partem*] rule is indicated by virtue of the enormous damage mining can do to the environment and ecological systems. What has to be ensured when application is made for the issuing of a mining licence is that development which meets present needs will take place without compromising the ability of future generations to meet their own needs. Our Constitution, by including environmental rights as fundamental, justiciable human rights, by necessary implication requires that environmental considerations be accorded appropriate recognition and respect in the administrative processes in our country. Together with the change in the ideological climate must also come a change in our legal and administrative approach to environmental concerns.[148]

The inclusion of a right to just administrative action in the Bill of Rights,[149] as further codified in the *Promotion of Administrative Justice Act* 3 of 2000 (PAJA), has significantly altered the manner in which these disputes are resolved. PAJA has clarified: what constitutes lawful, reasonable and procedurally fair administrative action;[150] the grounds on which administrative action can be challenged;[151] and the remedies available to the court in such proceedings.[152] Cumulatively, the above has proliferated the number of cases which have been brought to court by citizens seeking to challenge decisions by environmental authorities relating to: the promulgation of regulations;[153] the grant/failure to grant environmental permits;[154] the grant/failure

---

147. 1999 (2) SA 709 (SCA).
148. Para. G at 107.
149. S. 33.
150. Ss 2 and 3.
151. S. 6.
152. S. 8.
153. See, e.g.: *South African Shore Angling Association and Another v. Minister of Environmental Affairs* 2002 (5) SA 511 (SE).
154. See, e.g.: *BP Southern Africa (Pty) Ltd v. MEC for Agriculture, Conservation, Environment and Land Affairs* 2004 (5) SA 124 (WLD); *Earthlife Africa (Cape Town) v. Director General: Department of Environmental Affairs and Tourism* 2005 (3) SA 156 (C); *MEC for Agriculture v. Sasol Oil (Pty) Ltd and Another* 2006 (5) SA 483 (SCA); and *Fuel Retailers Association of Southern Africa v. Director-General: Environmental Management, Department of Agriculture, Conservation and the Environment, Mpumalanga Province, and Others* 2007 (6) SA 4 (CC).

to grant land development rights;[155] the allocation of rights to use natural resources;[156] and the use of various administrative enforcement measures such as directives and compliance notices.[157]

If one surveys these cases, it is evident that the judiciary does not generally shy away from its role to keep a check on the executive and set aside unlawful, unreasonable and procedurally unfair administrative action. The judiciary has recently even gone as far as replacing its decision for that of the executive.[158] In doing so, however, the judiciary needs to walk and respect the fine line between undue judicial deference and undue judicial activism. In the words of Hoexter, quoted by the Constitutional Court in *Bato Star Fishing (Pty) Ltd v. Minister Environmental Affairs & Others* (Bato Star):[159]

> [A] judicial willingness to appreciate the legitimate and constitutionally-ordained province of administrative agencies; to admit the expertise of those agencies in policy-laden or polycentric issues; to accord their interpretations of fact and law due respect; and to be sensitive in general to the interests legitimately pursued by administrative bodies and the practical and financial constraints under which they operate. This type of deference is perfectly consistent with a concern for individual rights and a refusal to tolerate corruption and maladministration. It ought to be shaped not by an unwillingness to scrutinize administration action, but by a careful weighing up of the need for – and the consequences of – judicial intervention.[160]

---

155. See, e.g.: *Corium (Pty) Ltd v. Myburgh Park Langebaan (Pty) Ltd* 1995 (3) SA 51 (C); *Oudekraal Estates (Pty) Ltd v. City of Cape Town and Others* 2004 (6) SA 222 (SCA); *Hentru Developers & Contractors CC v. Hanekom NO & Another* [2005] JOL 15650 (T); *City of Cape Town & Others v. Oudekraal Estates (Pty) Ltd and Others* Case No. 8112/2004 of 9 October 2007 (unreported judgment of Van Reenen J in the High Court of South Africa Cape Provincial Division); *Hangklip Environmental Action Group v. MEC for Agriculture, Environmental Affairs and Development Planning (Western Cape) and Others* 2007 (6) SA 65 (C); and *SLC Property Group (Pty) Ltd and Another v. Minister of Environmental Affairs and Economic Development and Another* Case No. 5542/2007 of 26 October 2007 (unreported judgment of Erasmus J in the High Court of South Africa Cape Provincial Division).
156. See, e.g.: *Bato Star Fishing (Pty) Ltd v. Minister Environmental Affairs & Others* 2004 (4) SA 490 (CC); and *Foodcorp (Pty) v. DDG, Department of Environmental Affairs and Tourism: Branch Marine and Coastal Management* 2006 (2) SA 191 (SCA).
157. See, e.g.: *Evans and Others v. Llandudno/Hout Bay Transitional Metropolitan Substructure and Another* 2001 (2) SA 342 (C); *Bareki NO and Another v. Gencor Ltd & Others* 2006 (1) SA 432 (T); *Khabisi NO and Another v. Aquarella and Others* 2008 (4) SA 195 (T); and *MEC: Department of Agriculture, Conservation and Environment and Another v. HTF Developers (Pty) Ltd* 2008 (2) SA 319 (CC).
158. *SLC Property Group (Pty) Ltd and Another v. Minister of Environmental Affairs and Economic Development and Another* Case No. 5542/2007 of 26 October 2007 (unreported judgment of Erasmus J in the High Court of South Africa Cape Provincial Division).
159. 2004 (4) 490 (CC) at para. 46.
160. C. Hoexter, 'The Future of Judicial Review in South African Administrative Law', *SALJ* 117 (2000): 501-502. Also cited by Cameron JA in *Logbro Properties CC v. Bedderson NO and Others* 2003 (2) SA 460 (SCA) at para. 21.

Notwithstanding the guidance provided by PAJA, the judiciary will need to continue fashioning rules to assist it in determining how far it can go without overstepping the line and thereby undermining the separation of powers doctrine entrenched within the Constitution. The fairly robust approach of the judiciary to date has, however, compelled administrators to exercise their functions in a far more open, transparent and participatory manner.

5.3   FACILITATING ACCESS TO INFORMATION

Another procedural issue which aims to promote transparent, accountable and effective environmental governance is that of granting access to information held by the State and citizens. Access to information is currently comprehensively regulated by the *Promotion of Access to Information Act* 2 of 2000 (PAIA) and NEMA[161] which effectively codify the right of access to information enshrined in the Constitution (section 32). Notwithstanding this comprehensive regulatory framework, several disputes have been referred to the courts, the outcomes of which reflect: the challenges faced in framing requests for information; the risks inherent in approaching the courts for relief; and the apparent skewed statutory protection afforded to commercial confidential information.

The case of *Trustees Biowatch Trust v. Registrar: Genetic Resources and Others* (Biowatch) epitomizes these challenges.[162] The applicant, an NGO opposed to GMOs, sought to obtain access to information held by the respondent, the government authority responsible for administering the *Genetically Modified Organisms Act* 15 of 1997 in South Africa. The applicant had on numerous occasions sought to obtain information from the registrar for GMOs regarding: what permits had been issued to release GMOs in South Africa; the location of trial sites; and details of risk assessments and public participation undertaken prior to issuing permits. The applicant did not receive a satisfactory response to its requests and therefore approached the court for relief relying principally on the right of access to information contained in the Constitution and NEMA. The respondent opposed the application on the basis that: the information sought constituted confidential information of current permit holders; and secondly, the nature of the requests was vague and vexatious and simply constituted a fishing expedition. Certain current permit holders such as Monsanto South Africa and Emergent Genetics USA joined the proceedings to protect their interests.

The court considered the constitutional right of access to information, together with PAIA[163] and NEMA, and concluded that the right was not absolute and had to be balanced with other rights.[164] In giving effect to this balance, the court considered the grounds of refusal prescribed under PAIA and NEMA, such as

---

161. S. 31 of NEMA provides for access to environmental information.
162. 2005 (4) SA 111 (T).
163. Act 2 of 2000.
164. Para. 35.

confidential trade secrets and commercial information, in relation to each of the applicant's requests and granted it access to the majority of the information it sought.[165] The court was in agreement that the nature of the requests for information was very broad and somewhat vague but that it was not in the interests of justice to exclude the requests on this basis given the constitutional dictates of openness and accountability.[166] The applicant was, however, ordered to pay the substantial legal costs of the permit holders who had joined the proceedings. The court held that these parties were effectively compelled to join the proceedings to protect their interests owing to the vague nature in which the applicant had framed its requests for information.[167]

A further case which considered the access to information regime was *Earthlife Africa (Cape Town Branch) v. Eskom Holdings* (Earthlife).[168] The applicant (an environmental NGO) sought to obtain access to information held by the respondent (ESKOM – South Africa's primary State-owned energy provider) relating to a proposed nuclear power plant that it was developing. The respondent had initially invoked the grounds of refusal prescribed in PAIA (that the information was sensitive, commercial and confidential in nature) and refused access. The applicant accordingly approached the court for relief. The court refused the applicant's application and similarly made a cost order against it. The court held that although the 'applicant... came to the court with noble intentions and with a noble cause', 'the applicant persisted in claiming access to all information sought' and 'made no concession whatsoever as to whether any portion of the information withheld might have been exempt information'.[169]

While the judiciary has provided some guidance regarding how to formulate requests for information and bring associated disputes to court, there still appears to be much uncertainty regarding how to frame requests where it is unclear what information is available. The judiciary will hopefully provide clearer guidance as more access to information disputes are brought before it in the future. However, the apparent tendency of the judiciary, as evident in the *Earthlife* and *Biowatch* cases discussed above, to 'penalize' failed applicants may unfortunately discourage future applications of this nature.

5.4 EXTENDING *LOCUS STANDI*

As has been illustrated above, South Africa's post-constitutional dispensation affords citizens liberal standing to bring matters to court where their constitutional

---

165. Paras 45-65.
166. Para. 66.
167. The Applicant's attempt to appeal this costs order failed: *The Trustees for the Time Being of the Biowatch Trust v. The Registrar: Genetic Resources and Others* Case No. A831/2005 undated (unreported judgment of Mynhardt J in the High Court of South Africa Transvaal Provincial Division).
168. [2006] (2) All SA 632 (W).
169. Para. 42.

rights (including the environmental right) have been threatened or infringed. In the *Woodcarb* case, the court went as far as granting an environmental authority *locus standi* to approach the court for an interdict to shut down a woodmill which was affecting the health and well being of a community residing in the area, even though alternate statutory remedies (namely criminal sanctions) were available.[170]

Notwithstanding this liberal framework, the courts have been reluctant to grant litigants *locus standi* in various circumstances. In *All the Best Trading CC t/a Parkville Motors and Others v. SN Nayagar Property Development and Construction CC and Others* (All the Best),[171] the applicants sought to prevent the respondents from constructing an allegedly illegal petrol filling station. The applicants attempted to found their *locus standi* on an infringement of the environmental right. In reality they were not operating out of a concern for the environment, but rather to prevent potential financial prejudice following the construction of a new filling station in the area.[172] The court considered the interest on which the applicants sought to rely and held that they did not have requisite standing to bring the matter to court. In doing so the court stated:

> The applicants do not indicate that they have an interest of an environmental nature that needs to be protected. They are, in essence, seeking to protect their commercial interests. Therefore, I am of the further view that the applicants' reliance upon the constitutional provisions is indeed misplaced since there is nothing in their papers to indicate that their complaint is the violation of their constitutional right to a clean environment.[173]

The courts have also on occasion strangely adopted very strict interpretations of relevant statutory frameworks to deny applicants standing in environmental matters. In *Raubenheimer NO v. Trustees Johannes Bredenkamp Trust* (Raubenheimer),[174] for example, the applicant sought an urgent interdict preventing the respondent from demolishing a historical house. The respondent had a permit to demolish the house which the applicant had not sought to appeal. The respondent challenged the *locus standi* of the applicant on the basis that he did not have a *bona fide* interest in the grant of the permit nor was he directly affected by it. The applicant averred that he 'had a direct interest in the move to prevent the demolition of the structure in that it formed "part of his social and cultural life" and he received "emotional and psychological satisfaction" from it'.[175] The court held that the applicant did not have a *bona fide* interest and that it 'was based on a purely sentimental and emotional attachment'.[176] Furthermore, in *Merebank Environmental Action Committee v. Executive Member of Kwa-Zulu Natal Council for*

---

170. *Supra* n. 113 at 161I-162A.
171. 2005 (3) SA 396 (T).
172. Para. F at 396.
173. Para. H-J at 400.
174. 2006 (1) SA 124 (CPD).
175. Para. E-F at 133.
176. Para. E at 137.

Agriculture and Environmental Affairs (Merebank)[177] a group of residents formed a committee to interdict a petroleum company constructing a gas pipeline through their neighbourhood. The court dismissed the application on the basis that the applicant lacked *locus standi* as a committee 'cannot conceivably be an association with *locus standi in judicio*'. The court appears to have adopted a very strict interpretation to the wording contained in section 38(e) of the Constitution in coming to its conclusion and clearly failed to take into account the broad *locus standi* provisions prescribed by NEMA.

Where an applicant fails to satisfy the court that a right enshrined in the Bill of Rights has been infringed or threatened, and cannot rely on the extended standing provisions prescribed by NEMA, the applicant will have to revert to the common law rules to found *locus standi*. As has been illustrated above, the rules effectively preclude public interest litigation. However, the courts have in an array of environmental cases recognized the constitutional imperative to develop the common law, including its rules on standing, in line with the Bill of Rights.[178] This bodes well for the future but appears to be wholly at odds with the unduly restrictive interpretation afforded to existing constitutional and statutory *locus standi* provisions in the *Raubenheimer* and *Merebank* cases discussed above.

5.5   LINKING LAND REFORM AND ENVIRONMENTAL PROTECTION

South Africa's previous apartheid policies resulted in the extensive and arbitrary deprivation of property from certain sectors of society. Land reform and the restoration of property rights are accordingly key priorities in South Africa. Tensions often arise where courts are called upon to decide on the restoration of environmentally sensitive areas to previously marginalized and disadvantaged communities. This was vividly illustrated in *In re Kranspoort Community* (Kranspoort),[179] where the court declared the applicant community entitled to restitution, but imposed certain conditions specifically aimed at preventing the unsustainable use of renewable resources situated on the land subject to the claim. In its rather cursory reference to environmental considerations and the environmental right, the court stated that:

> The effect of such depletion would be to prevent the younger members of the community from having equitable access to the restored asset [referring to the land and its renewable resources] in the future. As I [Dodson J] have said,

---

177. Case No. 2691/01 (D) (unreported case delivered by Majid J in the High Court of South Africa Durban and Coast Local Division).
178. See, e.g.: *Wildlife Society of Southern Africa and Others v. Minister of Environmental Affairs and Tourism of the Republic of South Africa and Others* 1996 (3) SA 1095 (Tk) at 1105A-B; and *Van Huyssteen NO and Others v. Minister of Environmental Affairs and Tourism and Others* 1996 (1) SA 283 (C) at 301G/H-302D/E.
179. 2000 (2) SA 124 (LCC). This case, notably, was heard in the Land Claims Court; a special court which specifically hears matters related to the restitution of land rights.

s 35(3) [of the *Restitution of Land Rights Act* 22 of 1994] empowers and obliges the Court to impose conditions which will ensure equal access to the restored asset by *all* members of the community, including younger members who will come to access the property in their own right in the future. This allows me to impose conditions aimed at eliminating the risk of such depletion. Such an interpretation of s 35(3) 'promotes the spirit purports and objects' of s 24(b) of the Constitution.[180]

The court added that even though the land in question was not a formally protected natural environment, uncontested evidence suggested ' . . . its *de facto* significance form an environmental perspective . . . [and that] . . . all of these conditions [including the environmental conditions] justify the imposition of appropriately formulated conditions in this matter aimed at the sustainable management of the farm'.[181]

Tensions between land restoration and environmental imperatives will no doubt proliferate in the future. The judiciary's willingness to create novel solutions for marrying these interests is encouraging. So too is its recognition of the need to create long-term solutions to facilitate not only intra-generational equity, but also inter-generational equity.

5.6   STATUTORY INTERPRETATION

Owing to the rapid emergence of South Africa's environmental regime, the courts are frequently called upon to interpret inherent anomalies which arise when authorities seek to implement them. The judiciary has, for example, been compelled to: delimit the ambit and procedural prerequisites for environmental remediation provisions;[182] determine the applicability of EIA legislation;[183] pronounce on the nature of statutory directives and liability to non-compliance;[184] and determine the

---

180. Para. 117 at 183.
181. Para. 118 at 184.
182. See for instance: *Evans and Others v. Llandudno/Hout Bay Transitional Metropolitan Substructure and Another* 2001 (2) SA 342 (C); *MEC: Department of Agriculture, Conservation and Environment and Another v. HTF Developers (Pty) Ltd* 2008 (2) SA 319 (CC); *Hichange Investments (Pty) Ltd v. Cape Produce Co. (Pty) Ltd t/a Pelts Products* 2004 (2) SA 393 (E); and *Khabisi NO and Another v. Aquarella and Others* 2008 (4) SA 195 (T).
183. See, e.g.: *Silvermine Valley Coalition v. Sybrand van der Spuy Boerderye and Others* 2002 (1) SA 478 (C); *Capital Park Motors CC and Another v. Shell South Africa Marketing (Pty) Ltd and Others* Case No. 3106/05 of 18 March 2005 (unreported judgment of the High Court of South Africa Transvaal Provincial Division); *BP Southern Africa (Pty) Ltd v. MEC for Agriculture, Conservation, Environment and Land Affairs* 2004 (5) SA 124 (W); *MEC for Agriculture, Conservation, Environment and Land Affairs v. Sasol Oil (Pty) Ltd & Another* 2006 (5) SA 483 (SCA); and *MEC: Department of Agriculture, Conservation and Environment and Another v. HTF Developers (Pty) Ltd* 2008 (2) SA 319 (CC).
184. See, e.g.: *Hichange Investments (Pty) Ltd v. Cape Produce Co. (Pty) Ltd t/a Pelts Products* 2004 (2) SA 393 (E); *Bareki NO and Another v. Gencor Ltd & Others* 2006 (1) SA 432 (T); *Minister of Water Affairs and Forestry v. Stilfontein Gold Mining Co. Ltd and Others* 2006 (5)

applicability of principles and objectives contained in various environmental laws.[185] Some of the more recent notable judgments are briefly discussed below.

Arguably, the most severe pollution in South Africa occurred prior to the enactment of the current comprehensive environmental governance regime. Liability for this historic pollution is a contentious issue which recently was subject to judicial scrutiny in *Bareki NO and Another v. Gencor Ltd and Others* (Bareki).[186] The first respondent operated an asbestos mine. When the mine was closed in 1985, the mine was not rehabilitated. The main applicant was a traditional leader acting in his own name and on behalf of the community living adjacent to the mine. The applicants alleged that the mine caused, and continued to cause, significant pollution (particularly as a result of dispersion of asbestos fibres) which was causing ill-health in the neighbouring community. They further argued that the first respondent and the State (the owner of the land in question) had failed to take reasonable measures, as prescribed in section 28 of NEMA, to contain or rectify the pollution or degradation of the environment.[187] One of the central issues was whether this statutory provision applied retrospectively to historical pollution.

The court referred to the presumption against retrospectivity which prevails in South African law. It held that the presumption is based on the principle of fairness in that 'individuals should have an opportunity to know what the law is and to conform their conduct accordingly'.[188] The court held that the wording of section 28 created strict or even absolute liability and did not afford the polluter any statutory defenses.[189] In the court's opinion, 'if the Legislature intended attaching new legal consequences to past conduct by creating severe strict liability retrospectively, one would have expected that such an intention would have been made clear'.[190] The retrospective application of NEMA, according to the court, would cause great unfairness and encroach on the rule of law by creating unreasonable strict or absolute liability.[191] Having considered the relevant statutory context, including the environmental right, the court held that applicants had failed to rebut the presumption and accordingly dismissed the application.[192]

SA 333 (W); *Minister of Water Affairs and Forestry v. Stilfontein Gold Mining Co. Ltd and Others* 2006 (5) SA 333 (W); and *Kebble and Others v. Minister of Water Affairs and Forestry* (2007) SCA 111 (RSA).

185. See, e.g.: *Minister of Public Works and Others v. Kyalami Ridge Environmental Association and Others* 2001 (7) BCLR 652 (CC); *Bato Star Fishing (Pty) Ltd v. Minister Environmental Affairs & Others* 2004 (4) SA 490 (CC); and *BP Southern Africa (Pty) Ltd v. MEC for Agriculture, Conservation, Environment and Land Affairs* 2004 (5) SA 124 (W).
186. 2006 (1) SA 432 (TPD).
187. S. 28 states that: 'Every person who causes, has caused or may cause significant pollution or degradation of the environment must take reasonable measures to prevent such pollution or degradation from occurring, continuing or recurring, or, in so far as such harm to the environment is authorised by law or cannot reasonably be avoided or stopped, to minimise and rectify such pollution or degradation of the environment.'
188. Para. B at 439.
189. Para. H at 440 to para. B at 441.
190. Para. I at 441.
191. Para. C at 442.
192. Para. C at 445.

This judgment has been criticized by various commentators owing to the courts failure to give effect to not only the express wording contained in NEMA, but also its national environmental management principles and the environmental right.[193] It would furthermore appear to preclude the ability of environmental authorities to address historic pollution until such time as the statutory framework is amended.

An interesting trilogy of cases which considered the interpretation and application of various statutory administrative measures in the mining and water pollution context was initiated by *Harmony Gold Mines v. Regional Director, Free State, Department of Water Affairs and Tourism and Another* (Harmony).[194] The applicant sought to challenge a statutory directive issued under the NWA which compelled it, inter alia, to extract large volumes of groundwater from its mine to prevent water pollution.[195] Several adjacent mining companies, whose mines were linked to that of the applicant through a series of underground tunnels, were issued similar directives. However, a couple of these mining companies had gone into liquidation and accordingly the applicant had been directed to contribute to the costs of extracting water from these adjacent mines which it did not own. The applicant sought to challenge the legality of the directive. It argued that the relevant statutory framework only enabled the authorities to direct the applicant to take measures to prevent pollution on its own land and not that of another person. The court, having considered the broader constitutional environment and the provisions of the NWA, held that the scope of the duty of care provision was wide enough to include taking measures on another's land. Although it agreed that ordinarily the cost of taking measures on land owned or controlled by another would be for these parties' account, it held that exceptional circumstances could exist where other parties could be compelled to collaborate to cover these costs. The court ruled that this was one of these exceptional circumstances and therefore dismissed the application.[196]

Notwithstanding the outcome of the above case, one mining company to which a statutory directive had been issued failed to comply with it. The State sought and obtained a court order compelling the mining company to do so. The mining company failed to comply with the court order and accordingly the State again approached the court, in *Minister of Water Affairs and Forestry v. Stilfontein Gold Mining Co. Ltd and Others* (Stilfontein),[197] for an order declaring the mining

---

193. See for instance: W. du Plessis & L.J. Kotzé, 'Absolving Historical Polluters from Liability through Restrictive Judicial Interpretation: Some Thoughts on Bareki NO v. Gencor Ltd', *StellLR* 18 (2007): 161-193; and Kidd, *supra* n. 144, 7.
194. (2006) SCA 65 (RSA).
195. S. 19 states that: '(1) An owner of land, a person in control of land or a person who occupies or uses the land on which – (a) any activity or process is or was performed or undertaken; or (b) any other situation exists, which causes, has caused or is likely to cause pollution of a water resource, must take all reasonable measures to prevent any such pollution from occurring, continuing or recurring.'
196. Para. 34-36.
197. 2006 (5) SA 333 (WLD).

company, and four directors of the company, to be in contempt of court. The respondent alleged, inter alia, that the directives were so vague and unintelligibly worded that it could not comply with them. It further argued that this was the reason for many of the directors resigning just prior to the matter being heard by the court. The court held that: the directives were sufficiently clear and therefore capable of implementation; the mining company and its directors were in contempt of court; and issued fines against them. Evidently frowning upon the strange timing of the directors' resignation, the court stated:

> I have not come across a case, in the corporate history of this country, where all the directors of a listed company resigned at once. Not surprising then that I could find no case law in this country that dealt with this situation, nor was I able to find such a state of affairs in the English case law. This is probably because this is simply not done within the corporate world.[198]

The court added that this was 'unacceptable' and that the directors could not 'be allowed to merely walk away because it is convenient for them to do so'.[199] In a telling statement, the court concluded that:

> The object of the directives is to prevent pollution of valuable water resources. To permit mining companies and their directors to flout environmental obligations is contrary to the Constitution, the Mineral Petroleum [Resources] Development Act and to the National Environmental Management Act. Unless courts are prepared to assist the State by providing suitable mechanisms for the enforcement of statutory obligations, an impression will be created that mining companies are free to exploit the mineral resources of the country for profit, over the lifetime of the mine; thereafter they may simply walk away from their environmental obligations. This simply cannot be permitted in a constitutional democracy which recognises the right of all citizens to be protected from the effects of pollution and degradation. For this reason too, the . . . respondents cannot be permitted to merely walk away from the company, conveniently turning their backs on their duties and obligations as directors.[200]

This remarkable decision was overturned by the Supreme Court of Appeal in *Kebble v. Minister of Water Affairs* (Kebble).[201] The court, in what can only be described as a superficial and unsubstantiated judgment, held that the statutory directives were unclear, incapable of implementation; and accordingly the company and its directors could not be held to be in contempt of court.[202] It is regrettable that the approach of the High Court was overturned in the Supreme Court of Appeal,

---

198. Para. F-G at 348.
199. Para. B at 351.
200. Para. D-H at 352.
201. [2007] SCA 111 (RSA).
202. See L.J. Kotzé & N. Lubbe, 'Silent Spring Revisited? The Stilfontein Drama in Three Parts', paper presented at the Annual IAIAsa/ELA conference (Bela Bela, August 2008) (on file with the authors).

as the former had the potential to significantly alter the South African landscape of corporate environmental liability.

It is always open to the recipient of a statutory directive to challenge its legality on the basis that the necessary jurisdictional facts were not present prior to its issue. In the recent case of *Khabisi NO and Another v. Aquarella and Others* (Aquarella),[203] the court held that the recipient cannot, however, simply ignore a directive which he/she believes to be invalid; or to raise it as a collateral challenge when the issuing authority seeks to enforce the directive. This should significantly bolster authorities' enforcement efforts.[204]

As should be evident from the above analysis, the track record of the judiciary in interpreting various aspects of South Africa's contemporary environmental regime has been somewhat chequered. In some instances, such as the *Stilfontein* and *Khabisi* cases, the courts have shown a willingness to facilitate improved environmental governance by extending the ambit, and confirming the status of, various administrative measures. In others, such as the *Gencor* and *Kebble* cases, the courts have unfortunately undermined potentially powerful statutory tools for facilitating improved environmental governance. Fortunately, laws are living instruments and subject to amendment and whilst the latter judgments have been subject to criticism, one positive result is that they have compelled the legislature and executive to think very carefully regarding the wording and terminology used in laws, regulations and administrative notices.

5.7   CRIMINAL ENFORCEMENT

The South African environmental regime relies heavily on criminal measures to facilitate compliance and enforcement and contains 'satisfactory' and in some instances even 'severe' penalties for those who commit environmental crimes.[205] It is very difficult to determine the extent to which the penalties have been imposed by the courts as these matters usually come before Magistrates' Courts whose decisions are not reported. Kidd opines that with the exception of the fishing industry,[206] insufficient penalties are generally imposed by the courts.[207]

---

203. 2008 (4) SA 195 (T).
204. T. Winstanley, 'Chapter 9: Administrative Measures', in Paterson & Kotzé (eds), *supra* n. 4.
205. M.A. Kidd, 'Chapter 10: Criminal Measures', in Paterson & Kotzé (eds), *supra* n. 4. For a further discussion on the use of criminal measures to facilitate environmental compliance and enforcement in South Africa see: M.A. Kidd, 'Sentencing Environmental Crimes', *SAJELP* 11 (2004): 54-57; M.A. Kidd, 'Environmental Crime: Time for a Rethink in South Africa?', *SAJELP* 5 (1998): 188-191; and C. Loots, 'Making Environmental Law Effective', *SAJELP* 1 (1994): 17-22.
206. See e.g. *S v. Packereysammy* 2004 (2) SACR 169 (SCA); and *S v. Van Dyk* 2005 (1) SACR 35 (SCA).
207. Kidd, *supra* n. 205.

While it appears that fines and imprisonment have been employed by the courts with some success, the judiciary has been very reluctant to make use of many available 'alternative' criminal sanctions prescribed in South Africa's contemporary environmental laws such as: fines for continuing offences; compensation orders; reparation orders; fines equivalent to the object of the crime; fines equivalent to advantage gained; forfeiture; community service; revocation of authorizations; recovery of prosecution costs; employee liability; and director liability.[208] These alternative sanctions will no doubt receive increasing judicial attention as the 'novelty and mystery' surrounding their use wears off over time. This process be expedited by recent judicial training initiatives undertaken by DEAT during the course of the past two years, and the anticipated increased number of prosecutions brought to court following the creation of the EMI, an inspectorate specifically tasked with facilitating improved environmental compliance and enforcement and investigating environmental offences.[209]

5.8	COMMON LAW REMEDIES

In South Africa, common law remedies continue to play an important role in environmental governance and are frequently invoked where suitable alternate statutory remedies are absent. Common law remedies that are of particular relevance to environmental matters include nuisance, neighbour law, and the law of delict. These remedies, effectively administered by the judiciary, enable aggrieved citizens and authorities to halt unlawful environmentally deleterious action by way of an interdict and theoretically recover any patrimonial loss caused by such action. The law of nuisance has been successfully invoked to prevent air pollution,[210] offensive odours,[211] water pollution,[212] light pollution,[213] noise[214] and land contamination.[215] Neighbour law has similarly been invoked to bring an end to noise pollution[216] and water pollution.[217] There is, however, a dearth of

---

208. *Ibid.* See for instance NEMA (s. 34) and NWA (ss 152-154).
209. For further information on these training initiatives and the Environmental Management Inspectorate see Craigie et al., *supra* n. 103.
210. See *Gibbons v. SA Railways and Harbours* 1933 CPD 521.
211. See *Winshaw v. Miller* 1916 CPD 439.
212. See *Dreyer v. Cloete* (1877) 7 Buch 142; and *Trill v. Claremont Municipality* (1904) 21 SC 362.
213. See *Robert George Tiffin v. Jeremy Edward Woods NO* Case No. A324/2006 of 26 April 2007 (unreported judgment of the High Court of South Africa Cape Provincial Division).
214. See *Holland v. Scott* (1882) 2 EDC 307; *Graham v. Dittmann and Son* 1917 TPD 288; *Prinsloo v. Shaw* 1938 AD 570; *De Charmoy v. Day Star Hatchery (Pty) Ltd* 1967 (4) SA 188 (D); *Nelson Mandela Metropolitan Municipality v. Greyvenouw CC* 2004 (2) SA 81 (SE); and *Laskey and Another v. Showzone CC and Others* 2007 (2) SA 48 (C).
215. *Savoy House (Pty) Ltd v. Salisbury City Council* 1959 (2) SA 645 (SR).
216. *Gien v. Gien* 1979 (2) SA 1113 (T).
217. *Rainbow Chicken Farms (Pty) Ltd v. Mediterranean Woollen Mill (Pty) Ltd* 1963 (1) SA 201 (N).

jurisprudence relating to the recovery of 'environmental damages' by way of the law of delict.

Notwithstanding the fact that South Africa's contemporary statutory framework has largely supplanted the common law as the principal basis of environmental law in South Africa, it continues to play a role largely owing to its flexible nature and ability 'to respond to the unique facts applicable to a specific dispute'.[218] As highlighted by Summers, its future role is, however, somewhat undermined by many inherent procedural and substantive constraints, evidentiary obstacles and the fact that most remedies are founded on the protection of individual proprietary interests as opposed to public and/or environmental interests.[219] The judiciary is, however, under a duty to apply and develop the common law remedies in the light of the rights enshrined in the Constitution, including the environmental right. The manner in which the judiciary responds to this duty remains to be seen. Furthermore, it must be remembered that the judiciary can only deliberate those matters brought before it and accordingly its role could be frustrated by the reticence of litigants wishing to bring these often complex, costly, time-consuming and risky matters to court.

5.9   LITIGATION COSTS

As alluded to above, the cost of litigation frequently serves as a deterrent to potential litigants wishing to institute proceedings to protect and enforce environmental rights and interests. Fortunately, South Africa's framework environmental law, NEMA, affords the court discretion not to award costs against an applicant who fails to secure his/her relief sought if the court is of the opinion that the applicant acted reasonably out of a concern for the public interest, or in the interest of protecting the environment, and had made due effort to use other means reasonably available for obtaining the relief sought.[220] This provision theoretically encourages private and public litigants to have environmental disputes resolved by the courts.

The first case to consider these provisions was *Silvermine Valley Coalition v. Sybrand van der Spuy Boerderye* (Silvermine),[221] where the court stated that the principal test to be applied in the consideration of a cost award lies in 'whether . . . [the] applicant acted reasonably out of a concern for the public interest of protecting the environment and had made all due efforts to use other means reasonably available for obtaining relief sought'.[222] Having applied this test to the

---

218. For a comprehensive analysis on the contribution role of the common law to environmental governance see R. Summers, 'Chapter 13: Common Law Remedies for Environmental Protection', in Paterson & Kotzé 2009, (eds), *supra*. n. 4.

219. *Ibid.*

220. S. 32(2).

221. 2002 (1) SA 478 (CPD).

222. Para. J at 491.

facts before it, the court elected not to award costs against the applicant notwithstanding its failed application as it was of the opinion that:

> NGOs should not have the unnecessary obstacles placed in their way when they act in a manner designed to hold the State and indeed the private community accountable to the constitutional commitments of our new society, which includes the protection of the environment.[223]

In the *Biowatch* case, discussed above, the court elected not to apply section 32(2) of NEMA.[224] Even though the court found in favor of the applicant NGO as regards the main action (see discussion above), it held that:

> the manner in which some of its [Biowatch's] requests for information were formulated, as well as the manner in which the relief claimed in the notice of motion was formulated, has convinced me that it should not be granted a costs order in its favour in these circumstances . . . In my view the applicant should be ordered to pay Monsanto's costs.[225]

Section 32(2) NEMA was again invoked by an environmental NGO in *Wildlife and Environmental Society of South Africa v. MEC for Economic Affairs, Environment and Tourism, Eastern Cape and Others* (WESSA).[226] WESSA withdrew its application and did not, as is custom, tender to pay the respondents' costs. The respondents accordingly gave notice of their intention to apply for an order forcing the NGO to pay their wasted legal costs. The applicant opposed this application relying principally on section 32(2) of NEMA. The court stated that section 32(2) could feasibly be invoked where a litigant withdraws its application.[227] However, having considered the reasonableness of the applicant's conduct in launching the application, the court ruled that it had relied on fatally flawed expert evidence, rested on a fundamental misunderstanding, and had no prospects of success.[228] The court consequently, in its own words, 'regrettably' ordered the applicant to pay the wasted legal costs of the respondent.[229]

These judgments illustrate the willingness of the courts to readily apply the novel cost order provisions inherent in NEMA. However, the *WESSA* case makes it abundantly clear that a litigant should properly avail itself of all facts and secure solid evidence in support of its case prior to bringing the dispute to court. A failure to do so may well result in the litigant being lumped with a legal costs order even if it is able to establish that it was acting in the environmental interest. This would appear to be just and equitable and should encourage potential litigants to be well-prepared before approaching a court.

---

223. Para. C-D at 493. Own emphasis.
224. Para. D at 146.
225. Para. E-F at 146.
226. 2005 (6) SA 123 (E).
227. Para. J at 132 to para. B at 133.
228. Para. J at 140 to para. A at 141; para. C at 142; and para. H at 143 to para. I at 143.
229. Para. I at 143 to para. B at 144.

6   CONCLUSION

The above critical analysis of relevant environmental cases confirms that the South
African judiciary is clearly playing a significant role in environmental governance.
It has demonstrated a clear willingness to grapple with the elements of, and challenges posed by, South Africa's fledging environmental regime by seeking to: give
content to the environmental right; define the mandate of environmental authorities; facilitate administrative justice; promote access to environmental information; extend *locus standi* in environmental matters; interpret anomalies in
environmental legislation; link land reform and environmental matters; facilitate
criminal enforcement; and apply and develop common law remedies to resolve
environmental disputes.

   However, if one takes a holistic view of all the relevant environmental cases
which have come before the courts in the past decade, one can conclude, in the
words of Kidd, that the judiciary's performance is:

> rather 'chequered' in environmental cases, which suggests that the judiciary needs
> to become more attuned to environmental law. I call this process, for purposes of
> this note, 'greening the judiciary'. What I mean by this is not that judges must
> decide all environmental cases in a way that favours the environment, but that
> they must correctly consider, interpret and apply the relevant environmental law,
> and give environmental considerations appropriate deliberation.[230]

Many of the challenges and opportunities for 'greening the judiciary' have been
addressed in the comprehensive critical analysis of relevant jurisprudence undertaken
in part 5 of this chapter. There are, however, some more generic challenges and
opportunities for improving the role of the judiciary in environmental governance.

   The resolution of environmental matters currently falls to South Africa's
'ordinary' courts. The judges presiding over these 'ordinary' courts are traditionally
generalists and do not have the requisite specialist skills and training to deal with
often technical environmental disputes. This is no doubt the reason for several of the
questionable judgments handed down in environmental matters in recent times.
Whilst several laudable initiatives have been undertaken to subject various members of the judiciary to environmental legal training, it would appear unreasonable
and unfeasible to expect all members of the judiciary to be experts in the area.

   Furthermore, South Africa's entire justice system is under significant strain.
Courts are faced with rising caseloads, diminishing budgets and shrinking
capacity. One needs look no further than the current rate of violent crime in
South Africa to realize that something is amiss in the country's judicial system.
Understandably, a large proportion of current judicial capacity has been directed to
deal with criminal matters such as murder, rape and armed robbery; causing delays
in the resolution of environmental matters. A massive injection of capacity and
resources into the flailing judicial system is essential to ensuring future effective
justice, including environmental justice, in South Africa.

---

230. Kidd, *supra* n. 144, 1.

One interim measure available to the government to facilitate the more speedy resolution of environmental matters is to extend the current jurisdiction of the Magistrates' Courts to hear such matters as they are currently predominantly heard by the overburdened 'higher' courts. However, perhaps a far more effective manner to achieve the same end and simultaneously improve the quality of judicial decisions in environmental matters is to re-establish the specialist environmental court in South Africa. It is unclear why there is currently such little political support for its re-establishment in the light of the existence of other specialist domestic courts hearing labour, commercial and land reform disputes.

Notwithstanding these challenges, the judiciary, with the Constitution nestled safely under its arm, had clearly embarked on the road to becoming an integral role player promoting environmental governance for sustainability in South Africa. The road will no doubt take many twists and turns but as one author has stated:

> The path to our destination is not always a straight one. We go down the wrong road, we get lost, we turn back. Maybe it doesn't matter which road we embark on. Maybe what matters is that we embark.[231]

BIBLIOGRAPHY

Bosman, C., L.J. Kotzé & W. du Plessis. 'The Failure of the Constitution to Ensure Integrated Environmental Management from a Co-operative Governance Perspective'. *SA Public Law* 19 (2004): 411-421.

Bray, E. 'Legal Perspectives on Global Environmental Governance: South Africa's Partnership Role (Part 2)'. *Journal of Contemporary Roman-Dutch Law* 3 (2005): 357-373.

Couzens, E. 'NEMA: A Step Closer to Coherence?'. *South African Journal of Environmental Law and Policy* 6 (1999): 13-19.

Craigie, F., P. Snijman & M. Fourie. 'Environmental Compliance and Enforcement Institutions'. In *Environmental Compliance and Enforcement in South Africa: Legal Perspectives*, edited by A.R. Paterson & L.J. Kotzé. Juta, 2009.

Currie, I. & J. de Waal. *The Bill of Rights Handbook*. Lansdowne: Juta, 2005.

DEAT. 'National State of the Environment Report 2006'. <www.ngo.grida.no/soesa/nsoer/>, 20 November 2008.

DEAT. *National Air Quality Management Programme – Initial State of the Air Report*. Pretoria: Department of Environmental Affairs and Tourism, 2006.

DEAT. *National Climate Change Response Strategy*. Pretoria: Department of Environmental Affairs and Tourism, 2004.

DME. 'South Africa's Mineral Industry (2006/2007)'. <www.dme.gov.za/minerals/sami_ 2005.stm>, 20 November 2008.

---

231. B. Hall, *Northern Exposure*: *Rosebud* (Studio City, CA: Pipeline Productions, 1993).

Du Plessis, A.A. The Fulfillment of the Constitutional Environmental Right in the Local Sphere of Government. LLD thesis, North-West University, Potchefstroom, South Africa, forthcoming.

Du Plessis, W. & L.J. Kotzé. 'Absolving Historical Polluters from Liability through Restrictive Judicial Interpretation: Some Thoughts on Bareki NO v. Gencor Ltd'. *Stellenbosch Law Review* 18 (2007): 161-193.

Du Plessis, W. & J.G. Nel. 'An Evaluation of NEMA based on a Generic Framework for Environmental Framework Legislation'. *South African Journal of Environmental Law and Policy* 8 (2001):1-37.

Dugard, J. *International Law: A South African Perspective*. 3rd ed. Cape Town: Juta, 2005.

Feris, L. 'Compliance Notices – A New Tool in Environmental Enforcement'. *Potchefstroom Electronic Law Journal* 3 (2006):1-18. <www.puk.ac.za/fakulteite/regte/per/issue06v3.html>, 20 November 2008.

Feris, L. 'Constitutional Environmental Rights: An Underutilised Resource'. Unpublished paper presented at the 5th Annual IUCN Academy of Environmental Law Colloquium. Parati, Brazil, June 2007.

Field, T-L. 'Realising the National Environmental Management Act's potential to bring polluters to book'. *South African Law Journal* 121 (2004):772-784.

Glazewski, J. *Environmental Law in South Africa*. 2nd ed. Durban: LexisNexis Butterworths, 2005.

Glazewski, J. 'The environmental right'. In *South African Constitutional Law: The Bill of Rights*, edited by M.H. Cheadle, D.M. Davis & N.R.L. Haysom. Durban: LexisNexis Butterworths, 2002.

Hall, B. *Northern Exposure: Rosebud*. Studio City, CA: Pipeline Productions, 1993.

Hoexter, C. 'The Future of Judicial Review in South African Administrative Law', *South African Law Journal* 117 (2000): 484-509.

Kidd, M.A. 'The Constitutional Court's Dilution of NEMA: Minister of Public Works and Others v. Kyalami Ridge Environmental Association and Another'. *South African Journal of Environmental Law and Policy* 8 (2001): 119-127.

Kidd, M.A. 'Sentencing Environmental Crimes'. *South African Journal of Environmental Law and Policy* 11 (2004): 53-57.

Kidd, M.A. 'Environmental Crime: Time for a Rethink in South Africa?'. *South African Journal of Environmental Law and Policy* 5 (1998): 181-191.

Kidd, M.A. 'Greening the Judiciary'. *Potchefstroom Electronic Law Journal* (2006): 1-15. <www.puk.ac.za/fakulteite/regte/per/issue06v3.html>, 20 November 2008.

Kidd, M.A. 'Criminal Measures'. In *Environmental Compliance and Enforcement in South Africa: Legal Perspectives*, edited by A.R. Paterson & L.J. Kotzé. Juta, 2009.

Kidd, M.A. *Environmental Law*. Cape Town: Juta, 2008.

King Committee on Corporate Governance. *King Report on Corporate Governance for South Africa*. Parklands: Secretariat, King Committee on Corporate Governance, 2002.

Kotzé, L.J. 'Promoting Public Participation in Environmental Decision-making through the South Africa Courts: Myth or Reality?'. Unpublished paper presented at the UNITAR-Yale Conference on Environmental Governance and Democracy, University of Yale. New Haven, May 2008.

Kotzé, L.J. 'The Judiciary, the Environmental Right and the Quest for Sustainability in South Africa: A Critical Reflection'. *Review of European Community and International Environmental Law* 16, no. 16 (2007): 298-311.

Kotzé, L.J. *A Legal Framework for Integrated Environmental Governance in South* Africa. Nijmegen: Wolf Legal Publishers, 2006.

Kotzé, L.J. & N. Lubbe. 'Silent Spring Revisited? The Stilfontein Drama in Three Parts'. Paper presented at the Annual IAIAsa/ELA conference. Bela Bela, August 2008.

Kotzé, L.J., et al. *South African Environmental Law through the Cases*. Durban: LexisNexis Butterworths, 2008.

Loots, C. 'Making Environmental Law Effective'. *South African Journal of Environmental Law and Policy* 1 (1994): 17-33.

Nel, J.G. & W. du Plessis. 'Unpacking Integrated Environmental Management – A step closer to effective co-operative governance'. *SA Public Law* 19 (2004):181-190.

Orr, J. 'South Africa'. In *The Judicial Institution in Southern Africa: A Comparative Study of Common Law Jurisdictions*, edited by L. van de Vijver. Cape Town: Siber Ink, 2006.

Paterson, A.R. & L.J. Kotzé (eds). *Environmental Compliance and Enforcement in South Africa: Legal Perspectives* (Juta, 2009).

Soltau, F. 'The National Environmental Management Act and Liability for Environmental Damage'. *South African Journal of Environmental Law and Policy* 6 (1999):33-41.

Statistics South Africa. *Census 2001: Investigation into appropriate definitions of urban and rural areas for South Africa – Discussion document*. Pretoria: Statistics South Africa, 2003.

Summers, R. 'Common Law Remedies for Environmental Protection'. In *Environmental Compliance and Enforcement in South Africa: Legal Perspectives*, edited by A.R. Paterson & L.J. Kotzé. Juta, 2009.

Thompson, H. *Water Law: A Practical Approach to Resources Management and the Provision of Services*. Cape Town: Juta, 2006.

Van Reenen, T.P. 'Constitutional Protection of the Environment: Fundamental (Human) Right or Principle of State Policy?'. *South African Journal of Environmental Law and Policy* 4 (1997): 269-289.

White Paper on the Conservation and Use of South Africa's Biodiversity (GN 1095) *Government Gazette* No. 18163 of 28 July 1997.

Winstanley, T. 'Administrative Measures'. In *Environmental Compliance and Enforcement in South Africa: Legal Perspectives*, edited by A.R. Paterson & L.J. Kotzé. Juta, 2009.

Winstanley, T. 'Entrenching Environmental Protection in the new Constitution'. *South African Journal of Environmental Law and Policy* 2 (1995): 85-97.

World Conservation Monitoring Centre. *Global Biodiversity Status of the Earths Living Resources.* London: Chapman & Hall, 1992.

Wynberg, R. 'A decade of biodiversity conservation and use in South Africa: Tracking progress from Rio Earth Summit to the Johannesburg World Summit on Sustainable Development'. *South African Journal of Science* 98 (2002): 233-243.

TABLE OF LEGISLATION

Cape Land Use Planning Ordinance 15 of 1985
Constitution of the Republic of South Africa 200 of 1993
Constitution of the Republic of South Africa, 1996
Development Facilitation Act 67 of 1995
Environment Conservation Act 73 of 1989
Genetically Modified Organisms Act 15 of 1997
Intergovernmental Relations Framework Act 13 of 2005
KwaZulu-Natal Nature Conservation Management Act 9 of 1997
Magistrates' Court Act 32 of 1944
Mineral and Petroleum Resources Development Act 28 of 2002
Mpumalanga Nature Conservation Act 10 of 1998
National Environmental Management Act 107 of 1998
National Environmental Management: Air Quality Act 39 of 2004
National Environmental Management: Biodiversity Act 10 of 2004
National Environmental Management: Integrated Coastal Management Bill 2007
National Environmental Management: Protected Areas Act 57 of 2003
National Environmental Management: Waste Management Bill 2007
National Heritage Resources Act 25 of 1999
National Nuclear Regulator Act 47 of 1999
National Water Act 36 of 1998
Nuclear Energy Act 46 of 1999
Promotion of Access to Information Act 2 of 2000
Promotion of Administrative Justice Act 3 of 2000
Water Services Act 108 of 1997

TABLE OF CASES

All the Best Trading CC t/a Parkville Motors and Others v. SN Nayagar Property Development and Construction CC and Others 2005 (3) SA 396 (T)
Bamford v. Minister of Community Development and State Auxiliary Services 1981 (3) SA 1054 (C)
Bareki NO and Another v. Gencor Ltd & Others 2006 (1) SA 432 (T)
Bato Star Fishing (Pty) Ltd v. Minister Environmental Affairs & Others 2004 (4) SA 490 (CC)

BP Southern Africa (Pty) Ltd v. MEC for Agriculture, Conservation and Land Affairs 2004 (5) SA 124 (WLD)

Capital Park Motors CC and Another v. Shell South Africa Marketing (Pty) Ltd and Others Case No. 3106/05 of 18 March 2005 (unreported) High Court TPD

Capital Park Motors CC and Another v. Shell South Africa Marketing (Pty) Ltd and Others [2007] JOL 20072 (T) (unreported)

City of Cape Town & Others v. Oudekraal Estates (Pty) Ltd and Others Case No. 8112/2004 9 October 2007 (unreported) High Court CPD

Corium (Pty) Ltd v. Myburgh Park Langebaan (Pty) Ltd 1995 (3) SA 51 (C)

Dalrympie v. Colonial Treasurer 1910 TS 372

De Charmoy v. Day Star Hatchery (Pty) Ltd 1967 (4) SA 188 (D)

Diepsloot Residents v. Landowners' Association and Another 1994 (3) SA 338 (AD)

Director Mineral Development, Gauteng Region and Another v. Save the Vaal Environment and Others 1999 (2) SA 709 (SCA)

Director of Education Transvaal v. McCagie 1918 AD 616

Doctors for Life International v. Speaker of the National Assembly and Others 2006 (12) BCLR1399 (CC)

Earthlife Africa (Cape Town Branch) v. Eskom Holdings Ltd [2006] 2 All SA 632 (W)

Earthlife Africa (Cape Town) v. Director General: Department of Environmental Affairs and Tourism 2005 (3) SA 156 (C)

Eskom v. Rini Town Council 1992 (4) SA 96 (E)

Evans and Others v. Llandudno/Hout Bay Transitional Metropolitan Substructure and Another 2001 (2) SA 342 (C)

Foodcorp (Pty) v. DDG, Department of Environmental Affairs and Tourism: Branch Marine and Coastal Management 2006 (2) SA 191 (SCA)

Fuel Retailers Association of SA (Pty) Ltd v. Director-General Environmental Management Mpumalanga and Others 2007 (10) BCLR 1059 (CC)

Gien v. Gien 1979 (2) SA 1113 (T)

Government of the Republic of South Africa and Others v. Grootboom and Others 2001 (1) SA 46 (CC)

Graham v. Dittmann and Son 1917 TPD 288

Hangklip Environmental Action Group v. MEC for Agriculture, Environmental Affairs and Development Planning (Western Cape) and Others 2007 (6) SA 65 (C)

Harmony Gold Mines v. Regional Director, Free State, Department of Water Affairs and Forestry and Another [2006] (4) All SA 366 (W)

Hentru Developers & Contractors CC v. Hanekom NO & Another [2005] JOL 15650 (T)

Hichange Investments (Pty) Ltd v. Cape Produce Company t/a Pelts Products 2004 (2) SA 393 (E)

Holland v. Scott (1882) 2 EDC 307

HTF Developers (Pty) Ltd v. Minister of Environmental Affairs and Tourism and Others 2007 (5) SA 438 (SCA)

In re Kranspoort Community 2000 (2) SA 124 (LCC)

Kebble v. Minister of Water Affairs [2007] SCA 111 (RSA)

Khabisi NO and Another v. Aquarella and Others 2008 (4) SA 195 (T)

Lascon Properties (Pty) Ltd v. Wadeville Investment Co. (Pty) Ltd and Another 1997 (4) SA 578 (W)

Laskey and Another v. Showzone CC and Others 2007 (2) SA 48 (C)

Laskey and Another v. Showzone CC and Others 2007 (2) SA 48 (C)

Laugh it Off Promotions CC v. SAB International (Finance) BV t/a Sabmark International (Freedom of Expression Institute as Amicus Curiae) 2006 (1) SA 144 (CC)

Logbro Properties CC v. Bedderson NO and Others 2003 (2) SA 460 (SCA)

MEC for Agriculture, Conservation, Environment and Land Affairs v. Sasol Oil (Pty) Ltd & Another 2006 (5) SA 483 (SCA)

MEC for Economic Affairs Environment and Tourism v. MacKay Bridge Farm CC [1996] 3 All SA 340 (SE)

MEC: Department of Agriculture, Conservation and Environment and Another v. HTF Developers (Pty) Ltd 2008 (2) SA 319 (CC)

Merebank Environmental Action Committee v. Executive Member of Kwa-Zulu Natal Council for Agriculture and Environmental Affairs Case No. 2691/01 (D) (unreported) High Court D&CLD

Milani v. South African Medical and Dental Council 1990 (1) SA 899 (T)

Minister of Health and Welfare v. Woodcarb (Pty) Ltd and Another 1996 (3) SA 155 (NPD)

Minister of Health v. Drums and Pails Reconditioning CC t/a Village Drums and Pails 1997 (3) SA 867 (N)

Minister of Public Works and Others v. Kyalami Ridge Environmental Association and Others 2001 (7) BCLR 652 (CC)

Minister of Water Affairs and Forestry v. Stilfontein Gold Mining Co. Ltd and Others 2006 (5) SA 333 (WLD)

Nelson Mandela Metropolitan Municipality v. Greyvenouw CC 2004 (2) SA 81 (SE)

Nelson Mandela Metropolitan Municipality v. Greyvenouw CC 2004 (2) SA 81 (SE)

Oudekraal Estates (Pty) Ltd v. City of Cape Town and Others 2004 (6) SA 222 (SCA)

Patz v. Greene & Co. 1907 TS 427

Petro Props (Pty) Ltd v. Barlow and Others 2006 (5) SA 160 (W)

Prinsloo v. Shaw 1938 AD 570

Rainbow Chicken Farms (Pty) Ltd v. Mediterranean Woollen Mill (Pty) Ltd 1963 (1) SA 201 (N)

Rainbow Chicken Farms (Pty) Ltd v. Mediterranean Woollen Mill (Pty) Ltd 1963 (1) SA 201 (N)

Raubenheimer NO v. Trustees Johannes Bredenkamp Trust 2006 (1) SA 124 (CPD)

Robert George Tiffin v. Jeremy Edward Woods NO Case No. A324/2006 26 April 2007 (unreported) High Court CPD

S v. Packereysammy 2004 (2) SACR 169 (SCA)

S v. Van Dyk 2005 (1) SACR 35 (SCA)

Savoy House (Pty) Ltd v. Salisbury City Council 1959 (2) SA 645 (SR)

Silvermine Valley Coalition v. Sybrand van der Spuy Boerderye 2002 (1) SA 478 (CPD)

SLC Property Group (Pty) Ltd and Another v. Minister of Environmental Affairs and Economic Development and Another Case No. 5542/2007 26 October 2007 (unreported) High Court CPD

South African Shore Angling Association and Another v. Minister of Environmental Affairs 2002 (5) SA 511 (SE)

The Trustees for the Time Being of the Biowatch Trust v. The Registrar: Genetic Resources and Others Case No. A831/2005 (unreported) High Court TPD

Trustees, Biowatch Trust v. Registrar: Genetic Resources and Others 2005 (4) SA 111 (TPD)

Verstappen v. Port Edward Town Board and Others 1994 (3) SA 569 (D)

Wildlife and Environmental Society of South Africa v. MEC for Economic Affairs, Environment and Tourism, Eastern Cape and Others 2005 (6) SA 123 (E)

Wright and Another v. Cockin and Others 2004 (4) SA 207 (EC)

ABBREVIATIONS

CPD	Cape Provincial Division
D&CLD	Durban and Coast Local Division
DEAT	Department of Environmental Affairs and Tourism
DME	Department of Minerals and Energy
DWAF	Department of Water Affairs and Forestry
ECA	Environment Conservation Act
EIA	Environmental Impact Assessment
EMI	Environmental Management Inspectorate
GMO	Genetically Modified Organism
NEMA	National Environmental Management Act
NGO	Non-governmental Organization
NWA	National Water Act
PAIA	Promotion of Access to Information
PAJA	Promotion of Administrative Justice Act
TPD	Transvaal Provincial Division
WESSA	Wildlife and Environmental Society of South Africa
WSSD	World Summit on Sustainable Development

Chapter 19
Eritrea

Zerisenay Habtezion

1   INTRODUCTION

Still rising from the ashes of war, Eritrea is a country that is not blessed with natural resources, especially terrestrial resources. Its environment is fragile, challenged by an assortment of natural and anthropogenic factors. The role of the country's judiciary, as well as other relevant institutions in environmental governance, reflects these challenges.

 Like most African States, Eritrea is a colonial creation. Originally Italy's first colony, present-day Eritrea has also previously been occupied by the Turks and the Egyptian Pashas.[1] Following the defeat of the Italians in the Horn of Africa by the British, the latter soon established a protectorate over Eritrea. In 1950, the United Nations resolved, in a notorious verdict, to federate Eritrea with Ethiopia, which was put into effect in 1952.[2] By 1962, Ethiopia abrogated the federal status and

---

1. See generally: F. Nahum, 'The Enigma of Eritrean Legislation', *J. Eth. L.* 9, no. 1 (1973): 308; J. Firebrace, *Eritrea: Never Kneel Down: Drought, Development and Liberation in Eritrea* (Trenton, NJ: Red Sea Press, 1986), 17; and G. Trevaskis, *Eritrea, A Colony in Transition: 1941-1952* (London: OUP, 1960).
2. General Assembly Resolution 390 (V), UN GAOR, 5th Session, Supp. No. 20, UN Doc. A/1775 (1950). For a description of this process, see B. Boutros-Ghali, *The United Nations and the Independence of Eritrea*, The United Nations Blue Book series, vol. XII (NY: Department of Public Information, 1996), 9-11.

Louis J. Kotzé and Alexander R. Paterson (eds), *The Role of the Judiciary in Environmental Governance: Comparative Perspectives*, pp. 603–630.
© 2009 Kluwer Law International BV, The Netherlands.

annexed Eritrea, triggering the longest armed struggle for independence in Africa.[3] Eritrea gained its virtual independence in 1991 and formal independence in 1993 following an internationally monitored referendum. The country is still in a no-war no-peace state of affairs owing to renewed conflicts with its former foe, Ethiopia.

The history of war and conflict has had a significant toll on the country's economy, infrastructure and human resources.[4] Its impact on natural and cultural heritage is no less significant, indeed if not more so.[5] Much still remains to be done in terms of the move towards constitutionalism and the building of many institutions, including a strong and independent judiciary. Adding insult to injury, recurrent droughts compound prevalent poverty and environmental deterioration.[6] One of the overwhelming challenges that Eritrea faces in its drive to reconstruct its economy, is the need to rehabilitate the nation's degraded environment.[7] Among the many institutions that are expected to play a pivotal role in this regard, is the judiciary.

This chapter considers the role that Eritrea's fledgling judiciary is playing in protecting the environment and promoting the sustainable use of the nation's natural resources, with specific focus on the forestry and wildlife sectors. The survey specifically: considers the main environmental challenges in Eritrea; highlights the relevant laws, policies, institutions and governance structures of direct and indirect relevance to the environment; provides a brief history of the Eritrean judiciary, elaborating on its evolution, status and current structure; provides an analysis of various court decisions relating to forestry and wildlife from two of the country's six administrative regions, namely the Gash Barka Region and Northern Red Sea Region; and presents a critical survey of the judiciary's role in environmental governance in light of the case law analysis. This critique specifically considers the following issues: the absence of relevant environmental legislation governing certain sectors; jurisdictional issues; structural constraints; judicial capacity constraints; and a lack of public awareness and capacity to initiate environmental litigation. Noteworthy interventions by the judiciary in the absence of supportive institutional and/or legal frameworks are also addressed. The chapter concludes by considering the major challenges facing the judiciary to assist Eritrea in moving towards sound environmental governance, and the opportunities available to the judiciary to facilitate this process.

---

3. Boutros-Ghali, *supra* n. 2, 13.
4. GoE, Macro Policy (Asmara: The Government, 1994), hereafter Macro Policy.
5. For the impact on cultural heritage, see: Z. Habtezion, 'Heritage Governance in Eritrea: Reality and Choices', in *Archaeology of Ancient Eritrea*, ed. P. Schmidt, M.C. Curtis & Z. Teka (Trenton, NJ: Red Sea Press, 2007), 349-351.
6. See generally: Macro Policy, *supra* n. 4; GoE, National Environmental Management Plan for Eritrea (Asmara: The Government, 1995), hereafter NEMP-E; and GoE, State of the Environment Report (Asmara: The Government, 2006), hereafter SoE Report.
7. NEMP-E, *supra* n. 6.

2   MAIN ENVIRONMENTAL CHALLENGES

2.1   INTRODUCTION

The fragility of Eritrea's environment, both in a quantitative and qualitative sense, directly impacts on the sustainability of the country's future development. Soil erosion, deforestation, depletion of water resources, ecosystem degradation, loss of biodiversity and the projected impact of climate change, stand out as critical environmental issues which present enormous challenges to achieving food security and poverty alleviation.[8] The survival, or to employ a more restrained language, *sustainable development* of the nation, can only be ensured if proper measures are taken to protect its terrestrial and aquatic resources.[9] For purposes of this chapter, emphasis is placed on forestry and wildlife resources, although questions of biodiversity depletion and land degradation are also addressed.

2.2   DEFORESTATION AND LAND DEGRADATION

Forest is estimated to have covered about 30% of the nation's landmass a century ago.[10] This figure dwindled to 11% by 1952,[11] and 5% by 1960.[12] Today, closed and open degraded forest covers less than 1% of the land area while bush land, albeit with arguably significant biodiversity, covers roughly 60% of the country. At current rates of deforestation and if sustainable forest management practices are not properly adopted, the few remaining forests and woodlands will rapidly degrade.[13]

Various interrelated factors are said to have contributed to the decline of the nation's forest resources with the principal causes being: land clearing for commercial and subsistence agriculture; consumption of wood for fuel;[14] construction of *Hidmos*

---

8. See: SoE Report, *supra* n. 6, and GoE, Rio+10 Country Report (Asmara: The Government, 2002), 1. Hereafter Rio+10 Country Report.
9. The coast has not been exposed to major development and the upshot of this is that the marine environment is, by and large, in relatively better shape when compared to the terrestrial environment. 'The Eritrean marine and coastal environment is characterized by an array of diversified ecosystems: coral reefs, mangroves, sea grass beds, sandy and muddy flats, all important for fisheries activities and offering a significant tourism potential. The inter-tidal and near-shore zones support a diverse range of marine and terrestrial species and are key areas of ecological and economic importance.' GoE, State of the Coast Report (Unpublished: 2006) Item 1.4.
10. GoE, National Action Plan (Asmara: The Government, 2002), 63. Hereafter NAP.
11. See: NEMP-E, *supra* n. 6, and E. Bein et al., *Useful Trees and Shrubs in Eritrea*, Technical Handbook No. 12 (Nairobi, SIDA Regional Soil Conservation Unit, 1996).
12. NAP (2002), *supra* n. 10.
13. UNEP, 'African Environmental Outlook', <www.unep.org/dewa/Africa/>, 21 September 2008. Hereafter AEO.
14. Forests and woodlands are the main source of fuel for the majority of the households which have significantly contributed to deforestation and declining forest quality. Currently, annual *per capita* energy consumption in Eritrea totals 0.2 tons of oil equivalents. About 96% of energy consumed by households is biomass. See Rio+10 Country Report, *supra* n. 8.

(traditional houses in the highland area);[15] drought; and land clearing for military purposes.[16] Deforestation has a direct correlation with the country's other key environmental ailment, land degradation, and it is currently estimated that approximately 63% of land in Eritrea is degraded to varying degrees.[17] Land degradation has, in turn, significantly lowered the current and/or potential capacity of the nation's land to produce essential goods and services,[18] and coupled with inadequate and erratic rainfall, is largely responsible for the annual 0.5% decline in the nation's crop yields.[19]

2.3   WILDLIFE DEPLETION

Historically, Eritrean forests, woodlands and pastoral savannahs hosted a wide diversity of wildlife species.[20] In the course of the past few decades, this diversity of species has been considerably depleted owing to persistent drought, war, neglect, and the conversion of natural habitats for agriculture and grazing.[21] Conflicts between wildlife conservation and human development remain in certain areas, which may exacerbate the current crises.[22]

---

15. A research project jointly conducted by the University of Asmara and the Ministry of Agriculture on the impact of the construction of a traditional house in highland/rural Eritrea (the *Hidmo*), found that these houses require about 14.4 pillars, 11.4 beams, and 145.2 cross-beams leading to the cutting of a large number of mature trees. Moreover, 'Growing demand for firewood and charcoal in the urban areas and the declining standard of living has exasperated the rapid deforestation and land degradation.' See K. Mengsteab, 'Eritrea's Land Reform Proclamation: A Critical Appraisal', *ESR* 2, no. 2 (1998): 5-6.
16. In Eritrea, forest resources have been indiscriminately devastated by increased agriculture, fuel wood gathering, charcoal burning, commercial logging for timber production, traditional house construction, overgrazing, inadequate tenure policy, recurrent droughts and other underlying causes including war, rural poverty and the state of the economy. See generally: GoE, National Action Plan (Unpublished: 2006); NEMP-E, *supra* n. 6; and Bein, *supra* n. 11.
17. The arid and semi-arid lands of Eritrea are characterized by low, unreliable and erratic rainfall patterns. Soil erosion (the annual net rate of soil loss from croplands is estimated at 12 tons/ha/year), the accelerated depletion of vegetation cover due to increased agriculture in fragile ecosystems and overgrazing, and exacerbate land degradation in these areas are all matters of grave concern. Given that agricultural activity is almost the sole source of income for more than 80% of Eritrea's population, land degradation poses a serious challenge to Eritrea's economy. See: GoE, 3rd National Report on the Implementation of the UNCCD (Asmara: MoA, 2004), <www.unccd.int/cop/reports/africa/national/2004/eritrea-eng. pdf>, 21 September 2008; and AEO, *supra* n. 13.
18. J. Bojö, Land Degradation and Rehabilitation in Eritrea: Working Paper 1 (Washington, DC: World Bank, 1996).
19. NAP (2002), *supra* n. 10.
20. *Ibid.*
21. *Ibid.*
22. As a notable example is cited the Gash Barka region where there have been numerous incidents of destruction of banana plantations by elephants, and the Semenawi Bahri region, were leopards are taking increasing numbers of sheep and goats. Interview with A. Yohannes, DoE Ministry of Land, Water and Environment expert on biodiversity and Eritrea's focal person for the CBD, 17-18 December 2007.

There is a shortage of reliable information to accurately quantify the status and/or rate of Eritrea's biodiversity demise. Various recent studies have fortunately shown that following Eritrea's independence in 1991, the wildlife population in some parts of the country is reviving.[23] This data is, however, confined to high profile species and relatively little is known about the current status of invertebrates, reptiles, amphibians and other less prominent species.[24] Given the apparent uniqueness and richness of Eritrea's biodiversity,[25] the introduction of special conservation measures would appear prudent.

2.4 OTHER

A range of other environmental problems exist in the country including: water scarcity, air pollution and, perhaps to a lesser extent, marine and land pollution.

Water scarcity is a grave problem in Eritrea. Located in the drier parts of Africa, the country is not endowed with adequate water resources. Rainfall is very low and erratic in its duration and geographical spread. Water shortages for human, agricultural, and industrial consumption are acute and the problem is exacerbated by inefficient water use, storage and service delivery.[26]

With a coastline of approximately 1,216 km, territorial waters and a continental shelf of over 50,000 km², Eritrea's marine environment is vulnerable to all sorts of marine pollution ranging from oil,[27] sewage, solid waste, pesticides, and toxic metals.[28] Owing to Eritrea's low level of industrial growth and development,

---

23. NEMP-E, *supra* n. 6, SoE Report, *supra* n. 6, AEO, *supra* n. 13.
24. Yohannes, *supra* n. 22.
25. A total of 126 mammal species and 577 species of birds (320 of which are resident, 195 migrant and approximately fifty recorded as breeding in Eritrea) have been identified in Eritrea. GoE DoE, Eritrea's National Biodiversity Strategy and Action Plan: Biodiversity stocktaking Assessment Report (Asmara: The Government, 1999). A total of ninety reptiles and nineteen amphibian species have also been recorded for Eritrea, including two possible endemic reptiles and one possible endemic amphibian. In the absence of a national checklist, a number of site-specific checklists are included in one list of almost 700 plant species which indicates that considerable plant diversity may persist in human-altered landscapes. *Ibid.* Eritrea is also home to eleven endangered tree species of recorded medicinal value. Given that the majority of the Eritrea's population relies on traditional medicine, the loss of such medicinal species will adversely affect the rural poor. See Rio+10 Country Report, *supra* n. 8.
26. NEMP-E, *supra* n. 6, 40-46.
27. Given that most of the vessels that pass through the Red Sea are oil tankers, the coast of Eritrea remains vulnerable to major oil spills and leakages. *Ibid.*
28. *Ibid.*, 30. Among the coastal and marine environmental problems confronting Eritrea, are those that have a direct and indirect effect on human health. Of particular concern are a range of natural and synthetic organic contaminants, and their entry into the coastal zone. Problems are compounded by the Red Sea's small tidal change, low wave energy, and limited water movements. Currently, there is no comprehensive law on marine pollution in Eritrea.

industrial air pollution[29] and land pollution[30] do not currently pose potential vexing challenges. However, because of the situation of a number of existing industries within residential areas, pollution disputes will no doubt arise in the near future. In addition, rapid increase in private vehicle ownership causes concerns to increasingly mount over vehicle emissions.[31]

3   THE LEGAL AND INSTITUTIONAL MILIEU FOR
           ENVIRONMENTAL GOVERNANCE

3.1   THE ERITREAN LEGAL SYSTEM

The Eritrean legal system originates from a complex array of sources including: the system inherited from its colonialists; the customs of its people; and other traditions developed from codes of conduct and methods of adjudication used by the Eritrean Peoples' Liberation Front (EPLF) during the war for independence. This array of sources has translated into a complex legal system which includes: the Constitution of Eritrea (Constitution),[32] which although adopted in 1997, is yet to be implemented; transitional laws (which incorporate pre-independence laws of the EPLF); revised Ethiopian laws (which are the result of the transplantation of continental law); customary laws; Shari'a laws; and laws enacted in the post independence era. Customary and Shari'a laws have limited application; both in terms of the legal subjects and/or the objects they govern. In addition, a number of post-independence proclamations, published in the Official Gazette of Eritrean

---

29. It is noteworthy that indoor air pollution is a worrisome form of pollution in rural Eritrea. 'The extensive use of biomass (wood, crop residues and dung) in cooking coupled with the use of open stoves in rural areas poses a considerable health problem. This can lead to high exposures to pollutants such as carbon monoxide and polycyclic aromatic hydrocarbons (PAHs). Women and children who spend a lot of time indoors are particularly threatened. Biomass burning has been identified by the WHO as the major indoor air pollution in the world. In Eritrea the situation is believed to be critical. Further study is required before mitigation measures can be defined to solve the problem.' *Ibid.*, 34.

30. 'Industrial pollution' is used in this context to cover industrial solid and liquid waste. For a summary of the nature of industrial waste in the capital and major towns, see NEMP-E, *supra* n. 6, 35-36.

31. G. Yohannes, Motor vehicle pollution in Eritrea: Unpublished Paper (Asmara: University of Asmara, 2003), 3-8. 'Within the last 10 years the number of registered vehicles in Eritrea has risen from 18,500 in 1994 to more than 50,000 in mid 2003.' This data does not include vehicles purchased by the Eritrean Defense Force, Police Force, Air Force and Navy. Moreover, automobiles which are not in use or properly registered are not included in these statistics. Around 40% of these vehicles are thought to run on diesel. A report prepared by the DoE in the year 1997 points to the fact that vehicle emissions may be the cause of wide-spread disease in urban areas. The GoE DoE, State of the Environment-Eritrea: Pilot Report (Asmara: Ministry of Land Water and Environment, 1997), 29-30. Hereafter SoE-E.

32. *Constitution of Eritrea* 1997.

Laws, also are in force. At the lowest tier of the legal hierarchy are an array of regulations, administrative acts and directives issued by the various ministries and government agencies.

3.2 THE CONSTITUTIONAL FRAMEWORK

In terms of the Constitution, the government is responsible for: regulating all land, water and natural resources; ensuring their management in a balanced and sustainable manner and in the interest of future generations; and creating appropriate conditions for securing the participation of people to safeguard the environment.[33] Public participation is also one of the seven 'democratic principles' enshrined in the Constitution and according to which Eritrea must 'guarantee its citizens broad and active participation in all political, economic and cultural life of the country'.[34] The government of Eritrea will accordingly be compelled, when the Constitution comes into force, to manage its 'natural resources', which include forestry and wildlife resources, in a manner consistent with the principles of sustainable management, inter-generational equity, and public participation.

3.3 RELEVANT ENVIRONMENTAL LAWS

Eritrea's environmental law regime is relatively undeveloped and contains no framework environmental law.[35] The government has, in the course of the past ten years, promulgated a limited array of sectoral laws of direct and indirect relevance to environmental regulation. These include the: *Forestry and Wildlife Conservation and Development Proclamation* (2006);[36] *Fisheries Proclamation* (1998);[37] *Tourism Proclamation* (2006);[38] *Proclamation to Promote the Development of Mineral Resources* (1995);[39] *Proclamation on Petroleum Operations* (2000);[40] revised *Petroleum Operations Proclamation* (2000);[41] *Free Zones*

---

33. *Ibid.*, Art. 8(3).
34. *Ibid.*, Art. 7.
35. Government is seeking to draft a framework environmental law and three attempts have been made by the Ministry of Land, Water and Environment to do so. The first draft of the code was undertaken in 1996 (comprising ninety articles); the second in 2000 (comprising eighty-three articles); and the third in 2002 (comprising sixty-seven articles). The code is yet to be finalized.
36. *Forestry and Wildlife Conservation and Development Proclamation* 115 of 2006.
37. *Fisheries Proclamation* 104 of 1998. See also: *Fishery Product Proclamation* 105 of 1998; Foreign Fishing Vessel Regulation *LN* 38 of 1998; Fishery Product Regulation *LN* 40 of 1998; Regulations to amend the Fishery Product Regulations *LN* 71 of 2003.
38. *Tourism Proclamation* 152 of 2006.
39. *Proclamation to Promote the Development of Mineral Resources* 68 of 1995.
40. Revised Regulations on Petroleum Operations *LN* 45 of 2000.
41. *Revised Proclamation to Govern Petroleum Operations LN* 108 of 2000.

Proclamation (2005);[42] and the *Land Proclamation* (1994).[43] Various relevant draft proclamations have also been published and these include: the Draft Eritrean Environmental Proclamation (2002);[44] the Draft Proclamation on Biological Diversity (1997);[45] and the Draft Integrated Coastal Area Management (ICAM) Proclamation (2007).[46] Owing to the fact that this chapter primarily focuses on Eritrea's regime regulating wildlife and forestry, as it is the most current and comprehensive environmental regime in Eritrea, the subsequent analysis primarily considers the scope and ambit of the *Forestry and Wildlife Conservation and Development Proclamation*.

The *Forestry and Wildlife Conservation and Development Proclamation* governs forests,[47] wildlife,[48] woodlots,[49] and wildlife products.[50] It provides, among others, for: the establishment of protected areas;[51] the prescription of a national action plan for forestry and wildlife resources;[52] the development of management plans;[53] the designation of protected areas and riverine forest areas;[54] watershed management and the creation and management of community and private woodlots;[55] a permitting system for the sustainable use of these resources;[56] environmental impact assessment (EIA);[57] prohibited and permitted activities;[58] public participation;[59] the establishment of the Forestry and Wildlife Advisory Board composed of public and private actors;[60] and the prescription of offences and penalties.[61]

---

42. The *Eritrean Free Zones Proclamation* 115 of 2001.
43. *Proclamation to Reform the Land Tenure in Eritrea, to Determine the Manner of Exploiting Land and for Purposes of Development and National Reconstruction and to Determine the Powers and Duties of the Land Commission* No. 58 of 1994.
44. *Draft Environmental Proclamation of Eritrea* 2002.
45. *Draft Proclamation on Biological Diversity* 1997.
46. *Draft Integrated Coastal Area Management (ICAM) Proclamation* 2007.
47. Defined as: '...a community of trees and associated living organisms growing in a well-defined area, excluding wildlife', Proclamation 115 of 2006, *supra* n. 36, Art. 2.
48. Defined as: '...all types of wild animals, excluding fish and other marine living organisms' (Art. 2).
49. Defined as: '...a group of any number of trees' (Art. 2).
50. Defined as: '...anything derived from wildlife, including bushmeat, horns, teeth, bones, claws, skins, hair, eggs, feathers and ivory' (Art. 2).
51. Art. 16.
52. Art. 10.
53. Art. 11.
54. Art. 15.
55. Art. 24.
56. The detailed permitting procedures are prescribed in Regulations for the Issuance of Forestry Permits *LN* 111 of 2006 and Regulations for the Issuance of Wildlife Permits *LN* 112 of 2006.
57. Art. 14 read with GoE, National Environmental Assessment Procedures and Guidelines (Asmara: The Government, 1999).
58. Arts 19, 25, 27 and 29.
59. Art. 15.
60. Art. 5.
61. Art. 35.

In addition to the above national environmental laws, Eritrea has also acceded to numerous international environmental agreements.[62] In line with Article 32(4) of the Constitution, these international instruments need to be approved and enacted in domestic legislation before they can have the effect of binding legal instruments in Eritrea. National laws are thus required to incorporate and/or implement these instruments.

As should be evident from the above analysis, Eritrea's environmental regime is relatively undeveloped. The Constitution, which includes key environmental provisions, is yet to be implemented. Eritrea's framework environmental code, together with key environmental proclamations, remains in draft form. Although various sectoral environmental laws have been enacted in the course of the past few years, these only regulate certain aspects of Eritrea's pressing environmental concerns and the majority have not been subject to judicial scrutiny. In light of this legislative vacuum, several relevant environmental policies which have been introduced during the course of the past few decades, have played an important role in guiding environmental governance in Eritrea.

3.4   RELEVANT POLICY INSTRUMENTS

Although not legally binding, environmental policies, plans and programmes can play an important role in environmental governance through guiding State action and decision-making and informing the formulation of relevant legislation. As with legislation, these policies, plans and programmes may be framework in nature, of general relevance to the environment; or sectoral (i.e. only of relevance to specific environmental issues). Eritrea has developed both these forms of policy instruments.

The National Environmental Management Plan for Eritrea (NEMP-E),[63] introduced in 1995, addresses major environmental issues, inclusive of forestry

---

62. These include: United Nations Framework Convention on Climate Change (1992) 31 *ILM* 848; Kyoto Protocol (1997) 37 *ILM* 22; Convention on Biological Diversity (1992) 31 *ILM* 818; Cartagena Protocol on Biosafety (2000) 6 *ILM* 1027; United Nations Convention to Combat Desertification in Countries Experiencing Serious Drought and/or Desertification (1994) 33 *ILM* 1328; Convention on International Trade in Endangered Species of Wild Fauna and Flora (1973) 46 *ILM* 1178; Convention on the Conservation of Migratory Species of Wild Animals (1980) 19 *ILM* 11; Rotterdam Convention on the Prior Informed Consent Procedure for Certain Hazardous Chemicals and Pesticides in International Trade (1999) 38 *ILM* 1; Vienna Convention on the Protection of the Ozone Layer (1987) 26 *ILM* 1516; Montreal Protocol on Substances that Deplete the Ozone Layer; Stockholm Convention on Persistent Organic Pollutants (2001) 40 *ILM* 532; Basel Convention on the Control of Transboundary Movements of Hazardous Wastes and their Disposal (1989) 28 *ILM* 567; and International Plant Protection Convention, 1997.
63. NEMP-E, *supra* n. 6. Part 1 provides an overview of the plan and considers environmental and developmental prospects for Eritrea within a broader international context, including the United Nations Conference on Environment and Development (UNCED). Part 2 addresses the major environmental and development issues confronting Eritrea. Part 3 defines major steps and

and wildlife conservation, and sets out possible policy choices, alternatives and an order of State priorities. The NEMP-E proposes a specific institutional structure for its implementation, namely an Eritrean Agency for the Environment, and identifies key priorities in the context of forestry and wildlife resources. With regard to the former, priorities include: establishment of fuel wood and pole plantations; development of alternative energy resources; afforestation and soil conservation; area closure for natural regeneration; development of conservation, education for improving public awareness; improvement of land use and husbandry; and development of forestry research.[64] In relation to the latter, priorities include: conservation education; institutional capacity building; the establishment of terrestrial and marine protected areas; the establishment of botanical gardens, zoological gardens and an animal orphanage; the protection of biodiversity; and participation of local people in conservation activities.[65]

The NEMP-E is complemented by an array of additional policies. The first is the Eritrean National Code of Conduct for Environmental Security (ENCCES),[66] which was adopted as part of the NEMP-E and sets out a series of commitments relating to the sustainable development of natural resources, sustainable management of waste, and regional and global cooperation in environmental matters. The second is the National Biodiversity Strategy and Action Plan (NBSAP),[67] adopted in 1998, which documents what is currently known about Eritrea's biodiversity;[68] provides an overview of relevant Eritrean policy and legislation dealing with biodiversity;[69] sets out the principal components of the strategy and describes, inter alia, the main activities which are considered to be essential elements for ensuring effective biodiversity conservation and sustainable use in Eritrea.[70] Third, the Eritrean Macro-Policy (Macro Policy),[71] published in 1994 and which provided the most important statement guiding national development between 1994 and 1998, compelled the government to afford proper attention 'to potential environmental consequences of investment decisions'.[72] More specifically, it requires the government to consider a number of factors when making investment-related decisions, including: the environmental consequences of proposed investment; appropriate agricultural land use and planning to reduce land degradation;

---

responses involved in an integrated environmental and development planning process. Part 4 examines in detail the requirements for implementation of the NEMP-E and its associated project activities, institutional prerequisites, and financial and human resources.

64. NEMP-E, *supra* n. 6, 68.
65. *Ibid.*, 84.
66. NEMP-E, *supra* n. 6, Annex, xii. Adopted at the Environmental Conference, Asmara (February 1995).
67. GoE, National Biosafety Strategy and Action Plan (Asmara: Department of Environment, 1998).
68. *Ibid.*, 7-20.
69. *Ibid.*, 25-27.
70. *Ibid.* (See s. 6 for terrestrial biodiversity, s. 7 for marine biodiversity and s. 8 for agricultural biodiversity).
71. Macro Policy, *supra* n. 4.
72. *Ibid.*, Item 6.10.

the regulation of the use of water for domestic, industrial and agricultural purposes; the prevention of water pollution; cooperation with other coastal States to prevent and fight marine pollution; and the establishment of proper industrial and urban waste disposal systems.[73] Fourthly, the revised National Economic Policy Framework and Program for the Years 1998-2000 (NEPFP),[74] which provides a framework for implementation of the Eritrean macro-policy, lists among its goals the adoption of appropriate environmental protection legislation and sets out 'restoration, enhancement and preservation of Eritrea's ecological integrity' as one of four major priorities.[75]

The final key policy document is the Agricultural Sector Policy and Strategy Framework (ASPSF),[76] completed in 2002 and which is, in effect, the interim policy framework for the Eritrean agricultural sector pending completion of a comprehensive agricultural policy. It is noteworthy that Part 2 of the ASPSF specifically notes the link between Eritrea's structural food deficit and its limited natural resources, and that it accordingly integrates environmental considerations into the policy's mission and medium term objectives.[77] The ASPSF also identifies the need to halt the decline and promote the restoration of the nation's forestry and wildlife resources.[78] Promoting community involvement, reinforcing legislation, building regulatory capacity and improving planning procedures are highlighted as key areas requiring attention.[79]

These national policy documents have cumulatively, in the absence of a comprehensive environmental legislative framework, proven essential in guiding State action and decision-making of environmental relevance. It must be emphasized, however, that these policy frameworks are not an adequate substitute for legislation, the latter which creates binding rights and obligations. Although having proven to be a useful tool in raising the profile of environmental concerns in Eritrea, and forming the contextual framework for future environmental legislation, a comprehensive environmental law regime now needs to be drafted and implemented. As has been alluded to above, the current legislative vacuum is slowly being filled by the promulgation of various environmental related proclamations and the current drafting of many others. This bodes well for the creation of a comprehensive Eritrean environmental law regime in future.

---

73. *Ibid.*, Item 16.
74. GoE, National Economic Policy Frameworks Programme for the Years 1998-2000 (Asmara: The Government, 1998).
75. *Ibid.*, 33-37.
76. Ministry of Agriculture, *Agricultural Sector Policy and Strategy Framework* (Asmara: The Government, 2002).
77. *Ibid.*, 10.
78. *Ibid.*, 49-50.
79. *Ibid.*

3.5   GOVERNANCE STRUCTURES

Until such time as the Constitution comes into force, three laws currently prescribe the structure, powers and functions of the government of Eritrea. The *Proclamation to Determine the Structure, Powers and Functions of the Government of Eritrea*,[80] sets out the general powers and functions of the executive, legislature and the judiciary; Legal Notice No. 14 of 1993[81] details the powers and functions of the various organs of the Executive; and Legal Notice No. 16 of 1994[82] reforms certain aspects of Legal Notice No. 37 of 1993.

These three laws were implemented shortly after Eritrea's formal independence, and unfortunately the level of detail regarding the powers and functions of the different organs of State leaves a lot to be desired. These outdated laws have also not kept abreast of the myriad institutional changes that have taken place during the past decade. Owing to their outdated nature and lack of legal specificity, organs of State have been compelled to interpret, define and/or refine their roles the way they deem fit, within the parameters of the above three laws.

In summary, there are two main ministries of relevance to the environment. The first is the Ministry of Agriculture which is formally mandated to: ensure food security through improved farming; develop animal husbandry; encourage and support the production of raw materials necessary for industry; encourage and support the production of agricultural produce for export; regulate wildlife conservation and use; improve national ecology, and control desertification; control the import and export of agricultural produce and animals; establish quarantine facilities; and establish agricultural colleges.[83] The second is the Ministry of Land, Water and Environment, established in 1996, which has incorporated the roles of the Eritrean Environment Agency (which was set up following the adoption of the NEMP-E),[84] the Land Commission established under the Land Proclamation,[85] and the Water Resources Division which was extracted from the original Ministry of Energy, Mines and Water Resources (now the Ministry of Mines and Energy). Owing to the fact that this ministry has been comprehensively restructured subsequent to the prescription of the enabling statutory framework highlighted above, its powers and functions have unfortunately not been specifically spelled out in legislation. Nonetheless, it currently plays a key role in coordinating and integrating environmental governance in Eritrea.

One additional key institution is the Department of Environment (DoE), which falls under the Ministry of Land, Water and Environment. As with the

---

80. *Proclamation to Determine the Structure, Powers and Functions of the Government of Eritrea* No. 37 of 1993.
81. Regulations to Determine the Powers and Functions of Ministries, Authorities and Offices of the GoE *LN* 14 of 1993.
82. Regulations to Determine the Powers and Functions of Ministries, Authorities and Offices of the GoE (Amendment Legislation) *LN* 16 of 1994.
83. *Ibid.*, Art. 2(9).
84. NEMP-E, *supra* n. 6.
85. See GoE, *supra* n. 43.

ministry, the department has, since its establishment, 'been engaged in defining its role and responsibilities within the framework of the overall government policy'.[86] The role of the department is generally perceived to be one of coordinating the activities of all government bodies of relevance to, or which impact on, the environment; and specifically, 'in collaboration with other relevant agencies of government and the private sector', to act as the lead agent in 'protecting, restoring and enhancing the environment' and 'developing standards, and taking steps to ensure that environmentally sustainable practices are pursued in Eritrea's economic endeavors'.[87] The role of the department no doubt will be clarified in the proposed Draft Proclamation on the Environment when it is eventually completed.

4 AN OVERVIEW OF THE JUDICIAL SYSTEM

4.1 HISTORIC OVERVIEW

History demonstrates that long before the arrival of Eritrea's Italian colonizers, a number of Eritrean communities already had local customary laws and customary judicial institutions and laws.[88] These laws dealt with land rights, criminal offences, marriage, divorce, inheritance and procedures for the resolution of disputes.[89] They were mainly local-specific (with each tribe or clan prescribing its own laws and procedures), lacked coherence, and failed to differentiate between criminal and civil cases. According to these customary laws, disputes were traditionally presided over by a respected elder; in most cases a village chief, who was selected by two arbitrators appointed by the parties to the dispute. The appointment of the 'judge', the selection of the arbitrators, and the resolution of the dispute, was accordingly largely a consensual affair. Owing to the fact that no delineation was made between criminal and civil cases, the 'plaintiff' ordinarily requested redress in monetary or other proprietary terms, or asked for a 'judicial' decision to enforce or protect a right.[90]

During the Italian colonial period, a centralized system of modern codified laws, courts, prosecution, and prisons was established, although it was deeply

---

86. In addition to developing environmental regulatory frameworks and policies, the DoE has been engaged in the following activities: collecting, synthesizing and distributing data; promoting the active participation of government and non-government agencies and the general public in the proper conservation and sustainable use of environmental resources; introducing environmental education into the national curriculum; cooperating with national, regional and international organizations in the conservation and proper use of the environment; and introducing and enforcing environmental laws at national and sectional levels. SoE Report, *supra* n. 6, 95.

87. NEPFP 2000, *supra* n. 74, 33-37.

88. EPLF, *Heghen Higawunetin Ab Hebreteseb E'rtra* [Law and Legality in the Eritrean Community] (Asmara: EPLF, 1992), 3.

89. EPLF, *Compilation of Papers for Conference of the Research and Information Centre on Eritrea* (Asmara: EPLF, 1998), 1.

90. *Ibid.*, 2.

rooted in racism and was primarily entrenched for colonial ends.[91] Jurisdiction was generally decided based on nationality.[92] Five institutions were charged with the adjudication of criminal cases, namely: the *Guidice Della Colonia;* the *Residenti;* the *Tribunale del Commissariato; Corte di Assise;* and the Appellate Court for Italians.[93] With regard to civil cases, jurisdiction was allocated among several institutions. The colonial government had the power to identify and adjudicate over 'collective disputes' including disputes between clans or villages.[94] In other cases, the authorities having jurisdiction varied between village or clan heads, district or tribal chiefs, the *Commissari*, the *Residenti*, the Shari'a courts, the Judge of the Colony, and the Appeal Court of Italian East Africa in Addis Ababa.[95]

During the Second World War, Eritrea was occupied by British forces. Although the British found the existing judicial system to be highly complex, they were bound by the provisions of the Hague Convention of 1907, which prohibited the occupying authority from making changes to existing institutions and laws in the occupied enemy territory.[96] Hence, they established a 'standing military court' with jurisdiction over all penal cases involving both British and Italian law and the 'native courts' having authority over civil and penal cases involving Eritreans.[97] To facilitate the

---

91. *Ibid.*, 3.
92. Trevaskis, *supra* n. 1, 27. According to Trevaskis, four types of laws were administered during the Italian colonial regime: the Italian Penal Code, which applied to all inhabitants of the territory regardless of their nationality; the Italian Civil Code which extended to all civil issues where at least one of the parties was an Italian citizen; the Shari'a or Islamic law applicable in certain civil issues where the parties were Moslem; and the Eritrean customary law, which was enforced in civil cases between Eritreans.
93. *Ibid.* The *Guidice della Colonia* had jurisdiction over all issues concerning Europeans. The *Residenti* had authority over all non-serious cases involving Eritreans and other non-Europeans. The *Tribunale del Commissariato* investigated serious cases where non-Europeans were implicated. The *Corte di Assise* tried the most serious cases involving non-Europeans. The Appellate Court heard civil and criminal appeals for Italians.
94. *Ibid.*
95. *Ibid.*, 27-28. Trevaskis recounts that civil cases between Eritreans of the same religion and community were under the authority of the appropriate village or clan chief. The chief was therefore, for practical purposes, the court of first instance. The court of second instance was the district or tribal chief, and an appeal from the tribal chief's decision lay within the jurisdiction of the *Residenti*. In the case of a dispute arising between Eritreans of different religious or community backgrounds, it was decided by the *Residenti*. Shari'a courts considered certain cases between Eritrean Moslems, while the judge of the colony presided over civil cases between Europeans. Appeals from Shari'a courts were heard by Shari'a courts themselves, whereas appeals from the Italian judge were reviewed by the governor.
96. *Ibid.*, 28-29.
97. *Ibid.*, 28. According to Trevaskis, the standing military court was composed of British officers who sat either individually or as panels; and the Native Courts were composed of Eritrean chiefs and notables, with the same jurisdiction in civil issues as the *Commissari* or the *Residenti* and with limited jurisdiction in penal cases. The British and the Native Courts disposed of most of the cases involving Eritreans and the authority of the Italian courts was restricted to some penal cases and cases involving Italians. At a later stage the Native Courts replaced the *Residenti* and the Appeal Court for Italian East Africa was dissolved and replaced by the Italian Court of Civil and Criminal Appeal for Italians. Appeals from non-Europeans went to the chief administrator.

transfer of power at the end of the British administration, a special committee composed of a United Nations commissioner, British legal officers and Italian judges drafted a constitution, authorizing the establishment of an Eritrean supreme court, a high court of justice and district courts.[98]

In 1952, the United Nations federated Eritrea with Ethiopia. The federation brought about a new constitution for Eritrea, but the existing judicial organization was otherwise left intact.[99] Ethiopia later abrogated the federal arrangement and Eritrea was annexed as Ethiopia's fourteenth province. By doing so, Ethiopia imposed the use of its laws in Eritrea and completely banned the application of Eritrean customary law. The remnants of this event are still reflected in Eritrea's legal system as the Ethiopian Code of Civil Procedure has been adopted by Eritrea as a Transitional Code of Civil Procedure.[100] During the time of Ethiopian occupation, the court structure, from the lowest to the highest court, was as follows: village courts, *woreda* (regional) courts, *awraja* (sub-regional) courts, the high court, and the Supreme Court.[101]

During the armed struggle for independence, customary laws were applied in the areas under the control of the EPLF.[102] With the expansion of liberated areas and the stabilization of administration in these areas, the EPLF set up semi-judicial departments which were in charge of the administration of justice. In 1987, the EPLF managed to establish the Department of Justice which drafted civil and criminal codes along with their procedural codes.[103] These were applicable in the 'liberated areas'.

4.2 CURRENT COURT STRUCTURE

Eritrea's judicial system mirrors the reality of the country; i.e. it is still in the process of (re-)construction. Court structures and hierarchies are yet to complete their metamorphosis but certain trends can be discerned from Eritrea's fledgling judicial system.

The highest court in Eritrea is currently the High Court established in terms of the *Eritrean Transitional Administration of Justice Proclamation* No. 1 of 1991; the first law to be passed following Eritrea's independence. The High Court is presided over by the president, or otherwise known as the Chief Justice, who is the

---

98. *Ibid.*, 122-123. Chiefs and sub-chiefs were denied their judicial powers and were allowed to act as arbiters only. The application of customary laws henceforth dwindled.
99. Nahum, *supra* n. 1, 309. Art. 96 of the Eritrean Constitution that was introduced with the United Nations brokered federation stated that 'Laws and regulations which were in force in 1 April 1941, and have not since been replaced by the administrating authority and the laws and regulations enacted by that Authority, shall remain in force ... '.
100. *Civil Procedure Code of Ethiopia* 1960.
101. EPLF, *supra* n. 88, 3.
102. *Ibid.*, 6-7.
103. Although the EPLF's Central Committee had approved the texts and in liberated areas, judges were selected and given training, their laws were not applied as independence ensued. *Ibid.*, 6-7.

highest judicial officer in the country.[104] The High Court has jurisdiction over both civil[105] and criminal matters.[106] Although environmental matters do not expressly fall within the purview of the High Court, it has jurisdiction over all appeals from lower courts which may involve environmental, forestry and wildlife matters. Situated below the High Court tier, are two additional court structures; regional courts and community courts. The civil and criminal jurisdiction of the regional courts[107] and community courts[108] diminishes as one descends the hierarchy of Eritrea's court structure.

Two further court structures exist in Eritrea. First, Eritrea has established military courts which adjudicate on criminal matters committed by or against military personnel, and crimes jointly committed by a member of the military and a civilian.[109] The military court is two tiered, comprising of the military high court and the military lower court.[110] Right of appeal from the military court is to the High Court. Second, Eritrea has established a Special Court in 1996 by the *Special*

---

104. *Eritrean Transitional Administration of Justice Proclamation* 1 of 1991, Art. 7(1).
105. The High Court has exclusive jurisdiction to hear a range of special cases relating to the formation, dissolution and liquidation of bodies corporate, negotiable instruments, bankruptcy, maritime law, insurance policies, patents and copyright and trademarks, expropriation and collective exploitation of properties, nationality, filiation, *habeas corpus*, and liabilities of public servants for acts done in the discharge of official jurisdiction. In addition, it has jurisdiction to try all suits regarding movable property, where the amount involved exceeds 250,000 Nakfa; and immovable property, where the amount involved exceeds 500,000 Nakfa. (Art. 2(b) of *Amendment Proclamation* 25 of 1992 as amended by Proclamation 113 of 2003).
106. As regards criminal matters, the High Court has jurisdiction to try certain serious offences which entail rigorous punishment. (Art. 3(1)(a) of *LN* 3 of 1991, issued to amend the *Transitional Criminal Procedure Code Amendment Proclamation* 5 of 1991, gives the High Court the jurisdiction to try various serious offences listed in the *Transitional Penal Code of Eritrea* 1957.
107. In civil matters, regional/district courts have jurisdiction when the amount or value of the subject-matter of the suit, in case of movable property, is above 50,000 Nakfa but does not exceed 250,000 Nakfa; and in case of immovable property, is above 100,000 Nakfa and less than 500,000 Nakfa. In addition, the regional courts have jurisdiction to try civil matters whose subject matter cannot be expressed in money (such as change of name and agency) as long as these matters do not fall within the exclusive jurisdiction of the High Court (Art. 2(a) of *LN* 3 of 1991). In criminal matters, the regional/district court has jurisdiction to try all criminal offences other than those which are within the exclusive jurisdiction of the High Court or community court.
108. The community court has jurisdiction over civil suits regarding movable property not exceeding 50,000 Nakfa and regarding immovable property not exceeding 100,000 Nakfa (Art. 5 of Proclamation 132 of 2003). In respect of criminal matters, it has jurisdiction over specific petty crimes listed in the *Transitional Penal Code of Eritrea* 1957, such as intimidation, assault, minor acts of violence, slight offences against honor, and minor damage on property by cattle (Art. 8 of Proclamation 132 of 2003).
109. These offences include: a breach of duty to perform military service; abuse of military duty; desertion; mutiny; insubordination; capitulation; sabotage; and attacks on members of the armed forces. See generally Art. 2(9) of *Amendment Proclamation* 25 of 1992 and Arts 296-353 of *Transitional Penal Code Eritrea* 1957.
110. Art. 4(2).

Court Establishment Proclamation No. 85 of 1996. The role of this Special Court is to hear cases related to theft, embezzlement and corruption.[111] However, the unique nature and administration of this court is such that, while technically a court, it is not ordinarily regarded as part of the judicial structure.[112] Shari'a courts also operate in the field of family law, with limited application.

Final appeals from the civil and military courts,[113] together with review proceedings,[114] are heard by the appellate bench of the High Court. When adjudicating cases of first appeal from the High Courts, the bench is composed of the president of the High Court and four other judges who did not preside over the case at hand; in the case of a second appeal from lower civil courts, it is composed of three judges.[115] Although falling within the structure of the High Court, the appellate bench has assumed the form of a *quasi*-Supreme Court owing to the permanent assignment of certain judges to it since 2007.[116]

In addition to the military court and the appellate bench of the High Court, there currently are five High Courts, thirty-six regional courts and 683 community courts engaged in the administration of justice in Eritrea.

5	ANALYSIS OF SIGNIFICANT ENVIRONMENTAL JUDGMENTS

5.1	INTRODUCTION

Eritrea's judiciary, as noted above, is very much in the process of creation. Currently, it is plagued by chronic capacity constraints, in both a qualitative and quantitative sense, and its role is further undermined by the fact that Eritrea's environmental regime is similarly at the embryonic stage of development. The judiciary's role in

---

111. Art. 2.
112. The special court has a distinct administration to the other courts. The Ministry of Defense is responsible for overseeing its establishment. Management of this special court is entrusted to the chairman of the court who may submit budgetary requests directly to the government and hire employees independent of the Ministry of Defense and any other governmental agency. (Art. 7 and Art. 2(3)).
113. Art. 7(5) of *Proclamation* 1 of 1991 read together with Arts 2(3) and (4) of *Amendment Proclamation* 25 of 1992. The latter amends *Proclamation* 1 of 1991, the *Transitional Civil Procedure Code Amendment Proclamation* 3 of 1991, and the *Transitional Criminal Procedure Code Amendment Proclamation* 5 of 1991.
114. Art. 7(6) of *Proclamation* 1 of 1991. The review of a judgment is given of right to any party in a civil matter who considers himself/herself aggrieved by a court order (from which an appeal lies or does not) where: (a) subsequently to the judgment, he/she discovers a new and important matter, such as forgery, perjury or bribery, which after the exercise of due diligence, was not within his/her knowledge at the time of the judgment was granted; and (b) had such matter been known at the time of the judgment was granted, it would have materially affected the substance of the original court order. Art. 6(1) of *Transitional Civil Procedure Code of Eritrea* 1957 as amended.
115. See Arts 2(3) and (4) of *Amendment Proclamation* 25 of 1992.
116. Interview with A. Habtemariam, High Court Judge, Asmara Eritrea, 20 September 2007.

environmental governance is therefore currently rather limited with the majority of judgments comprising of criminal prosecutions for breaching one of Eritrea's few environmental laws. This part of the chapter considers a sample of court judgments of relevance to the protection of Eritrea's forestry and wildlife resources, being the sector in respect of which Eritrea's most comprehensive and contemporary environmental legislation exists. Cases from two of the six administrative regions in the country are considered, namely: the Northern Red Sea Region (specifically the regional court of Ginda'e) and the Gash Barka Region (the Agordat, Barentu and Af'abet regional courts).[117] The analysis is divided along temporal lines: the first part focuses on cases which were heard prior to the introduction of the *Wildlife and Forestry Conservation and Development Proclamation*;[118] and the second part on those heard after its introduction.

5.2   Pre-Proclamation No. 155 of 2006

In the absence of dedicated environmental legislation, the established practice of the Eritrean judiciary was to apply Italian and/or Ethiopian colonial law. In the context of forestry and wildlife, this was the outdated *Wildlife Proclamation* No. 192/1980, inherited from Ethiopia.

In *Public Prosecutor* v. *Kalifa Mohammed Ali and Others*,[119] two forest guards appointed to guard a particular forest, were charged with cutting down fifteen trees in the same forest. The court found them guilty and sentenced them to various fines ranging from 4,000 Nakfa to 1,000 Nakfa.[120] Interestingly, in handing down the sentence, the court took into account extenuating socio-economic factors pleaded by the accused.[121] Strangely, no aggravating factors, to the effect that the accused were forest guards and had breached their duty to protect the forest, were presented by the public prosecutor.

In *Public Prosecutor v. Mohammed Seid Idris and Others*,[122] the first accused was charged with cutting forty live *eucalyptus* trees and transporting them with a view to selling the trees. Three co-accused were charged with buying seventeen 'fruits' of the crime. All the accused pleaded guilty, and the prosecutor submitted an array of aggravating circumstances for consideration by the court in its sentencing deliberations, namely: in respect of the first accused, that he had cut live trees which Eritrea's people and the government had invested heavily in their protection; and in respect of the three co-accused, that they had bought live specimens. The accused were sentenced and fines were imposed ranging from 5,000

---

117. These regions have been selected as they contain Eritrea's biodiversity hot spots.
118. *Forestry and Wildlife Conservation and Development Proclamation* (*supra* n. 36).
119. Gindae Regional Court File No. 193 of 2004.
120. 15 Nafka are the equivalent of US$1.
121. The extenuating circumstances pleaded were personal, such as social and financial problems of the defendants.
122. Gindae Regional Court File No. 191 of 2004.

Nakfa to 2,500 Nakfa, the former apparently being the highest fine levied by any court in the country for a forestry related offence.[123] The sentence is also in stark contrast to the lesser sentences previously handed down by the same court for similar offences.[124]

Courts have not, however, limited their sanctions to the imposition of fines. In *Public Prosecutor v. Mulugeita Belay*,[125] the accused was found guilty of cutting 1,350 palm trees. During sentencing, the court considered the fact that 'the palm tree is difficult to replace' and sentenced the defendant, a commercial farmer, to six months imprisonment and a fine of 1,000 Nakfa.[126] This case involves the largest land clearing exercise in violation of laws protecting forestry resources, and is frequently cited by the Ministry of Agriculture as evidence of the court's diminished tolerance of environmental offenders. The approach of the courts to forestry-related offences is unfortunately far from consistent. This is illustrated in *Public Prosecutor v. Weldensae Tewelde and Others*[127] where the accused were found guilty of cutting a significant number of trees,[128] and they were only penalized with fines ranging between 1,000 Nakfa and 4,000 Nakfa.

Wildlife issues provide a somewhat different picture in Eritrea. Of the twenty environmental cases surveyed by the author, only two involved harm to wildlife which is indicative of the contrasting human threats posed to wildlife and forestry

---

123. The conclusion is based not only on the cases surveyed, but also interviews with judges in relevant courts, prosecutors and legal advisors to the Ministry of Agriculture. Interviews with judges T. Ghebrekrstos (Ginda'e) and A. Yohanness (Massawa) of the Northern Red Sea Region, during September 2007, and public prosecutors A. Berhane and T. Teklemariam, during December 2007. Interview with T. Mogos, Legal Advisor, Ministry of Agriculture, during September 2007.

124. In *Public Prosecutor v. Omar Mohammed Mahmud* (Gindae Regional Court File No. 189/04), the same court punished a person found guilty of cutting forty trees with a fine of 2,000 Nakfa.

125. Agordat Regional Court File No. 11/03.

126. Before the coming in to effect of the *Forestry and Wildlife Conservation and Development Proclamation* (*supra* n. 36), the Gash-Barka regional administration of the Ministry of Agriculture attempted to adopt administrative directives that would effectively impose a fine on offenders corresponding to the number and nature of the trees cut. To illustrate, an individual palm tree was valued 1,000 Nakfa and in the matter of *Public Prosecutor v. Mohammed Seid Idris and Others* the offender would have been fined 1,350,000 Nakfa. These directives were dropped by the regional courts and have even led to at least two prosecutions of officers of the Gash-Barka regional administration. See *Public Prosecutor v. Kesete Yohanness and Others* (Tekombia Prosecution File No. 136/04) in which two members of the Gash-Barka regional administration who fined twenty-eight individuals 1,500 Nafkas each for 'abuse of power' under the *Transitional Penal Code of Eritrea*. See further *Public Prosecutor v. Fitsum Abraham* (Goled'j Prosecution File No. 114/03) in which an officer of the Gash Barka regional administration was accused of 'abuse of power' for issuing a person allegedly cutting trees and making eighteen sacks of coal with a fine of 14,000 Nakfa. Both cases against members of the Gash Barka regional administration are pending.

127. Barentu Regional Court File No. 137/05.

128. The first accused was found guilty of cutting 190 *Zeziphus Spina-christi* and eight *Acacia Seyal*; the second accused sixty-six *GABA*, eight *Acacia Seyal* and six palm trees; the third accused 163 *Zeziphus Spina-christi* and six *Acacia Seyal*; and the fourth accused fifteen *Zeziphus Spina-christi*, eight *Acashia Laeta*, three *Acacia Seyal* and five *Balanites Aegyptiaca*.

resources in Eritrea. In both wildlife cases, the harm to wildlife was caused by military personnel. In the first case, *Public Prosecutor v. Captain Teklemariam Abraha and Others*,[129] the four accused were commanders who authorized their respective troops to kill eleven *kudus* (antelope) and destroy various trees. The court deferred the case to the Ministry of Defence and in the absence of any meaningful response from them, suspended the case in February 2006. In a subsequent case which never reached the court, a military regiment was alleged to have killed twenty-five *kudu* for food. The public prosecutor was advised, four years after the commission of the offence, to drop the case owing to the difficulties in identifying the individual offenders where the crime was committed by a military regiment.

5.3   POST-PROCLAMATION No. 155 OF 2006

The year 2006 was significant for environmental governance in Eritrea, as it saw the introduction of the country's most comprehensive and dedicated environmental law; the *Wildlife and Forestry Conservation and Development Proclamation* (2006). A number of cases have already been brought before the courts under this proclamation.

In *Public Prosecutor v. Senait Kifle and Uqbasenbet Menghisteab*,[130] the first accused was charged with cutting down sixty-eight protected trees to rebuild her house without the necessary permit issued under the Proclamation.[131] The second accused was charged with abusing his official duties by issuing a permit to the first accused.[132] Both defendants were found guilty of their respective offences. As in most cases in Eritrea, no aggravating circumstances were pleaded by the public prosecutor, while extenuating circumstances were pleaded and considered by the court. The court, having considered the extenuating circumstances, penalized the first and second accused to a fine of 1,500 Nakfa and 700 Nakfa respectively. A similar trend regarding the failure on the part of the prosecution to lead evidence in aggravation of sentence and the court to issue stringent penalties, is evidenced in a number of recent judgments such as: *Public Prosecutor v. Musa Osman Hussein*;[133] *Public Prosecutor v. Mr Said Ali Nur*;[134]

---

129. Akurdet Regional Court (Gash Barka Region) File No. 324/05.
130. Gindae Regional Court File No. 52/07.
131. Art. 20(b) of the Proclamation prohibits the cutting of trees without a permit.
132. Art. 414 of the *Transitional Penal Code of Eritrea* 1957, deals with 'abuse of power'.
133. Gindae Regional Court File No. 14/07. In this case, the accused was found guilty of cutting approximately forty protected trees and was sentenced to a fine of a mere 900 Nafka. No extenuating factors were placed before the court for consideration.
134. Gindae Regional Court File No. 13/07. In this case, the accused was charged and found guilty of cutting forty live *Balanites Aegyptiaca* trees and of charcoal burning. The court, taking into consideration his personal mitigating factors, sentenced him to a fine of 1,000 Nakfa.

Public Prosecutor v. Ms Nghisti Tekeste Hineshum;[135] and *Public Prosecutor v. Mr Ibrahim Hamed Ahmed.*[136]

In the context of wildlife protection, a similar pattern of cases and sentencing trends is evident. In *Public Prosecutor v. Mohammed Ali Mohammed Abdela and Others*,[137] for example, the accused, a member of the military, was found guilty of killing two *kudu*. No aggravating factors were pleaded by the prosecution and the accused was fined a mere 1,000 Nakfa.

6   CRITICAL SURVEY

In a bid to tackle the major environmental challenges facing the country, including those posed to its wildlife and forestry resources, the government has undertaken an array of measures in the past decade including the promulgation of key environmental policies and laws. However, the existing environmental law regime is still very much in its infancy and the absence of a comprehensive environmental legal framework has constrained the role of the judiciary in environmental governance. In addition, significant resource, capacity constraints, and a lack of political will on the part of both judges and prosecutors, appear to have undermined the ability of the judiciary to proactively engage in environmental governance prior to and following the promulgation of the *Wildlife and Forestry Conservation and Development Proclamation* (2006). This is evident in the following trends discerned from the cases discussed above.

First, the courts in the regions subject to review, have been very lenient in their sentencing of environmental offences. In terms of the *Wildlife and Forestry Conservation and Development Proclamation* (2006), the court is empowered to impose significant penalties including imprisonment of up to three years and/or a fine not exceeding 10,000 Nakfa.[138] Interestingly, the court must order 'the offender to make good the damage resulting from his violation of the provisions of this Proclamation'.[139] Furthermore, the penalty may increase where the offence is committed in respect of any endangered forestry and wildlife species listed in annexes to the Proclamation.[140] What is noteworthy from the cases surveyed is that, with the exception of *Public Prosecutor v. Mulugeita Belay*, the courts have failed to sentence

---

135. Gindae Regional Court File No. 43/07. In this case, the accused was charged with clearing shrub on her property without a permit. The accused pleaded guilty and the court, after having considered her mitigating factors, sentenced her to a fine of 1,500 Nakfa

136. Gindae Regional Court File No. 122/07. In this case, the accused was charged with cutting two live *Sesban* and one *Balanites Aegyptiaca*, and of making three sacks of charcoal from them. He was sentenced to a fine of 600 Nakfa.

137. Akurdet Regional Court File No. 151/07.

138. Art. 34(2).

139. Art. 34(3).

140. *Ibid.*

offenders to imprisonment and have generally levied fines of less than 2,000 Nakfa; well below the upper limit of 10,000 Nakfa. Furthermore, although the courts have in the majority of cases ordered the confiscation of cut trees, it is unclear why they have not ordered the offenders to remedy the environmental damage caused by their action. In light of the above, it would appear that the empowering legal framework has not been fully understood or effectively applied by the judiciary and the prosecutor's office;[141] a sentiment acknowledged by various prosecutors.[142]

Second, and related to the above, is the general failure on the part of the prosecution to plead aggravating factors in the sentencing process. This is in stark contrast to the offenders who consistently, and successfully, plead factors in mitigation of sentence. It would appear that the prosecutors, having secured the conviction, are satisfied with whatever sentence is handed down by the court. This is compounded by the failure on the part of the prosecution to seek to appeal the very lenient sentences handed down by the courts of first instance.

7　　　　　　　THE WAY FORWARD

There appears to be a number of perquisites for mitigating the above trends inherent in Eritrea's recent environmental jurisprudence, and in entrenching the Eritrean judiciary as a key role player in the country's environmental governance effort.

The first relates to the prescription of a comprehensive environmental law regime. Although having promulgated the *Wildlife and Forestry Conservation and Development Proclamation* in 2006, similar legislative reforms are required in many other environmental fields to regulate land degradation, pollution and the depletion of other natural resources. In the context of wildlife and forestry, the *Wildlife and Forestry Conservation and Development Proclamation* (2006) overcomes many of the institutional and legislative *lacunae* which were prevalent prior to its introduction by: introducing mechanisms to clarify competing mandates and facilitate co-operative governance;[143] establishing the Forestry and Wildlife Advisory Board with members drawn from the public and private actors;[144] and prescribing procedures for public participation and input in the preparation and revision of the national action plan, management plans and pertinent regulations.[145]

---

141. Interview with Mr S. Beyn, head of Environmental Division, Ministry of Agriculture, on 11 October 2007.
142. Interview with Mr A. Berhane, head of Gash Barka Regional Prosecution Office, on 5 December 2007.
143. Prior to its introduction, overlapping mandates blurred state responsibility over wildlife and forestry resources where clashes of interest existed between the Ministry of Land, Water and Environment and the Ministry of Agriculture. The *Wildlife and Forestry Conservation and Development Proclamation* (*supra* n. 36) expressly mandates the Ministry of Agriculture with the task of developing, conserving and regulating forestry and wildlife resources.
144. Art. 5.
145. Art. 15.

Notwithstanding these improvements, one significant issue which remains unresolved is the issue of 'administrative offences' and remedies. In earlier drafts of the Proclamation, there was a proposal to empower inspectors to issue spot fines, thereby effectively easing the burden on the judiciary and simultaneously empowering the environmental authorities to assess damage and impose penalties where appropriate. This proposal, however, was rejected by the Ministry of Justice owing to concerns about potential abuse of the procedure by environmental authorities. The prescription of a schedule of offences and appropriate penalties could provide one mechanism for overcoming the judiciary's current misunderstanding of what constitute appropriate sentences for environmental offences. In this regard, the Ministry of Agriculture is in the process of preparing a list of offences and penalties for specified forestry and wildlife offences.[146] When formally promulgated, this list should aid judges in matching the appropriate sanction to the offence on a case-by-case basis.

Notwithstanding the prescription of a comprehensive environmental law regime, what is further required is the sensitization and appropriate training of the judiciary, prosecutors and enforcement authorities. In the absence of such training, misunderstanding and misconceptions about the current and any future environmental law regime will prevail. This needs to be further complemented by increased human and financial resources available to the judiciary and relevant government authorities. Current capacity constraints are chronic, as the following figures from the two jurisdictions considered in this chapter indicate: in the Gash Barka Region, there are only fourteen judges and five prosecutors; in the Northern Red Sea Region, there are only twelve judges and five prosecutors. Of the twenty judges, ten hold LLB degrees, while the remaining sixteen are high school graduates with basic 'on the job' legal training. Of the ten prosecutors, eight hold LLB degrees and two have not even completed high school. The majority of judges and prosecutors holding LLB degrees are recent graduates with very limited experience in environmental matters. The Ministry of Justice has acknowledged these problems and has mapped out an aggressive recruitment and training programme, including the establishment of a legal training centre. The integration of environmental legal training within this broader training programme could significantly improve the role of the judiciary in environmental governance. The benefits of this process may be undermined, however, by Eritrea's apparent inability to retain skilled citizens and a lack of basic mechanisms and resources to facilitate their functions.[147]

A further key area requiring priority attention is creating public awareness and participation in environmental governance. Although public participation is expressly recognized in the *Wildlife and Forestry Conservation and Development*

---

146. Interview with Beyn, *supra* n. 141.
147. The lack of vehicles, for example, is significantly hampering the work of prosecutors in gathering essential evidence. Interview with Berhane, *supra* n. 142.

Proclamation (2006), civil society currently plays an almost non-existent role in reporting environmental offences or bringing these offences to court. Facilitating public participation could go someway to alleviating the current capacity and resource constraints plaguing environmental authorities and prosecutors. An interesting development in this regard, is the bid by concerned nationals to establish a so-called 'Friends of the Eritrean Elephant Association', a non-profit, non-governmental organization (NGO) which is in the process of formal registration. It is hoped that the successful registration of this environmental NGO may facilitate the establishment of similar organizations, thereby potentially increasing the role of civil society in the broader environmental governance effort.

A final opportunity for improving the role of the judiciary in environmental governance in Eritrea, is improving the political will of government authorities, prosecutors and the judiciary to more efficiently investigate and prosecute environmental offences. Securing the support of the executive appears to be a *sine qua non* for effective environmental governance in Eritrea, where the legislature is yet to develop and the judiciary suffers from various frailties. In this regard, the Ministry of Agriculture has been the champion as evidenced by its advocacy for and ultimate introduction of the *Wildlife and Forestry Conservation and Development Proclamation* (2006).

8   CONCLUSION

It is trite that objectively, the judiciary can play a significant role in environmental governance. However, what should be evident from this chapter's analysis of the Eritrean judiciary, and particularly its decisions relating to forestry and wildlife resources, is that its role is still in its infancy and is constantly evolving to reflect Eritrea's economic and political transition. This evolution has significantly impacted on the judiciary's structure, jurisdiction, manpower, political agenda and available resources. Ongoing evolution provides opportunities for change and in the Eritrean context, numerous opportunities and pre-requisites exist for improving the role of the Eritrean judiciary in environmental governance. In summary, these include: building political will; prescribing a comprehensive environmental regime; capacity building and training for the judiciary and the prosecution; providing the judiciary and the prosecution with the necessary capacity and resources; and improving civil society participation.

As it stands, the most glaring toll on Eritrea's environment is arguably attributable to the military's development and defense activities. This is worrying given the limited jurisdiction of the High Court and regional courts to pronounce on these activities, and the reticence of the military courts to sanction their own personnel. Resolving these jurisdictional gaps therefore appears to be a final key prerequisite for entrenching the Eritrean judiciary as a force in the country's environmental governance effort.

BIBLIOGRAPHY

Bein, E., et al. *Useful Trees and Shrubs in Eritrea.* Technical Handbook No. 12. Nairobi, SIDA Regional Soil Conservation Unit, 1996.

Bojö, J. Land Degradation and Rehabilitation in Eritrea: Working Paper 1. Washington, DC: World Bank, 1996.

Boutros-Ghali, B. *The United Nations and the Independence of Eritrea.* The United Nations Blue Book series, vol. XII. New York: Department of Public Information, 1996.

EPLF. *Compilation of Papers for Conference of the Research and Information Centre on Eritrea.* Asmara: Eritrean Peoples' Liberation Front, 1998.

EPLF. *Heghen Higawunetin Ab Hebreteseb E'rtra.* Asmara: Eritrean Peoples' Liberation Front, 1992.

Firebrace, J. *Eritrea: Never Kneel Down: Drought, Development and Liberation in Eritrea.* Trenton, NJ: Red Sea Press, 1986.

GoE. 3rd National Report on the Implementation of the UNCCD. Asmara: Ministry of Agriculture, 2004. <www.unccd.int/cop/reports/africa/national/2004/eritrea-eng.pdf>, 21 September 2008.

GoE. National Biosafety Strategy and Action Plan. Part 1. Asmara: Department of Environment, 1998. <www.cbd.int/doc/world/er/er-nbsap-01-p1-en.pdf>, 21 September 2008.

GoE. National Biosafety Strategy and Action Plan. Part 2. Asmara: Department of Environment, 1998. <www.cbd.int/doc/world/er/er-nbsap-01-p2-en.pdf>, 21 September 2008.

GoE. Macro Policy. Asmara: The Government, 1994.

GoE. National Action Plan. Asmara: The Government, 2002.

GoE. *National Action Plan.* Unpublished: 2006.

GoE. National Economic Policy Frameworks Programme for the Years 1998-2000. Asmara: The Government, 1998.

GoE. National Environmental Assessment Procedures and Guidelines. Asmara: The Government, 1999.

GoE. National Environmental Management Plan. Asmara: The Government, 1995.

GoE. Rio+10 Country Report. Asmara: The Government, 2002.

GoE. State of the Coast Report. Unpublished, 2006.

GoE. State of the Environment Report. Asmara: The Government, 2006.

GoE DoE. Eritrea's National Biodiversity Strategy and Action Plan: Biodiversity stocktaking Assessment Report. Asmara: The Government, 1999.

GoE DoE. State of the Environment-Eritrea: Pilot Report. Asmara: Ministry of Land Water and Environment, 1997.

Habtezion, Z. 'Heritage Governance in Eritrea: Reality and Choices'. In *Archaeology of Ancient Eritrea,* edited by P. Schmidt, M.C. Curtis & Z. Teka. Trenton, NJ: Red Sea Press, 2007.

Mengsteab, K. 'Eritrea's Land Reform Proclamation: A Critical Appraisal'. *Eritrean Studies Review* 2, no. 2 (1998): 1-18.

Ministry of Agriculture. *Agricultural Sector Policy and Strategy Framework.* Asmara: The Government, 2002.

Nahum, F. 'The Enigma of Eritrean Legislation'. *Journal of Ethiopian Law* 9, no. 1 (1973): 308-331.

Trevaskis, G. *Eritrea, A Colony in Transition: 1941-1952.* London: Oxford University Press, 1960.

UNEP. 'African Environmental Outlook'. <www.unep.org/dewa/Africa/>, 21 September 2008.

Yohannes, G. Motor vehicle pollution in Eritrea: Unpublished Paper. Asmara: University of Asmara, 2003.

TABLE OF LEGISLATION

Civil Procedure Code of Ethiopia 1960
Constitution of Eritrea 1997
Draft Environmental Proclamation of Eritrea 2002
Draft Integrated Coastal Area Management Proclamation 2007
Draft Proclamation on Biological Diversity 1997
Eritrean Free Zones Proclamation 115 of 2001
Fisheries Proclamation 104 of 1998
Fishery Product Proclamation 105 of 1998
Fishery Product Regulation *LN* 40 of 1998
Foreign Fishing Vessel Regulation *LN* 38 of 1998
Forestry and Wildlife Conservation and Development Proclamation 115 of 2006
Revised Proclomation to Govern Petroleum Operations 108 of 2000
Proclamation to Determine the Structure, Powers and Functions of the Government of Eritrea 37 of 1993
Revised Proclomation to Promote the Development of Mineral Resources 68 of 1995
Proclomation to Reform the Land Tenure in Eritrea, to Determine the Manner of Exploiting Land and for Purposes of Development and National Reconstruction and to Determine the Powers and Duties of the Land Commission 58 of 1994
Regulations for the Issuance of Forestry Permits *LN* 111 of 2006
Regulations for the Issuance of Wildlife Permits *LN* 112 of 2006
Regulations to amend the Fishery Product Regulations *LN* 71 of 2003
Regulations to Determine the Powers and Functions of Ministries, Authorities and Offices of the GoE *LN* 14 of 1993
Regulations to Determine the Powers and Functions of Ministries, Authorities and Offices of the GoE *LN* 16 of 1994
Revised Regulations on Petroleum Operations *LN* 45 of 2000
Tourism Proclamation 152 of 2006
Transitional Criminal Procedure Code Amendment Proclamation 5 of 1991
Transitional Penal Code of Eritrea 1957

TABLE OF CASES

TABLE OF INTERNATIONAL INSTRUMENTS

Montreal Protocol on Substances that Deplete the Ozone Layer (1987) 26 *ILM*
    1541
Rotterdam Convention on the Prior Informed Consent Procedure for Certain
    Hazardous Chemicals and Pesticides in International Trade (1999) 38 *ILM* 1
Stockholm Convention on Persistent Organic Pollutants (2001) 40 *ILM* 532
United Nations Convention to Combat Desertification in Countries Experiencing
    Serious Drought and/or Desertification (1994) 33 *ILM* 1328
United Nations Framework Convention on Climate Change (1992) 31 *ILM* 849
Vienna Convention on the Protection of the Ozone Layer (1987) 26 *ILM* 1516

ABBREVIATIONS

AEO	African Environmental Outlook
ASPSF	Agricultural Sector Policy and Strategy Framework
CBD	Convention on Biodiversity
DoE	Department of Environment
EPLF	Eritrean People's Liberation Front
ENCCES	Eritrean National Code of Conduct for Environmental Security
GoE	Government of Eritrea
ICAM	Draft Integrated Coastal Area Management
LN	Legal Notice
NAP	National Action Plan
NBSAP	National Biodiversity Strategy and Action Plan
NEMP-E	National Environmental Management Plan for Eritrea
NEPFP	National Economic Policy Framework and Program
NGO	Non-governmental Organization
SoE	State of Environment
UNCED	United Nations Conference on Environment and Development
UNEP	United Nations Environmental Programme

Index

ENERGY AND ENVIRONMENTAL LAW & POLICY SERIES

1. Stephen J. Turner, *A Substantive Environmental Right: An Examination of the Legal Obligations of Decision-makers towards the Environment.* 2009. ISBN: 978-90-411-2815-7
2. Helle Tegner Anker, Birgitte Egelund Olsen & Anita Rønne (eds.), *Legal Systems and Wind Energy: A Comparative Perspective.* 2009. ISBN: 978-90-411-2831-7
3. David Langlet, *Prior Informed Consent and Hazardous Trade: Regulating Trade in Hazardous Goods at the Intersection of Sovereignty, Free Trade and Environmental Protection.* 2009. ISBN: 978-90-411-2821-8
4. Louis J. Kotzé and Alexander R. Paterson (eds.), *The Role of the Judiciary in Environmental Governance: Comparative Perspectives.* 2009. ISBN 978-90-411-2708-2